FileMaker Pro 2.0/2.1 Bible

FileMaker Pro 2.0/2.1 Bible

By Dr. Steven A. Schwartz

IDG Books Worldwide, Inc.
An International Data Group Company
San Mateo, California ◆ Indianapolis, Indiana ◆ Boston, Massachusetts

Macworld™ FileMaker Pro 2.0/2.1 Bible

Published by
IDG Books Worldwide, Inc.
An International Data Group Company
155 Bovet Road, Suite 310
San Mateo, CA 94402

Text, art, and software compilations copyright © 1994 by IDG Books Worldwide. All rights reserved. No part of this book, including interior design, cover design, and icons, may be reproduced or transmitted in any form, by any means (electronic, photocopying, recording, or otherwise) without the prior written permission of the publisher.

Library of Congress Catalog Card No.: 94-77749

ISBN: 1-56884-201-5

Printed in the United States of America

10 9 8 7 6 5 4 3 2 1

1B/QY/RW/ZU

Distributed in the United States by IDG Books Worldwide, Inc.

Distributed in Canada by Macmillan of Canada, a Division of Canada Publishing Corporation; by Computer and Technical Books in Miami, Florida, for South America and the Caribbean; by Longman Singapore in Singapore, Malaysia, Thailand, and Korea; by Toppan Co. Ltd. in Japan; by Asia Computerworld in Hong Kong; by Woodslane Pty. Ltd. in Australia and New Zealand; and by Transworld Publishers Ltd. in the U.K. and Europe.

For general information on IDG Books in the U.S., including information on discounts and premiums, contact IDG Books at 800-434-3422 or 415-312-0650.

For information on where to purchase IDG Books outside the U.S., contact Christina Turner at 415-312-0633.

For information on translations, contact Marc Jeffrey Mikulich, Foreign Rights Manager, at IDG Books Worldwide; FAX NUMBER 415-286-2747.

For sales inquiries and special prices for bulk quantities, write to the address above or call IDG Books Worldwide at 415-312-0650.

For information on using IDG Books in the classroom, or for ordering examination copies, contact Jim Kelly at 800-434-2086.

Limit of Liability/Disclaimer of Warranty: The author and publisher of this book have used their best efforts in preparing this book. IDG Books Worldwide, Inc., International Data Group, Inc., and the author make no representation or warranties with respect to the accuracy or completeness of the contents of this book, and specifically disclaim any implied warranties or merchantability or fitness for any particular purpose, and shall in no event be liable for any loss of profit or any other commercial damage, including but not limited to special, incidental, consequential, or other damages.

Trademarks: FileMaker Pro is a registered trademark of Claris Corporation. All brand names and product names used in this book are trademarks, registered trademarks, or trade names of their respective holders. IDG Books Worldwide is not associated with any product or vendor mentioned in this book. Macworld is a registered trademark of IDG Communications, Inc.

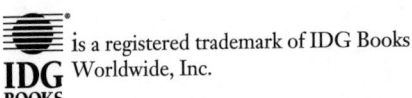 is a registered trademark of IDG Books Worldwide, Inc.

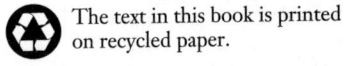 The text in this book is printed on recycled paper.

About the Author

In 1978, Dr. Steven Schwartz bought his first microcomputer, a new Apple II+. Determined to find a way to make money with it, he began writing software reviews, BASIC programs, and user tips for *Nibble* magazine. Shortly thereafter, he was made a Contributing Editor.

Over the past 16 years, Steven has written hundreds of articles for more than a dozen computer magazines. He currently writes for *Macworld* and *Multimedia World*. He was also a founding editor of *Software Digest*, as well as Business Editor for *MACazine*. From 1985 to 1990, he was the Director of Technical Services for Funk Software.

Steven is the author of eighteen books, including *Macworld Guide to ClarisWorks 2* and *Macworld ClarisWorks 2.0/2.1 Companion* (IDG Books Worldwide), *The 9–to–5 Mac* (Hayden Macintosh Library), *Help! The Mac Answer Book* (Alpha Books), and a series of popular game tip books from Prima Publishing and COMPUTE Books.

Steven has a Ph.D. in psychology and presently lives in the Arizona desert with his family, where he writes books, consults on game development issues, and complains about the heat.

ABOUT IDG BOOKS WORLDWIDE

Welcome to the world of IDG Books Worldwide.

IDG Books Worldwide, Inc., is a subsidiary of International Data Group, the world's largest publisher of business and computer-related information and the leading global provider of information services on information technology. IDG was founded more than 25 years ago and now employs more than 5,700 people worldwide. IDG publishes more than 200 computer publications in 63 countries (see listing below). Forty million people read one or more IDG publications each month.

Launched in 1990, IDG Books is today the fastest-growing publisher of computer and business books in the United States. We are proud to have received 3 awards from the Computer Press Association in recognition of editorial excellence, and our best-selling ...*For Dummies* series has more than 7 million copies in print with translations in more than 20 languages. IDG Books, through a recent joint venture with IDG's Hi-Tech Beijing, became the first U.S. publisher to publish a computer book in the People's Republic of China. In record time, IDG Books has become the first choice for millions of readers around the world who want to learn how to better manage their businesses.

Our mission is simple: Every IDG book is designed to bring extra value and skill-building instructions to the reader. Our books are written by experts who understand and care about our readers. The knowledge base of our editorial staff comes from years of experience in publishing, education, and journalism — experience which we use to produce books for the '90s. In short, we care about books, so we attract the best people. We devote special attention to details such as audience, interior design, use of icons, and illustrations. And because we use an efficient process of authoring, editing, and desktop publishing our books electronically, we can spend more time ensuring superior content and spend less time on the technicalities of making books.

You can count on our commitment to deliver high-quality books at competitive prices on topics customers want to read about. At IDG, we value quality, and we have been delivering quality for more than 25 years. You'll find no better book on a subject than an IDG book.

John Kilcullen
President and CEO
IDG Books Worldwide, Inc.

IDG Books Worldwide, Inc., is a subsidiary of International Data Group. The officers are Patrick J. McGovern, Founder and Board Chairman; Walter Boyd, President. International Data Group's publications include: **ARGENTINA'S** Computerworld Argentina, Infoworld Argentina; **AUSTRALIA'S** Computerworld Australia, Australian PC World, Australian Macworld, Network World, Mobile Business Australia, Reseller, IDG Sources; **AUSTRIA'S** Computerwelt Oesterreich, PC Test; **BRAZIL'S** Computerworld, Gamepro, Game Power, Mundo IBM, Mundo Unix, PC World, Super Game; **BELGIUM'S** Data News (CW) **BULGARIA'S** Computerworld Bulgaria, Ediworld, PC & Mac World Bulgaria, Network World Bulgaria; **CANADA'S** CIO Canada, Computerworld Canada, Graduate Computerworld, InfoCanada, Network World Canada; **CHILE'S** Computerworld Chile, Informatica; **COLOMBIA'S** Computerworld Colombia, PC World; **CZECH REPUBLIC'S** Computerworld, Elektronika, PC World; **DENMARK'S** Communications World, Computerworld Danmark, Macintosh Produktkatalog, Macworld Danmark, PC World Danmark, PC World Produktguide, Tech World, Windows World; **ECUADOR'S** PC World Ecuador; **EGYPT'S** Computerworld (CW) Middle East, PC World Middle East; **FINLAND'S** MikroPC, Tietoviikko, Tietoverkko; **FRANCE'S** Distributique, GOLDEN MAC, InfoPC, Languages & Systems, Le Guide du Monde Informatique, Le Monde Informatique, Telecoms & Reseaux; **GERMANY'S** Computerwoche, Computerwoche Focus, Computerwoche Extra, Computerwoche Karriere, Information Management, Macwelt, Netzwelt, PC Welt, PC Woche, Publish, Unit; **GREECE'S** Infoworld, PC Games; **HUNGARY'S** Computerworld SZT, PC World; **HONG KONG'S** Computerworld Hong Kong, PC World Hong Kong; **INDIA'S** Computers & Communications; **IRELAND'S** ComputerScope; **ISRAEL'S** Computerworld Israel, PC World Israel; **ITALY'S** Computerworld Italia, Lotus Magazine, Macworld Italia, Networking Italia, PC Shopping, PC World Italia; **JAPAN'S** Computerworld Today, Information Systems World, Macworld Japan, Nikkei Personal Computing, SunWorld Japan, Windows World; **KENYA'S** East African Computer News; **KOREA'S** Computerworld Korea, Macworld Korea, PC World Korea; **MEXICO'S** Compu Edicion, Compu Manufactura, Computacion/Punto de Venta, Computerworld Mexico, MacWorld, Mundo Unix, PC World, Windows; **THE NETHERLANDS'** Computer! Totaal, Computable (CW), LAN Magazine, MacWorld, Totaal "Windows"; **NEW ZEALAND'S** Computer Listings, Computerworld New Zealand, New Zealand PC World, Network World; **NIGERIA'S** PC World Africa; **NORWAY'S** Computerworld Norge, C/World, Lotusworld Norge, Macworld Norge, Networld, PC World Ekspress, PC World Norge, PC World's Produktguide, Publish& Multimedia World, Student Data, Unix World, Windowsworld; IDG Direct Response; **PAKISTAN'S** PC World Pakistan; **PANAMA'S** PC World Panama; **PERU'S** Computerworld Peru, PC World; **PEOPLE'S REPUBLIC OF CHINA'S** China Computerworld, China Infoworld, Electronics Today/Multimedia World, Electronics International, Electronic Product World, China Network World, PC and Communications Magazine, PC World China, Software World Magazine, Telecom Product World; IDG HIGH TECH BEIJING'S New Product World; IDG SHENZHEN'S Computer News Digest; **PHILIPPINES'** Computerworld Philippines, PC Digest (PCW); **POLAND'S** Computerworld Poland, PC World/Komputer; **PORTUGAL'S** Cerebro/PC World, Correio Informatico/Computerworld, Informatica & Comunicacoes Catalogo, MacIn, Nacional de Produtos; **ROMANIA'S** Computerworld, PC World; **RUSSIA'S** Computerworld-Moscow, Mir - PC, Sety; **SINGAPORE'S** Computerworld Southeast Asia, PC World Singapore; **SLOVENIA'S** Monitor Magazine; **SOUTH AFRICA'S** Computer Mail (CIO),Computing S.A.,Network World S.A., Software World; **SPAIN'S** Advanced Systems, Amiga World, Computerworld Espana, Communicaciones World, Macworld Espana, NeXTWORLD, Super Juegos Magazine (GamePro), PC World Espana, Publish; **SWEDEN'S** Attack, ComputerSweden, Corporate Computing, Natverk & Kommunikation, Macworld, Mikrodatorn, PC World, Publishing & Design (CAP), Datalngenjoren, Maxi Data,Windows World; **SWITZERLAND'S** Computerworld Schweiz, Macworld Schweiz, PC Tip; **TAIWAN'S** Computerworld Taiwan, PC World Taiwan; **THAILAND'S** Thai Computerworld; **TURKEY'S** Computerworld Monitor, Macworld Turkiye, PC World Turkiye; **UKRAINE'S** Computerworld; **UNITED KINGDOM'S** Computing /Computerworld, Connexion/Network World, Lotus Magazine, Macworld, Open Computing/Sunworld; **UNITED STATES'** Advanced Systems, AmigaWorld, Cable in the Classroom, CD Review, CIO, Computerworld, Digital Video, DOS Resource Guide, Electronic Entertainment Magazine, Federal Computer Week, Federal Integrator, GamePro, IDG Books, Infoworld, Infoworld Direct, Laser Event, Macworld, Multimedia World, Network World, PC Letter, PC World, PlayRight, Power PC World, Publish, SWATPro, Video Event; **VENEZUELA'S** Computerworld Venezuela, PC World; **VIETNAM'S** PC World Vietnam

Acknowledgments

I am grateful to the many people who offered their encouragement and support throughout this project, including Clint Hicks, my assistant for this project; John Faylen and Jay Lee (Claris Corporation); Pat Seiler, the best copyeditor in the business; Kristin Cocks, Janna Custer, and Megg Bonar (IDG Books Worldwide); and my agent and friend, Matt Wagner (Waterside Productions) for understanding that I'm a writer, not an infinite number of monkeys.

The following individuals were kind enough to provide helpful tips and templates that were used in the book or provided on the disk:

- Lara Cool, Bill Swagerty, and Max Pruden, Claris Technical Support
- Mark Wall, Green Mountain Software
- Bill Taube, Database Associates, Inc.
- Kevin J. Jundt, author of Acid Jazz
- Dave Applegate, author of DayPlan
- Bill Goodman, Cyclos

(The Publisher would like to give special thanks to Patrick J. McGovern, without whom this book would not have been possible.)

Credits

Publisher
David Solomon

Managing Editor
Mary Bednarek

Acquisitions Editor
Janna Custer

Production Director
Beth Jenkins

Senior Editors
Tracy L. Barr
Sandra Blackthorn
Diane Graves Steele

**Associate
Production Coordinator**
Valery Bourke

Associate Acquisitions Editor
Megg Bonar

Project Editor
Kristin A. Cocks

Editors
Pat Seiler
Kathy Simpson

Editorial Assistant
Laura Schaible

Technical Reviewer
Jay Lee

Production Quality Control
Steve Peake

Production Staff
Tony Augsburger
J. Tyler Connor
Kent Gish
Angie Hunckler
Drew R. Moore
Carla Radzikinas
Patricia R. Reynolds
Kathie Schnorr
Gina Scott
Robert Simon

Proofreader
Kathleem Prata

Indexer
Anne Leach

Book Design
University Graphics

Contents at a Glance

Introduction 1

Part I: The Fundamentals 7
Chapter 1: What is a Database? 9
Chapter 2: Macintosh Essentials 25
Chapter 3: FileMaker Pro Basic Operations 71

Part II: Database Design Basics 93
Chapter 4: Creating Your First Database: Address Book 95
Chapter 5: Defining Fields 147
Chapter 6: Layouts 189
Chapter 7: Setting Preferences 223

Part III: Working with Databases 233
Chapter 8: Using Browse Mode: Viewing, Entering , Editing, and Deleting Records 235
Chapter 9: Searching for Records 269
Chapter 10: Sorting Records 293
Chapter 11: Using the Spelling Checker 313
Chapter 12: Reports 335
Chapter 13: Printing 343

Part IV: Intermediate Topics 365
Chapter 14: Calculations and Computations 367
Chapter 15: Automating FileMaker Pro 403
Chapter 16: Exchanging Data 447
Chapter 17: Creating and Using FileMaker Pro Templates 465
Chapter 18: Documenting and Designing Help Systems for Your Database 473

Part V: Advanced Topics 487
Chapter 19: Linking Databases 489
Chapter 20: Sharing and Protecting Data 507
Chapter 21: Developing Databases for Others 525

Part VI: Appendixes 541
Appendix A: Installing FileMaker Pro 2 543
Appendix B: Installing the FileMaker Pro 2.1 Update 553
Appendix C: Keyboard Shortcuts 557
Appendix D: Resources 565
Appendix E: FileMaker Pro Limitations 569
Appendix F: Installing and Using the FileMaker Pro Bible Disk 571

Index 581

License Agreement 623

Reader Response Card ....Back of Book

Table of Contents

Introduction 1
    Why FileMaker Pro? 1
    About This Book 2
    Whom This Book Is for 2
    How This Book Is Organized 3
    Part I: The Fundamentals 3
    Part II: Database Design Basics 3
    Part III: Working with Databases 3
    Part IV: Intermediate Topics 3
    Part V: Advanced Topics 3
    Conventions Used in This Book 4
    How to Use This Book 4
        For the beginner 5
        For the more experienced Mac user 5
        For an owner of a previous version of FileMaker Pro 6
    Macworld FileMaker Pro 2.0/2.1 Bible Disk 6

Part I: Fundamentals 7

CHAPTER 1

What Is a Database? 9
    Paper Databases vs. Computer Databases 11
        Limitations of paper databases 11
        Advantages of computer databases 12
        When should you use a database program? 13
    Flat-File and Relational Databases 14
    Introducing FileMaker Pro 15
        Understanding layouts 16
        Understanding layout parts 19
        Understanding modes 20
    Getting "The Big Picture" 21
        Home uses for FileMaker Pro 22
        Business uses for FileMaker Pro 22
    Concepts and Terms 24

CHAPTER 2: Macintosh Essentials 25
- Starting Up and Shutting Down 25
- The Macintosh Desktop 28
- Using the Mouse 32
  - Using the mouse to select items 33
  - Using the mouse to choose menu commands 34
  - Double-clicking 36
- Basic Text Editing 38
  - Entering text 38
  - Selecting text 38
  - Deleting text 39
  - Copying text 40
  - Pasting text 40
- Working with Windows 41
- Dealing with Dialog Boxes 43
  - Common dialog box elements 44
  - File dialog boxes 46
    - Disk and folder navigation 47
    - Opening a file 50
    - Saving a file 50
- Switching between Running Programs 50
  - Switching programs under System 6 (using MultiFinder) 51
  - Switching programs under System 7 52
- A Printing Primer 53
  - Using the Chooser 54
  - The meaning of the Print and Page Setup options 55
    - Page Setup options 56
    - Unique ImageWriter options 57
    - Unique LaserWriter options 58
    - Print options 59
- The Importance of Backups 61
  - Making backup copies from the desktop 63
  - Making backup copies by using the Save As command 64
  - Making backup copies by using FileMaker Pro's Save a Copy As command .. 65
  - Making backup copies by using a backup program 66
- System 7 Bonus: Making Aliases 67
- Concepts and Terms 68

CHAPTER 3: FileMaker Pro Basic Operations 71
- Starting Up 71
- Quitting 74
- File-Handling Procedures 75
  - Opening, creating, and closing databases 75
  - Saving files 77
  - Making a backup copy of a file 78
  - Automatic backups 81

Issuing Commands 84
Using Tools and Palettes 86
Concepts and Terms 91

Part II: Database Design Basics 93

CHAPTER 4: Creating Your First Database: Address Book 95

Step 1: Create a New Database 97
Step 2: Define Fields 98
Step 3: Set Field Options 101
Step 4: Design the Data Entry Layout 104
   Altering the layout parts 104
   Adding graphics 105
   Setting field attributes 107
      Text attributes 107
      Field borders 110
      Field formats 111
   Setting the dimensions for and placing fields 112
      Manually sizing and placing objects on the layout 112
      Using the Size windoid to size and place layout objects 115
   Adding the finishing touches 118
      Naming the layout 119
      Setting the final size of the layout 120
      Adding a box around the Category field 121
      Ungrouping the background graphics 121
Step 5: Design a Report Layout 123
   Resizing the fields 126
   Formatting the header 127
   Formatting the footer 128
Step 6: Create the Scripts 129
   The script definition process 130
   The Address Book scripts 131
      The Show Companies script 131
      The Show Individuals script 135
      The Show All script 136
      The Find Businesses script 136
      The Find Friends script 137
      The Find Relatives script 137
      The Sort by Company, Last Name script 138
      The Phone Directory (by Last Name) script 138
      The Phone Directory (by Company) script 139
   Assigning scripts to buttons 140
Step 7: Set Document Preferences 142
Concepts and Terms 145

CHAPTER 5: Defining Fields 147

- Setting Field Definitions 147
  - All about field types 149
    - Text fields 150
    - Number fields 151
    - Date fields 152
    - Time fields 153
    - Picture and Sound fields 154
    - Calculation fields 155
    - Summary fields 156
- Setting Field Entry Options 163
  - Auto-entry options 165
    - Creation Date, Creation Time, Modification Date, Modification Time, Creator Name, and Modifier Name 166
    - Serial number 168
    - Data 169
  - Data verification options 170
    - Not empty 170
    - Unique 170
    - An existing value 171
    - Of type 171
    - From . . . To 171
  - Repeating fields 172
  - Value lists 174
  - Lookups 176
- Modifying Field Definitions, Names, and Options 180
  - Adding new fields by starting from scratch 180
  - Duplicating existing fields 181
  - Changing field names 182
  - Deleting a field and its data 182
  - Setting field options for existing fields 184
  - Changing a field definition 184
  - Changing or deleting options for a field 186
- Concepts and Terms 187

CHAPTER 6: Layouts 189

- Understanding Layouts 190
  - Layout Mode 190
  - Creating a layout: an example 192
- Using the Predefined Layout Styles 193
  - Standard layouts 194
  - Columnar layouts 195
    - Working with columns outside columnar layouts 197
    - Changing or removing a column setup 199
    - Label layouts 199
    - Envelope layouts 202

Making Layouts Suit Your Needs 203
  Duplicating a layout 203
  Reordering layouts 203
  Renaming a layout 204
  Deleting a layout 204
Making Your Own Layouts 205
  Working with layout parts 205
    Body 205
    Header 206
    Footer 206
    Summary parts 206
  Adding a layout part 206
  Modifying parts 208
    Resizing 208
    Reordering 209
    Changing types and options 210
    Changing the positions of part labels 210
    Deleting 210
  Adding items to a layout part 211
    Adding fields 211
  Using the measurement and alignment tools 212
    Formatting fields 212
    Formatting repeating fields 216
    Adding and modifying text 217
    Adding graphics 217
  Applying the finishing touches 218
    Aligning objects 219
    Grouping objects 220
    Other object commands 220
    Setting tab order for data entry 220
Concepts and Terms 222

CHAPTER 7

Setting Preferences 223

Working with the Preferences Dialog Box 223
Setting General Program Preferences 225
Setting Document-Specific Preferences 226
Using Memory Preferences to Set a Save Interval 230
Concepts and Terms 232

Part III: Working with Databases 233

CHAPTER 8
Using Browse Mode: Viewing, Entering, Editing, and Deleting Records 235
Browse Mode Basics 235
   Switching to Browse mode 236
   Using Browse mode tools and functions 237
      Using the layout pop-up menu to switch layouts 238
      Using the book icon to navigate among records 239
      Changing the magnification level 243
      Showing and hiding the status area 244
Data Entry and Editing 244
   Creating new records 244
   Entering data 245
      Using the data-entry and arrow keys 246
      Entering different types of data 247
      Working with value lists 257
      Copying and reusing data 261
      Entering the current date, time, or user name 263
   Editing records 264
   Deleting records 266
   Using the spelling checker 267
Concepts and Terms 268

CHAPTER 9
Searching for Records 269
Find Mode Basics 270
   Switching to Find mode 270
   Using Find mode tools and functions 270
Finding Records 272
   Matching all criteria 273
   Matching one criterion or another 275
   Matching different kinds of text 276
      Matching text exactly 276
      Finding text that's alphabetically above or below a value 278
      Using wildcard characters for partial matches 278
      Nonindexed (literal) text 278
More about Find Requests 279
   Creating Find requests 279
   Repeating and editing Find requests 279
   Deleting Find requests 280
Matching Special Items 281
   Matching values in a range 281
   Matching the current date 281
   Searching for empty fields 282

Table of Contents

Searching for values that exceed or are less than a given value	282
Searching for duplicates	283
Searching for invalid information	284
Omitting: Finding records that don't match the criteria	284
Working with Found Records	285
Omitting records from a found set	285
Swapping found sets with omitted records	287
Copying found sets	287
Deleting found sets	288
Replacing values in a found set	288
Concepts and Terms	291

CHAPTER 10 Sorting Records 293

About Sorting	293
Creating a Sort Order	296
Sorting on one field	298
Sorting on several fields	301
Modifying Sort Specifications	303
Changing sort fields	303
Changing the sort order	304
Additional Sorting Options	306
Using a value list for a sort	306
Setting an international sort order	307
Sorting by Summary fields	308
Unsort: Restoring the Original Record Order	310
Concepts and Terms	312

CHAPTER 11 Using the Spelling Checker 313

Setting Spell-Checking Options	313
Checking Your Spelling	315
Spell-checking on request	315
On-the-fly spell-checking	318
Installing a Dictionary	318
Working with User Dictionaries	320
Creating a user dictionary	320
Adding words to a user dictionary	321
Merging user dictionaries	324
Spelling Tips and Tricks	326
Creating a spelling list from existing FileMaker Pro databases	326
Extracting a custom dictionary from another program	329
Restricting spelling checks to a subset of fields	332
Concepts and Terms	333

CHAPTER 12 Reports 335

Report Design Essentials	335

Designing a layout	336
Selecting records to include in the report	337
Sorting the found set	337
Printing or previewing the report	337
Report Design Tips	338
Working with layout parts	338
Duplicating a report layout	339
Transferring layouts between databases	339
Concepts and Terms	341

CHAPTER 13
Printing 343

Setting Up	344
Selecting a printer with the Chooser	344
Using the Page Setup dialog box	346
Using a LaserWriter	347
Using a StyleWriter	350
Using an ImageWriter	351
Readying a Report	353
Selecting and sorting	353
Previewing before printing	354
Printing	355
The Print command	355
Printing in the background with PrintMonitor	359
Printing More Effectively	361
Troubleshooting	363
Concepts and Terms	364

Part IV: Intermediate Topics 365

CHAPTER 14
Calculations and Computations 367

About Calculation Fields	367
Available operations	368
Arithmetic operations	368
Logical operations	369
Text operations	370
Creating an expression	370
Creating a Calculation field	371
About FileMaker Pro's Built-In Functions	373
Data conversion functions	376
DateToText	377
NumToText	377

Table of Contents

- TextToDate ... 377
- TextToNum ... 378
- TextToTime ... 378
- TimeToText ... 379
- Date functions ... 379
  - Date ... 379
  - Day ... 380
  - DayName ... 380
  - DayofYear ... 380
  - Month ... 381
  - MonthName ... 381
  - Today ... 381
  - WeekofYear ... 381
  - Year ... 382
- Field functions ... 382
  - Average ... 382
  - Count ... 383
  - Extend ... 383
  - Last ... 383
  - Max ... 384
  - Min ... 384
  - StDev ... 385
  - Sum ... 385
  - Summary ... 385
- Financial functions ... 386
  - FV ... 386
  - NPV ... 387
  - PMT ... 387
  - PV ... 387
- The IF function: making logical decisions ... 388
- Mathematical functions ... 389
  - Abs ... 389
  - Exp ... 390
  - Int ... 390
  - Ln ... 390
  - Log ... 391
  - Mod ... 391
  - Pi ... 391
  - Random ... 392
  - Round ... 392
  - Sign ... 392
  - Sqrt ... 393
- Text functions ... 393
  - Exact ... 393
  - Left ... 394
  - Length ... 394
  - Lower ... 394
  - Middle ... 395
  - Position ... 395
  - Proper ... 395

Replace	396
Right	396
Trim	397
Upper	397
Time functions	397
Hour	397
Minute	398
Seconds	398
Time	398
Trigonometric functions	399
Atan	399
Cos	399
Degrees	399
Radians	400
Sin	400
Tan	400
Concepts and Terms	401

CHAPTER 15
Automating FileMaker Pro 403

Using ScriptMaker	404
Listing scripts in the Scripts menu	407
Running a script	408
Modifying a script	409
Renaming a script	409
Duplicating a script	410
Deleting a script	410
Editing a script	411
Script step reference	412
Script step options	412
Script step definitions	414
Attaching a Script to a Button	439
Using Advanced Scripting Procedures	441
Executing other scripts from within a script	441
Using Apple Events	442
Using QuicKeys with FileMaker Pro scripts	444
Using AppleScript	445
Concepts and Terms	446

CHAPTER 16
Exchanging Data 447

Moving Data to and from Other Places	447
About importing and exporting	447
Understanding file formats	448
Tab-separated text	448
Merge	449
Comma-separated text	449
BASIC	449
SYLK	449

DIF 449
WKS 449
DBF 449
Edition file 449
Importing Data from Other Sources 450
  Format selection 450
  Data cleanup 450
    Cleaning up data in a spreadsheet 451
    Converting return-delimited text 453
  How to import 454
Exporting Data 456
  Format selection 456
  Data cleanup 456
  How to export 457
    Exporting summary fields 458
    Performing a mail merge 458
Exchanging Data with PCs 459
  Moving data to and from FileMaker Pro for Windows 460
  Understanding the compatibility issues 460
Working with a Newton 462
Concepts and Terms 463

CHAPTER 17
Creating and Using FileMaker Pro Templates 465
Installing a Template 466
Reinstalling a Fresh Copy of a Template 466
Saving a Database as a Template 467
Working with a New Template 469
Concepts and Terms 471

CHAPTER 18
Documenting and Designing Help Systems 473
Suggested Help Topics 474
Different Approaches to Presenting Help Information 475
  Approach #1: A Read Me file 475
    TeachText and other text editors 475
    Stand-alone documents 476
    Word processing programs 477
    Paper-only documentation 477
  Approach #2: A help layout 478
  Approach #3: Script-guided help 482
Concepts and Terms 486

Part V: Advanced Topics 487

CHAPTER 19
Linking Databases 489
How Lookups Work 489
   Defining lookup fields 493
   An extended example 497
   More about lookups 500
Performing a Relookup 501
Automating a Relookup 503
Concepts and Terms 505

CHAPTER 20
Sharing and Protecting Data 507
Running FileMaker Pro on a Network 507
   Hosts and guests 508
      The host is in charge 508
      Guest activities 511
   Notes on cross-platform database sharing 512
Protecting Databases and Setting Access Privileges ...512
   Creating passwords 513
   Passing out passwords 516
   Modifying passwords 517
   Creating and deleting groups 517
   Setting, changing, and examining access privileges ...519
      Opening a database without a password 521
   Using a protected file 521
      Changing a password 522
Concepts and Terms 524

CHAPTER 21
Developing Databases for Others 525
Creating Shareable Templates 527
   Simplify the interface by using menus 527
   Creating a Navigation Menu 530
   Providing instant access via buttons and scripts 532
   Consider color and screen space 533
      Color 533
      Screen real estate 535
   Protecting a template 535
   Restricting access to features of shareware templates ...537
Using FileMaker Pro SDK 538
Concepts and Terms 539

Part VI: Appendixes 541

APPENDIX A

Installing FileMaker Pro 2 543
System Requirements 543
Using the Installer 544
    Performing an Easy Install 544
    Performing a Custom Install 546
    Selecting a different hard disk 548
Registering FileMaker Pro 2 552

APPENDIX B

Installing FileMaker Pro Updates 553
Updating to FileMaker Pro 2.1v2 553

APPENDIX C

Keyboard Shortcuts 557

APPENDIX D

Resources 565
Technical Support/General Help 565
Custom Programming and Vertical Applications 566
News Sources 566
Magazines: Additional Sources of Tips 567

APPENDIX E

FileMaker Pro Limitations 569

APPENDIX F

Installing and Using the FileMaker Pro Bible Disk 571
Disk Contents 573
About Shareware and Freeware 575
Shareware Registration Forms 576
    ACID JAZZ (1.2v1) 576
    Disclaimer 576
    Requirements 576

Index 581

License Agreement 623

Reader Response Card .... Back of Book

Introduction

Why FileMaker Pro?

FileMaker Pro is a mature database product. We're not talking about some company's latest brain child that is being foisted — bug-laden — onto an unsuspecting public. In its various incarnations and from its various publishers, it has been known as FileMaker, FileMaker 2, FileMaker IV, FileMaker Pro, and FileMaker Pro 2. FileMaker Pro has been around the block — and I've been in lock-step with it.

Unlike many computer products that are periodically "redefined" by having drastic changes made to the *user interface* (the way you interact with the program and perform different procedures) or to the program's *focus* (such as changing a simple text editor into a desktop publishing program), FileMaker Pro's versions have all shown a steady progression forward. This means that if you've used any version of FileMaker Pro — even one that is several years old — the information and experience you've gained has not been a waste of time. Much of your knowledge can be applied directly to the current version of the program.

Although I've reviewed computer programs for more than 15 years for magazines such as *Macworld, Multimedia World, Mac Home Journal, MACazine, Macintosh Business Journal,* and *Software Digest,* surprisingly few products exist that impress me so much that I've stuck with them over the years. FileMaker Pro is such a program. Apparently, much of the Macintosh community agrees with my assessment, because FileMaker Pro currently owns about 70 percent of the Mac database market. Because it's safe to assume that you own a copy of FileMaker Pro, you're in excellent company.

About This Book

The *Macworld FileMaker Pro 2.0/2.1 Bible* is a different kind of computer book. First, it's not a manual. Many people don't like computer manuals — perhaps because they feel obligated to read them from cover to cover to avoid missing something important, or because manuals are designed to explain how features work rather than how to put a program to work for you. The *Macworld FileMaker Pro 2.0/2.1 Bible* is not a book that you have to read. It's a book that I hope you'll *want* to read — because it provides easy-to-find, easy-to-understand explanations of the common tasks for which you bought FileMaker Pro in the first place. When you want to know how to use a particular program feature, you can use the extensive Table of Contents, or Index to quickly identify the section of the book that you need to read.

Second, although I hope that you'll find some of the material in this book to be entertaining, the primary mission of the *Macworld FileMaker Pro 2.0/2.1 Bible* is to inform. I want you to really understand how FileMaker Pro works and to be able to make it do exactly what you want it to do. No matter where you turn in this book, if you find yourself with a puzzled look on your face after reading a section, I haven't done my job.

Finally, the philosophy of this book — as well as the other books in the IDG Bible series — is that you don't want or need a handful of books to learn all about a computer program; one book should suffice. The *Macworld FileMaker Pro 2.0/2.1 Bible* is an all-in-one book that gives you a well-rounded knowledge of FileMaker Pro. You don't just learn *how* to perform an action; you also learn *when* and *why* you would perform that action. You can find almost anything you want to know about FileMaker Pro in this book.

Whom This Book Is for

The Macworld FileMaker Pro 2.0/2.1 Bible is for anyone who uses version 2 or 2.1 of FileMaker Pro:

❖ If you're a beginning FileMaker Pro user, step-by-step instructions help you get up to speed quickly with explanations of how to perform common (and not so common) FileMaker Pro features and procedures.

❖ If you're an intermediate or advanced FileMaker Pro user — someone who doesn't need much hand-holding — tips and insights in each chapter help you get the most from FileMaker Pro. You'll find the information provided in the QuickTips and Backgrounder sidebars to be handy tools for your FileMaker Pro toolbox.

How This Book Is Organized

Each chapter is self-contained. When you need to perform a particular FileMaker Pro task, scan the Table of Contents to locate the chapter that addresses your needs. You can also flip through the pages of the book to quickly find the chapter you need. *The Macworld FileMaker Pro 2.0/2.1 Bible* is divided into five Parts:

Part I: The Fundamentals

This part is a gentle introduction to database concepts, using the Macintosh, and essential FileMaker Pro concepts.

Part II: Database Design Basics

This part instructs you in using the various design tools to construct databases and to design different types of layouts.

Part III: Working with Databases

In this part, I explain what you need to know when you're ready to start working with a database: entering and editing data, searching for particular records, sorting, designing reports, and printing.

Part IV: Intermediate Topics

This part covers material that helps you make more productive use of FileMaker Pro. It isn't essential to learn about these features immediately, but you will want to tackle them after you're comfortable with the FileMaker Pro basics.

Part V: Advanced Topics

In this part is material that will interest more experienced FileMaker Pro users and would-be developers, including using lookups to link databases and tips for creating databases that you'd like to share (or sell) to others.

Conventions Used in this Book

The chapters in this book contain the following icons:

These sidebars offer insights into the feature or task being discussed, suggesting better or easier ways of accomplishing that task. Also look here for ways to better use the program features.

These sections offer in-depth information about the subject being discussed — information that is not necessarily vital to performing a task. Look here if you're interested in achieving a more well-rounded knowledge of FileMaker Pro .

Look for these icons for specific instructions — presented in the order in which you perform the them — that are needed to accomplish a particular task.

How to Use This Book

Far be it from me to tell you how to read this book. Reading and learning styles are all very personal. When I get a new computer program, I frequently read the manual from cover to cover before even installing the software. Of course, I'll be flattered if you read the *Macworld FileMaker Pro 2.0/2.1 Bible* the same way — but I'll be *surprised* if you do, too.

This book is written as a reference to "all things FileMaker Pro." When you want to learn about defining fields, there's a specific chapter to which you can turn. If you just need to know how to use the spelling checker, you can flip to the Table of Contents or the Index and find the pages where it's discussed. Most procedures are explained in step-by-step fashion, so you can quickly accomplish even the most complex tasks. So you can read this book as you would a novel, read just the chapters that interest you, or use it as a quick reference for when you need to learn about a particular feature or procedure.

For those who prefer a little more direction than "whatever works for you," some general guidelines are suggested in the following paragraphs — arranged according to your level of Mac expertise and previous FileMaker Pro experience.

However, I do have one general suggestion: *If at all possible, read this book with FileMaker Pro on-screen.* Sure, you can read about editing a user dictionary for the spelling checker while relaxing in the tub, but — unless you have exceptional recall — what you read will be more meaningful if you're sitting in front of the computer.

For the beginner

Although this book does discuss many of the basic concepts and procedures necessary for the beginning user to start working productively on the Macintosh (see Chapter 2), it is *not* a substitute for the documentation that came with your Mac. As you work on the desktop and begin experimenting with FileMaker Pro, you're bound to encounter additional Mac issues that are only touched on — or ignored altogether — in Chapter 2. When that happens — *and it will* — it's time to drag out the manuals for your Macintosh, printer, and system software, and see what you've missed. Once you fill in the gaps in your Mac education, you'll feel more confident and comfortable tackling FileMaker Pro and any other programs you eventually purchase.

If you're relatively new to the Mac, start by reading all of Part I. This will acquaint you with basic database concepts, the fundamentals of using the Mac, and the FileMaker Pro basics. Next, work through the tutorial presented in Chapter 4. This chapter gently leads you through the process of creating your first database, a full-featured Address Book in which you can record your business and personal contacts. Finish up by reading the remaining chapters of Part II (Chapters 5 through 7) and at least the next three chapters of Part III (Chapters 8 through 10). This will provide you with a sufficient grounding in FileMaker Pro concepts and features to enable you to tackle basic database projects. Then, as you find it necessary to explore additional program features, such as printing or creating calculations, you can just jump to the appropriate chapter.

The more advanced stuff is saved for Part IV and Part V. Although you'll eventually want to check out the material in those Parts, too, you'll note that I've purposely separated the advanced matters from the basics in order to keep new users from being overwhelmed.

For the more experienced Mac user

If you're familiar with databases, you can safely skip Chapters 1 and 2. The material in these chapters is very basic and is probably second-hand to you. If FileMaker Pro is your first database program, however, you should at least skim through the material in Chapter 1.

Chapter 3, is must reading for every FileMaker Pro user. Many FileMaker Pro tasks, such as using the tools, are discussed here.

Parts II and III are the real meat-and-potatoes chapters for new FileMaker Pro users. Many of the topics covered in these parts are at least touched upon on Chapter 4. After completing this tutorial chapter, you may feel sufficiently confident to tackle some of your own database projects. You can treat the remainder of the book as reference material and read as needed.

For an owner of a previous version of FileMaker

As mentioned earlier, FileMaker (in its various incarnations) has always worked basically the same. Through the years, however, new features and capabilities have been added. If you are familiar with an older version of FileMaker, you should pay particular attention to material in the following chapters:

- Chapter 15 discusses ScriptMaker and explains how to create auto-entry data fields.
- Chapter 16 explains the procedures for moving data between FileMaker Pro and other programs.
- Chapter 19 discusses FileMaker Pro's lookup capabilities, enabling you to automatically bring data from an external database into the current database.
- Chapter 20 tells how FileMaker Pro works on a network and explains how Publish & Subscribe (a feature introduced with System 7) is used.

Macworld FileMaker Pro 2.0/2.1 Bible Disk

Bound into this book is the *Macworld FileMaker Pro 2.0/2.1 Bible Disk*, an on-disk collection of ready-to-run FileMaker Pro templates, example databases, demos, and FileMaker-related utilities. Whether you just want to get up and running quickly, need some help with the more advanced topics covered in the book, or are looking for new ways to use FileMaker Pro, you're strongly encouraged to check out the disk.

Note: The Macworld FileMaker Pro 2.0/2.1 Bible Disk is neither a product of nor is it endorsed by Claris Corporation.

Part I
The Fundamentals

CHAPTER ONE

What Is a Database?

IN THIS CHAPTER

- Understanding essential database terminology
- Comparing paper databases and computer databases
- Looking at the differences between flat-file and relational database programs
- Understanding essential FileMaker Pro concepts and terms
- Learning some of the potential uses for FileMaker Pro

Before exploring FileMaker Pro, you need to understand what a database is. A *database* is an organized collection of information, usually with one central topic. In a computer database (as opposed to a paper database), the program that you use to enter and manipulate the data is called a *database program* or a *database management program*.

The word *organized* is a key part of this definition. Otherwise, a shoe box stuffed with business receipts may be considered a database. In general, if you may need to manually look at every scrap of data before finding the one for which you're searching, you don't have a database. You just have a shoe box full of stuff.

Even if you have never used a computer database, you are already familiar with plenty of examples of paper databases:

❖ Address books and business card files

❖ Employee records

❖ Recipe card files

❖ Telephone books

❖ Holiday greeting card lists

Every database — whether on paper, in a hand-held electronic organizer, or in a computer — is composed of records. A *record* contains all the information that has been collected on one individual or entity in the database. In the preceding examples, a record holds all the address data on one friend or business associate (address book or business card file), the employment information on one employee (employee records), the ingredients and cooking instructions for one recipe (recipe card file), the name, street address, and phone number for every person and business in the area (telephone book), and the name of one person or family whom you previously received a card from or intend to send a card to (holiday greeting card list).

Records are divided into fields. A *field* contains a single piece of information about the subject of the record. In an address database, for example, the fields may include first name, last name, address, city, state, zip code, and phone number. Figure 1-1 shows the relationship among the components of a database.

What distinguishes a database from any old hodgepodge of information is that the data within each record is *organized*. Fields are responsible for this organization. The fields appear in the same place on every record and are reserved for a particular type of information. In the example in Figure 1-1, the field for the last name is always in the upper-left corner of the address card, and it always contains a person's last name. No matter which address card you pull, you can be assured of finding a last name at that spot on the card.

Of course, in some paper databases, maintaining this level of organization can be difficult. When you are writing or typing an address card, for example, you may occasionally reverse the order of the last and first names or enter a company name in that location. Organization in informal paper databases comes exclusively from your own consistency — or lack of it.

When consistency is critical, such as when you are recording information on employees or filling out a customer invoice, records are often designed as forms. Spaces on the form have labels so that you always know which piece of information belongs where. You can still type a phone number in the space labeled "Social Security number," but at least the labels make catching and correcting mistakes easier. Forms help organize the data in much the same way that a computer-based database does. In fact, this type of paper database is frequently the basis for a computer database.

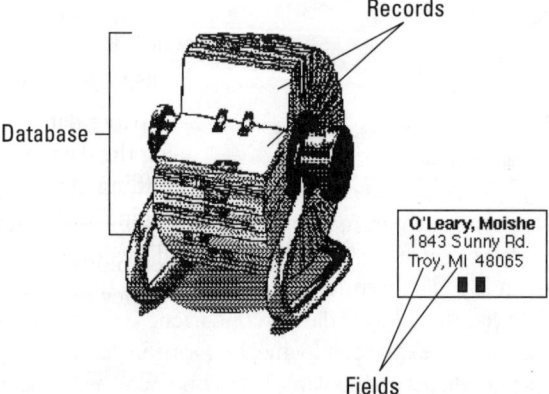

Figure 1-1: Every database is composed of records that contain fields. [Card file image from EPS Business Art, part of the ClickArt software series, courtesy of T/Maker Company.]

Paper Databases vs. Computer Databases

So what's wrong with paper databases? Many homes and businesses depend heavily on them. The following sections discuss some of the shortcomings of paper databases and explain how computer databases can avoid these limitations.

Limitations of paper databases

First, consider some of the shortcomings of paper databases:

❖ *It's easy to make data-entry errors.* When you are using a typeset form, nothing stops you from entering the wrong data in a field or forgetting to fill in a critical field, such as hire date or medical history.

❖ *Maintenance can be difficult.* For records to be easy to locate, they must be in some rational order. Whenever you return or add a record to a folder or filing cabinet, you have to be careful to place it in the correct spot. If you put the vendor file for Alpha Gamma Corp. in the *Q* folder, you may never find it again!

❖ *Updating records can be time-consuming.* Because of changes in information, such as addresses, phone numbers, and salaries, few databases are static. Updating a paper record may require several steps, including finding the record, erasing the old information, writing in the new information (or typing a whole new record), and returning the form to the filing cabinet. Making an across-the-board change — such as granting an incremental salary increase to all employees — can take a long time.

❖ *Sorting records, selecting subgroups of records, and creating reports are cumbersome tasks.* Your boss walks into your office and says, "We're thinking about putting in a day-care center. How many of our 149 employees have kids under the age of five?" Or you may be thinking of sending a direct-mail piece to your local customers. To determine printing and postage costs, you need to know how many customers are in the target zip code or are within a particular range of zip codes.

In either case, you have to examine every record in the paper database. Whenever a task requires sorting, organizing, or summarizing the data in a different way, you can look forward to a nightmare of paper shuffling. And when you're through, you have to restore all the records to their original order!

❖ *Sharing records is difficult.* When a supervisor borrows employee records, the office manager no longer has easy access to the records. They're no longer in the file drawer.

❖ *Information is hard to reuse.* If you want to use the information in a paper database for any purpose other than just reading it (addressing envelopes, for example), someone has to drag out the typewriter. (Unless you're creating a ransom note, photocopying an address and then taping it onto a letter is considered bad form.)

Advantages of computer databases

Computer databases, on the other hand, offer the following benefits:

❖ *Entering error-free information is easier.* Most database programs include many features that speed data entry. Setting *default values* for some fields can save an incredible amount of typing time and ensure that information is entered consistently. (Using *CA* as the default entry for a state field, for example, ensures that you don't end up with records that variously contain *CA*, *Calif.*, and *California* in the same field.)

Other useful data-entry features include *auto-incrementing fields* (which automatically assign invoice or record numbers to new records), *field types* (which, for example, can prevent you from entering alphabetic information in a field that was designed to record salary data), *range checking* (which accepts only numbers within a particular range), and *required fields* (which warn you if you do not fill in a critical field).

❖ *You can easily add, delete, or change data.* Making a change to a record involves only bringing the record up on-screen, editing it, and then closing the file. Because you make all changes on a computer, you don't need to search through file drawers or hunt for an eraser. And if you need additional copies of a record, you can quickly print one. As you can see, the ease with which you can *manage data* is one of the key reasons for buying and using a database program, such as FileMaker Pro.

❖ *Finding records is simple.* A Search or Find feature enables you to jump directly to the record or records of interest.

❖ *You can specify criteria for sorting data.* Arranging records in a different order is as simple as issuing a Sort command. You can rearrange records in order of zip code, salary, record creation date, or any other field that is in the database. Most database programs also enable you to simultaneously sort by multiple fields. For example, you can sort a client database by city within each state.

❖ *You can work with discrete groups of records.* Using the database program's record selection tools, you can select a subgroup of records that is based on any criteria that you want. You may, for example, want to organize recipes according to their main ingredient or group employee records according to salary ranges or by department.

❖ *Database programs can perform calculations.* Current database programs frequently offer many of the same calculation capabilities that spreadsheet programs offer. Instead of using a hand calculator to compute the sales tax and total for an invoice, you can have a database program automatically make the computations for you. In addition to performing computations within individual records, database programs also can generate summary statistics across all records or for selected groups of records. For example, you can easily summarize the efforts of different sales teams by calculating sales totals and averages by region.

Chapter 1: What Is a Database?

❖ *Many people can simultaneously access the database.* If several people in a company need to view or modify the information in a database, you can use a database program (FileMaker Pro, for example) on a network.

❖ *You can readily use information for multiple purposes.* For example, you can use the address information in records to print mailing labels, envelopes, or a pocket-sized address book, as well as to create personalized form letters.

❖ *You can create custom reports.* Only you are in a position to decide which reports are essential to running your business, department, bowling league, or home. Accounting programs, for example, typically come with a limited number of predefined reports. In most database programs, you can create your own reports and lay them out in any format that meets your information needs. Because you can save report formats on disk, you can reuse a format whenever you want to generate a current report.

❖ *You can use data from one program in another program.* Most database programs can import and export data. *Importing* enables you to bring information into the database from other programs. For example, you may already have an address book program, desk accessory, or HyperCard stack in which you've recorded the addresses of friends and business associates. Rather than retyping those addresses in your database program, you can export them from the original program (creating a file that your database program can read) and then import them into a database.

Exporting, on the other hand, enables you to use fields and records in a database to create a file that other programs can read. For example, you can easily export database information so that a word processing program, such as MacWrite Pro or Microsoft Word, can use it to generate a mail merge. Similarly, you may want to export numeric data so you can graph it with a spreadsheet program, such as Microsoft Excel.

When should you use a database program?

Although the list of reasons why computer databases are superior to paper databases is lengthy, you also need to recognize that not every database is a good candidate for computerization. Specifically, when you are deciding between using a paper database and using a computer database, you need to ask yourself the following questions. (The more *yes* answers you give, the more reasons you have for using a database program.)

1. *Will the contents of individual records change frequently?* If the information for each record is not static and editing is often necessary, choose a computer database.

2. *Is much of the information repetitive?* As mentioned previously, database programs enable you to create default entries for fields. If much of the information that you'll enter is repetitive, using a database program can help you avoid unnecessary typing.

Part I: The Fundamentals

3. *Will the records need to be grouped or sorted in different ways?* Database programs can quickly sort and select records for even very large collections of data.

4. *Will calculations be necessary?* The more complex the calculations, the more you need a database program.

5. *Will printed output be required?* Unless photocopies are satisfactory, use a database program.

6. *Will reports be necessary?* Summarizing information is a task at which database programs excel. If your reports go beyond simple record counts, a database program may be the best choice.

Flat-File and Relational Databases

Techno Trivia: You can roughly classify every database program as either *flat file* or *relational*, according to the program's relational capabilities; that is, its ability to simultaneously draw information from more than one database on the basis of shared fields.

That explanation is quite a mouthful, isn't it? A couple of definitions and an example may make it easier to swallow:

❖ A *flat-file database* always consists of a single file. All fields that are required have to be contained within that data file.

❖ A *relational database* consists of two or more interrelated data files that have one or more key fields in common.

Instead of designing a single customer database that contains all your customer information (as you would in a flat-file database program), you might create several smaller databases. One could contain just customer addresses (Addresses), and another could hold information about the customers' previous orders (Orders). To link the records in the two databases, you could assign a unique identification number to each customer. By placing the I.D. field in both data files, you can relate the two sets of information. For example, you can generate a statement from the Orders database and instruct the program to pull the customer's mailing address from the Address database (see Figure 1-2).

Both types of database programs have advantages. Conceptually, flat-file database programs are easier to understand and to learn to use. All the important data is in a single file. If you need to record additional information, you just add more fields.

Because of the multi-file approach that relational database programs use, the files tend to be smaller and, hence, faster to work with for common tasks such as sorting and searching. Because of their power and flexibility, relational database programs are frequently used for large record-keeping projects or projects that have complex requirements.

Chapter 1: What Is a Database?

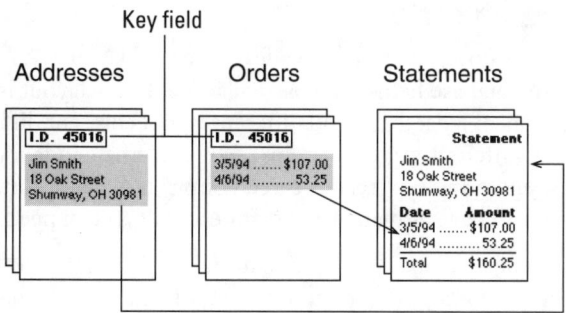

Figure 1-2: Relational database programs can create a report by extracting information from several files.

Learning to use a relational database program is difficult, however, because of the complexity of the relational concept and the fact that much of the program's power frequently comes from a programming language that you need to use to create advanced databases. In addition, designing relational databases often requires substantial planning. You must usually decide on the relational (or key) fields ahead of time and determine what data will be collected in each file. Unlike a flat-file database, a relational database is not easy to toss together.

Because this book is about FileMaker Pro, you may well be asking yourself where it fits into this classification scheme. The answer — as is often the case in discussions of computer programs — is that it's somewhere in between. Basically, FileMaker Pro is a flat-file database program with some relational capabilities. (Some people might call it a *semi-relational* program.) Specifically, you can use its Lookup feature to look up information in a secondary file and then use that information in the current file. Although FileMaker Pro is not as flexible or as speedy as most fully relational database programs, its ease of use makes up for those limitations.

Introducing FileMaker Pro

Even before you sit down to try out FileMaker Pro, it's important that you understand a few key concepts and features. Although all database programs have much in common with each other (as explained earlier in this chapter), FileMaker Pro has distinct ways of doing things that clearly distinguish it from other programs. (These differences explain — at least partially — why FileMaker Pro has long been the database program of choice for Macintosh users and is making great strides in the Windows world.) The remainder of this chapter provides an introduction to these key concepts and an explanation of how FileMaker Pro can effectively be used to tackle many database requirements — both in the business and home user arenas.

Part I: The Fundamentals

Understanding layouts

Much of FileMaker Pro's power comes from a feature called layouts. A *layout* is an arrangement of a set of database fields for a particular file. Every layout is a view or window into the contents of a database, and different layouts present different views (frequently using different groups of fields). You can create individual layouts for doing data entry, generating reports (on-screen or printed), and printing labels or envelopes. And you can have as many layouts for each file as you need.

Whenever you create a new database and define its fields, FileMaker Pro automatically generates a layout that is a standard arrangement of all the fields that you have defined (see Figure 1-3). If a quick-and-dirty database is all you need, you can use this layout to start entering data immediately.

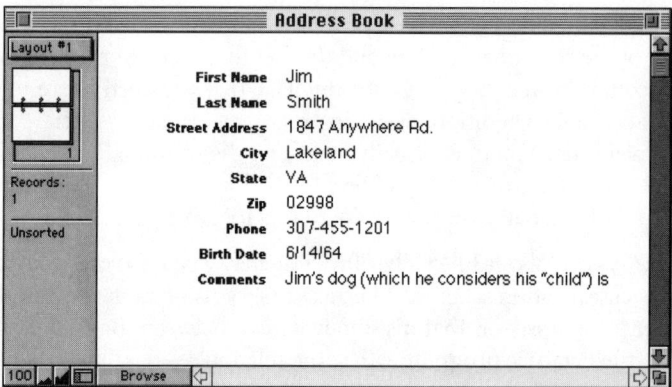

Figure 1-3: A standard database layout.

On the other hand, you can customize any layout by doing any of the following:

❖ Changing the placement of fields (to create a columnar report, for example)

❖ Eliminating fields from the layout that you do not want to display (you can still use them in other layouts)

❖ Removing some or all of the field labels or moving the labels to different positions (field labels are not attached to fields)

❖ Embellishing the layout by adding text and graphics and by modifying the font, style, color, pattern, or border for fields

❖ Adding or removing layout parts (which are explained later in this chapter) to eliminate parts that are not needed or to add new ones that display summary statistics or present information that repeats on every page

Chapter 1: What Is a Database?

Figure 1-4 shows a custom layout for the same database as the one shown in Figure 1-3. The data-entry screen is more attractive because of the rearrangement of the fields, changes in font sizes and styles, and the addition of color. The ability to produce custom layouts is one of the many features that attracts users to FileMaker Pro.

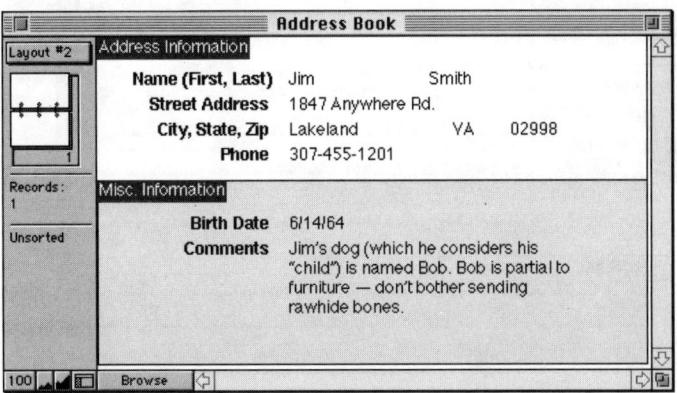

Figure 1-4: A custom layout.

Every layout that you create for a database is separate from every other layout, but it draws from the same set of fields. When you design a new layout, you select only the fields that you need. In a customer database, for example, you can use one layout to display invoice information, such as the customer's name, address, items or services purchased, and a total. A second layout may contain only name and address information that is formatted as a mailing label. You can create a third layout to print or display a client phone book that shows monthly purchase totals. Figure 1-5 shows three different layouts for the same database.

No practical restrictions limit the number of fields you can use in a layout. Data-entry screens, for example, frequently have many fields so that you can easily enter all important information for a record in a single layout. At the other extreme, a Help screen layout may contain only static text — no fields at all.

As you design layouts for a database, you may often need to create additional fields that are specific to a single layout. For example, a summary field that shows total sales by city may be helpful in a report layout but unnecessary (or pointless) in a data-entry or address label layout. Similarly, you do not have to include every field that you define in any layout at all. You may want to create a field to use only as a test for a calculation (determining whether another field is blank, for example) and not place it on any layout.

Keep in mind that data that you enter in one layout automatically appears in any other layouts that use those same fields. Although you can — and usually will — create an all-encompassing layout for data entry, you can use the other layouts for data entry too.

Part I: The Fundamentals

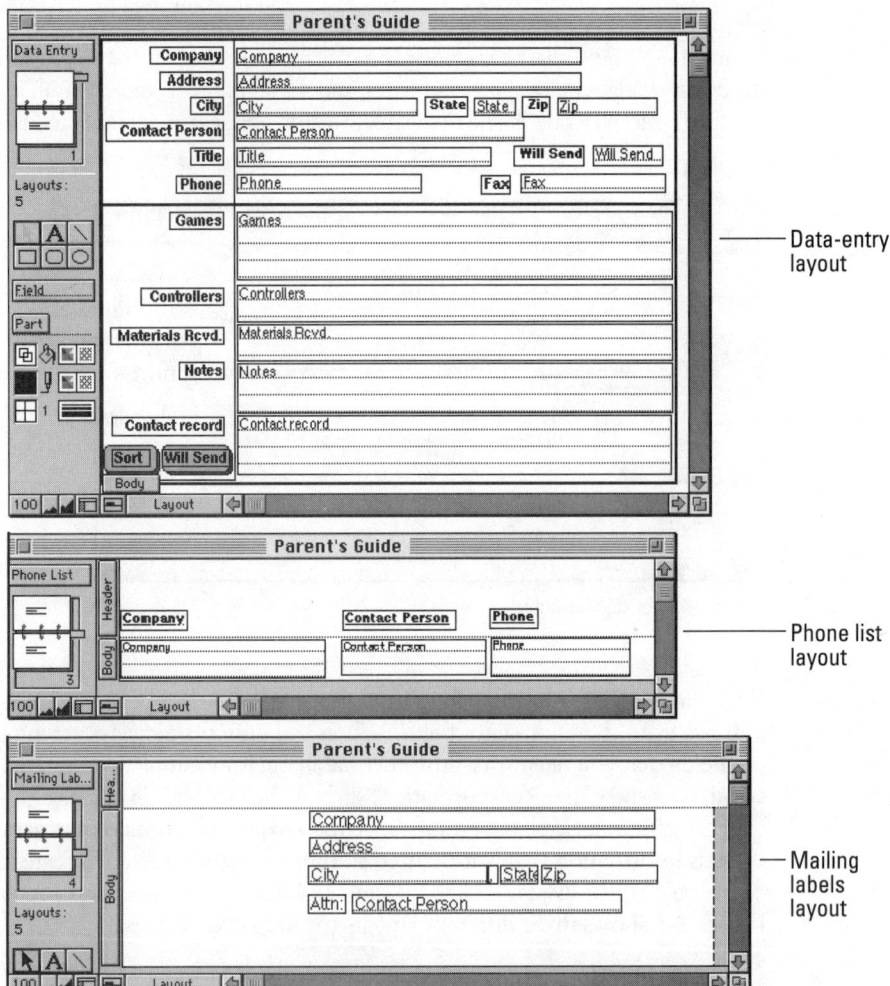

Figure 1-5: Layouts for data entry, a phone book, and mailing labels.

Because you can make new layouts whenever you like — even after a database contains records — you can design additional reports, labels, and data-entry screens as the need arises. And if you didn't originally remember to create a field that is critical to a new layout, you can just add fields as you need them.

Remember the following critical points about layouts:

❖ Every database can have as many different layouts as you need.

❖ Every layout can use as many or as few of the defined fields as you like.

- ❖ A database can have fields that are not included in any layout.
- ❖ As with the process of defining new fields, you can create or modify layouts whenever the need presents itself.

Understanding layout parts

Layouts are divided into parts. Like a word processing document, a layout can have, for example, a body, a header, and a footer. Each of these elements is a *part*. Every part can contain fields from the database, graphics, static text, and other embellishments. (As you will learn in Chapter 5, information in some parts is visible both on-screen and in reports, but you can see information in other parts only when you print a report or use the Preview command.)

The following layout parts are available to you in FileMaker Pro:

- ❖ *Title header and title footer:* This special header or footer appears only on the first page of a report, and substitutes for any other header or footer part that has been defined for the layout.
- ❖ *Header and footer:* Headers and footers appear at the top or bottom, respectively, of every page of a report or other type of layout. (If you create a title header or footer, it takes precedence on the first page of the report.) Page numbers, logos, and the current date are popular items to place in a header or footer.
- ❖ *Body:* Unlike the other layout parts, information in the body appears for every record in the database. For this reason, you normally place most fields in the body.
- ❖ *Sub-summaries:* You use sub-summary parts to summarize groups of related records after you have sorted the database by the contents of a particular field. For example, after sorting an address database by city, you can use a sub-summary field to display a count of records in each city. Sub-summaries can appear above or below each group of records, and they are visible only in *Preview mode* and in printed output. (Preview and other FileMaker Pro modes are discussed in the next section.)
- ❖ *Grand summaries:* Statistics that appear in a grand summary apply to all records that are currently visible (that is, they are being *browsed*). A grand summary can appear at the beginning (leading grand summary) or end (trailing grand summary) of a report, and it is visible only in Preview mode and in printed output.

When you first create a layout, it starts with only a body, header, and footer. You can remove unnecessary parts and add other parts as you like. Figure 1-6 contains a layout that has several parts. The figure illustrates the relationship between the layout and an on-screen preview of the report.

Part I: The Fundamentals

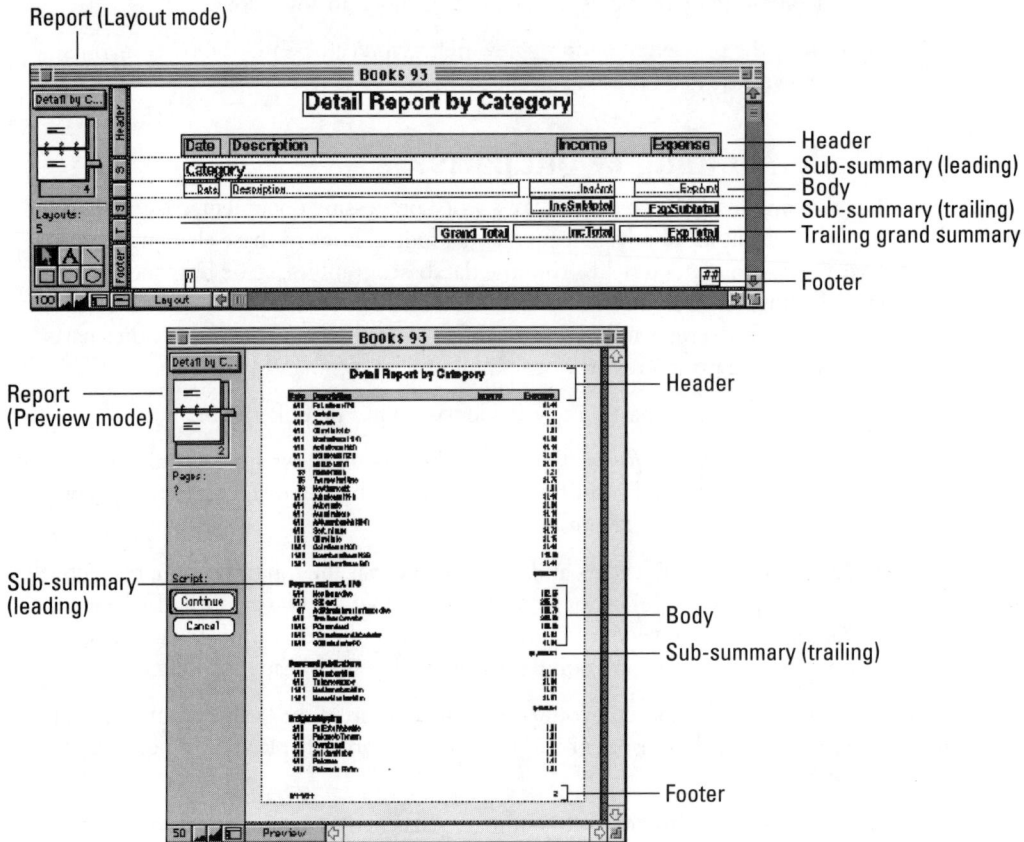

Figure 1-6: Layout parts (as defined in Layout mode and in Preview mode).

Understanding modes

FileMaker Pro has four modes of operation: Browse, Layout, Find, and Preview. The mode that you are in at any given moment governs the types of activities that you can perform:

- *Browse mode:* Use this mode to enter, edit, and delete records. (You perform all data entry in Browse mode.)

- *Layout mode:* You design, edit, or delete database layouts in Layout mode.

- *Find mode:* In Find mode, you can search for or hide records that meet criteria that you specify.

- *Preview mode:* Preview a report or layout on-screen (usually prior to printing) in the Preview mode.

Chapter 1: What Is a Database?

Preview Your Documents before Printing

When examining a report or other type of layout in Preview mode, whatever is shown on the preview screen is precisely what will be sent to the printer. If your printout doesn't look like what you expected, use Preview mode to check your changes until your printout is correct. This saves time and paper when printing to check layouts, labels, and reports, for example.

Thus, when you want to enter a new record, you first need to switch to Browse mode. To modify any portion of a layout (add or resize a graphic, for example), you have to be in Layout mode. If you're not sure what mode you're in, check the Mode indicator at the bottom of the database window.

Getting "The Big Picture"

Now that you understand what a database program is, what one can do, and how to determine when it's the right tool for the job, you may be facing a problem common to anyone who buys a new type of program. You probably wonder what *you* can do with FileMaker Pro. (Yes, many of us often purchase solutions before clearing defining the problems they were intended to solve.)

Although FileMaker Pro is a wonderful piece of technology, it's only as useful as *you* make it. And, like so many other things in life, understanding how something works is not the same as knowing *when* to use it. If you've ever taken an advanced math or statistics course, you understand what I mean. Memorizing formulas is not the same as knowing when they should be applied.

If you've already experimented with the sample files that are included with FileMaker Pro, it should be very obvious that they are not meant to serve all your database needs. (Neither are the templates included with this book, by the way.) Before long, you will be faced with the prospect of designing and using your *own* databases. And if you're new to databases, your biggest initial problem will not be learning how to use the program, but rather what to use it for.

To get you into the proper mind set, this chapter concludes with a list of uses to which FileMaker Pro can be put — some general and some very specific. Hopefully, these examples will give you some ideas for databases that you may want to create, moving you from the thinking stage to the doing stage.

Home uses for FileMaker Pro

❖ *Track a collection.* A database program is ideal for recording purchases and catalog values for any set of collectibles, such as stamps, coins, baseball cards, comic books, paintings, books, and wines. If you have a scanner, you can also include graphic images of the items in the database. (Stamp Want List — one of the templates on the enclosed disk — can be used as a starting point for your own collectibles database.)

❖ *Maintain a home inventory.* If you've ever had a large casualty loss due to a burglary, fire, or natural disaster, you understand the pressing need for documenting everything you own. An inventory database can be used to conveniently list your possessions, their serial numbers, and purchase date and cost. A similar database that merely lists insurance policies, credit cards, and other important documents (and their locations) can also be very useful.

❖ *Record credit card and checking account activity.* If you don't already have a home accounting program, you can use FileMaker Pro to create one for yourself. Every transaction (a check, deposit, charge, or payment) is treated as a separate record.

❖ *Never a lender be.* Do you have neighbors, friends, and relatives that are great at borrowing, but no so hot at returning items? Use a database to track what was lent, when, and to whom. By including a simple date calculation, you can automatically determine how long it has been since each item was lent, too. (Even if you don't throw this information in the borrowers' face — as in, "Bill, you borrowed my hedge clippers 47 days ago!" — at least you'll always know where your stuff is.)

❖ *Get a handle on your investments.* You just sold some stock. Do you remember what you paid for it? The IRS expects you to record this information in order to determine capital gains. With all its calculation capabilities, you can also use FileMaker Pro to calculate gains and losses (in dollars and percentages), number of days that a stock was held, and so on.

Business uses for FileMaker Pro

❖ *Automate your business forms.* Most businesses rely on forms, and many of these are perfect targets for databases. A petty cash voucher system is one example. Rather than just fill out a slip of paper that gets tossed into a cash box or file drawer, you can duplicate the voucher as a FileMaker Pro data entry form. Features such as date-stamping and assigning serial numbers can be automatically applied to each new voucher. And by creating appropriate report layouts, you can break down disbursements by different time periods, departments, or individuals.

Chapter 1: What Is a Database?

❖ *Improve your shipping records.* Rather than frantically search for a shipping receipt or bill of lading whenever a shipment goes awry, FileMaker Pro can help you keep track of incoming and outgoing shipments. The program's search capabilities make it easy to locate any shipment documentation that normally might just be tucked away somewhere in a file drawer. FileMaker Pro can also help you organize your receipts and create appropriate reports — grouping them and showing total shipments to each customer, for example.

❖ *Reuse existing customer data.* For many businesses, the customer list is its most valuable asset. Sadly, many businesses — both small and large — still have only paper records on their customers. Entering customer information into a database makes it possible to do mass mailings to announce sales, easily update and correct customer information (a change of address, for example), examine customer buying patterns, and determine when an additional sales call or purging from your list is necessary.

❖ *Track rental information.* Small businesses that do rentals are excellent candidates for FileMaker Pro. By creating appropriate formulas, scripts, and reports, you can instruct the program to find all rentals that are late, calculate late charges, and determine who your best customers are, for example.

❖ *Examine employee performance.* Although not the best choice for project tracking (there are many programs designed specifically for this task), you can certainly create a simple assignment-oriented database that records each assignment you hand out, due date, progress notes, and completion date. By adding fields for "quality of work," the database can help you perform (and document) the dreaded annual salary review.

❖ *Schedule company resources.* Conference rooms, audio-visual equipment, and other limited company resources are often in high demand. If you're the office manager, you may want to create a database of resource requests. By sorting by resource, date, and time, you can quickly flag duplicate requests.

CHAPTER 1: CONCEPTS AND TERMS

- Every database is composed of records, one per person or entity in the database. Records are divided into fields, which are each designed to hold one particular piece of information.

- A database program, such as FileMaker Pro, enables you to store information for rapid retrieval and organize the data in ways that are extremely cumbersome and time-consuming if attempted with a paper database.

- Paper databases are most useful when the data collected is relatively static. A database program is a better choice when data frequently changes, when you need to use the information for multiple purposes, or when you want to be able to print the information. A database program also is a better choice when you want to perform calculations or you need summary information or reports.

auto-incrementing field
A field that is automatically filled in by the database program when you create a new record. The entry in the field is based on an increment over the contents of that field in the previous record. This feature is very useful for generating new invoice numbers, check numbers, record numbers, and so on. See Chapter 5 for additional information on this capability of FileMaker Pro.

database
An organized collection of information, normally with one central topic.

database program (or database management program)
A program for entering, editing, and otherwise managing data records.

default value
A common value that is automatically entered in a field when you create a new record. Using a default value saves typing time and ensures that information is entered consistently.

export
To move a copy of selected data from one program to another. To ensure compatibility with the program that will receive the data, most programs that export data can write it in a number of different file formats. Importing data into and exporting from FileMaker Pro databases are discussed in Chapter 16.

field
Fields are the building blocks of which records are composed. Each database field is meant to store one particular type of information, such as a Social Security number or a birth date.

field type
Most database programs enable you to specify what kind of information can be entered in each field. Some common field types are text, numeric, date, time, and picture. The main reason for declaring field types is to enable the database program to screen for invalid data so that it can warn you if you have, for example, entered text in a numeric field.

Find
A command for locating a record or group of records based on criteria that you establish. For example, you may want to find the address record for Ames Corp. or identify the records of all salespeople who earned more than $40,000 last year. Most database programs enable you to set multiple criteria when performing a Find.

flat-file database
A flat-file database normally consists of a single file. Every field that is necessary has to be in that file.

import
To bring data from another program into the current program. Importing saves you the effort of needlessly retyping data.

lookup
A database feature that enables you to find (look up) information in a secondary database based on a request made in the primary database. For example, entering an inventory part number in one database can trigger a lookup of a price and description for that part in another database.

mail merge
Combining address and other personal or business information (usually from a database) with a form letter (usually created in a word processing program) to generate a series of "personalized" letters.

range checking
A database program feature that prevents input errors by making certain that each entry in a particular field is within acceptable ranges. For example, entries for student grades have to be between 0 and 4.

record
The basic unit of every database. All databases are composed of records, each storing information for a single entity, such as a person, catalog item, video tape, or recipe.

relational database program
A program in which shared key fields link information in multiple database files, enabling you to generate reports that are based on information from more than one database.

required field
A field that must contain data. Programs that support required fields warn or remind you if you leave such a field blank in the current record and then attempt to move to another record or save the file.

semi-relational database program
A database program that provides some — but not all — of the functionality of a fully relational database program. Such programs (FileMaker Pro, for example) frequently limit their relational capabilities to doing lookups in other files.

sort
To rearrange database records in a different order than the one in which they were originally entered. Most database programs can simultaneously sort on multiple fields. The more powerful database programs enable you to specify *key* or *index* fields — special sort fields that are automatically maintained by the program. Indexes are particularly useful for very large databases, where a normal sort would be extremely time consuming. (By default, FileMaker Pro indexes the contents of every field, which is why it executes Find commands so swiftly.)

CHAPTER TWO

Macintosh Essentials

- Starting up and shutting down the Macintosh
- Understanding the Macintosh desktop
- Using the mouse
- Editing text
- Working with windows
- Dealing with dialog boxes
- Printing

If you're new to the Macintosh, taking the time to get a firm grasp of Mac basics, such as understanding the desktop and using the mouse, can make using FileMaker Pro much easier. Chapter 2 is written especially for you. Although it covers much of the same material that's in the Macintosh owner's manual, this chapter stresses information that is essential for operating the Mac and running FileMaker Pro (as well as any other Macintosh program you'll ever use).

Even if you have a solid understanding of the basics, a fast read of this chapter may still be worthwhile. For example, the instructions on starting up and shutting down can save you an enormous amount of grief by preventing damage to the data on your hard disk. And the section on printing explains the meaning of those odd Page Setup options.

Starting Up and Shutting Down

You can start up and shut down the Mac in two ways — the right way or the wrong way. Starting up the correct way ensures that any external hard disks and tape drives are ready to go. Shutting down correctly makes certain that all the data that's floating around in the Mac's memory is properly written to the hard disk before you shut off the Mac and it's too late.

Problem: When his Mac had a single hard disk — one that was built into the Mac — Jim used to turn on the system by just hitting the On button on a power strip. Over time, Jim's storage needs grew, so he added an external hard disk. Now when he uses the power strip to turn everything on together, sometimes the external hard disk doesn't appear on the desktop.

Solution: External hard disks and similar devices need time to warm up before you turn on the Mac.

Problem: At the end of each work day, Bob shuts down his Mac by just cutting the power. (That's the same way he learned to shut down his PC.) For some reason, startups are now taking longer and longer, and sometimes the Mac does funny things.

Solution: Although simply turning off the power is the correct way to shut down a DOS-based PC, it's not the right way to turn off a Mac. The proper way to shut down the Mac is to select the Shut Down command from the Special menu. This gives your system a chance to do whatever "housekeeping" is necessary, such as noting which windows were open and the positions of icons, and giving the Mac a chance to save this information to your hard disk.

To start up the Macintosh, do the following:

1. **Turn on all external *SCSI* (Small Computer System Interface — pronounced *skuzzy*) devices that are connected to the Mac.**

   These devices normally include external hard disks, CD-ROM drives, tape drives, and scanners.

   A *SCSI device* is any device that is connected, either directly or in a chain, to the SCSI port on the back of the Mac. The icon that identifies the SCSI port is shown in Figure 2-1.

   Normally, you can turn other non-SCSI external devices on and off whenever you like. Check the manuals for such devices (printers and modems, for example) to be sure.

   If you don't have any external SCSI devices, you can move directly to Step 3.

Figure 2-1: The SCSI port icon.

2. **Wait for the external SCSI devices to warm up.**

   SCSI drives usually go through an audible power-up sequence. When they stop grinding, clanking, and making other interesting noises (usually within 20 to 45 seconds), they are ready to go.

3. **Flip the power switch on the back of the Mac or press the power key on the keyboard.**

   (For Macs so equipped, the power key is identified by an open triangle symbol.) The Mac goes through its normal start-up procedure.

Chapter 2: Macintosh Essentials

To shut down the Macintosh, follow these steps:

1. **When you're through with your Mac for the day, quit all programs that are currently running.**

   Normally, you do this by choosing Quit from the File menu and, optionally, saving any open files.

2. **At the desktop, choose Shut Down from the Special menu (see Figure 2-2).**

   Depending on the model of Macintosh that you have, it will either shut down automatically or display a message saying that you can now safely turn off the Mac.

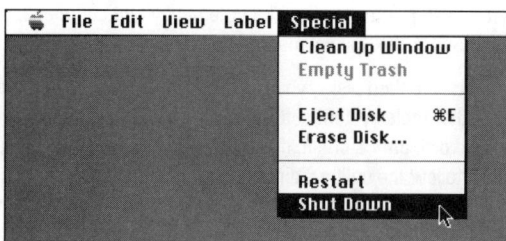

Figure 2-2: Choosing the Shut Down command

3. **If the Mac didn't shut off automatically in Step 2, you can turn its power off now by flipping its power switch to the Off position.**

4. **Turn off all external SCSI devices.**

   After you have used this procedure to shut down the Mac, you can safely turn off all external hard disks and other SCSI devices.

If you shut down the Mac by using any method other than choosing the Shut Down command (just turning off the power, for example), unfortunate consequences such as the following may result:

- ❖ Any newly created documents or data files that you did not save will be gone. Older files that you modified during the computing session but neglected to save will not contain your changes.

- ❖ If the Mac was in the process of writing information to your hard disk, that particular file may now be unreadable or contain erroneous data.

- ❖ The next time you turn on the Mac, the start-up process will take longer than usual. The system software will have to figure out what windows were open and where the various file and folder icons were located when you shut down so abruptly.

Part I: The Fundamentals

When You Can't Shut Down Normally

Sometimes you have no choice but to cut the power to the Mac or press the reset switch. An example of this situation is when the Mac crashes. (A *crash* is when the mouse pointer freezes, the current program no longer responds to the keyboard or mouse clicks, or a system crash dialog box appears, that shows a bomb icon. The Mac crashes when, for some reason, the current program or the Macintosh system software is so messed up that it's unable to continue.) In most cases, the only fix for a crash is to restart the Mac.

Sometimes, however, the Mac's "emergency quit" command can help you recover from a crash. Before giving up and pressing the Mac's reset switch, trying pressing ⌘-Option-Esc. A dialog box appears, offering you the option of forcing the current program to quit. If you successfully quit the program, you will lose any document changes that you haven't saved. However, the Mac may still be functioning well enough to enable you to save open files in other programs that are running. After you use the emergency quit command, you should quit all programs and select the Restart command in the Special menu.

Because a crash can occasionally wreak havoc with hard disks, you may want to use a utility program — such as Disk First Aid (free with your copy of the Apple system software), Norton Utilities, Public Utilities, or Central Point MacTools — to examine the hard disk after a crash. If any damage has occurred, these utilities may be able to correct it. (Be sure to carefully follow the utilities' directions. Used improperly, they can sometimes cause problems of their own.) Improved crash recovery is also an excellent reason for regularly backing up important data files, as discussed at the end of this chapter.

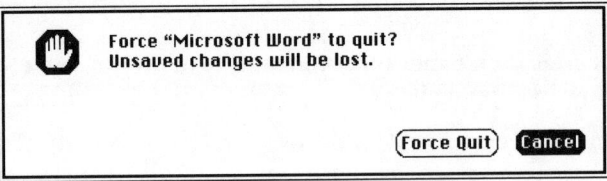

The Macintosh Desktop

When you first turn on the Mac, you see the *desktop*, which is sort of a Command Central for Mac operations. Here you perform many disk-related and file-related activities, such as making copies of disks and files, erasing disks, deleting files, formatting disks (preparing them so they're ready to receive data), creating folders in which to organize files, and selecting programs to run. Figure 2-3 points out some of the key components of the desktop.

Chapter 2: Macintosh Essentials

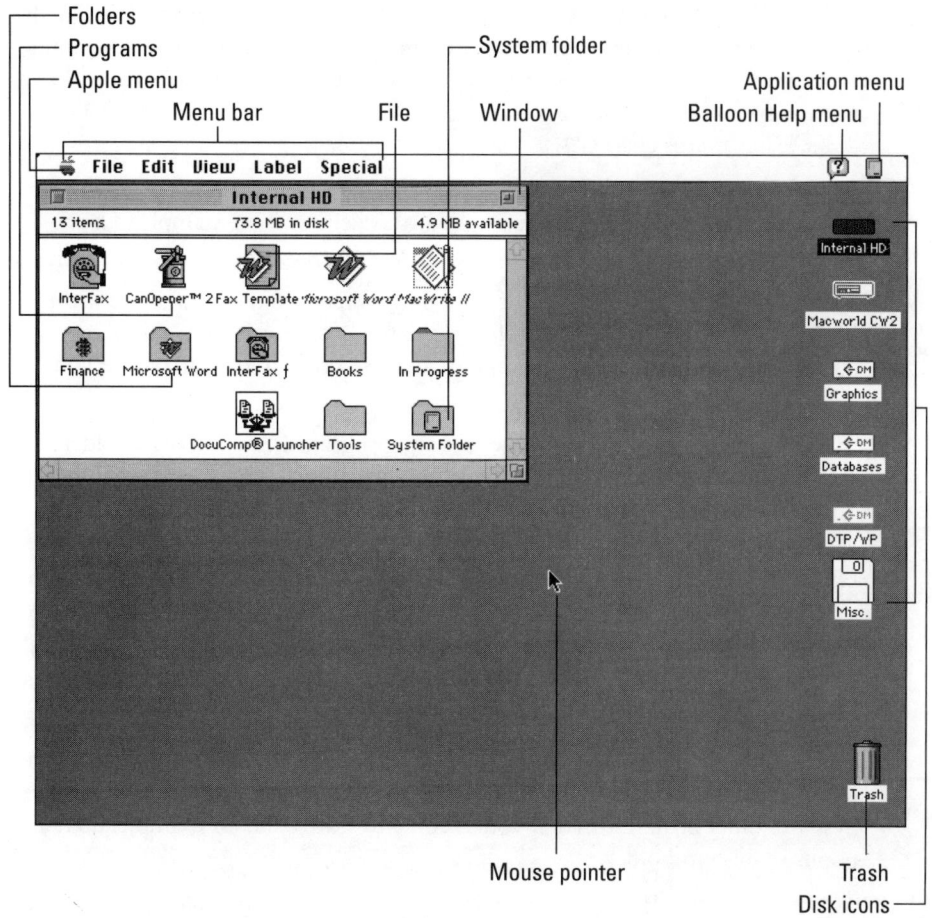

Figure 2-3: The Macintosh desktop.

- ❖ *Menu bar:* Whether you're at the desktop or working within a program, you always see a set of menus across the top of the screen. Click any menu name to view and select from the commands that appear.

- ❖ *Apple menu:* The apple icon sits atop a very special menu. Click it to examine and use desk accessories (mini programs) that you've installed. You sometimes invoke Help information for the current program from the Apple menu, too.

  In System 7, you also can put programs, important data files, and folders in the Apple menu by simply dropping their icons (or *aliases* of their icons) into the Apple Menu Items folder within the System Folder. (For information on creating aliases, see "System 7 Bonus: Making Aliases," at the end of this chapter.)

Part I: The Fundamentals

- *Window:* Any open disk or folder is represented by a rectangular window like the one shown for the Internal HD hard disk in Figure 2-3. When you are running a program such as FileMaker Pro, each document that you open also is enclosed in a window. (For more information about windows, see "Working with Windows," later in this chapter.)

- *Programs or applications:* A program (often called an *application*) is a set of instructions that performs a computer task. A word processor is an example of a program.

- *File:* A file contains information of some sort. Databases that you create within FileMaker Pro are files, as are preference data; help information; and other documents that come with the program, that are created for you, or that you create in different programs.

- *Folders:* You use folders to organize files and programs. You can place folders inside other folders, nested as deeply as you like, in order to achieve the level of organization that you desire. (On a PC, folders are called *directories* and *subdirectories*.)

- *System Folder:* The System Folder is a special folder that contains the Macintosh system software (the System, Finder, fonts, and other important files). When you, Apple, or your dealer installed the system software on your Mac, a System Folder was automatically created. The presence of a System Folder makes a disk *bootable* (that is, you can use it to start up the Mac).

  You must have only one System Folder per disk — whether it's a hard disk or a floppy. And only disks that have to be able to start up the Mac need to have a System Folder at all. Disks that you use only to store data, for example, do not require a System Folder.

- *Balloon Help menu:* If you are running System 7, you see this balloon icon. When you click it, a special menu appears that enables you to turn balloon help on or off. When balloon help is on and the mouse pointer moves over an object that has help information attached to it, a cartoon-style balloon that contains help information appears (see Figure 2-4).

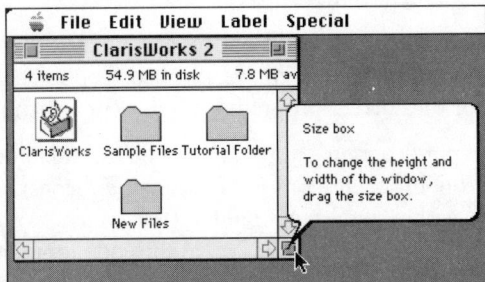

Figure 2-4: An example of balloon help.

Chapter 2: Macintosh Essentials

❖ *Application menu:* If you're running System 6 with *MultiFinder* or are using System 7, you see a tiny icon in the upper-right corner of the screen — whether you're at the desktop or are running a program. This icon is the Application menu, and you use it to switch between programs that are currently running.

With System 6, you switch between open programs by simply clicking the Application menu icon. Each time you click, the Mac cycles to the next open program.

If you are using System 7, click the Application menu icon to view a menu of the programs and desk accessories that are running. To switch to any of these programs or desk accessories, choose it from the Application menu (shown in Figure 2-5).

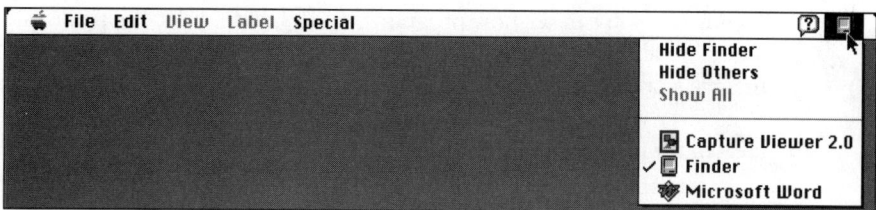

Figure 2-5: The Application menu (System 7 only).

❖ *Disk icons:* Every disk drive that is connected to the Mac — whether the drive is internal or external — is represented by an icon that appears on the desktop. Any disk that has a visible icon is referred to as *mounted*. Disk drives that use *removable* media (floppy drives, removable hard disk drives, and CD-ROM drives, for example) appear on the desktop only when a disk has been inserted into them. Note that floppy disks (such as Misc., in Figure 2-3) have icons that clearly distinguish them from hard disks.

You should note that some types of drives, such as tape drives, never appear on the desktop. The reason that tape drives do not appear on the desktop is that, normally, you cannot directly access them from the desktop. You need to run a special tape backup program to gain access to the information that's stored on the tape.

❖ *Trash:* The Trash can serves two purposes. First, if you want to *delete* a file (erase it), you drag its icon to the Trash and then choose Empty Trash from the Special menu. Second, to remove a disk from the desktop (usually a floppy, CD-ROM, or a removable hard disk), you drag its icon to the Trash. Unlike trashing a file, this procedure does not erase the disk. It merely removes its icon from the desktop and then automatically ejects the disk (floppy disks and CD-ROMs, for example) or enables you to manually remove other types of disks, such as removable hard disks.

❖ *Mouse pointer:* The mouse pointer (shaped like an arrowhead) tracks the position of the mouse. You use it to select objects in programs and to perform desktop activities such as dragging files to the Trash and choosing menu commands.

Almost everything on the desktop is represented by an *icon* (a pictorial symbol). In Figure 2-3, you can see how programs, folders, hard disks, floppy disks, and the Trash are all represented by icons. Programs and data documents have their distinctive icons assigned to them by the programmers who write the programs. Whenever you save a new document with a program, a special icon is automatically created for it.

Actions that you perform on icons affect the data files, programs, folders, or disks that they represent. On a PC running DOS, to copy a file to a directory on a different drive, you may type something like this:

```
C> COPY MEMO.DOC D:\WP\DOCS
```

To perform the same copy on a Mac, all you need to do is use the mouse to select the MEMO file and then drag it to where you want the copy to go. One simple action . . . nothing to type, no commands to remember. This visual, icon-oriented work environment is what makes the Macintosh so easy to use.

Using the Mouse

The mouse is key to most operations on the Mac. On the desktop, you'll see a tiny arrowhead-shaped pointer, which is known as the *mouse pointer*. The mouse pointer moves as you move the mouse. As you perform different actions on the Mac, you'll notice that the pointer frequently changes shape. When you are typing in a word processing document, for example, the pointer may appear as a straight vertical line. When you want to move the insertion point (to type somewhere else in the document), the pointer is shown as an I-beam. If you move the mouse pointer outside the document window, it changes into a pointer. When a program is performing a lengthy process (sorting a large database, for example), the pointer may change into an icon of a watch or a spinning beach ball. The pointer changes shape to indicate that you are performing a different type of operation.

The two basic operations that you perform with the mouse are *clicking* and *dragging*. All mouse operations involve one or both of these actions.

Chapter 2: Macintosh Essentials

To *click* means to press the mouse button once and then release it. To *drag*, you press and hold the mouse button while you move the mouse pointer to a different on-screen location. The following sections describe a few of the most common mouse maneuvers.

Using the mouse to select items

Launching programs, copying files, opening folders, pulling down menus, and almost everything else that you do on the desktop involves selecting items. You have to select an item before you can do anything with it. To select an item on the desktop (or an object in most programs), do the following:

1. **Move the mouse to position the pointer over the item that you want to select.**

2. **Click the mouse button once.**

   The item turns black to indicate that it has been selected. (When you are selecting an object in a program, a FileMaker Pro field in Layout mode, for example, small dots called *handles* may appear at the corners of the object to show that it is selected.)

To select multiple items on the desktop, follow these steps:

1. **Hold down the Shift key and click once on each item that you want to select.**

   — or —

1. **Click once outside the area where the items are located and, while continuing to hold down the mouse button, drag a rectangle around or through the items that you want to select (see Figure 2-6).**

   The rectangle, which is composed of tiny dots, is called a *marquee*.

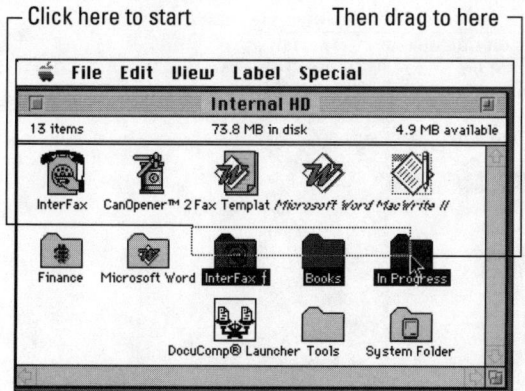

Figure 2-6: Dragging to select.

Part I: The Fundamentals

This technique is an example of dragging. Again, to drag, you move the mouse while holding down the mouse button. When you are working on the desktop, you need to make sure that the selection rectangle touches each item that you want to include in the selection. In some programs, however, you need to make sure that items are completely *surrounded* by the marquee.

Using the mouse to choose menu commands

Another common example of dragging is choosing menu commands — both on the desktop and within programs. To choose a menu command, follow these steps:

1. **Move the mouse until you position the pointer over the menu that you want to open.**
2. **Click the menu name (File or Edit, for example) and continue to hold down the mouse button.**

   The menu name turns black, and the menu drops down, exposing the commands that the menu contains. (Note that some of the commands in the figure are grayed out — meaning that they cannot currently be chosen.)

3. **While continuing to hold down the mouse button, drag the pointer down until the command that you want to choose is *highlighted* (that is, until it turns black).**
4. **Without moving the mouse, release the mouse button.**

   The command executes.

   If you change your mind and decide *not* to choose a command, continue to hold down the mouse button while you drag the pointer away from the menu area, as shown in Figure 2-7. Then release the mouse button. As long as a command is not highlighted when you release the mouse button, the command does not execute.

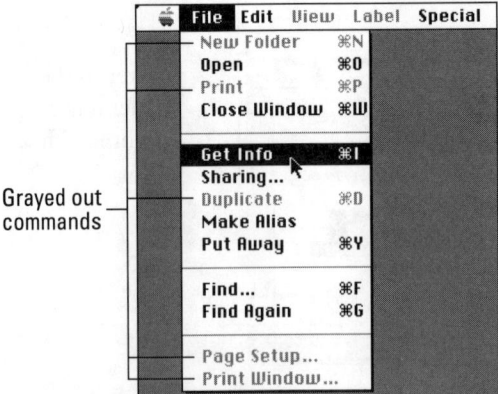

Figure 2-7: Selecting a menu command.

Chapter 2: Macintosh Essentials

If you browse through some menus, you'll notice that some commands are *grayed out* (gray). You cannot choose commands when they are grayed out; the pointer merely slides over them without highlighting them. Usually, grayed-out commands are irrelevant to the current state of the program or the desktop. For example, the Empty Trash command in the Special menu is grayed out if the Trash is empty. A program's Save command may be grayed out if you don't have a file open or if you have just saved a file.

Some programs also have *hierarchical menus* (also known as *pop-up menus* or *submenus*) that are often indicated by a triangle symbol. The Spelling command in FileMaker Pro's Edit menu is an example of this type of menu. When you choose such a command, another menu appears with a set of commands from which you can choose.

To choose a command from a hierarchical or pop-up menu, do the following:

1. **Move the mouse until you position the pointer over the menu that you want to open.**

2. **Click the menu name (FileMaker Pro's Edit menu, for example) and continue to hold down the mouse button.**

   The menu name turns black, and the menu drops down, exposing the commands that it contains.

3. **While continuing to hold down the mouse button, drag the pointer down until the hierarchical command that you want to choose is highlighted (Spelling, for example).**

   The list of choices for the command appears usually to the left or right of the menu.

4. **Drag the mouse pointer into the set of pop-up commands and highlight the one you want.**

5. **Without moving the mouse, release the mouse button. The pop-up command executes.**

Dialog boxes (discussed in "Dealing with Dialog Boxes," later in the chapter) also may incorporate pop-up menus. An example of a pop-up menu in a dialog box can be seen when choosing FileMaker Pro's Save a Copy as command from the File menu (see Figure 2-24).

Part I: The Fundamentals

Keyboard Shortcuts for Menu Commands

Both on the desktop and within programs, some menu commands list an unusual propeller-like symbol that is followed by a letter, number, or character. This symbol is the *Command* symbol, and it appears on most keyboards as ⌘ or . In addition to choosing these menu commands with the mouse, you can use the Command-key combination that is shown in the menu to issue the command directly from the keyboard — without using the mouse. For example, on the desktop, you can close the active window by holding down the Command key and pressing W. You can request information about a file by selecting it and pressing ⌘-I. Most program manuals refer to these Command-key combinations as *keyboard shortcuts*, *keyboard equivalents*, or *Command-key equivalents*.

Some programs, particularly the more powerful ones like FileMaker Pro, also use the Shift key in combination with the Command key to expand the number of keyboard shortcuts that the program offers. In FileMaker Pro, ⌘-D creates a duplicate of the current record, and Shift-⌘-D pops up the Define Fields dialog box. Some programs also define operations for the *function keys* (labeled F1 through F15 at the top of some keyboards). The operations assigned to different key combinations can vary widely from one program to the next. Refer to the program manuals for information about the keyboard shortcuts.

Although you never *have* to use keyboard shortcuts, the more experienced you become with a program, the more likely you are to begin using the shortcuts. For instance, using ⌘-S to execute FileMaker Pro's Sort command is considerably quicker than taking your hands off the keyboard and reaching for your mouse to choose the same command from a menu.

Double-clicking

Some Mac operations require a *double-click*, rather than a single click. You can double-click a program icon on the desktop to run the program. Double-clicking a document icon normally launches its creating program and then automatically opens the file for you. Double-clicking a word in a word processor selects the entire word for further editing, such as changing the font or text style. In many programs, double-clicking an object displays a dialog box that you can use to modify that object. In a charting program, for example, double-clicking a graph element may bring up a color and pattern dialog box.

To double-click an object, do the following:

1. **Position the pointer over the icon, object, or text item.**
2. **Rapidly press the mouse button twice in succession.**

Some programs support other mouse commands, such as clicking and dragging while holding down a modifier key (⌘, Shift, or Option). In some word processors, triple-clicking selects an entire sentence or paragraph. Check the program manuals for details.

Chapter 2: Macintosh Essentials   37

Getting the Mouse to Recognize Double-Clicks

If you find that the Mac isn't responding correctly to double-clicks, you're probably taking too much time between clicks — making the Mac think that you've executed two single clicks rather than one double-click. You can adjust double-click speed in the Mouse control panel by performimg the steps that follow this sidebar.

To adjust the double-click speed, follow these steps:

1. **Choose Control Panels from the Apple menu.**
2. **Under System 6, click the scroll bar until you see the Mouse icon and then click the icon to select it.**

   — or —

2. **Under System 7, double-click the Mouse control panel icon.**
3. **If you tend to click slowly, select the option on the left by clicking its radio button.**

   The Mouse control panel, shown in Figure 2-8, supports three double-click speeds. The middle option is normal speed, and the one on the right is the fastest setting.

4. **Close the control panel by clicking the close box in the upper-left corner.**

   Any changes that you've made take effect immediately.

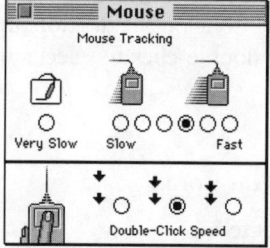

Figure 2-8: The Mouse control panel.

Part I: The Fundamentals

Basic Text Editing

Whether you are typing in a word processing, spreadsheet, or database document, entering text in a dialog box, or simply renaming an icon, the Mac has its own distinctive conventions for text editing. This section contains the essentials of text editing.

Entering text

The most basic activity in any program that includes text is entering the text. To enter text, do the following:

1. **Move the pointer to where you want to begin typing.**

2. **Click once.**

   The pointer positions itself where you clicked.

3. **Begin typing.**

Selecting text

Before you can act on text (cut it, change the font or style, and so on), you first have to select the text. You can select it in two different ways. After positioning the pointer at either the start or end of the intended selection, do one of the following:

❖ Drag to complete the selection.

❖ Press the Shift key and then click at the other end of the selection.

The selected text — like a selected menu command — is highlighted, as shown in Figure 2-9. You can extend a text selection by pressing Shift again and clicking in an area beyond the selection.

Many programs also offer additional text-selection shortcuts. One shortcut that you can use almost anywhere — including in editing done on the desktop, in dialog boxes, and in FileMaker Pro data fields — is to double-click to select a word. To select a word, follow these steps:

1. **Position the pointer over the word.**

   (You can position the pointer *anywhere* over the word.)

2. **Double-click, and the entire word is selected.**

Chapter 2: Macintosh Essentials

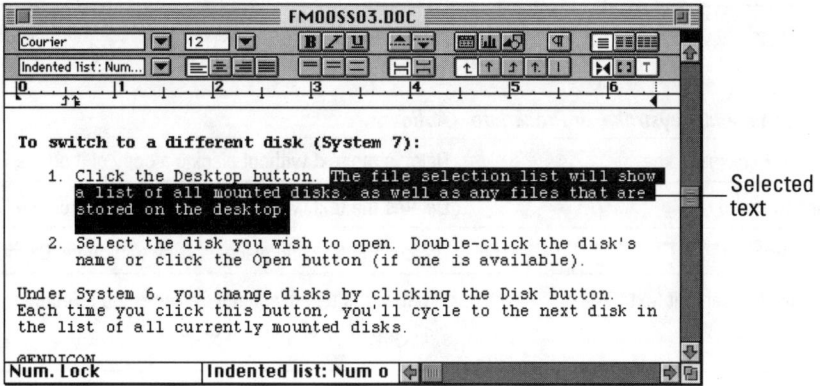

Selected text

Figure 2-9: Selected text.

About the Macintosh Clipboard

Text or objects that you copy (⌘-C) or cut (⌘-X) are copied to the *Clipboard*, a temporary storage area in the Mac's memory. Whatever you have copied or cut remains in the Clipboard and is available for pasting (⌘-V) until you either cut or copy something else or shut down the Mac.

You can paste the contents of the Clipboard elsewhere in the same document, in a different document, or even in a document that you create in another program. Because of this capability, you'll frequently use the Paste commands to move information from the Clipboard to another document in the same program or a different program.

Deleting text

You can delete individuals characters by positioning the pointer in the text and then pressing the Delete or Backspace key. Each time you press the key, you delete the character to the immediate left of the pointer. Although this approach is fine for eliminating typos and other small strings of text (and is how you may have learned to correct errors on a typewriter), the Mac provides several more powerful and efficient means for deleting bigger text segments.

To delete a larger section of text (a phrase, sentence, or paragraph, for example), use one of the text selection methods described previously and then issue one of the commands or perform one of the procedures listed in Table 2-1:

Table 2-1
Procedures for Deleting Text

Menu Command, Keystroke, or Procedure	Action
Delete or Backspace key	Deletes the text without placing a copy of it on the Clipboard
Clear command	Deletes the text without placing a copy of it on the Clipboard
Cut command (⌘-X)	Deletes the text and places a copy of it on the Clipboard
Type the replacement text	Whatever is typed instantly replaces the selected text without placing a copy of it on the Clipboard

If you don't intend to reuse the text, the deletion method doesn't matter. If you want to paste the text into another spot in the document, into a different document, or into another program, use the Cut command (⌘-X).

Note that some programs also enable you to use a key marked *Del* to delete text. (This key does not appear on all keyboards.) When its use is supported by the program, the Del key deletes the character to the immediate *right* of the pointer, which is the opposite of the function that the Delete and Backspace keys perform.

Copying text

To copy selected text, press ⌘-C or choose Copy from the Edit menu. In many programs, you also can use this command to copy selected objects. A copy of the text or object is stored in the Clipboard and is immediately available for pasting. For example, to avoid a little typing, you can copy address information from a FileMaker Pro database record and then paste it into a letter that you're writing in your word processing program. You should note that because the copied text remains in the Clipboard until you Copy or Cut something else to replace it, you can paste the copied material *repeatedly* if you like — making several copies of a picture of a tree to create your own forest, for instance.

Pasting text

After you have copied or cut some text to the Clipboard, you can paste it into a document in the same program or in a different program.

To paste text, do the following:

1. **Move the pointer over the area where you want to paste the text.**
2. **Click once to position the pointer.**
3. **Select Paste from the Edit menu (or press ⌘-V).**

    The contents of the Clipboard are pasted at the current pointer location.

The procedure for pasting an object is similar to the procedure for pasting text. Note, however, that some programs may not have an option that you can use to specify the *location* in which you want the object to be pasted.

Working with Windows

No matter what kind of work you're doing on the Mac, chances are good that you're doing it in a window. A *window* is a rectangular box that presents information. Program documents, such as word processing files and databases, are displayed in windows. When you double-click a disk or folder icon on the desktop, the files and other folders that it contains are displayed in a window. The system software communicates with you by placing information in windows such as *alert boxes* (which present warnings that you must acknowledge — for example, a notification that you're running out of memory) and *dialog boxes* (which offer choices for handling a situation or the opportunity to set options). For more information on alert boxes and dialog boxes, see "Dealing with Dialog Boxes," the next section of this chapter.

Windows come in all shapes and sizes. Figure 2-10 shows examples of common types of windows. (*Windoids* have begun to appear in the last few years. Programs frequently use these miniature windows to display palettes for setting colors, gradients, patterns, sizes, and the positions of objects.)

Regardless of the type of window, working with them requires only that you understand what their various components do and how to interact with them. The parts of a typical window are shown in Figure 2-11, and an explanation follows.

- ❖ *Title bar:* The horizontal bar at the top of a window that shows the name of the window's contents (a filename or a dialog box's function, for example). You can move a window that has a title bar by dragging the title bar.

- ❖ *Close box:* Click this small box in the window's upper-left corner to close the window. (In many programs, you also can choose a Close command in the File menu or press ⌘-W.)

- ❖ *Size box:* Drag in the box in the lower-right corner of a window to change the size of the window.

- ❖ *Zoom box:* Click this box in the upper-right corner of a window to expand the window to its maximum size. A second click returns the window to its original size.

Part I: The Fundamentals

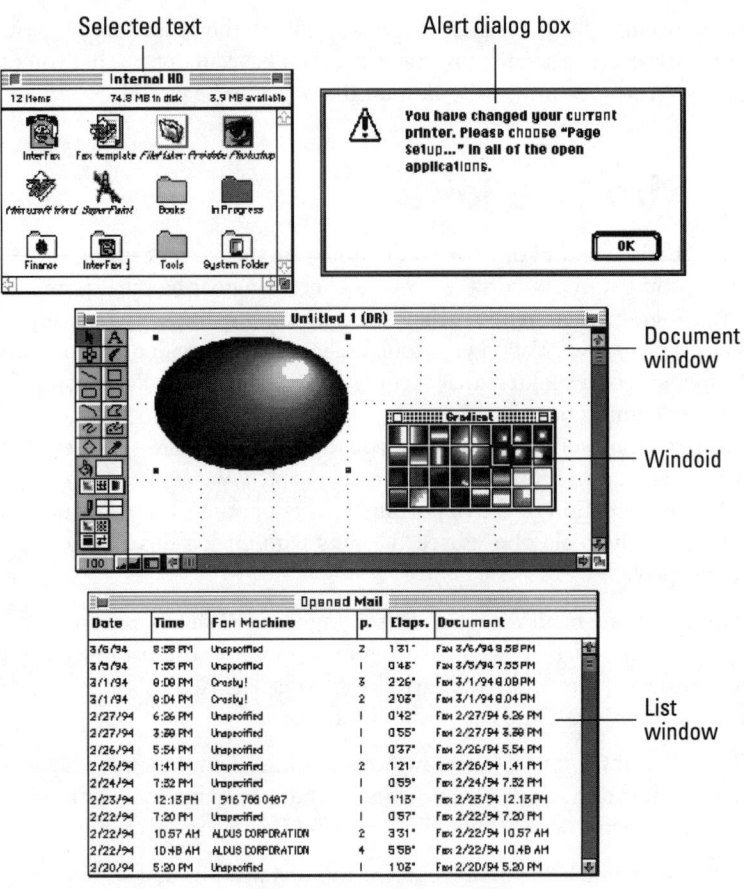

Figure 2-10: Some types of windows that you may encounter

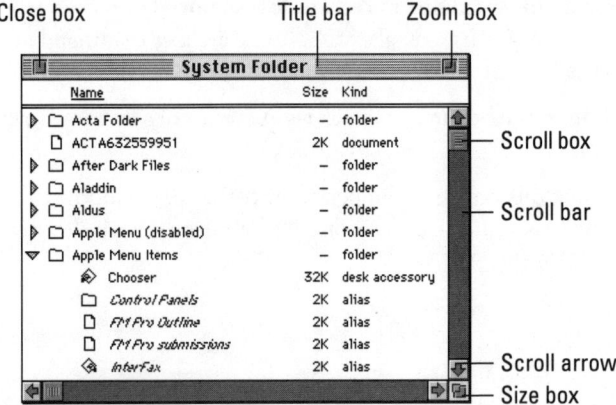

Figure 2-11: Window components.

Chapter 2: Macintosh Essentials

❖ *Scroll bar:* A rectangular bar along the right or bottom of a window. Clicking or dragging in the scroll bar changes your view of the document.

❖ *Scroll box:* The box in a scroll bar. The position of the scroll box in the scroll bar indicates the position of what's in the window relative to the entire document. Dragging the scroll box causes the document's contents to scroll opposite to the direction dragged.

❖ *Scroll arrow:* An arrow at either end of a scroll bar. When you click a scroll arrow, the scroll box moves toward the arrow you're clicking, but the window's contents move in the opposite direction. This is to simulate the movement of the window itself, rather than the contents of the window. For example, if you click the down-arrow, it seems that the window is moving down the page; therefore, the contents of the window move up. Positioning the mouse pointer over a scroll arrow and pressing and holding down the mouse button moves a document continuously (as though you had clicked the arrow repeatedly).

Keep in mind that programmers are free to include or exclude window components as their needs dictate. You'll frequently find program windows that contain some, but not all, of the standard components. Not all windows have a close box, for example. The key, however, is that when you encounter a new type of window, the elements that *are* present should work the same and appear in the same location as they do in other windows with which you're already familiar.

Dealing with Dialog Boxes

Whether you're selecting menu commands from the desktop or working in a program such as FileMaker Pro, you'll frequently be confronted by dialog boxes. A *dialog box* is a special window in which you select options, answer questions, and communicate choices to programs and the system software. At its simplest, a dialog box may present a single question and buttons for Yes, No, and Cancel or for OK and Cancel. To respond to such a dialog box (see Figure 2-12), click the button that corresponds to your choice.

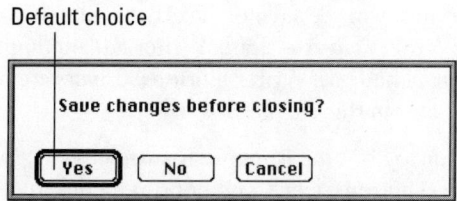

Figure 2-12: This dialog box may appear if you close a document before saving changes. Note the thick border around the default option.

Part I: The Fundamentals

Dialog Box Shortcuts

In almost any dialog box, you can select buttons by using two keyboard shortcuts. To select the Cancel option, press ⌘-. (period). To accept the default option (the button surrounded by the thick border), press either Return or Enter. (*Techno Trivia:* In some programs, you can also type the first letter of a choice to select a dialog box element. When you get tired of dragging your mouse around, try it and see what happens!)

Perhaps the simplest form of dialog box is the *alert box*. An alert box warns about a potentially dangerous situation or reports an error or an important event that has just occurred. Figure 2-13 is an example of an alert box. Typically, an alert box has a single button. After reading the message, click the button to dismiss the alert box.

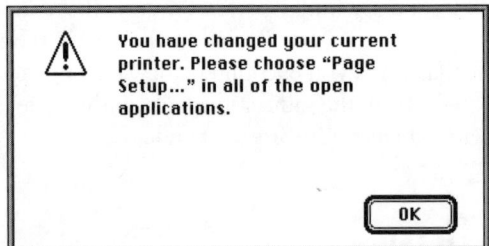

Figure 2-13: An alert box.

Some dialog boxes enable you to set multiple options at one time. The Text Format dialog box in FileMaker Pro is an example of such a dialog box.

Common dialog box elements

To see some of the common features that are included in dialog boxes, examine the Page Setup dialog box. Choose Page Setup from the File menu to display the dialog box. If you have a LaserWriter, you see a dialog box that is like the one shown in Figure 2-14. (Newer LaserWriter *drivers* — LaserWriter 8.0 and higher — use a different Page Setup dialog box. The LaserWriter 8 printer drivers are discussed in detail in "A Printing Primer," later in this chapter.)

The LaserWriter Page Setup dialog box incorporates many elements, such as radio buttons, text boxes, check boxes, buttons, icons, and pop-up menus, that are common in dialog boxes. Here's how each element works:

Chapter 2: Macintosh Essentials

- *Radio buttons:* Radio buttons present a group of mutually-exclusive choices. That is, only one radio button can be selected at a time. In the Page Setup dialog box, paper size choices are presented as radio buttons.

  To select a radio button option, click once in the circle beside your choice. A black dot appears in the radio button to denote that the item has been selected. Notice that when you choose a radio-button item, the previously selected radio button will change to an empty circle to indicate that it is no longer selected.

- *Text boxes:* A text box is a box in which you type an entry. The Reduce or Enlarge box is an example of a text box. In most cases, you also can use standard editing techniques, such as cutting and pasting, in text boxes.

- *Check boxes:* Like radio buttons, check boxes are presented as a group. However, the items are not mutually exclusive; you can select as many as you like. Clicking in a check box toggles the current state of the box. If it was checked, it becomes unchecked. If it was unchecked, it becomes checked.

- *Icons:* Dialog boxes occasionally use icons to display options. In Figure 2-14, two icons — one normal and one sideways — show portrait and landscape paper orientations. This pair of icons is mutually exclusive. To select one, you merely click the appropriate icon. It turns black to show that it has been selected.

- *Pop-up menus:* The Tabloid radio button on the far right incorporates a pop-up menu, as indicated by the triangle symbol. After you click the box surrounding the arrow, a new set of options appears. While holding down the mouse button, select one of the items in the pop-up menu and then release the mouse button. The radio button will be selected and show the new option that you've chosen.

- *Buttons:* Rather than setting options, buttons in dialog boxes are action elements. You click one to change the dialog box (presenting more choices, as in the case of the Options button) or to select a final action (OK or Cancel, for example). You exit from a dialog box by clicking a button.

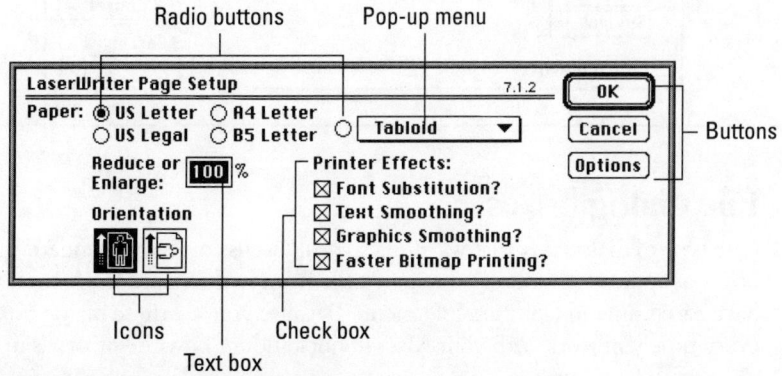

Figure 2-14: The LaserWriter Page Setup dialog box.

Part I: The Fundamentals

Techno Trivia: Modal and Modeless Dialog Boxes

Every dialog box can be classified as modal or modeless. A *modal dialog box* is one that you must respond to immediately. If you try to click outside the dialog box, return to the desktop, open a desk accessory, or switch to another running program, the Mac beeps at you. Until you respond to the dialog box and dismiss it (usually by clicking one of its buttons), you cannot do anything else. Such dialog boxes are called *modal* because, when one is presented, you are in dialog box mode. Other modes, such as editing your document, are unavailable to you. Alert dialog boxes (notifying you that your printer is out of paper, for example) and file dialog boxes (seen whenever you choose a program's Open or Save As commands, for instance) are examples of some common modal dialog boxes. Like most programs, FileMaker Pro relies heavily on modal dialog boxes.

On the other hand, you can leave modeless dialog boxes on-screen while you work. They are called *modeless* because you can respond to them or do something else. Microsoft Word's Find dialog box is an example of a modeless dialog box. As with a standard document window, you can freely switch back and forth between the Find dialog box and a document window without ever being obligated to close either window. The accompanying figure shows examples of both types of dialog boxes.

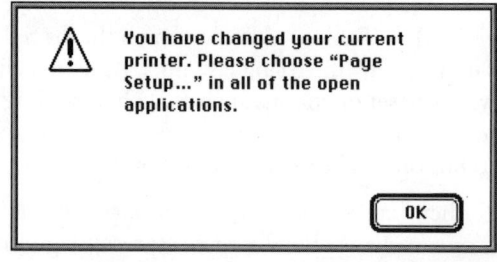

File dialog boxes

One type of dialog box that warrants special discussion is the standard file dialog box that appears whenever you open a file from within a program or choose the Save As command from the File menu. Because you see these dialog boxes almost every time you work with your Mac, understanding how they work is important.

Chapter 2: Macintosh Essentials

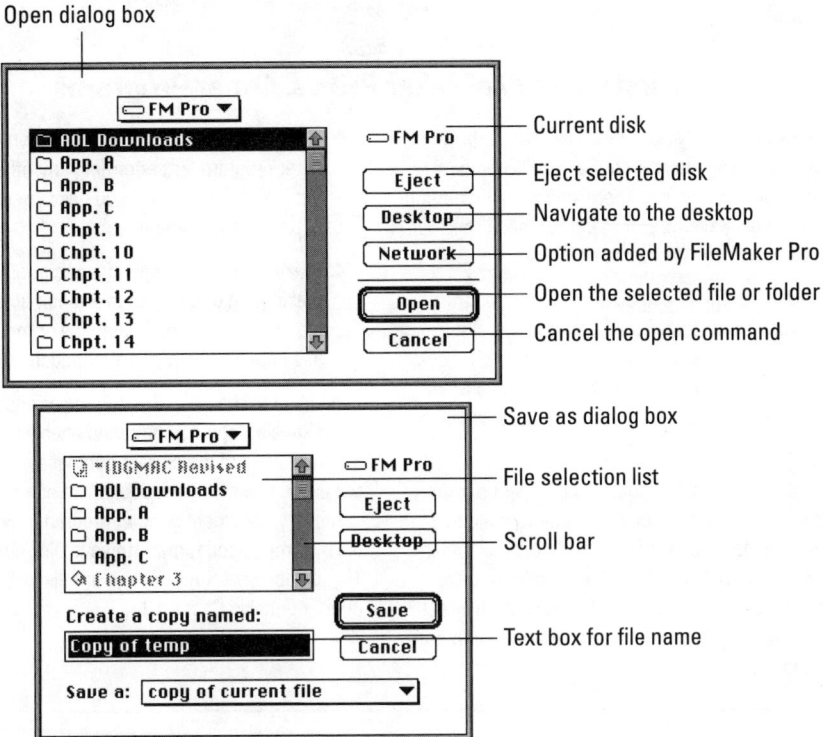

Figure 2-15: Examples of file dialog boxes (System 7).

Figure 2-15 shows FileMaker Pro's Open and Save a Copy As file dialog boxes. These examples contain all the elements of the standard Open and Save As file dialog boxes in System 7. (In System 6, the Desktop button is replaced by a Disk button, but in other respects, the options work the same way.) Note that FileMaker Pro adds a few special elements to these dialog boxes, including the Network button in the Open dialog box and the pop-up menu in the Save a Copy As dialog box.

Using either of these dialog boxes is a two-step process. First, you navigate to the disk and folder from which you want to open or save the file. Second, you open or save the file.

Disk and folder navigation

When you choose Open or Save a Copy As from FileMaker Pro's File menu, one of the dialog boxes shown in Figure 2-15 appears. The disk and folder that are displayed are normally the most recent ones used by the program in the session. When you save a copy of a file that was opened during the session, its original disk and folder are usually selected for you. In many instances, however, you'll want to change to a different disk or folder.

Part I: The Fundamentals

Saving Files: FileMaker Pro vs. Other Programs

If you examine FileMaker Pro's File menu, you'll quickly notice an important difference when compared to other programs. There's no Save command, and the usual Save As command has been replaced by a Save a Copy As command.

Let's talk about the Save command first. In other programs, you choose Save to save a new file to disk or to update an existing disk file with changes you've just made to it. FileMaker Pro has no Save command because it automatically saves all your changes as you make them.

Selecting the Save As command in other programs enables you to save a copy of the current file to a different folder or disk than the file's original folder and disk. The command provides a safe to make copies of a file while keeping the original file intact. This is particularly useful when performing either of the following tasks:

❖ Creating a complex spreadsheet, writing a computer program, or performing any other computer activity in which you need "generational" copies of a document

❖ Making a backup copy of a document before making major changes to it (such as deleting many records from a database or modifying assumptions on which a spreadsheet is based)

In addition to the usual Save As functions, FileMaker Pro's Save a Copy As command enables you to create a clone of the current database file (a copy of the file sans data — the equivalent of a template or stationery document in other programs) or save the file in compressed format (to save disk space). These additional Save options are discussed in greater detail in Chapter 3.

To switch to a different disk (System 7), follow these steps:

1. **Click the Desktop button.**

   The file selection list shows a list of all mounted disks, as well as any files or folders that are stored on the desktop.

2. **Select the disk you wish to open.**

3. **Double-click the disk name.**

— or —

3. **Select the disk name and click the Open button.**

When running System 6, you change disks by clicking the Disk button. Each time you click this button, you cycle to the next disk in the list of all currently mounted disks.

Chapter 2: Macintosh Essentials

To switch to a different floppy or other removable disk, perform the following steps:

1. **Select the currently inserted floppy or removable disk, as described in the preceding sets of steps.**

   If you want to use a particular floppy or removable disk and no disk is currently in the drive, go directly to Step 3.

2. **Click Eject.**

   The floppy pops out. (In the case of some types of removable hard disks, such as a SyQuest, the disk is merely unmounted from the desktop. You can then manually remove the disk from its drive.)

3. **Insert the disk that you intend to use.**

4. **If the new disk is not automatically selected for you, double-click its name in the file selection list or select the disk's name and click the Open button.**

After choosing the correct disk, you'll frequently need to change to a different folder. To navigate to a lower (more deeply nested) folder on the current disk, do the following:

1. **Select a folder in the file selection list.**

   To move quickly through a list that is larger than the window, click the scroll bars.

2. **Double-click the folder name or select the folder name and click the Open button.**

To navigate to a higher (less deeply nested) folder on the current disk, do the following:

1. **Click the current folder pop-up above the file selection list.**

   A list of folders that are higher in the hierarchy appears.

2. **While continuing to hold down the mouse button, drag to select the folder that you want to open.**

Part I: The Fundamentals

A System 7 Shortcut

If you are running System 7, you can use a shortcut to move up through the folder hierarchy. Click the name of the current disk (in this case, Databases). Each time you click it, you automatically move up one level in the folder hierarchy.

Opening a file

After you select a disk and folder, you open the desired file by selecting it in the file list and taking one of the following actions:

❖ Double-click its filename.

❖ Click the Open button (or press Return or Enter).

The file is then loaded into the program.

Saving a file

Similarly, after you have chosen a program's Save As command (or FileMaker Pro's Save a Copy As command) and have navigate to the disk and folder where you want to save the file, you complete the save process by typing a filename in the text box and clicking the Save button.

If you enter the name of a file that already exists on the selected disk and folder, you see a new dialog box that asks the question *Replace existing (filename)?* Click Replace to overwrite the old file. Click Cancel if you decide to save the file with a different name, to a different disk, or in a different folder.

Switching between Running Programs

If you are running System 7 or running System 6 with MultiFinder, you can run several programs at the same time. The number of programs is limited only by the amount of *RAM* (Random-Access Memory) installed in the Mac. Simultaneously running several programs is often useful because you can easily copy and paste material from one program into another program. For example, you can copy address lines from a FileMaker Pro database and then paste them into the address section of a letter or envelope in a word processing program.

Chapter 2: Macintosh Essentials

Fast File Selection

Many times, the file list in file dialog boxes can be quite lengthy. Although you can use the scroll bars, box, and arrows to move through the list, the Mac provides some useful keyboard shortcuts.

Press the up- or down-arrow key
You can scroll to the filename quickly without using the mouse. To open a folder or file, press Return or Enter when it is highlighted.

Press the Page Up, Page Down, Home, or End key (Apple Extended keyboard only)
Although these keys do not select files or folders, they do move through the list. Page Up and Page Down are the equivalent of a single click in the scroll bar. Home and End display the beginning and end of the file list, respectively.

Type the first letter or two of the filename
The list automatically scrolls to the first matching entry. For example, to open a file named Memo, press M. The list displays the first filename that begins with *M*. If no name starts with *M*, the next filename that follows alphabetically is selected. If you type fast enough, you can string several letters together as a search string. If you have many files that begin with *M*, for example, typing **ME** will locate the Memo file more precisely.

The method that you use to switch from one running program to another depends on the version of the system software that is installed in the Mac. (The *system software* is a set of files provided by Apple Computer. It enables the Mac to run programs, manage the desktop, and display windows and graphics. In short, the system software is what gives the Mac its personality, as well as its ability to do things.)

If you're not sure which version of system software you have, return to the desktop and pull down the *Apple menu* (the menu that is at the far left side of the menu bar and is topped by the Apple icon).

❖ If you're running a version of System 6, the first menu option in the Apple menu is About the Finder.

❖ If you're running a version of System 7, the first menu option in the Apple menu is About This Macintosh.

Switching programs under System 6 (using MultiFinder)

With System 6 and MultiFinder (See "Turning on MultiFinder"), you can switch between the programs that are running by performing any of the following actions:

Part I: The Fundamentals

- Click once in any open window that belongs to the program to which you want to switch.

- Pull down the Apple menu. At the bottom of the menu, the names of open programs are listed. Select the name of the program to which you want to switch.

- On the desktop, find the icon of the program to which you want to switch. Icons for running programs are displayed as dimmed patterns. (See Figure 2-16). To switch to that program, double-click the dimmed icon.

Figure 2-16: A dimmed program icon.

- A tiny icon that represents the program that is currently active is in the upper-right corner of the menu bar. The Finder, for example, is indicated by a tiny Macintosh. To switch programs, click the tiny icon. Each time you click, the Mac cycles to the next running program.

After you perform one of these actions, the new program becomes *active* (its windows move to the front layer of the screen, and its menu bar replaces the menu bar of the previously active program or of the Finder, whichever was last active).

To run more than one program at a time under System 6, you need to be using the MultiFinder component of the system software. If MultiFinder is not running, you can turn it on by following these steps:

1. **Return to the desktop, and choose Set Startup from the Special menu.**

   The Set Startup dialog box appears.

2. **At the top of the dialog box, click the radio button marked MultiFinder.**

3. **Click OK to close the dialog box.**

The next time you turn on or restart the Mac, MultiFinder will be active. If you later want to turn MultiFinder off, repeat these steps but click the Finder button in Step 2.

Switching programs under System 7

When you are running System 7, the procedure for switching between open programs is a little different. You can use any of the following methods:

Chapter 2: Macintosh Essentials

- Click once in any open window of the program to which you want to switch.

- Like System 6, System 7 displays a tiny icon that represents the currently active program in the right-hand corner of the menu bar. You do not click it, however, to cycle through the running programs. The icon is the top of the Application menu. When you click the icon, a menu appears that lists all running programs, as shown in Figure 2-17. A check mark shows the program that is currently active. To switch to another program, choose it from the Application menu.

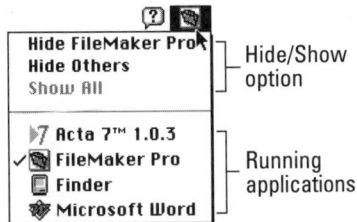

Figure 2-17: System 7's Application menu lists the names of all programs that are currently running.

- On the desktop, find the icon of the program to which you want to switch. (Icons for running programs are displayed as dimmed patterns, as shown in Figure 2-16.) To switch to that program, double-click the dimmed icon.

You can instantly return to the Finder desktop by clicking in any open area of the desktop.

A Printing Primer

Printing is one of the most basic computer operations. Although printing is usually a straightforward process (you choose Print from the File menu and then click the Print button), things can quickly become muddled when you have several printers, are printing over a network, or are trying to decipher the meaning of the various Print and Page Setup options.

Preparing to print requires three actions:

1. Selecting a printer in the Chooser desk accessory.

2. Setting options in the Page Setup dialog box.

3. Setting options in the Print dialog box.

Part I: The Fundamentals

Using the Chooser

You use the Chooser desk accessory (see Figure 2-18) to select the printer or other device (such as a fax modem) to which the next print job will be sent. Subsequent print jobs will continue to go to that device until you select a different one in the Chooser.

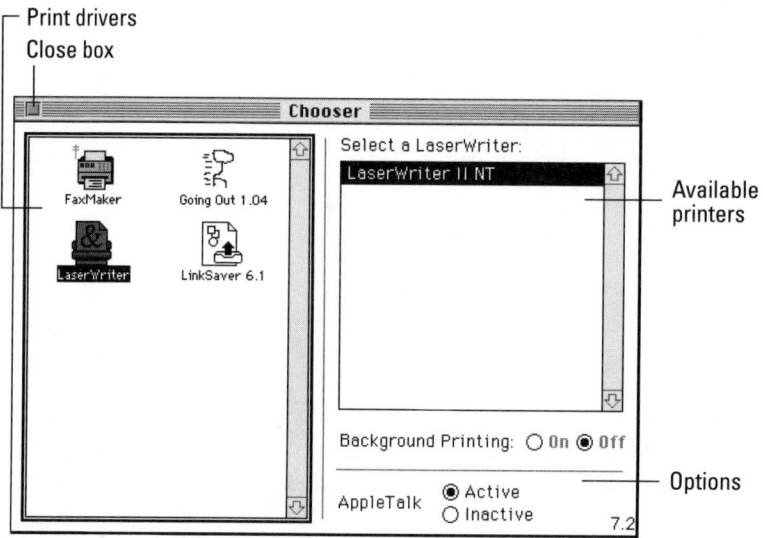

Figure 2-18: The Chooser desk accessory.

To select a printer, do the following:

1. Select Chooser from the Apple menu.

The left side of the Chooser window displays all print drivers that are installed in the System Folder. (In System 6, they're stored loose in the System Folder. In System 7, they're stored in the Extensions folder within the System Folder.) Although most Chooser drivers are for printers, other programs and utilities may also supply drivers that redirect printing. In Figure 2-18, for example, FaxMaker is a driver for a fax modem. When selected, FaxMaker intercepts all Print commands and converts the current document to fax format for transmission to a fax machine.

You also may see drivers for printers that you do not own or that are not connected to the Mac or the network. When you install the system software on the Mac, the default installation procedure installs all Apple printer drivers. You may want to throw out the ones that you don't need.

2. **In the left side of the window, click once to select the driver for your printer.**

   In the right side of the window is a list of printers that can use the selected driver.

3. **Click to select the printer to which you want to send the next print job.**

   If you are on a network, you may be able to choose from several printers, including printers that are not directly connected to your Mac. (Note that a printer must be *on* in order for it to appear in the list.)

4. **Set options for the printer.**

   The particular options that are listed vary according to the type of printer that you select. See the printer manual for a list of the printer's capabilities and the meaning of the options. (In the case of drivers for Apple printers, refer to the manual that came with the system software or the program in which the driver was distributed.)

5. **To record the changes you make, click the close box in the upper-left corner of the Chooser window.**

   If you've just changed printer types in the Chooser, the Mac will remind you to check the Page Setup options to make sure that they're correct for the new printer. Choose Page Setup from the File menu on the desktop or from within any program to check the settings and, if necessary, change them.

The meaning of the Print and Page Setup options

Whether you're printing from the desktop, from within FileMaker Pro, or from another program, you need to understand the Print and Page Setup dialog box options. The Page Setup dialog box deals with paper and image issues: size, rotation, scaling, and similar options. The Print dialog box governs the print quality, the number of copies, the page range, and the paper source.

When You Always Use the Same Printer

If you have only one printer that you always use, you can select it once in the Chooser and then never have to use the Chooser again until you want to change options. The only exception to this rule is when you install or reinstall the system software. Doing so usually leaves the Mac without a selected printer.

Note that the Print and Page Setup options that are discussed in the following sections are the *default* options — options you see in every Print and Page Setup dialog box. In addition to these options, many programs modify the Print and Page Setup dialog boxes to offer program-specific choices. Refer to program manuals for descriptions of these additional options. Special options that appear in FileMaker Pro are discussed in Chapter 13.

Page Setup options

Page Setup options are document-specific. When you establish Page Setup options for a document — setting it to print in landscape orientation, for instance — and then save the document, the Page Setup settings are saved, too. The next time you print the document, it will automatically print in landscape mode.

Normally, you need to adjust the Page Setup options only when you want to do one of the following tasks:

❖ Select a new printer in the Chooser.

❖ Print on a different paper type or size, such as an envelope or legal-sized paper.

❖ Change the orientation of the printout (from portrait to landscape or vice versa).

Figure 2-19 shows the Page Setup dialog boxes for three of the most common Apple printers: the LaserWriter, ImageWriter, and StyleWriter. (If you have a non-Apple printer that came with its own printer driver, the Page Setup options may differ somewhat from the options in these dialog boxes. Refer to the printer manual for an explanation of the options.)

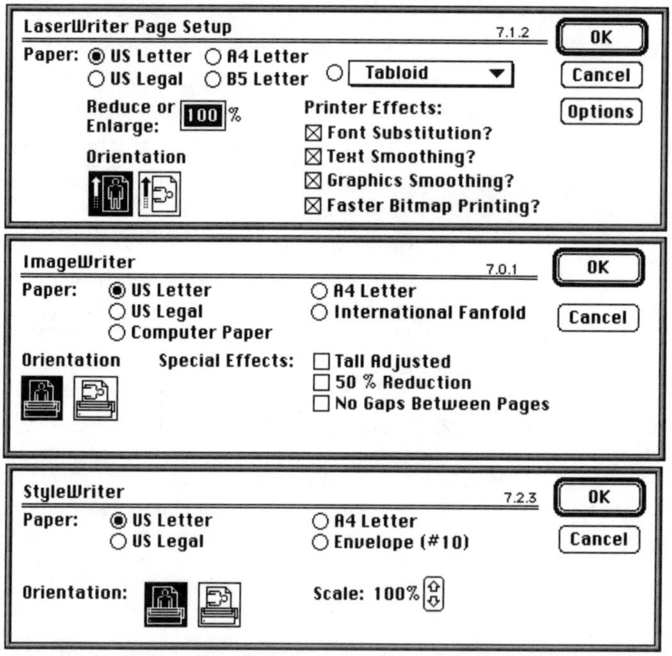

Figure 2-19: Page Setup dialog boxes for three common printers.

Chapter 2: Macintosh Essentials

The three Page Setup dialog boxes have the following options in common:

❖ *Paper sizes:* At the top of each dialog box is a set of radio buttons for several paper sizes. Select the option that's correct for the paper that you intend to use.

Although most printing is done on standard 8.5 x 11-inch paper (US Letter), some of the other options that you may encounter are A4 Letter (8.5 x 11.67-inch paper, a popular European size for letters); B5 letter (7 x 10-inch paper, another European paper size used for correspondence); Computer Paper (standard 15 x 11-inch fan-fold computer paper, a popular choice for ImageWriter printers); and Tabloid (11 x 17-inch paper that, because of its large size, is normally supported only by special laser printers).

If you have a LaserWriter or another printer that uses the LaserWriter driver, be sure to check the contents of the Tabloid pop-up menu. It contains choices for envelope printing, as well as for other special paper types and sizes.

❖ *Orientation icons:* All Macintosh printers can print documents in two orientations: *portrait* (right-side up) and *landscape* (sideways). You print most documents in portrait mode, which is represented by the first orientation icon. If a document is too wide to fit within the eight or so printable inches of standard letter paper, click the landscape icon. Landscape mode is also useful for addressing envelopes.

❖ *Reduction and scaling options:* Occasionally, you may want to change the size of what you're printing — either to make it fit on one page or to take up more room on the page. This option is available for many printers, but it may come with restrictions. PostScript printers, such as LaserWriters, generally enable you to specify any percentage for reducing or enlarging an image. ImageWriters, on the other hand, offer only two choices: full size or 50 percent reduction.

Some options are specific to a particular printer. The following sections discuss these unique options.

Unique ImageWriter options

The ImageWriter Page Setup dialog box contains these unique options:

❖ *Tall Adjusted:* Select this option when you are printing graphics. It adjusts for the difference between the resolution of the ImageWriter and the resolution of the Mac's screen.

❖ *No Gaps Between Pages:* When you are printing to continuous-form computer paper, making a continuous printout is sometimes useful. Spreadsheets and program listings, for example, are often printed this way.

Part I: The Fundamentals

Unique LaserWriter options

The LaserWriter Page Setup dialog box contains these unique options:

- *Font Substitution:* When this option is checked, PostScript fonts (Times, Helvetica, and Courier) are automatically substituted for their lower-resolution counterparts (New York, Geneva, and Monaco). Unless you routinely use ImageWriter fonts to format documents, you usually don't need to check this option. (On the other hand, leaving it checked doesn't hurt.)

- *Text Smoothing:* This option minimizes jagged edges when you are printing non-PostScript fonts.

- *Graphics Smoothing:* This option minimizes jagged edges on graphics images.

- *Faster Bitmap Printing:* When this option is checked, bitmapped images are pre-processed for faster printing. However, this option was apparently intended to be used only with the original LaserWriter and LaserWriter Plus printers (very old Apple printers). Checking this option for more recent printers can actually slow the printing or prevent some images from printing at all.

If you click the Options button in the LaserWriter Page Setup dialog box, another group of settings appears (see Figure 2-20). The Apple *dogcow* image on the left side of the dialog box changes to show the effects of options that you select on this screen. (I'll bet you didn't know that *dogcow* was a computer term — or even a word, for that matter.)

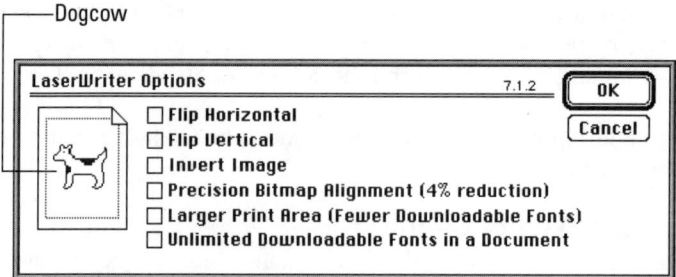

Figure 2-20: Additional LaserWriter Page Setup options.

- *Flip Horizontal:* This option reverses the page from left to right.

- *Flip Vertical:* This option reverses the page from top to bottom (so the image is upside down).

- *Invert Image:* This option reverses blacks and whites in the image.

Chapter 2: Macintosh Essentials

The LaserWriter 8 Driver

The new LaserWriter 8 driver adds two elements to the Page Setup dialog boxes. First, clicking the dogcow picture makes the dialog box display information about the currently selected paper size and print margins. Second, the Page Setup dialog box contains a new Layout pop-up menu. Clicking this menu enables you to print one, two, or four document pages on each piece of paper.

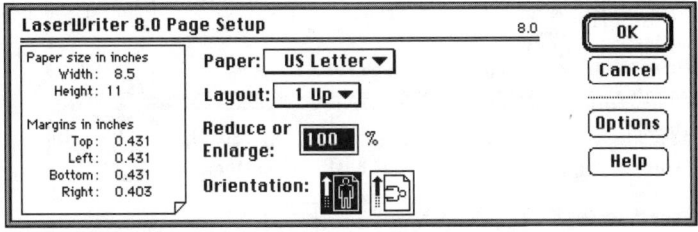

❖ *Precision Bitmap Alignment (4% reduction):* Choose this option if you want the printout to precisely match the original bitmapped image. The printout is printed at 288 dots per inch, exactly four times the Mac's screen resolution of 72 dots per inch.

❖ *Larger Print Area (Fewer Downloadable Fonts):* This option enlarges the printable area slightly at the expense of having fewer *downloadable* (nonresident) fonts available to the document.

❖ *Unlimited Downloadable Fonts in a Document:* This option enables you to print a document that contains a large number of fonts that must be *downloaded* (transmitted to the printer). Printing time may increase substantially.

Print options

As explained above, since most printing is done using the default settings in the Print and Page Setup dialog boxes, you can choose the essential settings very quickly. Thus, the final (and often only) steps in printing are to choose Print from the File menu, set print options, and click the Print button — skipping the Page Setup dialog box completely. Figure 2-21 shows the standard Print dialog box for each of the three printers discussed previously.

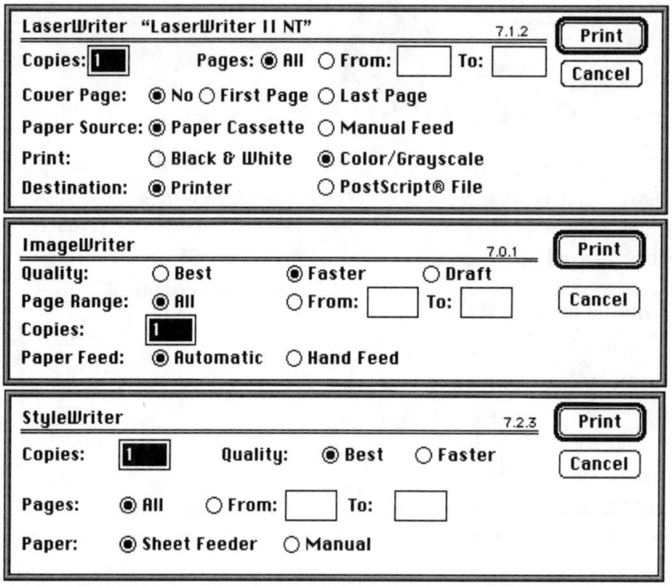

Part I: The Fundamentals

Figure 2-21: Print dialog boxes for the Apple LaserWriter, ImageWriter, and StyleWriter printers.

You use the various options to do the following:

❖ *Copies:* Specify the number of copies of the document that will be printed.

❖ *Page Range (Pages):* Determine whether the entire document will be printed (if you click the All radio button) or only a subset of the pages will be printed (type a page range).

❖ *Quality (Print):* Different printers provide different quality settings. Normally, the lower the quality, the faster the document will print.

On an ImageWriter, choose Draft to use the printer's built-in font and ignore fonts that are set in the document. On a LaserWriter, choose Black & White to produce a two-tone printout and Color/Grayscale to use a halftone process that produces shades of gray.

❖ *Paper Source (Paper Feed, Paper):* This option determines where the paper will be drawn from during printing. Select Hand Feed if you want to insert cut-sheet paper into an ImageWriter and Automatic when you want to use continuous-form computer paper. The other choices are self-explanatory.

The LaserWriter Print dialog box offers several unique options, as follows:

❖ *Cover Page:* You set a cover page when you want the first or last page to provide identifying information about the print job: the user's name, the application, the document name, the date, the time, and the printer. This feature is most useful for distinguishing the owner of different print jobs on a shared network printer.

Chapter 2: Macintosh Essentials

❖ *Print:* This option is similar to the Quality choice that is offered for other printers. Depending on the printer's capabilities and the quality of graphics output that you desire, select Black & White (the best choice for a document that contains only text) or Color/Grayscale (the best choice when printing graphics that contain color or shades of gray).

The LaserWriter 8 printer driver adds another option: Calibrated Color/Grayscale. For printers that support PostScript Level 2 (check your printer manual), this option attempts to precisely match the colors shown on your monitor with those used in the printed output.

❖ *Destination:* Normally, you choose Printer. This option sends the current print job to the printer and then produces printed output. You use the PostScript File or File option to create a *PostScript file* from the document; nothing is sent to the printer.

Creating a PostScript file is sometimes useful when you are preparing a document for printing at a service bureau. A PostScript file contains nothing but programming code (in the PostScript language). PostScript printers can interpret this code and use it to produce printed document pages. The original program is not required to print a PostScript file. To *dump* (send) a PostScript file to your printer, you need a utility such as LaserWriter Font Utility (included with the System 7 software).

❖ *PostScript Errors (LaserWriter 8 printer driver only):* When a PostScript print job fails, most users don't have the vaguest idea what went wrong. (The usual result of most PostScript errors is simply that nothing prints!) This new option (see Figure 2-22) enables you to see error messages, either summarized on-screen or printed in detail.

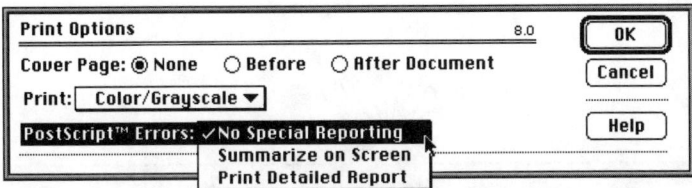

Figure 2-22: These LaserWriter 8 print options are displayed when you click Options in the Print dialog box.

The Importance of Backups

Backing up (or *making a backup*) is the process of making an extra copy of important files. Although some people think that their Mac is immune to disaster, such an idea is foolhardy. Here are just a few of the ways that you can lose critical data files:

Part I: The Fundamentals

- You throw a folder that you no longer need into the Trash, only to discover that you threw away the wrong folder.

- While cleaning your desk, someone bumps your Mac or your hard disk. The bump results in a *head crash*, a catastrophic event that renders the disk inoperable.

- The hard disk's power supply dies. Although your data is still intact, you have no way of getting at it until the hard disk is repaired. How long can your business survive without access to that information?

- You borrow a disk from a friend, not realizing that it is infected with a computer virus. The first time that you run a program from the disk, it erases every file on your hard disk while pretending to do something useful.

- A *real* disaster occurs. A fire or theft leaves you with a smoking or missing Mac, and your data goes along for the ride.

To be safe, you should always have one or more duplicate copies of every important data file on your system. Even if you can't afford a special backup device, such as a tape drive or removable cartridge system, you can always back up your data on floppies. Whenever you make significant changes to an important file, save it to your hard disk and then copy it onto a floppy, too.

You can make backup copies of files in several different ways. The following methods are common:

- Copying files on the desktop
- Using the Save As command within a program (or the Save a Copy As command in FileMaker Pro)
- Using a backup program

Saving Multiple Generations of a File

If you need to keep multiple generations of a file that you're working on (a budget proposal or a worksheet that you're designing over a period of time, for example) name each draft something slightly different. You may want to use a numbering scheme (such as Budget 1, Budget 2, and so on) or add the date to the end of the filename (such as Budget 8/4/94, Budget 8/9/94). This procedure will keep you from inadvertently saving over any of the earlier drafts.

Making backup copies from the desktop

You can make a duplicate copy of any file that appears on the desktop. The method that you use depends on whether you want to place the copy on the same disk as the original file or on a different disk.

To make a duplicate of a file on the same disk, do the following:

1. **To select the file that you want to duplicate, click its icon once.**
2. **Choose the Duplicate command from the File menu (or press ⌘-D).**

   A copy of the file is created.

3. **If necessary, rename the file.**

   Click the filename once. It becomes highlighted, and it is surrounded by a box. Use normal text-editing procedures to edit or replace the name.

   Note that the name must be different from the names of all other files in that particular folder or at that level of the disk. For example, you cannot have two files named Memo at the *root* (top) level of a disk.

Usually, you place the backup copy on a *different disk* — another floppy or hard disk, for example. The most common reason for making a backup is to protect a file; a backup gives you a copy to use if the original file or its disk becomes damaged. Placing the copy on a different disk provides greater protection than having two copies on the same disk. Disks *can* fail, you know.

To copy a file to another disk, follow these steps:

1. **Make sure that the destination disk for the copy appears on the desktop.**

   If necessary, insert the destination disk (a floppy or removable hard disk, for example) or use whatever utility you normally use to *mount* the disk (make it appear on the desktop).

2. **Select the file that you want to copy by clicking its icon once and, while holding down the mouse button, drag the file to the destination disk's icon.**

   Note that when you drag a file onto a disk icon, the copy is automatically placed at the top (root) level of the disk. If you'd rather place the copy in a particular folder on the destination disk, replace Step 2 with Steps 2a and 2b.

2a. **Double-click the destination disk's icon to open a window for that disk, and double-click the appropriate folder icons on the disk to make the destination folder appear.**

2b. **Select the file that you want to copy by clicking its icon once and, while holding down the mouse button, drag the file to the folder on the destination disk.**

Part I: The Fundamentals

3. **Release the mouse button.**

   An exact duplicate of the file is created for you.

Making backup copies by using the Save As command

In most programs, the File menu contains a pair of commands for saving files. Choosing the Save command when a document is open automatically replaces the old copy of the document with the new version. If you have never saved the document, a dialog box appears that enables you to name the new file and specify where you want to save it. The same dialog box appears when you choose the Save As command (see the following set of steps on using the Save As command to make a backup copy). You also can use the Save As command to save copies of a document to the same disk or a different disk.

To save a file using the Save As command, do the following:

1. **From within a program, choose the Save As command from the File menu.**

   The Save As dialog box appears, as shown in Figure 2-23.

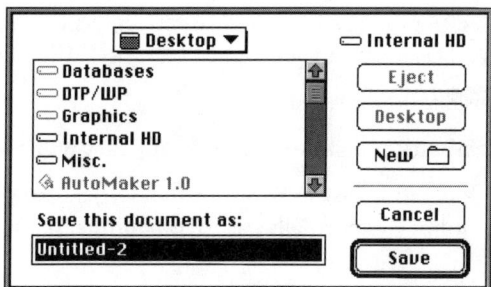

Figure 2-23: The Save As dialog box.

2. **Negotiate to the drive and folder in which you want to save the file.**
3. **If you want to change the name of the file (or the default filename that is proposed for a new file, such as Untitled), type the new name in the text box.**
4. **Click the Save button.**

   The file is saved as directed.

Chapter 2: Macintosh Essentials

Making backup copies by using FileMaker Pro's Save a Copy As command

As mentioned above, FileMaker Pro does not have a Save command or a Save As command. To avoid data loss, FileMaker Pro automatically saves any changes that you make as you work in a database. Although this approach is obviously beneficial as far as the security of your data is concerned, it also has a drawback. If you make a change to the data or the database design by deleting records, fields, or layouts, you cannot revert to the previous state of the database unless you have a backup copy.

In addition to other methods of making a backup copy (making copies from the desktop and using a backup program), FileMaker Pro provides a Save a Copy As command that you can use to make a duplicate copy of the database that you are currently using. To use the Save a Copy As command, follow these steps:

1. **Choose Save a Copy As from the File menu.**

   The Save a Copy As dialog box appears, as shown in Figure 2-24.

Figure 2-24: The Save a Copy As dialog box.

2. **Navigate to the drive and folder where you want to save the copy.**

3. **Optionally, you can change the filename that FileMaker suggests for the copy (Copy of *filename*).**

   The pop-up menu at the bottom of the dialog box offers three options: copy of current file, compressed copy (smaller), and clone (no records).

4. **To make a normal backup copy, choose the first option (copy of current file).**

   The other options are discussed in Chapter 3.

5. **Click the Save button.**

   A copy of the file is saved.

Part I: The Fundamentals

Making backup copies by using a backup program

If you want to make the backup process more manageable, you can choose one of the many good commercial backup programs. The following programs from Dantz Development Corp. (510-849-0293) are my favorites:

❖ DiskFit Direct (for creating backups on floppy disks and removable cartridges)

❖ DiskFit Pro (floppy and removable cartridge backups, plus server and scheduled backup support)

❖ Retrospect, which is shown in Figure 2-25 (floppy, tape, and removable cartridge backups; server support; scheduled backups; compression; and data encryption)

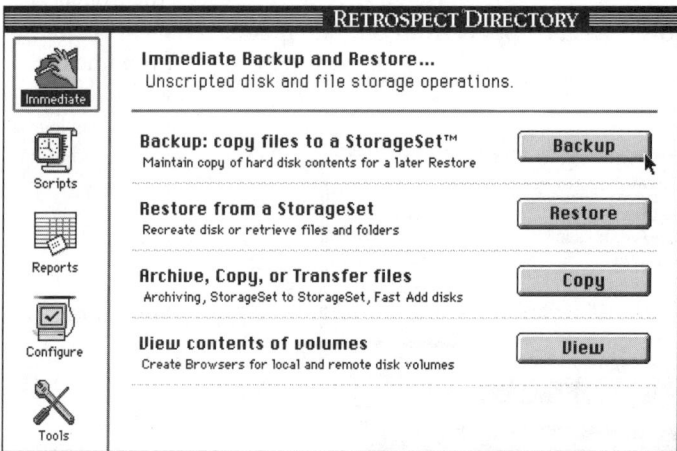

Figure 2-25: Retrospect takes the backup process to new levels of simplicity while maintaining flexibility.

Backing up the Hard Disk

In addition to providing extra features, backup programs make backing up the entire hard disk as easy as backing up only important data files. Having a full backup of the hard disk makes restoring the entire disk a snap if the need arises (following the disk's total destruction, for example).

System 7 Bonus: Making Aliases

Although understanding the following material is hardly a "Macintosh essential," you'll find this information is extremely helpful. It explains how to use aliases, one of System 7's most powerful, easy-to-use features.

If you're running System 7 and have favorite programs or documents that you use frequently, *aliases* (file, folder, or disk stand-ins) offer speedy access to files without the usual folder-sifting. An alias is a tiny 1 – 2K file that represents another file, folder, or disk. When you double-click an alias of a program, the program that it represents launches or, in the case of a disk or folder alias, a window with the contents of that disk or folder appears on the desktop.

You can place aliases anywhere you like. The desktop is one popular spot. When you pop them into the Apple Menu Items folder (inside the System Folder), you can launch programs and open current project documents by simply choosing the alias file from the Apple menu. As a practical example, if you find that there are particular FileMaker Pro databases that you regularly use, you can make aliases of them and place them on the desktop or in the Apple Menu Items folder so you can launch them on a moment's notice. Similarly, you can make an alias of the folder in which your databases are stored, giving you direct access to *any* of your most important files.

To create an alias, follow these steps:

1. **On the desktop, use the mouse to select the program, document, folder, or disk for which you want to make an alias.**

   If you want quick access to FileMaker Pro, for example, select its icon.

2. **Choose Make Alias from the File menu.**

   The alias icon appears. (Note that names of aliases are in italic.)

   As with other files, you can rename an alias, if you want to. (I usually eliminate the "alias" part of the filename because it makes the name unnecessarily long. Besides, the name is already in italic, so you can easily identify it as an alias.)

3. **Place the alias wherever you like.**

   No matter where you place it, the alias maintains its link with the original program, document, folder, or disk that it represents.

   If, for example, you want to add the alias to the Apple menu, open the System Folder and then drag the alias icon into the Apple Menu Items folder. The alias appears on the Apple menu immediately.

CHAPTER 2 CONCEPTS AND TERMS

- There are right and wrong ways to start up the Mac and shut it down.
- When you are not working in a program, you spend much of your time on the Mac desktop. You manipulate files and disks and organize documents within folders on the desktop.
- The mouse pointer changes its shape to match the operation that you are performing.
- All mouse operations involve clicking, dragging, or a combination of these actions.
- You can double-click to launch programs, open documents, or select a word in most documents and text boxes. If the Mac doesn't respond consistently to double-clicks, you can adjust the double-click speed in the Mouse control panel.
- You need to follow special procedures for editing and selecting text on a Mac. After you learn them, however, you can apply them on the desktop and within almost every program.
- The Clipboard is an area in memory that stores the most recent text or object that you have copied (⌘-C) or cut (⌘-X). The contents of the Clipboard remain intact and available for pasting (⌘-V) until you copy or cut something else or until you turn off the Mac.
- Although window types can vary dramatically from one program to the next, adapting to new windows is easy when you understand what the different window components do.
- Some dialog boxes convey important messages from programs and the system software. Other dialog boxes enable you to set program options.
- You use file dialog boxes to open and save documents from within programs. Some programs, such as FileMaker Pro, alter these dialog boxes by adding their own options.
- Readying a document for printing consists of three steps: selecting a printing device in the Chooser desk accessory, specifying Page Setup options, and setting Print options. As with file dialog boxes, some programs change the options presented in the Page Setup and Print dialog boxes.
- You should make a point of making regular copies (backups) of important data files. In many cases, the value of the information that is stored in a Mac is many times that of your hardware and programs.
- System 7 users can create aliases of important files, folders, or disks. Aliases enable you to quickly find and launch important programs and documents without forcing you to reorganize your hard disk or make multiple copies of the files.

alert box
A program or system software dialog box that notifies you that something important has occurred or is about to happen.

alias
A System 7 stand-in for a program, file, folder, or disk. Double-clicking an alias results in the same action that would occur if you double-clicked the original icon.

Apple menu
The menu at the far left side of the menu bar. Under System 6, the Apple menu was reserved for desk accessories (small programs that you could use while you were running another program). Under System 7, you can place almost anything in the Apple menu, including frequently-used programs, documents, folders, and control panels.

Application menu
Found at the upper-right corner of the menu bar (System 7 only), this menu lists all programs that are currently running and enables you to freely switch from one program to another. The top half of the Application menu enables you to temporarily hide some or all of the programs, relieving some of the desktop clutter.

balloon help
When the mouse pointer is passed over a program or system software object, menu item, or icon that has help information attached to it, a cartoon-style help balloon appears (System 7 only).

button
A push-button style object in dialog boxes. You click it to select, confirm, or cancel an action.

check box
A small box that is associated with an option in a dialog box. Clicking the box changes the state of the option from selected to deselected (and vice versa). Normally, you can choose multiple check boxes.

Chooser
The control panel that you use to select a printer or other "printing" device (such as a fax modem) and, in some cases, to set options for that device.

(continued on the next page)

Chapter 2: Macintosh Essentials

click
To press the mouse button once and then immediately release it.

Clipboard
A temporary area in memory that stores a copy of the object or text that was most recently copied or cut.

close box
The tiny box in the upper-left corner of some windows that, when clicked, closes or dismisses the window and any document that it contains.

crash
The cessation of functioning by a computer or a program. Signs that a computer has crashed include system crash dialog boxes (which contain a bomb symbol), as well as keyboard and mouse lock-ups.

desktop
The main work area on the Macintosh.

dialog box
A special type of window that programs and the system software use to present information or to enable you to make choices.

drag
To hold down the mouse button while moving the mouse pointer.

double-click
To press the mouse button twice in rapid succession.

emergency quit command
A keyboard command (⌘-Option-Esc) that you can use to force a program to quit. You can sometimes use this command of last resort to escape from a program that has locked up or crashed.

file
Any named, ordered collection of information that is stored on disk. Programs, documents, and system software components (such as the Finder) are examples of files.

folder
A holder of documents, applications, and other folders on the desktop. A folder is the equivalent of a directory or subdirectory on a DOS (PC) system.

keyboard shortcut
Keys that you press to execute a program or system command, as an alternative to selecting a command from a menu. It is also called a *keyboard equivalent* and a *Command-key equivalent*.

menu
A list of choices, presented by a program, from which you can select an action. Menus appear when you click menu titles in the menu bar. You choose commands by dragging through the menu and releasing the mouse button while a command is highlighted.

menu bar
In a program or at the desktop, the horizontal strip at the top of the screen that contains the menu titles.

modal dialog box
Any dialog box that you need to respond to before you can continue working.

modeless dialog box
A dialog box that you can leave open while you attend to other work; it does not require an immediate response or dismissal.

mouse pointer
An on-screen indicator that moves in response to movements that you make with the mouse or another pointing device. The mouse pointer changes its shape to reflect the activity that you are performing.

MultiFinder
A first-generation multitasking operating system for Macintosh computers that enables you to have several applications open at the same time, including background applications that you can use to perform one task while the computer performs another. Optional in System 6, MultiFinder capabilities became an integral feature of System 7.

pop-up menu (or hierarchical menu)
A menu in which one or more menu items contain a submenu.

printer driver
A piece of software that enables the system software and programs to communicate with a printing device.

radio button
In dialog boxes, buttons that present a series of mutually-exclusive options or settings (for example, enabling or disabling background printing).

reset switch
A hardware switch or button that causes the Mac to go through its start-up sequence. (See the owner's manual for the availability and location of the switch or button.)

scroll arrow
The arrow icon at either end of a scroll bar. When you click the arrow, the window's contents move in the opposite direction of the arrow.

scroll bar
A rectangular bar along the right side or bottom edge of a window. Clicking or dragging in a scroll bar changes your view of the window's contents. Document windows and large text fields often have scroll bars.

scroll box
The box in a scroll bar. The position of the scroll box indicates the position of what is in the window relative to the entire document.

SCSI (pronounced skuzzy)
Small Computer Systems Interface. Enables devices, such as hard disks, CD-ROM drives, and tape drives, to be connected in series to the Macintosh.

Shut Down
Command in the Special menu that you use to shut down the Mac and devices that are connected to it.

(continued on the next page)

(continued from the previous page)

size box
A box in the lower-right corner of some active windows. Dragging the size box changes the size of the window.

system software
Software that supports application programs by managing system resources, such as memory and input/output devices.

template (or stationery document)
A partially completed document that serves as a starting point for other documents. In a word processing program, for example, you might make a memo template that contains appropriate headers and text formatting, making it simple for you to create each new memo without unnecessarily having to retype basic text. The equivalent document in FileMaker Pro is known as a *clone* and is created using the Save a Copy As command.

text box
A rectangular area in a dialog box or program that presents information that you can edit. A common example is the space provided for a filename in Open and Save dialog boxes.

title bar
The horizontal bar at the top of a window that shows the name of the window's contents. You can move the window by dragging its title bar.

zoom box
A tiny box in the upper-right corner of some windows. Click the zoom box to expand the window to its maximum size. A second click returns the window to its original size.

CHAPTER THREE

FileMaker Pro Basic Operations

- Starting up and quitting FileMaker Pro
- Performing common file-handling procedures
- Issuing commands
- Using FileMaker Pro's tools and palettes

In Chapter 1, you learned that FileMaker Pro is a mode-oriented program. That is, the mode that you're in (Browse, Layout, Find, or Preview) determines the types of operations that you can currently perform. Now that you understand the fundamental FileMaker Pro concepts of modes and layouts, you're ready to explore the basic — yet essential — program procedures for performing common operations: running and quitting the program, handling files, issuing commands, and using the layout and status tools.

As in the previous two chapters, Chapter 3 is intended primarily for new users of FileMaker Pro. Even if you consider yourself an intermediate or advanced user, this chapter is still worth a quick skim — just in case something important may have slipped past you.

Starting Up

Before you can do anything with FileMaker Pro, you have to run the program. From the desktop, you can start up FileMaker Pro — and most other programs, for that matter — in several ways. Regardless of the method that you choose, however, only two results are possible:

❖ FileMaker Pro runs, and you see a file dialog box where you can either choose a database to open or create a new database (see Figure 3-1).

❖ FileMaker Pro runs, and one or more preselected databases are simultaneously opened for you.

Part I: The Fundamentals

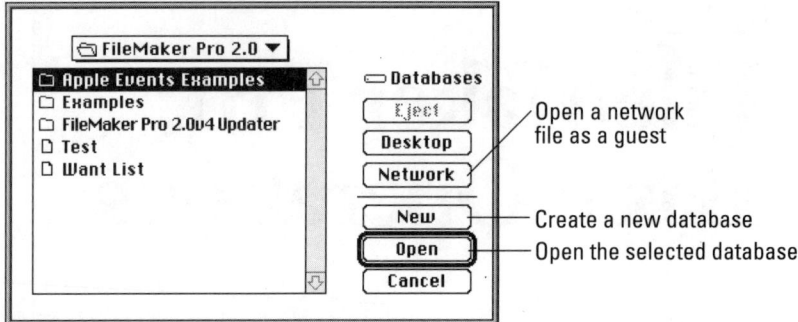

Figure 3-1: This file dialog box appears after the opening screen.

Note: When books, magazines, or manuals discuss *starting up* a program, they sometimes use the terms *run* and *launch*. All three terms mean the same thing.

The method that you use to launch FileMaker Pro depends on whether you also want to simultaneously open one or more databases.

To launch FileMaker Pro without opening an existing database, do the following:

1. **Locate the FileMaker Pro icon on the desktop (see Figure 3-2).**

   If the program is stored on a disk whose window is closed, double-click the disk icon to open its window. Similarly, if the program is stored in a folder that is not presently open, double-click the folder to display its contents. Similarly, Continue opening folders as necessary until you see the FileMaker Pro icon.

   Tip: If you don't feel like double-clicking to open disks or folders, you also can open them by selecting them and then choosing Open from the File menu or pressing ⌘-O.

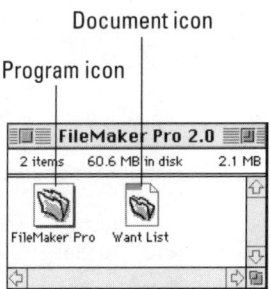

Figure 3-2: The FileMaker Pro program icon and a document icon.

2. **Double-click the FileMaker Pro program icon.**

— or —

Chapter 3: FileMaker Pro Basic Operations

2. **Click once to select the FileMaker Pro program icon and then choose Open from the File menu or press ⌘-O.**

   FileMaker Pro loads into memory and presents you with a file dialog box (see Figure 3-1).

3. **Click the appropriate button in the file dialog box.**

   You can create a new database (New), open an existing database (Open), open a network file as a guest (Network), or dismiss the dialog box (Cancel) by clicking the appropriate button.

   The New and Open options work the same whether you select them in the file dialog box or choose their commands from the File menu later in the computing session. The Network option is discussed in Chapter 20.

Dealing with the initial file dialog box, however, can be a nuisance. If the database you want to work with already exists, you can simultaneously launch FileMaker Pro and open a database file by following these steps:

1. **Locate the file icon of the database you want to open (see Figure 3-2).**
2. **Double-click the database file icon.**

   — or —

2. **Click once to select the database file icon and then either choose Open from the File menu or press ⌘-O.**

   FileMaker Pro launches, and the database is automatically opened.

If you want, you can simultaneously launch FileMaker Pro and open *several* databases, as follows:

1. **Locate the file icons of the databases you wish to open.**

   To simultaneously open more than one database, all of the database files have to be on the same disk and in the same folder (or in the root directory of the same disk).

2. **Drag to select all the databases of interest.**

   — or —

2. **Click one of the databases to select it and then, while holding down the Shift key, click the additional databases that you want to open.**
3. **Choose Open from the File menu or press ⌘-O.**

   FileMaker Pro launches, and all the selected databases are automatically opened.

Try as you might, you cannot use the double-click method to open several database files at the same time. The moment that you double-click a file icon, all of the other previously selected icons cease to be selected. When you are opening multiple files from the desktop, you have to use the Open command instead of double-clicking.

FileMaker Pro and Memory Usage

When you launch FileMaker Pro and open a database, the entire database is not always loaded into memory. FileMaker Pro uses a *disk-caching* scheme, loading only the data that it requires at the moment (based on your Find requests, the layout in use, and so on). When the program needs to display additional records or a different layout, it reads the information in from disk, replacing the data that was previously in memory with the new data. This way, you can open a 10MB FileMaker Pro database with a Mac that only has 5MB of *RAM* (Random Access Memory), for example. Disk caching is common to many database programs.

An important consequence of this disk-caching scheme is seen when using FileMaker Pro with a portable computer, such as a PowerBook. With large databases, you can expect more disk accesses than normal, which will shorten the battery life. Unless you can plug your portable computer into a wall outlet (rather than run it from its battery), you are well-advised to restrict your work to smaller databases or use larger databases sparingly — closing them as soon as you've accomplished the task at hand.

Quitting

When you're ready to end a FileMaker Pro session, choose Quit from the File menu (or press ⌘-Q). Any open data files are closed as part of the Quit process. And because FileMaker Pro automatically saves changes to files as you work with them, you don't need to issue any Save commands. (For more information on how FileMaker Pro saves data, see "Saving Files," later in this chapter.)

FileMaker Pro and the Power Switch

As explained in Chapter 2, the proper way to shut down your Mac is to select the Shut Down command from the Special menu. Just as it's a bad idea to simply cut the power instead of using the Shut Down command, turning off the juice is also a poor substitute for using a program's Quit command. Although FileMaker Pro does indeed save your work automatically and even has a command that can be used to recover a damaged database file, don't take unnecessary risks with your data. Unless circumstances beyond your control prevent doing so (a crash, lightning strike, or your puppy yanks out the Mac's power cord), you should always use the Quit command to conclude a FileMaker Pro session.

Chapter 3: FileMaker Pro Basic Operations

File-Handling Procedures

While you are working in FileMaker Pro, you may want to open additional database files, create new files, close files, or make a backup copy of a database that you are using. The information in this section explains how to perform these common procedures.

Opening, creating, and closing databases

You use the File menu or a keyboard shortcut to open a database, create a new database, or close a database. To open an existing database, follow these steps:

1. **Select Open from the File menu (or press ⌘-O).**

    A standard file dialog box appears (see Figure 3-3).

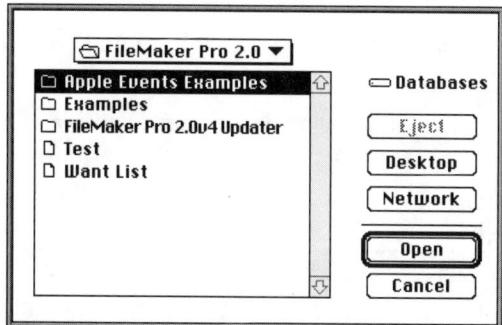

Figure 3-3: The file dialog box that appears when the Open command is issued.

2. **Navigate to the drive and folder where the database file is stored.**

    For help selecting a file to open, see "Dealing with Dialog Boxes" in Chapter 2.

3. **Open the file by double-clicking its filename or by selecting the filename and then clicking the Open button.**

    As mentioned previously, you can have several FileMaker Pro databases open at the same time, if you like. To open additional databases, simply repeat these steps.

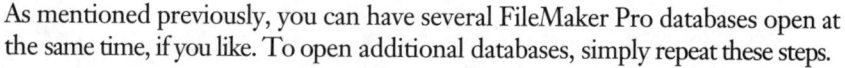

To create a new database file, do the following:

1. **Choose New from the File menu.**

    A standard file dialog box appears, as shown in Figure 3-4.

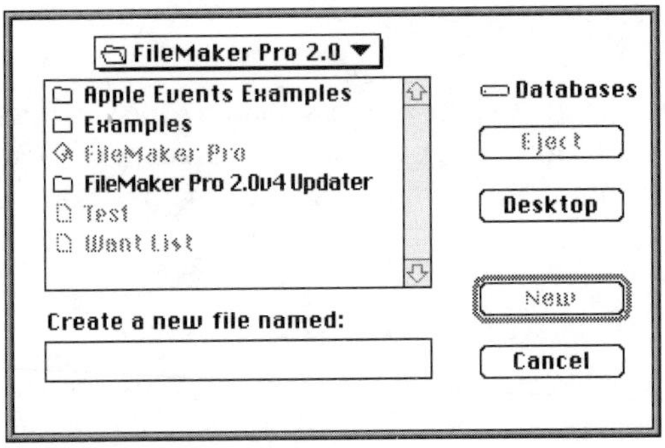

Part I: The Fundamentals

Figure 3-4: The New File dialog box.

2. Navigate to the drive and folder where you want to store the new database file.
3. Enter a name for the file in the "Create a new file named" text box and then click New.

   The Define Fields for *database name* dialog box appears, as shown in Figure 3-5.

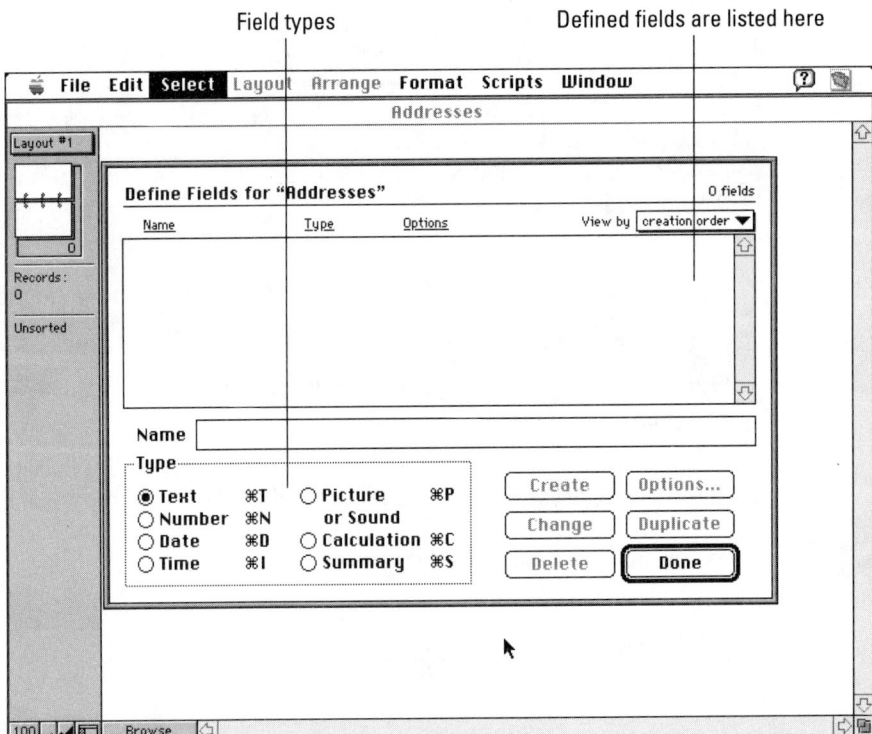

Figure 3-5: The Define Fields dialog box.

Chapter 3: FileMaker Pro Basic Operations

4. Define the necessary fields and click Done.

A standard layout is created for you, the first record of the database is displayed, and you are switched into Browse mode — ready to enter data for the first record. (The details of defining fields and designing layouts are covered in Chapters 5 and 6.)

When you're through working with a database, you can close its file by performing any of the following actions:

1. Choose Close from the File menu (or press ⌘-W).

— or —

1. Click the file's close box, which is in the upper-left corner of the document window.

— or —

1. Choose Quit from the File menu (or press ⌘-Q). Quitting automatically closes any open database files and records any unsaved changes.

When you are working in FileMaker Pro, remember that you do not have to close *any* files. You can have as many open files as will fit in available memory.

Saving files

In most Macintosh programs, the procedure for saving a new file or for saving changes that you've made to an older file is to choose the Save or Save As command from the File menu. In FileMaker Pro, however, you do not use these methods. In fact, if you examine the File menu (see Figure 3-6), you'll note that it does not have Save and Save As commands. Those commands are missing because FileMaker Pro automatically saves changes as you work with a file. And when you close a file or quit the program, you never see a dialog box asking whether you want to save your changes. The program has already saved them.

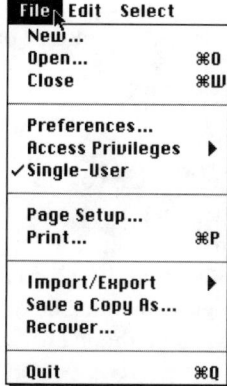

Figure 3-6: FileMaker Pro's File menu.

Note: You can exert some control over when FileMaker Pro saves files. Choose the Preferences command from the File menu and click the Memory icon in the left side of the Preferences dialog box. Then tell FileMaker to save only during idle time or every so many minutes. The latter option is most useful if you are a PowerBook user. By setting the minutes between saves to a relatively high number, you can conserve battery power by reducing the frequency of hits on the internal hard disk or floppy drive. Select a setting with which you're comfortable. For instance, if you choose 15 minutes as the save period, you are risking up to 15 minutes worth of data in the event that your Mac crashes before the data is saved. Don't worry about quitting before the time is up, however. As mentioned earlier, FileMaker Pro automatically saves all data when you quit.

Because the integrity of your data is of paramount importance, FileMaker Pro's approach to saving goes a long way toward reducing the risk of data loss. The only negative side to auto-saving is that FileMaker Pro saves *all* changes — both good and bad — that you make to a database. For example, if you experiment with a layout, FileMaker Pro records the changes. Two options are available for recovering from inadvertent changes:

- Immediately choose the Undo command from the Edit menu (or press ⌘-Z).
- Create a backup of the file before you make any major changes (as discussed in the next section, "Making a backup copy of a file").

The Undo command has two limitations. First, you can undo only the most recent modification that you have made to the database. (The wording of the Undo command automatically changes to reflect the most recent action that you can undo.) For example, if you delete some text from a field and then type information into another field, you cannot undo the deletion. Second, some commands simply cannot be undone. When you can't use the Undo command, it changes to Can't Undo. Actions that cannot be undone include using most of the Delete commands, such as Delete Record, Delete Found Set, Delete Layout, and the Delete command in the Define Fields dialog box.

The moral is that relying on the Undo command to save you from major mistakes can *be* a major mistake. The only safe approach is to keep backups of important files to ensure that you can recover from even the most horrendous mistake or computer calamity.

Making a backup copy of a file

Don't trust computers! Do I have your attention now? Although you may have spent thousands of dollars on your Macintosh and programs, they are not infallible. Regardless of how many times they hear this, most new computer users appear to feign deafness. Then one morning, they wake up to find that their hard disk has bit the dust, their kids messed up and threw out the folder that contained the family's financial records, or a thief has walked off with the Mac. Without a backup of your important data, you're right back at square one.

Chapter 3: FileMaker Pro Basic Operations

Because your data and layouts are important to you, FileMaker Pro provides several ways to make backup copies. In the event that something happens to the original file, you can use its backup copy to get it up and running again. In addition to using the backup procedures provided by FileMaker Pro, you can make copies by using the Finder or a commercial backup program (described in Chapter 2).

In particular, you may want to make a backup copy of a file for the following reasons:

❖ As a general precaution against data loss due to user error, hardware failure, or software problems (a crash, for example)

❖ When you are planning to make a major change to a database, such as deleting records or modifying a layout

❖ When you want to create a database template, either to give to someone else or to save for your own use

You can make an exact duplicate of a database file (containing all the data and layouts) from the Finder, using a commercial backup program, or from within FileMaker Pro. However, you can make *templates* (databases without data) only from within FileMaker Pro.

To duplicate a FileMaker Pro database file from within FileMaker Pro, do the following:

1. **In FileMaker Pro, open the database that you wish to copy.**
2. **Select Save a Copy As from the File menu.**

   A file dialog box appears, as shown in Figure 3-7.

Figure 3-7: This dialog box enables you to save a copy of a FileMaker Pro database in any of three formats.

3. **Click the Save a: pop-up menu and select the type of file that you want to create.**

You choose from the following types:

- *Copy of current file:* Use this choice when you want an exact duplicate of a file, including all the layouts and data that it contains.
- *Compressed copy (smaller):* This choice produces a usable copy of a database, but the copy is compressed to save disk space. This option is particularly useful when you are *archiving* a database (storing it for posterity or as a backup) or when a database is a bit too large to fit on a floppy disk.
- *Clone (no records):* Select this option when you want to create a template from the database. All formulas, field definitions, and layouts are retained in the new file, but it contains no records.

4. **In the "Create a copy named" text box, FileMaker Pro proposes a name for the copy, using the following convention:**

   Copy of *current filename*

   If you like, you can change the name.

5. **Using standard file dialog box procedures, navigate to the disk and folder in which you want to save the copy.**

   (See "Dealing with Dialog Boxes" in Chapter 2 for additional information.)

More about Clones

A FileMaker Pro *clone* is the equivalent of a template or stationery file that you create in most other programs. It's an empty database, ready for you to begin adding records. Unlike icons for templates or stationery files that you create in other programs, however, the icon for a clone looks exactly like the icon for any other FileMaker Pro database file, so recognizing that it's a clone is difficult. And because it's not a *real* template or stationery file, when you open a clone, you aren't opening a copy of it — you're opening the actual file. Any data that you add to the clone is automatically saved as part of the file. If you want to preserve the clone, make a copy of it (or make a second clone) and make changes to the copy rather than to the original.

Clones are particularly useful when you have databases that you routinely need to start over from scratch (for example, a bookkeeping database that you clear monthly or annually), when you want to experiment with a layout, or when you want to provide a template for other users but don't want them to have your data.

When you open a clone for the first time, the bulk of the screen is blank. You can't see the fields or graphics elements that you painstakingly added to the original layouts. To begin using the file, choose New Record (⌘-N) from the Edit menu. After a record is created, the fields and designs immediately appear.

Chapter 3: FileMaker Pro Basic Operations

6. Click Save (or press Enter or Return).

The copy is saved in the format that you selected.

Automatic backups

If you're worried about making inadvertent changes to a database or concerned that something catastrophic may happen to a database, you can create a FileMaker Pro script that automatically creates a backup every time you open the database. A copy of the script is added to the Scripts menu so that you can instantly create backups during a session, too.

To create an automatic backup script, follow these steps:

1. Launch FileMaker Pro and open the database.

2. Choose ScriptMaker from the Scripts menu.

The Define Scripts dialog box appears (see Figure 3-8). The dialog box displays all scripts that have been defined for the database.

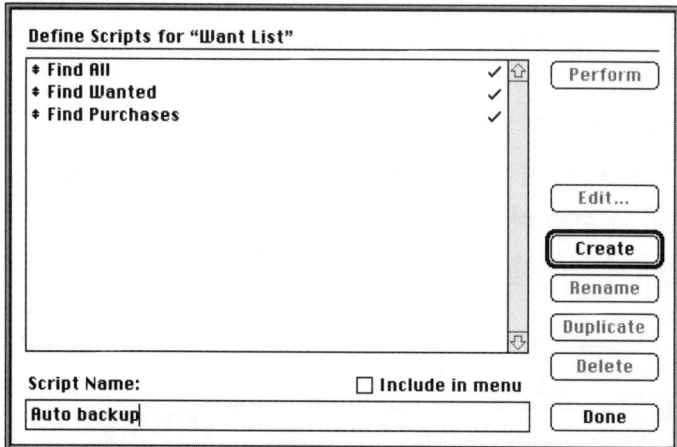

Figure 3-8: The Define Scripts dialog box.

3. Type a name for the script in the Script Name box.

If the Include in menu check box does not contain a check mark, click once in the box to add the check mark.

4. Click Create to define the script.

The Script Definition dialog box appears, as shown in Figure 3-9.

Part I: The Fundamentals

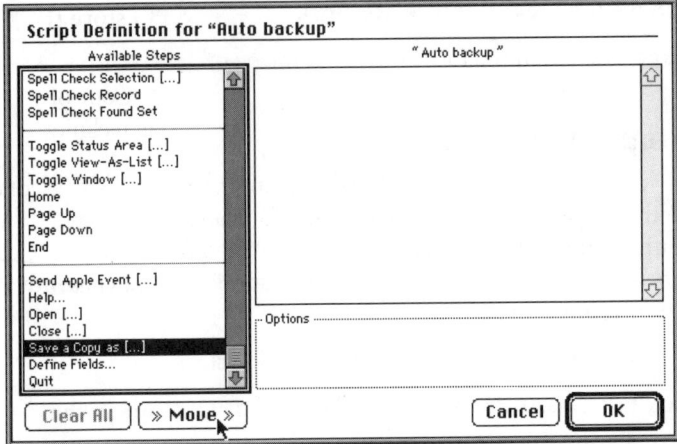

Figure 3-9: The Script Definition dialog box.

5. **Click Clear All to clear the script definition list on the right side of the dialog box.**
6. **Scroll down the Available Steps list until the choice Save a Copy as [...] appears.**
7. **Select Save a Copy as [...] and then click the Move button.**

   The script step is copied to the script list on the right.

8. **Click the Specify File button.**

   A standard file dialog box appears, as shown in Figure 3-10.

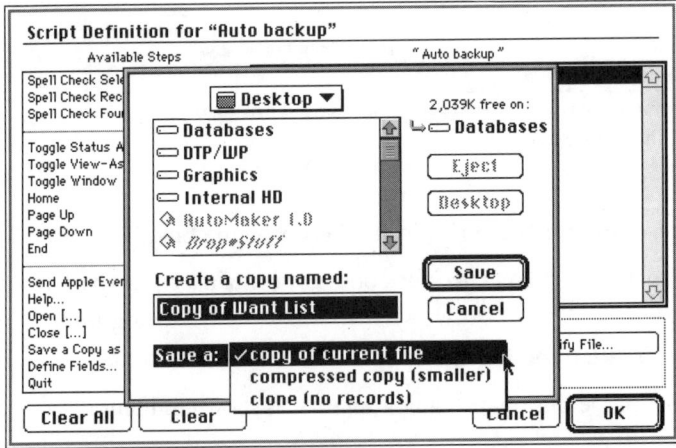

Figure 3-10: You specify the name, location, and type of backup file in this dialog box.

Chapter 3: FileMaker Pro Basic Operations

9. **Navigate to the drive and folder where you intend to store the backup files made by the script.**

    By default, FileMaker Pro offers to name the backup file Copy of *filename*, but you can change the name of the file using normal editing techniques.

10. **At the bottom of the dialog box, click the Save a: pop-up menu and choose either copy of current file or compressed copy (smaller).**

    Either option will save a complete copy of the database, including all records, layouts, and field definitions. If disk space is at a premium, you may prefer to use the latter option.

11. **Click the Save button.**

12. **To complete the script, click OK and then click Done in the dialog boxes that appear.**

    A backup copy is created, and the script is added to the bottom of the Scripts menu.

13. **To make the script execute automatically whenever you open the database file, choose Preferences from the File menu.**

    The Preferences dialog box appears, as shown in Figure 3-11.

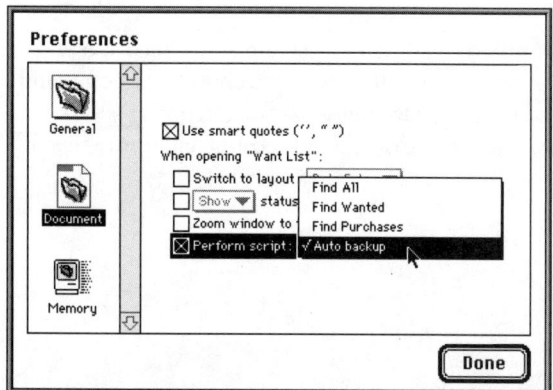

Figure 3-11: The Preferences dialog box.

14. **Click the Document icon in the left side of the dialog box and click the Perform script check box in the right side of the dialog box.**

15. **Choose the automatic backup script from the pop-up list that appears (Auto backup, in this case).**

Part I: The Fundamentals

16. **Click Done.**

    The changes are recorded, and the dialog box disappears.

Keep the following in mind when you are using this backup script:

- Each time a new backup is created, it writes over the previous backup file. If you need to keep multiple generations of backups, you should return to the desktop and manually rename the backup before or at the end of each FileMaker Pro session.

- Remember that the backup file is an exact copy of the original. Thus, it also contains the automatic backup script. If you ever need to use the backup file, be sure to rename it before opening it in FileMaker Pro. Otherwise, an error dialog box will appear, informing you that FileMaker was unable to create a backup (because the script is attempting to make a copy of the currently open database, using its own name).

Issuing Commands

Issuing commands in FileMaker Pro is no different from issuing them in any other Macintosh program. For those of you who are new Mac users, the following discussion will be helpful.

To issue a command in FileMaker Pro — to create a new record or add formatting to a field, for example — you can use the mouse to choose the command from a menu, or if the command has a *keystroke equivalent*, you can press a special combination of keys. Figure 3-12 shows an example of selecting a command from a menu.

Figure 3-12: Selecting a command from a menu.

Chapter 3: FileMaker Pro Basic Operations

Some menu commands are gray. These *grayed-out* commands are not presently available, usually because they are not relevant to the operation that you are attempting to perform. For example, when you're in Browse mode, all commands in the Layout menu are grayed-out. This is because the Layout commands can only be executed when you are in Layout mode. Grayed-out commands become available only when they are relevant to the current state of the database and what you are doing at the moment.

To choose a menu command, do the following

1. **Click the menu title that contains the command that you want to issue.**

   The menu drops down, exposing the commands within it.

2. **While continuing to hold down the mouse button, drag the pointer until the command that you want to issue is *highlighted* (turns black).**

3. **Release the mouse button.**

   The command executes.

A strange propeller-shaped symbol and a letter follow some of the commands that are in the figure in the following sidebar. The ⌘ symbol represents the Command key (shown on most keyboards as ⌘ or). You can issue any menu command that is followed by a letter, number, or symbol without using the mouse or the menus. Such a command is said to have a *keyboard shortcut*, a *keyboard equivalent*, or a *Command-key equivalent* (all three terms mean the same thing).

To issue a keyboard shortcut, follow these steps:

1. **Press and hold the modifier key (or keys) that precedes the letter, number, or symbol in the menu.**

   The modifier keys that FileMaker Pro uses include the Shift, Option, and Command keys. They are called *modifier keys* because they have an effect only when you press them in combination with a letter, number, or symbol key. They *modify* the meaning of that key. Figure 3-13 shows the symbols used to represent these keys.

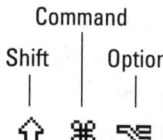

Figure 3-13: Modifier key symbols as displayed in FileMaker Pro menus.

2. **While holding down the modifier key(s), press the letter, number, or symbol key that completes the keyboard shortcut.**

   The command executes.

Part I: The Fundamentals

Overcoming keystroke conflicts caused by utilities

If using a keyboard shortcut produces an unusual effect (a dialog box appears that seems to have nothing to do with FileMaker Pro, for example), you probably have a utility running in the background that is conflicting with FileMaker Pro. Many background programs are constantly scanning for the particular key combination that activates them. On my system, for example, attempting to execute the keyboard shortcut for Define Fields (Shift-⌘-D) results, instead, in the launching of DiskTop — a file-manipulation utility.

Several options are available for overcoming conflicts of this sort:

❖ Reconfigure the utility so that it responds to a different key combination.

See the utility's manual for instructions. Assuming that reconfiguration is possible, this is the best solution. To avoid additional conflicts, try to choose key combinations that are unlikely to conflict with your main programs. You can avoid many conflicts by using the Control key as the modifier key rather than the Command, Option, or Shift keys.

❖ If you cannot reconfigure the utility, turn it off when you are using FileMaker Pro. Again, see the manual for details.

No matter how helpful utilities are, few of them are as critical as the work that you do in a major application, such as a database, word processing program, or spreadsheet. If a utility gets in the way, temporarily shut it down. If you can't reconfigure it or shut it down, get rid of it.

❖ When a conflict occurs, restrict yourself to using FileMaker Pro's menus to select the command.

This solution is better than nothing, but not by much. It may remind you of this old joke:

Patient: "It hurts when I do this."

Doctor: "Well, then don't do that!"

Using Tools and Palettes

This section provides a brief introduction to the tools and palettes that are available in FileMaker Pro. Later chapters describe them in detail.

Figure 3-14 shows FileMaker Pro in Layout mode. This figure shows all tools except the few that are specific to Find mode.

❖ *Layout pop-up menu* (available in all modes): Click this icon to display a menu of the names of all layouts that have been created for the current database. Selecting a different layout from the menu switches to that layout.

❖ *Book:* In Browse mode, you use the book to switch to different records. In Layout mode, you use it to switch to different layouts. In Find mode, you use it to switch between multiple find requests.

Chapter 3: FileMaker Pro Basic Operations 87

Commands with ellipses and arrows

If you browse through FileMaker Pro's menus, you'll notice that two unusual elements are tacked onto the end of some commands: ellipses and arrows.

An *ellipsis* is a series of three dots. They indicate that the command displays a dialog box to which you have to respond (see the second set of commands in the Format menu, for example). In contrast, menu commands that do not have ellipses are executed immediately.

A right-facing arrow that follows a menu command (see the top set of commands in the Format menu) indicates that the command is accompanied by a *hierarchical menu* (also called a *pop-up menu* or *submenu*). When the mouse pointer slides over one of these menu commands, another menu pops out to the side of the original menu. You need to continue to hold down the mouse button while you move the pointer and highlight the appropriate command in the submenu. Then release the mouse button to choose the command.

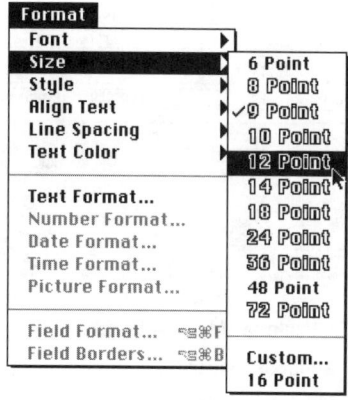

- ❖ *Tool palette* (Layout mode only): Clockwise from the top left, these tools are used to select objects (pointer), add or edit text (A), draw lines (line), draw ovals and circles (oval), draw rounded rectangles and rounded squares (rounded rectangle), and draw rectangles and squares (rectangle).

- ❖ *Field and part tools* (Layout mode only): These tools enable you to place additional fields and parts on a layout.

- ❖ *Fill and pen controls* (Layout mode only): You use the fill controls to set fill colors and patterns for objects. You use the pen controls to set line and border colors. Figure 3-15 shows the pop-up palettes that appear when you click the fill, pattern, or line width controls.

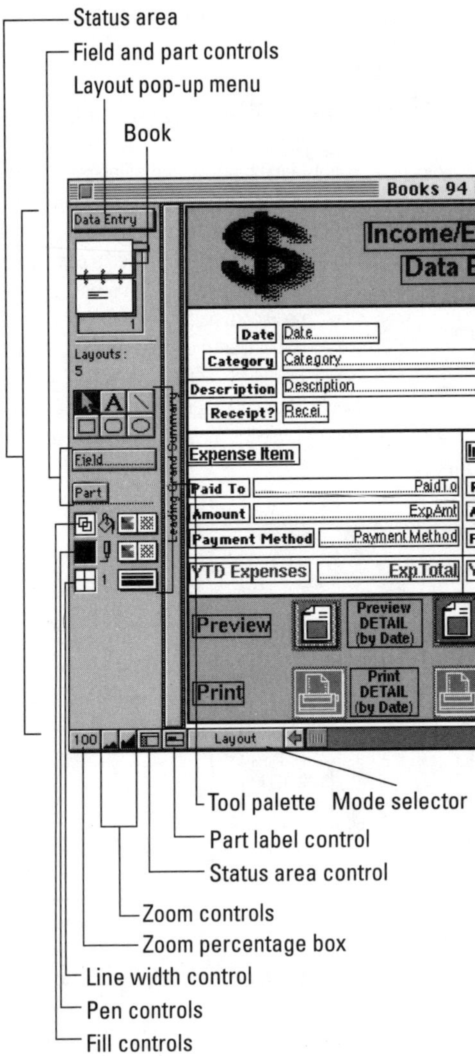

Part I: The Fundamentals

Figure 3-14: The FileMaker Pro tools and palettes.

Labels: Status area; Field and part controls; Layout pop-up menu; Book; Tool palette; Mode selector; Part label control; Status area control; Zoom controls; Zoom percentage box; Line width control; Pen controls; Fill controls.

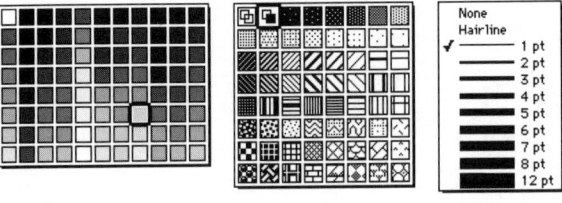

Fill palette — Pattern palette — Line width pop-up menu

Figure 3-15: Select a color, pattern, or line width by clicking in these palettes.

Chapter 3: FileMaker Pro Basic Operations

- *Line width control* (Layout mode only): The line width control enables you to set the thickness of any line (in points).

- *Zoom percentage box* (all modes): This box shows the current zoom level (enlarges or shrinks your view of what's on-screen). Click it to switch between 100 percent and the current zoom level.

- *Zoom controls* (all modes): Click the left icon to reduce the size of the view and provide a bird's eye perspective. The current zoom percentage is reduced by one-half. Click the right icon to increase the document's zoom (magnification) level. The current zoom percentage is doubled.

- *Status area control* (all modes): Click to show or hide the entire status area, including all tools.

- *Part label control* (Layout mode only): Click to switch between displaying layout labels horizontally and displaying them vertically.

- *Mode selector* (all modes): The mode selector displays the current mode. Click to display a pop-up menu (see Figure 3-16) that enables you to switch between the four program modes: Browse, Layout, Find, and Preview.

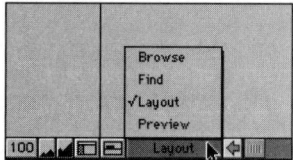

Figure 3-16: The Mode pop-up menu.

In Find mode, a few special tools are introduced, as shown in Figure 3-17. In addition, you use the book to switch between multiple find requests.

- *Omit check box* (Find mode only): Check this box to exclude records from the found set that match the find criteria. For example, if the criterion is Sales > 100000, you create a found set of records that includes everyone *except* salespeople with sales of more than $100,000.

- *Symbols pop-up menu* (Find mode only): Instead of typing conditional symbols and special characters when you are entering find criteria, you can select them from this pop-up menu.

- *Find button* (Find mode only): Click this button when you are ready to execute a find request (or multiple find requests).

 **Part I: The Fundamentals**

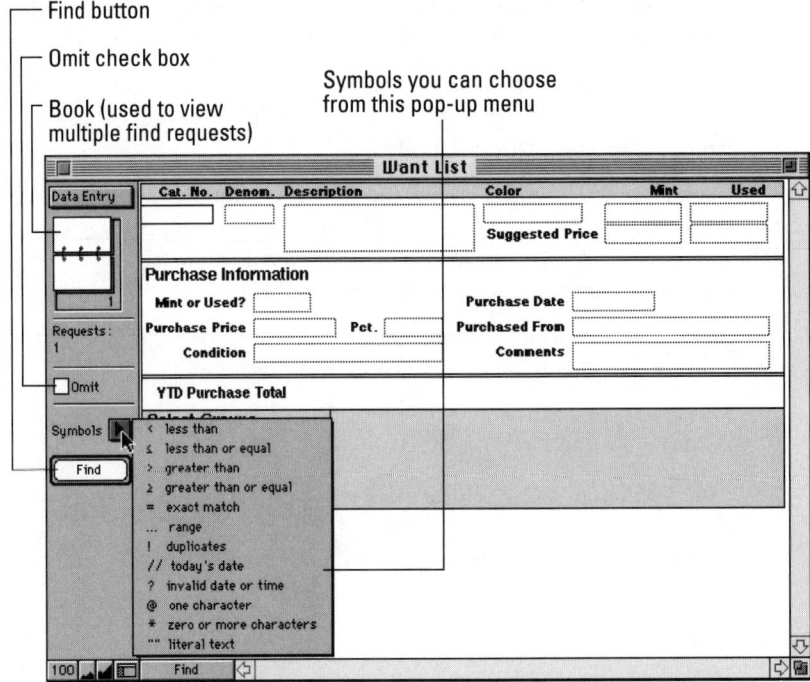

Figure 3-17: The tools in Find mode.

Chapter 3: FileMaker Pro Basic Operations

CHAPTER 3 CONCEPTS AND TERMS

- Layouts are arrangements of database fields. Different layouts enable you to view and present information in different ways. You can have as many layouts for a database as you like.
- Layouts are divided into sections called *parts*. Depending on the parts in which you place fields, text, and objects, they will be printed once for every record in the database (body), only at the top or bottom of each report page (header or footer), only at the top or bottom of the first report page (title header or title footer), once before or after each group of records sorted on the sort-by field (leading or trailing sub-summary), or once before or after all of the records being browsed (leading or trailing grand summary).
- You do all work in FileMaker Pro in one of four modes: Browse, Layout, Find, and Preview. For example, you can enter data only when the database is in Browse mode. If you're ever unsure of the current mode, check the Mode indicator at the bottom of the database window.
- Ordinary business or home users do not need to be concerned about FileMaker Pro's limitations unless their databases are enormous (greater than 32MB) or extremely complex (requiring more than 14 open files at the same time).
- Double-clicking a database icon on the desktop is the quickest way to launch FileMaker Pro and simultaneously open the database.
- Changes that you make to a database are automatically saved for you. If you want to protect a database, you can use the Save a Copy As command to make a backup copy.
- You can issue commands by choosing from menus and, in some cases, by pressing keyboard shortcuts.

Apple menu
The menu at the far left side of the menu bar. Under System 6, the Apple menu only displays desk accessories. In System 7, it also can contain programs, documents, control panels, and *aliases* (stand-ins for programs, documents, folders, or disks). (See Chapter 2 for additional information about aliases.)

application menu (System 7 only)
The tiny icon in the upper-right corner of the menu bar that, when clicked, displays a menu of all currently running programs. Using the application menu, you can switch among programs and selectively hide or reveal programs.

backup
An exact copy of a file.

back up
To create a duplicate of one or more files.

clone
An exact copy of a previously-created FileMaker Pro database that is stripped of all records.

file dialog box
Any dialog box that is designed to enable file-handling tasks, such as opening, saving, importing, and exporting files. Unlike most dialog boxes, file dialog boxes frequently have no title.

hierarchical menu (also pop-up menu, submenu)
A secondary menu that pops up when a menu command is selected.

keyboard shortcut (also keyboard equivalent, Command-key equivalent)
The keystrokes required to issue a menu command from the keyboard.

layout
A particular arrangement of fields, text, and graphics for a FileMaker Pro database. You can use a layout for viewing records, entering data, and generating printed and on-screen reports. A database can have multiple layouts.

mode
A state of a FileMaker Pro database in which you can perform only one global type of activity. The four modes are Browse, Find, Layout, and Preview.

modifier key
Any key on the keyboard that, when pressed in combination with another key, modifies the meaning of the second key. On a Macintosh keyboard, modifier keys include Shift, Option, ⌘, and — on some keyboards — Control.

MultiFinder (System 6 only)
A first-generation multitasking system software component that enables you to run multiple programs simultaneously. Using MultiFinder was optional in System 6, but its capabilities were made an integral part of System 7.

open
To load a copy of a document from disk into a program. You also can open desktop windows for disks and folders (by double-clicking the icon that represents them).

save
To store a current copy of a document on disk.

script
One or more commands associated with a specific database that FileMaker will execute automatically or when instructed by the user to do so.

ScriptMaker
The FileMaker Pro component that you use to design scripts.

Part II
Database Design Basics

CHAPTER FOUR

Creating Your First Database: Address Book

IN THIS CHAPTER

- Designing a full-featured database
- Creating and formatting fields
- Using graphics in layouts
- Mastering layout tools that enable you to place, resize, and align objects
- Designing multiple layouts for data entry and reports
- Sorting and searching for records
- Creating scripts and assigning them to buttons and the Scripts menu
- Setting preferences for a database

When I first conceptualized this chapter, I imagined walking you through the steps of creating a simple FileMaker Pro database. But the more I thought about it, the more pointless that approach seemed. The purpose of this book is to give you a solid understanding of FileMaker Pro's features and capabilities, not just a quick glimpse of them. So this chapter took a dramatic turn.

Instead of helping you design a simple database, this chapter steps you through the creation of a full-featured database called Address Book, a database that has graphics, multiple layouts, buttons, scripts, and reports. Figure 4-1 shows the data-entry layout for the completed database and points out a few of its features.

Part II: Database Design Basics

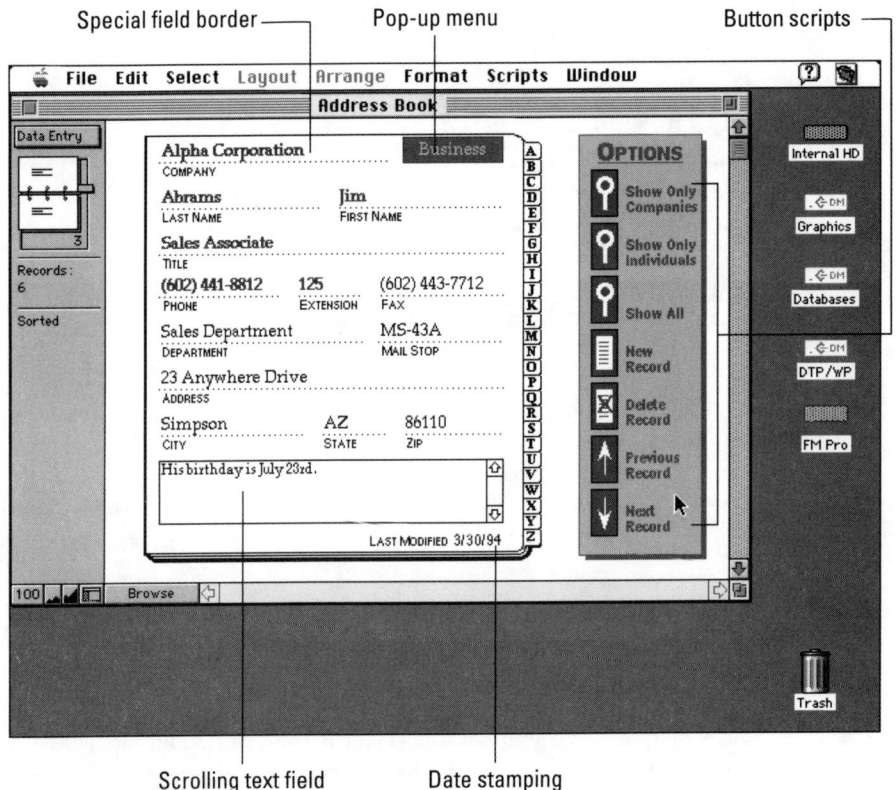

Figure 4-1: The data-entry layout for Address Book.

Constructing your own version of Address Book introduces you to the following FileMaker Pro tasks:

❖ Setting field types and choosing field options

❖ Creating pop-up menu fields, required fields, auto-entry fields, and scrolling text fields

❖ Adding formatting to text, including fonts, sizes, styles, alignments, and colors

❖ Creating field borders

❖ Using layout tools to size and place fields, field labels, and other objects precisely

❖ Using graphics in layouts and grouping and ungrouping objects

Chapter 4: Creating Your First Database: Address Book

❖ Creating a report layout that has automatic date-stamping and page number-stamping in the footer

❖ Designing scripts and assigning them to buttons or to the Scripts menu

The purpose of this extended exercise is to help you become familiar with many of the important functions of FileMaker Pro while you create a database that you may actually want to use. After you finish making the database, you will have at least a passing familiarity with how FileMaker Pro works and what its many capabilities are. Later chapters provide in-depth instructions on using the program features that this chapter discusses.

The *Macworld FileMaker Pro 2.0/2.1 Bible Disk* includes two templates for the database: Address Book and Address Book — Graphics. If you haven't already done so, install the database templates on your hard disk. See Appendix F for instructions.

Address Book is the finished database. Before launching into this tutorial, you may want to play with Address Book to see what you are going to accomplish. Address Book — Graphics contains the background graphics and buttons that you use to make the database more attractive.

Designing a database that does exactly what you want it to do (collecting the proper data and presenting it in ways that meet your specific needs) is seldom a linear process. Unless you spend an inordinate amount of time planning a database before you begin the actual construction work in FileMaker Pro, you are likely to add more fields, delete some fields that — in retrospect — you don't need, design additional reports, and tweak the layout (trying out different fonts and alignments, for example). In the design process, you'll repeatedly bounce between Layout, Browse, and Preview modes, as well as in and out of ScriptMaker.

Like most tutorials, however, this one is in a format that is step by step and linear. But don't be fooled. This relatively simple database took me a full day to construct, and the process was far from linear. Thus, don't be surprised if the process that you go through in designing your own databases doesn't match the Step 1⇨Step 2⇨Step 3 approach that you find in this chapter. (Of course, planning does help. The more time you spend deciding which fields, reports, and scripts you need; how to format fields; and what you want the layouts to look like, the faster the creation process will go.)

Step 1: Create a New Database

If FileMaker Pro isn't already running, double-click the FileMaker Pro icon to launch the program. To begin the process of creating the database, choose New from the File menu. The file dialog box shown in Figure 4-2 appears.

Part II: Database Design Basics

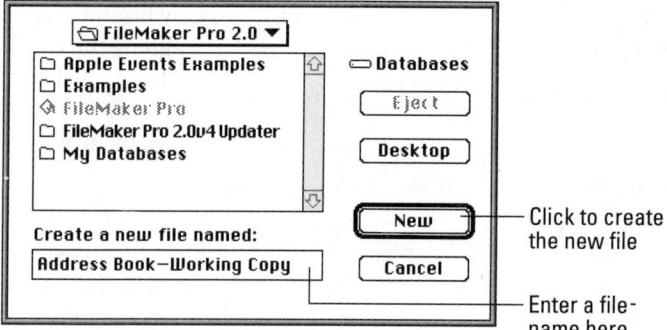

Figure 4-2: Creating a new database.

Select the disk drive and folder in which you want to store the new database, enter a name for it (**Address Book — Working Copy**, for example), and click New. The Define Field dialog box appears, as shown in Figure 4-3.

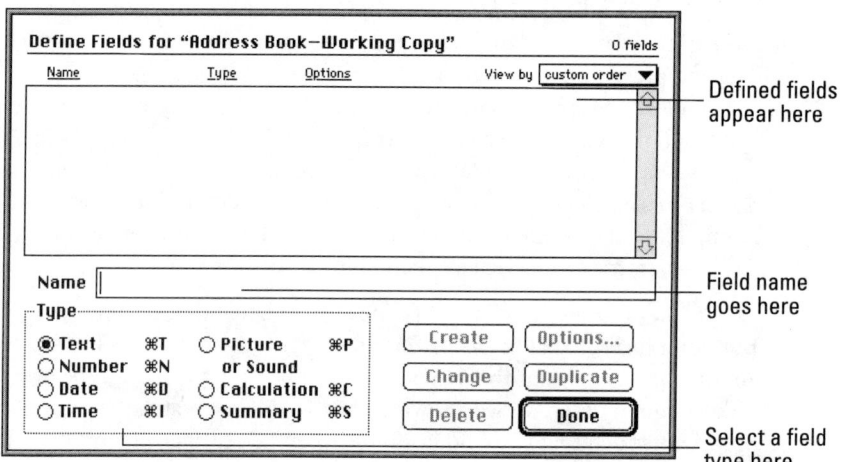

Figure 4-3: The Define Fields dialog box.

Step 2: Define Fields

As with any new database, the first task is to define the fields that the database will use to store and present the data. You need to define a database field before you can use it. A field definition consists of the field's name, the type of information that the field will contain (text, number, date, time, picture or sound, calculation, or summary), and any special options that you want to set for the field.

Chapter 4: Creating Your First Database: Address Book

Defining fields often requires several steps. You normally begin by defining all the fields that you think you will need. In the process of designing the database, however, you often discover that you should have created additional fields initially or find that you don't need some of the fields that you have defined. Making a change in the fields is not a problem. You can add them or remove them as the need arises, even after you create records and enter data.

To keep things simple, there are only two field types used in the Address Book database: text and date. Table 4-1 lists the database fields that you need to define.

Table 4-1
Field Definitions for Address Book

Field Name	Type	Options	Field Contents
First Name	Text		First name of contact
Last Name	Text		Last name of contact
Title	Text		Person's title, if any
Company	Text		Company affiliation
Department	Text		Department
Mail Stop	Text		Mail stop
Address	Text		Street address
City	Text		City
State	Text		State
Zip	Text		Zip code
Phone	Text		Area code and phone number
Extension	Text		Phone extension
Fax	Text		Area code and fax number
Category	Text	Required Value, Value List	Classification for the record
Comments	Text		Notes
Last Modified	Date	Modification Date	Date the record was last altered

Note that you usually think of several of these fields — Phone, Extension, Fax, and Zip — as containing numbers. In Address Book, however, these fields are text fields rather than number fields. In FileMaker Pro, you define a field as a number for the following reasons:

Part II: Database Design Basics

❖ You intend to use the contents of the field in a calculation.

❖ You want to restrict the contents of the field to numbers only.

Because you are not going to base a calculation on any of these four fields and because they can legitimately contain letters or special characters — such as (619) 443-5555, 1-800-SUCCESS, and N9B 3P7 — it makes better sense to treat them as text than to define them as number fields.

You need to set options for only two fields, Category and Last Modified. Although you can set field options when you are defining the field, for this example you define the fields first and then set the field options.

To define the first field, type **First Name** in the Name text box. Note that the moment you begin typing, the Create button becomes selectable. Because Text is already chosen as the field type and you are not assigning any options to the field, click the Create button. The field is added to the scrolling list at the top of the dialog box (see Figure 4-4).

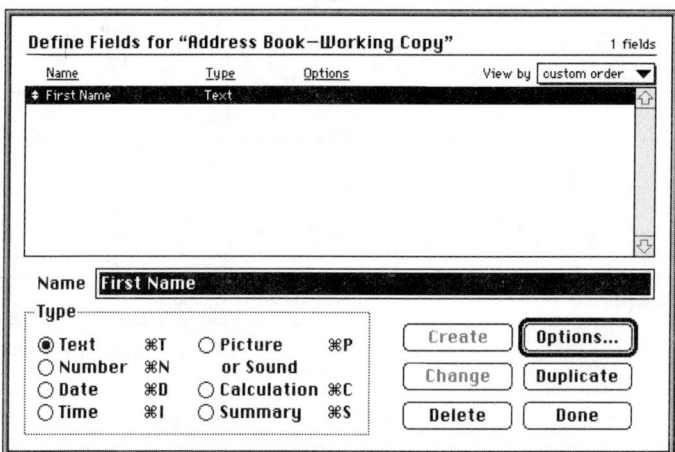

Figure 4-4: Defining the first field.

To create the Last Name field, type **Last Name** in the Name text box and click Create again. Continue this process, defining every Text field in Table 4-1 through the Comments field.

Finally, create the Last Modified field. Type **Last Modified**, choose Date as the field type, and click Create. The Last Modified field automatically stores the date that each record was last modified, giving you an idea of how current the information is.

Chapter 4: Creating Your First Database: Address Book

Speeding up the Field Definition Process

You can make the field definition process go faster by pressing Return or Enter after you type each field name. Whenever the Create button, or any other button in a dialog box, is surrounded by a thick line, you can choose it by pressing Return or Enter. Of course, you can still click the button with the mouse if you prefer.

Step 3: Set Field Options

You can use various FileMaker Pro field options to automatically enter information (such as the current date or a serial number), verify that only appropriate data has been entered, create repeating fields (entries in an invoice, for example), or present a pop-up list of values for a field. As examples of these capabilities, you define options for two fields: Last Modified and Category.

With the Last Modified field still selected, click the Options button. The Entry Options for Date Field "Last Modified" dialog box appears, as shown in Figure 4-5. (Note that regardless of the field for which you are setting options, the dialog box always looks the same. The name of the dialog box changes, however, to reflect the name and type of field for which you are setting options.) Choose Modification Date from the pop-up menu, as shown in Figure 4-5. Then click OK to return to the Define Fields dialog box.

Figure 4-5: Setting an option for the Last Modified field.

Part II: Database Design Basics

When the database is finished, use the Category field to assign a general classification to every record: Business, Friend, or Relative. (Even if you would prefer other classifications, please use these for the example. You can change them to something more appropriate later.)

Make Category a *required field* — one that cannot be empty. When you are doing data entry, if you attempt to leave a record without first making a Category choice, FileMaker Pro displays a warning.

Follow these steps to set options for the Category field:

1. **In the Define Fields dialog box, select the Category field and then click Options.**

   The Entry Options for Text Field "Category" dialog box appears.

2. **In the Verify that the field value is section of the dialog box, click the not empty check box.**

3. **Click the Use a pre-defined value list check box near the bottom of the dialog box.**

   Because no value list has been defined for the field, the Display Values for "Category" dialog box automatically appears (see Figure 4-6). Any values that you enter in this dialog box will appear as a pop-up menu when you click or tab into the Category field. The order in which you type the values is the order in which they will appear.

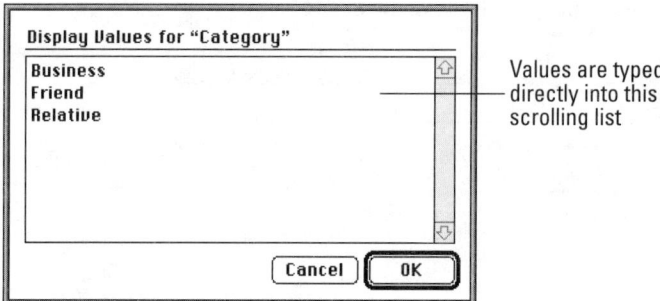

Figure 4-6: Creating a value list.

4. **Type the three lines of text that are shown in the Display Values for "Category" dialog box in Figure 4-6, pressing Return after typing the first and second values.**

Chapter 4: Creating Your First Database: Address Book

5. **After you enter the values, click OK to accept them and click OK again to return to the Define Fields dialog box.**

After you have defined all the fields and set their options, click Done. A *standard layout* is automatically created for you, as shown in Figure 4-7. As you can see, a standard layout is a vertical arrangement of all the database fields. Each field includes a label that matches whatever you named the field in the Define Fields dialog box.

If you were interested in only a quick-and-dirty database, you could stop right here. Address Book — Working Copy is ready to receive data. Instead, in the next step you rearrange the fields, add field formatting, and include some graphics to make this layout more visually appealing.

If you'd like to learn more about defining fields, see Chapter 5.

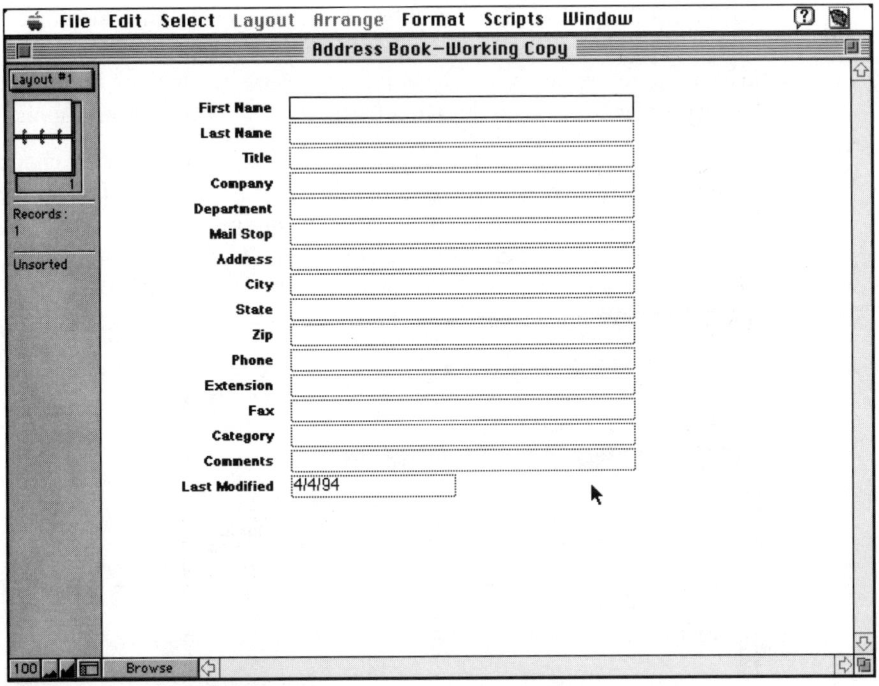

Figure 4-7: A standard layout.

Step 4: Design the Data Entry Layout

If you want to carry the Data Entry layout beyond the functional stage — all the way to attractive and pleasant to use — you may find that you spend more time on this task than on any other database development task. Frankly, however, not every database is worth the extra effort. Many databases, such as those intended only for your personal use, need never evolve beyond the functional stage. A database that you use daily or one that you intend to distribute to others, on the other hand, should look good and contain scripts that make performing common tasks easy. In this step, you do some of the work that's required to create an attractive layout.

Altering the layout parts

Normally, the standard layout that FileMaker provides is a good starting point for a custom layout such as the one you are going to create for Address Book. Because I know the height of the graphics that you are going to place in the background, however, I'll save you a little grief by having you change the size of the layout before you add the graphics and arrange the fields. Specifically, you'll remove the header and footer layout parts (because they serve no purpose in the Data Entry layout) and enlarge the body layout part (to make room for the graphics and fields).

To delete the unnecessary layout parts, switch to Layout mode by choosing Layout from the Select menu and then choose Define Parts from the Layout menu. The Define Parts dialog box appears, as shown in Figure 4-8. To remove the header part, select Header and click the Delete button. Then delete the footer part, too. Finally, click Done to close the dialog box. You return to the layout and see that it now contains only one part — the body.

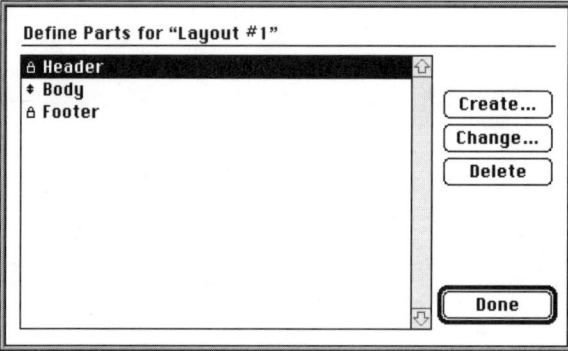

Figure 4-8: The Define Parts dialog box.

The body needs to be about 5.5 inches high. If you don't see a ruler down the left side of the layout, choose the Rulers command from the Layout menu. To increase the height of the body, drag the Body part indicator down until you reach the 5.5-inch mark.

Adding graphics

Next, add the background graphics. They're stored in the file named Address Book — Graphics. Having the graphics in place enables you to more easily arrange the fields so they fit correctly. (After you begin to create your own databases, you can design your own graphics in any graphics program, buy ready-made graphics called clip art, or if you don't intend to resell the databases you can copy graphics from files that you obtain from user groups and on-line information services.)

Follow these steps to transfer graphics from Address Book — Graphics to Address Book — Working Copy (or whatever you named the database you are creating):

1. **Choose Open from the File menu and choose the database that contains the graphics (Address Book — Graphics, in this case).**

   The file opens.

2. **Choose Layout from the Select menu and then click to select the graphics.**

   Note that because the database opens in Browse mode, you can see the graphics when you open it, but you can't select them. You have to be in Layout mode to copy or otherwise manipulate elements in a layout.

   Because the graphics have been *grouped* (so you can work with them as a single unit instead of as the mass of little images that they really are), clicking anywhere within the graphics selects everything. (When an object is selected, a black dot called a *handle* appears at each of the objects four corners, as shown in Figure 4-9.) Later you will use the Ungroup command so you can deal with the graphics elements individually.

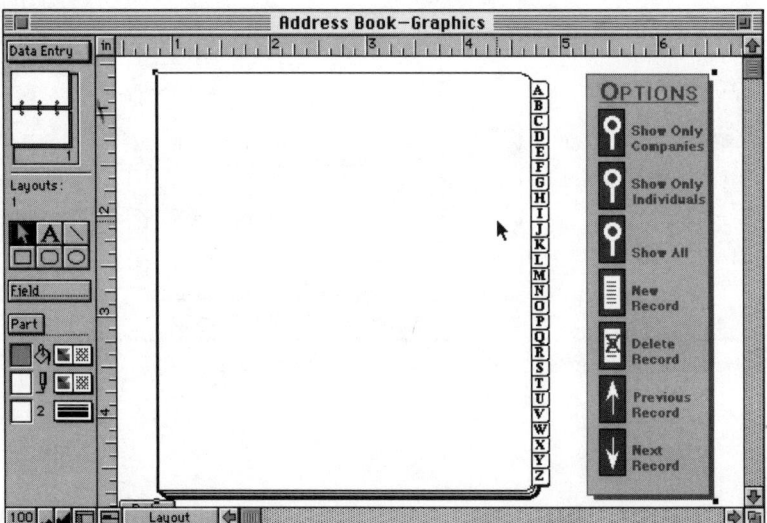

Figure 4-9: The Address Book — Graphics database.

Part II: Database Design Basics

3. **Choose Copy from the Edit menu (or press ⌘-C).**

   A copy of the graphics is stored in memory (in the Macintosh Clipboard).

4. **Choose Close from the File menu.**

5. **Open the destination file — the one that will receive the copied graphics.**

   If your copy of the Address Book — Working Copy database isn't already open, choose Open from the File menu, choose the Address Book — Working Copy database, and click Open.

6. **Switch to Layout mode by choosing Layout from the Select menu (or by pressing ⌘-L).**

7. **Choose Paste from the Edit menu (or press ⌘-V).**

   The graphics are pasted onto the layout.

8. **Because you want the graphics to appear *behind* the data fields instead of obscuring them, choose Send to Back from the Arrange menu (or press Shift-⌘-Option-J).**

9. **Then drag the graphics so they approximately match the placement shown in Figure 4-10.**

Figure 4-10: Address Book — Working Copy, with the graphics in place.

Chapter 4: Creating Your First Database: Address Book

Setting field attributes

Instead of immediately moving the fields and labels to their final resting place on the layout, use the initial stacked format to select and assign text attributes (font, size, style, alignment, and color) as well as field borders, as described in the following sections.

Text attributes

All the field labels are displayed in the finished database with the same font and format, so start by selecting them. To select multiple fields, first select the Pointer tool by clicking its icon in the Tools palette. Then do either of the following:

❖ Drag a selection rectangle that completely surrounds the fields of interest.

❖ Hold down the Shift key and click every field that you want to include in the selection.

You also can combine the two approaches. In this case, though, because the field labels are all stacked in a nice, neat column, the first approach is simplest. The selected fields should look like the ones in Figure 4-11.

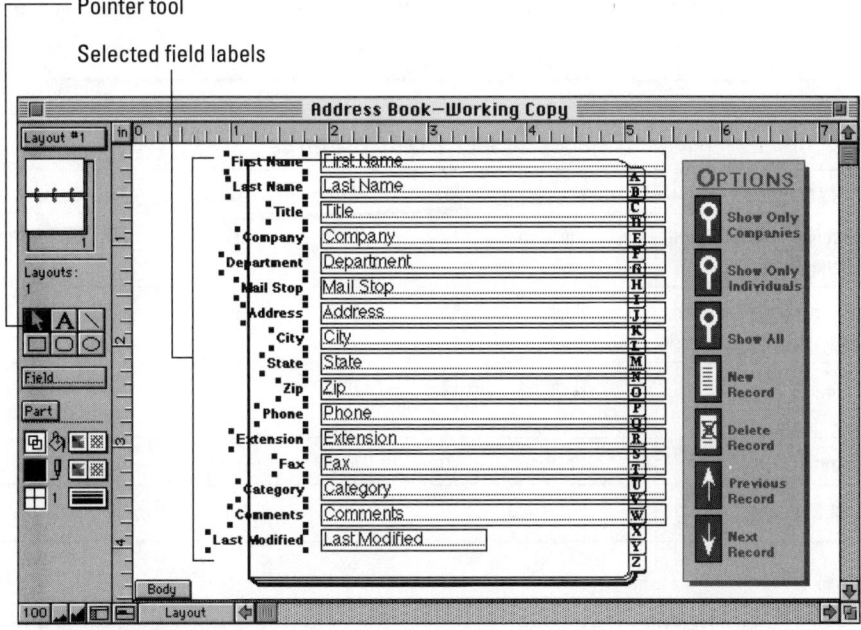

Figure 4-11: Selecting the field labels.

Part II: Database Design Basics

The format for each of the *field labels* is left-aligned, 9-point Helvetica, with small caps. With the field labels still selected, choose the following commands from the appropriate submenus of the Format menu:

- Choose Helvetica from the Font submenu. (If Helvetica does not appear as a choice in the Font submenu, choose another font.)
- Choose 9 from the Size submenu.
- Choose Bold or Plain Text from the Style submenu. (Either command will remove the boldface that was assigned by default to the field labels.)
- Choose Small Caps from the Style submenu.
- Choose Left from the Align Text submenu.

Next, format the fields. In the layout, each field appears as a rectangle surrounding a field name. As you apply different formatting attributes to a field, the field name automatically changes to reflect the new attributes.

Select individual fields or groups of fields as described in Table 4-2 and apply the designated formats. Each column in Table 4-2 corresponds to a text attribute command in the Format menu. Working with a single row of the table at a time is easiest.

Table 4-2
Field Text Attributes

Field Name(s)	Font	Size	Style	Align Text	Text Color
First Name, Last Name, Title, Phone, Extension	Palatino	12	Bold	Left	Dark blue Company,
Department, Mail Stop, Address, City, State, Zip, Fax	Palatino	12	Plain	Left	Black
Category	Palatino	12	Plain	Center	Faint blue
Comments	Palatino	10	Plain	Left	Black
Last Modified	Helvetica	10	Plain	Left	Black

Showing you which colors to use for the field text is easier than expecting you to guess. Figures 4-12 and 4-13 illustrate the process of picking a text color, as well as the specific colors that you should choose.

Chapter 4: Creating Your First Database: Address Book

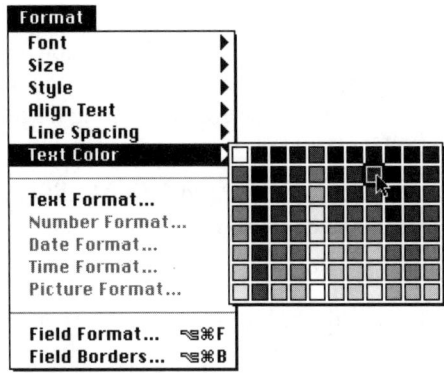

Figure 4-12: Select this color for the First Name, Last Name, Title, Company, Phone, and Extension fields.

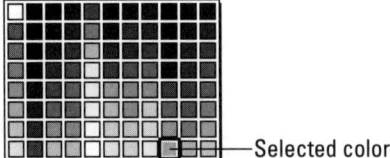

Figure 4-13: Select this color for the Category field.

Choosing Several Text Format Options at One Time

Try this shortcut for making several different Format menu selections: After you select each field or group of fields, choose Text Format from the Format menu. In the Text Format dialog box that appears (see the accompanying figure), you can simultaneously set all the text formats for the selected fields.

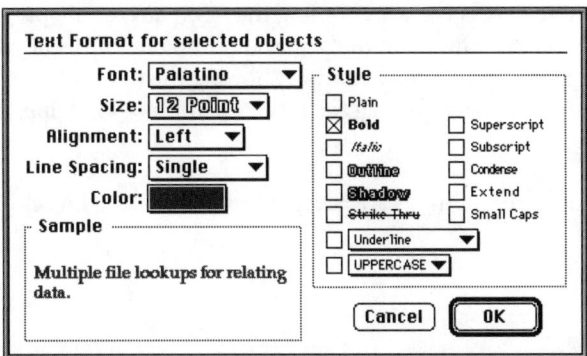

Part II: Database Design Basics

Field borders

If you take another peek at the finished version of Address Book shown in Figure 4-1, you'll note that many of the fields have a dotted line as a bottom border. Although FileMaker Pro does not have a specific feature for creating dotted lines, you can use the trick described in the following steps:

1. **Select all fields except Category, Comments, and Last Modified. (Be sure to select only the fields — not the fields labels.)**

2. **Choose Field Borders from the Format menu.**

    The Field Borders for selected objects dialog box appears, as shown in Figure 4-14.

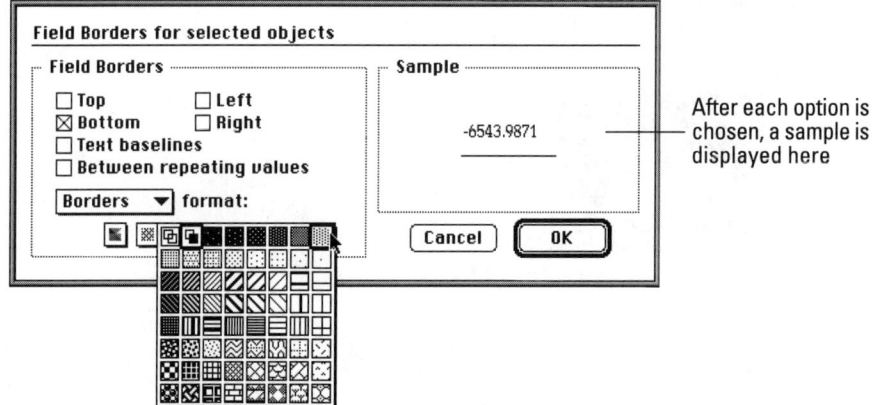

Figure 4-14: Selecting a pattern for a bottom border.

3. **Click the Bottom check box.**

4. **At the bottom of the dialog box, click the pattern pop-up menu (the second icon from the left) and choose the pattern shown on the right side of the pop-up menu in Figure 4-14.**

    You'll note that as you are choosing the new pattern, the previous pattern (the solid fill on the left side of the pattern pop-up menu) is still selected. When you release the mouse button, a sample showing the dotted-line pattern appears in the Sample box — replacing the former pattern (a solid line, in this instance).

5. **Click OK.**

    The new border settings are accepted, and the dialog box closes.

Chapter 4: Creating Your First Database: Address Book

Field formats

The Format menu has a few commands that you haven't used in the Address Book database. The final option that you are going to use is the Field Format command. You use it in this database to make the Comments field into a scrolling text window, but you can use it to add a vertical scroll bar to any standard field. This feature is particularly useful when you want to store a great deal of text in a relatively small area on a layout.

Follow these steps to create a scrolling text window for the Comments field:

1. **Select the field on the layout (in this case, the Comments field).**
2. **Choose Field Format from the Format menu.**

    The Field Format for "Comments" dialog box appears, as shown in Figure 4-15).

Figure 4-15: The Field Format dialog box.

3. **Be sure that the Standard field radio button at the top of the dialog box is selected and then click the Include vertical scroll bar check box.**
4. **Click OK.**

    The dialog box closes, and a vertical scroll bar is added to the right side of the selected field.

Setting the dimensions for and placing fields

The last two major field-arrangement tasks are resizing the fields and placing them in their proper places on the layout. You can alter the size of fields, field labels, and graphics objects on a layout in two ways:

❖ Manually — by selecting an object and dragging one of its handles in the appropriate direction

❖ Precisely — by entering one or more dimensions in the Size windoid

To see the tiny Size window (see Figure 4-16), choose Size from the Layout menu.

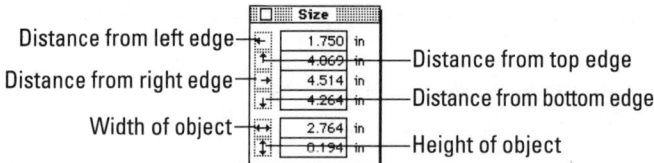

Figure 4-16: The Size windoid enables you to see and change the dimensions and location of any selected object.

Because your task in this tutorial is to duplicate the layout shown in Figure 4-1, rather than make a rough approximation of it, you can use the Size windoid to avoid all the manual dragging and resizing. However, because most of the databases that you'll design from scratch won't have a template that you're attempting to match, you also need to explore the manual method.

Manually sizing and placing objects on the layout

So that you'll have some fields with which to work, start by selecting the following fields and their field labels: First Name, Last Name, and Title. Choose Copy from the Edit menu and then choose Paste. Duplicates of these fields and labels will appear on the layout. With these objects still selected, drag them to the right until they cross the vertical dashed line that marks the page break. Moving the objects to this area gives you plenty of room to experiment without fear of disturbing the "real" fields, labels, and graphics.

When you finish trying out the manual sizing and placement procedures, be sure to select the duplicate fields and labels that you created and remove them by pressing Delete.

Before modifying any of the duplicate objects, you may want to turn on some of the tools in the Layout menu. For example, the Align to Grid command simplifies creating equal-sized fields and arranging them in a uniform manner. The T-Squares tool also can help you make sure that fields are properly aligned with one another — in straight rows and columns. You also may want to choose Text Objects from the Show submenu of the Layout menu. This command places a

Chapter 4: Creating Your First Database: Address Book

bounding box around every field label and text object on the layout and enables you to more easily determine visually whether these objects are correctly positioned and in alignment with other objects.

Next you can begin to experiment with manually changing field sizes. Whether you're working with a field, a label, or another layout object, you always begin by selecting the object. (A selected object has a black dot called a *handle* at each of its corners.) To change a field's size or shape, drag any handle to a new location. Dragging options include the following:

- ❖ *Dragging:* The normal dragging procedure enables you to change the height, width, or both dimensions as you drag. (If the Align to Grid feature is on and you're reasonably careful, you can relatively easily make sure that only one dimension changes.)

- ❖ *Shift-dragging:* If you press the Shift key as you drag, you restrict size changes to one dimension — horizontal or vertical. When you want to keep all text fields the same height, this technique is ideal for ensuring that only the field's width changes.

- ❖ *Option-dragging:* Depending on the shape of the object you're resizing, pressing the Option key as you drag restricts the object's final shape to a square, a square with rounded corners, or a circle.

Manually *placing* an object is also a simple task. Click anywhere within the center of the object and drag it to a new spot on the layout. As you drag, FileMaker Pro displays an outline of the object (as shown in Figure 4-17) so that you can easily see the object's precise location before you release the mouse button.

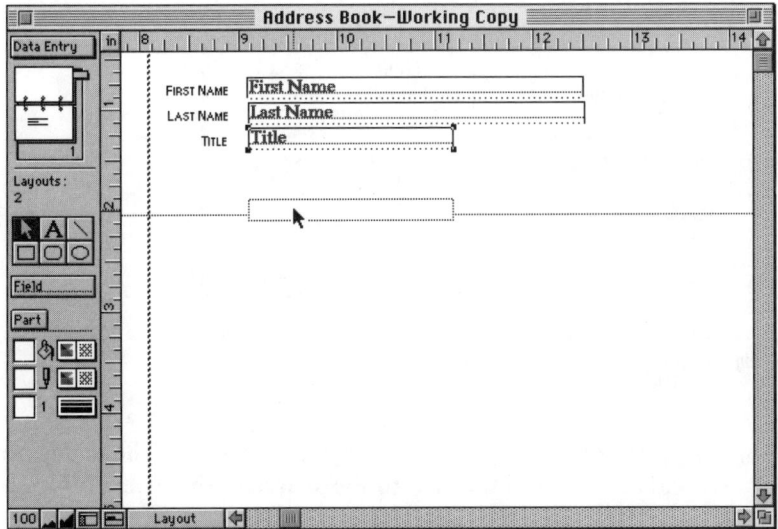

Figure 4-17: Dragging a field to a new location.

Part II: Database Design Basics

Nudging an Object

You can nudge any selected field, label, or other object slightly by pressing any arrow key. This technique works even when the Align to Grid command is in effect.

After resizing and rearranging the fields and labels, you also may want to try out FileMaker Pro's alignment commands. To keep things nice and uniform, you can use Alignment and Align Objects to align the edges of any group of fields or to align fields and their labels, for example. These commands are especially helpful when you have nudged several objects with the arrow keys or have been aligning objects by using the "eyeball method" — as in: "Hmm . . . Looks like the First and Last Name fields are lined up now."

The steps in this box describe how to align selected objects:

1. **Select the objects that you want to align with each other by selecting the Pointer tool and then drawing a selection rectangle around the objects, Shift-clicking the objects, or using a combination of the two selection methods.**

2. **Choose Alignment from the Arrange menu.**

   The Alignment dialog box appears (see Figure 4-18).

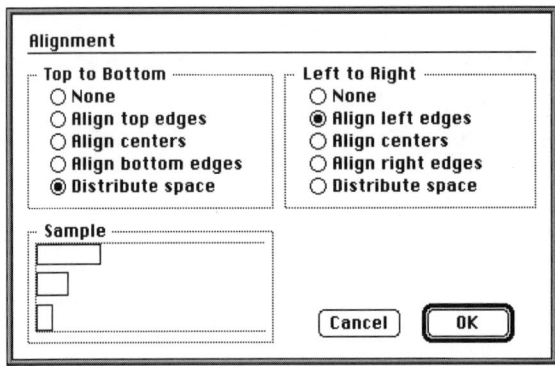

Figure 4-18: The Alignment dialog box.

3. **Select one option from the Top to Bottom area of the dialog box and a second option from the Left to Right area of the dialog box.**

   As you choose options, the Sample area of the dialog box shows what effect your choices will have on the selected objects.

4. Click OK.

The dialog box closes, and FileMaker Pro executes the alignment options. If the result is not what you intended, you can restore the objects to their previous locations by immediately choosing Undo Align from the Edit menu (or pressing ⌘-Z).

The options that you choose in the Alignment dialog box remain in effect until you choose new options or until you quit the program. These options are also the ones that will be used when you choose the Align Objects command from the Arrange menu (or press ⌘-K). Unlike the Alignment command, Align Objects is executed immediately on the selected objects. No dialog box appears.

If you want to become more familiar with the process of manually sizing and placing fields, refer to Figure 4-1 and attempt to match the field widths and placements visually as best you can. When you're done, use the information in Tables 4-3 and 4-4 in the next section to see how well you have done and to correct any mistakes you have made.

Using the Size windoid to size and place layout objects

You can use the Size windoid (refer to Figure 4-16) to perform the following functions:

❖ Determine the exact location and dimensions of any object on a layout

❖ Move an object to a precise location

❖ Change the dimensions of an object

Instead of using the Alignment command to arrange several fields in a perfect column, for example, you can select each field and then enter the same distance from the left edge of the page in the first text box in the Size windoid. Also, by clicking several objects one-by-one, you can check to make sure that they are all exactly the same distance from a particular edge or that they are all the same height or width.

In this tutorial, however, your use of the Size windoid is a bit unorthodox. You combine the second and third uses of the Size windoid from the preceding list to precisely size and place every field and label on the layout — and you do both at the same time. Using the Size windoid in this manner is very much like having a robot slave who happily and mindlessly pushes the fields around the page for you.

Although this exercise doesn't have a practical application — after you start designing your own databases, that is — it does serve two important purposes. First, it enables you to quickly match the placement of fields and labels with those in the finished Address Book database. Second, it makes you an expert on using the Size windoid. When you have a real need for it, you won't have to flip through the manual or this book to see how the Size windoid works.

Part II: Database Design Basics

To resize and place the fields and labels, read the following instructions for using the Size windoid and then, using the information in Tables 4-3 and 4-4, enter the appropriate numbers in the windoid's text boxes to size and place the fields and field labels, respectively.

1. **If the Size windoid is not visible, choose Size from the Layout menu.**

   The Size windoid appears (see Figure 4-16). If you want to change the measurement units for the Size windoid, click one of the units to the right of any number entry in the windoid. Each mouse click chooses one of the three possible measurement units: inches, centimeters, and pixels.

2. **Select the object whose placement or size you want to modify.**

   Handles (black dots) appear at the object's corners to show that it is selected.

3. **To change the position of the selected object, type numbers into any of the top four text boxes in the Size windoid.**

   In order, these boxes represent the object's distance from the left, top, right, and bottom edges of the layout area. To execute the changes, press Tab or Return to move to the next text box, press Enter to stay in the same text box, or use the mouse to click in a different text box.

   You can precisely set the location of any object by specifying any pair of vertical and horizontal units, as in distance from left and distance from top, or distance from right and distance from bottom, for example. As you make changes to the chosen pair of units, the numbers in the other pair automatically change to reflect the object's new location.

4. **To change the dimensions of the selected object, type numbers into the bottom two text boxes: width and height.**

5. **To execute the changes, press Tab or Return to move to the next text box, press Enter to stay in the same text box, or use the mouse to click in a different text box.**

For example, to set the size and location of the First Name field and the other fields in the database, follow these steps:

1. **Using the Pointer tool, select the First Name field.**

2. **In the Size windoid, type the numbers shown in the First Name row of Table 4-3.**

   Move from one text box to another by pressing Tab or Return or click in each box with the mouse. When you're through, the Size windoid should look like the one in Figure 4-19.

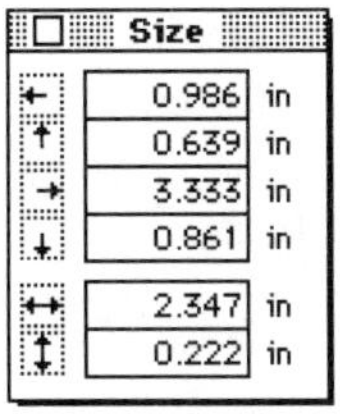

Chapter 4: Creating Your First Database: Address Book

Figure 4-19: The entries for sizing and placing the First Name field.

3. **Next, without closing the Size windoid, individually select each field and one-by-one enter the appropriate settings from Table 4-3.**

Table 4-3 lists the size and placement for the fields in the Address Book database. Note that the Height dimension remains constant for most of the fields. This consistency is natural, because most fields contain data that is formatted with the same font and size.

Table 4-3 Field Size and Placement (all dimensions are in inches)				
Field Name	**Left Edge**	**Top Edge**	**Width**	**Height**
First Name	2.819	1.097	1.681	.222
Last Name	.986	1.097	1.681	.222
Title	.986	1.556	3.514	.222
Company	.986	.639	2.347	.222
Department	.986	2.431	2.097	.222
Mail Stop	3.236	2.431	1.264	.222
Address	.986	2.889	3.514	.222
City	.986	3.347	1.514	.222
State	2.667	3.347	.681	.222
Zip	3.486	3.347	1.014	.222
Phone	.986	1.972	1.264	.222
Extension	2.403	1.972	.681	.222
Fax	3.236	1.972	1.264	.222
Category	3.528	.639	.931	.222
Comments	.986	3.806	3.514	.639
Last Modified	3.986	4.528	.514	.194

Table 4-4 contains the data that you need to position all the field labels. It does not include Width and Height dimensions because every label is already the correct size. Because neither the Comments nor the Category field has a field label in the final layout, remove these two labels by selecting them and pressing Delete. Then, one-by-one, select each field label in Table 4-4 and enter its pair of placement figures in the Size windoid.

Table 4-4 Field Label Placement (all dimensions are in inches)		
Field Label	**Left Edge**	**Top Edge**
First Name	2.819	1.319
Last Name	.986	1.319
Title	.986	1.778
Company	.986	.861
Department	.986	2.653
Mail Stop	3.236	2.653
Address	.986	3.111
City	.986	3.569
State	2.667	3.569
Zip	3.486	3.569
Phone	.986	2.194
Extension	2.403	2.194
Fax	3.236	2.194
Last Modified	3.125	4.542

Adding the finishing touches

In designing the data entry layout, only a few minor tasks remain:

❖ Naming the layout

❖ Setting the final size of the layout

❖ Adding a box around the Category field

❖ Ungrouping the background graphics

Chapter 4: Creating Your First Database: Address Book

Naming the layout

Layout #1 is the default name assigned to the first layout created for a database. Because this database will have more than one layout, giving each layout a more descriptive name is preferable. The following steps describe how to assign a name to a layout:

1. **Choose Layout from the Select menu.**

2. **If the database has more than one layout, switch to the layout that you want to rename by choosing its current name from the layout pop-up menu in the upper-left corner of the document window.**

   (At this point, Address Book has only a single layout, so this step is unnecessary.)

3. **Choose Layout Options from the Layout menu.**

   The Layout Options dialog box appears (see Figure 4-20). The current name of the layout is shown in the Name text box.

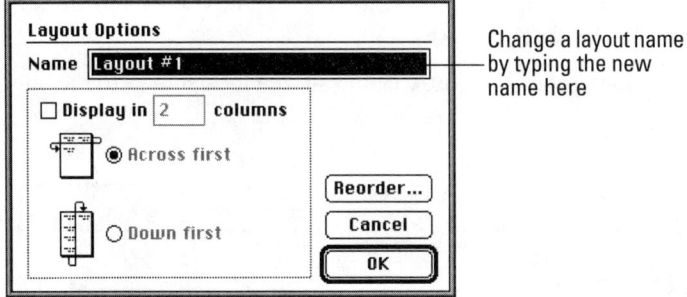

Figure 4-20: The Layout Options dialog box.

4. **Type the new name for the layout and then click OK.**

   In this example, type **Data Entry.**

You do not have to assign a name to a layout at any specific time. You can assign and change layout names whenever the mood strikes you. However, because some FileMaker Pro scripts refer to layouts by name, setting layout names early in the design process — and certainly before you begin to create any scripts — is the best method.

Part II: Database Design Basics

Setting the final size of the layout

Because you will use the Data Entry layout only for data entry and you will never use it to view more than one record at a time, the layout will look better if you eliminate all unnecessary white space that surrounds the graphics. To eliminate the unnecessary white space, do the following:

1. **Change to Layout mode (choose Layout from the Select menu or press ⌘-L).**
2. **Choose Select All from the Edit menu (or press ⌘-A).**

   This command selects all the objects on the layout (in this case, the fields, field labels, and the background graphic).

3. **Drag the objects so that their edges are closer to the top and left edges of the layout.**
4. **Click the Body part indicator and drag it upward to remove any unnecessary space.**
5. **If you like, you can drag the window's size box to match the size of the Data Entry layout.**

   Your version of the Data Entry layout should look similar to the one shown in Figure 4-21.

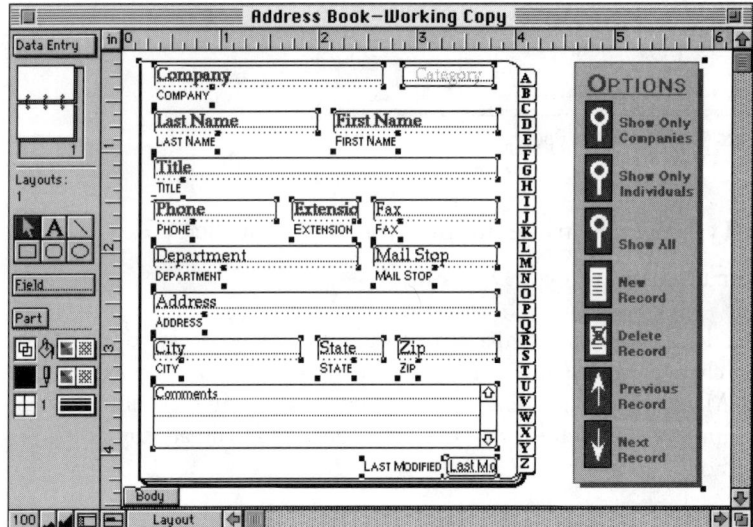

Figure 4-21: The resized Data Entry layout.

Chapter 4: Creating Your First Database: Address Book

Adding a box around the Category field
Because the text for the Category field is set in a light-colored font, adding a colored graphics box around the field enables you read the text easily and makes the field stand out. To create a box, follow these steps:

1. **Switch to Layout mode (choose Layout from the Select menu or press ⌘-L).**

2. **Click the Box tool in the Tools palette.**

3. **In both the Fill color and Pen color pop-up palettes, select the color shown in Figure 4-22.**

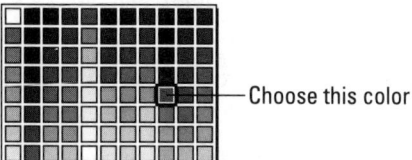

Figure 4-22: Choose this color for both the Fill and Pen color.

4. **Drag to create the box around the Category field.**

5. **With the box selected, choose Send Backward from the Arrange menu (or press Shift-⌘-J).**

   Issuing this command moves the box behind the text field, making the text clearly visible.

6. **As necessary, move and resize the box so it fits snugly around the Category field.**

This technique can be used to create a background for *any* object on a layout. An alternative procedure for making a contrasting background for either a field or a field label is to simply select the field or label and then choose a color from the Fill color pop-up menu in the Tools palette.

Ungrouping the background graphics
To make manipulating the background graphics safer when you were in the design phase of creating the Data Entry layout, the graphics were initially *grouped*. (To group objects, you switch to Layout mode, select the graphic elements to be grouped, and then choose the Group command from the Arrange menu). Grouping enables you to treat two or more individual graphic elements as a single entity. As a result, you can move the graphics without fear of leaving some elements behind, and you can apply a formatting command that simultaneously affects all the graphic elements in the group.

After you *ungroup* the graphics, you can treat each graphic element, such as the buttons in the control palette, individually. You can move one element or assign a script to one element, for example.

Follow these steps to ungroup previously grouped objects (in this case, the background graphics):

1. **Change to Layout mode by choosing Layout from the Select menu (or pressing ⌘-L).**

2. **Select the graphic element that you want to ungroup.**

   Because all the graphics form a single group, click anywhere in the background graphic (the control palette on the right, for example). Handles appear at the corners of the graphic to show that it is selected.

3. **Choose the Ungroup command from the Layout menu (or press Shift-⌘-G).**

   Every element in the selected object that was previously grouped is now displayed with its own handles, showing that it is now ungrouped.

Although you will later assign scripts that will interact with the Data Entry layout, the design work is now done. The layout that you just created should look very much like the one shown in Figure 4-23. For more information on designing and modifying layouts, see Chapter 6.

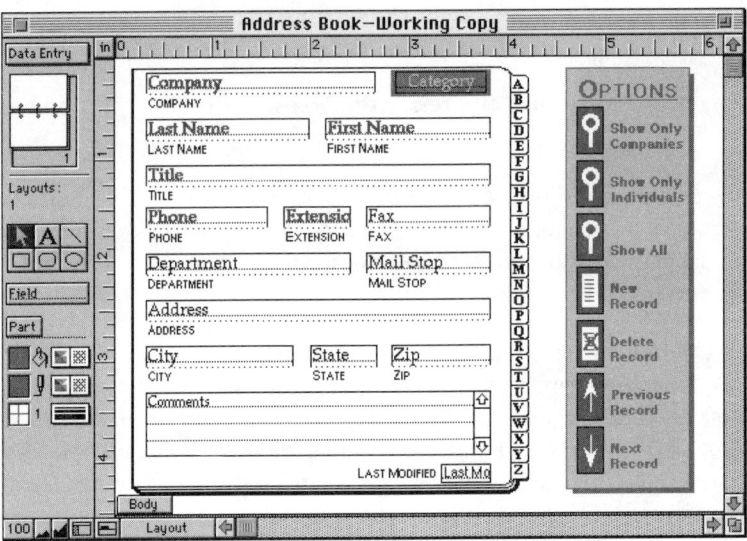

Figure 4-23: The finished Data Entry layout.

Step 5: Design a Report Layout

Although the Data Entry layout is excellent for its intended purpose (entering address and contact information), most users wouldn't have much interest in using this layout to create reports. (If you're curious, open the finished Address Book database, make sure that the Data Entry layout is selected, and then choose Preview from the Select menu. Preview mode shows what you would get if you were to print the current layout. As you can see, only two records fit on a page, and the information in each record is arranged in exactly the same way as it looks when you're in Browse mode — pretty, but hardly functional.)

Unless you have designed an all-purpose layout for a database, you're usually better off creating one layout for data entry and other layouts for reports. As an example of the kinds of reports that you can produce from the Address Book database, you next create a layout that prints a phone directory. Phone Directory is a columnar report layout. As with most such layouts, you can print reports that you generate from it or view them on the monitor. The finished layout looks like the one in Figure 4-24.

Figure 4-24: The completed Phone Directory layout.

Preselecting Text Formatting Settings

Whenever you enter Layout mode and set a new font, style, color, or so on, without first selecting a field or object to which the formatting will be applied, those formatting options become the new defaults. The next field, label, or object that you create will automatically use those preselected settings. Thus, you can use this trick to preselect the text formatting for the fields and save yourself the trouble of having to manually reformat each field after FileMaker Pro generates the layout.

To preselect the text formatting, enter Layout mode, make sure that no field or object is selected in the current layout (Data Entry), and choose the following settings in the Format menu:

- ❖ Font: Palatino
- ❖ Size: 10
- ❖ Style: Plain Text
- ❖ Align Text: Left
- ❖ Text Color: Black

Finally, set the Fill and Pen colors in the Tools palette to white.

Part II: Database Design Basics

To create the preliminary Phone Directory layout, follow these steps:

1. **Change to Layout mode by choosing Layout from the Select menu (or pressing ⌘-L).**

2. **Choose New Layout from the Edit menu (or press ⌘-N).**

   The New Layout dialog box appears, as shown in Figure 4-25.

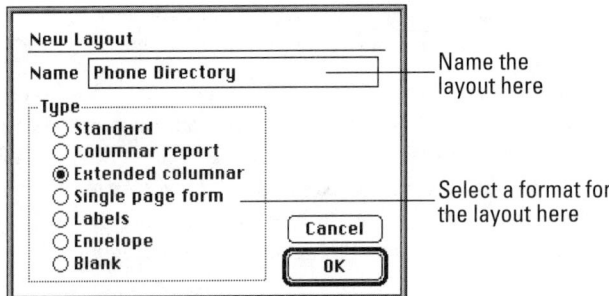

Figure 4-25: The New Layout dialog box.

3. **Type a name for the layout in the Name text box.**

   (In this case, type **Phone Directory**.)

   Instead of accepting the default name for the layout (Layout #2, in this example) or naming it later in the process as you did with the Data Entry layout, you name this layout when you create it.

4. **Click the Extended columnar radio button.**

   FileMaker Pro 2 can automatically generate two types of columnar reports: columnar and extended columnar. The only difference between the two layouts is the manner in which FileMaker places the fields when it creates the layout.

   In a columnar report layout, fields do not exceed the width of a single page. If the fields don't initially fit, FileMaker automatically wraps them into as many rows as are needed. In an extended columnar layout, FileMaker assumes that you don't care how wide the layout is and simply arranges all the field columns in a single continuous row. Because this format is going to be the final format for the report (you'll change the size of the fields as necessary to make them fit), the Extended columnar layout is the best format to choose.

5. **Click OK.**

   FileMaker presents the Set Field Order dialog box (see Figure 4-26).

Chapter 4: Creating Your First Database: Address Book

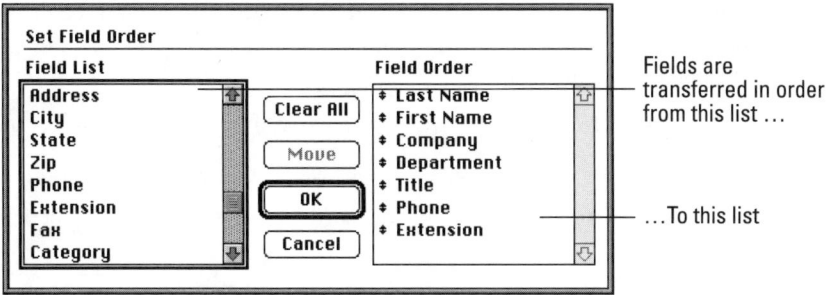

Figure 4-26: The Set Field Order dialog box.

6. **Select fields in the left side of the dialog box, click Move to transfer them to the Field Order list on the right, and when you have finished, click OK.**

   The Set Field Order dialog box has two functions. You use it to select the initial set of fields that you want to appear in the layout, and you also specify the order in which the fields appear. For the Phone Directory layout, select and move the following fields (in order): Last Name, First Name, Company, Department, Title, Phone, and Extension.

   The report layout is generated, as shown in Figure 4-27.

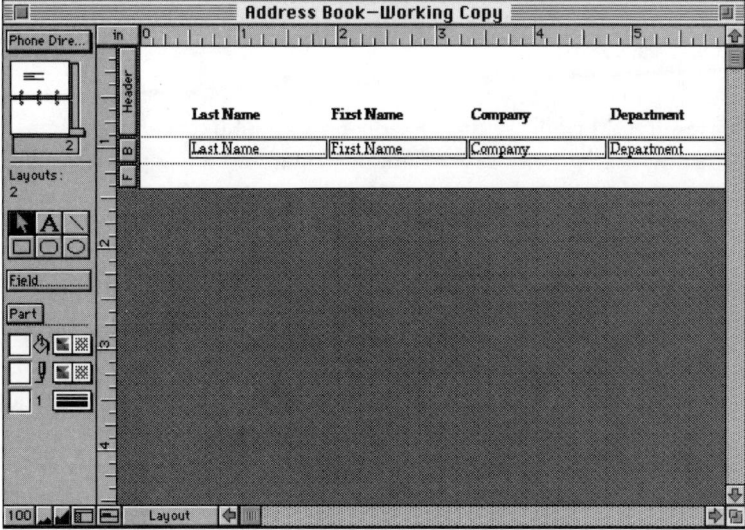

Figure 4-27: The tentative layout for the Phone Directory report.

If you scroll the Phone Directory layout from side-to-side, you see that it extends beyond the current page width by about 2.75 inches. Several possible solutions are available for this problem:

- Set printing for *landscape mode* (sideways), using the Page Setup command.
- Remove some of the fields.
- Change the layout by reducing the size of some fields and sliding them to the left.

Although using either of the first two approaches is an easy way to resolve the width problem, assume that you have your heart set on producing a phone directory report that you can print in portrait mode and that you want it to include every one of the originally chosen fields. Proceed with the third option — reducing field sizes and sliding them left so that they fit within the width of a single page.

Resizing the fields

Try using the "eyeball/best approximation" approach to manually resize and move the fields so they fit on the layout. You can use Figure 4-24 as a rough guideline to how wide the fields should be. (Unless you're feeling adventuresome, though, leave the column headings/field labels where they are. In the next section, you learn an easy way to move them.)

When you alter the width of each field, hold down the Shift key as you drag. Doing so assures that only one dimension of the field will change — the width, in this case. Because you prespecified the font to be used in every field, the *height* of each field is already correct.

When you're through manually resizing and shuffling the fields to the left, check your results against the settings for the Size windoid that are shown in Table 4-5. Please note that no settings are right or wrong. As long as you have left sufficient room for each field to display its intended contents, the layout is fine. However, if the data from any record doesn't fit within a field's new dimensions (the database may contain an extra-long company name, for example), the extra characters will be *truncated* (chopped off) when the report is printed. When setting field widths, err on the plus side if possible.

As before, to examine or alter the dimensions or placement of any field, select the field on the layout and then check its size and location in the Size windoid.

Table 4-5
Field Dimensions (Inches)

Field Name	Distance from Left Edge	Field Width
Last Name	.514	.903
First Name	1.431	.736
Company	2.181	1.486
Department	3.681	1.403
Title	5.097	1.403
Phone	6.514	1.153
Extension	7.681	.403

Formatting the header

In a columnar report, the field labels for the columns are normally placed in the header rather than in the body layout part. That way, when you scroll the report on-screen or print it, you can be assured that the column headers (the field labels) are always visible. To format the field labels, you need to do the following:

❖ Move the field labels downward, placing them closer to the body of the report (because I think they look better that way)

❖ Align each field label with its matching field

To move the field labels closer to the body, drag a selection rectangle around all of them and then press the down-arrow key five or six times. This technique moves all the field labels exactly the same distance.

To align each label with its matching field, follow these steps:

1. **Select a field and its matching label by Shift-clicking the two elements.**
2. **Choose Alignment from the Arrange menu.**
3. **Set options in the Alignment dialog box as shown in Figure 4-28. (In the Top to Bottom area, choose None; in the Left to Right area, choose Align left edges.)**

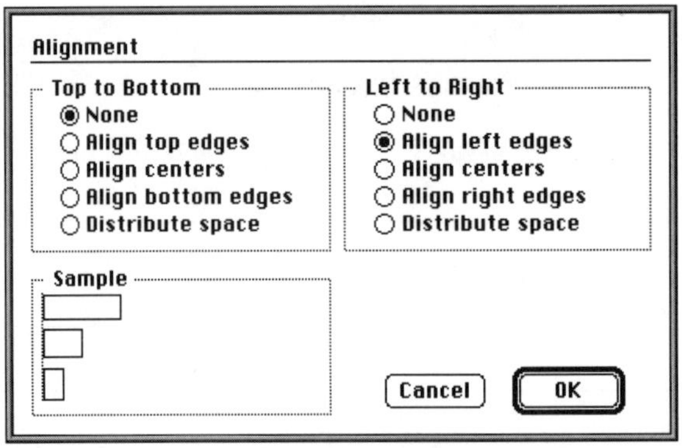

Figure 4-28: Match the settings in this dialog box.

4. **Click OK.**

   The dialog box closes, and the two fields are aligned.

After you set the proper alignment options, you can quickly align the remaining fields and labels by selecting each pair and pressing ⌘-K (the keyboard shortcut for Align Objects).

The labels now have only one thing wrong with them: some of them are too long or too close to the next label. Select the Text tool (the uppercase *A*) from the Tools palette and change the wording of the three labels that are too long:

❖ Change Last Name to Last

❖ Change First Name to First

❖ Change Extension to Ext.

Finally, the report could use a label of its own — a title, that is. Select the Text tool again, click near the top center of the Header part, and type **Phone Directory.** Then select the Pointer tool, click the Phone Directory text, and, using commands in the Format menu, set the text to 24-point Palatino Bold. As the last step, drag the text and place it near the top center of the header.

Formatting the footer

Like every other layout generated by FileMaker Pro, this one already has space reserved for a footer. Although the Data Entry layout doesn't need a footer, footers are often useful in report layouts. They can be used to present any information that you want to see on any page, such as a page number, date, name of the database, or the name of the user who created the report. To complete the Phone Directory layout, you will add a date-stamp and a page number place holder to the footer.

Chapter 4: Creating Your First Database: Address Book

To add the date-stamp, choose Date Symbol from the Paste Special submenu of the Edit menu. The date symbol, a pair of slashes (//), appears in the layout. Select the Pointer tool and drag the date symbol to the left edge of the layout, directly under the Last Name field.

To add automatic page-numbering to the footer, select the Text tool and type **Page** somewhere in the footer. Then choose Page Number from the Paste Special submenu of the Edit menu. The page number symbol, a pair of pound signs (##), appears in the layout. Using the Pointer tool, drag both the word *Page* and the page number symbol to the right edge of the layout. Leave a little space between *Page* and the place holder for the page number to keep them from running together when real page numbers are inserted.

Finally, to make the information in the footer stand out from the body of the report, use the Pointer tool to select all three items (the date symbol, the *Page* text, and the page number symbol) and press Shift-⌘-B (the keyboard shortcut for making text boldface). When you print the Phone Directory layout or view it in Preview mode, the date and page number symbols will automatically be replaced by the current date and the appropriate page numbers.

For more information on working with layout parts, see Chapter 6.

Step 6: Create the Scripts

Strictly speaking, you could quit right here and still have an extremely functional database. But by adding scripts that automate many of the database operations, you can transform this functional database into an easy-to-use, time-conserving database. Carefully chosen scripts can eliminate an enormous amount of wasted effort. For example, what's the point of constantly re-creating a particular Find request or set of Sort instructions when all you have to do is design a tiny script that performs these actions at the touch of a button?

Because the term *script* smacks of programming, many users shy away from the ScriptMaker feature. The simple but powerful scripts presented in this section show you what you have been missing and demonstrate just how easy ScriptMaker is to use. And no programming is required!

Address Book uses scripts in two ways: some are assigned to buttons, and others are available only as commands in the Scripts menu. Furthermore, some of the scripts contain several steps, and some execute only a single command. By looking at the ways in which scripts are incorporated into this database, you can get a good idea of the kinds of things that you can do with scripts in your own databases.

Revealing a Script's Sort and Find Instructions

You can easily reveal the Sort and Find instructions that are used in scripts contained in other people's databases. Perform the script and then immediately choose the Sort (⌘-S) and Refind (⌘-R) commands.

When you are examining the Sort and Refind requests, *performing* the Sort or Refind isn't necessary or desirable. You simply use these commands to determine what options the creator of the database set for the scripts. You can exit the Sort dialog box by clicking Done and exit the Refind request by choosing Browse mode from the Select menu (or by pressing ⌘-B).

The script definition process

When creating a script, the first step is to use menu commands to perform all the actions that the script will eventually handle. Doing so "sets up" the database so that all necessary command options are already selected. That is, while you are executing the steps that you intend to include in the script, you set, for example, the correct Sort, Find, Page Setup, Print, Export, and Import options. Setting these options is essential because you cannot specify Sort fields, Find logic, Print options, or settings for other commands as you create the script. In fact, the following methods are the only ones that you can use to set options for commands used in scripts:

❖ Instruct the script to present a dialog box that enables the user to verify the settings or enter different ones.

❖ Instruct the script to use the command settings that were in effect at the moment when the script was created.

If you are creating a generic Sort, Find, or Export script, the former approach works well. Each time the script step is executed, you can enter the appropriate settings in the dialog box that appears.

In many cases, though, you want scripts to perform steps that have preset options. For example, you may create a script that switches to a particular layout, finds only the records of employees who have arrived late for work more than three times in the last month, sorts the found records by salary, sets printing for landscape mode, and then prints the resulting report. Although you can instruct FileMaker Pro to present a dialog box for each of the last four actions (Find, Sort, Page Setup, and Print), doing so is a waste of time. Because you intend to use the same options every time you execute this script, incorporating the command options within the steps of the script is much simpler. Doing so adds consistency to the script's performance, and it ensures that no matter who runs the script (such as a temporary worker who is sitting in for you), the result is always the same.

Chapter 4: Creating Your First Database: Address Book

After creating the necessary scripts, you'll assign some of the scripts to the buttons in the background graphics. Other scripts will be available only as commands in the Scripts menu.

The Address Book scripts

Address Book contains nine scripts. Some are attached to buttons, others appear in the Scripts menu, and one is a special-purpose script that is used only as a step in another script. Each script is described in detail in the pages that follow. The first script, Show Companies, contains a complete walk-through of the script creation process. After creating the Show Companies script, you should have little difficulty creating the other scripts.

Before you start creating scripts, spend a few minutes entering some sample records for the database. You can more easily determine whether your scripts are working correctly if you have records in the database. (To create a new record, enter Browse mode and choose New Record from the Edit menu.) Be sure that your records contain a sampling of all three Categories (Business, Friend, and Relative) and that some records include a Company name and some do not. When you're ready to use your own data with the copy of Address Book that you have created (or with the finished template that's on the *Macworld Filemaker Pro 2.0/2.1 Bible Disk*), you can delete the dummy records.

The Show Companies script

This script limits visible records to those that have an entry in the Company field. Because FileMaker Pro does not have a Find symbol that enables you to search for a field that is not empty, the Find request has to do things the hard way. That is, it checks to see whether the Company field is blank and then omits all such records. The result is that only records that contain something in the Company field are displayed.

You are interested in looking at records sorted by company, so Company is selected as the first sort field. Because you may have several records for the same company, the records are further sorted by Last Name. Thus, all the personnel from a particular company will be listed in alphabetical order according to last names.

Follow these steps to create a script that sorts records by companies and last names:

1. **If the Data Entry layout isn't currently displayed, choose Data Entry from the layout pop-up menu in the upper-left corner of the document window.**

2. **Choose Find from the Select menu (or press ⌘-F).**

   A Find request form appears (see Figure 4-29).

Part II: Database Design Basics

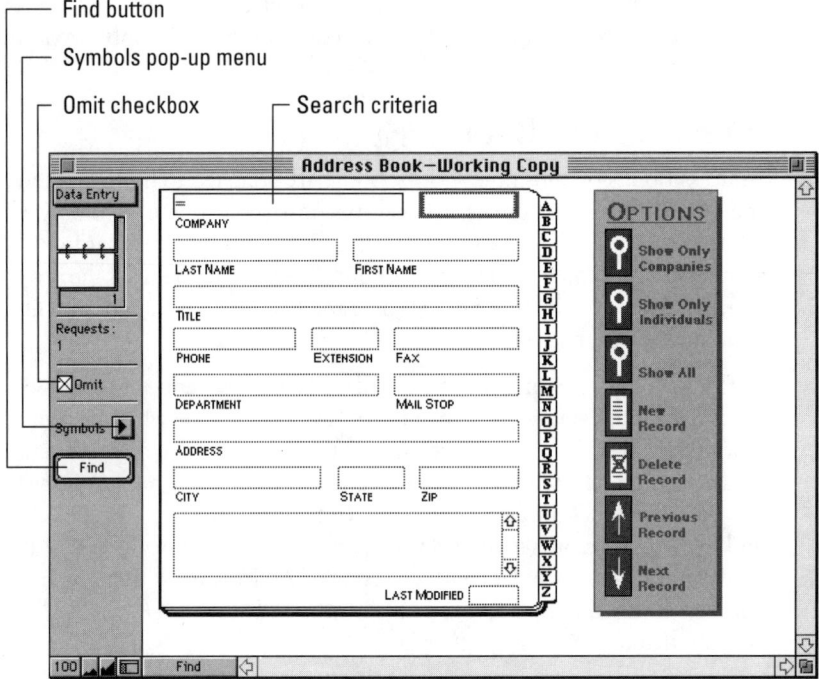

Figure 4-29: A Find request form.

3. **Enter an equal sign (=) in the Company field, as shown in Figure 4-29, and click the Omit check box.**

   The equal sign stands for *exact match*. No characters follow the equal sign, so you are looking for records that contain nothing in the Company field (that is, records in which this field is blank). You can type the equal sign or choose it from the Symbols pop-up menu.

4. **Click Find.**

   The search executes.

5. **Choose Sort from the Select menu (or press ⌘-S).**

   The Sort Records dialog box appears, as shown in Figure 4-30.

Chapter 4: Creating Your First Database: Address Book

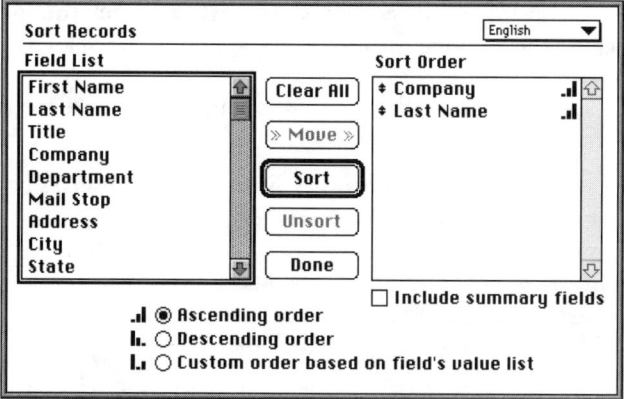

Figure 4-30: The Sort Records dialog box.

6. **In the Field List, choose Company as the first sort field and then click Move to add the field to the Sort Order list.**

7. **Choose Last Name as the second sort field and then click Move to add the field to the Sort Order list.**

8. **Click Sort.**

   The database is sorted by the two fields.

   You have completed the preparatory steps for creating the Show Companies script. Next, you build the actual script.

9. **Choose ScriptMaker from the Scripts menu.**

   The Define Scripts dialog box appears (see Figure 4-31).

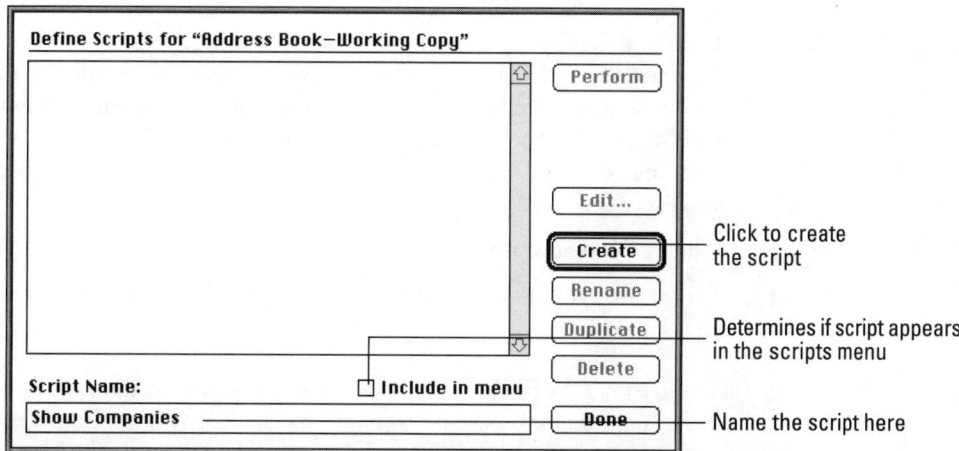

Figure 4-31: To create a new script, enter a name for it in the Define Scripts dialog box and then click Create.

10. **Type** Show Companies **in the Script Name text box, click the Include in menu check box to remove the check mark, and then click Create.**

    Because this script will be attached to a button, there is no need to also list it in the Scripts menu.

    The Script Definition dialog box appears, listing FileMaker Pro's best guess at the steps that will be needed (see Figure 4-32).

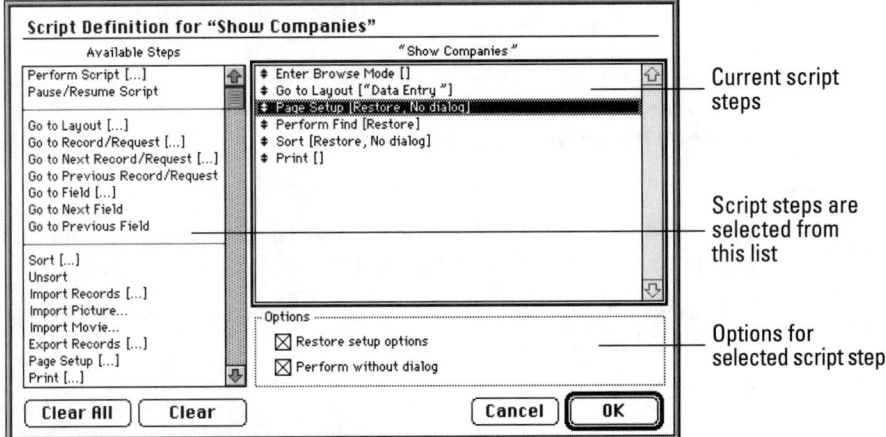

Figure 4-32: The Script Definition dialog box.

11. **In the list of included script steps (on the right side of the dialog box), select the Page Setup step and then click the Clear button to remove this step.**

12. **Do the same to remove the Print step.**

    Because this script has nothing to do with printing, you can eliminate both the Page Setup step and the Print step. (Although the Page Setup step can affect the on-screen and printed appearance of the layout, this database is always used with the standard portrait-mode Page Setup options. Because you are not going to change the Page Setup, you do not need to restore these settings each time you execute the script.)

13. **Click OK to accept the script definition.**

14. **When the Define Scripts dialog box reappears, click Done to return to the database.**

    Table 4-6 shows the final steps in the Show Companies script. Details for some of the steps are listed in the second column (Special Instructions/Comments). You will create the remaining scripts for the database by following the instructions presented in the explanatory text and the tables.

Note that any text in brackets that is shown as part of a script step is an option that you specify when you add or edit that script step (Perform Find [Restore], for example.) Available options are always shown at the lower-right corner of the Script Definition dialog box, either as check boxes or as pop-up menus. Quotation marks around text indicate that it refers to a specific layout, file, field, or script name.

Table 4-6
The Show Companies Script

Script Step	Special Instructions/Comments
Enter Browse Mode []	
Go to Layout ["Data Entry"]	
Perform Find [Restore]	= in Company field; Omit box checked
Sort [Restore, No dialog]	Sort by Company, Last Name

The Show Individuals script

Table 4-7 shows the steps in the Show Individuals script. The Find command in this script is very straightforward, particularly when you compare it to the Find request used in the Show Companies script. To find records of *individuals* (records that have no entry in the Company field), you search for Company fields that are empty (=).

Sorting is done by Last Name only. Because these records are for people who have no company affiliation, also sorting by Company is pointless. If you expect that the database will contain records for several individuals who share the same last name, you can modify the Sort request by adding First Name as a second sort field.

Table 4-7
The Show Individuals Script

Script Step	Special Instructions/Comments
Enter Browse Mode []	
Go to Layout ["Data Entry"]	
Perform Find [Restore]	= in Company field
Sort [Restore, No dialog]	Sort by Last Name

The Show All script

Table 4-8 shows the steps in the Show All script. The purpose of this script is to make all of the records visible (same as issuing a Find All command) and then sort them by Company and Last Name. Note that the Find All command does not use a Find layout to perform a search. Choosing the Refind command will *not* display instructions relevant to a Find All command. Instead, Refind shows the most recent regular Find request performed for the database — which has absolutely nothing to do with the Find All command.

**Table 4-8
The Show All Script**

Script Step	Special Instructions/Comments
Enter Browse Mode []	
Go to Layout ["Data Entry"]	
Find All	
Sort [Restore, No dialog]	Sort by Company, Last Name

The Find Businesses script

Table 4-9 shows the steps in the Find Businesses script. This script finds all records for which you have chosen Business in the Category field pop-up menu. Although the Find Businesses script serves a purpose similar to that of the Show Companies script, it finds all records that you have identified as being a Business, rather than relying on the contents of the Company field. Many self-employed people, for example, operate a business out of their home but have no company name. Similarly, you also may have records that list home addresses of your business contacts. (Although the records may not contain a company name, you still consider them business contacts.) The Find Businesses script will locate all of these records.

The found records are sorted by Company and then by Last Name. Because your business contacts may or may not have a company name, also sorting them by Company is important. Records without a company name (the Company field is blank) will appear first in the sorted database.

You can choose this script from the Scripts menu by placing a check mark in the Include in menu check box in the Define scripts dialog box. Because this script is the first one added to the Scripts menu, FileMaker Pro assigns it a keyboard shortcut of ⌘-1.

Table 4-9
The Find Businesses Script

Script Step	Special Instructions/Comments
Enter Browse Mode []	
Go to Layout ["Data Entry"]	
Perform Find [Restore]	"Business" in Category field
Sort [Restore, No dialog]	Sort by Company, Last Name

The Find Friends script

Table 4-10 shows the steps for the Find Friends script. This script finds all records for which you have chosen Friend in the Category field pop-up menu. The found records are sorted by Last Name only. Although you also can sort by Company name, you have identified the individuals in these records as being personal friends rather than business contacts, so you'll be able to locate them more easily if they're alphabetized by Last Name rather than by Company.

You can choose this script from the Scripts menu (place a check mark in the Include in menu check box in the Define scripts dialog box), and you can execute it by pressing ⌘-2.

Table 4-10
The Find Friends Script

Script Step	Special Instructions/Comments
Enter Browse Mode []	
Go to Layout ["Data Entry"]	
Perform Find [Restore]	"Friend" in Category field
Sort [Restore, No dialog]	Sort by Last Name

The Find Relatives script

Table 4-11 shows the steps for the Find Relatives script. This script works exactly like the Find Friends script described in the preceding section, but it finds only the records for which you have chosen Relative in the Category field pop-up menu. The found records are sorted by Last Name only.

Part II: Database Design Basics

You can choose this script from the Scripts menu (place a check mark in the Include in menu check box in the Define scripts dialog box), and you also can execute it by pressing ⌘-3.

Table 4-11 The Find Relatives Script	
Script Step	Special Instructions/Comments
Enter Browse Mode []	
Go to Layout ["Data Entry"]	
Perform Find [Restore]	"Relative" in Category field
Sort [Restore, No dialog]	Sort by Last Name

The Sort by Company, Last Name script

This utility script performs only one action. It sorts the database by Company and Last Name. Its only purpose is to be part of the two Phone Directory scripts that are described in the next two sections. (A script that is executed by another script is known as a *sub-script*). Thus, you will neither assign it to a button nor place it in the Scripts menu.

Follow the steps in this box to create the script that will sort the database by Company and Last Name:

1. **Perform a Sort, using Company and Last Name as the sort fields.**

2. **Choose ScriptMaker from the Scripts menu.**

3. **Type** Sort by Company, Last Name **in the Script Name text box, click to remove the check mark in the Include in menu check box, and then click Create.**

4. **Click the Clear All button.**

5. **In the Available Steps list, double-click the Sort [...] step.**

6. **Accept the default settings: Sort [Restore, No dialog].**

7. **Click OK and then click Done.**

The Phone Directory (by Last Name) script

Table 4-12 shows the steps for the Phone Directory (by Last Name) script. This script prints a phone directory that is alphabetized by Last Name only. As in the Show Individuals script, if your database will contain records for several individuals who share the same last name, you may want to modify the Sort instructions by adding First Name as the second sort field.

Chapter 4: Creating Your First Database: Address Book

When printing, the script uses the Page Setup and Print options that were in effect when the script was created and prints without displaying a dialog box. Thus, it is important to turn the printer on before you execute the script.

Just before creating the script, choose both the Page Setup and Print commands from the File menu and make sure that they are set for normal defaults: portrait mode (right-side up), U.S. Letter paper, 1 copy, Pages: All, and Records being browsed. (If you are using a dot-matrix printer rather than a laser or ink-jet printer, you may need to change options to indicate an appropriate paper type for your printer.)

After printing the phone directory, the script automatically returns to the Data Entry layout and then performs the Sort by Company, Last Name script (displaying all records and sorting them by Company and Last Name).

You can choose this script from the Scripts menu — place a check mark in the Include in menu check box. You also can execute it by pressing ⌘-4.

Table 4-12
The Phone Directory (by Last Name) Script

Script Step	Special Instructions/Comments
Enter Browse Mode []	
Go to Layout ["Phone Directory"]	Switch to the Phone Directory layout
Find All	Use all records
Sort [Restore, No dialog]	Sort by Last Name
Page Setup [Restore, No dialog]	
Print [No dialog]	
Go to Layout ["Data Entry"]	
Perform Script [Sub-scripts, "Sort by Company, Last Name"]	Sort by Company, Last Name

The Phone Directory (by Company) script

Table 4-13 shows the steps for the Phone Directory (by Company) script. This script and the Phone Directory (by Last Name) script are different in two small ways. First, this script sorts by Company and Last Name rather than only by Last Name. Thus, the list is alphabetized by Company and, within each company, employees are listed alphabetically according to their last names. Second, because the Sort command arranges the database in the same order that it needs to be in after the script is finished, you don't need to perform another sort as the final script step.

Part II: Database Design Basics

When creating this script, see the instructions presented for the Phone Directory (by Last Name) script to set the Page Setup and Print options.

This script can be chosen from the Scripts menu — place a check mark in the Include in menu check box — and can also be executed by pressing ⌘-5.

Table 4-13
The Phone Directory (by Company) Script

Script Step	Special Instructions/Comments
Enter Browse Mode []	
Go to Layout ["Phone Directory"]	Switch to the Phone Directory layout
Find All	Use all records
Sort [Restore, No dialog]	Sort by Company, Last Name
Page Setup [Restore, No dialog]	
Print [No dialog]	
Go to Layout ["Data Entry"]	

For more help with designing and editing scripts, see Chapter 15.

Assigning scripts to buttons

After you define all the scripts, you can attach several of them to the graphic buttons in the Data Entry layout. Any object on a layout can be made into a button by simply attaching a script or script step to the object. Whenever a button is clicked, the attached script or script step is instantly performed. Many users find it more convenient to click a button than to pull down the Scripts menu and select a script. (Note, however, that there is nothing to prevent you from attaching the same script to a button *and* adding the script to the Scripts menu.)

Follow these steps to assign a script to a button:

1. **Switch to Layout mode (choose Layout from the Select menu or press ⌘-L).**
2. **Using the Pointer tool, select the button or object to which you want to attach the script.**
3. **Choose Define Button from the Scripts menu.**

   The Define Button dialog box appears, as shown in Figure 4-33.

Chapter 4: Creating Your First Database: Address Book

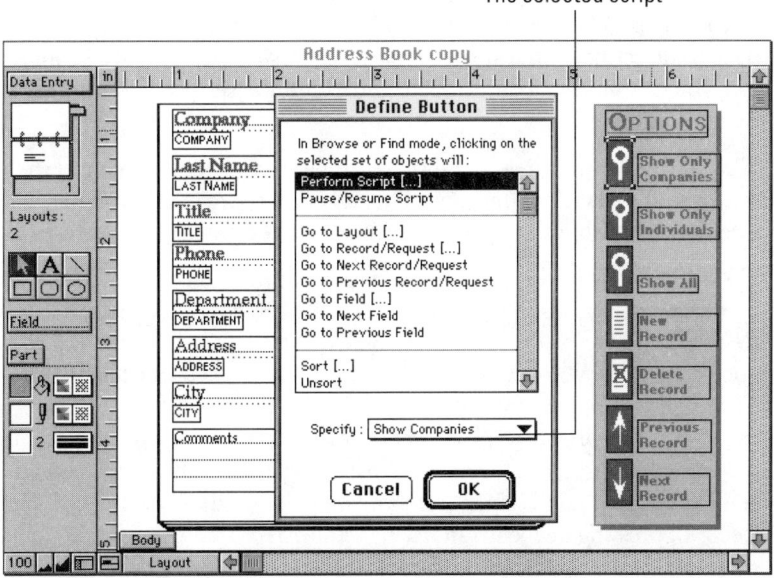

Figure 4-33: The define button dialog box.

4. **Select Perform Script [...] and choose the specific script in the Specify pop-up menu.**

5. **Click OK.**

FileMaker Pro assigns the script (or action) to the button that you selected.

Use this procedure to attach scripts to the top three buttons in the Data Entry layout, as indicated in Figure 4-34.

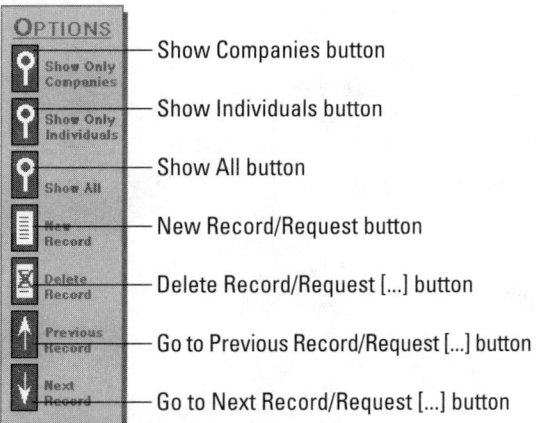

Figure 4-34: Attach the Show Companies, Show Individuals, and Show All scripts to the buttons shown.

You have not yet created scripts for the last four button icons (New Record, Delete Record, Previous Record, and Next Record) because you can control each button by a single script step. Instead of using ScriptMaker to design a script for each button, you can simultaneously create and assign the scripts by using only the Define Button command.

The button definition process is very similar to the one that you use to assign scripts to the first three buttons. The only difference is that you select a specific FileMaker Pro function in Step 4 instead of choosing a script to be performed.

To assign functions to the remaining four buttons, select each button and assign the following actions to them (in order): New Record/Request, Delete Record/Request [...], Go to Previous Record/Request [...], and Go to Next Record/Request [...]. After you have selected these actions and you switch to Browse mode, clicking these four buttons creates a new record, deletes the current record, switches to the previous record in the current sort order, and switches to the following record in the current sort order, respectively. Of course, you also can execute these commands by choosing menu commands (New Record, Delete Record), pressing keyboard shortcuts (⌘-N, ⌘-E), and clicking book pages in the status area. Because these functions are common, however, providing them as buttons is a thoughtful touch.

Note that the Delete Record/Request [...] script step has an option that enables you to delete records without having to respond to a dialog box that asks whether you are sure that you want to delete the record. Unless you're a very careful computer user, however, you should not set this option. If, in a moment of carelessness, you click the Delete Record button when you mean to click the New Record or Previous Record button, the record will be deleted instantly. Unfortunately, you cannot use the Undo command to restore deleted records, but the Delete dialog box may help you avoid deleting records by mistake.

For more information about attaching scripts to buttons, see Chapter 15.

Step 7: Set Document Preferences

To complete the Address Book database, you can add one last option to make the database even easier to use. You can specify *start-up actions* that will occur whenever you open the database. Specifically, you will make the Data Entry layout automatically appears, regardless of the layout you last used.

Follow these steps to set database start-up actions:

1. **Choose Preferences from the File menu.**

   The Preferences dialog box appears (see Figure 4-35).

Chapter 4: Creating Your First Database: Address Book

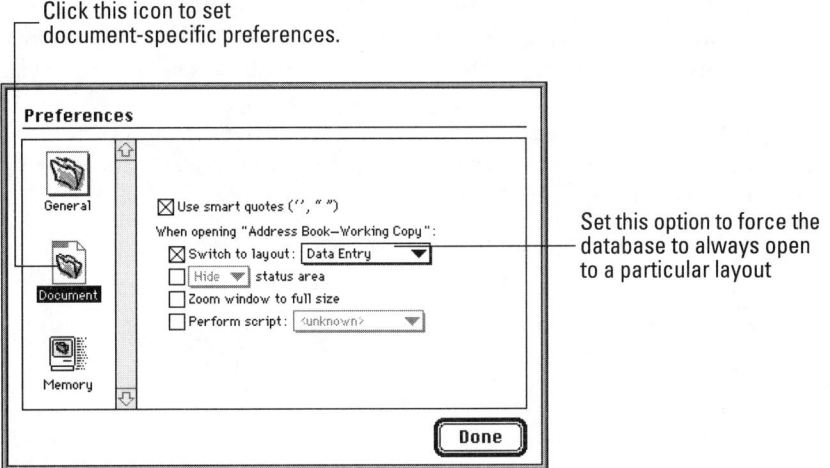

Figure 4-35: The Preferences dialog box.

2. **To set preferences for the current database, click the Document icon.**

   Only preferences relevant to the current document are displayed.

3. **Set document preferences.**

   In this instance, click the Switch to layout check box and choose Data Entry from the pop-up layout menu to have the database always open to the Data Entry layout.

4. **Click Done.**

   The Preferences dialog box closes, and the changes are recorded.

By choosing Data Entry from the Switch to layout pop-up menu, you ensure that the database will automatically open in the Data Entry layout, regardless of the layout that you were in when you last closed the database. Because the primary purpose of Address Book is entering, editing, and viewing address records, you can save a little time and effort by making sure that the Data Entry layout always appears when you first open the database.

Depending on your work habits and who the intended users of the database happen to be, you may want to set some other preferences, too. For example, if you prefer to do all your record navigation by clicking the Previous and Next Record buttons, you may want to click the Preferences check box for Hide status area. If you want the database to always expand to the full width of the screen, you can click Zoom window to full size. This option can be very helpful if you're distributing a database to many users who have monitors that are different sizes.

Note, however, that most people have their own preferences concerning the size of database windows and whether the status area should be shown or hidden. I, for example, like to reduce each window to the smallest possible size that still shows all the elements of the current layout. Keep in mind, too, that FileMaker Pro always remembers how you last set the status area and the size of the window. Leaving these two preferences off enables users to set these preferences to their liking — instead of forcing them to accept your preferences.

For additional information on setting preferences, see Chapter 7.

Chapter 4: Creating Your First Database: Address Book

CHAPTER 4 CONCEPTS AND TERMS

- Creating a database can be as simple as defining fields and then using the default (standard) layout that FileMaker provides. However, taking the time to enhance the database by creating custom layouts, adding graphics, and designing scripts can greatly improve the database's functionality and ease-of-use.

- Each field in a database is a specific type. The field type determines the kind of information that the field can contain, such as text, numbers, or pictures.

- You can resize and move fields as necessary. You also can apply different formatting options (fonts, styles, and colors, for example) to fields.

- A database can have as many different layouts as are needed to collect and display the data in the ways that you want. For example, creating one layout specifically for entering and editing data and other layouts for generating reports and mailing labels is not unusual. Every layout draws on the same information contained in the database; it simply arranges the data in a different way.

- Scripts enable you to automate common and not-so-common database procedures. ScriptMaker sets many script options for you by watching the actions that you perform.

- You can use graphic or text objects on a layout as buttons. When you click a button, it executes the script that has been attached to it.

auto-entry field
A database field that FileMaker Pro automatically fills in for each new record.

button
A user-created object, in a FileMaker Pro database layout, that has a script attached to it. Clicking the button makes the script action(s) occur.

field type
Set in the Define Fields dialog box, a field type specifies the type of information that a particular field is intended to collect and display.

group
A set of objects that you have applied the Group command to so that you can treat them as a single entity rather than as a collection of objects in the layout.

handle
In Layout mode, the black dot that appears at each corner of an object when it has been selected.

layout
An arrangement of database fields, labels, and graphics. FileMaker Pro databases can contain multiple layouts.

layout parts
The major sections in a database layout. Depending on the purpose of the layout, it may contain a body, header, footer, and summary parts, for example.

preferences
Program-specific or document-specific settings that you use to established preferred program and document behaviors.

required field
A database field that must contain an entry for the record to be considered complete.

script
One or more database-specific instructions that you want FileMaker Pro to execute, often without user intervention.

windoid
A tiny, special-purpose window that is typically provided as a user-control tool. The Size tool is an example of a windoid.

 **Part II: Database Design Basics**

CHAPTER FIVE

Defining Fields

- Understanding field types
- Creating calculation and summary formulas
- Setting and modifying data-entry options for fields

As explained in Part 1 of this book, fields are the building blocks from which databases are constructed. In this chapter, you learn all about defining fields, selecting types for them, and setting field options.

Setting Field Definitions

Until you define fields for a database, you cannot store data in the database. After you select the disk drive and folder in which you want to store the new database and give the database a name, the next step is to define the fields. The process of defining a field includes the following:

❖ Naming the field

❖ Setting a *type* for the field (the type of information that the field will store)

❖ Setting options for the field (data validation procedures, auto-entry options, value lists, lookups, and so on)

The first two steps, naming the field and selecting a data type for the field, are required. Setting options, naturally enough, is optional. You create all fields in the Define Fields dialog box (shown in Figure 5-1).

Part II: Database Design Basics

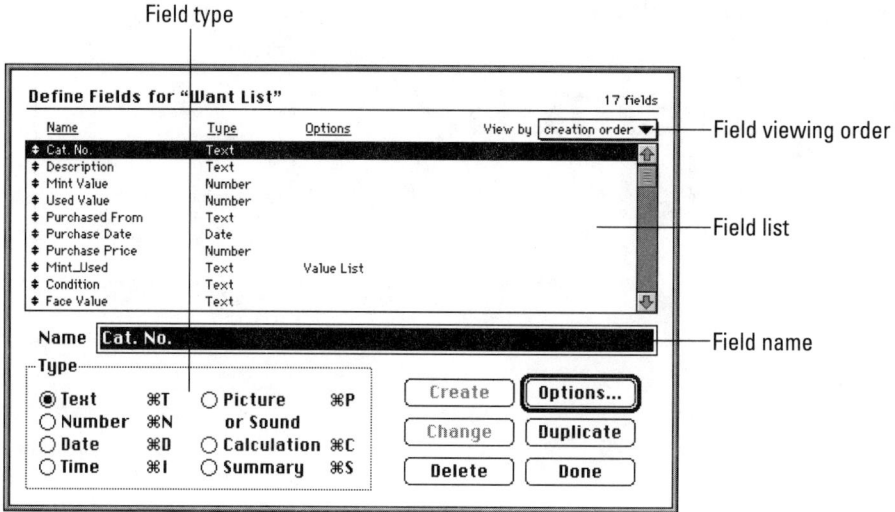

Figure 5-1: The Define Fields dialog box.

You reach the Define Fields dialog box in one of two ways:

❖ *Choose New from the File menu.* When you create a new database file, the Define Fields dialog box automatically appears after you name the database.

❖ *Choose Define Fields from the Select menu (or press Shift-⌘-D).* When you want to create new fields or examine, edit, or delete existing field definitions, choose the Define Fields command.

Follow these steps to define a field:

1. **For a new database, choose New from the File menu and then enter a filename for the database in the standard file dialog box that appears.**

— or —

1. **For an existing database, choose Define Fields from the Select menu (or press Shift-⌘-D).**

   In either case, the Define Fields dialog box appears.

2. **Type a name for the new field (up to 60 characters) in the Name box.**

   If you think that you may want to use the field in a calculation formula, be sure that the name does not contain a number, period, comma, quotation mark, math symbol, logical keyword (AND, OR, NOT), or the name of a FileMaker Pro built-in function. (Refer to Chapter 14 for the names of FileMaker Pro functions.) Such symbols and words will be improperly interpreted as being part of the formula. To prevent such nasty occurrences, FileMaker Pro routinely warns you if you enter an improper name (see Figure 5-2).

Chapter 5: Defining Fields

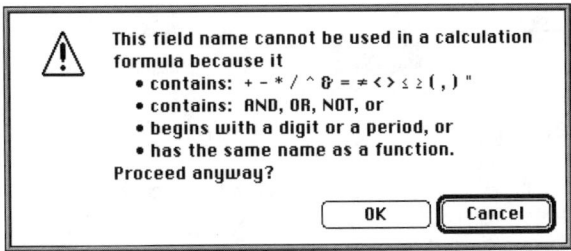

Figure 5-2: This warning appears if you enter an improper field name.

3. **Click a radio button to select a data type for the field.**

   Field types are explained in "All about field types," later in the chapter.

4. **Click Create.**

   If you select Calculation or Summary as the field type, another dialog box appears in which you can specify the formula or type of summary information that you want. For any other field type, the basic definition process ends when you click Create.

5. **To define additional fields, repeat Steps 2 through 4 and then click Done when you are through defining fields.**

After you create a field, you can set options for it, as described in "Setting Field Entry Options," later in this chapter.

When a you create a database (by choosing New from the File menu), you normally begin by defining all its fields. You should note, however, that you are not locked in to this set of fields. You can later add new fields, delete fields, set and change field options, or even change field types (from Number to Text, for example). You can change field definitions at any time by choosing Define Fields from the Select menu (or pressing Shift-⌘-D). For additional information, see "Modifying Field Definitions, Names, and Options" at the end of this chapter.

All about field types

Before defining fields, you need to understand *field types*. The field type determines what kind of data you can enter and store in a field. Number fields, for example, store numeric data. Because Number fields contain numbers, you can use them to perform calculations, such as COMMISSION = SALE * .05.

Breaking up Complex Fields

When you are defining fields for a database, think seriously about dividing complex fields into their logical components. For example, instead of defining a single Name field, you may want to define Title, First Name, and Last Name fields. The latter approach makes sorting by last name simple. If you attempt to sort a single Name field, on the other hand, FileMaker Pro will list everyone alphabetically by their first name or — worse yet — by their title, such as Mr., Dr., or Ms.

Using different fields for Title, First Name, and Last Name also makes doing a mail merge easy. You can create the salutation by combining the Title and Last Name fields, as in

    Dear <Title> <Last Name>:

rather than

    Dear <Name>:

Thus, instead of saying "Dear Dr. John Abrams:," a form letter would read "Dear Dr. Abrams:."

As you can see, combining several specific fields is much easier than attempting to dismantle and work with a single general field. Plan ahead.

FileMaker Pro has seven field types from which you can choose: Text, Number, Date, Time, Picture/Sound, Calculation, and Summary. You need to specify a type for every field that you create. Each field must be defined as being one — and only one — type.

In order to improve the speed of executing Find requests, FileMaker Pro keeps track of data that has been entered in each field and maintains an index for the field. Depending on the field type that you assign to a field, FileMaker Pro indexes all data for that field, only part of the data, or no data at all, as Table 5-1 summarizes and the following sections describe.

Text fields

A Text field can store any type of information: text, numbers, and other characters. With a maximum of 64,000 characters, Text fields are ideal for handling large amounts of information, such as comments and notes. Searching for any word in a Text field is easy because FileMaker Pro automatically indexes every word in Text fields — not just the first one, for example. Because you can enter anything in a Text field, a majority of database fields are defined as Text fields.

Number fields

Although its name implies otherwise, you can also enter anything in a Number field — text and symbols, as well as numeric characters. Number fields, however, have greater restrictions than Text fields have. They can contain a maximum of only 255 characters, and you have to enter data as a single line. If you attempt to press Return when you are typing an entry in a Number field, FileMaker Pro beeps and ignores the Return. Because the numeric information in Number fields is readily accessible for use in formulas and computations, the contents of Number fields are frequently used as the basis for Calculation fields, which are discussed later in this chapter.

Only the first 122 numeric characters (numbers, decimal points, or signs) in a Number field are indexed. Text and other characters are ignored. If you enter both text and numbers in a Number field, individual numbers in the field are concatenated to form a single number. As an example, suppose that you have entered the following address in a Number field:

```
23 East Elm Street, Apt. #7
```

For indexing purposes, FileMaker Pro treats this field as if it contains the number *237*. It appends a *7* to the end of the number *23*. This method of operating also affects searches (performed with the Find command). If you enter 23 or 7 as the search string, the search will fail. Similarly, because the text in a Number field is not indexed, searching for Elm also fails. On the other hand, searching for 237 — the concatenated numbers — successfully finds this record.

This discussion of concatenation leads to an important point. If you think that you will need to enter both text and numeric information in a field, you may be happier if you define it as a Text field rather than as a Number field. If you're just interested in making sure that only legitimate numbers can be entered into a numeric field, you have to set the "of type Number" option for the field. See "Setting Field Entry Options," later in this chapter, for instructions.

Table 5-1
Field Type Specifications

Field Type	Field Content and Restrictions	Indexed Information
Text	Up to 64,000 characters of any sort	Every word
Number	Up to 255 characters (must be on one line)	First 122 characters
Date	One date (8 characters) between year 1 and 3000	Entire date
Time	One time (8 characters)	Entire time
Picture or Sound	One picture, QuickTime movie, or sound	Not indexed
Calculation	One formula with a text, numeric, date, or time result	Calculation result (amount of data indexed corresponds to the formula result type chosen)
Summary	Result of one summary function	Not indexed

Part II: Database Design Basics

Changing the Field Order

A field list appears in several FileMaker Pro dialog boxes, such as the Define Fields and Sort dialog boxes. By default, fields appear in the list in the order in which you created them. Working with this list may be easier if you establish a new order for fields. To change the field order, choose one of the following four options that are found on the View by pop-up menu in the upper-right corner of the Define Fields dialog box and are shown in the accompanying figure:

View by: creation order / field name / field type / custom order

❖ **Creation order:** Fields are listed in the order in which they were created.

❖ **Field name:** Fields are sorted alphabetically by field name.

❖ **Field type:** Fields are grouped by type (Text, Number, and so on). Within each type, the fields are presented in creation order.

❖ **Custom order:** You manually move one or more fields to a new position in the list. This process is described in the following step-by-step instructions.

The following steps describe how to create a custom field order:

1. **In the Define Fields dialog box, move the pointer over the name of the field that you want to move.**

   When the pointer moves over the beginning of a field name, it changes to a two-headed arrow.

2. **With the two-headed arrow visible, click to select the field, drag the field up or down in the list, and release the mouse button when the field is where you want it to be.**

   As soon as you move a single field, the View by pop-up menu automatically shows that the custom order setting has been selected.

   Repeat these steps for any additional fields that you want to move. Note that even if you switch back and forth between several different field order views, when you next choose the custom order view, all the manual modifications that you made to the field order are restored.

Date fields

Date fields are reserved for dates. Each date can contain up to eight characters plus separators (MM/DD/YYYY), and the entire data is indexed as a single string. When you type dates, you must use only numbers and the following separators: slash (/), dash (-), period (.), or space. Thus, all the following dates are proper FileMaker Pro dates: 3/14/95, 3-14-95, 3.14.95, and 3 14 95. Leading zeroes (as in 03/14/95) are optional. The year portion of the date must be between 1 and 3000.

When you enter the month or day part of a date, you can use one or two digits. You can enter any year in the current century with either two or four digits (4-15-*95* or 4/15/*1995*, for example). To enter other years, do the following:

Chapter 5: Defining Fields

For a Year in the Range...	Enter This...
1 – 9	A single digit in the year's place (**4,** for example)
10 – 99	Four digits (the year preceded by two zeroes, as in **0057**)
100 – 999	Three or four digits (**756** or **0756,** for example)
1000 – 1899	Four digits — the actual year (**1847,** for example)
1900 – 1999	Two or four digits (**94** or **1994,** for example)
2000 – 3000	Four digits (**2017,** for example)

The manner in which the date is *displayed*, on the other hand, is determined by the format that you have set for the field by using the Date Format command (see Chapter 6). Note that when you base a Find request on the contents of a Date field, you have to enter a date that is in keeping with the restrictions for entering a date.

Entering the Year Automatically

Here's a way to avoid some typing. When you enter a date for the current year, you don't have to include the year at all. If you type 4/17, for example, FileMaker Pro fills in the current year for you.

Time fields

Like Date fields, a Time field can hold one time (up to eight characters in length), and it is indexed as a single string. You can enter times as hours (5); hours and minutes (5:12); or hours, minutes, and seconds (5:12:43). When you enter data in a Time field, you have to separate the parts of the time with colons (see Figure 5-3). Leading zeros are optional (both 5:07 and 5:7 are acceptable, for example). You also can append AM or PM to the end of a time string. You can set a display format for a Time field by using the Time Format command (see Chapter 6).

> The time in this field must be hours, hours and minutes, or hours, minutes and seconds and should look like "11:47:33 AM".
>
> [OK]

Figure 5-3: The correct way to enter a time.

Picture and Sound fields

A Picture/Sound field can store one of three types of material: a picture, a QuickTime movie, or a sound. You can play movies and sounds from within the database by double-clicking the field in which either type of data is stored. You can copy pictures and QuickTime movies and paste them into the field, or you can import them by using the Import/Export submenu in the File menu. (See Chapter 16 for instructions.) You can copy and paste sound clips into a Picture/Sound field, or you can record them directly into the field if you have the necessary hardware. Figure 5-4 shows a record that contains a movie.

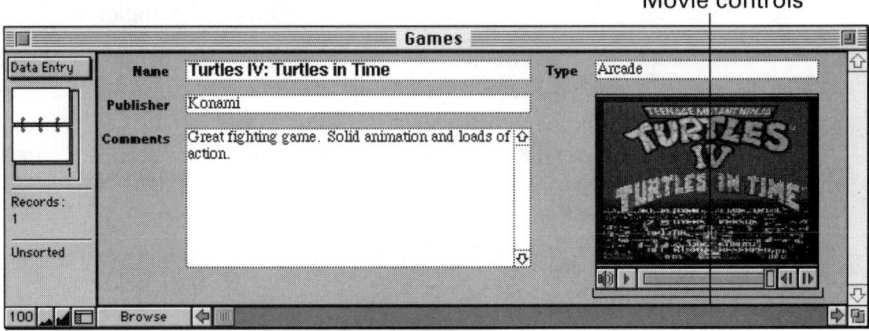

Figure 5-4: A QuickTime movie in a Picture/Sound field.

Why Put Movies or Sounds in a Database?

Uses for pictures in databases are obvious. Employee ID photos (in an employee database), pictures of personal property (in a household inventory database), and images of houses (in a real estate database) are three good examples. But why would you want to store sounds in a database? Pasting an interesting sound effect into a record may prove entertaining, but using sound this way is pointless. More appropriate uses of sounds include the proper pronunciation of someone's name, recorded comments that are relevant to the record (notes or explanations, for example), or music samples in a database for a CD collection.

Thinking of sensible uses for movies also can be a head-scratcher. In a customer service database, you could use a movie that shows how to make specific repairs. In a travel-related database, you might include short movie clips that show major points of interest. Most Macintosh users, however, will never create their own QuickTime movies. What few movies they do have often come with other programs. Thus, another possible use is to create a database that catalogs the QuickTime movies that you have and serves as a type of movie viewer.

Keep in mind, though, that if the original movies are scattered across a series of CDs, each time you attempt to play the movie in FileMaker Pro, you will need to insert the appropriate CD. As in other applications, the movies aren't actually stored in the database. FileMaker Pro merely keeps track of each movie's original location. If the appropriate disk isn't mounted when you attempt to play a particular movie, FileMaker Pro asks you to insert the disk.

Chapter 5: Defining Fields

Information in a Picture/Sound field is not indexed, so you cannot do a Find based on the contents of the field. Of course, this limitation makes sense because the information in the field isn't labeled in any way — there's nothing to search for. If you want to search for a particular picture, sound, or movie, create a separate Text field to store a name or set of keywords that describe the picture, sound, or movie, and then base your Find request on the contents of the Text field.

Calculation fields

Calculation fields perform numeric, text, date, or time calculations within each record. A calculation can include constants, any of FileMaker Pro's built-in functions, and references to other fields, as well as any combination of these items. The ability to perform calculations elevates a database from a nicely arranged stack of note cards to a powerful provider of information that is often not obvious when you just flip through records. Calculations unleash the real power of FileMaker Pro. For example, you can use any word processing program to type an invoice. But an invoice database that has Calculation fields also can automatically total the purchases, compute the sales tax, and show you the number of days that a payment is overdue.

You specify the formula for a Calculation field in the Options dialog box, which appears automatically when you select Calculation as the field type. You need to specify the result type for each Calculation field. A result can be text, a number, a date, or a time.

Here are some simple examples of the types of calculations that you can perform:

Formula	Result Type	Explanation
Commission = SalesTotal * .08	Number	Multiply the value in the SalesTotal field by 0.08 to compute a salesperson's commission
Name = First & " " & Last	Text	Concatenate each person's first and last name to show the full name (First and Last are separated by a space)
Hours = EndTime – StartTime	Time	Compute the amount of time spent on a particular task
Days Until Due = DueDate - Today	Number	Subtract today's date (Today) from the due date to determine the number of days that remain

To avoid erroneous results, FileMaker Pro will not allow you to modify the contents of a Calculation field. To emphasize this fact, Calculation fields are automatically skipped when you tab from field to field. However, if you want to *copy* the contents of a Calculation field, you can click the field and then choose Copy from the Edit menu (or press ⌘-C).

Chapter 14 presents the details of creating formulas for Calculation fields, as well as descriptions and explanations of FileMaker Pro's built-in functions.

Summary fields

Instead of performing calculations within each record as Calculation fields do, Summary fields perform calculations across records. For example, in a database that tracks customer purchases, you may define a Summary field named Grand Total to total all the purchases by all customers.

A Summary field is based on the contents of a single Number, Date, Time, or Calculation field, and it summarizes the records that you are currently browsing. When all records are visible, the Grand Total field provides the total of all purchases by all customers. If, on the other hand, you issue a Find request to restrict the visible records to only customers from Boston, the Grand Total field shows total purchases by Boston customers rather than by the entire database.

You can place Summary fields in any layout part: header, body, footer, and so on. If you place a Summary field in a sub-summary part and you sort the database by a particular field, you can generate group statistics, such as computing the average rainfall for cities in country A, country B, and so on. (Chapter 6 discusses sub-summary and other layout parts.)

FileMaker Pro automatically recalculates Summary fields whenever necessary. When you change the contents of a field on which a summary is based, it recalculates the summary. Similarly, when the set of browsed records changes, it also re-calculates the summary.

Functions for Summary fields include total, average, count, minimum, maximum, standard deviation, and fraction of total. Defining Summary fields is discussed in the next section.

As it does with Calculation fields, FileMaker Pro prevents you from tabbing into a Summary field. But you can click a Summary field and copy its contents. Summary fields are not indexed, nor can you base a Find on the contents of a Summary field.

Defining Calculation and Summary fields

You can completely define all field types, except Calculation and Summary fields, by just naming them, selecting a field type, and clicking Create. The following sets of step-by-step instructions explain how to define these two types of fields.

Follow these steps to define a Calculation field:

1. **In the Define Fields dialog box, type a name for the new field (up to 60 characters) in the Name box.**
2. **In the Type section of the dialog box, click the Calculation radio button (or press ⌘-C).**
3. **Click Create.**

    The Options for Field "*Calculation field name*" dialog box appears (see Figure 5-5).

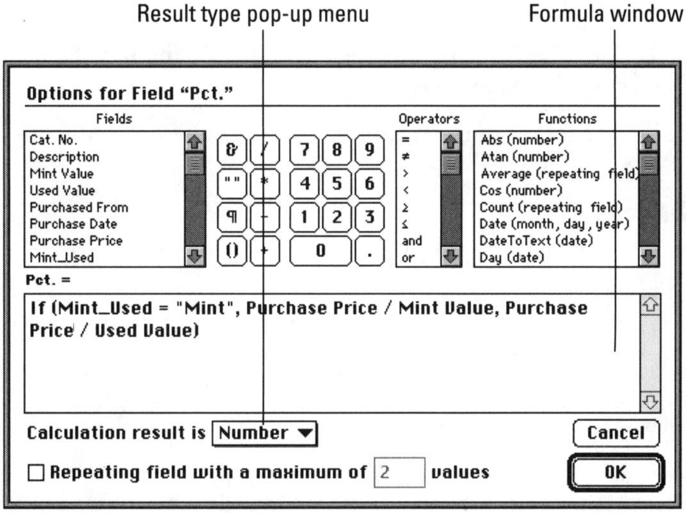

Chapter 5: Defining Fields

Figure 5-5: Create a formula for the Calculation field in this Options dialog box.

4. **Enter the formula for the field in the scrolling text box in the center of the dialog box.**

   You can select field names, numbers, special symbols, operators, and functions by clicking the appropriate items in the upper part of the dialog box. You also can type directly into the formula definition box.

5. **Choose a result type for every formula.**

   You have to choose a result type for each formula. Choose Text, Number, Date, or Time from the Calculation result pop-up menu.

6. *Optional:* **If you want this field to be a repeating field, click the Repeating field check box and type a number for the maximum number of repeats that you want the field to have.**

   (See "Repeating fields," later in this chapter, for more information.)

7. **Click OK.**

   FileMaker Pro evaluates the formula and reports any errors that it detects. When the formula is correct, it returns you to the Define Fields dialog box.

8. **Click Done when you are through defining fields.**

The process of creating Calculation fields is explained in greater detail in Chapter 14, where definitions and examples for each of the built-in functions are also provided.

Part II: Database Design Basics

Follow these steps to define a Summary field:

1. **In the Define Fields dialog box, type a name for the new field (up to 60 characters) in the Name box.**
2. **In the Type section of the dialog box, click the Summary radio button (or press ⌘-S).**
3. **Click Create.**

    The Options for Summary Field *"Summary field name"* dialog box appears, as shown in Figure 5-6.

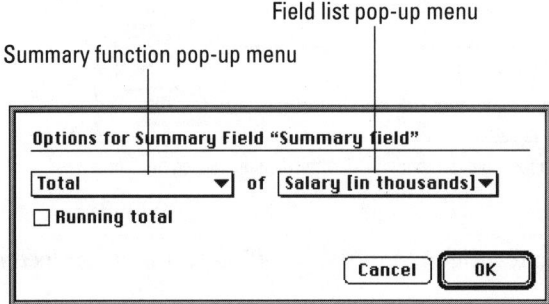

Figure 5-6: Select a summary function in this Options dialog box.

4. **Choose a summary function from the summary function pop-up menu.**

    See the next section for a description of the available summary functions and their options.

5. **From the field list pop-up menu, select a field on which to base the summary.**
6. *Optional:* **At the bottom of the dialog box, many of the summary functions provide an option that you can select by clicking the check box and, if required, choosing a field from the option's pop-up menu.**

    The type of option depends on the particular summary function.

7. **Click OK to accept the definition or Cancel to ignore the settings that you have selected.**

Table 5-2
Summary Functions and Options

Summary Function	Option
Total	Running total
Average	Weighted by *field name*
Count	Running count
Minimum	None
Maximum	None
Standard deviation	None
Fraction of total	Subtotaled when sorted by field *x*

Understanding summary functions

Table 5-2 lists the available summary functions and their options.

The following descriptions of the summary functions and their options can help you select the most appropriate function for any Summary field:

❖ *Total/Running total:* The Total function totals a chosen field across all records that are being browsed.

   Example: In a database in which you record household expenses, you can create a Total Summary field that shows total expenses to date for the entire database. You can place the Total Summary field in a sub-summary part and then sort by Expense Category to calculate separate totals for each type of expense.

   Select the Running Total option if you prefer to see a cumulative total for the field as you flip from one record to another. To calculate subtotals for groups of records, place this Summary field in a sub-summary part and then sort by the appropriate field.

❖ *Average/Weighted by* field name: This function calculates a simple numeric average of a selected field for the records being browsed. Place this Summary field in a sub-summary part if you want to calculate group averages.

   Example: If bowling scores of 112, 142, and 175 were being summarized, the average displayed would be 143 — the sum of the scores (429) divided by the number of scores (3).

   If the Weighted by *field name* option is checked, instead of computing a simple average, the statistic is weighted by another field of your choice.

Example: In the Want List database on the *Macworld FileMaker Pro 2.0/2.1 Bible Disk*, one Calculation field displays the percentage of catalog value at which each stamp was purchased (see Figure 5-7). If you were to use the Average summary function to compute the average percentage, the result would have little meaning because, from a monetary standpoint, purchases for hundreds of dollars would be treated equally to purchases for pennies. Weighting the average by purchase price, on the other hand, gives greater importance to the more expensive purchases.

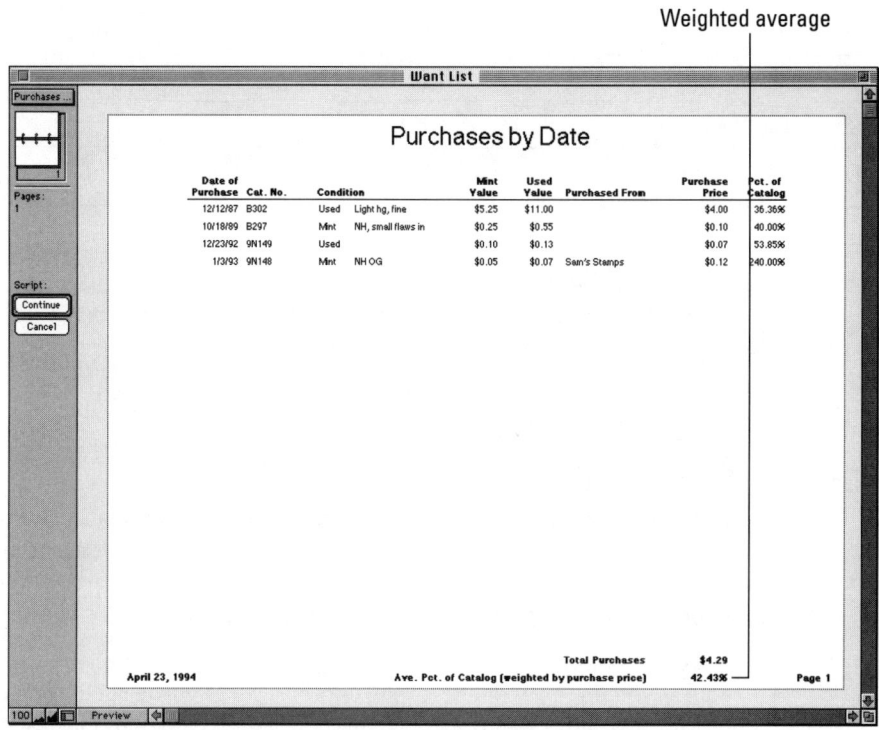

Figure 5-7: An example of an Average when weighted by summary function.

❖ *Count/Running count:* Placed in any part other than a sub-summary, a Count shows the number of records that contain any value in the selected field across the records that are currently being browsed. That is, the count is incremented by 1 for every field that is not blank. This function is considerably more useful when you place it in a sub-summary part, however, where it shows how many qualifying records are in each group (after being sorted by the appropriate field).

Example: To determine how many records have an entry in the Address field, place a Count Summary field in any layout part other than a sub-summary. The Count then shows the number of records from which you can create usable mailing labels. If you create a Count Summary field based on a field that is always filled in, place it in a sub-summary part, and then sort by the appropriate field, you can get an accurate count of the number of members in each sub-group.

A Running Count is also more informative when you place it in a sub-summary part, where it shows the cumulative number of records in each group (after being sorted by the appropriate field). When you place a Running Count in another layout part, it simply matches the record numbers — as in 1, 2, 3, 4, and so on.

❖ *Minimum:* When placed in any part other than a sub-summary, the Minimum function shows the smallest value for the chosen field across all records being browsed. When you place it in a sub-summary part, this function shows the smallest value for the chosen field for each group of records being browsed.

Example: In a software inventory database, a Minimum Summary field can show you the cheapest program in the lot. If you perform a Find on a particular software category, the field displays the least expensive program of that type. Placed in a sub-summary part and then sorted by software category, the Summary field shows the least expensive program for every type of software, on a category-by-category basis.

❖ *Maximum:* When placed in any part other than a sub-summary, the Maximum function shows the largest value for the chosen field across all records being browsed. When placed in a sub-summary part, this function shows the largest value for the chosen field for each group of records being browsed.

Example: In a software inventory database, a Maximum Summary field can show you the most expensive program in the lot. If you perform a Find on a particular software category, the field displays the most expensive program of that type. Placed in a sub-summary part and then sorted by software category, the Summary field shows the most expensive program for every type of software, on a category-by-category basis.

❖ *Standard deviation:* This function computes a statistic called a standard deviation for the chosen field across all records being browsed. The Standard deviation shows how widely the values summarized vary from one another.

Example: You can use a Standard deviation function in a student database to see how much the students' heights or grades vary. Place the same field in a sub-summary part and then sort by age, grade, or teacher name, for example, to get the same information separately for each group.

Part II: Database Design Basics

❖ *Fraction of total/Subtotaled when sorted by field* x: When placed in any part other than a sub-summary, this function shows the portion of the total for a field that can be accounted for by each record. When placed in a sub-summary part, the function shows the portion of the total for a field that can be accounted for by each group rather than each record. If the Subtotaled when sorted by field option is checked and you sort the database by the selected field, the Fraction of total figures are fractions of each group rather than of all visible records; that is, the Fraction of total figures within each group will add up to 1.0 (or 100 percent).

Example: In a household expense database, place this field in any layout part other than a sub-summary to determine the fraction of total expenses that each transaction accounted for. Place the same field in a sub-summary part and then sort by Expense Category to see the fraction of the category that can be attributed to each expense item.

More Help with Summary Functions

If you're having trouble making sense of Summary fields, how the different functions work, and when you should use them, the quickest path to understanding is to create a test file and try out the various options. You can use Summary File Tester, a sample file on the *Macworld FileMaker Pro 2.0/2.1 Bible Disk*.

Summary File Tester contains only six records and consists of the following four fields:

❖ City — a Text field

❖ Age — a Number field

❖ Salary [in thousands] — a Number field

❖ Summary field — a Summary field

The same Summary field appears in two places in the database — in the body and in a trailing sub-summary part (at the bottom of each record). That way, you can determine the correct layout part in which to place your *own* Summary fields. The figure shows a record from Summary File Tester in which City is the sort field.

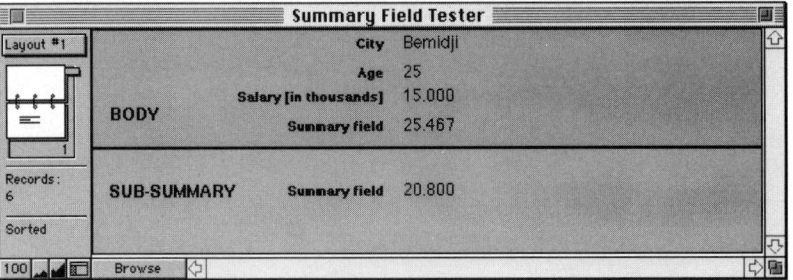

Chapter 5: Defining Fields

To see how each summary function and option works, open Summary Field Tester and do the following:

1. **Choose the Define Fields command from the Select menu (or press Shift-⌘-D).**

   The Define Fields dialog box appears (refer to Figure 5-1).

2. **Select Summary field in the list of defined fields and click Options.**

   The Options for Summary Field "Summary field" dialog box appears.

3. **Choose a different option from the summary function pop-up menu or alter the status of the check box, if one appears at the bottom of the dialog box.**

   Leave the field list pop-up menu alone (reading "Salary [in thousands]").

4. **To dismiss the dialog boxes, click OK and then Done.**

   If the status area shows that the records are Unsorted or Semi-Sorted, choose the Sort command from the Select menu (or press ⌘-S). The Sort dialog box should show that the database will be sorted by City, which is the sort field set for the sub-summary part. Click Sort or press Return or Enter to execute the sort.

   Repeat these steps as often as you like, testing a different summary function or option each time. After each definition has been completed, flip through the records to see what the Summary field is summarizing, both in the body and in the sub-summary part.

Setting Field Entry Options

In addition to selecting a type for each field, you can set many other options:

❖ *Data auto-entry:* You can set options that automatically enter the creation or modification date or time for each record, the name of the user who created or last modified the record, a serial number, or a default value into the chosen field.

❖ *Data validation:* Depending on the options chosen, you can require that a field not be left blank, that the value entered must be unique, that the value already exist in another record, that data be of a particular type, or that entries fall within a specific range.

❖ *Repeating values:* This option enables you to enter multiple values in what normally would be considered a single field. In an invoice database, for example, you can define Quantity, Item Description, Price, and Extended Price fields, each of which can receive up to ten values.

Part II: Database Design Basics

❖ *Present a list of values from which to choose:* Choosing this option causes a user-defined list of values to appear when someone tabs into or clicks the field. For example, you can create a value list for a Payment Method field that lists all the payment methods (such as specific credit cards, checks, cash, and traveler's checks) that your store accepts as payment for services and goods. In addition to speeding data entry for the field, this option helps ensure that each entry is spelled correctly and worded consistently.

❖ *Look up data values in another file:* When data is entered into a lookup field, FileMaker Pro automatically looks up information in another file and then copies that data into one or more fields in the current file. Using this option in an inventory database, you could enter a part number into a field. FileMaker Pro would then open the second database file that you specified; find the part name, description, color, and unit cost for the part; and then transfer a copy of that information to the first database. Because of the complexity of this concept, lookups are covered separately in Chapter 19.

The following steps present the general procedure for setting options for a field. Instructions for setting specific kinds of field options are in the sections that follow.

1. **Choose Define Fields from the Select menu (or press Shift-⌘-D).**

   The Define fields dialog box appears (refer to Figure 5-1).

2. **In the field list, select the field for which you want to set options.**

   — or —

2. **If the field doesn't already exist, define the field by following the instructions for defining fields, presented earlier in this chapter.**

3. **Click Options (or double-click the name of the field in the field list).**

4. **Set options and click OK to return to the Define Fields dialog box.**

5. **To set options for additional fields, repeat Steps 2 through 4. Click Done when you are through setting options.**

When you select a Text, Number, Date, Time, or Picture/Sound field in the Define Fields dialog box and then click Options, the Entry Options dialog box in Figure 5-8 appears. Note that the title of the dialog box changes to reflect the name and data type of the selected field. The specific options that you can set also vary with the data type of the field. For example, you cannot select any of the auto-entry or data validation options for a Picture/Sound field.

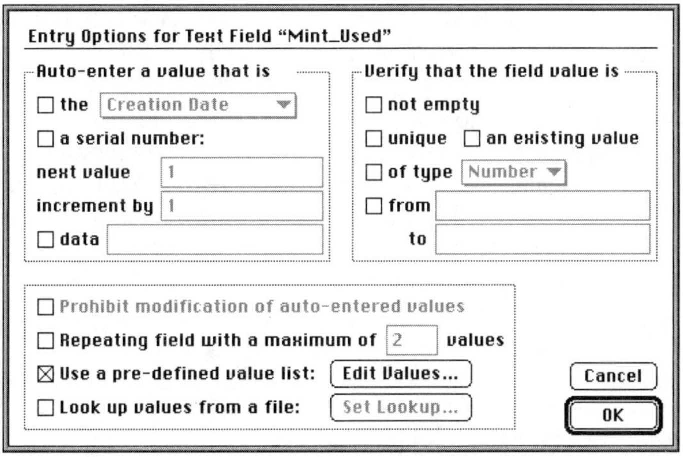

Figure 5-8: The Entry Options dialog box.

You should note that setting entry options for a field after the field contains data can sometimes cause problems. FileMaker Pro does not warn you about existing records that, as a result of the field type change, now contain invalid data. You have to find and correct them yourself. The following Find request symbols are helpful in performing this task:

Find Symbol or Operation	Action
=	Find empty fields
!	Find duplicate values
value1 … *value2*, and click the Omit check box	Find values that fall outside of the range

You also can search for invalid dates and times by entering a question mark (?) in a Date or Time field. However, because the contents of these fields are automatically restricted to valid dates and times, this type of search is necessary only if you have converted a field to a Date or Time field from some other field type (a Text field, for example).

Auto-entry options

The portion of the Entry Options dialog box labeled "Auto-enter a value that is" contains options that provide for the automatic entry of several types of information in a field when you initially create the record or when you later modify the field. The various auto-entry options are discussed in the following sections.

Part II: Database Design Basics

Creation Date, Creation Time, Modification Date, Modification Time, Creator Name, and Modifier Name

Click the first check box in the Auto-enter a value that is section of the Options dialog box (see Figure 5-9) to instruct FileMaker Pro to automatically enter the record's creation date, creation time, modification date, modification time, creator name, or modifier name. The specific choices that appear in the pop-up menu depend on the type of the field for which you are setting options. If you are defining options for a Date field, for example, you can select only the Creation Date and Modification Date options. Other options are grayed-out (dimmed).

Figure 5-9: Setting an automatic date, time, creator, or modifier stamp for a field.

Selecting Creation Date or Creation Time causes FileMaker Pro to automatically enter the appropriate data as each new record is created. When these options are set, you can tell how old each record is, so you have an idea of whether the record is up to date.

Note that if you define a Creation Date, Creation Time, or Creator Name field *after* the database already contains records, the field will be left blank in existing records. You may want to manually enter this information for the old records.

Modification Date and Modification Time show when a record was last modified. FileMaker Pro automatically enters the appropriate value when you finish editing a record and you press Enter or switch to a different record. If you're interested only in how current a record is — as opposed to when it was originally created — use the Modification Date option. When a new record is created, the Modification Date is the *same* as the Creation Date.

Chapter 5: Defining Fields

Performing Automatic Time Calculations

If you do time billing, you can use Creation Time and Modification Time together to track time spent on the phone with a client or time spent working on a project. For example, when a client calls, immediately create a new record. The Creation Date (Date), Creation Time (Start Time), and Modification Time (End Time) are automatically filled in for you. Total Time is calculated by subtracting Start Time from End Time. When the record is created, the result of this formula is initially zero (0).

Enter the client's name. When the call ends, press Enter to complete the record. The Modification Time is then automatically updated to reflect the current time, and Total Time is recalculated to show the actual length of the call.

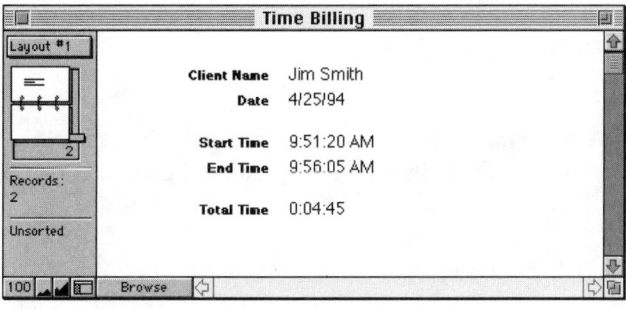

Creator Name and Modifier Name show who created or last modified the record, respectively. These field options are extremely helpful in a multi-user environment.

The Creator Name and Modifier Name are read from information entered in the Sharing Setup control panel (System 7) or the Chooser desk accessory (System 6). If the Creator and Modifier Name fields in your database are always blank, you need to tell your system who you are.

In System 7, follow these steps to identify yourself to your Mac:

1. **Choose Control Panels from the Apple menu.**

   The folder in which your control panels are stored appears on the desktop.

2. **Double-click the icon named Sharing Setup.**

   The Sharing Setup control panel opens.

3. **Type your name or other identifying information in the Owner Name box in the Network Identity section of the window, as shown in Figure 5-10.**

Part II: Database Design Basics

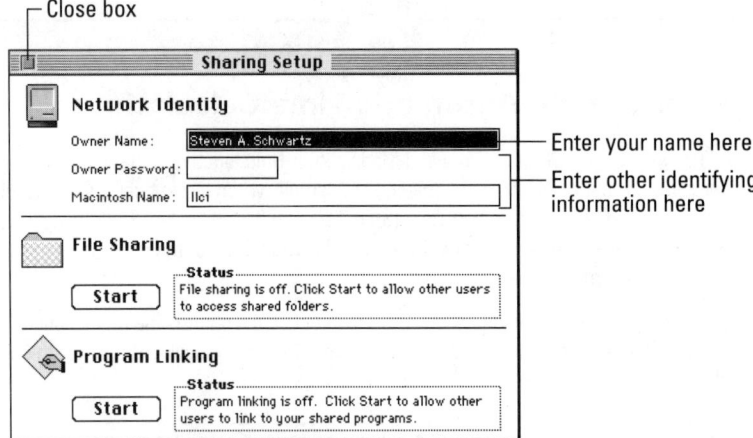

Figure 5-10: Identifying your Mac (System 7).

4. To close the window and save your changes, click the close box in the upper-left corner of the Sharing Setup control panel.

In System 6, follow these steps to identify yourself:

1. **Select the Chooser desk accessory from the Apple menu.**

2. **Type your name or other identifying information in the User Name box.**

3. **To close the Chooser and save the changes, click the close box in the upper-left corner of the Chooser window.**

Serial number

You use this option to automatically enter a number that increments by a set amount for each new record. For example, you can use this option to create invoice and statement numbers.

The following steps describe how to create a Number field in which FileMaker Pro automatically enters serial numbers using the increment that you specify.

1. **Select a Number or Text field in the Define Fields dialog box and click Options.**

2. **Click the "a serial number" check box.**

3. **In the "next value" box, enter the starting serial number.**

   This number will be assigned to the next new record that you create.

4. In the "increment by" box, enter a number for the amount that you want each new serial number to increase over the previous serial number.

5. Click OK to return to the Define Fields dialog box.

Note that a serial number does not have to be a simple number. For example, you can set the starting serial number (next value) as A27B-1000. In a mixed text and number entry such as this one, FileMaker increments the serial number by using the right-most number string and ignoring other numbers in the string. In this example, assuming that the increment was 1, the next serial numbers would be A27B-1001, A27B-1002, and so on.

Data

The Data option enables you to specify a piece of data that you want to have entered automatically for every record. As such, this option is excellent for creating a default entry for a field. For example, in an employee database, often employees live in the same city. By using the name of this city as auto-entry data, you can save some typing. If you create a record for an employee who lives in a *different* city, you can edit the name of the city in that record (unless you have set the option for Prohibit modification of auto-entered values as part of the field's definition. This option is described in the sidebar "Protecting Auto-Entered Values").

Protecting Auto-Entered Values

To protect auto-entered values, you may want to check the Prohibit modification of auto-entered values option in the bottom section of the dialog box. Setting this option prevents you and other users of the database from inadvertently altering the contents of an auto-entry field.

You need to set this option for each field that you want to protect. If you later discover that you need to edit one or more of the auto-entered values for a particular field, return to this screen, remove the check mark from the Prohibit modification of auto-entered values option, edit the fields as necessary, and then restore the check mark.

Data verification options

The options in the Verify that the field value is section are for data validation. They govern the types of information that must, may, or may not be entered in a chosen field.

You need to keep two important things in mind when you create a verification/validation option for a field. First, you can set verification options only for Text, Number, Date, and Time fields. Second, even with a verification option set, FileMaker Pro gives you (or any other person who may be using the database) the option of overriding the validation requirements. If you leave a required field blank or enter text in a number-only field, for example, you see a dialog box like the one in Figure 5-11.

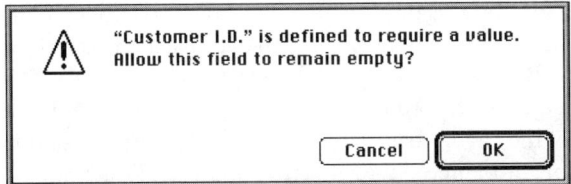

Figure 5-11: A warning that a required field has not been filled in.

Although this approach offers maximum flexibility, it also limits the usefulness of the validation options. If someone else will do data entry for you or if the database will be shared over a network, remember that other users can override the validation requirements. (If you want to stop someone from overriding the warnings, you can set access privileges for the file. See Chapter 20 for details.)

Not empty

Click this check box to create a *required field* (one that must not be empty). In many databases, you will have essential fields that render a record worthless if their data is left blank. In a customer database, for example, you cannot send out bills if the Name, Address, or City fields for a customer are blank. If you attempt to switch to another record without filling in a required field, FileMaker Pro displays a warning.

Unique

The unique option requires every record in the database to have a different value for the field. FileMaker Pro warns you if you enter a value that already exists in another record. Often, customer or record identification numbers must be unique.

When determining whether an entry is unique, FileMaker Pro ignores punctuation, capitalization, and word order. Thus, it considers *Steve Schwartz* and *schwartz, steve* to be identical.

Chapter 5: Defining Fields

When to Use the "An Existing Value" Option

From the explanation of the "an existing value" option, you may think that you should add it only after a database contains many records. In fact, the opposite is true. This option causes a warning dialog box to appear if you enter a value that has never been used for the field, and, as usual, you can override the warning and accept the value. Thus, if you add this entry option when you first create the database, you can specify the allowable entries as you enter records. If you set this option for a Company Name field, for example, you can ensure that every company name is always entered exactly the same way. (However, sorting the database periodically to check the accuracy of your mental notes concerning the companies that you've already entered is still a good idea.)

An existing value

Use this option to ensure that every value that is entered in a particular field matches a value in that field in another record. Essentially, this entry option is the opposite of the Unique option.

When determining whether one entry matches another, FileMaker Pro ignores punctuation, capitalization, and word order. Note, too, that the unique and existing value entry options are mutually exclusive. For any given field, you can set only one of these options.

Of type

Use this option to indicate that only a number, date, or time is an acceptable entry for the field. Assigning this option is the way to ensure that only numbers are entered in Number fields, for example. (Note that a number can include a decimal separator, thousands separator, sign, and parentheses.)

As with the other data validation options, the user can still override the warning dialog box that appears when the wrong type is entered. To keep users from overriding the warning, you must also set access privileges for the database (as described in Chapter 20).

From ... To ...

Select this option to specify an allowable range for a Text, Number, Date, or Time field. Enter the lowest acceptable value in the from box and the highest acceptable value in the to box. (Note that text is handled alphabetically. You can enter the letters *A* and *F* to restrict acceptable entries to text strings that begin with the letters *A*, *B*, *C*, *D*, *E*, and *F*, for example.)

Part II: Database Design Basics

Using the "Of Type Number" Option with a Numeric Range

For numeric ranges, you also may want to set the "of type Number" entry option (discussed in the preceding section). This setting ensures not only that the value will be in range, but also that it will be the proper data type — a number. (In order to get precisely the type of validation you require, it is not uncommon to select two or more validation options that work in concert with each other.)

Repeating fields

Although most fields are intended to handle only one piece of data, you may sometimes want to use a single field to handle multiple bits of information. This type of field is called a *repeating field*.

In older, less capable database programs, you often had to handle repeating fields the hard way. For example, to create an eight-line invoice, you had to define eight separate Quantity, Item Description, Unit Price, and Extended Price fields. Calculations based on these fields were cumbersome to create, as in ExtPrice1 + ExtPrice2 + ExtPrice3.... The FileMaker Pro invoice shown in Figure 5-12, on the other hand, was created by defining a single field for each of the following: Quantity, Item Description, Unit Price, and Extended Price. Then the repeating field option was assigned to each field. You can set any type of field to repeat, except for Summary fields.

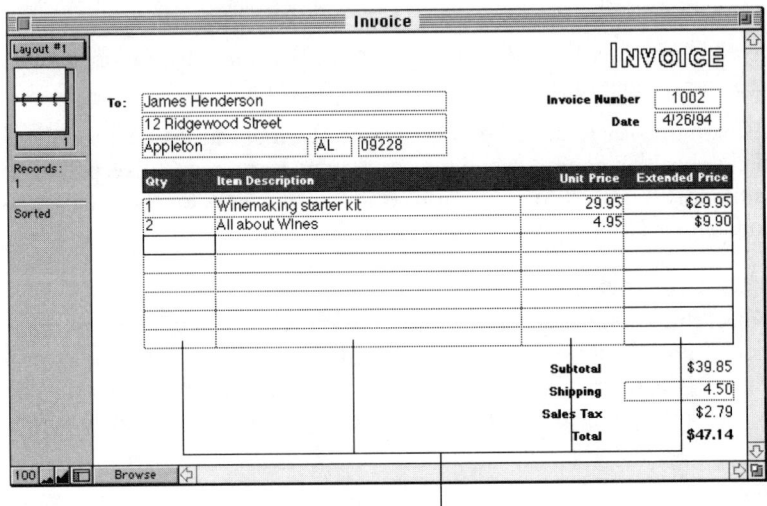

Four repeating fields:
Quantity, Item Description, Unit Price, and Extended Price

Figure 5-12: Repeating fields in an invoice database.

Chapter 5: Defining Fields

Follow these steps to set the repeating field option for a field:

1. **Choose the Define Fields command from the Select menu (or press Shift-⌘-D).**

   The Define Fields dialog box appears.

2. **From the scrolling field list, select the Text, Number, Date, Time, Picture/Sound, or Calculation field that you want to define as a repeating field.**

3. **Click Options.**

   An Options or Entry Options dialog box appears. (The specific dialog box that appears depends on the type of field that you choose.)

4. **Click to place a check mark in the option marked "Repeating field with a maximum of *x* values" and enter the maximum number of repetitions in the number box.**

   The number is simply the upper limit of repetitions that the field can store. You set the number of repetitions that are *displayed*, on the other hand, by switching to Layout mode and choosing the Field Format command from the Format menu (described in Chapter 6).

5. **Click OK to return to the Define Fields dialog box.**

6. **Repeat Steps 2 through 5 for additional fields that you want to define as repeating fields.**

7. **Click Done to record the changes and return to the database.**

Several built-in functions are intended expressly for the purpose of performing computations on repeating fields. You are already familiar with many of them, such as Total and Average, from the discussion in this chapter concerning summary functions (see "Defining Calculation and Summary fields"). For calculation purposes, you can use the Extend function to treat a nonrepeating field as though it repeats.

You need to be aware of a few important facts about repeating fields:

❖ Regardless of the number of repetitions that are visible on the current layout, FileMaker uses *all* repetitions in calculations.

   For example, if you alter an invoice layout that shows eight line items so that it shows only five, FileMaker also will consider the other three line items when it calculates the Sum (repeating field) function. If you really want to keep the additional entries from being included in the calculation, you can delete them.

Part II: Database Design Basics

- When conducting a sort that is based on a repeating field, FileMaker uses only the first entry in the sort.

- Other database programs may not correctly handle a FileMaker export that contains repeating fields.

Value lists

If you have been impressed by the pop-up menus used in many programs, you will be equally impressed to learn that FileMaker Pro 2 enables you to create the same type of choice lists for your database fields.

You determine the values that appear in the list. Depending on the format that you select for a field, the list is presented as a pop-up menu, a pop-up list, a set of check boxes, or a set of radio buttons. When you tab into or click a field that is formatted as a pop-up list or a pop-menu, the list or menu appears automatically. Even if a field has an associated value list, you can still type different information in the field.

Follow these steps to create a value list for a field:

1. **In the Define Fields dialog box, select the Text, Number, Date, or Time field of interest and then click Options.**

2. **In the Options dialog box that appears, click the option for Use a predefined value list.**

   A check mark appears in the check box, and the Value List dialog box appears, as shown in Figure 5-13.

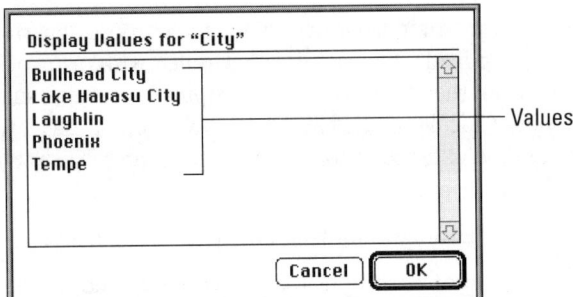

Figure 5-13: A typical value list.

3. **Type entries for the value list, pressing Return after each entry except the last one.**

   (If you press Return after the final entry, you will end up with an extra blank line at the end of the list.)

Chapter 5: Defining Fields 175

Note that FileMaker Pro does not have an option to alphabetize the values. If you want them in a particular order, you have to type them in that order. You also can change their order by cutting and pasting them.

You can type a hyphen (-) on any line to generate a dashed line in pop-up menus and lists or a blank space between radio buttons and check boxes.

4. **Click OK when you are done creating the value list, click OK again to leave the Entry Options dialog box, and then click Done to leave the Define Fields dialog box.**

To set a display format for the value list, follow these steps:

1. **Change to Layout mode by choosing Layout from the Select menu (or pressing ⌘-L).**
2. **If the field with the associated value list isn't already on the layout, add it to the layout by dragging a field object onto the layout and selecting the name of the field in the New Field list that appears.**
3. **Select the field with the associated value list by clicking the field.**

   Handles appear at the corners of the field to show that it is selected.

4. **Choose Field Format from the Format menu (or press ⌘-Option-F).**

   The Field Format dialog box appears, as shown in Figure 5-14.

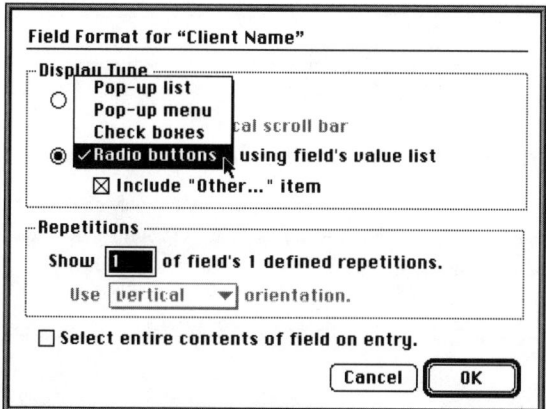

Figure 5-14: The Field Format dialog box.

5. **In the Display Type section of the dialog box, click the radio button labeled "*format style* using field's value list" (if it isn't already selected) and then choose the display format that you want from the pop-up menu.**

6. *Optional:* If you select any format other than Pop-up list, you can click the check box for Include "Other…" item to add a choice marked "Other…" to the pop-up menu, check boxes, or radio buttons.

   An Other… choice facilitates the entry of data that is not present in the field's value list.

7. Click OK to record the changes or Cancel to leave the formatting the way it was.

Lookups

The lookup field option instructs FileMaker Pro to look up information in a second database and copy it into the current database. When you create several databases that share some common element (perhaps they all make use of address information), you can minimize the amount of duplicate data entry that is required by instructing each of these databases to automatically extract the address information from the Address database.

A lookup is the only the *relational* function that FileMaker Pro can perform (referred to in Chapter 1). Note that a lookup is a one-way function. Data is copied from another file into the current file, much like importing field information but affecting only the current record rather than the entire database.

Selecting Multiple Radio Buttons

If you format a value list field as a set of check boxes, you can select multiple options when you enter data in the field. And although radio button options are mutually exclusive in most programs (you can normally choose only one from a set), you can select multiple radio buttons by holding down the Shift key as you click each one.

Chapter 5: Defining Fields

The following steps describe how to create a lookup field:

1. **Choose Define Fields from the Select menu (or press Shift-⌘-D).**

   The Define fields dialog box appears.

2. **Select or create a field to receive the copied (lookup) data and click Options or double-click the field name in the field list.**

   The field type must be Text, Number, Date, Time, or Picture/Sound.

3. **Click the Look up values from a file option in the Entry Options dialog box that appears.**

   A standard file dialog box appears.

4. **Select the FileMaker Pro file from which you intend to extract the lookup information and click Open.**

   Whenever a lookup is performed, the second file is automatically opened for you as part of the lookup process.

   The Lookup Value dialog box appears (see Figure 5-15). Information relevant to the lookup file is displayed on the left side of the dialog box; information concerning the current file is displayed on the right side.

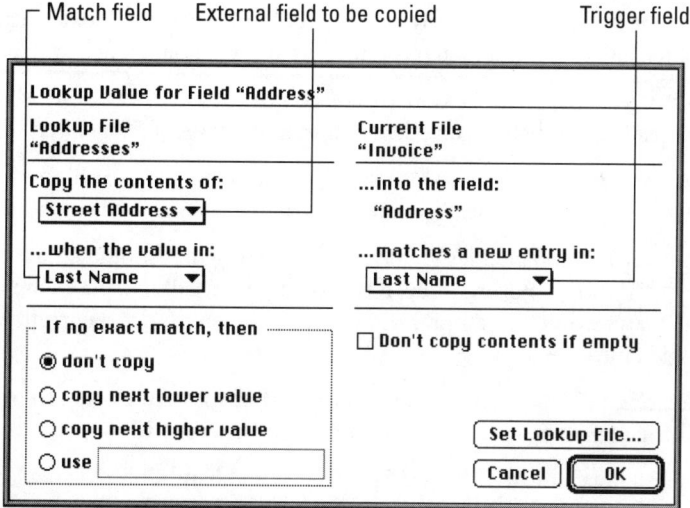

Figure 5-15: The Lookup Value dialog box.

5. **Select the name of the field that you want to copy into the current database.**

   The pop-up menu labeled "Copy the contents of" contains a list of all fields in the lookup file (the external database). You select the field from this menu.

   When the lookup is executed, the contents of the selected field are copied into the current field, which is shown on the right side of the dialog box. (In the example, Street Address will be copied from the lookup file into the Address field in the current file, as shown in Figure 5-15.)

6. **Using the final pair of pop-up menus, select the match fields from the two databases.**

   FileMaker Pro will compare these fields to determine whether a match exists between the two databases.

7. **In the section of the dialog box labeled "If no exact match, then," you need to tell FileMaker Pro what to do if it doesn't find an exact match. Options include the following:**

   ❖ *Don't copy:* This option is the default and, in most cases, it is exactly what you want. Rather than copying erroneous data, the field is left as is.

   Note that after a lookup executes, you can still edit the contents of the field into which data was copied. If you ever edit the *trigger field* (the field in the current database that initiates the lookup), however, the lookup will be executed anew; and if a match is found, your edited data will be replaced.

   ❖ *Copy next lower value:* Choose this option to copy the next lower value (numerically or alphabetically, depending on the type of data stored in the field).

   ❖ *Copy next higher value:* Choose this option to copy the next higher value (numerically or alphabetically, depending on the type of data stored in the field).

   ❖ *Use:* This option enables you to specify a string that should be used when no match is found. For example, if the lookup is based on a phone number and the search comes up empty, you can have the text, "Not a current customer," copied into the field.

8. *Optional:* **Click the Don't copy contents if empty check box to avoid copying information from a blank field into the current file.**

   In the example shown in Figure 5-15, if you had hand-entered an address in the Address field, selecting this option would prevent the address from being replaced by a blank address from the external file.

9. **Click OK to accept the options you have just set or click Cancel to ignore the new settings.**

10. **Repeat Steps 2 through 9 to define additional lookup fields, as desired, and click Done when you're ready to close the Define Fields dialog box and return to the database.**

Choose the Match Field Wisely

When you are selecting a field on which to base a lookup, you'll be much happier if you choose one that is unique, such as a customer ID number, Social Security number, or telephone number. If, for example, you use the contents of the Last Name field as what you're attempting to match (as I've done in the instructions for creating a lookup field), you will run into problems if you have several people who share the same last name. No matter how many times you execute the lookup, you'll find only the first person who has that particular last name.

Here are some other important factors to keep in mind when you are creating and using lookups:

- To determine whether a match has been found, FileMaker Pro compares only the first 20 characters in the match fields. It ignores word order, punctuation, and capitalization, as well as any text that is contained in a Number field.

- If the data in the external database changes, a lookup that you previously performed may now contain data that is out of date. To correct this situation, you can instruct FileMaker Pro to perform the lookup again by tabbing into the field that is used to trigger the lookup and choosing the Relookup command from the Edit menu.

    Note that unlike a regular lookup, which is performed for only the current record, a relookup is performed for all records that are being browsed.

- You can select any FileMaker Pro file in which to do a lookup, including the current file.

    This technique can be extremely useful with any database that contains multiple records for the same customer, client, or subject. As an example, an invoice database can look for a Customer ID among the existing records and then, if a match is found, fill in the fields of the mailing address for you.

Because a lookup is a complex concept for many users to grasp, an entire chapter is devoted to the topic (see Chapter 19).

Using Lookups to Fill in Multiple Fields

At first glance, you may not think that you can trigger a lookup that will copy multiple fields to the original database. As the example in the instructions for creating a lookup field (earlier in this chapter) shows, when a match is located, the lookup copies the contents of only one external field into one field in the current database.

The solution is to individually define a lookup for *every* field that you want to copy, using the same trigger field for each lookup. For example, to copy an entire address, begin by identifying a unique field, such as the Social Security number, the phone number, or a customer identification number. Then create a separate lookup for each field in the address (First Name, Last Name, Address, City, State, and Zip) using the same trigger and match fields in each lookup definition (the Social Security number, for example). When you enter the information in the trigger field during data entry, FileMaker will perform all the lookups simultaneously. Although FileMaker will appear to be doing only one lookup, in fact, it will perform half a dozen of them.

Modifying Field Definitions, Names, and Options

A few capabilities of the Define Fields dialog box remain unexplored (and unexplained). As previously mentioned, FileMaker Pro 2 enables you to add, change, or delete field definitions and options whenever you like. You also can rename fields. And to speed the process of creating fields, FileMaker Pro lets you duplicate existing field definitions. The step-by-step instructions in this section explain how to perform all these tasks.

Adding new fields by starting from scratch

The following steps describe how to add new fields when you are starting from scratch.

1. **Choose Define Fields from the Select menu (or press Shift-⌘-D).**

   The Define fields dialog box appears.

2. **Type a name for the new field (up to 60 characters) in the Name box.**

   If you think that you may want to use the field in a calculation formula, be sure that the name does not contain a number, period, comma, quotation mark, math symbol, logical keyword (AND, OR, NOT), or the name of any FileMaker Pro built-in function. Such symbols and words will be improperly interpreted as being part of the formula.

Chapter 5: Defining Fields

3. **Click a radio button to select a data type for the field.**

4. **Click Create.**

   If you select Calculation or Summary as the field type, another dialog box appears in which you can specify the formula or type of summary information that you want. For any other field type, clicking Create concludes the basic definition process.

5. **To create additional fields, repeat Steps 2 through 4 and click Done when you are through defining fields.**

Duplicating existing fields

To save time, you may want to duplicate some existing fields — particularly fields that have complex options that you want to avoid having to reenter. After you duplicate a field, editing and renaming the new field is a simple matter (see the instructions for renaming a field, later in this section).

For example, in an invoice or statement database, you might have a series of repeating fields that you use to record each line item (such as Quantity, Description, Unit Cost, and Extended Cost). You'd use separate Calculation fields to compute the total for each of the Cost fields. After defining a formula for the first Calculation field as *Sum (Unit Cost)*, you could duplicate the field definition and, in the formula, simply replace *Unit Cost* with *Extended Cost*.

To duplicate an existing field, follow these steps:

1. **Choose Define Fields from the Select menu (or press Shift-⌘-D).**

   The Define fields dialog box appears.

2. **Select the field that you want to duplicate and click the Duplicate button.**

   FileMaker Pro creates an exact duplicate of the field and names it *original field name* Copy. For example, if the field to be duplicated is named Comments, the duplicate is named Comments Copy. Additional duplicates of the same field are named Comments Copy2, Comments Copy3, and so on.

3. *Optional:* **To rename the duplicate field, select the field in the scrolling field list, type a new name in the Name box, and click Change.**

4. *Optional:* **To change any of the options for the duplicate field, select the field and click Options.**

5. **To duplicate additional fields, repeat Steps 2 through 4 and click Done when you are through duplicating fields.**

Part II: Database Design Basics

Replacing One Field with Another

Has this ever happened to you? After carefully selecting, placing, resizing, and setting attributes for fields on a layout, you discover that one of the fields wasn't the right one. Rather than deleting the errant field and then adding the correct one, you can use this trick to redefine the field as a different field.

Switch to Layout mode, hold down the Option key, and double-click the field you want to redefine. The New Field windoid (the list of defined fields) appears. Select a replacement field from the list and click OK. Redefining the field preserves its original placement on the layout, as well as its dimensions and formatting attributes.

Changing field names

Unless you give a great deal of thought to field names when you design databases, you'll find that the names you choose for some fields can sometimes stand a little improvement. Feel free to change field names to ones that are more appropriate. FileMaker Pro 2 automatically adjusts field labels, sort instructions, and other references to the field (in calculation formulas, for example).

Follow these steps to give a field a different name:

1. **Choose Define Fields from the Select menu (or press Shift-⌘-D).**

   The Define fields dialog box appears.

2. **Select the field that you want to rename.**

   The field name appears in the Name box.

3. **Type a new name in the Name box and click Change.**

   FileMaker Pro renames the field and automatically adjusts any references to the field in Calculation field formulas, Summary fields, or scripts to reflect the new field name. If, when you originally created the field, you accepted and placed the default label for the field, FileMaker Pro also changes the label to match the new field. Field labels that you have manually edited or typed from scratch, on the other hand, are unaffected.

4. **To rename additional fields, repeat Steps 2 and 3. Click Done when you are through renaming fields.**

Deleting a field and its data

The more you work with a particular database, the more familiar you become with the data it was designed to collect. If you decide that you no longer need a particular field (or perhaps that you should never have included it in the first place), follow these steps to delete the field and the data it contains:

Chapter 5: Defining Fields

1. **Choose Define Fields from the Select menu (or press Shift-⌘-D).**

   The Define fields dialog box appears.

2. **Select the field that you want to delete and then click the Delete button.**

   One of two dialog boxes appears. The normal dialog box simply asks whether you're sure you want to delete the field and its contents (see Figure 5-16).

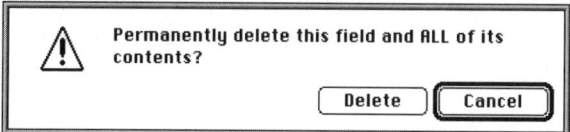

Figure 5-16: This dialog box appears when you attempt to delete most fields.

If the field is referenced in a Calculation or Summary field, the second dialog box appears (see Figure 5-17), explaining that you cannot delete the field. To delete such a field, you first have to edit the appropriate Calculation and Summary fields so that they no longer reference the field that you intend to delete. Then you can delete the field.

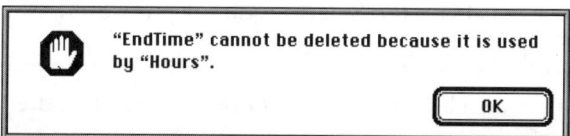

Figure 5-17: This dialog box appears if you attempt to delete a field that is referenced in a Calculation or Summary field formula.

3. **In the normal dialog box (shown in Figure 5-16), click the Delete button to delete the field or click Cancel if you change your mind.**

4. **To delete additional fields, repeat Steps 2 and 3. Click Done when you are ready to return to the database.**

As the dialog box in Figure 5-16 warns, *deleting a field eliminates the field and all the data for the field.* You cannot undo this deletion. If you may later need the data, make a backup copy of the file by choosing the Save a Copy As command from the File menu before you delete the field.

Part II: Database Design Basics

An Alternative to Deleting a Field

Instead of deleting a field, you can simply remove it from all layouts. Removing a field in this manner does not delete it. All data previously entered in the field remains intact. To be able to see the data, all you have to do is add the field back onto a layout. This approach makes the database larger than necessary, however, because it is still storing information that you may never use again. If you're *certain* that you no longer need to continue collecting the data for a field, the *best* approach is to make a backup copy of the original database, delete the field in the current version of the file, and then move on.

Setting field options for existing fields

You do not have to set field options when you first define a field. You can add them later as the need arises. (Note, however, that if you enter data before setting options for a field, you may need to go back and correct some of the earlier entries for the field.)

Follow these steps to set options for fields that you have already defined:

1. **Choose Define Fields from the Select menu (or press Shift-⌘-D).**

   The Define fields dialog box appears.

2. **Select the field for which you want to set options and click the Options button.**

   (You also can double-click any field in the list to move directly to the Options dialog box for that field.)

3. **In the Options dialog box that appears, set options as described in "Setting Field Entry Options," earlier in this chapter.**

4. **To accept the new options, click OK. To ignore the options you have selected, click Cancel.**

5. **To set options for other fields, repeat Steps 2 through 4. Click Done when you are through setting options.**

Changing a field definition

The following steps describe how to change a field definition:

1. **Choose Define Fields from the Select menu (or press Shift-⌘-D).**

   The Define fields dialog box appears.

Chapter 5: Defining Fields   185

2. Select the field you want to change.

3. To change the field's type, select a new type and click Change.

   If changing to the new field type involves any potential problems, FileMaker presents one of the dialog boxes shown in Figure 5-18. (The *particular* box that you see is related to the type of change that you want to make). The warning box contains information that you should consider before proceeding with the conversion. If a warning box appears, you may want to use the Save a Copy As command to make a backup copy of the database before you proceed.

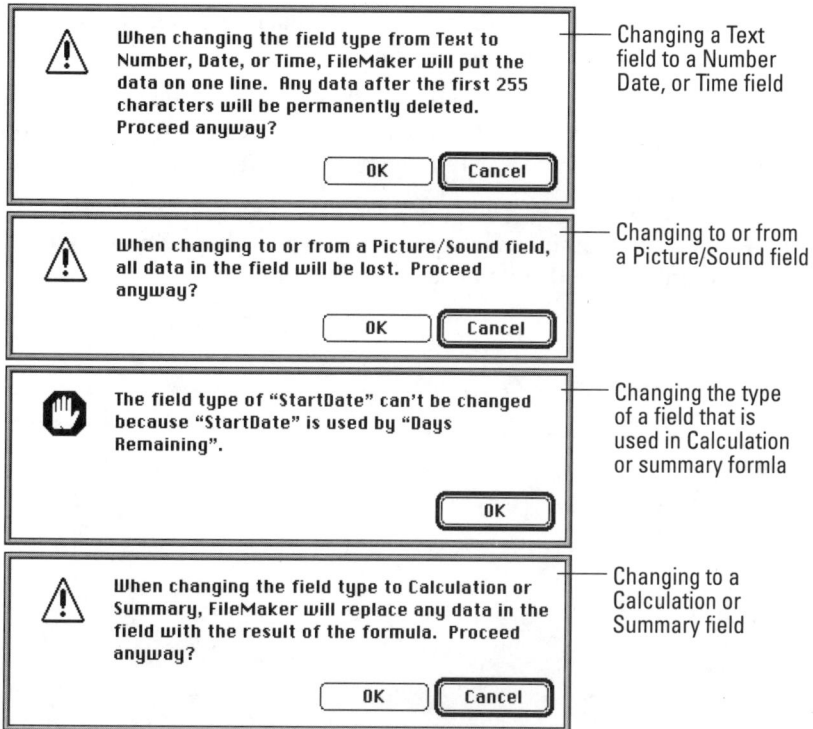

Figure 5-18: Warning boxes that may appear when changing a field type.

— or —

3. If the field to be changed is a Summary or Calculation field, click the Options button, select a new Summary function or edit the formula for the Calculation field, and click OK to accept the changes or Cancel to revert to the original settings.

4. To change additional field definitions, repeat Steps 2 and 3 for each field. When you are through, click Done to leave the Define Fields dialog box.

Part II: Database Design Basics

Changing or deleting options for a field

To change or delete options for a field, follow these steps:

1. **Choose Define Fields from the Select menu (or press Shift-⌘-D).**

    The Define fields dialog box appears.

2. **Select the field whose options you want to change and then click the Options button or double-click the field name in the field list.**

    An Options dialog box appears, appropriate to the data type of the field that you selected.

3. **Change the options that you want to change and then click OK to return to the Define Fields dialog box.**

    The means of changing options is always obvious. You can add or remove options by clicking check boxes, clicking buttons, making selections from pop-up menus, and using normal editing techniques (to change value lists and formulas, for example).

4. **To change options for other fields, repeat Steps 2 and 3. Click Done when you are through changing field options.**

Chapter 5: Defining Fields

CHAPTER 5 CONCEPTS AND TERMS

- FileMaker Pro offers seven field types: Text, Number, Date, Time, Picture/Sound, Calculation, and Summary. The type that you choose for a field determines the kinds of information that you can enter in the field.
- You can set auto-entry options for a field to instruct FileMaker Pro to automatically enter a value in the field whenever you create a new record or, in some cases, when you edit a record. By selecting the option labeled "Prohibit modification of auto-entered values," you can protect the contents of this type of field from inadvertent (or deliberate) modification.
- Data validation options help ensure that only acceptable values are entered for a field.
- You can alter the fields for a database at any time by changing their names, definitions, or options. You also can add new fields or delete existing fields.

Calculation field
A field type that is used to generate within-record computations. Formulas in Calculation fields can reference other fields, use FileMaker Pro's built-in functions, and contain constants.

field type
Specifies the type of information that can be stored in a particular field.

index
FileMaker Pro maintains this internal list of data that covers the contents of every Text, Number, Date, Time, and Calculation field. Indexes are responsible for the speed with which FileMaker Pro executes Find requests.

lookup
A field option that instructs FileMaker Pro to search an external database for a record that contains a match to the data entered in the current database. If a match is found, data from another field in the external database is automatically copied into a field in the current database.

Picture/Sound field
Fields of this type can be used to store graphics, QuickTime movies, or sound clips.

Relookup
A command in the Edit menu that causes all lookups for a database to be executed again (for every record currently being browsed). Choosing this command ensures that all lookup fields contain current data.

repeating field
A field option that enables a single field to store and display multiple values.

required field (not empty)
A field that must be filled in before finalizing the information for the record. The record is checked for completeness only when you press Enter; attempt to switch to a different record, layout, or mode; close the database; or try to quit FileMaker Pro while the database is still open.

Summary field
A field that statistically summarizes all records currently being browsed.

trigger field
A field in the current database that, when data is entered or modified, initiates a lookup.

unique field
A field that can contain only data that is not duplicated in any other record.

value list
A field option that causes a user-specified list of choices to be displayed when you click or tab into the field.

 **Part II: Database Design Basics**

CHAPTER SIX

Layouts

- Learning about layouts
- Working with FileMaker Pro's predefined layouts
- Creating layouts of your own
- Working with different layout parts
- Arranging fields in a layout
- Adding additional elements to a layout, including formatting, labels, and graphics

You may have everything from soup to nuts in a database, but it's a sure bet that you won't need all that information for every conceivable application. To print envelopes or mailing labels, for example, you need access to the name and address fields of each client in your database, but you don't need to see any information about how much each client has ordered from you. On the other hand, if you're preparing a summary of your recent sales figures, the exact names and addresses of clients who have ordered are of little importance. What you need to know is how much has been ordered, who was responsible for selling it, and what the total sales were.

In effect, you need a way to display only the database information that you need for a particular purpose, such as entering data, printing envelopes, examining help information, or viewing sales totals. FileMaker Pro gives you a powerful feature to do just that — the layout. A *layout* is a particular arrangement of all or a subset of fields in a database. You choose which fields are included in each layout and which ones aren't; you can arrange the fields in each layout to address a specific need (such as printing labels, entering data, or presenting a columnar report); you can add layout parts, such as a header and footer, to make some information repeat on every page, for instance; and you can include special items to help identify your layouts or make them more attractive (such as titles and graphics). You can have as many layouts for a given database as you like, one to suit every need. Your imagination — and the amount of hard disk space you have — are the only limits.

Understanding Layouts

A FileMaker Pro layout is composed of several elements. First are the various *layout parts*, which are the areas in which information is displayed. In a way, layout parts are like the parts of a blank sheet of paper intended for use in a printed report. Layout parts include the *header* and *footer*, which are used to display a title, page numbers, or other information that must appear on every page of a report; the *body*, which is used to display fields; and *summary parts*, which can enable you to present a running total of numerical data, such as total sales figures. The body is the only required part; the others are optional.

You place fields in the different layout parts, particularly the body. You can place a field in any layout that your database contains; you can even place fields more than once, if you like. You set the size of each field, and you can specify the form in which its data is displayed. You can, if necessary, add labels to identify the fields; the labels don't have to be the same as the fields' defined names. To jazz things up, you can add graphics. Finally, you can group and coordinate all these items, using a grid to keep items a standard distance from one another and using alignment options to make sure that the items are properly aligned.

Layout Mode

You accomplish all these actions in Layout mode, which is one of FileMaker Pro's four operational modes. (The others are Browse, Find, and Preview.) Switch to Layout mode, and you'll see a screen similar to Figure 6-1, which shows the Address Book database in Layout mode.

At the upper-left corner of the Address Book database is a pop-up menu, listing the layouts that have been defined. This menu enables you to choose an existing layout to edit. Below the pop-up menu is a book icon that also gives you access to available layouts. You click the book to page up and down through the available layouts. Below the book icon are a number of tools that you use to add or modify elements on a layout. Of particular interest are the field and part pop-up menus. You use these menus to add layout parts and to add fields to them.

Finally, at the right side of the window, you see the current layout. Notice the rules at the top and to the left of the layout; these rules help you align objects and show you how large your layout is becoming. The size and spacing of a layout are of greatest importance when you're preparing something to be printed, especially labels and envelopes.

Important features of Layout mode can be found in the Layout, Arrange, and Format menus. These menus contain commands to add items to layouts, arrange them, and specify how to display them. You'll learn more about these menus as the chapter progresses.

Chapter 6: Layouts

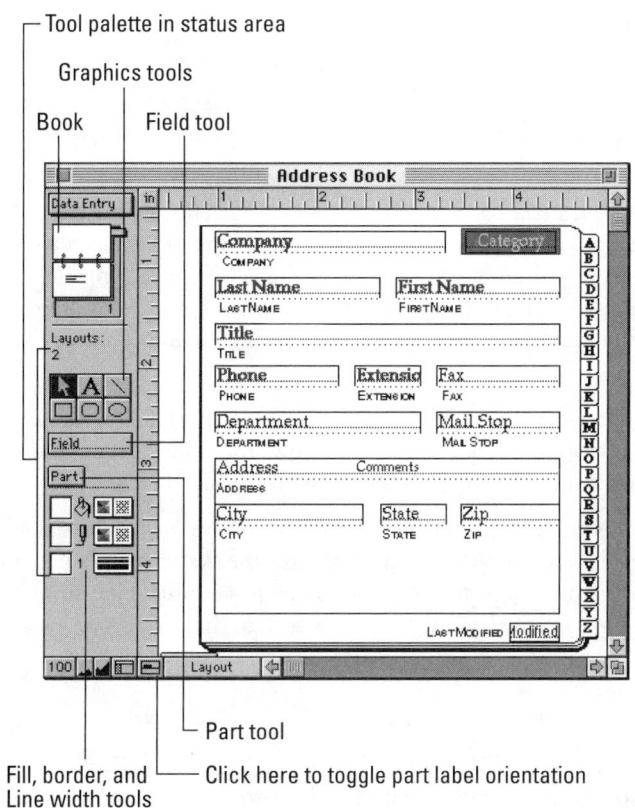

Figure 6-1: The Address Book database in Layout mode, data-entry layout displayed.

To switch to Layout mode, follow these steps:

1. **Launch FileMaker Pro, if it isn't already running.**
2. **Open the database in which you want to add, modify, or view layouts.**
3. **Choose Layout from the Select menu (or press ⌘-L).**
4. **From the layout pop-up menu in the upper-left corner of the window, choose the layout you want to view.**

— or —

4. **Click the book icon to page through the available layouts until the one you want appears.**

Creating a layout: an example

In looking through the various tools and options available in Layout mode, you might be somewhat overwhelmed. The process of designing and implementing a layout, however, really isn't difficult. The following example shows the steps involved.

Dave runs his own small consulting business from his house. Recently, he closed a deal on a new house. His new home includes, for the first time, a separate office space. Dave wants to announce his move to all his clients via a mailing, letting them know how to reach him at his new home office. He's already prepared an announcement to send. Now he wants to save a little time in preparing the envelopes.

Dave maintains a FileMaker Pro database with a separate record for each client, past and present. He realizes that the information in his Clients database could be used to print envelopes. What's more, he knows that FileMaker Pro includes an Envelopes layout that he can adapt for use with the Clients database.

First, Dave prepares a rough sketch just to show where his database fields should go in his new envelope layout. (In fact, he prepares the sketch on a blank envelope.) Next, he follows these steps to bring the Envelopes template into his Clients database and to adapt the layout to the structure of that database:

1. **With his Clients database open, Dave chooses Layout from the Select menu.**

   This command switches him to Layout mode.

2. **Dave chooses New Layout from the Edit menu.**

   The New Layout dialog box appears (see Figure 6-2 later in this chapter).

3. **Dave clicks the Envelope radio button to select that form of layout.**

4. **Dave enters a name for his layout, calling it Client Mailing.**

5. **Dave clicks OK.**

   A dialog box appears, in which he must select fields to put in his new layout.

6. **Dave selects the fields he wants to use in the Client Mailing layout, clicking the Move button for each field.**

7. **Dave clicks OK when he finishes selecting fields.**

   The new layout appears with the chosen fields in place.

8. **Dave arranges the fields so that the envelope will look good when printed.**

   His rearranging includes moving some fields and changing the size and position of others.

9. **Dave adds his new return address as a text object.**
   His new layout now is ready to use in preparing the mass mailing.

Chapter 6: Layouts

The preceding example is simple, but it does show the basic steps involved in creating a layout. Using these predefined layout styles is the easiest way to get started designing your own layouts.

Using the Predefined Layout Styles

When you define fields for a new database, FileMaker Pro creates your first layout for you. This layout, referred to simply as Layout #1, contains all the fields in your database. The fields appear in the order in which you defined them, labeled with their field names. You can immediately use this layout for data entry and viewing, if you like.

To view data in other ways, you must add more layouts. FileMaker Pro includes six predefined layouts that you can use as starting points. In addition, the program includes a blank layout form you can use when you want to design a layout from scratch. The predefined layouts are listed and explained in Table 6-1 below.

Table 6-1
FileMaker Pro Predefined Layout Styles

Layout Name	Purpose
Standard	Shows one record per screen, with all fields displayed in the order in which they were defined.
Columnar Report	Fields are displayed left to right in columns, with one record per line. Fields that don't fit on one line are wrapped to the next line.
Extended Columnar	Same as Columnar Report, but fields aren't wrapped; all fields are displayed on one line, no matter how long.
Single Page Form	One record per screen; no header or footer.
Labels	Fields formatted for small area, for use with mailing labels.
Envelope	Fields formatted for small area, for use with business envelopes.
Blank	A blank layout that you can use to create custom layouts.

To create a new layout, you choose the New Layout command from the Edit menu. (This command is available only when you're in Layout mode.) Choosing this command (or pressing ⌘-N) brings up the New Layout dialog box, shown in Figure 6-2.

Part II: Database Design Basics

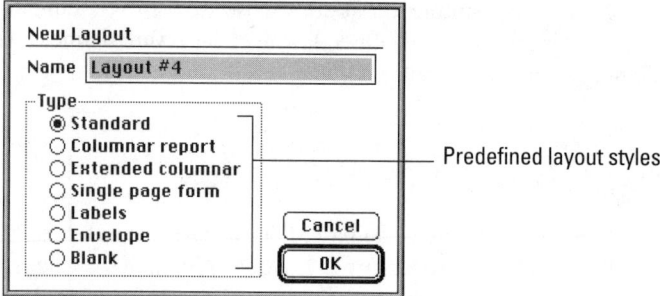

Figure 6-2: The New Layout dialog box.

FileMaker Pro fills in the layout name for you, but—because its choice isn't very descriptive—you can type a layout name of your own choosing instead. Then click a radio button to select the style of layout you want to use. Click OK to finish. At this point, you may or may not proceed to another dialog box, depending on whether all fields in the database or only a selected subset will appear in the new layout. Label and Envelope layouts, for example, use only the fields that you specify.

Follow these steps to create a new layout based on a predefined layout style:

1. **Determine what sort of layout you want to use and what fields you need to display.**

2. **With the appropriate database open in FileMaker Pro, switch to Layout mode by choosing Layout from the Select menu (or by pressing ⌘-L).**

3. **Choose New Layout from the Edit menu (or press Ô-N).**

   The New Layout dialog box appears.

4. **Type a name for the new layout.**

5. **Choose the layout style you want to use by clicking the appropriate radio button.**

6. **Click OK to create the layout.**

For most layout types, FileMaker Pro creates your layout immediately. For layout types that use a limited set of the fields available in the database, you must choose which fields to use, as explained in the following sections.

Standard layouts

The Standard predefined layout is the same one that FileMaker Pro creates as a data-entry layout when you define fields for a database. In this layout, one record is displayed at a time. In addition to the body area, where the record is displayed, the layout includes blank headers and footers; each of these elements is a layout part. (You'll learn more about parts later in the "Layout Parts" section.)

All the fields in your database are automatically included in a Standard layout. The fields appear, top to bottom, in the order in which they were defined. Fields are labeled with their field names. Figure 6-3 shows a standard layout.

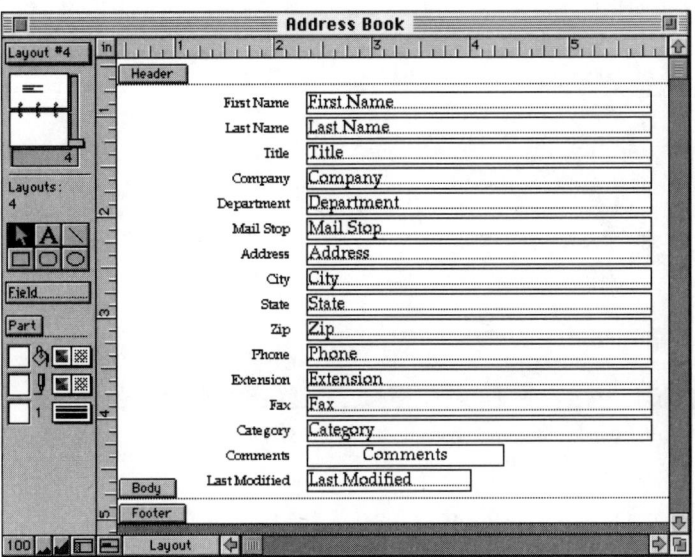

Figure 6-3: A Standard layout for the Address Book database.

You should note that the Single Page Form layout is the same as the Standard layout, except that a Single Page Form layout doesn't have a header or footer part. Later in this chapter, you'll learn how to add items to these layout parts and how to rearrange and alter the fields shown in any layout, including increasing the field's size and changing its format.

Columnar layouts

FileMaker Pro offers two kinds of *columnar* layouts (in which fields are displayed in columns across the page). In a Columnar Report layout, FileMaker Pro attempts to fit all fields on a single line but wraps excess fields to the next line. In a Extended Columnar layout, FileMaker Pro displays all fields on a single line, no matter how wide the line is. Columnar layouts are frequently used to produce reports.

Figure 6-4 shows an Extended Columnar layout for the Address Book database.

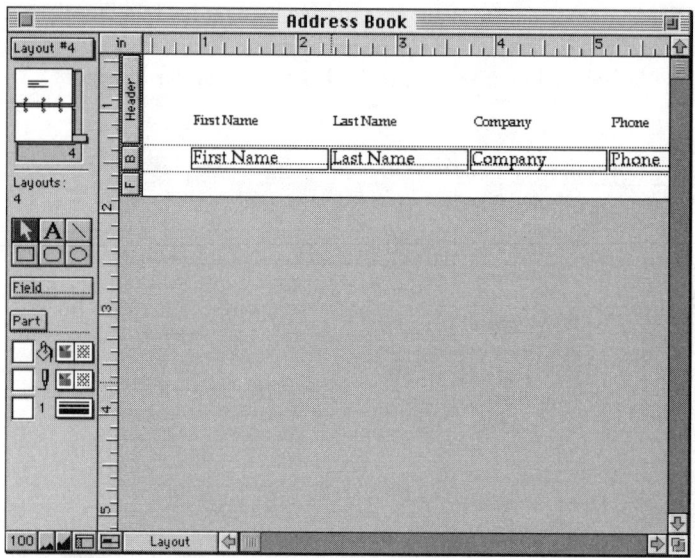

Figure 6-4: An Extended Columnar layout for the Address Book database.

Only the fields that you specify appear in a columnar layout. When you create a columnar layout, the Set Field Order dialog box appears, asking you to specify which fields should appear in the layout and in what order across the page (see Figure 6-5).

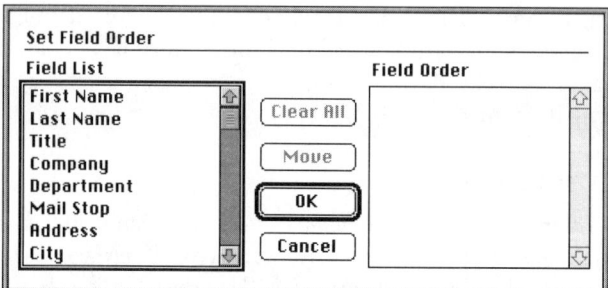

Figure 6-5: The Set Field Order dialog box.

The names of the fields in your database appear in the list on the left side of the dialog box. The currently selected fields and their order in the layout appear in the list on the right side of the dialog box. (In Figure 6-5, no fields have been selected yet.) The buttons in the center allow you to specify which fields to use.

Chapter 6: Layouts

 Follow these steps to define a columnar layout and to use the Set Field Order dialog box:

1. **Within the appropriate database in FileMaker Pro, switch to Layout mode.**
2. **Choose New Layout from the Edit menu (or press ⌘-N).**

   The New Layout dialog box appears.
3. **Type a name for the layout.**
4. **Click the Columnar report or Extended columnar radio button.**
5. **Click OK.**

   The Set Field Order dialog box appears.
6. **Click the name of the field that you want to appear first in the layout (as the leftmost column).**
7. **Click the Move button to move this field to the Field Order list.**
8. **Repeat Steps 6 and 7 for all fields that you want to use in the layout.**
9. **To change the order of fields after you move them to the Field Order list, drag a field's name up or down to another position; repeat for each field whose order you want to change.**
10. **To remove a field from the Field Order list, select its name in the Field Order list and then click Clear.**

    (The Move button changes to Clear when you select a field in the Field Order list.)
11. **To remove all fields and start over, click Clear All.**
12. **When you finish adding fields, click OK.**

    FileMaker Pro creates the layout with the fields you specified in the order you specified.

Working with columns outside columnar layouts

At times, you may want to view or print a conventional layout to columnar form — when you want to keep the field display the same but want to see more than one record at a time. One simple way to do this is to choose View as List from the Select menu. You can also use columns to accomplish this task. To add columns to a layout, choose Layout Options from the Layout menu. Choosing this command brings up the Layout Options dialog box (see Figure 6-6).

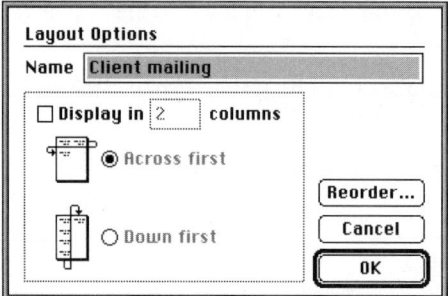

Figure 6-6: The Layout Options dialog box.

Click the Display in check-box to choose to display columns; then indicate how many columns you want to use by typing a number in the text box. Finally, specify how records will fill the columns. The Across first option fills each column across the page before proceeding to the next row; the Down first option fills an entire column on a page and then moves to the top of the next column. The first option is good for printing labels and for use whenever you want to conserve paper; the second option is more appropriate for phone directory listings, among other things.

To change an existing layout to a columnar layout, follow these steps:

1. **In the appropriate database, switch to Layout mode.**
2. **From the layout pop-up menu, choose the layout that you want to change to columnar format.**

   The appropriate layout appears on-screen.
3. **Choose Layout Options from the Layout menu.**

   The Layout Options dialog box appears.
4. **Click the Display in checkbox to select that option and enter the number of columns in the text box.**

   (Remember that the more columns you use, the less space you have for each column.)
5. **Specify whether you want to fill columns across or down by clicking the appropriate radio button.**
6. **Click OK to modify the layout.**

You should note that in addition to specifying columns, you can use the Layout Options dialog box to change the order of fields in a layout and to change a layout's name.

Chapter 6: Layouts

Changing or removing a column setup

You also can use the Layout Options dialog box to alter an existing column setup. To change the number of columns in a layout and to change the manner in which columns are filled, follow these steps:

1. **In the appropriate database, switch to Layout mode.**
2. **From the layout pop-up menu, choose the layout that you want to change.**

    The appropriate layout appears on-screen.

3. **Choose Layout Options from the Layout menu.**

    The Layout Options dialog box appears.

4. **Enter the new number of columns in the text box.**
5. **Specify whether you want to fill columns across or down by clicking the appropriate radio button.**
6. **Click OK to modify the layout.**

Follow these steps to remove columns from a layout and revert to a Standard layout:

1. **In the appropriate database, switch to Layout mode.**
2. **From the layout pop-up menu, choose the layout that you want to change.**

    The appropriate layout appears on-screen.

3. **Choose Layout Options from the Layout menu.**

    The Layout Options dialog box appears.

4. **Click the Display in checkbox to deselect that option.**
5. **Click OK to modify the layout.**

Label layouts

Another of FileMaker Pro's predefined layout styles allows you to print labels. You can specify any of the supported Avery label formats, or you can create your own label. See Chapter 12 for more information on label layouts and on creating your own labels.

When you use the Label layout style form to create a new layout, the Label Setup dialog box appears, asking you to specify what type of label to use (see Figure 6-7).

Part II: Database Design Basics

Choose from among the available preset labels

Figure 6-7: The Label Setup dialog box.

This dialog box contains two radio-button options: one for using the predefined Avery label formats, and the other for entering custom measurements. The latter procedure can be tricky if you don't have much experience in working with label stock.

One thing that you probably will want to do is change the format of the fields in your Label layout, making some fields larger and some fields smaller, and dragging others to different positions. (You'll learn how to do all those things for *any* layout a little later in this chapter.)

Follow these steps to define a layout based on one of the predefined Avery label formats:

1. **In the appropriate database within FileMaker Pro, switch to Layout mode.**
2. **Choose New Layout from the Edit menu (or press ⌘-N).**

    The New Layout dialog box appears.

3. **Enter a name for the new layout.**
4. **Click the Labels radio button to select that option.**
5. **Click OK.**

    The Label Setup dialog box appears.

6. **Specify the Avery-label part number for the label stock you want to use.**

    Choose this number from the pop-up menu in the upper-right corner of the dialog box.

Chapter 6: Layouts

7. Click OK.

The Set Field Order dialog box appears.

8. Make any necessary changes in this dialog box.

9. Click OK to finish defining the label layout.

If you know a couple of fairly simple rules, you can create laser labels from scratch. First, the height of the header in your layout should equal the distance from the top of the label sheet to the top of the first row of labels. Second, when entering the dimensions in the Label Setup dialog box, set the height to match the label's *vertical pitch* (the distance from the top of the first row of labels to the top of the second row). Set the width to match the label's *horizontal pitch* (the distance from the left edge of one label to the left edge of the next label).

Dot-matrix printers are already able to handle almost any conceivable style of label. Because laser printers are designed only to accept reasonably-sized *sheets* of labels, it's more likely that you may encounter an unusual label size that is specific to lasers.

You can use the following steps to create a new label layout for a laser printer.

1. Choose Layout from the Select menu.

2. Choose Page Setup from the File menu.

The Page Setup dialog box appears.

3. Click the Options button, choose the Larger Print Area option, and then click OK.

4. Choose New Layout from the Edit menu.

The New Layout dialog box appears.

5. Choose Label Layout as the layout type, and then click OK.

6. Enter the height and width for the labels, as well as the number of labels across, and then click OK.

7. Select the fields to be placed on the labels.

8. Choose the Size command from the Layout menu.

The Size windoid appears.

9. Click the Header part label to select it; then in the size window, click the fourth value down to select it and enter the header height (the distance from the top of the label sheet to the top of the first row of labels).

10. Move and resize fields in the layout as needed.

Before you print your labels, it's a good idea to do a test printout using a normal piece of paper. Take the test printout and place it under or over a sheet of the labels. (The "eyeball" test is one of the best ways to see if the label data is printing in the correct spot on each label—and is a considerably cheaper than running *real* labels through your printer.) If necessary, adjust the label layout until you achieve an acceptable match between the test printout and the labels.

Envelope layouts

Like Dave, the home-office-based consultant, you easily can create layouts to address standard business envelopes. Figure 6-8 shows an envelope layout prepared for the Address Book database.

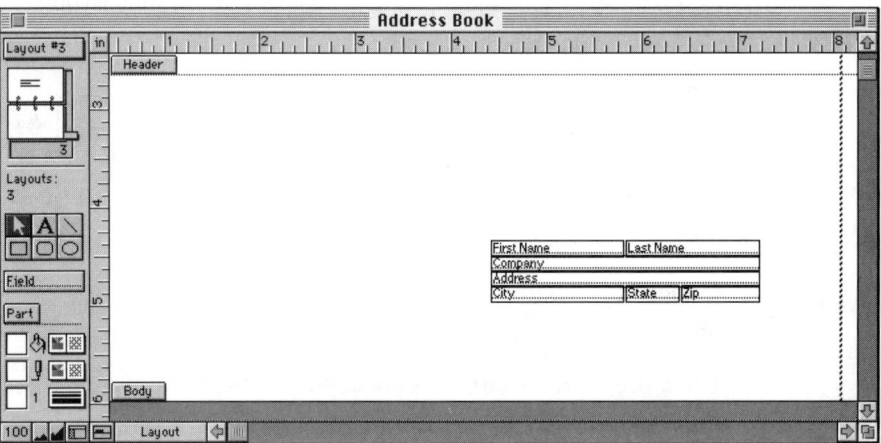

Figure 6-8: An envelope prepared for use with the Address Book database.

Follow these steps to define an Envelope layout:

1. **In the appropriate database within FileMaker Pro, switch to Layout mode.**
2. **Choose New Layout from the Edit menu (or press ⌘-N).**

   The New Layout dialog box appears.
3. **Enter a name for the new layout.**
4. **Click the Envelope radio button to select that option.**
5. **Click OK.**

   The Set Field Order dialog box appears.
6. **Make any necessary changes in this dialog box.**
7. **Click OK to finish defining the label layout.**

Notice that the fields in your new envelope may not appear in the exact way you want to print them. When you create an envelope, each field is the same size, in order from top to bottom, starting at the appropriate print position. Your return address also will be missing. You can drag fields to new positions, change the size of fields by dragging their size boxes, and add text items (such as your return address). All these operations are detailed later in this chapter, in the section "Making Your Own Layouts."

Making Layouts Suit Your Needs

You can perform several fundamental operations on existing layouts to make those layouts better meet your current needs. You can use an existing layout as the basis for a new one, preserving the old while modifying the new. You can change the display order in a layout, and you can give the layout a new name. You also can get rid of layouts that no longer serve your purposes. All these layout operations are discussed in the following sections.

Duplicating a layout

To create a new layout that differs only slightly from an existing one, often the easiest method is to clone the existing layout and make small changes to the copy. One example is using a business-envelope layout to create a layout for a greeting card envelope. The layout for the greeting card envelope has the same fields as the layout for the business envelope, but the body of the greeting card layout must have different dimensions that match the size of the envelope. You can preserve the fields while changing their positions and the dimension of the overall layout.

To duplicate a layout for use as a starting point for a new layout, follow these steps:

1. **Open the FileMaker Pro database that contains the layout you want to duplicate.**
2. **Switch to Layout mode.**
3. **Choose the layout you want to duplicate by selecting it from the layout pop-up menu.**
4. **Choose Duplicate Layout from the Edit menu.**

    The duplicate layout appears, with the word *Copy* appended to its name.

5. **Edit the layout copy as desired.**

Reordering layouts

In the layout pop-up menu, layouts are displayed in the order in which you created them. This order, however, may not be what you want. For example, you may want to display at the top of the layout pop-up menu the layouts you use most frequently.

Part II: Database Design Basics

To change the order in which layouts are displayed in the pop-up menu, follow these steps:

1. **In the appropriate FileMaker Pro database, switch to Layout mode.**
2. **Choose Layout Options from the Layout menu.**

   The Layout Options dialog box appears.
3. **Click the Reorder button.**

   The Reorder Layouts dialog box appears.
4. **Drag layout names into the desired order.**

   To make a layout first in the list, for example, click and drag its name to the top of the list.
5. **Click OK to put the new order into effect.**

   You return to the Layout Options dialog box.
6. **Click OK to finish changing layout options.**

Renaming a layout

Particularly when you create new layouts by duplicating existing ones, you may want to give layouts new names. (Layout #1, for instance, isn't very informative.) You can use the Layout Options dialog box to give a layout a new name.

Follow these steps to rename a layout:

1. **In the appropriate FileMaker Pro database, switch to Layout mode.**
2. **Choose the layout that you want to rename from the layout pop-up menu.**
3. **Choose Layout Options from the Layout menu.**

   The Layout Options dialog box appears.
4. **Type a new name for the layout in the Name text box.**
5. **Click OK.**

Deleting a layout

A layout may no longer be useful for several reasons. The layout may not have been exactly what you wanted, for example; you may have created it just to test certain FileMaker Pro layout features, with no real intention of putting the layout to use. Or you may no longer require the kind of report for which the layout was designed. Whatever the case, you can get rid of layouts that you no longer want or need, eliminating them from the layout pop-up menu.

Chapter 6: Layouts

Follow these steps to eliminate a layout:

1. **In the appropriate FileMaker Pro database, switch to Layout mode.**
2. **Choose the layout you want to delete from the layout pop-up menu.**
3. **Choose Delete Layout from the Edit menu (or press ⌘-E).**

   An alert box appears, asking you to confirm that you want to delete the layout.

4. **Click the Delete button in the alert box.**

   FileMaker Pro removes the layout from your database.

Making Your Own Layouts

As you saw in the discussion of preparing labels and envelopes, there's much more to creating layouts than just cloning a template and tossing in a few fields. You may want to put fields in different positions in the layout; you may want certain fields to print only at the top or bottom of a page, or only after a group of sorted records. Further, you may want to apply formatting to different fields and to add extra objects, such as field labels and graphics. FileMaker Pro's Layout mode has tools that enable you to do all these things and more.

Working with layout parts

All FileMaker Pro layouts are divided into parts. Parts control how and when data appears. When you change to Layout mode, each part is labeled by name in the layout. The available parts are described below.

Body

Every layout normally has a body. The layout body is displayed once for each record. If you have fields that you want to see in every record you view, you should put those fields in the layout body. If you open several databases from the *Macworld FileMaker Pro 2.0/2.1 Bible* disk and then switch to Layout mode, you'll note that the bulk of the fields usually appear in the body of the layout. (If you don't want to see detailed data for each record, you can remove the body from a layout, as long as you leave some other part—particularly a sub-summary part).

Single-page layouts
As a rule, FileMaker Pro displays the body of one record at a time, unless you choose the View as List command from the Select menu. When you print, FileMaker Pro tries to fit as many records on a page as it can. If the next record body won't fit on a page, the entire record is carried to the next page—unless you specify otherwise, telling FileMaker Pro to break parts across pages. You do this by using the Part Definition dialog box (described later in this chapter).

Multipage layouts

If you prefer, you can extend a single layout body over two or more pages. To do so, you simply make the body very long, changing its length by dragging its name (Body) downward on the layout. FileMaker Pro then displays a dashed line to show where the page breaks. Place the fields that you want to appear on the first page above the dashed line; put fields for the second page below the dashed line.

Header

FileMaker Pro displays the header at the top of every page. The header is always visible in Browse mode. At printing time, the header is printed at the top of each page. Use headers for column headings, report titles, and so on. You also can specify a *title header* that prints only on the first page of a report.

Footer

FileMaker Pro displays the footer at the bottom of every page. The footer is always visible in Browse mode. At printing time, the footer is printed at the bottom of each page. You also can specify a special *title footer* that prints only on the first page of a report.

Summary parts

Summary parts are powerful parts that you use to print information that summarizes a range of records. You use summary parts to display information calculated by summary fields. A *summary field*, in effect, adds all the values in one field for a given group of records and displays the total. You can place a summary part before the body (*leading summary*) or after it (*trailing summary*). To learn more about using Summary fields and summary parts, see Chapter 5.

Sub-summaries

Sub-summary parts are used to print a summary of values for records sorted by a specific field. A sub-summary of total sales by salesperson, for example, would show the sales subtotal for each salesperson in a database. For this feature to work, the database must first be sorted by salesperson.

Grand summaries

Grand summaries are used to print a summary of values for all records that currently are being browsed, regardless of their sort order. For example, you could display the grand total of sales for all salespeople in a database.

Adding a layout part

You use the Define Parts command to add a part to a layout. Alternatively, you can click the Part tool and drag it onto the layout. If you use the former approach, you see a dialog box like the one shown in Figure 6-9.

Chapter 6: Layouts

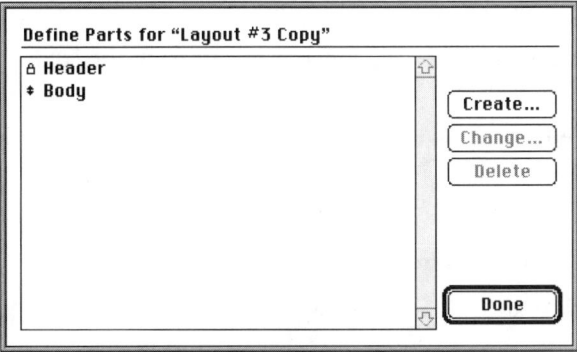

Figure 6-9: The Define Parts dialog box.

This dialog box shows all parts that are currently used in the layout. To add a new part, click the Create button. The Part Definition dialog box appears, as shown in Figure 6-10. (You go directly to this dialog box if you simply drag a new part onto the layout, as described above.)

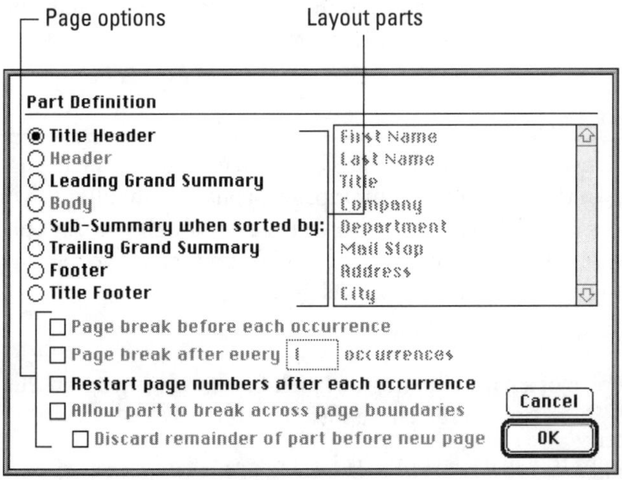

Figure 6-10: The Part Definition dialog box.

Click the appropriate radio button to specify the type of part you're adding; buttons are dimmed for parts that already exist or that aren't appropriate for the type of layout that you're modifying. Below the radio buttons are check box options for page numbering and page breaks.

Follow these steps to add a new part to a layout:

1. **In Layout mode, choose the appropriate layout from the layout pop-up menu.**
2. **Choose Define Parts from the Layout menu and, when the Define Parts dialog box appears, click Create**

— or —

2. **Drag the Part tool across to the layout.**

   In either case, the Part Definition dialog box now appears.
3. **Click the radio button for the part you want to add.**

   If the button is dimmed, the part already exists or isn't appropriate to the layout that you chose.
4. **Click any desired page-numbering and page-breaking options.**
5. **Click OK.**

   If you began this process by dragging a part onto the Layout, you are immediately returned to Layout mode.

   If you began this process by choosing the Define Parts command, you return to the Define Parts dialog box. Click Done to return to Layout mode.

Modifying parts

You can change existing parts in several ways. You can, for example, change a part's size, as you saw in the discussion on multipage layouts. Within limits, you can change the order in which parts appear on a page (although you can't put a header below the body or a footer above it, for example). You can move the part labels out of your way. And, if necessary, you can delete a part.

Resizing

To change the size of a part, you drag its label. Part labels appear on the left side of the layout area. The name of the part appears in its label.

Follow these steps to make a layout part larger or smaller:

1. **Switch to Layout mode and choose the appropriate layout from the layout pop-up menu.**
2. **Locate the label for the part that you want to resize.**

   (The label contains the part's name.)
3. **Click and drag the part label in the appropriate direction: up to make the part smaller, or down to make it larger.**
4. **Release the mouse button when the part is the size you want.**

Chapter 6: Layouts

You should notice that FileMaker Pro allows you to drag a part until you come to some other object — a field in another part, for example. To drag past an object, (text, graphic, or a field) you need to hold down the Option key while you drag.

You also can set the size of a part by choosing the Size command from the Layout menu. This command allows you to set the part's dimensions precisely. Choosing the Size command brings up a small window (called a *windoid*) like the one shown in Figure 6-11.

Figure 6-11: The Size windoid.

The Size windoid includes dimensions for the top, bottom, left and right margins of a part and for the part's width and height.

To specify a part's size precisely, follow these steps:

1. **In Layout mode, choose the appropriate layout from the layout pop-up menu.**
2. **Click the label of the part that you want to resize.**
3. **Choose the Size command from the Layout menu.**

   The Size windoid appears.

4. **Enter the desired dimensions in the appropriate text boxes.**
5. **Click the Size windoid's close box to dismiss it.**

Reordering

Within limits, you can change the order in which layout parts appear in a layout. Headers always go at the top and footers at the bottom; otherwise, you can move parts at will. You can change part order in two ways: by using the Define Parts dialog box, or by holding down the Shift key while you drag a part's label.

To use the Define Parts command to change the order of parts, follow these steps:

1. **In Layout mode, switch to the layout that contains the parts you want to reorder.**
2. **Choose Define Parts from the Layout menu.**

   The Define Parts dialog box appears.

3. **Drag part names to their new locations.**

   (A part name with a lock icon next to it cannot be moved.)

4. **Click Done.**

Changing types and options

You also can change a part's type, and you can reset certain options for the parts. You make such changes in the Part Definition dialog box.

Follow these steps to change a part's type and/or options:

1. **In Layout mode, switch to the layout that contains the part you want to modify.**

2. **Locate the label for the part you want to change and double-click the label to open the Part Definition dialog box for that part.**

3. **Click to make the changes you want.**

   (Options that are dimmed are not available.)

4. **Click OK.**

Changing the positions of part labels

Part labels are useful in Layout mode when you want to resize, move, or modify a part. These labels may get in your way, however. To toggle labels to vertical position, click the part-label control at the bottom of the Layout window. This control appears just to the left of the mode pop-up menu — which is labeled *Layout* when you're in Layout mode.

Deleting

You can delete a layout part in any of three ways, depending on whether the part contains objects of any sort. If the part is empty, you can resize it to nothing. Otherwise, you can select the part's label and press the Delete key, or you can delete the part from the Define Parts dialog box. If a part contains objects, you'll see an alert box when you try to delete it, because any objects in the part will be deleted with the part. (Any fields that are removed from the part in this manner can be added back to the layout using the Field tool. However, other objects, such as graphics or static text, will have to be recreated if you find that you still need them.)

To recover a part that you deleted with the Delete key, choose Undo from the Edit menu (or press ⌘-Z) immediately after deleting it. Part deletions accomplished within the Define Parts dialog box, on the other hand, *cannot* be recovered with the Undo command.

Chapter 6: Layouts

Follow these steps to delete a part by using the Define Parts command:

1. **In Layout mode, switch to the layout that contains the part you want to delete.**
2. **Choose the Define Parts command from the Layout menu.**

   The Define Parts dialog box appears.
3. **Select the name of the part to be deleted.**
4. **Click the Delete button.**
5. **If the alert box appears, click Delete to simultaneously delete the part and remove any objects that the part contains or click cancel if you change your mind.**

   Remember that deletions performed in this manner cannot be undone.
6. **Click Done in the Define Parts dialog box.**

Adding items to a layout part

You now know enough about layout parts to create neat, well-ordered, appropriately sized, blank layout parts. However, the purpose of any layout part is to display information rather than blank space. You must add objects to the parts. *Objects* include fields, field labels, text, and graphics. To add objects, you use the tools in the Tool palette on the left side of the Layout-mode window. Additional options for placing, arranging, and formatting objects appear in the Layout, Arrange, and Format menus.

Adding fields

Probably the most important objects in any layout are the fields. You have seen how to add fields at layout-creation time. The Standard layout automatically places every field that has been defined for the database. With the Label, Envelope, and columnar layouts, you specify which fields to place, as well as the order in which they are placed. You can also add a field to any layout at *any* time, even if the field didn't exist when you created the layout.

You add fields by using the Field tool. This tool appears in the center of the layout tool palette and is labeled *Field*.

Follow these steps to add a field to a layout part:

1. **In Layout mode, switch to the layout to which you want to add the field.**
2. **Drag the field tool across to the appropriate layout part and position.**

   The New Field dialog box appears.
3. **Click the name of the field you want to add.**
4. **Click OK.**

Using the measurement and alignment tools

The Layout menu includes many tools related to using rulers in Layout mode. Using these tools makes it easy to accurately place or arrange fields, labels, and graphics on the layout — even when you're doing it manually by dragging the objects.

- ❖ **Ruler Lines.** You can display on the layout screen dotted lines that correspond to lines on the rulers. Use these lines to check layout spacing. Choose Ruler Lines from the Layout menu to toggle the lines on and off.

- ❖ **T-squares.** These are solid vertical and horizontal lines. You can drag the lines to move them. Use T-squares to precisely position an object relative to the rulers. Choose T-Squares from the Layout menu to toggle these lines on and off.

- ❖ **Grid**. FileMaker Pro maintains an invisible grid that corresponds to current ruler settings. If the grid is on, objects being moved or resized move in increments, snapping to the nearest grid intersection. Choose Align to Grid from the Layout menu to toggle the grid on and off.

- ❖ **Ruler Settings.** To change the spacing and units for the grid and ruler, choose Ruler Settings from the Layout menu and make the appropriate settings in the Ruler Settings dialog box.

- ❖ **Rulers.** Rulers appear at the top and left edges of the layout area. Choose the Rulers command from the Layout menu to toggle the rulers on and off.

Formatting fields

It's a pretty safe bet that with few exceptions, a field doesn't come into a layout in the exact form in which you want it. The field may be too small or too large, for example. You also may want to add things to a field to spice it up, such as borders or a fill pattern. Fortunately, these changes are easy to make.

Size and position

One of these simplest things to change is a field's position; just click the field to select it and drag it where you want. Changing a field's size also is easy. When you click a field to select it, *handles* (small dark boxes) appear at all four of the field's corners. Drag any handle to change the field's size. Changing the size of a field, of course, alters the amount of room you have to display data. A field such as State, which probably contains a two-letter abbreviation, can be made quite small; you would want to give more room to fields such as Company and Address. (Note that this same technique is also used to resize *any* object, such as graphics, field labels, and text objects.)

Chapter 6: Layouts

To change a field's size or position, follow these steps:

1. **In Layout mode, switch to the layout that contains the field that you want to modify.**
2. **To move the field, click and drag the field to the desired location.**
3. **To change the field's size, click to select it and then click and drag a handle until the field is the desired size.**

Borders

Although fields are displayed in Layout mode with boxes around them, these boxes appear only for your convenience in moving and resizing the fields. If you want borders to appear around a field when you browse or print (when you are actually using the database, that is), you must *create* the borders. You create borders by using the Field Borders dialog box, which is shown in Figure 6-12.

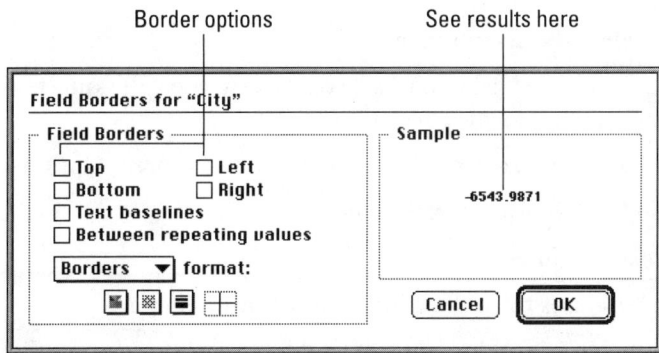

Figure 6-12: The Field Borders dialog box.

Follow these steps to add borders to a field:

1. **In Layout mode, switch to the layout that contains the field to which you want to add borders.**
2. **Click to select the appropriate field.**

   If there are additional fields to which you'd like to apply the same border options, you can select them all by Shift-clicking them.

3. **Choose Field Borders from the Format menu (or press Option-⌘-B).**

   The Field Borders dialog box appears.

4. **Click the appropriate check box options for the borders you want to add.**

Part II: Database Design Basics

5. **Choose Borders from the dialog box's pop-up menu.**
6. **Choose the desired color, pattern, and line width for the borders from the pop-up menus at the bottom of the dialog box.**

    The effects of your choices appear in the Sample box on the right side of the dialog box.

7. **Click OK.**

Baselines

You may want the contents of a field to be underlined. FileMaker Pro refers to such an underline as a *baseline*. As with borders, you add baselines by using the Field Borders dialog box.

Follow these steps to add baselines to a field:

1. **In Layout mode, switch to the layout that contains the field to which you want to add baselines.**
2. **Click to select the appropriate field.**

    If there are additional fields to which you'd like to apply the same border options, you can select them all by Shift-clicking them.

3. **Choose Field Borders from the Format menu (or press Option-⌘-B).**

    The Field Borders dialog box appears.

4. **Click Text Baselines.**
5. **Choose Baselines from the dialog box's pop-up menu.**
6. **Choose the desired color, pattern, and line width for the baselines from the pop-up menus at the bottom of the dialog box.**

    The effects of your choices appear in the Sample box on the right side of the dialog box.

7. **Click OK.**

Fill Patterns

To add a little color, you can add a fill color and/or pattern to a field — whether the field has a border or not. In Browse mode, the color/pattern appears behind the field's data.

You can specify a fill color or pattern in two ways. The first way is to use the Fill tools in the Tool palette (there is a bucket icon to the left of these tools). If no field is currently selected when you choose a color and pattern with these tools, the color and pattern become the default fill color/pattern. If you now add a field, that field automatically uses the new fill pattern and color. (You can also set default formatting options by simply Command-clicking on any field or text object. Then whenever you create a new field or text object, the new defaults will automatically be applied.)

Chapter 6: Layouts

Alternatively, you can use the Field Borders command to select a fill for a field by following these steps:

1. **In Layout mode, switch to the layout that contains the field to which you want to add a fill color or pattern.**
2. **Click to select the field.**
3. **Choose Field Borders from the Format menu (or press Option-⌘-B).**

    The Field Borders dialog box appears.

4. **Choose Fill from the dialog box's pop-up menu.**
5. **Choose the desired color and pattern for the fill from the pop-up menus at the bottom of the dialog box.**

    The effects of your choices appear in the Sample box on the right side of the dialog box.

6. **Click OK.**

Scroll bars

If you don't make a field large enough to begin with, all the contents of the field may not be visible. You could simply click and drag to make the field bigger, but this method may not produce the effect you want — especially if room in your layout is limited, such as when you're designing a layout for use only on-screen and not for printing. To make it possible to view the additional contents of a field, you can add scroll bars to the field. These scroll bars enable you to scroll a field and view data that cannot be displayed, just as you can with a window. You add scroll bars by using the Field Format dialog box, shown in Figure 6-13.

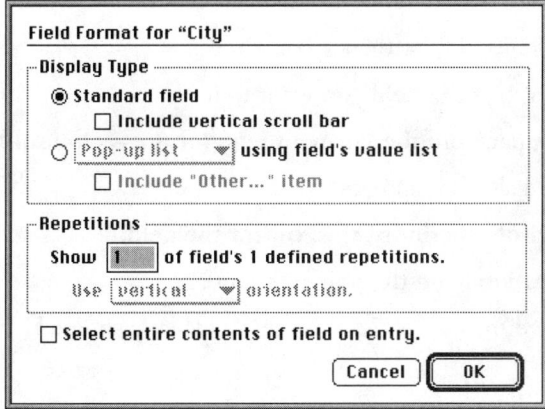

Figure 6-13: The Field Format dialog box.

Part II: Database Design Basics

To add scroll bars to a field, follow these steps:

1. **In Layout mode, switch to the layout that contains the field to which you want to add scroll bars.**
2. **Click to select the field.**
3. **Choose Field Format from the Format menu (or press Option-⌘-F).**

    The Field Format dialog box appears.

4. **Click the Include vertical scroll bar option.**
5. **Click OK.**

Deleting a field
To delete a field from a layout, click to select it and then press the Delete key. If you find that you've simply added the wrong field to a layout, there's a better approach to correcting this problem than just deleting the errant field and then adding the right one. You can swap one field for another.

In Layout mode, hold down the Option key while double-clicking the field. The New Field dialog box appears and presents a list of all fields that have been defined for the database. Choose the replacement field from the field list. All formatting options that you set for the old field are automatically applied to the new field.

Formatting repeating fields
As you learned in Chapter 5, some fields can contain more than one entry. Such fields are called *repeating fields*. In an invoice database, for example, you might have a repeating field named Price, which would contain the price of each item in an order. You set up a repeating field to contain a specific maximum number of values, but you don't have to display all those values in a layout. Use the Field Format dialog box to set this and other options for repeating fields.

To format a repeating field, follow these steps:

1. **In Layout mode, select the field you want to format.**
2. **Choose Field Format from the Format menu (or press Option-⌘-F).**

    The Field Format dialog box appears.

3. **Enter the number of repetitions to show for the field.**
4. **Choose an orientation from the pop-up menu.**

    Choose Vertical to display repetitions in a single column; choose Horizontal to display repetitions in a row.

5. **Click OK.**

Adding and modifying text

To identify items in a layout, you can add extra text. You can add text as a title for a report layout and place it in the header, for example. You can put an automatic page number and a data stamp in the footer. You can create custom field labels for all the fields displayed in the body. A wide range of formatting options are available for such text. You can use different fonts, sizes, and colors.

You add text by using the Text tool (the letter *A* in the Tool palette). When you click this tool, the mouse pointer changes to an insertion bracket. Click to position the bracket where you want the text to appear and then type the text. Text appears with the current default attributes for font, size, color, and so on, but you can change all these attributes at any time.

To change the formatting of existing text, change to Layout mode, use the Pointer tool to select the text object that you want to change and then select the desired Font, Size, Style, Align Text, Line Spacing, and Text Color options from the Format menu.

To edit existing text, use the Text tool to select the text; position the insertion point inside the text box and use the standard editing keys to modify the text.

Besides adding standard text items, you can paste in special items such as the current time and date, an automatic page number, or your username.

To insert special text, such as an automatic page number, follow these steps:

1. **In Layout mode, click the Text tool.**
2. **Click to position the insertion point where you want the special text to appear.**
3. **From the Paste Special submenu of the Edit menu, choose one of the following options: Current Date, Current Time, Current User Name, Date Symbol, User Name Symbol, Page Number, or Record Number.**

Adding graphics

FileMaker Pro offers a couple of ways to add graphical elements to a layout. You can create simple graphics — including ovals, squares, and lines — directly in the program. You also can add graphics created in other programs, such as logos or elaborate illustrations.

You create simple graphics by using the Line, Rectangle, Rounded Rectangle, and Oval tools in the Tool palette. Each tool is identified by an icon that shows the result of using that tool. To bring graphics and/or movies in from other programs, you use the Import/Export command. You can read more about importing and exporting in Chapter 16.

Part II: Database Design Basics

To add a graphical element, such as a line, oval, or rectangle, follow these steps:

1. **In Layout mode, switch to the layout to which you want to add the element.**
2. **Use the Fill, Border, and Line Width tools to set the appropriate style for the new element.**
3. **Click the tool that represents the element you want to add.**
4. **Position the tool on the part to which you want to add the graphic, and then drag until you create an element that's the desired size.**
5. **To change formatting for an object, click the object to select it and then set the appropriate options with the Fill, Border, and Line Width tools.**
6. **You can drag an object to change its position and drag its handles to change its size.**

You can create special objects by holding down the Option key as you drag with any of the tools. When Option is pressed, the Rectangle and Rounded Rectangle tools create squares; the Oval tool creates circles; and the Line tool is restricted to straight horizontal, vertical, or 45-degree lines.

Of course, more complex graphics are better created in a graphics program. You can import a graphical element created in another program by following these steps:

1. **In Layout mode, switch to the layout to which you want to add the graphic.**
2. **Choose Import/Export from the File menu, and then choose Import Picture from the submenu.**

   The Import Picture dialog box appears.
3. **Choose the format of the graphic from the pop-up menu at the bottom of the dialog box.**
4. **Find the graphic's name in the list and click to select it.**
5. **Click Open.**

   The graphic appears on the current layout.
6. **Drag the graphic to the appropriate position in the layout and use the graphic's handles to change its size, if necessary.**

Applying the finishing touches

Even after you add all the desired elements to a layout, the layout may not be perfect. If object alignment is a problem, you can correct it easily. You also can group objects so that you can move them as a unit. You can even set the order in which fields are filled during data entry.

Chapter 6: Layouts

Aligning objects

By choosing the Alignment command from the Arrange menu (or pressing ⌘-K), you can align objects with other objects. If you have a vertical list of field, you can use this command to perfectly align one edge of each of the fields and field labels, for example.

Follow these steps to align two or more objects:

1. **In Layout mode, select the objects that you want to align.**

   (You can hold down the Shift key to select additional objects after the first.)

2. **Choose Alignment from the Arrange menu (or press Shift-⌘-K).**

   The Alignment dialog box appears (see Figure 6-14).

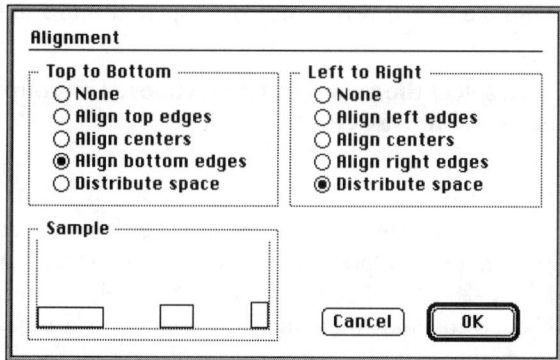

Figure 6-14: The Alignment dialog box.

3. **Choose the Top to Bottom and Left to Right options that you want to use.**

   The effects of your choices appear in the Sample box in the lower-left corner of the dialog box.

4. **Click OK.**

   The alignment settings are applied to the selected objects. If you find that you have made an error, you can correct it by immediately selecting the Undo Align command from the Edit menu.

If you later want to apply the same alignment settings to a different group of objects, just select the objects and choose the Align Objects command from the Arrange menu (or press ⌘-K).

You also can have FileMaker Pro snap objects to a grid automatically by choosing Align to Grid from the Layout menu (or pressing ⌘-Y). This option makes field and label placement extraordinarily simple.

Grouping objects

To make it easier to move several aligned objects to a new position without messing up their alignment, you can group the objects. FileMaker Pro treats grouped objects as though they were a single object.

To group several objects, follow these steps:

1. **In Layout mode, select the objects that you want to group.**

   (Hold down the Shift key to select additional objects after the first.)

2. **Choose Group from the Arrange menu (or press ⌘-G).**

   FileMaker Pro groups the objects, which are now displayed with a single set of handles.

3. **To ungroup objects, select the group and then choose Ungroup from the Arrange menu (or press Shift-⌘-G).**

Other object commands

You also can change the order in which objects are displayed back to front by choosing the Bring to Front (Shift-Option-⌘-F), Send to Back (Shift-Option-⌘-J), Bring Forward (Shift-⌘-F), and Send Backward (Shift-⌘-J) commands from the Arrange menu. These commands are particularly useful for placing background graphics behind fields or other graphics, for instance.

And if you want to make sure that a particular object isn't moved by mistake, you can lock it in place by choosing the Lock command from the Arrange menu (or pressing ⌘-H). To unlock an object, so you can change its size, position, attributes, and so on, choose Unlock from the Arrange menu (or press Shift-⌘-H).

Setting tab order for data entry

Finally, you can set the order in which the you move from field to field when the Tab key is pressed. Although this has no effect on the *appearance* of the layout, it can often be the difference between an easy-to-use layout and one that is annoying to use. The default order is left to right and top to bottom. You can change this order and even omit fields from the tab order, if you want. To change tab order, you choose the Tab Order command from the Arrange menu.

To change the tab order, follow these steps:

1. **In Layout mode, choose Tab Order from the Arrange menu.**

   The Tab Order dialog box appears (see Figure 6-15).

Chapter 6: Layouts

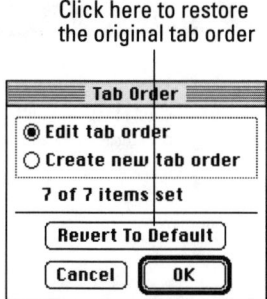

Figure 6-15: The Tab Order dialog box.

2. **Click the appropriate radio button to specify whether you want to edit the existing tab order or create a new one.**

3. **Edit the numbers in the arrows that appear next to each field in the layout to specify the tab order for fields.**

   Enter **1** in the arrow for the field that is to be first, and so on.

   — or —

3. **If you select New Tab Order, all the numbers disappear; click the arrows in the order in which you want the related fields to appear.**

4. **To omit a field from the tab order, leave its arrow blank.**

   When the user presses the Tab key, those fields will be skipped.

5. **Click OK to save the new tab order or click Cancel if you change your mind.**

At any time during this process, you can revert to the tab order that FileMaker Pro originally set for the layout by clicking Revert to Default.

Part II: Database Design Basics

CHAPTER 6 — CONCEPTS AND TERMS

- FileMaker Pro supports the use of multiple layouts, allowing you to specify what fields to display and how to format them.
- Layouts can be based on any of several predefined layout styles, including layouts for columnar reports, Avery labels, and business envelopes.
- Layouts have parts, including headers, footers, bodies, and summaries.
- Layout parts can include a number of objects, such as fields, text, and graphics. Objects can be aligned and moved as a group.

Avery
A manufacturer of specialized stock for printing a wide variety of labels, including labels for floppy disks, address labels, and so on.

body
A layout part that contains the main record information.

layout
A specialized arrangement of fields and graphical elements, intended to serve a specific purpose.

summary field
A type of field used to sum the information in the same field across many records.

CHAPTER SEVEN

Setting Preferences

- Customizing FileMaker Pro's operation
- Setting startup actions for a database
- Setting Memory preferences to optimize the use of batteries in a portable Macintosh

Not everyone likes to work the same way (some of us are morning people, and others are night owls, for example). The same holds true for using FileMaker Pro. The way that you prefer to create database layouts, enter data, and work with a database may differ significantly from the way that your neighbor performs the same tasks. Fortunately, you can set preferences to customize the way that you work with the program in general and the way that you work with individual databases in particular. If you work on a portable Macintosh, you also can conserve battery power by setting a preference that specifies the time interval for automatically saving changes.

You need to know that these preferences exist, how to set them, and how to change them when necessary. For example, you may find yourself working on someone else's computer or with a database that another person created. If the other person's computer or setup behaves differently from yours, you benefit from knowing that the differences are likely due to alternative preferences and that you can easily change them to match your normal way of working. (Be considerate, though. If you change the preferences on someone else's Mac, put them back as you found them when you're through.)

Working with the Preferences Dialog Box

You set all preferences by using the Preferences command in the File menu. Choosing this command makes the Preferences dialog box appear, as shown in Figure 7-1.

Part II: Database Design Basics

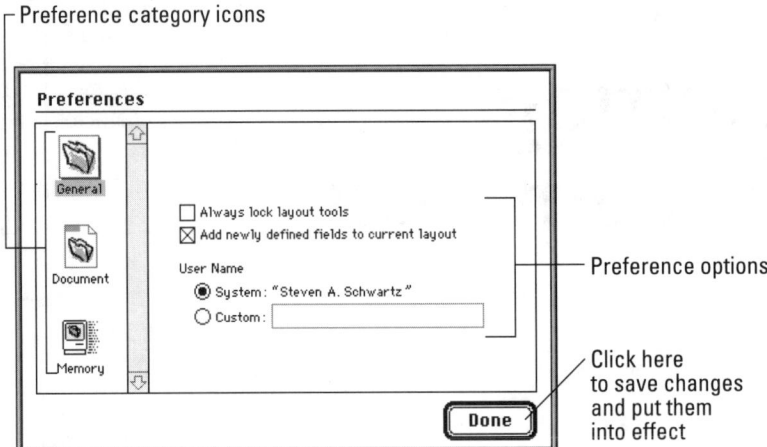

Figure 7-1: The Preferences dialog box.

On the left side of this dialog box are three category icons. You choose an icon to indicate the sort of preferences that you want to set. *General preferences* refer to those that govern how FileMaker Pro behaves as a whole. *Document preferences* apply only to the current database document, and you can set them differently for each database. The *Memory preferences* category enables you to adjust the frequency with which FileMaker saves data to disk.

Follow these steps to set preferences:

1. **Choose Preferences from the File menu.**

   The Preferences dialog box appears (refer to Figure 7-1).

2. **Determine which category of preferences you want to set (General, Document, or Memory) and click the corresponding icon at the left side of the dialog box.**

   The options in the right side of the dialog box change to ones appropriate to the selected category.

3. **Make the desired changes by clicking and by selecting options from pop-up menus.**

4. **Click another category icon to make changes in that category.**

   —or—

4. **Click Done to put changes into effect and dismiss the Preferences dialog box.**

Chapter 7: Setting Preferences

The following sections discuss the specific options that you can set in each category: General, Document, and Memory.

Note that unlike many dialog boxes in which you make choices, the Preferences dialog box doesn't have a Cancel button. Normally, pressing Cancel discards all changes and dismisses the dialog box. If you select some options in the Preferences dialog box and then change your mind, you have to manually restore the options to their previous settings.

Setting General Program Preferences

The General preferences category provides options that govern overall program behavior. This category contains the following options:

❖ *Always lock layout tools:* This option sets how tools behave when you're designing or modifying layouts. By default, FileMaker Pro automatically switches back to the Pointer tool after you have performed an operation with any other tool. Although this way of operating enables you to quickly select an item after you modify it, this feature can be annoying if you routinely perform several operations in a row with the same tool. When the Always lock layout tools box is checked, FileMaker Pro keeps the same tool selected until you choose a different tool or press the Enter key.

❖ *Add newly defined fields to current layout:* This option determines whether new fields that you define will automatically be added to the current layout. By default, FileMaker Pro is set to add them. To be able to define new fields without automatically placing them on the current layout, click to remove the check mark from this option. You will have to add new fields that you define manually (by dragging them onto the layout).

❖ *User Name:* This option governs whether FileMaker Pro uses the system user name or a name that you supply in the dialog box. The default is to use the system name, which is set in the Chooser in System 6 and in the Sharing Setup control panel in System 7. Click the System radio button to use this name or click the Custom radio button and enter another name in the box beside the button. (Note that if the system name is currently blank — shown as an empty pair of quotation marks — you haven't identified yourself to the Mac. Step-by-step instructions in Chapter 5 tell you how to set the system user name.)

You can paste the user name into a field with the Paste Special command, automatically enter it in a field by setting an appropriate auto-entry option, or use it in scripts.

Part II: Database Design Basics

Note that you can create scripts that use the user name. For example, you may want to create a script that finds data that is specific to a given individual, such as locating all telephone orders taken by Ken Summers. Instead of creating a separate script for every possible person, you can have FileMaker Pro use the custom user name. To find information for a different person (another telemarketer, for instance), you merely change the custom user name in the Preferences dialog box before running the script. See Chapter 15 for more information about scripts.

Setting Document-Specific Preferences

In addition to setting preferences for FileMaker Pro as a whole, you can set certain preferences individually for each database that reflect the way that you intend to use that database. For instance, you can set a start-up action for a given database by setting a preference that it should automatically open to a particular layout or run a special script. Obviously, you wouldn't want all databases to run a sort script when they're opened, but you certainly might want *one* of your databases to do so. That's why FileMaker provides Document preferences in addition to the General preferences.

Every database can have different Document preferences. The five Document preferences that you can set are described in the following list. The first governs data entry; the remaining four specify the actions that FileMaker Pro automatically performs each time you open the database. As with other FileMaker Pro preferences, you can change these preferences whenever you like.

- *Use smart quotes:* This option sets FileMaker to use curved open and closed quotation marks rather than straight quotation marks (" ' and " " vs. ' ' and " "). The former characters are commonly referred to as *curly quotes* and are generally favored — mainly because they look more professional.

  The "smartness" belongs to the program. FileMaker Pro 2 contains a set of rules that determines when to use a left quote and when to use a right quote. When the Use smart quotes box is checked and you press the single and double quotations mark key to the immediate left of the Return key, the appropriate curly quote character is typed. Note that this preference option has no effect if the font that you're using doesn't contain symbols for the curved quotes; straight quotes will be used instead.

- *Switch to layout:* This option specifies a particular layout to display when the database is opened. If you do not set this option, the database opens to whatever layout was active when you last closed the database.

  This option is most helpful in two situations. First, many databases are menu-driven. Instead of a normal data-entry screen, a database might contain a menu of buttons that enables the user to select which portion of the database or function he wants to perform — data entry, report printing, and label generation, for example. By setting the menu layout as the opening screen, we can ensure

Chapter 7: Setting Preferences

that new users won't be confused by starting in a different (possibly foreign) section of the database each time.

Second, many databases are designed so that they revolve around one basic screen. For example, the Address Book database discussed in Chapter 4 has a data entry layout as the central screen. Since most of the work a user will do is on that layout, it makes good sense to open automatically to that particular layout.

❖ *Show/hide status area:* This option sets FileMaker Pro to display or hide the status area (the area on the far left side of the document window in which the book icon, tools, and other database controls are normally shown). When the status area is hidden, more room is available for displaying records. Hiding the status area is particularly useful when you are working with large layouts or using a Mac that has a small screen. Regardless of the option that you choose, you can change between showing and hiding the status area whenever you like by clicking the Status area control at the bottom of the database window (see Figure 7-2).

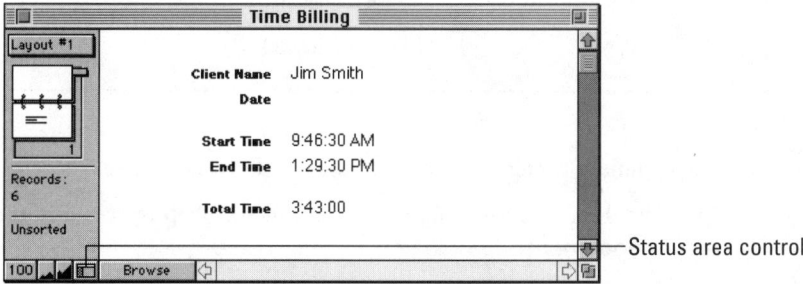

Figure 7-2: Click the Status area control button to toggle between showing and hiding the status area.

❖ *Zoom window to full size:* This option automatically sets the size of the database's window to the maximum size allowable for the particular Macintosh display (monitor) on which the database is opened. This option can be useful when you are creating templates for other people to use, especially when you know nothing about their monitors. In the case of a layout that is designed on a large screen, selecting this option ensures that the layout won't open partially on and partially off a smaller screen. (Note, however, that many users prefer to set window sizes themselves.)

❖ *Perform script:* This option automatically performs the selected script when the database is opened. For instance, you can perform a script that opens to a particular record (other than the first one), assures that the records are sorted in a desired order, or automatically prints a daily report. See Chapter 15 for more information about scripts.

Part II: Database Design Basics

Manually Entering Curly Quotes

In some databases (ones that refer to measurements in feet or inches, for example), using smart quotes may not be to your advantage. If this option is checked, you cannot enter straight quotations marks (' and "). If you find that you frequently need to use straight quotes in a particular database, the best approach is to remove the check mark from the Use smart quotes setting. When you need curly quotes, you can enter them manually, as explained in the following table. (As a bonus, you also can use the instructions in the table to produce curly quote characters in other programs that don't provide a smart quotes preferences setting.)

Type This . . .	*To Produce This Curly Quote Character* . . .
Option-[	" (double left quote)
Shift-Option-[	" (double right quote)
Option-]	' (single left quote)
Shift-Option-]	' (single right quote)

To set Document preferences for a database, follow these steps:

1. **Open the database for which you want to set preferences and make it the current document.**

   To make a database the current document, click anywhere in the database's window or select its name from the Window menu. If you have only one database open, it is — by definition — the current document.

2. **Choose Preferences from the File menu.**

3. **Click the Document icon.**

   The dialog box changes to show only document-specific preferences (see Figure 7-3).

4. **If you want to use plain, straight quotes, remove the check mark from the Use smart quotes check box by clicking the check box.**

   To use smart/curly quotes, leave the option checked. (Use smart quotes is the default.)

5. **Click the Switch to layout box to choose a layout that the database will automatically switch to each time it is opened and then select a layout from the pop-up menu.**

   The pop-up menu lists all layouts that you have created for the current database. If this option is unchecked (default), the database opens to the layout that was displayed the last time you closed the database.

Chapter 7: Setting Preferences

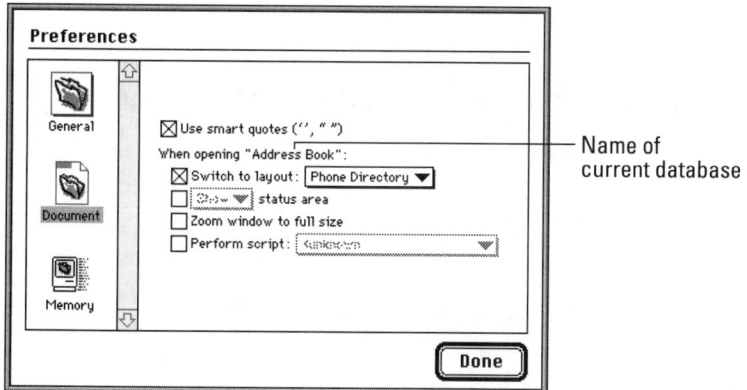

Figure 7-3: Setting individual document preferences.

6. **To hide the status area display, click the Show/hide status area box and choose Hide from the pop-up menu.**

   — or —

6. **To automatically show the status area, click the Show/hide status area box and choose Show from the pop-up menu.**

   The default is to match the condition of the status area (shown or hidden) when the database was last closed.

7. **Click the check box for Zoom window to full size if you want the database to open a window that matches the size of the current monitor.**

   Leave the option unchecked to have the window open at the size that you were using when you last closed the database (default).

8. **Click the Perform script check box to have FileMaker Pro automatically execute a particular script every time you open the database and then choose the script from the pop-up menu to the right of the option.**

   Leave the option unchecked if you don't want a script performed (default).

9. **Click Done.**

   FileMaker Pro saves the new settings, and they will be in effect the next you open the database.

The Power User's Guide to Preferences

Setting a startup script with the Perform script preference option is the best way to exert control over a database. Scripts enable you to have FileMaker Pro automatically perform any of the following actions when the database is opened:

❖ Make sure that the database is sorted in a particular order.

❖ Select a subset of records with which to work or make certain that all records are visible.

❖ Perform a Relookup so that all fields contain current data.

❖ Open to a report layout and automatically print a current copy of the report.

For an example of a startup script that automatically creates a backup file each time you open a particular database, see Chapter 3.

Using Memory Preferences to Set a Save Interval

Memory preferences control the manner in which FileMaker Pro saves data to disk. As you work, FileMaker Pro saves data in two ways: by using the memory cache and by copying new data to the disk that contains the original database document. The *cache* is a special part of RAM (Macintosh memory) that is set aside for FileMaker's use. Changes are accumulated in the cache until it is full or until an opportune moment arises (that is, when the system is idle). At this point, changes are flushed from the cache and saved to disk.

This way of operating is fine for desktop machines. On laptops, however, it can waste battery power. One of the most energy-consuming aspects of laptop operation is powering up and running the disk drives. For this reason, the drives are frequently powered down and kept idle when data isn't being read from or written to them. If FileMaker Pro is set to save all changes to disk during idle time, however, it can keep the drives running more often and longer than normal and thus decrease the amount of work time that you get from a single battery charge. To prevent such power waste, you can specify that FileMaker Pro save only after a given interval — perhaps once every 10 or every 30 minutes.

Note that setting a save interval involves a significant trade-off. The longer the interval you choose, the less battery power is consumed, but the more data you put at risk. If you suffer a crash between saves, you may lose everything that is in the cache. This problem is not significant if you're just using the database to look up information or if you're making only limited changes. Note, however, that even if you set a relatively long save interval, FileMaker Pro will still save if the cache fills before the interval is reached.

Chapter 7: Setting Preferences

Follow these steps to set a save interval:

1. **Choose Preferences from the File menu.**
2. **Click the Memory icon.**

   The dialog box changes to show the Memory preferences (see Figure 7-4).

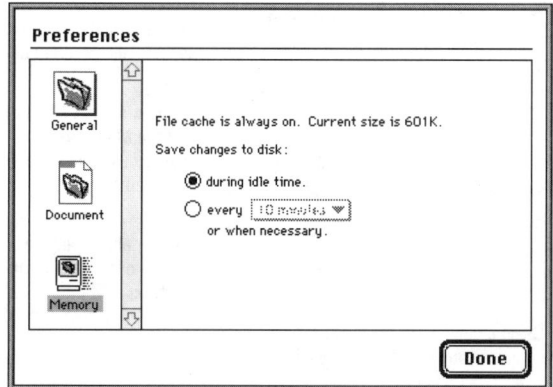

Figure 7-4: Setting the save interval to conserve battery power.

3. **Click the every . . . or when necessary radio button.**
4. **Choose the desired interval from the pop-up menu.**

   Remember that longer intervals are riskier to data, but they save more power.

5. **Click Done.**

   The new save interval is recorded and put into effect.

   If you later change your mind and want to set a different save interval, simply repeat these steps. If you decide that you'd rather just save new data as soon as possible, choose the Memory icon again and click the during idle time radio button (default).

Part II: Database Design Basics

CHAPTER 7 CONCEPTS AND TERMS

- You can customize how FileMaker Pro operates, as well as the startup actions of individual database documents, by using the Preferences command in the File menu.
- Selecting the Smart Quotes option instructs FileMaker Pro to automatically substitute curved left and right quotation marks for the usual straight quotation marks. However, using this option makes entering foot and inch symbols (straight quotation marks) difficult.
- You can select a script to execute every time you open a specific database document.
- You can save battery power on a portable Macintosh (a PowerBook, for example) by specifying the frequency with which FileMaker Pro saves data to disk.

default
The initial, "factory setting" for a changeable value. This setting determines how an option behaves if you never change the setting.

preferences
Option settings that govern how certain aspects of a program behave.

RAM
Random Access Memory. The memory that the Mac uses to run programs, use desk accessories, temporarily store data, and so on.

script
A user-defined sequence of commands and actions that automates FileMaker Pro tasks.

cache
An area in the computer's memory that is set aside for temporarily storing data that is on its way to and from a disk. Using a cache can greatly speed up operation because RAM is much faster to access than a disk.

Part III
Working with Databases

CHAPTER EIGHT

Using Browse Mode: Viewing, Entering, Editing, and Deleting Records

- Accessing Browse Mode
- Switching among layouts
- Navigating among and viewing records
- Adding and deleting records
- Entering and editing data in records
- Restrictions on entering data in different types of fields
- Entering data in fields that present a value list
- Reusing data from previously entered records

Browse Mode Basics

After you create a database, you naturally want to begin using it to store and work with information. Think of the Address Book database in Chapter 4, for example. You would start by entering address data for all of your correspondents. With that done, you could get a glimpse of the entire database by switching to the Phone Directory layout. If you learned that one of your contacts had moved, you could flip through the records, find the appropriate one, and modify the information in the address fields. And when you wanted to enter address data for a new contact or decided that you no longer needed one of the records, you could add or delete records. It's all in a day's work for a typical database.

To perform these operations — entering and editing data, adding and deleting records, flipping through records, and viewing data in different layouts — you need to be in Browse mode. This mode is one of the four FileMaker Pro operational modes that are discussed in Chapter 1. (The other three modes are Find, Layout, and Preview.) As the name suggests, you use Browse mode to casually flip through a database record by record, examining, and modifying data as you go.

You also have to be in Browse mode to *omit* records (temporarily hide them) or to sort records. Because you usually omit records in conjunction with a Find request, this topic is discussed in Chapter 9. Sorting is covered in Chapter 10.

Note that you can be in only one mode at a time. Determining which mode you are in is easy. In the Select menu, the current mode has a check mark next to it, as shown in Figure 8-1. The name of the current mode also appears in the mode selector pop-up menu at the bottom of the database window (also shown in Figure 8-1).

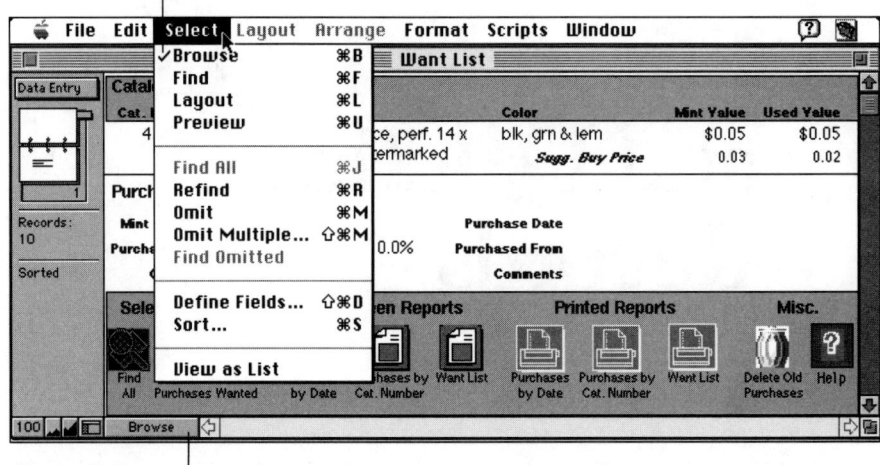

Figure 8-1: The current mode is indicated both in the Select menu and in the mode selector pop-up menu.

Switching to Browse mode

Regardless of the mode you're currently in, you can switch to Browse mode in two ways:

❖ By choosing the Browse command from the Select menu (or pressing ⌘-B)

❖ By choosing Browse from the mode selector pop-up menu at the bottom of the database window

You also switch to other modes (Find, Layout, and Preview) by selecting the mode from one of these menus.

Note that when you first open a database, FileMaker Pro automatically displays it in Browse mode. Opening the database in Browse mode is convenient, because browsing is what you do most.

Chapter 8: Using Browse Mode

Using Browse mode tools and functions

Figure 8-2 shows the Address Book database (discussed in Chapter 4) in Browse mode. You can see that fewer tools are visible than in Layout mode — the mode in which you designed the database. In addition, the Layout and Arrange menus are *dimmed*, so you cannot choose commands from these menus while you are in Browse mode.

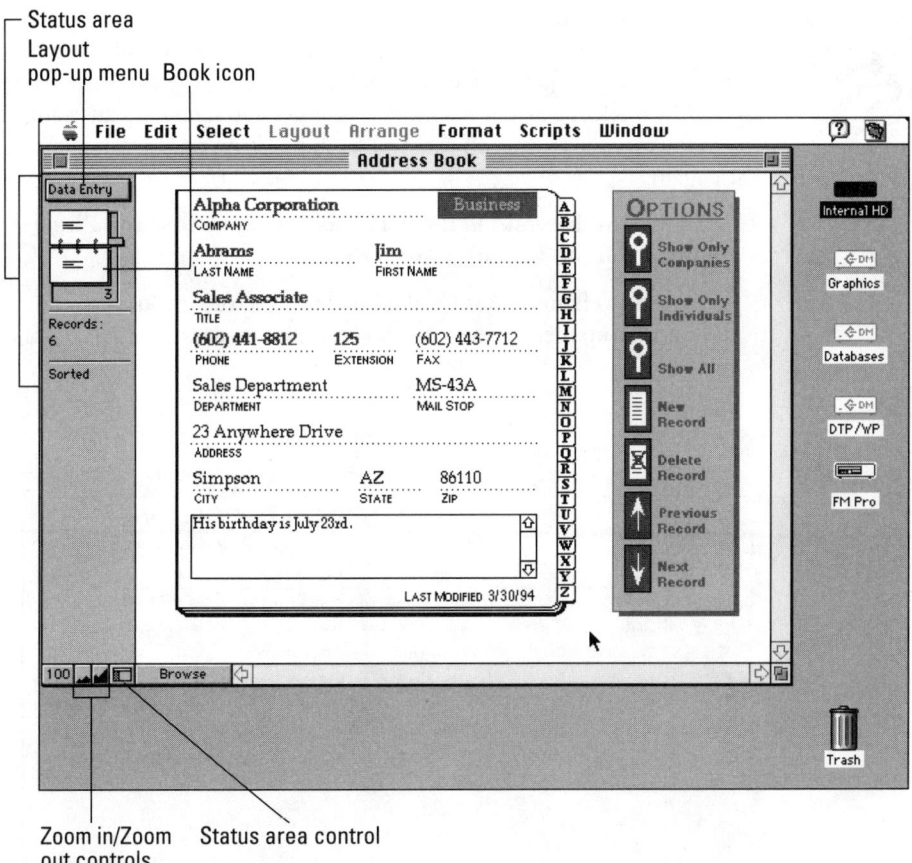

Figure 8-2: The Address Book database in Browse mode.

Part III: Working with Databases

Using the layout pop-up menu to switch layouts

The importance of layouts in FileMaker Pro is stressed throughout this book. As you will recall, a *layout* is a particular arrangement of database fields. Because no single way of displaying fields is equally useful for all tasks, having several layouts for a given database is not unusual. For example, a layout that makes entering data easy may not be the best one for displaying data when you want to look something up or generate a report. You can change layouts in Browse mode at any time.

In the upper-left corner of the window, above the status area, is the layout pop-up menu (see Figure 8-3). You use this menu to determine which layout is currently displayed and to switch between available layouts for the database. To switch layouts, you select a layout from the layout pop-up menu. As an example, you use the following steps to switch the Address book from one layout to another and then back again.

1. **With the Address Book database displayed, choose the Phone Directory layout from the Layout pop-up menu.**

   The display changes to show the Phone Directory layout (see Figure 8-3). The layout pop-up menu shows that you have changed to a new layout.

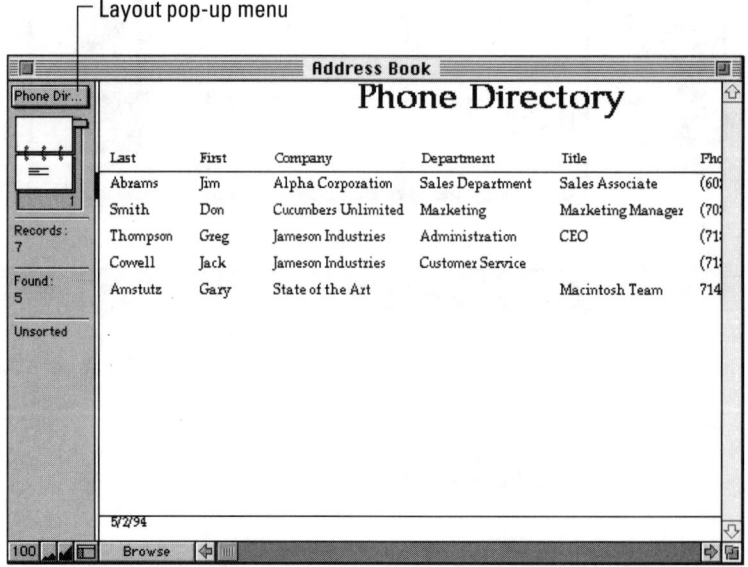

Figure 8-3: The Phone Directory layout from the Address Book database.

2. **Choose the Data Entry layout from the layout pop-up menu to switch back again.**

Chapter 8: Using Browse Mode

Keep in mind that different layouts may require different amounts of screen space in order to be fully displayed. When changing from one layout to another, you may sometimes need to resize the database window.

Note: If you want to, you can specify an opening layout for each database. Instead of opening to the layout that was displayed when you last closed the database (which is the default), FileMaker displays the opening layout that you set in the Preferences dialog box. For instructions on setting an opening layout, see Chapter 7.

Using the book icon to navigate among records

Below the layout pop-up menu is the book icon (see Figure 8-4). In Browse mode, you use the book to navigate among records to select the next one you want to work with or view. (Note that the book has different functions in other modes. In Find mode, for example, you use it to switch between multiple Find requests.)

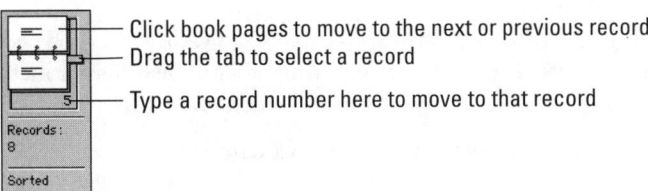

Figure 8-4: The book icon.

In Browse mode, the navigation operations that you can perform by using the book include the following:

❖ Flipping from one record to the next or the previous record (by clicking pages of the book)

❖ Quickly moving to the first or last record (by dragging the tab on the side of the book to the top or bottom)

❖ Moving to an approximate position in the database (by dragging the tab on the side of the book)

❖ Moving to a specific record (by typing a record number in the area below the book)

The tab on the right side of the book shows the approximate position in the database of the record that is currently displayed. The number below the book shows the exact position of the current record. The first record in the database is record number 1, the second is record number 2, and so on. The area below the book shows the total number of records that are currently in the database, the number of records that are being browsed (if all records aren't presently visible), and whether the database has been *sorted* (arranged in a particular order). In the example in Figure 8-4, the fifth record out of eight is currently displayed, and the database is in sort order.

Part III: Working with Databases

Search Suggestions

One common thing to do with a database is to look up individual records. After all, the purpose of a database is to store information for later retrieval. Although you can locate and examine records in several ways (many of which are discussed in later chapters), frequently, you just flip through records one at a time until you find the one you want.

Note: Flipping through records, however, can be tedious when you are working with a very large database. (See Chapter 9 for quicker, more efficient search methods.) Some things that you can do to make this process easier are to switch to a layout that shows more than one record at a time, such as the Phone Directory layout for the Address Book database, or to display the records in the current layout as a list (see the sidebar, "Browsing without Using the Book," later in this chapter).

The following step-by-step instructions explain the various methods of navigating through the database. If you want to experiment with the different methods, you can use the Address Book database or any other database that's handy.

Moving to the next or previous record in a database

You can use the book icon or keyboard shortcuts to move forward and backward in a database one record at a time.

1. **To move forward in a database, click the lower half of the book.**

   Each click switches to the next record in the current sort order, making it the current record. The book tab moves down slightly, and the new record is displayed.

   — or —

1. **To move backward through a database, click the upper half of the book.**

   Each click switches to the previous record in the current sort order, making it the current record. The book tab moves up slightly, and the new record is displayed.

2. **Continue clicking until the desired record appears.**

FileMaker Pro 2 also provides a pair of keyboard shortcuts that you can use to move to the next or previous record. To go to the next record, press ⌘-Tab. To go to the previous record, press Shift-⌘-Tab or Option-⌘-Tab.

Moving to the first record in a database

Follow these steps to move to the first record in a database:

1. **Click the book tab and drag upward until it reaches the top of the book.**

2. **Release the mouse button.**

Chapter 8: Using Browse Mode

— or —

1. **Click the record number indicator directly below the book to select it.**
2. **Press 1 and then press Return or Enter.**

   You can type any number to move directly to a particular record. Although you normally won't know specific record numbers, you will always know the first one.

   The first record in the database becomes the current record. You can tell that you're at the first record because the top half of the book icon is blank. As usual, the record number (1, in this case) is displayed below the book.

   Note that if the current layout displays one record per screen (such as the Data Entry layout in the Address Book database), only the first record is visible. If you have chosen View As List from the Select menu, as is often done in reports, a small vertical bar marks the current record in the list (refer to Figure 8-3.)

Moving to the last record in a database

Follow these steps to move to the last record in a database:

1. **Click the book tab and drag downward until it reaches the bottom of the book.**
2. **Release the mouse button.**

   The last record in the database becomes the current record.

— or —

1. **Click the record number indicator directly below the book to select it.**
2. **Type a large number and press Return or Enter.**

   As long as the number is greater than or equal to the number of records that are currently being browsed, the last record is displayed, and it becomes the current record.

Who's on First?

The particular database record that is first and the one that is last depends on whether the database has been sorted and by which field or fields. For example, the first record originally entered in Address Book may have been the one for Don Smith.

If you sort the database by Last Name, the new first record may be that of Jim Abrams. See Chapter 10 for more information on sorting and how it affects a database.

Part III: Working with Databases

When the last record is selected, the bottom of the book is blank — showing that no records follow the current one. As always, the record number is displayed immediately below the bottom book page.

Note that, regardless of the record navigation method that you use, if you attempt to move up past the first record or down past the last record, nothing happens.

Moving to a specific record in a database

You also can move to a specific record number if you happen to know, for example, that the record that you want is the fourth one down.

Follow these steps to move to a specific record number:

1. **Click the record number indicator below the book to select it.**

   — or —

1. **If no record is currently selected, press the Escape key (Esc).**

   In either case, the record number indicator changes to inverse video to show that it is selected.

2. **Type the number of the record that you want to examine.**

3. **Press Return or Enter.**

   The corresponding record appears on the screen and becomes the current record.

Browsing without Using the Book

You can completely bypass the book when you are browsing records by choosing View as List from the Select menu. In list view, all records are displayed as a continuous scrolling list, and you use the scroll bar at the side of the database window to change the view of the records. Reports and data-entry screens that have limited fields are often displayed and worked with in list view. If you have an Apple Extended keyboard (or an equivalent keyboard from another manufacturer), you also can use the following keys to move through the database:

Key	Effect
Home	Move to the first record
End	Move to the last record
Page Up	Move up one screen
Page Down	Move down one screen

Note that these commands are purely for navigation and *looking* at records. If you want to add data to or edit the current data in a record, you must *select* the record by clicking anywhere inside it.

If list view isn't the view you normally use for this layout, choose View as List from the Select menu to remove the check mark when you're done. The display reverts to the original one record per screen.

Chapter 8: Using Browse Mode

When you are browsing a database, you usually have all of its records at your disposal. Sometimes, however, you may want to view only a subset of the records. To view a subset, you can issue a Find request. A Find request restricts visible records to those that match the Find criteria (Salary < $50,000, for example). For more information about working with subsets of records, see Chapter 9.

Changing the magnification level

Below the status area (at the bottom of the database window) are three tools that enable you to change your view of the database by zooming in or out — that is, by changing the magnification level. You can use zooming to get a bird's-eye view of a complex layout or report or to concentrate on a particular section of a record. Although these tools are more useful in Layout mode, you can use them in Browse mode, too.

The current magnification is shown as a percentage: 100 means that the database is shown actual size, 200 means that it's twice the normal size, and so on. Clicking the number toggles the display between 100 percent and the most recently selected zoom level. You use the pair of buttons to the right of the magnification percentage to zoom out (decrease magnification) and zoom in (increase magnification), respectively. Each time you click one of the buttons, the magnification is decreased or increased by a factor of two. Thus, to decrease magnification from 100 percent to 25 percent, as shown in Figure 8-5, click the first button twice.

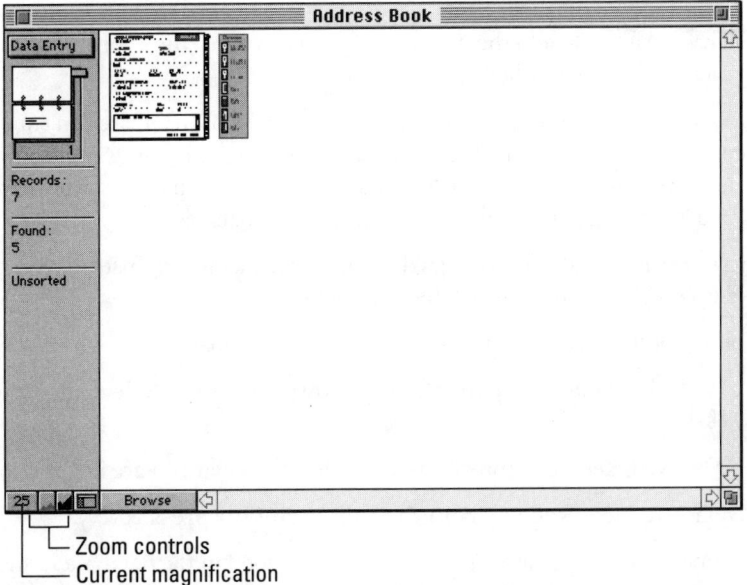

Figure 8-5: Address Book zoomed to 25 percent.

Showing and hiding the status area

To the right of the zoom controls is the status area control. This button, which works as a toggle, enables you to hide or show the status area. Hiding the status area gives you more room in which to display the database. Click the status area control to hide the status area; the current layout takes over the entire window. Click the status area control again to display the status area and regain access to the tools.

Finally, to the right of the status area control button, is the mode pop-up menu. As mentioned earlier in this chapter, you can use this menu to switch from one operational mode to another.

Data Entry and Editing

Perhaps the most important uses of Browse mode are entering and editing data. As you work with FileMaker Pro, you'll discover that a wealth of commands and techniques have been provided to make data entry and editing as simple as possible.

Creating new records

Few databases are static entities that you just browse through once in a while. Whether you've just finished designing a database or are working with one that you've had around for years, you'll want to add new records to it at some point. For example, a new business or personal contact requires a new record in your Address Book database. After you add the new record, you can enter the appropriate information in each of the record's fields.

Note that the exact way in which you add records to a database can sometimes depend on the way in which the database was designed. For example, in the Data Entry layout for Address Book (see Figure 8-2), you can click a New Record button to activate a script that adds a new record to the database.

However, most database layouts don't have such a button. Instead, you choose the New Record command from the Edit menu.

Follow these steps to create a new record for a database:

1. **With the database open, choose Browse from the Select menu (or press ⌘-B).**

   The New Record command is available only when you are in Browse mode.

2. **Choose New Record from the Edit menu (or press ⌘-N).**

   A new record appears on-screen, and it is added in the database immediately after the current record. Unless you have set auto-entry options for some fields (see Chapter 5), the record is blank.

Chapter 8: Using Browse Mode

Note that if the addition of the new record destroyed an existing sort order (the indicator below the book icon reads "Semi-sorted"), you can restore order to the database by sorting again, as discussed in Chapter 10.

Entering data

A blank record isn't of much use. After adding a record, you need to enter the appropriate information in it. Usually, you enter the information by typing it. First, of course, you need to select the field in which you want to enter data.

You enter information one field at a time. The *current field* is the one in which you can presently enter and edit data. The current field is surrounded by a solid border; borders around all other fields are dotted. The current field also contains the *insertion point*, a blinking vertical line that is sometimes called the cursor. Figure 8-6 shows a new record in a database named Games.

Note that the position of the insertion point in the field is determined by the alignment that has been set for the field (using the Align Text submenu of the Format menu). When a field is left-aligned, the insertion point appears on the left side of the field. When right-aligned — as numbers frequently are — the insertion point is on the right side of the field.

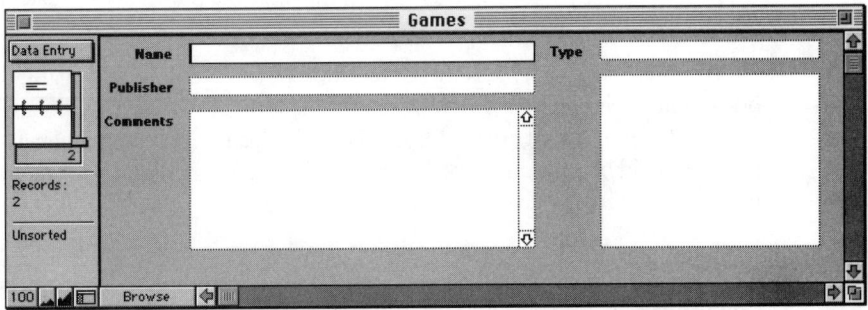

Figure 8-6: A new record, ready for data to be entered. The current field is Name.

Creating Multi-Word Index Entries

As part of its record-keeping routine, FileMaker Pro creates a separate index for each database field. The index consists of every word or value entered in each Text, Time, Date, Number, and Calculation field.

If you want an entire phrase or group of values to serve as an index entry, press Option-spacebar between each word or value in the phrase.

To enter data in another field, you first need to make it the current field. You can either click the field with the mouse or tab into the field by pressing the Tab key. Pressing Tab moves you forward through a record one field at a time. Pressing Shift-Tab moves you back to the previous field. To make a field the current field, do the following:

1. **Find the desired field on the layout.**
2. **Click in the field to select it.**

   The field's border becomes solid, and the insertion point moves into the field.

   — or —

2. **Press Tab and/or Shift-Tab until the desired field is selected.**

   The field's border becomes solid, and the insertion point moves into the field.

   When you press the Tab key, the insertion point moves through the fields from left to right and top to bottom. You can redefine the tab order by choosing the Tab Order command from the Arrange menu. See Chapter 6 for details.

Note that you cannot tab into a Summary or Calculation field (because you cannot edit or manually enter data in these types of fields; the only permissible action in these fields is copying the contents). To move into a Summary or Calculation field, you click it with the mouse.

To complete a record, press the Enter key, choose New Record again, or use the book icon to change to a different record. As long as you haven't violated any data validation options that are set for one of the fields in the record (such as leaving a required field blank), the record is immediately evaluated by FileMaker Pro. If you have committed any errors, you will be notified.

Keep in mind that you can enter data in any layout in which fields are displayed — including layouts for reports or mailing labels, for example. Of course, because some layouts show different sets or subsets of fields, data entry is more convenient in some layouts than in others. Regardless of which layout you use when entering or editing data, the new data is recorded in all layouts in which that same field appears. For example, the Address Book database has two layouts: Data Entry and Phone Directory. Adding or changing the text in a record's Company field in the Phone Directory layout simultaneously changes the text in the Company field in the Data Entry layout.

Using the data-entry and arrow keys

As you're entering data, remember which keys actually enter data and which ones merely move the insertion point — either within a field or between fields. The former are called *cursor-control keys*. The latter are usually referred to as *arrow keys*.

Chapter 8: Using Browse Mode

The data-entry keys
Data-entry keys do what their name suggests. When you press a data-entry key, a corresponding character of data is entered in a field at the insertion point. The data-entry keys consist of the letters *a* through *z*, the numerals *0* through *9*, the punctuation keys, and these same keys pressed in combination with Shift, Option, and Option-Shift. Return also acts as a data-entry key. Pressing Return ends the current line and adds a new line to the field. (Number fields, however, do not accept a Return. You need to enter all numbers on a single line within the field.)

The arrow keys
You use the data-entry keys to add information to a record, but you use the cursor-control keys to move within and between fields. Table 8-1 lists the arrow keys and their functions.

Table 8-1
Cursor-Control Keys

Key(s)	Function
Tab	Move to the next field
Shift-Tab	Move to the previous field
Up-arrow key	Move up one line in the current field, if possible; otherwise, do nothing
Down-arrow key	Move down to the next line in the current field, if possible; otherwise, do nothing
Left-arrow key	Move one character position left in the current field, if possible; otherwise, do nothing
Right-arrow key	Move one character position right in the current field, if possible; otherwise, do nothing

After you master the arrow and data-entry keys, entering data is relatively straightforward. FileMaker Pro supports the text-entry, arrow, and editing functions that you have already learned in other programs (such as pressing Delete to remove the previous character and using the Cut, Copy, and Paste commands). Keep in mind, however, that some field types and definitions may restrict the range of acceptable data that you can enter, as described in the next section.

Entering different types of data
In FileMaker Pro, you can select one of seven different data types for each field, as discussed in Chapter 5. The field types are Text, Numeric, Date, Time, Picture/Sound, Calculation, and Summary. You can neither enter nor edit data in Calculation and Summary fields. The following sections describe data entry and editing in the remaining five types of fields. (If you need additional help in determining what kinds of information can and cannot go into the different field types, see Chapter 5.)

Part III: Working with Databases

Typing Special Characters

You use the Option and Option-Shift key combinations to type special characters, such as foreign language characters and symbols. For example, to type a bullet (o), you press Option-8. If you want to find out where many of those special characters are hiding — the ones that aren't visible on the keyboard — you can use a desk accessory such as Key Caps from Apple Computer (included with every copy of the system software) or a more advanced utility such as KeyFinder. KeyFinder is part of the Norton Utilities for Macintosh from Symantec Corporation.

As you press Shift, Option, or Option-Shift, Key Caps shows the characters that you can type by pressing a particular letter, number, or punctuation key in combination with the modifier key or keys that you're holding down. (A *modifier key* is any key that changes the meaning of the normal key. In regular typing, the modifier keys are Shift and Option. The Control and Command modifier keys — if supported — are under program control and are usually reserved for issuing commands from the keyboard and similar functions.) You can copy any character created in Key Caps and then paste it into the current document.

KeyFinder is much easier to use and more powerful than Key Caps. It shows at a glance every character that's available in a particular font. After you click the desired symbol, KeyFinder tells you what keys to press to create that symbol in your document. (Undefined characters are shown as boxes.) As with Key Caps, you can copy any character created in KeyFinder and paste it into the current document.

If you need to move a database between the Macintosh and Windows versions of FileMaker Pro or if you are using a database on a mixed PC and Mac network, be sparing with your use of special characters. In most cases, these characters will not translate appropriately from one platform to the other. See Appendix C for details.

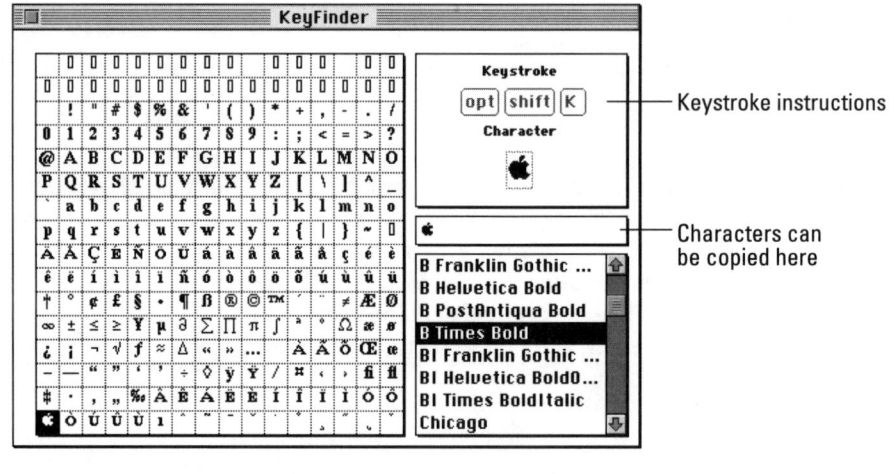

Chapter 8: Using Browse Mode

Note that any formatting that you set for a field is applied after you enter the data and move to another field.

Text fields

Text fields can contain any kind of character data, including text, numbers, and other characters. A single Text field can accept up to 64,000 characters of text.

When you enter information into a Text field, if you exceed the size of the field (as designed in Layout mode), the field automatically expands downward to accommodate the excess text. When you leave the field, it reverts to its original size, and the extra text is hidden from view. To see all the information that's stored in the field, you have to click or tab into the field (see Figure 8-7). If you want to use the field's contents in a printed report, be aware that whatever you normally see on-screen is also what will appear in the report; that is, if the contents of the entire field are not visible, you are well-advised to expand the field as necessary in Layout mode or edit the field's contents before printing.

Number fields

FileMaker Pro ignores nonnumeric data in a Number field when it is performing calculations based on the field, executing Find requests based on the field, and recording index entries for the field. Number values can consist of up to 255 characters, and you have to type them on a single line; no Returns are allowed. Any numeric formatting that you have set for the field (with the Number Format command) is applied only to the numeric parts of data within the field.

If a number exceeds the width of its field, it displays as a question mark (?). You can see the entire number by clicking the field or tabbing into it. (Note that a question mark also appears in a Calculation or Summary field if the formula cannot be evaluated or if it results in a divide-by-zero error.)

Although you can enter any kind of characters in a Number field, restricting the field to numeric data may be helpful — particularly if someone else will be doing the data entry. To restrict the field to numeric data, set the Verify that field is of type Number option when you are defining the number field. See Chapter 5 for instructions.

Time fields

When entering data in a Time field, you can use either the standard 12-hour format or the 24-hour military time format. When you type values, you need to use colons to separate the hours, minutes, and seconds (for example, 1:00 PM or 13:00:00). In 12-hour format, if you leave off the AM/PM designation, FileMaker Pro assumes that you mean AM. If you simply enter the number 7, for example, FileMaker interprets the 7 as 7:00 AM. Unlike with Number fields, you have to leave any extraneous, non-time related data out of a Time field. FileMaker Pro accepts only legitimate times.

Part III: Working with Databases

Figure 8-7: Text overflow in a field.

Date fields

Date fields are similar to Time fields. The maximum length of a Date field is eight characters — six for the month, day, and year, plus two separators. On a U.S. Mac, you enter dates in month-day-year format (12/31/95, for example). If the database was created on a system that used an international format for dates (day-month-year, for example), you have to use that same format when you enter dates. Regardless of the date format, leading zeroes (as in 04/07/95) are optional. You use the Date Format command to set a different display format for the date. However, this command affects only how the date is displayed in the record, not how you enter it.

Chapter 8: Using Browse Mode

You can separate the parts of the date with any non-numeric character, such as a slash or dash. If you use only two digits for the year, FileMaker assumes that you mean the current century. If you omit the year altogether, FileMaker assumes that you mean the current year (per the system clock). As with Time fields, you have to leave any extraneous, non-date related data out of a Date field. Only legitimate dates are accepted.

You should note that in Time and Date fields, you can edit auto-entry times or dates (information that's taken from the system clock) unless the Prohibit modification of auto-entered values option is selected as part of the field's definition. See Chapter 5 for details.

Note: Under recent versions of System 7, you can use the Date & Time control panel to set an international date or time format for programs such as FileMaker Pro to use.

Text fields
Picture/Sound fields can contain still images, sounds, or movies. Working with Picture/Sound fields is a little more complicated than working with Text or Number fields. In the case of movies and sounds, the Macintosh needs to have special capabilities that are provided in software, hardware, or a combination of the two.

You can use a variety of methods to insert pictures, sounds, and movies into a Picture/Sound field:

❖ You can import pictures and movies by using commands in the Import/Export submenu of the File menu.

❖ If you have an appropriate program or system utility that can open a picture, movie, or sound, you can copy or cut the picture, movie, or sound to the Clipboard and then paste it into the Picture/Sound field. Current versions of Apple's Scrapbook desk accessory, for example, can be used to store all three types of material.

❖ If your Mac has a microphone, you can use the Sound control panel to record sounds directly into the field.

These procedures are explained in the following sets of step-by-step instructions.

Follow these steps to insert a picture or a movie into a field:

1. **Switch to Browse mode by choosing Browse from the Select menu (or by pressing ⌘-B).**

2. **Make the Picture/Sound field the current field by clicking or tabbing into it.**

3. **Choose the Import/Export submenu from the File menu and then drag across to select the appropriate command.**

Part III: Working with Databases

Choose Import Picture for a still graphic or Import Movie for a QuickTime movie. One of the dialog boxes shown in Figure 8-8 appears.

4. **If the desired picture or movie isn't shown in the file list in the dialog box, use normal file navigation techniques to move to the disk and folder that contain the desired picture or movie.**

   For help with file navigation, see Chapter 3.

5. **Select the picture or movie that you want to insert.**

   If you want to insert a movie, you can click the Show Preview check box in the Import Movie dialog box to see a frame of the movie before you import it.

6. **Click Open to place the picture or movie in the field.**

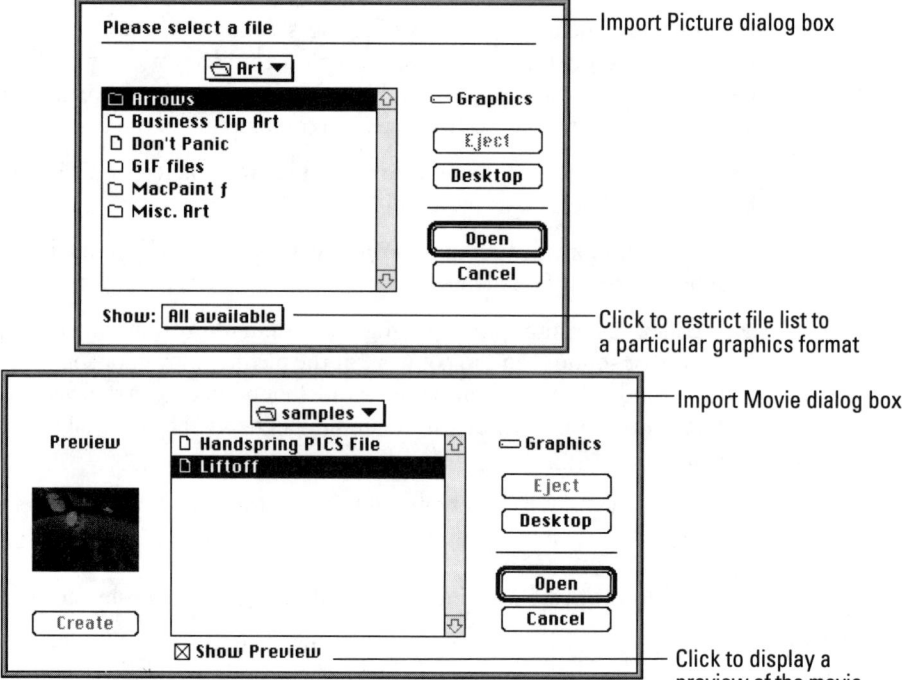

Figure 8-8: The Import Picture and Import Movie dialog boxes.

Chapter 8: Using Browse Mode

You also can copy a picture, movie, or sound and paste it into a field, as described in the following steps:

1. **Open the program that contains the picture, sound, or movie that you want to copy.**

2. **Within the program, open the item that you want to copy, select it, and then choose Copy from the Edit menu or press ⌘-C to copy the item to the Clipboard.**

3. **Exit the program.**

4. **Open the FileMaker Pro database into which you want to copy the picture, sound, or movie.**

5. **Select the Picture/Sound field that you want to copy the picture, sound, or movie into, making that field the current field.**

6. **Choose Paste from the Edit menu (or press ⌘-V).**

You also can record sounds directly into a Picture/Sound field if you have a Macintosh that is equipped with a microphone and have the Sound control panel installed. (The Sound control panel is part of the Macintosh system software.)

Follow these steps to record a sound directly into a field:

1. **Double-click the Picture/Sound field into which you want to record. The Sound Record dialog box appears (see Figure 8-9).**

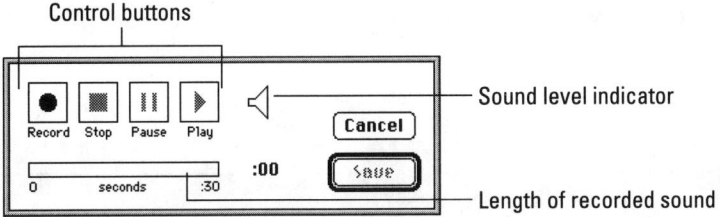

Figure 8-9: The Sound Record dialog box.

The Sound Record dialog box appears. You click the control buttons at the top of the box to record, stop recording, play back the recording, and pause the playback. A bar below the Control buttons indicates the length of the recording (the maximum is 10 seconds). An icon that looks like a speaker indicates the sound level. Sound volume is indicated by displaying curved lines to the right of the speaker icon; the more line, the louder the sound.

Part III: Working with Databases

2. When you are ready to record, click Record.
3. Speak or otherwise direct sound into the microphone.
4. When you are done recording, click Stop.
5. Click Play to listen to the sound that you recorded.

Playing back stored sounds or movies is simple. To play back a sound, just double-click the field in which it is stored. To play back a movie, click the Play/Stop button on the movie's frame (as shown in Figure 8-10) or double-click the movie itself. To stop playback, click the movie once or click the Play/Stop button again. Other movie controls enable you to change the playback volume and step forward or backward through the movie one frame at a time.

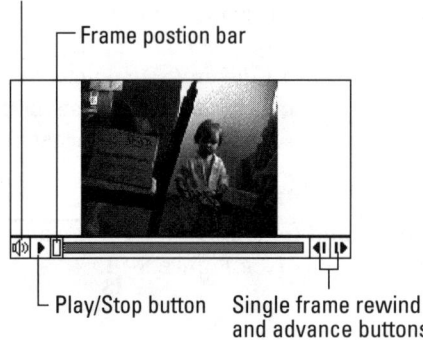

Figure 8-10: A movie and its control bar.

How FileMaker Stores Sounds, Pictures, and Movies

No matter how many times you use the same picture, movie, or sound item in a FileMaker Pro database, it is actually stored only once in the file. Each database maintains a library of sounds, graphics, and movies that are associated with Picture/Sound fields. This approach saves considerable disk space.

Chapter 8: Using Browse Mode   255

About QuickTime

QuickTime is an Apple system extension that offers a set of tools and standards for creating, editing, storing, and playing moving pictures with sound on the Macintosh. An important part of QuickTime is its ability to play movies on any Mac. The more recent versions of QuickTime even support Macs that have black-and-white displays.

QuickTime movies require a great deal of disk space. For example, the 19-second movie that is shown in Figure 5-5 (Chapter 5) occupies over 6MB of space! Getting video data into a Macintosh requires special hardware, such as the Radius Video Spigot (a video capture card). Although you can use simple utility programs to capture and edit movies, serious QuickTime work requires serious, multicapability software, such as Adobe Premiere. Because of the storage, hardware, and software requirements, movie making is out of the reach of many users. If you don't want to create your own movies, prerecorded QuickTime movies are available as commercial products. And movies are not unusual in CD-ROM programs.

Table 8-2 lists and explains the graphics and sound file formats that FileMaker Pro supports. A *format* is a specific method for storing a particular kind of data.

Table 8-2
Supported Graphics and Sound Formats

Format	Description
TIFF (Tag Image File Format)	A still graphics format; images can be color or gray scale; compressed versions are supported, but they may not be compatible with all programs; also supported by other computer systems, such as IBM. (Note that between the Mac and PC, there are many varieties of TIFF. Not all are supported.)
PICT	A Macintosh-specific graphics format (perhaps the most common format available for the Mac)
MacPaint	An older Macintosh black-and-white graphics format, now falling into disuse
EPS or EPSF (Encapsulated PostScript)	A graphics format for detailed drawings; favored by illustrators; the quality of the graphic depends on the output device
SND 1 and SND 2	Macintosh sound formats; requires a microphone (to record sounds) and the Sound Control Panel
MooV	QuickTime movie; requires System 6.0.8 or higher and the QuickTime extension

Part III: Working with Databases

Dealing with Lost Movies

When you copy or import a QuickTime movie into a Picture/Sound field in FileMaker Pro, a link is created to the original movie. The actual movie data is not copied into the database. Using this method saves disk space, but it also has important consequences. If you delete the original movie or move the database to another Mac without also supplying a copy of the movie, the link will be broken, and FileMaker Pro won't be able to play the movie. Note, however, that you will be given an opportunity to insert the disk that contains the movie. If you think that the movie is on a different disk that is already *mounted* (displayed on the desktop), you can tell FileMaker Pro where to find the movie or ask the program to search for the movie. If the movie is nowhere to be found, the contents of the Picture/Sound field are changed to a still picture. If you eventually locate the movie or transfer a new copy of it to your hard disk, the next time you open the database that references the movie, the link is reestablished.

The following steps describe how to copy sounds in the Sound control panel:

1. **Close all programs that are currently running.**

   You cannot modify the System file if programs are running.

2. **Drag the icon for the sound file onto the System file.**

   The System file is inside the System Folder on the start up hard disk.

   If the sound file is on the same hard disk as the System file, the sound file is moved into the System file. If the sound file is on a different hard disk than the System file, the sound file is merely copied into the System file.

3. **Open the Sound control panel, as shown in Figure 8-11.**

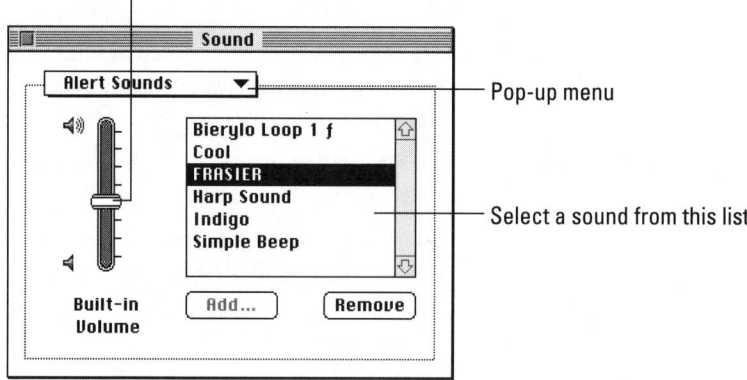

Figure 8-11: The Sound control panel.

Chapter 8: Using Browse Mode

The Alert Sounds portion of the Sound control panel lists the names of all sounds that are currently installed in the System file. (If Alert Sounds is not displayed, choose it from the pop-up menu.)

4. **Select the sound that you want to copy and choose Copy from the Edit menu (or press ⌘-C).**

   A copy of the sound is placed on the Clipboard.

5. **Close the Sound control panel by clicking its close box in the upper-left corner.**

6. **Open the FileMaker Pro database in which you want to paste the sound.**

7. **Select the Picture/Sound field in the desired record and choose Paste from the Edit menu (or press ⌘-V).**

   The sound is pasted into the field.

8. **If you want to paste additional sounds into the database, leave the database open, open the Sound control panel again, and continue to copy and paste.**

9. **To restore the System file to its original condition, double-click its icon.**

   A list of installed sounds appears.

10. **Select the icon for the sound that you previously inserted and drag it out of the System file and back to its original location.**

    — or —

10. **If the sound was copied into the System file rather than moved there (see Step 2), drag the sound icon into the Trash instead.**

11. **To finish the process, close the System file.**

Working with value lists

Not all data has to be typed or imported. Using the Field Format command, you can format fields to display as pop-up lists or menus, as well as sets of radio buttons and check boxes (see Figure 8-12). These fields help speed data entry by providing a list of choices from which you can select. The list of user-defined choices is called a *value list*. Any of these four formats except pop-up lists also can have an Other choice appended to it. For information on attaching a value list to a field, see Chapter 5.

Part III: Working with Databases

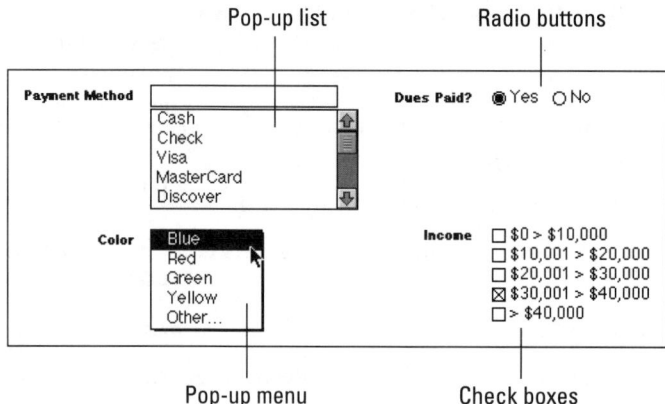

Figure 8-12: Examples of fields formatted as a pop-up list, a pop-up menu, radio buttons, and check boxes.

The following sets of step-by-step instructions describe how to make a choice from different kinds of value lists.

Choosing an item from a pop-up list

When you click or tab into a field formatted as a pop-up list, a scrolling list of values appears, similar in appearance to a list that you'd find in most dialog boxes (such as the Define Fields dialog box). To choose an item from a pop-up list, follow these steps:

1. **Click or tab into the field that contains the pop-up list.**

   The list automatically expands.

2. **Select the item of interest by double-clicking the choice or by clicking it once and pressing Return.**

   The choice is selected and the insertion point moves to the next field.

   — or —

2. **If you want to enter a response that is not included in the value list, ignore the list and click once in the field, type a different response, and then press the Tab key to move to the next field.**

You also can use the arrow keys to choose a particular item. The up-arrow and left-arrow keys move up in the list; the down-arrow and right-arrow keys move down in the list. In addition, you can type the first letter or two of a value to quickly select that item. Complete your selection by pressing Return.

Chapter 8: Using Browse Mode

Choosing an item from a pop-up menu

When you click or tab into a field formatted as a pop-up menu, a traditional pop-up menu appears. Unlike using a pop-up list, you cannot manually enter a value that is not in the menu unless you have included an "Other_" menu choice. To choose an item from a pop-up menu, follow these steps:

1. **Click or tab into the field that contains the pop-up menu.**

   Initially, the field is blank.

2. **Click the blank box to expose the pop-up menu and then drag to select your choice.**

   — or —

2. **To record a choice that is not listed in the menu, choose Other from the pop-up menu.**

   The Other dialog box appears, as shown in Figure 8-13.

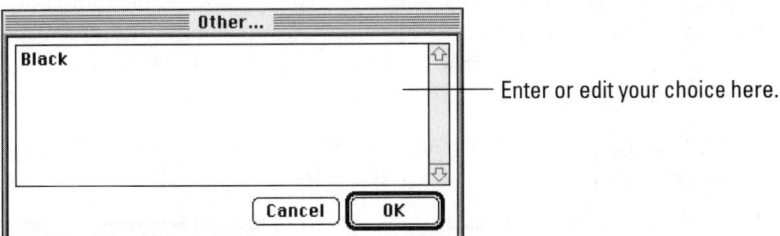

Figure 8-13: The Other dialog box.

Unlike with pop-up lists, you can enter a choice that does not appear in a pop-up menu only if you included an Other value when you set the field format.

3. **Type your choice and click OK to accept it.**

   Your choice now appears in the field.

Choosing an item from a group of radio buttons

To choose an item from a group of radio buttons, follow these steps:

1. **Click or tab into the field that contains the radio buttons.**

2. **To select a particular button, you can click the button once, select the button by using the arrow keys and then pressing Return or the spacebar, or select the button by typing the first letter or two in the choice's name and then pressing Return or the spacebar.**

When selected, the radio button blackens.

— or —

2. **To record a choice that is not listed as a radio button, click or otherwise select the Other radio button.**

   The Other dialog box appears, as shown in Figure 8-14.

   Unlike with pop-up lists, you can enter a choice that does not appear as a radio button only if you included an Other value when you set the field format.

3. **Type your choice and click OK to accept it.**

   Remember that although an alternative choice is recorded, you cannot see it on the layout. You see only that Other has been selected. To determine the exact wording of your choice, click the Other radio button again. The Other dialog box appears, showing what you originally typed as your choice.

Note that although radio buttons are normally used in most Macintosh programs to present mutually-exclusive choices, you can select multiple radio buttons, if you want to. Just press Shift as you make your selections. Note, however, that sorts, calculations, or summaries that are based on a field with multiple choices can produce strange results.

Choosing an item from a group of check boxes

To choose an item from a group of check boxes, follow these steps:

1. **Click or tab into the field that contains the check boxes.**

2. **To select a particular check box, do one of the following:**

   ❖ Click the check box once

   ❖ Select the check box by using the arrow keys and then press Return or the spacebar

   ❖ Select the check box by typing the first letter or two in the choice's name and then press Return or the spacebar.

   When selected, a check box is marked with an *X*.

— or —

2. **To record a choice that is not listed as a option, click or otherwise select the Other check box.**

   The Other dialog box appears, as shown in Figure 8-14.

   Unlike with pop-up lists, you can enter a choice that does not appear as a check box only if you included an Other value when you set the field format.

Chapter 8: Using Browse Mode

3. **Type your choice and click OK to accept it.**

   Remember that although the alternate choice is recorded, you cannot see it on the layout. You just see that Other has been selected. To determine the exact wording of the choice, click the Other check box again. The Other dialog box appears, showing what you originally typed as your choice.

In daily life (market research surveys, for example), multiple choices are frequently allowed when check boxes are used for items — as in "Check all that apply." To check more than one box in a FileMaker Pro database, just hold down the Shift key as you click each item's check box. Note, however, that sorts, calculations, or summaries that are based on a field with multiple choices can produce strange results.

Changing a value in a value list
To change a value that you have previously selected from a value list, use the following procedures:

- *Pop-up lists and pop-up menus:* Select a different item.
- *Radio buttons:* Click a different radio button. The previously selected button or buttons become deselected.
- *Check boxes:* Each check box works as a toggle. Click to reverse the state of any given check box.

To change a value that you have manually typed in a pop-up list field or an Other choice that you've selected in a pop-up menu, radio button, or check box field, use normal editing techniques.

Copying and reusing data
If you have already typed a particular piece of data somewhere else — either within or outside the current database — you can use it again without having to retype it. The simplest method is to select the data in another record, another field, or in another program (such as a word processor or graphics program), copy it to the Clipboard, and then paste it into a database field. (If you'd rather *move* data from one field or record to another, use the Cut command rather than the Copy command.)

Note that you also can copy the contents of a field that is formatted as a value list (pop-up list, pop-up menu, radio buttons, or check boxes). Simply select the field and choose Copy from the Edit menu. When you Paste (⌘-V), the appropriate information will appear in the field.

Copying data from a field index

You also can reuse data that you have previously typed in the database by selecting it from the index that FileMaker Pro maintains for the field. Each index consists of all of the words and numbers that you have entered in that field. You can use the index to make sure that a particular value is always entered in the same form in every record in which it appears. In a customer database, for example, you can use this technique to ensure that you don't have half a dozen different entries for the same company name (such as Apple, Apple Inc., Apple Computer, and Apple Computer Inc.).

To enter data from a field index, follow these steps:

1. **Select the field into which you want to enter data, making it the current field.**

   If the field is currently empty, skip to Step 3.

2. **If the field currently contains data, you can either replace all or part of that data or append the new information to the existing data.**

   To replace existing data, select the data.

   To append the new information to the existing data, click in the field to position the insertion point where you want the new data to be pasted.

3. **Choose the Paste Special submenu from the Edit menu and drag across to the From Index command (or press ⌘-I).**

   The View Index dialog box appears, as shown in Figure 8-14.

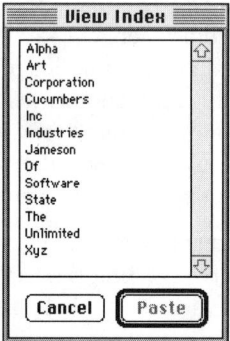

Figure 8-14: The View Index dialog box.

4. **In the View Index dialog box, select the item that you want to insert by typing the first few characters of the item's name or using the arrow keys or mouse to select the item directly.**

5. **Click Paste to insert the item in the current field.**

Chapter 8: Using Browse Mode

Duplicating a field from a previous record

If data in the current field will be exactly the same as in the corresponding field in the last record you entered or edited, you don't have to retype it. You can copy it directly into the new field by using the Paste Special Last Record command. (Think of this command as a "ditto" command.)

To duplicate a field from a previous record, follow these steps:

1. **Make sure that the last record that you entered or changed has the data you want to copy.**

2. **Select the field into which to copy data.**

3. **Choose the Paste Special submenu of the Edit menu and drag across to From Last Record (or press ⌘-' [apostrophe]).**

    The data from the corresponding field in the last record that you modified is immediately entered in the current record.

Creating a duplicate record

Sometimes working with a duplicate record is preferable, especially if you want to enter a new record that is very similar to an old one. In the Address Book database, for example, you may have a new contact at a company that you have dealt with before. Your previous contact still works there, so you don't want to modify that person's record. Instead, you can duplicate the record and then edit the duplicate.

To create a duplicate record, follow these steps:

1. **Select the record that you want to duplicate.**

2. **Choose Duplicate Record from the Edit menu (or press ⌘-D).**

    A duplicate record is added to the database and becomes the current record. You can now edit the duplicate.

Entering the current date, time, or user name

You can insert the current date, current time, or the current user's name into a field by choosing the appropriate menu command.

To insert the current date, time, or user name into a field, follow these steps:

1. **Select the field that you want to insert data into, making it the current field.**

2. **Choose the Paste Special submenu from the Edit menu and then drag across to the appropriate option: Current Date, Current Time, or Current User Name.**

    ❖ Choosing Current Date (or pressing ⌘— [hyphen]) inserts the current system date.

- Choosing Current Time (or pressing ⌘-; [semicolon]) inserts the current system time.

- Choosing Current User Name (or pressing Shift-⌘-N) inserts the name of your Macintosh (set with the Chooser in System 6 or the Sharing Setup control panel in System 7). If you have set a custom user name in FileMaker Pro's Preferences dialog box, the custom name is used instead. See Chapter 7 for additional information on setting preferences.

Editing records

No one would claim that, once entered, a given record's data is valid forever. Information needs to be updated from time to time. In the case of the Address Book database, for example, people often move, change jobs, and get new titles or phone numbers. You can edit the corresponding fields in the records for these individuals to keep them up to date. You also can eliminate records if you no longer need the data they contain.

All of these changes are easy to make. In a nutshell, editing an existing record involves locating the correct record, moving into the first field that you want to edit, changing the data in it, and then repeating this process until you have made all desired changes. The procedures discussed previously in this chapter, as well as the way that the data-entry, arrow, and text-editing keys work, apply to the process of editing data, too.

Note: Keep in mind that you also can edit data that is entered automatically, such as the date and time, unless you have set the option for Prohibit modification of auto-entered values as part of the field's definition. See Chapter 5 for details.

When you are entering or editing data in a field that contains text, the normal editing keys that are supported in most programs that you are already familiar with are also supported in FileMaker Pro. In addition to using the data-entry keys discussed previously, you also can use the keys, commands, and procedures listed in Table 8-3 in the entry/editing process.

Editing a Picture/Sound Field

The editing keys and commands that are listed in Table 8-3 also apply to Picture/Sound fields. Because you cannot selectively choose a part of the contents of a Picture/Sound field, however, you simply select the field (by clicking it or tabbing into it) and then execute the editing command or keystroke. For example, to delete a movie, picture, or sound, you select the field and then press the Delete key.

Chapter 8: Using Browse Mode

Table 8-3
Editing Techniques

Key, Command, or Procedure	Function
Delete	Deletes the character to the left of the insertion point or, if text is selected, deletes the selection
Del (Apple Extended or equivalent keyboards only)	Deletes the character to the right of the insertion point or, if text is selected, deletes the selection
⌘-X or Cut (Edit menu)	Deletes the current selection within a field and places a copy of it on the Clipboard
Clear (Edit menu)	Deletes the current selection within a field without placing a copy of it on the Clipboard
⌘-C or Copy (Edit menu)	Copies the current selection within a field and places a copy of it on the Clipboard
⌘-V or Paste (Edit menu)	Pastes the contents of the Clipboard into a field at the current insertion point
⌘-A or Select All (Edit menu)	Selects the entire contents of the current field
Double-click	Selects the current word within a field
Triple-click	Selects the current line within a field
Quadruple-click	Selects all text within the current field

The following step-by-step instructions list the general procedures for modifying a record:

1. **With the database open, find the record that you want to modify and make it the current record.**
2. **Click to select the first field to modify.**
3. **Edit, using normal editing procedures.**

   Remember that you can Cut, Copy, and Paste as needed.

4. **Tab to the next field that you want to modify, or click it with the mouse. Continue editing in this manner until you have made all changes that you want to make.**

   As you edit and move from field to field, FileMaker Pro evaluates the changes. If it discovers an error, it notifies you.

5. **To complete the editing, press Enter or move to another record.**

Part III: Working with Databases

Replacing Data in Multiple Records

Keep in mind that you can replace data in several records at the same time by using the Replace command. One handy use of this command is to reorder and renumber serialized records that have gotten out of order when you have imported records from other sources. Because the Replace command is best used on a limited group of records, rather than on a whole database, coverage of this topic is postponed until the next chapter, where finding and selecting groups of records are discussed.

Deleting records

No amount of editing can save a record that has served out its useful life. Here's how to get rid of old records by deleting them:

1. **Locate the record that you want to delete and make it the current record.**
2. **Choose Delete Record from the Edit menu (or press ⌘-E).**

   An alert box appears, asking you to confirm that you want to delete the record.

3. **Click Delete to remove the record or click Cancel to dismiss the Alert box without deleting the record.**

Before you delete a record, think carefully about whether you need the information it contains. After you delete the record, it is gone for good. You cannot get it back by using Undo. The best rule is to make certain that the data is useless before you delete the record. If you plan on wholesale deletions, making a backup copy of the database before you delete the records is a good idea. Old data is sometimes useful, so erring on the conservative side is often best.

Mass deletions are often performed on *found sets*, which are groups of records that are identified by one Find request or a series of Find requests. For example, in a client database, you may want to delete records for any person or company that hasn't done any business with your firm in the last two or three years. After performing the appropriate Find, you can use the Delete Found Set command from the Edit menu to eliminate those records. The Delete Found Set command is discussed in Chapter 9.

Using the spelling checker

Depending on the kind of database that you are using, FileMaker Pro's spelling checker may be helpful. You can instruct the program to check spelling as you type or to check it on command (to examine a particular layout, record, group of records, or a text selection). You access the spelling checker and spelling options by choosing the Spelling submenu of the Edit menu, as shown in Figure 8-15. Using the spelling checker is covered in Chapter 11.

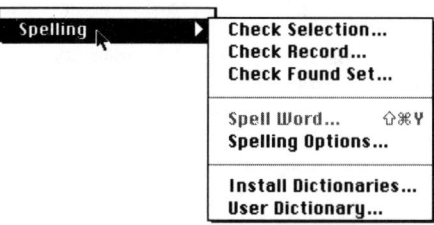

Figure 8-15: The Spelling submenu.

CHAPTER 8 — CONCEPTS AND TERMS

- You use Browse mode to view records within an existing database, to enter new records, and to modify or delete existing records.
- Databases can have different layouts to serve different purposes, such as data entry and data retrieval. You select layouts in Browse mode by using the Layout pop-up menu.
- You can display the records within a database one per screen or as a continuous scrolling list. The book icon enables you to move from one record to another, to an approximate position within the database, or to a specific record number. When a database is displayed in list form (View as List), the scroll bar functions similarly to the book icon.
- You use the data-entry and arrow keys to enter and edit character data. The former enter alphanumeric characters; the latter control the position at which newly-typed text is inserted.
- FileMaker Pro supports the use of picture, sound, and moving picture data in specific file formats. Only one copy of a given sound or picture is stored in the particular database's library, no matter how many records the sound or picture appears in.
- FileMaker Pro maintains an index for each database field. The index contains every word and number that has been entered in a particular field. Entries can be made into fields directly from the index to ensure the consistency of the database.

alphanumeric data
Information consisting of letters of the alphabet, numbers, or a mixture of the two (for example, *1911 Oak Street*).

arrow keys
Keys on a standard keyboard that, when pressed, move the insertion point within or between fields.

book
An icon in the status area. In Browse mode, you use the book to flip through database records.

current field
The database field that is presently selected (by tabbing or clicking into the field). Only the current field can be modified.

current record
The record that is presently selected. Only the current record can be modified.

data-entry keys
Keys on a standard keyboard that, when pressed, add data at the insertion point.

dimmed command
A menu command that cannot presently be selected — usually because it is irrelevant to the current operation. Dimmed items are also referred to as *grayed-out* and can appear in dialog boxes, as well as in menus.

index
A list of every word and value that has been entered in a single field across every record of the database.

insertion point
A blinking vertical line that indicates the point at which the next typed, pasted, or imported data will appear.

layout
In FileMaker Pro, a particular arrangement of fields. Unlimited layouts can be designed for each database, each with a different purpose. For example, some layouts may be used for data entry and others for generating printed or on-screen reports.

list view
Using the View as List command, you can display records in a continuous scrolling list rather than one record per screen.

modifier key
A key or keys that, when pressed in combination with a letter, number, or punctuation key, changes the meaning of the second key. When you are typing

CHAPTER NINE

Searching for Records

- Searching a database for specific information
- Using Find mode to create Find requests
- Tailoring Find requests to precise requirements
- Searching for special information, such as the current date and values within a range
- Working with found sets of records

In the last chapter, you learned how to use Browse mode to flip through records in a database. By now you should agree that this method works reasonably well when you're browsing within a small database, but that it is tedious and cumbersome when you are dealing with a database that contains many records. What's more, Browse mode is no help at all when you want to identify *groups* of records. In working with the Address Book database, for example, you may want to examine all your business contacts, excluding friends and relatives. At best, Browse mode will show you a screen of records displayed in a list.

Clearly you need a more efficient way to search for individual records. You also need a method for grouping records that share some specific characteristic — all records in the category "business contact," for example. FileMaker Pro provides these capabilities within Find mode, one of the program's four operational modes. Within Find mode, you can quickly search all records in a database for information that matches the contents of a field, such as a particular last name or a known telephone number. You also can have FileMaker Pro create groups of records that share a characteristic, such as all your business contacts or everyone within a certain telephone area code. Going well beyond simple searches, Find mode provides a number of powerful tools for locating and working with individual records and groups of records.

Find Mode Basics

Find mode does much more than make browsing through records easier. The immediate effect of a Find request is to change the set of records that you're currently browsing (that is, the ones that are visible). When you want to see only one particular record, you can search using a field that contains unique data, such as a particular social security number, phone number, inventory code, or customer identification number. You will also discover that a Find is often an important part of preparing reports. For example, in a Prospective Customer database, you may want a list of only your successes or clients for whom you have scheduled a follow-up. To produce such a list, you execute a Find and then print the report.

Switching to Find mode

As with Browse mode, you can switch into Find mode in two ways — regardless of the mode you're currently in:

❖ By choosing the Find command from the Select menu (or pressing ⌘-F)

❖ By choosing Find from the mode selector pop-up menu at the bottom of the database window

Using Find mode tools and functions

Figure 9-1 shows the Address Book database (discussed in Chapter 4 and provided on the *FileMaker Pro Bible Disk*) in Find mode. Find mode has more tools available than Browse mode has, but fewer tools than Layout mode has. The Layout, Arrange, and Format menus are dimmed because you cannot choose commands from these menus while you are in Find mode.

A number of tools that are available in Browse mode also are available in Find mode. You can switch to a different layout by using the Layout pop-up menu in the upper-left corner of the window, above the status area. You can change the current magnification at which the database is displayed by using the Zoom in and Zoom out buttons that are below the status area. You also can toggle the status area display itself by using the status area control button to the right of the Zoom in and Zoom out buttons. All of these controls work as they do in Browse mode, which is described in Chapter 8.

Chapter 9: Searching for Records

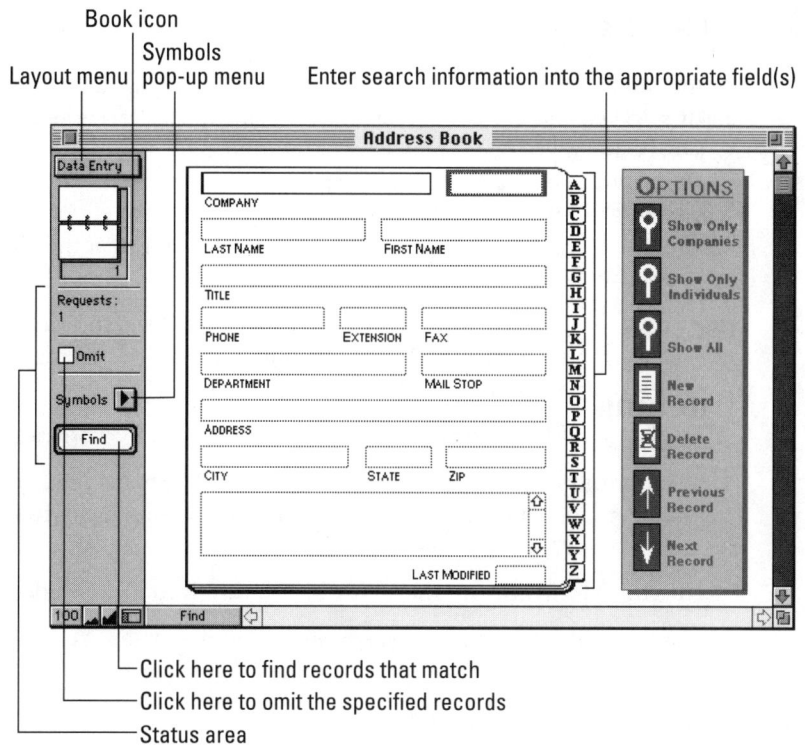

Figure 9-1: The Address Book database in Find mode.

An important part of Find mode is the Symbols pop-up menu (see Figure 9-2). This menu contains special symbols that enable you to design and implement custom searches. Using these symbols, you can search for values that are less than, equal to, or greater than a specified value, for example. You can search for all records that have an entry in the Last Name field that begins with the letter *H* or later in the alphabet. You also can look for ranges of values and for values that aren't valid. You'll learn more about these symbols in "Matching All Criteria," later in this chapter.

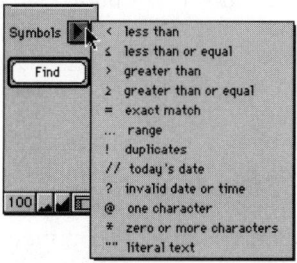

Figure 9-2: The Symbols pop-up menu.

Finding Records

Consider the following example. You work in the marketing department of a small company. While you were out to lunch with a client, your receptionist took a message for you and then left for lunch, too. Unfortunately, the receptionist's handwriting isn't very good, and you can't make out much more than that the caller's last name is Thompson and the call was urgent. You don't want to wait until the receptionist returns from lunch to find out who called and what the phone number is. What do you do?

Using FileMaker Pro and your Address Book database, you can search through all your contacts for a Thompson. An examination of the found records ought to give you an idea about who this anxious person is. Here's how you do it:

1. **First, launch FileMaker Pro and open the Address Book database.**

    The Data Entry layout appears, showing names and phone numbers. (If the database opens to a different layout, use the Layout pop-up menu to switch to the correct layout.)

2. **Using the Mode pop-up menu (or ⌘-F), switch to Find mode.**

    A blank record (called a *Find request*) appears on the screen. You enter the information for which you are searching into the Find request.

3. **Type Thompson in the Last Name field.**

4. **Click the Find button.**

    FileMaker Pro locates one record that has a last name beginning with Thompson. (When you type **Thompson,** FileMaker searches for all records having a last name that begins with those letters.) The set of all records that are identified as the result of a Find operation is known as the *found set*. Because only one record was found that matched your criteria, you call Mr. Thompson back to discover that he needs to place a large rush order with you and would have called a competitor if you hadn't responded so quickly.

This example of using Find mode shows the basic steps involved in locating specific records within a database. With the database open, you switch to Find mode and choose a layout that shows the information for which you want to search. You then enter the search information and click the Find button. Finally, you examine the found set.

Searches are performed on the contents of one or more fields in every record in a database. You can look for an exact match in a given field, such as all records that contain Thompson entries in the Last name field. You also can look for records that contain only partial matches (matching one set of criteria or another), as well as for records that contain specific pieces of information in two or more fields.

Chapter 9: Searching for Records

Note that as soon as you click the Find button, FileMaker Pro locates any matching records and then switches to Browse mode, displaying only the found set. The number of records in the found set is shown beneath the book icon. The rest of the records in the database are temporarily hidden from view. You then browse the found set as you would browse the entire database. To make all of the records visible again, choose the Find All command from the Select menu (or press ⌘-J).

Matching all criteria

The simplest kind of Find operation consists of searching for records that match all of one or more specific criteria. The preceding scenario — in which you combined a single-field search with manual browsing of the found set — is an example of using a single search criterion. You also can locate all Thompsons in Washington by using *two* criteria. All you need to do is enter information in each field on which you want to search. In the example, you would enter **Thompson** in the Last name field and **WA** in the State field before you clicked Find. To narrow the search even further, you can enter information in as many fields as you like.

Techno-trivia: This type of multifield search is called an *AND* search. When you type search instructions in multiple fields, you are asking FileMaker Pro to identify only those records that match *all* the criteria (Last Name = Thompson AND State = WA, for example).

Note that when you enter search criteria by simply typing some text or numbers into a field, FileMaker Pro not only locates records that exactly match the specified information but also finds records that contain a word that merely starts with this data. Thus, if you enter **Smith**, FileMaker Pro finds not only Smith, but also Smithy, Smithers, and Ogden Smith. You can restrict searches to exact matches if you want to (only a real Smith, for example). Refer to the section on "Matching Text Exactly," later in this chapter.

To perform a standard search in which you want FileMaker Pro to match one or more criteria in a single Find request, use the following steps. Note that this kind of Find is the simplest, as well as the one that you will use most often.

1. **In the database that you want to search, switch to a layout that shows all the fields that you want to use for the search.**

2. **Switch to Find mode by using the Mode pop-up menu, choosing Find from the Select menu, or pressing ⌘-F.**

    A blank Find request appears.

Part III: Working with Databases

3. **Enter the information for which you want to search in the appropriate field.**

   If you enter only a text string or a number, FileMaker Pro will find data that begins with that text string or number. Entering **80** in a Zip Code field, for example, will identify all records with zip codes that start with 80. If you like, you can include special search operators or symbols (as shown in Table 9-1). You can either type the symbol or select it from the Symbols pop-up menu (see Figure 9-2).

4. **To add more criteria, use the Tab key or the mouse to move to the next field that you want to use for the search and enter the information for which you're searching in this field.**

5. **Repeat Step 4 until you have set all search criteria.**

6. **Click the Find button or press Return.**

   The search executes and the found set, if any, is displayed.

   If FileMaker Pro doesn't locate any records that satisfy all of your Find criteria, a dialog box appears that informs you of this fact (see Figure 9-3). You can choose to Find again, using different criteria (Modify Find), or click Cancel to return to Browse mode.

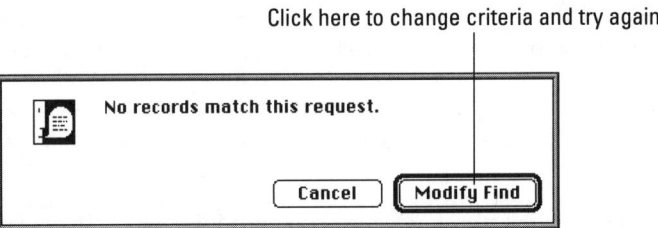

Figure 9-3: No matches were found.

Table 9-1
Find Symbols

Symbol	Meaning	Example
<	Less than	<50000 (finds persons who make less than $50,000 per year)
_	Less than or equal to	_5 (finds cities with annual rainfall that is less than or equal to 5 inches)
>	Greater than	>6/4/94 (finds any date after June 4, 1994)
_	Greater than or equal to	310:43 (finds any time that is equal to or later than 10:43)

(continued on the next page)

Chapter 9: Searching for Records

	Table 9-1 *(continued)*		
=	An exact match	=Kennedy (finds only records that exactly match this data)
...	Data within a range	80210...80218 (finds zip codes that fall within that range)
!	Duplicate values	! (entered in an ID field, selects all records with duplicate ID numbers)
//	Current date	// (selects all records with today's date in the chosen field)
?	Invalid dates or times	// (entered in a date or time field, finds all records with invalid dates or times)
@	Wildcard for a single character	B@nd (finds Band, Bend, Bind, and Bond)
*	Zero or more characters	B*S (finds BS, bats, and BUSINESS, for example)
" "	Literal text anywhere the field	"Homer" (finds Homer Simpson, Homer's Iliad, and Hi there, within Homer!)

As Table 9-1 illustrates, some symbols must precede the search string, others must surround it, and still others must be embedded within it. The proper use of each kind of search symbol or operator is discussed later in this chapter.

Matching one criterion or another

At times, you may want to search for all records that match any of two or more criteria. This kind of search is known as an *OR* search — as in: "Find all records that match this set of criteria OR that set." For example, you may want to find all Smiths who live in either California or New York. Such a search is quite different from trying to match all of several criteria. For an OR search, you have to fill out a separate Find request for each criterion by choosing New Request from the Edit menu before clicking the Find button. FileMaker Pro combines all the results of two or more Find requests into a single found set. This set combines all records that match any of the search criteria.

Individual Finds Are Not the Same as Multiple Find requests

Each time you switch to Find mode and issue one or more Find requests, two important things happen. First, regardless of which records are currently visible, FileMaker Pro considers *all* records in the search. Second, if you have created multiple Find requests, all requests are carried out at the same time. Thus, you have to use multiple Find requests in an OR search. If, instead, you conduct two separate Finds — the first looking for Smiths from California and the second searching for Smiths from New York — when the second search is executed, only the Smiths from New York appear in the found set. Remember, every Find starts from square one; the effects are not cumulative. On the other hand, a single Find that contains two Find requests — one for California Smiths and another for New York Smiths — will produce the desired results, showing you all Smiths who are from California *or* New York.

Use the following steps to perform a search for data that satisfies the criteria of at least one of several Find requests (an OR search):

1. **In the database that you want to search, switch to a layout that shows all the fields that you want to use for the search.**
2. **Switch to Find mode by using the Mode pop-up menu, choosing Find from the Select menu, or pressing ⌘-F.**

   A blank Find request appears.
3. **Enter the first criterion into the appropriate field.**
4. **If you want to use additional criteria for this Find request (Last Name = Jones and Salary < 25000, for example), tab to the appropriate fields and enter the criteria.**
5. **Choose New Request from the Edit menu (or press ⌘-N).**

   The database window is cleared and a new blank Find request form appears.
6. **Enter the criteria for this Find request into the appropriate field or fields.**
7. **Repeat Steps 5 and 6 until you have created all necessary Find requests.**
8. **Click the Find button or press Return.**

   All Find requests are evaluated, and the found set is presented.

Each time you click Find, all previous searches are cleared. If you want to repeat a search, you can choose the Refind command from the Select menu. You will learn more about performing multiple Find requests later in this chapter.

Matching different kinds of text

By using one of the special symbols that the Find command supports (see Table 9-1), you can make FileMaker Pro do more than locate matches for single words. For example, you can look for a specific text string, accepting no substitutes (Smith, but not Smithers, for example). You also can look for text that contains certain words or phrases. As an example, you can search an Address field for all instances of the word *Drive* — regardless of where the word falls within the field. You also can use this technique to look for pieces of text that aren't contained in the database's index, such as consecutive groups of letters (*mith*, for example). Note that such nonindex searches take much longer to perform, especially in large databases.

Matching text exactly

In a Find request, using the equal sign (=) in a field tells FileMaker Pro to look only for an exact match to the text that you have entered. For example, to find all customers whose last name is Smith, you enter **=Smith** in the Last name field. To locate an exact match to a phrase, you enter the phrase but precede each word by an equal sign (for example, **=Sammy =Smith**).

Chapter 9: Searching for Records

Some "Live" Examples

I realize that after you move beyond a simple one-field search, you can easily get confused. Remembering how to do AND and OR searches, how to look for duplicates, and so on may be difficult for you. Reading about Find mode isn't necessarily the best way to learn about it. You may find this mode easier to understand if you play with it by creating a series of Find requests and seeing what happens. The *FileMaker Pro Bible Disk* contains a folder named FM Pro Bible that includes a Find Examples database where you can see examples of many typical Find requests, each prepared as a script that you can execute with a button-click.

To use the Find Examples database, click any of the buttons on the Menu screen.

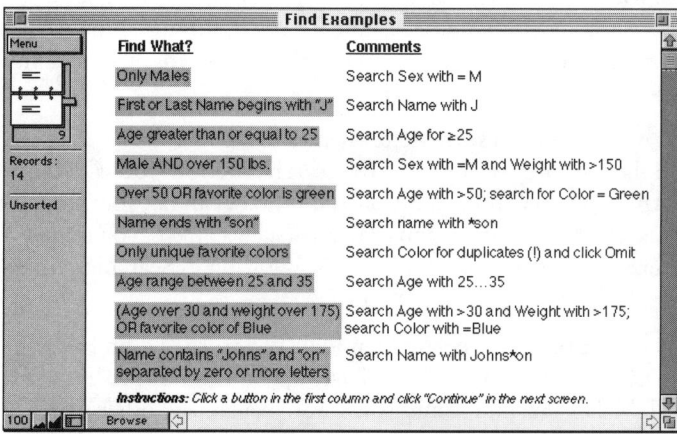

FileMaker Pro enters Find mode and displays another screen that shows the appropriate Find request (the list of Find requests is headed "Find Results"). Because the requests are displayed in list view (each line represents a separate Find request), you can see all the necessary requests on this single screen. After examining the requests, click the Continue button in the status area. The Find requests execute, and the results are displayed. To return to the menu screen, click the Go to Menu button at the bottom of the page.

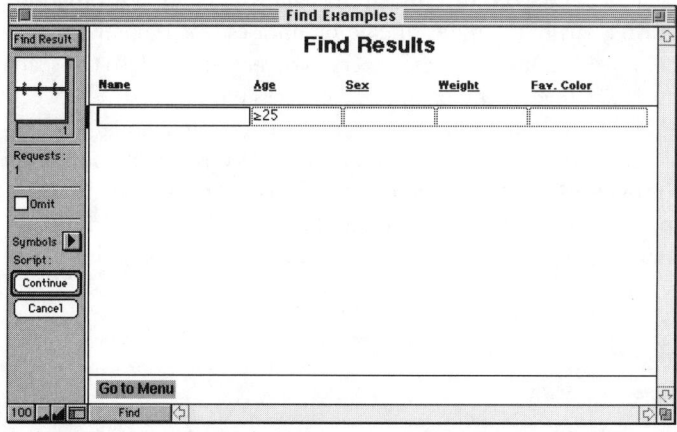

Finding text that's alphabetically above or below a value

You also can look for records that contain values that are less than, less than or equal to, greater than, or greater than or equal to a given value by using the appropriate mathematical symbols. For example, entering **Schwartz** in a Last Name field makes FileMaker Pro search for all last names that are either Schwartz or come alphabetically after Schwartz. To identify only those records for persons with a last name greater than but not including Schwartz (that is, those that come after Schwartz), you use the greater than symbol instead — as in **>Schwartz**.

Using wildcard characters for partial matches

You can search through all indexed items for records that contain a specific group of letters. To do so, you use wildcard characters to represent the missing letters. FileMaker Pro supports @ and * as wildcards. The former stands for a single character, and the latter represents a group of characters that is any length — including zero characters.

If, for example, you want to find all seven-letter names that begin with John, you use three @ signs in the last three positions of the search criterion (**John@@@**). Searching for this string of letters finds Johnson and Johnley but not Johnston. To find all values that start with a certain group of letters (such as *John*), you merely need to enter the exact group without any wildcards following it. Searching using **John** will find John, Johnson, Johnley, and Johnston.

You also can use the wildcard characters in the middle of a word. To find all last names that begin with Smith and end with the letter *n*, you enter **Smith*n** in the Last Name field. FileMaker Pro finds Smithson, Smithsonian, and other words that begin with Smith and end with n. Use the @ sign for words that differ by only a single character. Searching for Sm@th finds both Smith and Smyth, for example.

Nonindexed (literal) text

The preceding text search methods find only indexed text items. You will recall that the *index* is a special part of a FileMaker Pro database in which the program keeps a record of each separate word or value in the database. If you want to look for information that isn't part of the index (including phrases whose component words aren't separated by Option-Space characters), you have to enclose the search text in double-quotes. (When entering data, you can press Option-Space between words to force FileMaker Pro to index a phrase rather than the individual words that make up the phrase.) You can type the quotation marks directly, if you want to, but FileMaker Pro provides a simpler method. You need only choose literal text from the Symbols pop-up menu in the Find mode status area. Doing so immediately enters both open and close double-quotes and puts the insertion point between them.

More About Find Requests

Whenever you switch to Find mode and enter information on the blank form that appears, you're creating a Find request. FileMaker Pro enables you to manipulate Find requests in several ways. You can delete requests or repeat requests, perhaps editing them slightly to alter the search criteria. For example, if you looked for all Smiths from California one time, you could repeat the request and change CA to NY to find all Smiths from New York.

Creating Find requests

Creating a new Find request is easy. FileMaker Pro creates a Find request automatically when you first switch to Find mode so that you can use the request to enter search criteria. You may want to create additional requests, however, as in searching for information that matches one of several criteria (an OR search).

You have two options when you are creating additional Find requests. You can create an entirely new Find request from scratch (by choosing New Request from the Edit menu or pressing ⌘-N), or you can duplicate the current Find request and edit its contents. Until you click the Find button to execute the Find requests, you can use the book icon to page through all current Find requests — just as you use it in Browse mode to leaf through records and in Layout mode to view multiple layouts that you have designed.

Follow these steps to create one or more additional Find requests:

1. **To create a duplicate request, use the book icon to choose an existing Find request to use as a starting point.**
2. **Choose Duplicate Request from the Edit menu (or press ⌘-D).**

   A new Find requests appears that contains the same criteria as the one that was duplicated.

— or —

1. **To create a completely new request, choose New Request from the Edit menu (or press ⌘-N).**

   A new, blank Find request appears.

Repeating and editing Find requests

When you finish entering all the criteria for a Find request and then click the Find button, FileMaker Pro attempts to locate all matching records and then displays them to you in Browse mode as the found set. (If FileMaker Pro does not find any records, you can either modify and repeat the search or cancel the search and return to Browse mode.)

If you switch to Find mode again, FileMaker Pro erases the previous Find requests. However, you may not want to erase them. Odds are, if you are immediately switching back to Find mode, you may be able to use your previous Find requests as the basis for a new search. For example, if a search for Smiths in California doesn't yield results, you may want to go back and look for Smiths in Oregon. FileMaker Pro enables you to repeat the last search, preserving all Find requests that you defined within it. You can edit any or all of these Find requests to match the new requirements.

To repeat or modify the previous set of Find requests, follow these steps:

1. **Choose the Refind command from the Select menu (or press ⌘-R).**

   FileMaker Pro displays the previous set of Find requests.

2. **To simply repeat the last Find request(s), go directly to Step 6.**

   — or —

2. **Use the book icon at the top of the status area to move to the request that you want to edit, if any.**

3. **Use normal editing procedures to change the search criteria in the appropriate fields.**

4. **Repeat Steps 2 and 3 until all Find requests match your new requirements.**

5. *Optional:* **You also can add more requests to the set, duplicate any of the requests, or delete requests (as long as at least one will still remain) by choosing the appropriate commands from the Edit menu (New Request, Duplicate Request, and Delete Request, respectively).**

6. **Click the Find button or press Return.**

   The Find request or requests are executed.

Deleting Find requests

If one or more requests within the current set of Find requests don't meet your needs, you can get rid of them entirely.

To delete one or more Find requests, follow these steps:

1. **To delete all requests and start a Find from scratch, choose Find mode again (or press ⌘-F).**

   — or —

1. **To delete one or more specific requests, use the book icon to move to the request that you want to delete.**

Chapter 9: Searching for Records

2. **Choose Delete Request from the Edit menu (or press ⌘-D).**
3. **Repeat Steps 1 and 2 for each additional request that you want to delete.**

Matching Special Items

You can use Find mode to do more than just look for simple matches. Additional options are available in the Symbols pop-up menu in the status area (see Table 9-1). By using these symbols, you can find all records that have values between two extremes, such as two dates or two salaries. You also can use symbols to perform database maintenance by searching for erroneous or duplicate values and then eliminating the records that contain them.

Matching values in a range

You use the ellipsis symbol (...) to indicate values within a range. You can look for alphabetic values between two text strings, numeric values between two calculated or numeric items, or chronological values between two times or dates. For example, you can search for all records that have last names between Smith and Zane or for all records created between January 1 and December 31, 1994. In the former case, you enter **Smith...Zane** in the Last name field; in the latter case, you type **1/1/94...12/31/94** in the Date field.

To enter a range in a search field, separate the two values by typing three periods, pressing Option-; (semi-colon), or by choosing the... operator from the Symbols pop-up menu.

Matching the current date

Assuming that the system clock in your Macintosh is set correctly (to check the setting, choose the Alarm Clock desk accessory from the Apple menu or examine an appropriate control panel, such as General, General Controls, or Date & Time), you can easily search for records that match the current date, even if you don't happen to know it yourself. This feature is especially handy for inclusion in scripts because you don't need to enter specific information. Instead of having to recreate the script each time (changing the date from 10/5/94 to 10/13/94, for example), you can just instruct it to find today's date — whatever the date happens to be. See Chapter 15 for more information on scripts and their uses.

To find all values that contain the current date, follow these steps:

1. **Within Find mode, move the cursor to the date field in which you want to search.**
2. **Choose the today's date option from the Symbols pop-up menu or type a pair of slashes (//) directly into the field.**
3. **Click Find or press Return to execute the search.**

Searching for empty fields

Occasionally, databases get a bit mucked up. For example, you may create an extra record or two and forget to fill them in, or you may get interrupted and neglect to complete the current record. FileMaker Pro provides a way for you to look for all records that have no information in one or more fields. You simply enter an equal sign (=) — and nothing else — in that field. You can then correct or delete the errant records, as you like.

If you want to find all records that contain one or more blank fields, you need to create a separate Find request for each potentially blank field and then click Find. If you enter all potentially blank fields in a single Find request, FileMaker Pro will find only records in which *all* of these fields are blank. (Remember, when you specify multiple criteria in one Find request, you are conducting an AND search. All criteria must be satisfied in order for the record to be found.) Thus, records that have some fields blank and other fields filled in will not be identified. The correct procedure is to create multiple Find requests — one for each field that you want to check for blanks. (Although this procedure may sound as if it requires a great deal of work, it usually doesn't. In most cases, you want to screen for blanks in a small set of critical fields — those that, if left blank, would render the record useless.

Searching for values that exceed or are less than a given value

In the discussion of text searches, you saw that you can use the <, ≤, >, and ≥ symbols to find text that is alphabetically greater or less than a particular value. You also can use these symbols to find numeric, date, or time values. For example, to find all records dated on or after January 1, 1994, you enter ≥ **1/1/94**.

To match values that exceed or are less than a given value, follow these steps.

1. **Switch to Find mode.**
2. **Move to the field that you want to use in the search.**

Chapter 9: Searching for Records

3. **Choose the appropriate symbol from the Symbols pop-up menu (or type it directly into the field):**
   - ❖ **>** (greater than) to find all items that exceed the value entered
   - ❖ **≥** (greater than or equal to) to find all items that exceed or are exactly equal to the value entered
   - ❖ **<** (less than) to find all items that are smaller than the value entered
   - ❖ **≤** (less than or equal to) to find all items that are smaller than or exactly equal to the value entered

   Note that to type the **<** or **>** symbols, you need to press Option-, (comma) or Option-. (period), respectively.

4. **Type the search value.**
5. **Click Find or press Return to execute the search.**

Searching for duplicates

Find mode can also be used to help you perform another form of database maintenance. You can use it to identify records that have the same information in several fields. Although some people do have the same last names, for example, some such records may be duplicates. If you have checked your mail recently, you have undoubtedly noticed that some direct mail firms are sending you more than one copy of their catalog. They have a problem with duplicate database records — the ones that contain your name. FileMaker Pro has a special symbol that enables you to find all records that have duplicate information in one field. You can then browse these records and eliminate any duplicates.

To search for records that have identical contents in a given field, follow these steps:

1. **Switch to Find mode in the appropriate database.**
2. **Move to the field that you suspect is shared by two or more records.**
3. **Choose duplicates from the Symbols pop-up menu or type a single exclamation point (!).**
4. **Click Find or press Return to execute the Find.**

As when looking for empty fields (discussed previously), if you want to find all records that have duplicate values in one or more of several different fields, you need to create a separate Find request for each such field. Otherwise, you will find only records that match in all potential fields. (Check those catalog mailing labels again. In most cases, you will find that the labels aren't *exactly* the same. Your name may be slightly different on them, for example.) As a rule, you should include only one duplicates criterion in each Find request.

Searching for invalid information

Sometimes, you may find that time and date calculations do not yield valid results, particularly when you work with data that you have imported into FileMaker Pro from another program. FileMaker Pro provides a way to search for records that have invalid dates or times.

1. **Switch to Find mode.**
2. **Move to the date or time field that you suspect of harboring invalid values in some records.**
3. **Enter a question mark (?) or choose invalid date or time from the Symbols pop-up menu.**
4. **Click Find or press Return.**
5. **Examine each record and make the appropriate changes.**

Omitting: Finding records that don't match the criteria

When you are trying to narrow down a search for very specific kinds of records, you may find that a little "negative logic" is a easier to apply than the conventional kind. For example, suppose you want to find all your contacts in every state except California. You can create a separate Find request for each of the other 49 states, but doing so takes quite a while. As an alternative, you can enter **California** in the State field and then elect to omit the records that contain California from the found set. FileMaker Pro makes this task easy. Find mode has an Omit check box in the status area (see Figure 9-1). You click this check box to turn a conventional Find request into one that hides the found records and shows only the records that are left.

To omit records (find all records that do not match the search criteria), do the following:

1. **Switch to Find mode.**
2. **Enter the search criteria in the appropriate fields.**

    Recall that you will be leaving out of the found set all records that match these criteria.

3. **Click the Omit check box in the status area.**
4. **Click the Find button or press Return to execute the Find.**

In a series of Find requests, if you use the Omit option in some but not in others, you should put all Find requests that include the Omit option at the end of your list. FileMaker Pro works through all Find requests in the order that you specify. If you put Omit requests first, later Find requests will tend to wipe out their results.

Chapter 9: Searching for Records

For example, if you want to find all records of employees who are older than 25, or have a salary greater than $27,000, or are not from Houston, you create the following three Find requests, making sure that you create the request that uses the Omit option last:

>25 (in Age field)

>27000 (in Salary field)

=Houston (in City field) and Omit check box checked

Remember that whenever you issue multiple Find requests, you are conducting an OR search — looking for records that satisfy any one or more of the Find requests.

Working with Found Records

After you find records, you can do many things besides just browsing through them. Some of the operations that you can perform are intimately related to the reason that you found the records in the first place. For example, if you searched for duplicate records, you likely did so because you wanted to delete the duplicates. Another thing that you can do with found records is to copy them to the Clipboard and then paste them into another database or even into another program.

Omitting records from a found set

When working with a found set, you may sometimes want to temporarily hide some of the found records. For example, if you have just done a search to identify duplicate records, the found set contains both the original records that you want to keep and the duplicates. Before you can delete the duplicate records, you need to omit the originals from the found set by using the Omit or Omit Multiple commands. (Omitting records merely hide them from view, removing them from the found set. The records still remain in the database, however, and can be revealed with the Find All command.) After omitting the originals from the found set, you can delete the duplicates using the Delete Found Set command (discussed in "Deleting found sets from a database," later in this chapter).

To omit a specific record from a found set, follow these steps:

1. **Use the book icon in the status area to select the record that you want to omit.**

   If the layout is displayed in list view (View as List), you can click in any record to select it.

2. **Choose the Omit command from the Select menu (or press ⌘-M).**

   The specified record is removed from the found set; that is, it is hidden.

3. **Repeat Steps 1 and 2 for each additional record that you want to omit from the found set.**

Part III: Working with Databases

Omit Can Be Used with or without a Found Set

Although the Omit command is most frequently used with a found set (following a Find request), you can use it at any time to temporarily hide some records. In effect, such use of the Omit command manually creates the equivalent of a found set. Suppose, for example, that you are using Want List (provided on the *FileMaker Pro Bible Disk*) to prepare a list of stamps that you want to purchase from a mail-order dealer. After preparing the want list, you can use the Omit command to selectively eliminate several stamps — either because buying them would put you in the poorhouse or because you thought they were currently overpriced.

If a found set contains a range of consecutive records that you want to leave out, you can omit all of them with one command — Omit Multiple:

1. *Optional:* **If the records to be omitted are not grouped consecutively, you may be able to use a Sort command (⌘-S) to group them in the manner desired.**

   See Chapter 10 for information on sorting.

2. **Use the book icon in the status area to select the first record that you want to omit from the found set.**

   If the layout is displayed in list view (View as List), you can click in any record to select it.

3. **Choose the Omit Multiple command from the Select menu or press Shift-⌘-M.**

   The Omit Multiple Dialog box appears (see Figure 9-4).

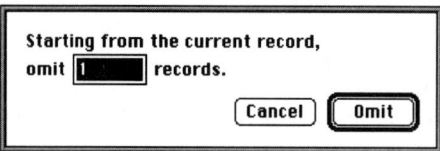

Figure 9-4: The Omit Multiple dialog box.

4. **Enter the number of consecutive records to omit in the dialog box.**
5. **Click the Omit button.**

   The records are omitted; that is, they are hidden from view.

Chapter 9: Searching for Records

If you want to restore all records omitted from a found set, simply use the Refind command to repeat the last Find request. You cannot restore omitted records directly, but you can use other methods to get them back, as you will learn in the next section.

Swapping found sets with omitted records

In the Want List example presented in the sidebar "Omit Can Be Used with or without a Found Set," you learn that you can use the Omit command to hand pick records that you want to remove from a found set. Sometimes, these omitted records are the ones that really interest you. In Want List, for example, you may want to prepare a list of all stamps that you have no interest in buying. Perhaps you want to take the list to stamp shows and to meetings with dealers to prevent yourself from buying something that you don't want or need. By using a special FileMaker Pro command called Find Omitted, you can make the omitted records the new found set. Find Omitted actually swaps the remaining records in the found set with the omitted ones. The omitted records then become the new found set.

Follow these steps to swap a remaining found set with records omitted from it:

1. **Use the Omit or Omit Multiple commands to mark records in a found set that you actually want to keep.**

2. **Choose the Find Omitted command from the Select menu.**

   Omitted records become the new found set, and the remaining records are omitted in their place.

Copying found sets

You can copy an entire found set of records to the Clipboard. From there, you can paste it elsewhere — into documents from other applications, for example. Information in each field is separated from other fields by <u>tabs</u>. Consecutive records are separated by Return characters.

Note that this procedure is a quick-and-dirty version of the Export command with tab-delimited as the selected format. The main difference is that you have less control over the particular fields that are copied and the order in which they are copied. Whatever layout is in effect when you issue the command determines the selected fields and their order.

To copy a found set to the Clipboard, follow these steps:

1. **Switch to Find mode, create a series of Find requests to locate all the records that you want to copy, and click Find.**

   The Find request or requests are executed.

2. **Press Option-⌘-C.**

   The found set is copied to the Clipboard in tab-delimited format.

Deleting found sets

Throughout much of this discussion, I have stressed that one major use for Find mode is to locate records that you want to delete from a database. After you have omitted records that you want to save from a found set, removing the remainder of the records from the database is easier.

Follow these steps to delete records in a found set:

1. **Enter Find mode (⌘-F) and create the Find requests that are necessary to identify the records that you want to delete.**

2. *Optional:* **Examine the found set and use the Omit command to leave out records that you do not want to delete from the database.**

3. **Choose Delete Found Set from the Edit menu.**

   An alert box appears, asking you to confirm that you want to delete the records in question.

4. **Click Delete to proceed or click Cancel to dismiss the alert box without deleting the records.**

   (You can also press Return to cancel.)

Caution: As with other Delete commands in FileMaker Pro, you cannot use the Undo command to undo the Delete Found Set command. Because you risk significant data loss if you make a mistake when you use this command, you may want to make a backup copy of the database by using the Save a Copy As command (described in Chapter 3) before you use the Delete Found Set command.

Replacing values in a found set

Another thing you can do with a found set is replace the contents of a single field in all found records at once (in much the same way as you use a word processor's Find/Replace command). After using Find requests to locate the particular records in which you want to make the replacement, you can use the Replace command to replace the contents of any single field with data that you specify.

This global replacement procedure is useful in many situations. Either of the following situations would be prime candidates for the Replace command:

❖ A company that is included in one of your databases has recently changed its name or moved to a new address. Search for the original name of the company and then use Replace to enter the new name (or the new address) in all found records. If the company had changed *both* its name and address, you could use two Replace procedures on the same found set; first the company name and then the address.

❖ A major kennel association reclassifies a particular breed of pooch as a "working dog." Search for all instances of that breed and then use Replace to change the classification for each of the found dogs.

Chapter 9: Searching for Records

Use the following procedure to replace the contents of one field in all records in the found set:

1. **Switch to Find mode (⌘-F), and use one or more Find requests to select the group of records whose contents you want to replace.**

   This creates the found set.

2. **In Browse mode, select the field you want to replace by tabbing into or clicking in the field.**

   It does not matter what record is currently displayed; any record in the found set will suffice.

3. **Enter the replacement text or value in the field.**

4. **Choose Replace from the Edit menu (or press ⌘-=).**

   The dialog box shown in Figure 9-5 appears.

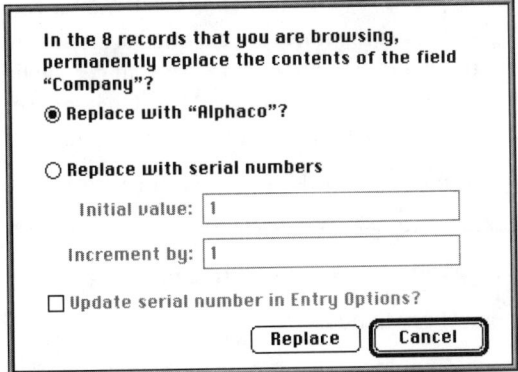

Figure 9-5: Use this dialog box to replace the contents of a field with a single text string or value.

5. **Select the ⌘ Replace with...⌘ radio button option.**

   The replacement text or value is shown within quotes (in Figure 9-5, the replacement text is "Alphaco").

6. **Click Replace.**

   The contents of the current field are replaced with the specified text string or value in all records in the found set.

As you can tell from looking at the dialog box shown in Figure 9-5, you can also use the Replace command to replace the contents of a field in the found set with serial numbers. This option is useful when, for example, you've imported a number of records into a database and have left gaps or otherwise thrown off the existing numbering scheme. You also can use the Replace command to *create* a record-numbering system where none existed before. Simply create a new field to hold the serial numbers, add it to a layout, issue a Find All command (⌘-J), select the field, and then issue the Replace command.

To replace the contents of a field in a found set with serial numbers, do the following:

1. **Switch to Find mode (⌘-F), and use one or more Find requests to select the group of records that you want to renumber.**

   This creates the found set.

2. **In Browse mode, select the field that you wish to reserialize by tabbing into or clicking the field.**

3. *Optional:* **Sort the database by one or more appropriate fields.**

   When the records are reserialized, numbers are assigned according to each record's position within the found set. The first record will get the first new serial number, for example. Using the Sort command (see Chapter 10), you can change the order of the records to a more meaningful arrangement.

4. **Choose the Replace command from the Edit menu (or press ⌘-=).**

   The dialog box shown in Figure 9-5 appears.

5. **Click the Replace with serial numbers radio button.**

   After this button has been clicked, the Initial value and Increment by text boxes can accept values.

6. **In the Initial value text box, enter the value for the new first serial number for the found set.**

7. **In the Increment by text box, enter the value by which each successive serial number should increase over the previous number.**

8. **Click Replace.**

As mentioned elsewhere in the book, a serial number can contain more than just numeric data. If your serial number is a mix of numbers and text, only the numeric portion of the field will change when the field is reserialized. Also, if the selected field was initially defined as an auto-entry field that would receive a serial number, you may wish to click the Update serial number in Entry Options? check box. After you reserialize the found set, checking this option instructs FileMaker Pro to note the last serial number used and to make sure that the next new record created continues the serialization sequence. (It updates the Next Value figure in the Entry Options dialog box for the serial number field.)

Chapter 10: Sorting Records

names are then arranged in order according to their first name. Thus, performing an ascending sort on Last Name and First Name would arrange the Jones records like this:

```
Jones, Abbie
Jones, Evan
Jones, Marcia
```

As you can see, adding First Name as the second sort field re-sorts all records that have the same Last Name.

After you apply the proper sorting options, browsing the database can be much easier — just as the alphabetic ordering of entries makes finding words in a dictionary or names in a phone book easier. What's more, you can organize a database so that using it away from your Mac is easy too. All you have to do is sort the database and then print a copy of the sorted records (see Chapter 13 for information on printing). In this chapter, you learn how to sort a database, set sorting options, and — if need be — restore the records to their original order.

More about Sorting

All computer systems contain data that has to be located from time to time. The rapidity with which this information can be located is of critical importance to the system's overall speed and efficiency. Because searching through ordered information is easier than searching through random information (both for the computer and for the computer's human users), the process of sorting has been and continues to be an important topic in computer science research.

One of the simplest sorting methods — frequently taught to beginning computer science students — is the *bubble sort*. In this sort method (or *algorithm*), each record is compared with the first record. If the two records are out of order, they are swapped, which causes the record that was being compared with the first record to become the new first record. After all records have been compared with the first record, the sort moves on to the second record and repeats the process. Every subsequent record is then compared with the second record. Swapping occurs if the two records are found to be out of order. The procedure continues for the third and every subsequent record down to the next-to-last record. Records are said to *bubble up* into the correct order (hence, the name of the algorithm).

The bubble sort works, but it consumes copious quantities of computing power and is very slow, especially when you use it with a large database. A more efficient method is the *binary sort,* which involves making comparisons within increasingly small subdivisions of the list that is being sorted. The binary sort uses far fewer steps for large databases than does the bubble sort. Other sort methods also exist.

You should note that the true storage order for a database is rarely (if ever) changed by a sort operation. Physically moving records to reflect a new database order is inefficient and unnecessary. Instead, the current sorted order of the database is often maintained within a separate list. This list shows which record is currently first, second, and so on. Normally, only this list (or *index*) is physically changed when a database is sorted.

Part III: Working with Databases

Creating a Sort Order

Prior to sorting a database, you need to make three basic decisions:

- *Whether to sort the entire database or sort only part of it:* By using Find requests, Omit commands, or Omit Multiple commands (see Chapter 9), you can restrict the visible portion of any database to a selected set of records. As with most FileMaker Pro commands, sorting affects only records that are currently visible.

- *The field or fields on which to sort:* Which fields you sort on depends on how you want to use the database. Use the field or fields that are presently of the greatest importance to you as the sort fields. For example, in a customer database, you may be concerned with sales totals. Sorting on the Total field enables you to easily see which customers are big buyers and which ones have recently bought little or nothing from you.

- *Whether records should be arranged in ascending, descending, or a custom order:* Text data is usually more useful when you sort it in ascending order. That is, you normally want to see the *A* entries first, rather than the *Z* entries. Numeric information, on the other hand, is frequently more useful when you view it in descending order. When you examine file sizes or cost figures, for example, your primary interest will often be in the largest files or the biggest dollar amounts.

    If you have defined a value list for a field, you can sort according to the order set in the value list. This is a great approach for organizing records in a specific order that is neither alphabetic nor numeric. For example, you may have a value list that consists of the department names of your company organized in a specific order. When you sort according to this value list (rather than alphabetically, as you normally might), you can assure that people in Administration will be listed before those in Accounting, for instance. See the section, "Additional Sorting Options," at the end of this chapter for details.

No matter how you organize a database's records, you sort by choosing the Sort command from the Select menu (or by pressing ⌘-S). The Sort Records dialog box appears, in which you can specify sorting options (see Figure 10-2).

In the Field List area on the left side of the Sort Records dialog box is a list of the fields by which you can sort the database. Eligible sort fields include all fields that you have defined for the database — not just the ones that appear on the current layout. Note, however, that you can choose Summary fields as sort fields only if you have checked the Include Summary fields check box (for details, see the "Sorting by Summary fields" section, near the end of this chapter).

Chapter 10: Sorting Records

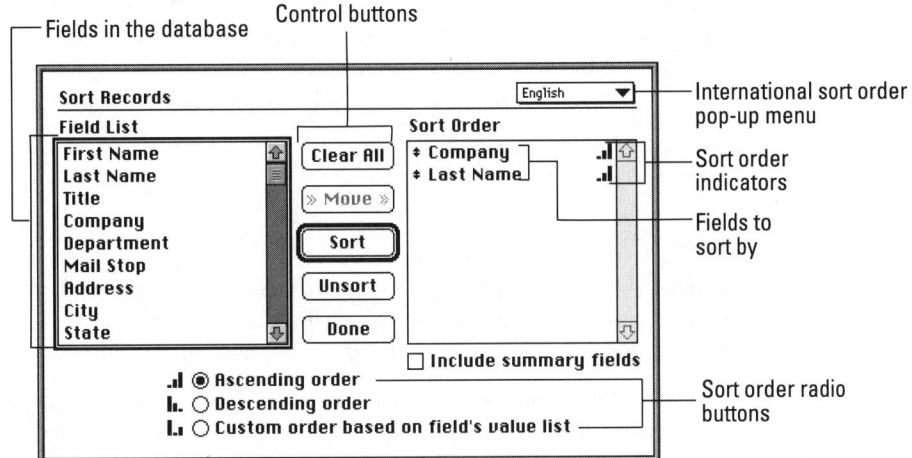

Figure 10-2: The Sort Records dialog box.

In the Sort Order area on the right side of the dialog box is a list of the currently chosen sort fields. The order in which the fields appear corresponds to the order in which the database will be sorted. In Figure 10-2, for example, the database will first be sorted by Company. Within each company, records will be re-sorted by each person's last name. An icon next to each field name in the Sort Order list indicates the sort order (ascending or descending). The icons correspond to the sort order options that are displayed at the bottom of the dialog box.

The buttons in the center of the dialog box enable you to control the Sort Order list. At the bottom of the dialog box are three radio buttons that you can use to specify, for each sort field, whether you want an ascending sort, a descending sort, or a sort based on the field's value list. The pop-up menu in the upper-right corner of the dialog box enables you to specify an international sorting convention, if desired (see the "Setting an international sort order" section, later in the chapter).

The following is a brief explanation of each component in the Sort Records dialog box:

❖ *Clear All*: This command removes all fields from the current Sort Order list. Use Clear All when you want to define a sort order from scratch and ignore any fields that are presently selected.

❖ *Move:* Click this button to copy the selected field from the Field List to the Sort Order list. Use Move to select each field by which you intend to sort.

- *Clear:* When you select a field in the Sort Order list, this button replaces the Move button. Click Clear when you want to remove the selected field from the Sort Order list. (Clear enables you to selectively remove fields from the Sort Order list. Use Clear All to remove all fields from the Sort Order list.)
- *Sort:* Click this button to sort the database according to the current specifications and options.
- *Unsort:* This command "undoes" any current sort operation and restores the records to their original order (that is, the order in which you entered them into the database). You seldom need to restore records to the original order — unless, of course, you originally created or imported the records in some meaningful order that you cannot duplicate by using a Sort command.
- *Done:* This command dismisses the Sort Records dialog box without sorting but preserves any changes that you have made to the sort specifications.
- *Include summary fields:* This check box specifies whether to include Summary fields as eligible sort fields. If it is not checked, Summary field names are grayed out (dimmed) — meaning that you cannot use them as part of the sort settings.
- *Ascending order:* Choosing this radio button sorts the selected field from the lowest value to the highest value ("A" to "Z," for example).
- *Descending order:* Choosing this radio button sorts the selected field from the highest value to the lowest value.
- *Custom order based on field's value list:* If you have prepared a value list as part of a field's definition (see Chapter 5), you can select this radio button option for that field. It instructs FileMaker Pro to use the order of the field's value list as the sort order for the field. The days of the week in chronological order may constitute such a value list. Using this value list, records sorted according to a Day field would appear in the order Sunday, Monday, Tuesday, and so on, rather than in ascending or descending alphabetical order.

Sorting on one field

The simplest and most common kind of sort is one that is based on a single field — sorting only by Zip Code, Invoice Total, Age, or Grade Point Average, for example. Depending on the complexity of their databases, many users find that the majority of their sorts use only a single sort field. The following steps describe how to sort on one field:

1. **Decide whether you want to sort the entire database or only selected records.**

Chapter 10: Sorting Records

2. Use the Find, Omit, and Omit Multiple commands to select the records of interest (see Chapter 9 for instructions).

   FileMaker sorts only those records that are currently visible (those that are being browsed).

   — or —

2. If you are currently browsing only a subset of records and want to sort the entire database, choose Find All from the Select menu (or press ⌘-J).

3. **Choose Sort from the Select menu (or press ⌘-S).**

   The Sort Records dialog box appears (refer to Figure 10-2).

4. **If the Sort Order list includes fields by which you do not intend to sort, click Clear All to remove them all or individually select each field and click Clear.**

   Note that if you have not sorted the database before, the Sort Order list will already be clear.

5. **In the scrolling Field List (on the left side of the dialog box), click the name of the field by which you want to sort.**

6. **At the bottom of the dialog box, click a radio button to indicate the sort order for that field.**

   ❖ Click Ascending order to start with the smallest numeric value and end with the largest, to sort words alphabetically (from *A* to *Z*), and to arrange times and dates chronologically.

   ❖ Click Descending order to start with the largest numeric value and end with the smallest, to sort words in reverse alphabetic order (from *Z* to *A*), and to arrange times and dates from most recent to oldest.

   ❖ Click Custom order based on field's value list to use a value list that you have defined for the field. (You can select this option only if you have already defined a value list for the chosen field.)

7. **Click Move to transfer the field to the Sort Order list.**

   — or —

7. **Double-click the field name to simultaneously select it in the Field List and move it to the Sort Order list.**

8. **Click Sort to sort the database in the specified order by the selected field.**

   When the sort is finished, the status area changes to show that the database has been sorted, as shown in Figure 10-3. The new first record in the sorted database appears in the document window.

Part III: Working with Databases

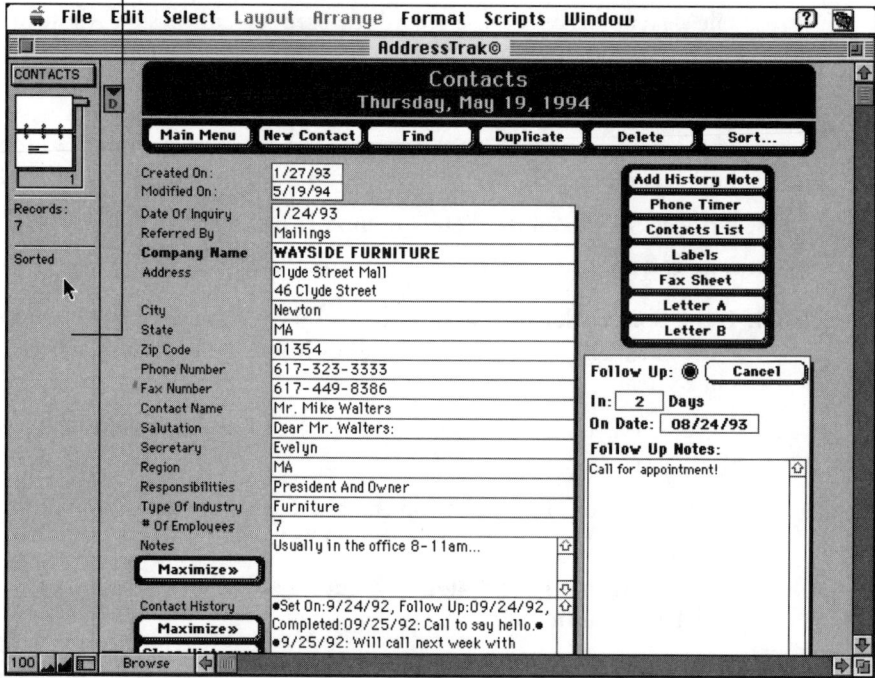

Figure 10-3: A sorted database.

Canceling a Sort Operation

Sometimes in the middle of a sort operation, you may decide that you want to sort on different fields than the ones you have chosen. Instead of waiting for FileMaker Pro to finish sorting the database, you can cancel the sort by pressing ⌘-. (period). This feature is especially helpful when the database is large and the sort operation is lengthy.

Sorting on several fields

As mentioned earlier in the chapter, sorting by a single field isn't always sufficient, particularly in a database in which several records may have the same value in the sort field. In such a case, you may want to further organize the records by specifying additional sort fields.

As an example, you may have several records for people who have the same last name. Sorting only by Last Name will leave the first names in whatever order the records were in when you originally entered them. (Can you imagine what a mess a metropolitan phone directory would be in if it were sorted only by last name? Try finding Jake Johnson in a 20-page listing of Johnsons!) Selecting First Name as the second sort field is often a smart move. And if you believe (or know) that in several instances people have the same last and first names, you can consider adding a third sort field, such as Phone Number, Address, or Age.

When specifying multiple sort fields, select them in the order of their importance. Fields further down in the Sort Order list are merely tie-breakers, as illustrated in Figure 10-4. Working with the Address Book database, you may decide that your main interest is in companies, rather than in people, and choose Company as the first sort field. If you have multiple contacts at various companies, you can use Last Name or Department as the second sort field. If the companies are very large, you also may want to select a third sort field, such as First Name.

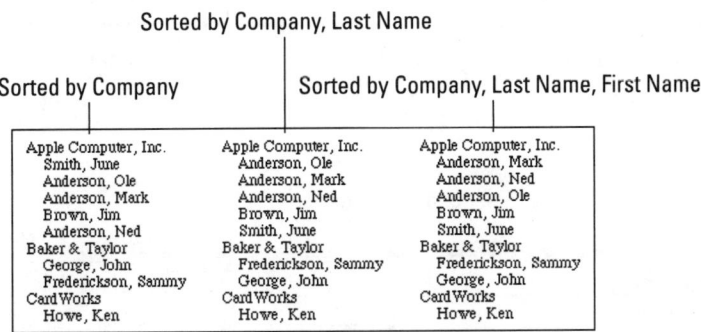

Figure 10-4: As additional sort fields are added, the ordering of the records becomes progressively more useful.

The following steps describe how to sort a database on multiple fields:

1. **Open the database and choose Sort from the Select menu (or press ⌘-S).**

   The Sort Records dialog box appears (refer to Figure 10-2).

2. **In the Field List, click to select the first field by which you want to sort.**

3. **At the bottom of the dialog box, click a radio button to indicate the sort order for that field.**

    ❖ Click Ascending order to start with the smallest numeric value and end with the largest, to sort words alphabetically (from *A* to *Z*), and to arrange times and dates chronologically.

    ❖ Click Descending order to start with the largest numeric value and end with the smallest, to sort words in reverse alphabetic order (from *Z* to *A*), and to arrange times and dates from most recent to oldest.

    ❖ Click Custom order based on the field's value list to use a value list that you have defined for the field. (You can select this option only if you have already defined a value list for the chosen field.)

4. **Click Move to transfer the field to the Sort Order section of the dialog box.**

5. **Repeat Steps 2 through 4 to move additional fields into the Sort Order list.**

6. **Click Sort.**

Note: If you discover that the fields in the Sort Order list are in the wrong order, you don't have to clear them and start over. You can rearrange the fields by simply dragging any of them to new positions in the list. To rearrange them, move the pointer over the double-headed arrow in front of any field name in the Sort Order list. When the pointer changes to a large double-headed arrow, click and drag the field to its new position (see Figure 10-5). Release the mouse button when the field is in the proper position within the list.

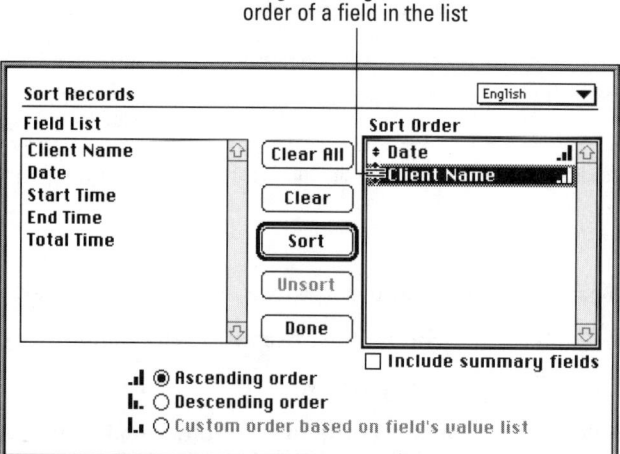

Figure 10-5: Changing the sort order by dragging a field to a new position in the list.

Chapter 10: Sorting Records

Sorting on Multiple Fields vs. Performing Multiple Sorts

Performing a sort that includes multiple sort fields is not the same as performing several successive sorts that use those same fields. Every sort always starts from the original record order — not from the order that is currently displayed on-screen.

For example, if you sort a database by Company and Last Name, the records are arranged in order according to Company. Within every company, records are further arranged alphabetically by the employees' last names. On the other hand, if you perform two sorts — the first by Company and the second by Last Name — each sort works independently of the other; that is, the effects are not cumulative. The first sort arranges records in Company order. The second merely arranges the records according to Last Name, completely ignoring the results of the initial sort.

Modifying Sort Specifications

After you define a sort for a database and set options, you may later decide that you want to change some of the options or perhaps sort on different fields. Although you can click Clear All in the Sort Records dialog box and then specify new sorting instructions from scratch, changing the appropriate options is often easier, as the following sections describe.

Changing sort fields

Depending on your current needs, you may want to change one or more of the fields by which you are sorting. When you are browsing through the Address Book database, for example, you may sometimes want to view the records in Company order and, at other times, want them arranged by Last Name. If you are printing mailing labels, you (or the post office) may prefer that the letters or post cards be sorted by Zip Code. When you are creating a monthly departmental report, you may want to organize the database by employee or project. When your sorting needs change, you can readily choose different sort fields, as the following steps describe:

1. **With the database document open, choose Sort from the Select menu (or press ⌘-S).**

    The Sort Records dialog box appears (refer to Figure 10-2).

Part III: Working with Databases

2. Remove any fields that you no longer need from the Sort Order list by selecting the field's name in the Sort Order list and then clicking Clear to remove it.

— or —

2. Click Clear All to remove all fields from the Sort Order list simultaneously.

3. In the Field List, click to select the first new field by which you intend to sort.

4. At the bottom of the dialog box, click a radio button to indicate the sort order for that field.

   ❖ Click Ascending order to start with the smallest numeric value and end with the largest, to sort words alphabetically (from *A* to *Z*), and to arrange times and dates chronologically.

   ❖ Click Descending order to start with the largest numeric value and end with the smallest, to sort words in reverse alphabetic order (from *Z* to *A*), and to arrange times and dates from most recent to oldest.

   ❖ Click Custom order based on the field's value list to use a value list that you have defined for the field. (You can select this option only if you have already defined a value list for the chosen field.)

5. Click Move (or double-click the field's name) to place the selected field in the Sort Order list.

6. Repeat Steps 3 through 5 for any additional sort fields that you want to use.

7. If the order of fields in the Sort Order list is incorrect, click and drag the field names to new positions in the list (as explained earlier in this chapter).

8. Click Sort to sort the database by the new fields.

Changing the sort order

Without changing the field or fields on which you are sorting, you can alter the sort order of any field to ascending, descending, or according to a value list that has been defined for the field. For example, in creating an in-house report on employees, you may perform an ascending sort by Salary or Employment Date and then decide that having the same sort in descending order is preferable.

Chapter 10: Sorting Records

The following steps describe how to change the sort order:

1. **With the database document open, choose Sort from the Select menu (or press ⌘-S).**

    The Sort Records dialog box appears (refer to Figure 10-2).

2. **Click the sort field's name in the Sort Order list to select it.**

    To modify a setting for any field, you first need to select the field.

3. **At the bottom of the dialog box, click a radio button to indicate the sort order for that field.**

    ❖ Click Ascending order to start with the smallest numeric value and end with the largest, to sort words alphabetically (from *A* to *Z*), and to arrange times and dates chronologically.

    ❖ Click Descending order to start with the largest numeric value and end with the smallest, to sort words in reverse alphabetic order (from *Z* to *A*), and to arrange times and dates from most recent to oldest.

    ❖ Click Custom order based on the field's value list to use a value list that you have defined for the field. (You can choose this option only if you have already defined a value list for the chosen field.)

4. **If you want to specify a different sort order for additional sort fields, repeat Steps 2 and 3.**

5. **Click Sort to re-sort the database according to the new order.**

The Need for Re-Sorting

FileMaker Pro tries to maintain the current sort order for a database, even when you add new records after you have sorted. Because it doesn't do a perfect job, however, you see Semi-sorted, rather than Sorted, in the status area. To ensure that all records are correctly sorted, you need to use the Sort command again after you add new records. FileMaker Pro records the last set of sort instructions that you use, so re-sorting the database is as simple as choosing the Sort command and then immediately pressing Return (the equivalent of clicking the Sort button).

Executing a Find request, on the other hand, has a more profound effect on the current sort order: It obliterates it. The new condition of the database is reported as Unsorted in the status area. Thus, you will usually want to re-sort the database following a Find request.

Additional Sorting Options

You can sort a database in more than one way. The Sort command offers additional capabilities, many of which are useful for tasks such as preparing reports. You can sort a database in the order defined in a field's value list, sort by Summary fields, sort in a way that makes the organization of records more useful for individuals in a different country, and restore the records to the order in which they were entered in the database.

Using a value list for a sort

Ascending and descending sorts aren't always appropriate. If you sorted the months of the year in ascending order, you would end up with an alphabetized list that started with April and August and ended with September — probably not what you had in mind. Sorting according to the order defined in a value list offers a way around such problems.

A *value list*, created as part of a field's entry options, displays the acceptable values for that field in a preset order. You can sort the database by any field that has an attached value list and substitute the order defined in the value list for the normal alphabetic, numeric, and chronological orders used by ascending and descending sorts.

To sort according to a value list, click the Custom order based on field's value list radio button in the Sort Records dialog box (refer to Figure 10-2). When you select this option, the order used for the sort matches the order in which the various values (entry options) appear in the value list. As shown in the example in Figure 10-6, a value list for a Payment Method field may list various payment methods according to their frequency of use. When the field is sorted, cash transactions will come first, checks will follow next, and individual credit card charges will appear last.

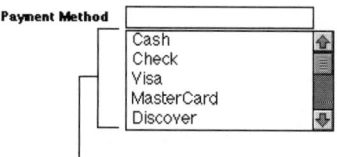

A value list for the
Payment Method field

Figure 10-6: Sorting by a field's value list is appropriate when you want records sorted in a special, predetermined order, rather than alphabetically, numerically, or chronologically.

Chapter 10: Sorting Records — 307

The Handling of "Other..." Choices

When you create a value list for a field, providing an "Other..." choice as a catchall is often helpful. In performing an ascending or descending sort on such a field, FileMaker Pro arranges the records in which "Other..." was selected according to the actual contents of the field. That is, it does not group all of them together as though they all contained the same value. On the other hand, when FileMaker Pro performs a Custom sort that is based on a field's value list, it groups all records in which "Other..." was chosen at the end of the database, followed only by records in which nothing was chosen for the field. (The procedure for adding an "Other..." choice to a value list is explained in Chapter 5.)

Setting an international sort order

Different countries follow different conventions for sorting data. Many countries use a non-Latin alphabet, for example; and other differences exist between countries that use the Latin alphabet. FileMaker Pro enables you to select an international sorting convention by choosing a language. The available languages appear in a pop-up menu in the upper-right corner of the Sort Records dialog box (see Figures 10-2 and 10-7).

Figure 10-7: Setting an international sort order.

To choose a sorting convention, click the pop-up menu, drag until you highlight the language of choice, and then release the mouse button. Note that the sort language is document specific. If you want to select any sort language other than English for your databases, you must set it individually for each database.

Part III: Working with Databases

Sorting by Summary fields

As you may recall from Chapter 5, a *Summary field* summarizes information from a single field across a series of records. For example, a Sale Total field may combine individual orders into one sales figure for all records that you are currently browsing.

When placed in a data-entry layout, the data in many Summary fields is the same, no matter which record you're currently viewing. For example, any Total or Average Summary field always shows the same total or average, regardless of which record is currently visible. For this reason, sorting by a Summary field makes more sense in a report layout than in a data entry layout, for example.

Here's a concrete example. Suppose you want to create a report that shows total sales for each member of your company's sales force. To accomplish this task, all you need to do is create a layout that contains a sub-summary part, define the part as being a "Sub-summary when sorted by Salesperson," and then place the Sale Total Summary field in the sub-summary part. To view the report, sort by Salesperson and then print or preview the report. (As explained in Chapter 6, you must sort before printing or switching to Preview mode if you want the information in the sub-summary part to display correctly.)

These steps accomplish two things. First, the sort specifications group sales by salesperson. All of Bob's sales are listed together, for example, instead of being scattered throughout the database. Second, adding the Summary field enables you to see an individual sales total for each salesperson. The report is shown in Figure 10-8.

Figure 10-8: The report generated when sorted by Salesperson.

Chapter 10: Sorting Records

Note, however, that what you have accomplished so far has been done without sorting by the Summary field. Although the salespeople are effectively grouped (all Marjorie's sales are listed together), arranging the groups in alphabetical order is not necessarily the most informative manner of presenting the data. If you add the Sale Total Summary field to the Sort Order list and sort the database again, the report becomes even more useful. As Figure 10-9 shows, not only are the records still grouped by salesperson, but they are arranged in order of increasing sales (Marjorie, Bob, and Jim).

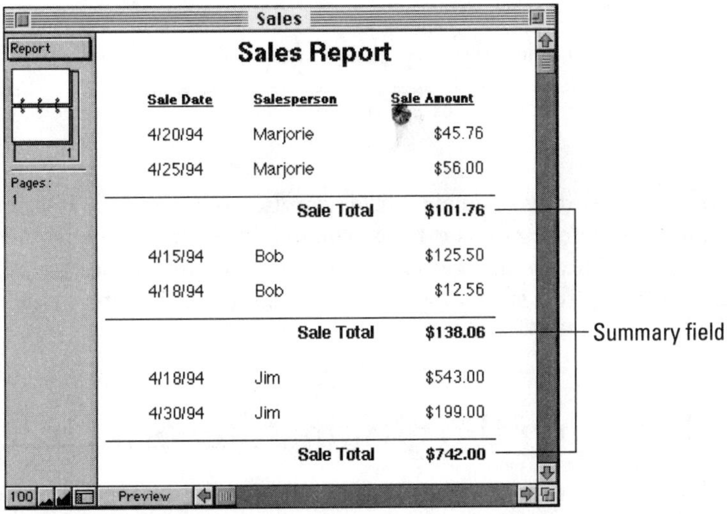

Figure 10-9: A report sorted by a Summary field.

To sort by one or more Summary fields, you need to set the Include summary fields option in the Sort Records dialog box (see Figure 10-10). Choose Sort from the Select menu (or press ⌘-S) and then click the Include summary fields check box in the Sort Records dialog box. Any Summary fields that are visible in the Field List change from being dimmed to being normal, selectable fields, and you can move the desired Summary fields into the Sort Order list. As with other sort fields, you can sort a Summary field in ascending or descending order. However, because you cannot create a value list for a Summary field, you cannot select the Custom sort option for such a field.

Part III: Working with Databases

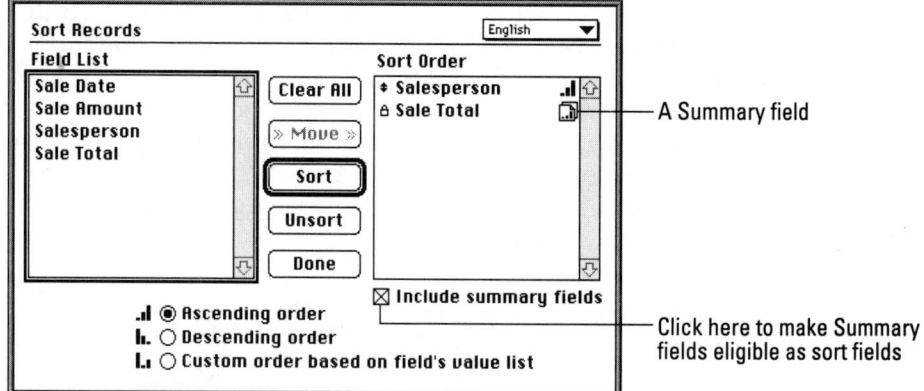

Figure 10-10: Enabling Summary fields to be included in a sort.

If you want to sort by a Summary field, you also need to include at least one non-Summary field among the sort fields. You should note that although the Summary fields always appear at the bottom of the Sort Order list, they are treated as the primary sort fields (that is, they have a higher precedence than non-Summary sort fields.)

Unsort: Restoring the Original Record Order

Nothing is forever. If you want to restore the records in a database to their original order — the order in which you entered them — you can easily do so by following these steps:

1. **Open the database and choose the Sort command from the Select menu (or press ⌘-S).**

   The Sort Records dialog box appears (refer to Figure 10-2).

2. **Click the Unsort button.**

   Records revert to being displayed in the order in which you entered them. (Note that this order is the actual order in which records are stored, even after you sort them.)

Remember that you do not need to Unsort before issuing a new Sort command. Every sort operates on the records in their original order (as you entered them in the database), not on the currently visible sort order.

Chapter 10: Sorting Records — 311

Special Sorting Tips and Considerations

Although the examples in this chapter concentrate on sorting the contents of Text and Number fields, you can sort records based on the contents of any field other than a Picture/Sound field. For example, sorting by date is frequently useful (when you are organizing a check register, for example). And if you were recording harness racing results, you might well want to sort by finish time. Calculation fields, such as sales totals, also are often useful as sort fields.

Here are some additional sorting tips that you may find helpful:

❖ If you need to sort on a Picture/Sound field, create an additional field (normally a Text field) that describes or names the picture, movie, or sound in the Picture/Sound field and sort on the text field instead.

❖ If you sort on a field that has been declared a repeating field, FileMaker bases the sort only on the contents of the first entry in the field.

❖ When you include a sort in a FileMaker Pro script, you don't need to sort the database before you define the script. Just set sort options and click Done in the Sort Records dialog box. You dismiss the dialog box without sorting but save the sorting instructions. (However, if you want to be certain that the sort results are as you intended, you may want to perform the sort anyway.)

CHAPTER 10 CONCEPTS AND TERMS

- Sorting is the process of arranging a group of records into a specific order. The mechanics of sorting is an important topic in computer science.
- A sort operation is based on the value of one or more fields in the records to be sorted.
- You can use any field type other than a Picture/Sound field as the basis for a sort.
- Sorting does not change the physical location of records in a database. Records are always stored in the order in which you entered them. As a result, you can easily restore the display order of records in a database to the order in which you entered them.
- Sorting is often an important step in preparing a database report.

algorithm
A series of steps for accomplishing a specific task.

ascending sort
A sorting order that starts with the smallest (or oldest) value and ends with the largest (or most recent) value. For numbers, values begin with the smallest value and proceed in numerical order. For text, values start with *A* and go through *Z*. Dates and times are sorted in chronological order. In fields that contain mixed data types (text, numbers, and characters), numbers come first.

descending sort
A sorting order that starts with the largest (or most recent) value and ends with the least (or oldest) value. An alphabetic sort in descending order begins with *Z*.

index
An internal list that many database programs maintain to show the sorted record order. Instead of physically rearranging records after a sort, the database keeps records in the same order and consults the index to display the records in the desired sort order.

report
A copy of selected information from a database, consisting of specified records in a certain layout, presented in a particular sort order.

sort
To arrange information in order, according to specific criteria.

sort order
The order in which a field is sorted. Every FileMaker Pro database field can be sorted in one of three sort orders: ascending, descending, or according to the field's value list (if one has been defined).

value list
A list of acceptable choices or values that are defined for a field. Using value lists can help speed data entry and ensure the consistency of information. Value lists can be displayed as pop-up lists, pop-up menus, radio buttons, or check boxes.

CHAPTER ELEVEN

Using the Spelling Checker

- Setting spell-checking options
- Checking spelling on the fly and on command
- Installing alternative dictionaries
- Creating, adding words to, and merging user dictionaries

The spelling checker provided with FileMaker Pro 2 includes a dictionary that is shared with all other Claris programs that use a spelling checker. Located in the Claris folder inside the System folder of the startup disk, the Main Dictionary file contains the spellings of approximately 100,000 words.

Of course, no dictionary that has been prepared for general use will contain the spellings of all of the words that are relevant to your business or your life. For example, you are not likely to find many company names, people's names, or technical terms in the Main Dictionary. Rather than having the spelling checker flag each of these items as a *questionable spelling* (the term that the spelling checker uses to indicate a word that it does not have in its dictionaries), you can create *user dictionaries* that contain other words that are important to you.

When you install FileMaker Pro, it creates the first user dictionary for you (appropriately enough, it's called User Dictionary). To start you off on the right foot, User Dictionary contains the spellings of three Claris products that didn't make it into the Main Dictionary: AppleWorks, ClarisWorks, and FileMaker.

Setting Spell-Checking Options

FileMaker Pro provides two ways for you to check spelling. You can check spelling on the fly (as you type, FileMaker Pro automatically checks each word against the words in the current main Dictionary and user Dictionary), or you can check spelling on request (FileMaker Pro examines the current record, set of found records, text selection, or layout only when you choose the appropriate command from the Spelling submenu). This type of spell checking is also referred to as *batch mode*. If you want spelling to be checked as you type, you have to set an option in the Spelling Options dialog box. The following steps describe how to set spell-checking options:

Part III: Working with Databases

1. Choose Spell Options from the Spelling submenu of the Edit menu.

   The Spelling Options dialog box appears (see Figure 11-1).

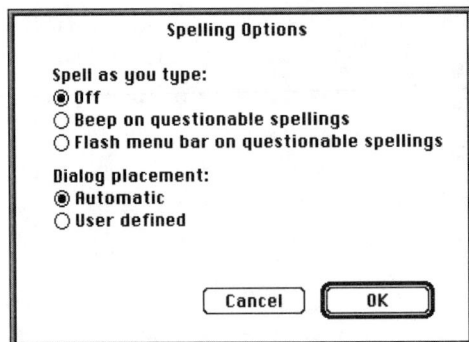

Figure 11-1: The Spelling Options dialog box.

2. If you want spelling to be checked as you type, click either of these two radio buttons:

   ❖ Beep on questionable spellings

   ❖ Flash menu bar on questionable spellings

   The advantage of checking as you type is that you can react immediately and correct the errors as the spelling checker discovers them. And you're still free to ignore the beeps or flashes if you would prefer to continue typing and make corrections later.

   If FileMaker Pro is currently set to check spelling as you type, you can switch to checking spelling on request by clicking the Off radio button.

3. Click the radio button labeled User defined in the Dialog placement option to specify a preferred location for the Spelling dialog box.

   After checking the box, the next time you spell check your database, you can place the spelling dialog where you want it. It will now be positioned there every time you need it.

4. To save changes that you make to the spelling options, click OK; to ignore the changes, click Cancel.

Checking Your Spelling

As mentioned previously, FileMaker Pro can check spelling in two ways: on the fly (checking as you type) or on request (examining a record, a group of records, a text selection, or labels in a layout only when you choose the appropriate command from the Spelling submenu). Because spell-checking on request is more common, it is discussed first.

Spell-checking on request

By selecting the appropriate command from the Spelling submenu of the Edit menu (see Figure 11-2), you can request that spelling be checked for any of the following:

❖ Currently selected text

❖ The current record

❖ The current set of Found (visible) records

❖ Labels in the current layout

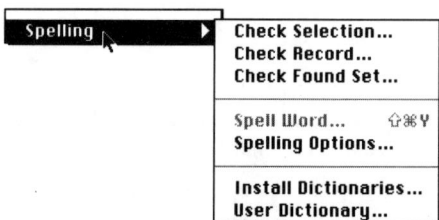

Figure 11-2: The Spelling submenu.

In preparation for a spell-checking session, you need to decide what you want to check and then follow the instructions for that kind of spell checking:

❖ *To check selected text:* In Browse mode (press ⌘-B), use normal text selection techniques to select text within a field. The amount of text can be as little as a single word or as much as the entire contents of the field. To begin the spelling check, choose Check Selection from the Spelling submenu of the Edit menu. The Check Selection command is particularly useful when you want to restrict a spell check to a single field rather than examine the entire record.

❖ *To check the current record:* In Browse mode (press ⌘-B), choose Check Record from the Spelling submenu of the Edit menu. The spelling of all data in all fields is checked. If you've just added a new record, for example, this command enables you to check just that record.

Part III: Working with Databases

❖ *To check the found set:* To restrict the spelling check to a subset of the records, issue a Find, Omit, or Omit Multiple command to select a group of records. If you prefer to check all records in the database, choose Find All from the Select menu (or press ⌘-J). (Following a Find request, the database automatically switches to Browse mode.) Choose Check Found Set from the Spelling submenu of the Edit menu. FileMaker Pro checks the spelling of all data in all fields of the visible (found) records. For more information on using Find mode and omitting or selecting records, refer to Chapter 9.

❖ *To check the current layout:* Select the layout of interest by choosing it from the layout pop-up menu in the upper-left corner of the database window, change to Layout mode (press ⌘-L), and then select Check Layout from the Spelling submenu of the Edit menu. (Note that the Check Layout command appears in the menu only when you are in Layout mode.) This command is most useful after you've designed a new layout or altered an existing one, and you want to make certain that all field labels and other static text on the layout is spelled correctly.

After you decide what you want to check, proceed with the spell-checking operation:

1. **Choose the appropriate command from the Spelling submenu (Check Selection, Check Record, Check Found Set, or Check Layout).**

    The Spelling dialog box appears (see Figure 11-3).

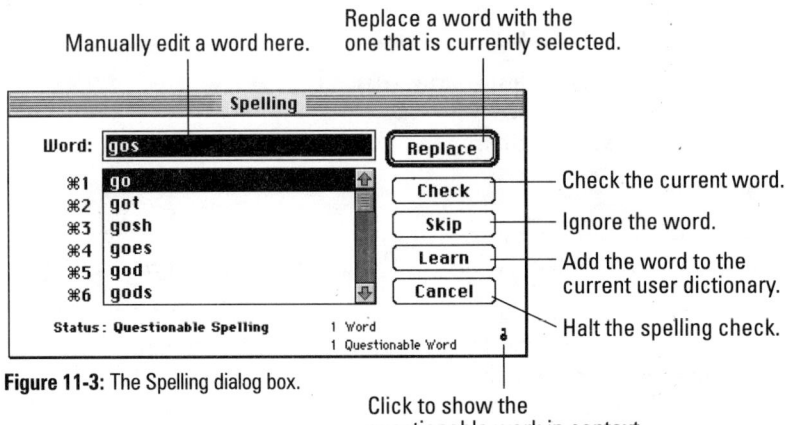

Figure 11-3: The Spelling dialog box.

The spelling checker identifies the first questionable spelling (if it finds one) and inserts a copy of it in the Word box of the Spelling dialog box.

If you prefer to see questionable words in context (within the sentence or phrase in which each one is embedded), click the tiny flag in the lower-right corner of the Spelling dialog box. In addition to appearing in the Word box, the word also appears in context at the bottom of the dialog box.

2. For each questionable spelling that the spelling checker identifies, perform one of these actions:

   ❖ **Replace button.** Use Replace to select a replacement word from the list of words that is provided. Either highlight the appropriate word and click Replace or type the word's Command-key equivalent (⌘-1 through ⌘-6). In either case, the questionable word is replaced by the selected word, and the spelling check continues.

   Note that in some cases, the spelling checker offers more replacement words than can fit on a single screen. You can use the scroll bar to see the additional word choices. Each time you scroll, the new words are assigned their own Command-key equivalents.

   ❖ **Skip button.** Click the Skip button to ignore the questionable word here and throughout the rest of text to be examined. You usually use Skip when you know that a word is spelled correctly, but you do not want to add it to the current user dictionary. For example, the last name Lundeen is not in the Main Dictionary, but, unless it's your last name or the name of an associate with whom you frequently correspond, you probably have no reason to add it to a user dictionary.

   ❖ **Learn button.** Click Learn to accept the word's spelling and add it to the current user dictionary. If you're certain that a word is spelled correctly and you want it to be known in future spell-checking sessions, click the Learn button. (A *user dictionary* records the spellings of words that you've added with the Learn command. By supporting user dictionaries, the spelling checker is not limited to just those words that are included in its *main* dictionary. The main and user dictionaries are discussed later in this chapter.)

   ❖ **Edit the word.** If you know the correct spelling of the questionable word, you can edit it within the Word box. Make the necessary edits and then click Replace. If you want to, you can check the edited word against the current dictionaries before clicking Replace. To check the word, finish your editing and click Check. Manual editing of questionable words is best done when you're in a rush or when the spelling checker does not offer the correct replacement word in its list.

3. Repeat Step 1 for each additional questionable spelling in the selected text, record, group of records, or layout.

4. After all words have been examined, click Done to conclude the spelling check.

   Keep in mind that you can click Cancel at any time during a spelling check to immediately halt the process.

Note that if you're working in a password-protected file or in a file in which you don't have access privileges for all fields, you may not be allowed to replace all questionable words. In those cases, the Replace button is labeled Next. Click Next to continue.

On-the-fly spell-checking

If you have set the Spelling Options to notify you of suspected spelling errors as they occur, FileMaker Pro automatically checks each word the moment you press the spacebar or type a punctuation mark (these actions normally signify the completion of a word). You can quickly check the most recent questionable spelling by doing one of the following:

❖ Choosing Spell Word from the Spelling submenu of the Edit menu

❖ Pressing Shift-⌘-Y

The normal Spelling dialog box appears (as shown in Figure 11-3), providing a list of possible replacements for the questionable word. Respond to the dialog box as you would in batch spell-checking mode (described previously). After you deal with the word, the dialog box disappears, and you can continue typing.

If you're sure that a flagged word is correct and you have no desire to add it to the current user dictionary (by using the Learn button in the Spelling dialog box), you're free to ignore the spelling checker's beep or flash. Similarly, if you know the correct spelling of a word, making the correction directly in the field is much faster than summoning the Spelling dialog box.

You should note that you cannot rely on this method of spell-checking to catch all errors. For example, if you move the mouse back into a word that has already been checked and edit it but make a spelling error in the process, FileMaker does not notify you that you have made an error. Thus, if you are unsure of your spelling skills, using both checking methods is a smart idea: check as you type and then recheck the entire record by choosing the Check Record command.

Installing a Dictionary

When you run a spelling check, you can have only one main and one user dictionary active at a given time. However, you can create as many other user dictionaries as you like.

The Install Dictionaries command enables you to switch between different main and user dictionaries as needs dictate. You can also use this command to let FileMaker Pro know that you've moved one or more dictionaries to a new location on your hard disk. Follow these steps:

Chapter 11: Using the Spelling Checker

1. **Launch FileMaker Pro 2 and open a database.**

   Unless a database is open, the Edit menu (which contains the Spelling commands) is disabled.

2. **From the Select menu, choose Browse (or press ⌘-B) or Layout (or press ⌘-L).**

   The Spelling commands are disabled in Find and Preview modes.

3. **Choose Install Dictionaries from the Spelling submenu of the Edit menu.**

   The Select Dictionary dialog box appears (see Figure 11-4).

4. **To install a main dictionary, click the Main radio button.**

   The currently installed main dictionary, if any, is indicated below the file list. (Most users normally leave the main dictionary supplied with FileMaker Pro as the installed one. The only times you might have to install a main dictionary are after you've removed the main dictionary by setting it to None, you've moved it to a different location on disk, or if Claris supplies you with a new main dictionary.)

5. **Select a main dictionary from the file list and click OK, or click None if you do not want to use a main dictionary.**

   — or —

4. **To install a user dictionary, click the User radio button.**

   The currently installed user dictionary, if any, is indicated below the file list.

5. **Select a different user dictionary from the file list and click OK; to avoid using a user dictionary, click None.**

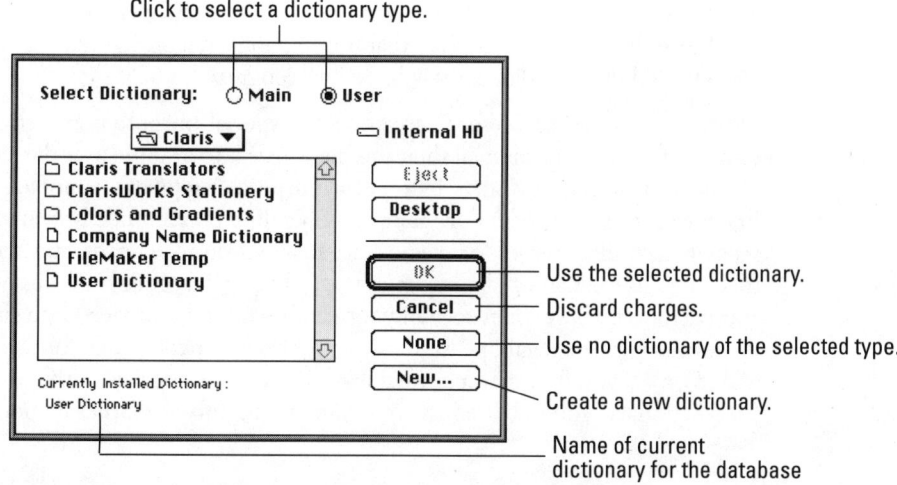

Figure 11-4: Select a dictionary to install from the Select Dictionary dialog box.

The steps that you need to follow to create a new user dictionary are presented in the section "Creating a user dictionary," later in this chapter.

Any user dictionary or main dictionary that you install is now used rather than the previous one. To return to the main dictionary or user dictionary that you previously used, repeat these steps and select the old dictionary.

Keep in mind that installing a different main dictionary or user dictionary does not globally affect every FileMaker Pro database. Instead, when you install a dictionary, it affects only the *current* database. Every database can have a different main dictionary and user dictionary installed. Whenever you close a file, FileMaker Pro makes a note of the last main dictionary and user dictionary installed for the file and automatically makes them available the next time you open the database.

Working with User Dictionaries

As discussed earlier in the chapter, user dictionaries contain spellings of words that you want FileMaker Pro (and any other Claris product that you own) to recognize as being spelled correctly. Although only one user dictionary can be active at a time, you can create as many of them as you like. This section discusses the procedures that are necessary for working with user dictionaries: creating user dictionaries, adding words to a user dictionary, and merging the contents of two or more user dictionaries.

Creating a user dictionary

FileMaker Pro automatically creates the first user dictionary for you during the installation process. For many users, this initial dictionary — called User Dictionary — will be the only user dictionary they ever create. Every new "Learned" word automatically gets added to that user dictionary, assuring that the same word encountered in other databases will also be recognized.

Other users, however, prefer to create several special-purpose user dictionaries instead of simply jamming all their unique words into a single user dictionary. (If you dedicate a user dictionary to a special purpose or type of terminology, you may find it easier to maintain.) For example, depending on your needs, you might create separate user dictionaries for medical, legal, and insurance terms, and another still that contains the names of companies with which you regularly do business. This approach works best when each of your databases can be serviced by a single user dictionary (just the legal one for database A, just the medical one for database B, and so on). If you find that many databases need to be checked with more than one user dictionary, you're better off combining them into one larger dictionary.

Chapter 11: Using the Spelling Checker

The following steps describe how to create a new user dictionary:

1. **Launch FileMaker Pro and open a database.**

   Unless a database is open, the Edit menu (which contains the Spelling commands) is disabled.

2. **From the Select menu, choose Browse (or press ⌘-B) or Layout (or press ⌘-L).**

   The Spelling commands are disabled in Find and Preview modes.

3. **Select Install Dictionaries from the Spelling submenu of the Edit menu.**

   The Select Dictionary dialog box appears (refer to Figure 11-4).

4. **Click New to create a new user dictionary.**

5. **In the file dialog box that appears, enter a name for the dictionary and click Save.**

   The new dictionary is created and becomes the current user dictionary.

Whenever you want to use one of the user dictionaries, follow the instructions in the section, "Installing a Dictionary," to make the dictionary of your choice the current user dictionary. In the next section, you will learn to add words to the new dictionary.

Adding words to a user dictionary

You can add words to a user dictionary in several ways:

- *Adding words as you go:* As you work with a database and perform on-the-fly or on request spelling checks, you can click Learn whenever FileMaker Pro finds an important word that it considers questionable. The advantage of this approach is that you add only words that are essential, because, by definition, they have already been encountered at least once in a checking session. The disadvantage is that until you have used FileMaker Pro for a fair amount of time, you have to add words frequently, interrupting the flow of the spelling checks.

- *Manually adding words:* You can use the User Dictionary command on the Spelling submenu to add new words individually. This option enables you to add key terms to a user dictionary without having to wait for them to be encountered in a spell-checking session.

- *Importing a word list:* You also can use the User Dictionary command in the Spelling submenu to import a list of words in Text-Only format that you want to add to a user dictionary en masse. This approach makes the most sense when you already have a list of terms prepared, perhaps as a user dictionary that you created in another program. Because such a list can contain *many* words, this is easily the fastest way to build a user dictionary. To be useful, however, you should carefully screen the contents of the word list beforehand to avoid having to later delete terms that are not needed.

Part III: Working with Databases

You already know how to use the Learn button to add words to a user dictionary. The following steps describe how to add or remove words manually:

1. **Launch FileMaker Pro and open a database.**

   Unless a database is open, the Edit menu (which contains the Spelling commands) is disabled.

2. **From the Select menu, choose Browse (or press ⌘-B) or Layout (or press ⌘-L).**

   The Spelling commands are disabled in Find and Preview modes.

3. **Choose User Dictionary from the Spelling submenu of the Edit menu.**

   The User Dictionary dialog box appears and presents a list of the words that the dictionary contains (see Figure 11-5).

4. **To add a word to the user dictionary, type the word in the Entry box and click Add.**

   If the word already exists in the user or main dictionary, FileMaker Pro informs you. Otherwise, the word is added to the user dictionary.

5. **To remove a word from the user dictionary, select the word in the word list and click Remove.**

   Note that you cannot *edit* words in the user dictionary. The procedure is to remove the old word and then add the replacement (spelled correctly, of course). As an alternative, you can select the misspelled word in the word list, edit it, choose Add, and then use the Remove command to eliminate the original word.

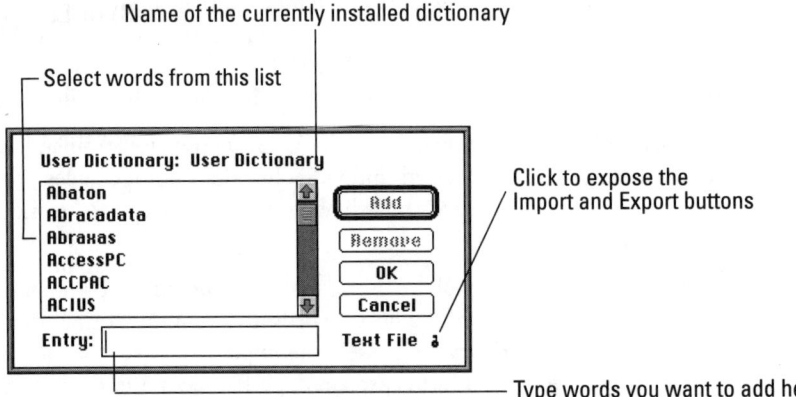

Figure 11-5: The User Dictionary dialog box.

Chapter 11: Using the Spelling Checker

6. **Repeat Steps 4 and 5 as desired.**
7. **To accept the additions and deletions, click OK.**

— or —

7. **To ignore all the changes you've made, click Cancel.**

   A dialog box appears, asking if you'd like to "Discard all changes to user dictionary?"

8. **To confirm that you want to ignore all changes, click Discard.**

   Otherwise, click Cancel to return to the User Dictionary dialog box.

Another way to add words to a user dictionary is to import a word list. FileMaker Pro can also export the contents of a user dictionary so it can be used in other programs. Whether you are importing or exporting a word list, the files are always in Text-Only format. On import, FileMaker Pro doesn't require that the words be set up in any particular way. As long as every word is separated from the next word by a space, tab character, or a Return, FileMaker will consider the word for inclusion in the user dictionary. On export, a user dictionary is written as a single paragraph, with every word separated from the next word by a space.

You should note that importing and exporting normally work hand-in-hand. You export data from one program so that it can be imported into and used by another program. Other FileMaker Pro import and export capabilities are discussed in Chapter 16. The following steps describe how to import and export a word list:

1. **Launch FileMaker Pro and open a database.**

   Unless a database is open, the Edit menu (which contains the Spelling commands) is disabled.

2. **From the Select menu, choose Browse (or press ⌘-B) or Layout (or press ⌘-L).**

   The Spelling commands are disabled in Find and Preview modes.

3. **Choose User Dictionary from the Spelling submenu of the Edit menu.**

   The User Dictionary dialog box appears and presents a list of the words that the dictionary contains.

4. **Click the tiny flag in the lower-right corner of the dialog box.**

   The dialog box expands, and Import and Export buttons appear, as shown in Figure 11-6.

Part III: Working with Databases

Figure 11-6: The expanded User Dictionary dialog box.

5. **To import a word list, click Import, select a text file to import from the file dialog box that appears, and click Open.**

   The words in the text file are compared to those in the main and user dictionaries. Any words that are not found are added to the current user dictionary.

   When the import is completed, a dialog box notifies you of this fact.

6. **Click OK to dismiss the dialog box and click OK a second time to dismiss the User Dictionary dialog box.**

   — or —

5. **To export a word list, click Export. In the file dialog box that appears, type a name for the file (or accept the one that is suggested), select a destination disk and folder, and click Save.**

   The entire contents of the user dictionary are saved as a one-paragraph text file. Each word is separated from the next word by a space.

   When the export is completed, a dialog box notifies you of this fact.

6. **Click OK to dismiss the dialog box and click OK a second time to dismiss the User Dictionary dialog box.**

Merging user dictionaries

Although being able to create as many special-purpose user dictionaries as you like is nice, switching from one dictionary to another can be a real pain. And if you aren't keeping careful track of which one you used last, chances are better than average that the wrong dictionary is currently installed.

If your user dictionaries aren't gigantic, you can make life simpler by just merging them into a single user dictionary that you use for most spell-checking sessions.

1. **Begin by creating a new user dictionary to hold the merged user dictionaries.**

Chapter 11: Using the Spelling Checker

Importing an Entire Document

During an import of a word list, FileMaker Pro discards any words that are already in the current main or user dictionary. Because the program isn't picky about the setup of the word list — just that it's in Text-Only format — you can use this fact to your advantage. You can take any word processing document, save a copy of it in Text-Only format, and then import the entire new document into the user dictionary. Any new terms that are encountered will be added to the dictionary; words that are already in the main or user dictionary (the bulk of them, in most cases) will be ignored.

Follow the steps listed in the section, "Creating a user dictionary," earlier in the chapter. (You can call this dictionary the "primary user dictionary.")

As an alternative, you may want to merge dictionaries into a user dictionary that already exists. If so, skip directly to Step 2.

2. **Select Install Dictionaries from the Spelling submenu of the Edit menu.**

   The Select Dictionary dialog box appears (refer to Figure 11-4).

3. **Click the User radio button, select the first user dictionary that you want to merge with the primary user dictionary, and click Open.**

   The dialog box closes, and the selected user dictionary becomes the current one.

4. **Choose User Dictionary from the Spelling submenu of the Edit menu.**

   The User Dictionary dialog box appears (refer to Figure 11-5).

5. **Click the flag at the bottom of the User Dictionary dialog box.**

   Import and Export buttons appear.

6. **Click Export.**

   A standard file dialog box appears.

7. **Select an output location and enter a name for the export file.**

   After you merge the export file with the primary user dictionary (after completing Step 15), you will have no further use for the export file. Although you can save it here to any disk and folder that you choose, you may want to save it to a spot where it's easy to find and delete, such as the *root* (top) level of the start-up hard disk.

8. **Click Save.**

   The export commences. When the export process is completed, a dialog box appears to notify you of that fact.

Part III: Working with Databases

9. Click OK to dismiss that dialog box and then click OK again to dismiss the User Dictionary dialog box as well.

10. Choose Install Dictionaries from the Spelling submenu of the Edit menu and then select the primary user dictionary (see Step 1) from the Select Dictionary dialog box that appears (refer to Figure 11-4).

11. Choose User Dictionary from the Spelling submenu of the Edit menu.

    The User Dictionary dialog box appears (refer to Figure 11-5).

12. Click the flag at the bottom of the User Dictionary dialog box.

    Import and Export buttons appear.

13. Click Import.

    A standard file dialog box appears.

14. Navigate to the disk and folder in which you saved the export file in Step 7, select the export file, and click Open.

    The import commences.

    After FileMaker Pro has successfully merged the two user dictionaries, a dialog box appears to notify you of that fact.

15. Click OK to dismiss that dialog box and then click OK again to dismiss the User Dictionary dialog box as well.

    If you want to merge additional user dictionaries with the primary user dictionary, repeat Steps 2 through 15.

Note: If you do any writing about Macintosh products or companies, you may find the user dictionary that's included on the FileMaker Pro Bible Disk helpful. Mac Dictionary is a user dictionary that contains approximately 300 names of Macintosh companies, products, and computing terms. To install it or merge it with an existing dictionary, follow the instructions presented in this chapter.

Spelling Tips and Tricks

This section examines several easily-mastered tricks for creating useful user dictionaries and working with the spelling checker.

Creating a spelling list from existing FileMaker Pro databases

Having a spelling checker that questions, for example, most company names, unusual last names, and technical terms wastes considerable time. Worse still, it encourages you not to use the spelling checker at all! (This is precisely why most

Chapter 11: Using the Spelling Checker

people go "Huh?" when they discover that a database program has a spelling checker. Since databases are often filled with proper nouns, spell-checking sessions can take forever.)

If you have been using FileMaker Pro for a while now, you may have already completed the first step toward creating one or more useful user dictionaries. In an address database (Address Book, for example), you may have collected dozens of company names and people's last names. In an inventory database, you may already have entered the precise spellings of most of the important parts that your company sells. A medical records database may contain the names of the majority of diseases that you treat. By using FileMaker Pro's Import/Export command, you can export the contents of these fields and create a text file that you can then import into a user dictionary.

The following steps describe how to create a word list from an existing database:

1. **Open the database from which you intend to extract the word list.**

2. **Choose Export Records from the Import/Export submenu of the File menu.**

   A file dialog box appears (see Figure 11-7).

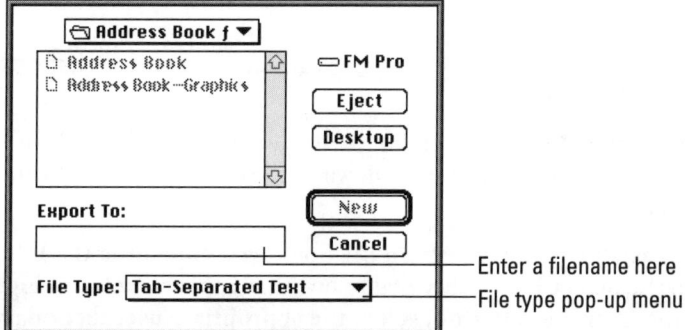

Figure 11-7: Name and select a type and location for the export file in this dialog box.

3. **Select a location for the export file, type a filename for it in the Export To box, set the File Type to Tab-Separated Text, and click New.**

   The Specify field order for export dialog box appears, as shown in Figure 11-8. It contains a list of all fields that have been defined for the database. If you have never exported data from this database, all fields will be checked.

Part III: Working with Databases

Figure 11-8: The Specify field order for export dialog box.

4. **Remove the check marks from fields that you do not want to export, make sure that the Don't format output radio button is selected, and then click OK.**

    Click once on any check mark to remove it. After you click OK, the export file is created.

    (As an example, if you were working with the Address Book database created in Chapter 4, you might select the following fields for export: Last Name, Company, and Comments.)

5. **Select Install Dictionaries from the Spelling submenu of the Edit menu, and in the Select Dictionary dialog box that appears (refer to Figure 11-4), click the User radio button, select the appropriate user dictionary from the file list, and then click OK.**

    These actions make current the user dictionary that will receive the word list.

6. **Choose User Dictionary from the Spelling submenu of the Edit menu.**

    The User Dictionary dialog box appears.

7. **Click the flag at the bottom of the User Dictionary dialog box.**

    Import and Export buttons appear at the bottom of the dialog box.

8. **Click Import.**

    A standard file dialog box appears.

Chapter 11: Using the Spelling Checker

Cleaning Up the Dictionary

As mentioned previously in this chapter, during an import, FileMaker Pro ignores words that are already contained in its main dictionary or in the current dictionary. You don't have to worry much about cluttering your user dictionary with needless words. As a sanity check, however, scanning the user dictionary and removing any words that are truly unnecessary is a good idea.

9. Navigate to the disk and folder in which you saved the export file in Steps 3 and 4, select the export file, and click Open.

    The import commences. When FileMaker Pro has successfully imported the word list, a dialog box appears to notify you of that fact.

10. Click OK to dismiss that dialog box and then click OK again to dismiss the User Dictionary dialog box as well.

Extracting a custom dictionary from another program

Most users have several programs that include spelling checkers. And although most programs also enable you to create one or more user dictionaries, these dictionaries may not be usable by other programs. For example, although I have two custom dictionaries that I developed for use with Microsoft Word, FileMaker Pro cannot read them, and I cannot use the Import command to merge them into another user dictionary. And because these custom dictionaries are not simple text files or any other recognizable format, I can't even open them as normal Word documents. (Like most custom dictionaries, the ones created in Word are stored in a proprietary format that often prevents their contents from being used by other programs.)

In designing its product line, Claris was kind enough to provide the ability to both export and import custom dictionaries as ordinary text files (often called *Text-Only files*). Although many programs enable you to import a word list (usually as a Text-Only file), few programs offer an export option.

But with a special program — CanOpener 2 from Abbott Systems — you can peer into virtually any file and display the text, picture, and sound resources stored in the file. If the word list that is contained in a custom dictionary is readable (many are), you can copy the list, paste it into a word processing document, and then import it into the current FileMaker Pro user dictionary.

Part III: Working with Databases

The following steps describe how to extract a word list from a foreign custom dictionary:

1. **Launch CanOpener 2, locate the foreign custom dictionary, and open it.**

   Be sure that you have selected Text as one of the resources to be displayed (see the top line of Figure 11-9).

2. **Examine each resource that is text.**

   If the word list is stored as a text resource, it will look something like the list in the lower part of the dialog box shown in Figure 11-9.

3. **Select Save As from the Item menu; in the standard file dialog box that appears (see Figure 11-10), enter a filename in the box labeled Save Text File As, select a location for the file, and click Save.**

   The list is saved as a Text-Only file.

Figure 11-9: A word list stored as a resource.

Chapter 11: Using the Spelling Checker

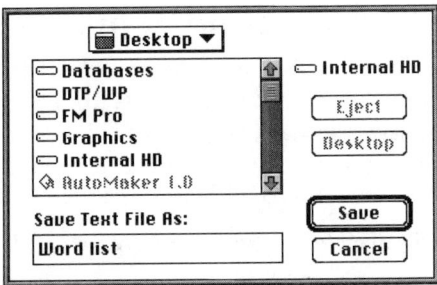

Figure 11-10: Saving a word list as a standard text file.

— or —

3. If the word list contains extraneous garbage, you may prefer to simply copy the words, paste them into a new word processing document, and then save the document in Text-Only format.

   Because you cannot edit the list in CanOpener 2, you will not see an insertion point. To select the words, double-click the first word and then Shift-click the last word in the list.

   You can now import the word list into a new or existing FileMaker Pro user dictionary, as described previously in the instructions for importing or exporting a word list.

Stand-Alone Spelling Checkers

If you don't feel like exploring the wonderful world of importing and exporting, you may want to consider another approach to spell-checking: buying a stand-alone spelling checker. Thunder 7 from BaseLinePublishing, for example, can check spelling in most programs. And because it comes with its own dictionary and enables you to create user dictionaries, you can remove the dictionaries that came with all of your other programs — freeing several megabytes of hard disk space in the process.

Restricting spelling checks to a subset of fields

Depending on the types of fields that you have created for a database, you may have no desire to check the spelling in every field (Check Record). Unfortunately, the only other option is to individually select and check one field at a time. Performing this task manually is time consuming. You can simplify the process by creating a FileMaker Pro script that selects and checks the fields one-by-one.

Figure 11-11 shows a sample script that checks the contents of two fields in a database. When the script executes, it selects the entire contents of the first field (Title) and executes the Check Selection command (from the Spelling submenu of the Edit menu). After the first field is checked, the second field (Comments) is selected, and the same procedure is used to check that field. Note that this script performs the spell check for only the current record.

To add more fields to such a script, you simply include additional pairs of Go to Field ["*field name*"] and Spell Check Selection [Select] script steps. Be sure that the Select entire contents check box is checked for each Spell Check Selection script step, as shown in Figure 11-11.

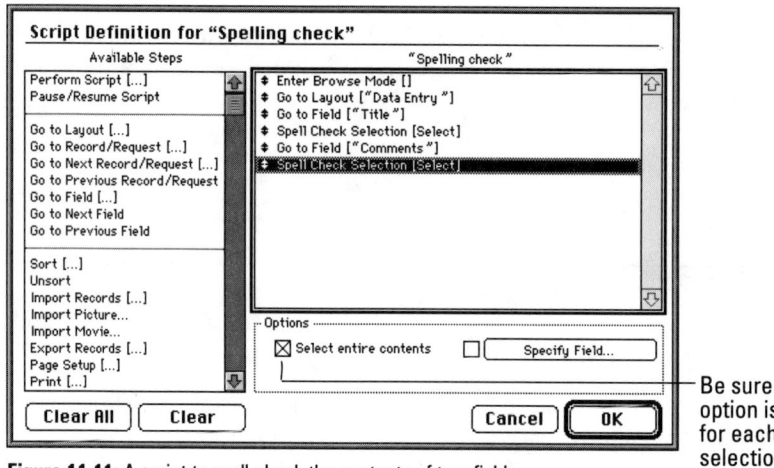

Figure 11-11: A script to spell-check the contents of two fields.

Be sure that this option is always set for each Spell Check selection script step

Chapter 11: Using the Spelling Checker

CHAPTER  CONCEPTS AND TERMS

- You can have spelling checked as you type or on request. You can check the spelling of any record, group of records, text selection, or set of layout labels.
- Only one main and one user spelling dictionary can be active at any given moment, but you may have more than one of each stored on disk and change between them as the need arises.
- Each database remembers the last main and user dictionary that was used with it. The next time you open the database, those same dictionaries will be active again.
- User dictionaries contain only the special or unusual words that you add to them. You add words by clicking the Learn button during a spelling check, by editing the user dictionary and manually typing the words, or by importing words from a standard text file.
- When FileMaker Pro imports a word list into a user dictionary, it checks each word against the contents of the current main dictionary and user dictionary and discards words that are already included.
- You can import a user dictionary that was created in another program into FileMaker Pro if the dictionary can be saved as a text file.

export
A procedure similar to saving a file, but it changes the format of the data so another program can read it.

import
A procedure similar to opening a file. Its purpose is to gather information that is saved in a different format — one that is not the native format of the program that will be opening the file.

questionable spelling
The term that FileMaker Pro's spelling checker uses to identify a word that is not contained in the current main and user dictionaries.

resource
Important program information, such as window definitions and icons, is often stored in the program as a resource. Defining such elements as resources enables a programmer to modify them easily without having to rewrite the program.

root
The top/highest level of any disk. When a disk icon is first opened, the root is the part of the disk that you first see.

text file (also called Text-Only file)
A file saved without formatting (a single font and no style or size options). The usual purpose of creating a pure text file is to enable it to be read by other programs or other types of computers.

Part III: Working with Databases

CHAPTER TWELVE

Reports

- How to create and produce a report
- Tips and tricks for designing report layouts

Perhaps the main reason that you enter data into a database is so that you can eventually get it back out in a neat, organized, informative fashion. You've seen how to locate information in a database by using Find mode and how to organize that information with the Sort command. You've even learned something about using layouts to view different arrangements of your data. What's been missing up to this point, though, is a discussion of putting all these procedures together to produce a real product that you can keep and share. When you select, sort, and format a group of records so you can print or view them on-screen, you're creating a report.

Report Design Essentials

A *report* is a summary of the data entered into a database, or an organized, collated view of the data. You don't necessarily have to print a report (you can use Preview mode to view it on-screen), but the process of creating a report is much the same whether you choose to print or not. You will learn more about printing in Chapter 13.

Preparing a report involves four steps:

- ❖ *Design a layout.* Create a layout that displays only the fields that you want to see. Make sure that the layout takes advantage of the available page space and that it is clearly presented. You use Layout mode to create and modify layouts (as explained in Chapter 6).

- ❖ *Find records to include in the report.* You don't always need to show the entire content of a database in a report; rather, your needs for the report will dictate the particular records to select. You may want to restrict your report to include only records in a certain time range; records associated with one or more individuals or organizations; or records with some specific property, such as overdue invoices. Records are selected in Find mode by creating Find requests or using related procedures (such as the Omit command).

- *Sort the records.* If they have never been sorted, records are presented in the order in which they were entered into the database. For report purposes, records often need to be arranged in some other order so that readers can locate particular records and make sense of the report as a whole. You arrange records in FileMaker Pro using the Sort command.

- *Printing.* When designing a report layout, it's important to keep your printing requirements and capabilities in mind, unless you intend to view the report only on-screen. Your choice of printer can affect the layout you use and how information must be arranged within that layout. Finally, certain kinds of information (such as Summary fields) appear only at preview or print time.

The following sections provide more information about these four essential steps in the report preparation process.

Designing a layout

When designing a report layout, you should ask yourself these questions:

- *What is the purpose of my report?* This is the key to determining what information to display; you should exclude anything that is not needed. In a phone directory created from an employee database, for example, you would not want to use a layout that also displayed information about employees' ages or Social Security numbers. If current layouts include extraneous information, you will either have to edit a duplicate of the most appropriate layout or design a new one especially for the report.

- *How much information can — and should — I put on a page?* You should make optimal use of the printed area, but not at the expense of the report's clarity. Allow an adequate amount of white space between records: slightly more space than FileMaker Pro normally places between fields in each record.

- *Is the report layout clear?* A report should be self-explanatory. A supervisor should be able to recognize its purpose immediately without having to ask for explanations. Fields and summary sections should be clearly labeled. And don't underestimate the importance of headers and footers for labeling and numbering each report page. The report's purpose can be further reflected in its title, printed in the header.

Once an appropriate report layout has been created, you can change to that layout at any time by simply selecting its name from the layout pop-up menu at the top of the status area. Because creating a report is a multi-step process (described earlier in this chapter), you may want to design a FileMaker Pro script that does the necessary preparatory work, changes to your report layout, and then prints the report for you. Scripts are discussed in detail in Chapter 15.

Chapter 12: Reports

Selecting records to include in the report

Finding records is perhaps the subtlest part of creating a report. What records do you need to display? Your choice likely will be based on the content of some field in the database. You may want to choose all records that have a certain value or range of values in that field — for example, all invoice records prepared during the third quarter of the current calendar year.

After you decide which records you want to include in the report, you can create one or more Find requests that locate those particular records — and *only* those records. After performing a Find operation or using another of FileMaker Pro's related commands (such as Omit), the remaining visible records are referred to as the *found set*. Whether you intend to print or preview your report on-screen, the records included in the report are always drawn exclusively from the found set. Refer to Chapter 9 for more information on finding records and working with found sets.

Sorting the found set

Unless they have previously been sorted, the records in the found set appear in the order in which they were entered into the database. To create a more meaningful order for the data, you can sort the found set.

Remember the fields that you used to find the records? You may want to sort the found set based on the contents of that same field. If the field contains names, the best thing may be to sort alphabetically. Or you may want to sort numerically, showing highest values first and lowest ones last. Such an order would be appropriate for a report on sales, in which you want to highlight the performances of your best salespeople.

Keep in mind that you can sort by more than one field. In the sales report example, you could sort records first by salesperson name and then by the amount of each sale. This produces a report in which each salesperson's sales are grouped, with the most prominent sale appearing at the top of the group. Refer to Chapter 10 for more information on sorting records.

If you're using a layout that includes at least one sub-summary part, you must sort by the field that you designated when you created the sub-summary; otherwise, the summary information won't appear in the report. For more information on this subject, refer to Chapters 5 and 6.

Printing or previewing the report

At this point, you have prepared a report. If you want to admire your work on-screen, you can switch to Preview mode (choose Preview from the Select menu or press ⌘-U). In fact, sometimes printing at all is a waste of paper. Many reports are simply something that you need to see once and then never again. It's often more convenient, and certainly faster, to simply review the report on-screen.

Part III: Working with Databases

To produce something that you can use to impress the boss, however, you will probably need to print the report. When designing a report that you intend to print, you should consider the following questions:

- *What type of paper will I be using?* This consideration is especially important when you're working with odd paper sizes or with special stock, such as mailing labels. You want your layout to fit on and to print properly on that paper. The paper that you use can dictate the size of the layout body, the distribution of fields in the layout, and whether you include headers and footers.

- *How long will the report be?* Short reports can use large type sizes; smaller sizes help conserve paper in longer reports. Don't choose type so small that it's difficult to read, though.

- *Do I have all the fields I need in my database?* If you want to summarize information in certain fields, you may need to define Summary and/or Calculation fields. You can use a Calculation field to convert data from one format to another format that is more appropriate for your report, for example (see Chapter 14).

See Chapter 13 for instructions on printing from FileMaker Pro.

Report Design Tips

That's all there is to it — presuming, of course, that you started with an appropriate and finely tuned report layout. If you didn't, you can remedy this situation by diving into the next section, which (in concert with Chapter 6) covers some of the important elements of creating a report layout.

Working with layout parts

Every layout part that you've defined for your report appears in a particular place when the layout is printed or viewed in Preview mode. Keep the following facts in mind when choosing parts for a report layout:

- A title header (if any) is printed once, at the top of the first page. If you make the title header a full page long, you have effectively created a cover sheet.

- A regular header (if any) prints at the top of every page. If you included a title header, the title header takes the place of the regular header on the first page.

- If a leading grand summary is part of the report, it prints above the body, before the contents of any records are printed. (For more information on grand and sub-summaries, see Chapter 5.)

- All of the found and sorted records are printed in the body. You can exclude the body part from a report if you want to print only summary information. This method is useful for getting total sales information from an invoices database, for example, when you aren't interested in seeing the contents of each invoice.

- If you have placed sub-summary parts below the body, each sub-summary prints once for each group of records with the same value in the When sorted by field that you used to create the sub-summary. You *must* sort the database with the Sort by field for a sub-summary part to actually appear and print. You can specify a page break before or after a sub-summary, forcing a break after each new group has been printed, for example.
- If the report contains a trailing grand summary, that summary prints below the body one time, after the contents of all records are printed.
- A title footer (if any) is printed one time, at the bottom of the first page.
- The regular footer (if any) prints at the bottom of every page. If you included a title footer, the title footer takes the place of the regular footer on the first page.

Duplicating a report layout

When you design a layout for a report, you can begin in either of two ways. You either can start from scratch by just choosing an appropriate predefined layout such as the Columnar Report or Extended Columnar, or you can duplicate and then modify an existing layout. The method you choose will depend on whether you already have a layout that is close to the final report that you envision.

For example, the Want List database on the FileMaker Pro Bible disk successfully reuses a report layout to present two different arrangements of the same data: purchases sorted by catalog number and purchases sorted by purchase date. After creating the first report layout, all that was needed to create the second was to:

- Create a duplicate of the layout (by choosing Duplicate Layout from the Edit menu or pressing ⌘-D).
- Edit the title in the header part of the duplicate layout to reflect the new sort order that will be used.
- Create a duplicate copy of the script that produces the original report, and then modify the duplicate script so it uses the correct sort instructions.
- Copy the button that is used to execute the original script, edit the button's name, and then attach the new script to the button.

Since many reports are often only a minor variation of another report, you'll find that using this approach enables you to quickly generate loads of informative reports with minimal effort, just the way most of us like it!

Transferring layouts between databases

You may have designed a good layout for a report, but that layout may happen to reside in a different FileMaker Pro database. If you used the same field names in both databases, you can transfer layout elements from the first database to the second. (Unfortunately, there's no way to transfer a layout as a whole.)

Part III: Working with Databases

Follow these steps to move layout elements from one database to another:

1. Open the database that contains the layout elements you want to copy.
2. Choose Layout from the Select menu (or press ⌘-L).
3. Choose the appropriate layout from the layout pop-up menu.
4. Choose Select All from the Edit menu (or press ⌘-A), and then choose Copy from the Edit menu (or press ⌘-C).

   All objects on the layout are selected and then copied to the Mac's Clipboard.

5. Open the database in which you want to use the layout.
6. Choose Layout from the Select menu (or press ⌘-L).
7. Choose New Layout from the Edit menu (or press ⌘-N).

   The New Layout dialog box appears.

8. Choose the Blank layout type, and click OK.
9. Drag the Body label so that the body is the same length as the body of the original layout.
10. Choose Paste from the Edit menu (or press ⌘-V).
11. Adjust layout parts and objects to the correct positions.

Note that any fields from the first (source) database that don't already exist in the second database aren't pasted as part of this operation. Use the Define Fields command in both database documents to check the compatibility of field names.

See Chapter 6 for more information on editing layouts.

Chapter 12: Reports

CHAPTER  CONCEPTS AND TERMS

- A report is a printed or on-screen copy of a selected group of records sorted in a specific order, arranged in a way that provides information that viewing individual records does not (and cannot).
- To prepare a report, the process typically includes selecting or designing an appropriate layout, choosing records to include using Find mode commands, arranging the records in a meaningful fashion with the Sort command, and then displaying the report on-screen with Preview mode or printing it with the Print command.

Clipboard
An area in the Mac's memory that is used to store the most recently copied (⌘-C) or cut (⌘-X) object or text string. The contents of the Clipboard can be pasted (⌘-V) into other locations on the same document, another document, or even in another application.

found set
The remaining visible (or browsed) records following a Find procedure, such as a Find request, Omit command, or Omit Multiple command.

CHAPTER THIRTEEN

Printing

- Setting page options for various printers
- Previewing a report before (or as an alternative to) committing it to paper
- Using the FileMaker Pro Print command
- Avoiding and solving printing problems

Having mastered the fine art of designing and producing reports from databases, you are no doubt eager to see your work realized on paper. This chapter takes you through the printing process step by step, from setting up a Macintosh to work with a particular printer through resolving certain problems that may crop up as you print.

Note that throughout this chapter, I discuss printing "reports." Although some of the procedures are indeed specific to reports, most can be applied equally to any type of FileMaker document you want to print, such as individual records, script definitions, and field definitions. And much of the general printing procedures can be applied equally to printing documents in other programs, too.

Printing a report involves three basic steps, each of which has at least a couple of elements:

1. *Setting Up:* You use Apple's Chooser desk accessory to select the printer that you want to use. After you select a printer, you select print options in the Page Setup dialog box within FileMaker Pro. You can omit the first part of this step if you always use the same printer; frequently, you can omit choosing the print options as well.

2. *Readying a Report:* With the database open, you select an appropriate layout, find the records that you want to include in the report, and sort the records. You then preview the report to make sure that it will print correctly. Previewing a report before printing is an excellent way to save paper.

3. *Printing:* After you are satisfied with the way a report looks in Preview mode, you send it off to the printer by using the Print command. You can choose from several options to control how a report prints.

   If all goes well, the end result of this process is a neatly printed report that contains just the information you need. Unfortunately, things do not always go well, which leads in some cases to Step 4.

4. *Troubleshooting:* If you don't get the results you want, you need to adopt a systematic approach to isolating and correcting the problem.

Setting Up

Before you begin a task, you need to do a certain amount of housekeeping. In the case of printing, you happen to be dealing with an outside entity from the Mac's point of view — namely, the printer. Thus, the first good housekeeping steps when you want to print involve making the printer known to the Macintosh and setting up FileMaker Pro so it prints correctly on the printer.

Selecting a printer with the Chooser

A wide variety of printers are available, but the Mac doesn't know which one you want to use until you tell it. Before you can print anything, whether in FileMaker Pro or any other program, you need to use the Chooser to select the printer that you want to use. The *Chooser* is a desk accessory, a program accessed via the Apple menu. It's Apple's way of putting you in touch with the various software programs, called *print drivers*, that your system has available to run printers. You can think of a print driver as a set of instructions that enables the Macintosh to communicate successfully with a printer and to get the printer to do what you want it to do: produce documents on paper.

Selecting the Chooser desk accessory from the Apple menu brings up a desk accessory window that is similar to the window shown in Figure 13-1. The appearance of the Chooser on your system may be different, depending on what print drivers you have installed.

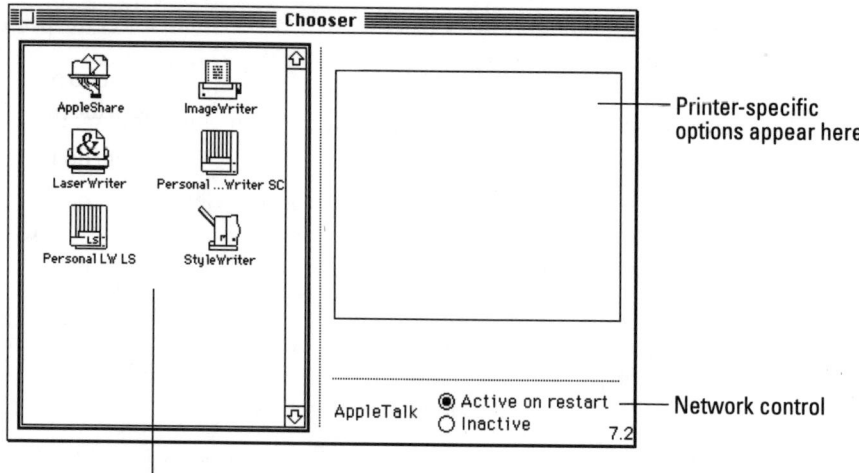

Figure 13-1: The Chooser desk accessory.

Chapter 13: Printing

On the left side of the window, you see a number of icons that represent, among other things, the print drivers that are currently installed on your Mac. You click the icon that is appropriate to the printer that you want to use. To the right is an area, blank in Figure 13-1, that contains options that are specific to the printer you have chosen. Below this area is the AppleTalk control. AppleTalk is a networking system — a way of stringing together computers and peripherals (such as printers) so that they can share information. Many laser printers require the use of AppleTalk.

To select a printer, follow these steps:

1. **Select the Chooser from the Apple menu.**

   The Chooser window appears.

2. **Click the icon that is appropriate to the printer that you want to use.**

3. **Click items in the right side of the window to set the appropriate options for the chosen print driver.**

   Following are the options available for three popular printers. If you have a different printer, the options may vary.

   - *LaserWriter:* Click to select which LaserWriter to use. Each available LaserWriter has a unique name. If no names are visible, no LaserWriters are connected to the Mac; or if any are connected, they are turned off. Click to turn Background Printing on or off. (See the section on PrintMonitor later in this chapter.)

   - *StyleWriter:* Click to select which port the StyleWriter is connected to on the back of the Macintosh. *Ports* are labeled jacks into which you plug peripheral cables.

   - *ImageWriter:* Click to select which port the ImageWriter is connected to on the Macintosh.

4. **If the selected printer is directly connected to your Macintosh, click the Inactive radio button in the AppleTalk section of the window.**

   Other than LaserWriters and similar printers, many printers do not require AppleTalk.

   — or —

4. **If the selected printer is on a network or always requires the AppleTalk option (as the Apple LaserWriters do, for example), click the Active radio button in the AppleTalk section of the window.**

   If you're unsure whether your printer requires the AppleTalk option, refer to the printer's documentation.

5. **Click the close box in the Chooser window to put your choice into effect and dismiss the window.**

Part III: Working with Databases

Using Chooser on a Network

If your Mac is connected to a network, you can select any printer that's on the network and currently turned on. When you choose a print driver (LaserWriter, for example), you will see the names of all LaserWriters that are on the network. Choose whichever one you want to use.

If you are connected to a network that is divided into AppleTalk zones, the Chooser window you see will look somewhat different from the one in Figure 13-1. An AppleTalk Zones area appears on the left side of the window beneath the installed print drivers. Before selecting the particular printer to which you intend to print, you must select the AppleTalk zone in which the printer is located. As you click different zone names, the names of the printers available in that zone will appear in the printer list on the right side of the window.

In the Chooser window, you should see an icon that is appropriate to the printer that you want to use. If not, you need to install the appropriate print driver software. This software should have come on a disk that accompanied your printer, and the printer's documentation should tell you how to install the software. The following procedure describes this task in general terms, but you should consult the printer documentation for specifics.

To install a print driver, follow these steps:

1. **Locate the print driver disk that accompanied the printer and insert it into the Macintosh's floppy disk drive.**
2. **Double-click the disk's icon to open it.**
3. **Locate the print driver icon for the printer and drag it to the System folder.**

   If you are running System 7, an alert box appears, informing you that you need to put the driver into the Extensions folder. Click OK to do so.

Using the Page Setup dialog box

The first thing that happens when you click the close box in the Chooser window is that the alert box shown in Figure 13-2 appears, telling you to change Page Setup for all applications that are open.

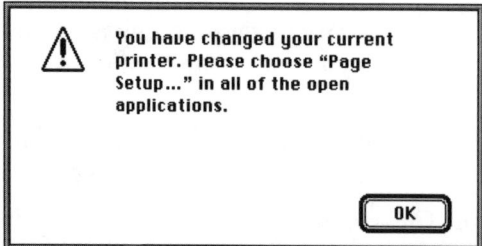

Figure 13-2: This alert appears whenever you select a different printer in the Chooser.

Chapter 13: Printing

After you click OK to send this alert box away, doing what it says to do is a good idea.

The Page Setup dialog box, which is not specific to FileMaker Pro, contains controls and options that you can use to adapt your specific printer to the kind of printed output that you want to produce. There is a different version of this dialog box for each of the main printer types. Options that are available depend on the printer and on the kind of paper that the printer supports. In any case, you access the Page Setup dialog box by choosing Page Setup from FileMaker Pro's File menu.

You should note that Page Setup options are document-specific rather than global. If you always want to print in landscape mode, for example, you will have to individually set that option for each document. Luckily, however, the most recent Page Setup settings used with a document are stored along with the document when the file is saved to disk.

Using a LaserWriter

Choosing Page Setup when you are working with any laser printer that uses the LaserWriter print driver brings up a dialog box that is similar to the one shown in Figure 13-3.

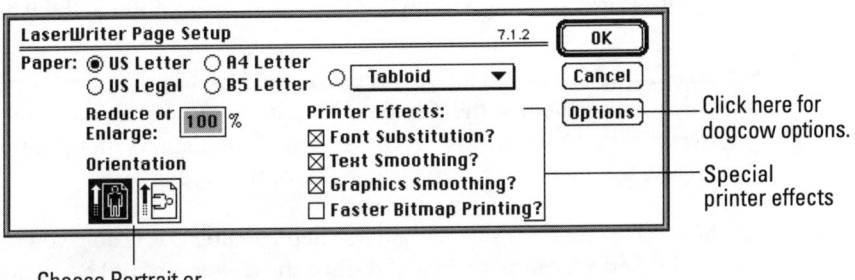

Figure 13-3: The Page Setup dialog box for a LaserWriter.

In the upper-left corner, you see radio buttons for the predefined paper sizes that you can use with the printer. (A4 and B5 are European standards that are not widely used in the United States and Canada.) The pop-up menu to the right of the B5 Letter button provides additional paper options. The sizes of paper that you can use depend on which printer you choose.

Below the paper size radio buttons is a text box into which you can enter a magnification factor. You may find this option handy if you are having trouble fitting records onto a page. For best results, you should restrict your choices to values that can evenly be divided by two. Such values work best because most laser printers have resolutions of 300 or 600 dots per inch. If you scale by an odd factor, the dots will have to be apportioned fractionally, occasionally yielding poor results.

Below this text box are buttons that control the orientation of the paper. There are two choices: portrait and landscape. You choose the icon on the left for portrait mode, in which text prints in the normal way. You choose the icon on the right for landscape mode, in which text prints across the long dimension of the paper (sideways, you might say). Landscape mode, like magnification, is handy for fitting wide records or reports onto a single sheet of paper. You also print envelopes in landscape mode. (Doing so pulls them through the printer lengthwise. Trying to print them in portrait mode almost invariably results in paper jams.)

To the right of the paper control buttons are check box options for special printer effects. You set most of them once and never change them, but nothing prevents you from fiddling with them any time you want. The options include the following:

- *Font Substitution:* This option enables the Macintosh to supply a different font to the laser printer if the laser version called for in a document isn't available in the system. If this box isn't checked, the Mac will use the *bitmap* version of the font (the one you see on the screen). Results will be substandard, and printing will take longer.

- *Text Smoothing:* With this option checked, the Mac applies a special algorithm to text to smooth off jaggies, those diagonal, staircase-looking edges that mar the appearance of text. Checking this option slows printing a small amount.

- *Graphics Smoothing:* This option is similar to Text Smoothing, but it applies to graphics.

- *Faster Bitmap Printing:* This option causes the Mac to preprocess bitmap images before sending them to the printer. This option is important only for the earliest LaserWriters. (Apple's most recent version of the LaserWriter print driver—currently 8.1.1—doesn't even include this option.)

The buttons on the right side of the Page Setup dialog box enable you to put your changes into effect, cancel them and dismiss the dialog box, or choose additional options. To see the additional options, click the Options button. You see a dialog box like the one in Figure 13-4.

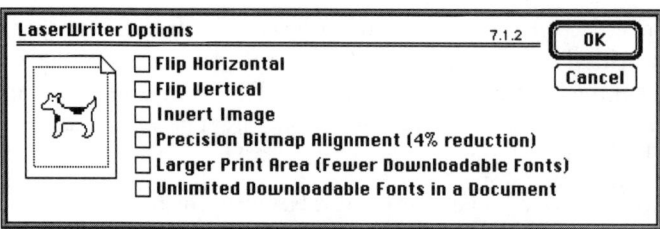

Figure 13-4: Additional printing options for use with LaserWriters.

Chapter 13: Printing

The LaserWriter Options dialog box offers a number of features:

- *Flip Horizontal:* When this option is checked, the page is inverted left to right, producing a mirror image.
- *Flip Vertical:* Choosing this option inverts the page top to bottom.
- *Invert Image:* This option swaps black to white and white to black.
- *Precision Bitmap Alignment (4% reduction):* This option attempts to reconcile the mathematical difficulties of printing a 72 dot-per-inch (dpi) bitmap on a 300 dpi printer. In essence, it causes printing at 288 dpi; hence the 4% factor. (300 - 288 = 12 = 4% x 300).
- *Larger Print Area (Fewer Downloadable Fonts):* This options expands the area available for printing. Laser printers, as a rule, aren't capable of printing all the way to the edge of a page, nor within a certain distance of the top or bottom. Checking this option enlarges the area, at the expense of printer memory, and hence, room for fonts.
- *Unlimited Downloadable Fonts in a Document:* This option enables the Macintosh to supply as many fonts to the printer as the current print job requires. It can slow down printing considerably for documents that use a large number of different fonts in different styles — which is a design no-no anyway.

At the left side of the dialog box, a small icon of an animal (a *dogcow*, to be precise) shows the effects of the current settings. Figure 13-5 is an example of how the dogcow demonstrates the settings.

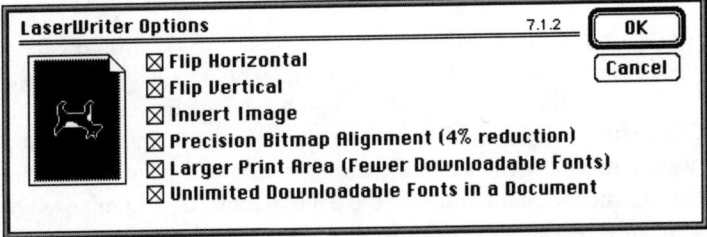

Figure 13-5: The dogcow image reflects the cumulative effects of the selected options.

After you set all of the Page Setup options, you are ready to print.

Part III: Working with Databases

Moving Up to LaserWriter 8

If you're ready to expand your printing horizons, it may be time for you to move up to the latest LaserWriter print driver; namely, LaserWriter 8. An option in the new Page Setup dialog box enables you to print 2-up and 4-up pages, in addition to a normal 1-up page. There's a Print dialog box option that allows you to select black-and-white, color/grayscale, or calibrated color/grayscale printing. And, unlike earlier versions of the LaserWriter print driver, LaserWriter 8 can display messages (either on-screen or in a detailed printed report) when a PostScript error occurs. LaserWriter 8 (currently 8.1.1) can be obtained free from most on-line information services.

Using a StyleWriter

Choosing Page Setup when you have selected a StyleWriter printer displays a dialog box like the one shown in Figure 13-6.

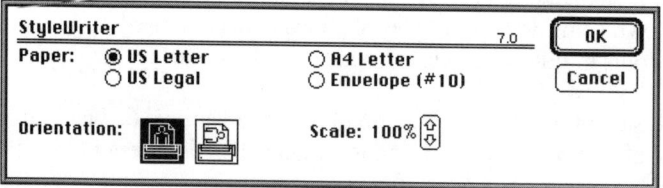

Figure 13-6: The Page Setup dialog box for a StyleWriter.

Toward the center of the dialog box are radio buttons that you use to select the four types of paper supported by a StyleWriter. Below them are icons to control the orientation of the paper you select. You have two choices: portrait and landscape. You choose the icon on the left for portrait mode, in which text prints in the usual way. You choose the icon on the right for landscape mode, in which text prints across the long dimension of the paper (sideways, you might say). The latter is good for fitting wide records or reports onto a single sheet of paper.

To the right of the paper orientation buttons is a double-arrow button that controls the magnification. Click the down arrow to have the document print smaller than normal. Click the up arrow to move the size back up (you can't go past 100%). Each click of an arrow changes the magnification factor by 20%.

Click the OK button to put changes into effect. Click Cancel to dismiss the dialog box without taking action.

After you set all the Page Setup options, you're ready to print.

Using an ImageWriter

Invoking the Page Setup command when you're using an ImageWriter or another dot-matrix printer that uses the same driver brings up a dialog box that resembles the one in Figure 13-7.

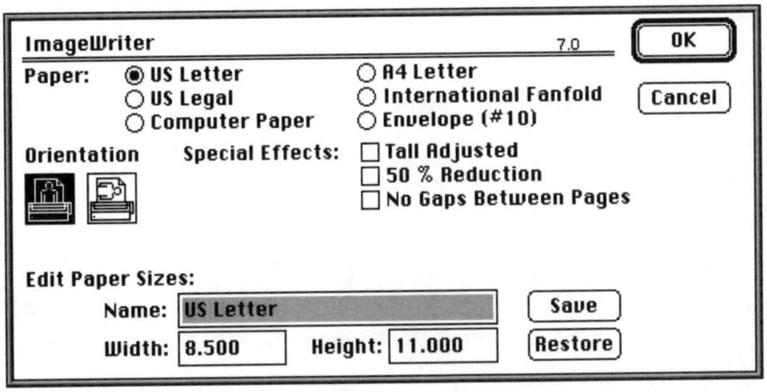

Figure 13-7: The Page Setup dialog box for an ImageWriter.

At the top of this dialog box are radio buttons that you click to indicate what kind of paper you want to use. Note, in particular, the Computer Paper option. You choose this option when you're working with fan-fold, tractor-feed paper. This paper is the kind that has perforated, detachable edges that have holes in them to guide the paper through the printer.

Below the paper size radio buttons are icons that control the paper's orientation. You have two choices: portrait and landscape. You choose the icon on the left for portrait mode, in which text prints in the usual way. You choose the icon on the right for landscape mode, in which text prints across the long dimension of the paper (sideways, you might say). The latter is good for fitting wide records or reports onto a single sheet of paper.

To the right of the paper orientation icons are three check boxes that offer special printer effects:

- *Tall Adjusted:* Choose this option whenever you are printing graphics. It tells the printer to print the same number of dots per inch horizontally and vertically. If you neglect to choose this option, circles will look like elongated ovals on your printouts, for example.

- *50% Reduction:* This is the only magnification option that is available for an ImageWriter printer. It reduces everything to half its normal size.

- *No Gaps Between Pages:* This option is useful only when you are using continuous feed computer paper. It eliminates top and bottom margins, printing everything on one long sheet. It is especially good for printing banners or spreadsheets in landscape mode.

Below these check boxes are a set of text boxes that you can use for editing the sizes of the standard paper choices to create a custom paper choice. Enter the width and height of the paper (in inches) into the relevant text boxes. Click Save to make the changes. Click Restore to go back to the original dimensions for the chosen paper.

Click OK to put your changes into effect. Click Cancel to take no action and dismiss the dialog box.

Note that the ImageWriter printer is no longer in production, having been discontinued in favor of the StyleWriter, which is much quieter, produces higher-quality printouts, and costs about the same. You can't stop progress. Even so, a great many ImageWriters are still in service, and Apple is still including print drivers for them with every new release of its system software.

No matter what printer you're using — whether it's the latest thing or an old standby — you set page options for your printer in the same way. The following procedure describes in general terms how to use the Page Setup dialog box for almost any printer:

1. **Open the database that you intend to print.**
2. **Choose Page Setup from the File menu.**

    You see the Page Setup dialog box for the printer you have selected in the Chooser.

3. **Click the relevant radio button to select the size of paper that you are using.**

    The standard choice in the United States is US Letter (8 1/2" x 11" paper).

4. **Choose the paper orientation.**

    Click the left icon, which has an image of an upright torso, to choose portrait mode. Portrait mode is the standard way of printing. Click the right icon, which has an image of a sideways torso, to choose landscape mode. Landscape mode prints sideways on the paper, which is good for wide records and reports.

5. **Select a magnification level to use if you want to adjust the number of records on a page, or leave this option at 100% to print at the standard size.**
6. **Choose any special printer effects that are relevant to your print job.**
7. **Click OK.**

If you always intend to print information from this database on the same kind of paper, in the same orientation, and at the same size, you need to configure Page Setup only once. You do not need to choose it every time you want to print a report. Remember, however, that the Page Setup options you just selected are specific to this database; they have no effect on how any other database document will print.

Readying a Report

With the preliminaries out of the way, you can get down to brass tacks. Before you can print a report, you need to prepare the report. You learned all about reports in Chapter 12, but you can refresh your memory of the basics by reading the following sections.

Selecting and sorting

You will seldom print the entire contents of a database. To print most operational databases, you would hog a printer the whole day and spend most of your time feeding it paper. And you wouldn't be too popular with your coworkers or with whoever orders supplies. Actually, the only reason to print the entire contents of most databases is to have a paper, back-up copy of the file's contents in case disaster strikes. Even then, several strategically located disk copies of the database are probably much more useful in case of an emergency.

Printing only a selection of the information that is contained in a database is much more common than printing the entire database. Which records you choose depends on the nature of your report. Consider an example: Susan is head of marketing at a small company. She has access to a FileMaker Pro database that contains records for each sales transaction. Among the fields in this database is one for the salesperson who is responsible for the transaction. Susan isn't confident that one of her charges, Guy, is doing very well lately, so she would like to check up on him.

All Susan needs to do is open the Sales database and issue a Find request to locate all records in which Guy's name appears in the Salesperson field. She uses Find mode, putting =Guy =Smith into the Salesperson field on the Find request. To restrict things further, she also places ≥1/1/94 in the Date field to limit the search to sales from the current calendar year.

After using Find to select a relevant group of records, the next step is to arrange them in a useful order. Susan uses the Sort command to arrange the records in descending order based on the amount of each sale. This sort puts the largest transaction first. Finally, Susan chooses a layout that shows only the information she needs and doesn't omit anything important. In this case, she selects a layout that includes a Summary field, one that will show the total of Guy's sales this year (so she won't have to add them up manually).

Following are the general steps necessary to prepare a report from a database:

1. **Within FileMaker Pro, open the database that contains the information from which you want to prepare a report.**

2. **Use Find mode to issue one or more Find requests to locate the records that you want to use as part of the report.**

3. **Use the Sort command from the Select menu (or press ⌘-S) to arrange the found set in a convenient order.**

Part III: Working with Databases

4. From the layout pop-up menu, choose a layout that contains all the information that you want and eliminates extraneous data.

5. Preview or print the report.

Previewing before printing

More paper has been wasted because of minor problems with a document's exact appearance than because of any other problem — with the possible exception of typographical errors on the first page of a re´sume´. Much of this paper waste could be avoided if folks took the time to check out documents on-screen prior to printing them. Admittedly, checking them isn't always easy (or even possible) in all Macintosh application programs. FileMaker Pro, however, includes a Preview mode that enables you to see the potential results of any print job.

To switch to Preview mode, choose it from the Mode pop-up menu or from the Select menu (or press ⌘-U). You see a view that is similar to Figure 13-8, which shows the Phone Directory layout of the Address Book database in Preview mode.

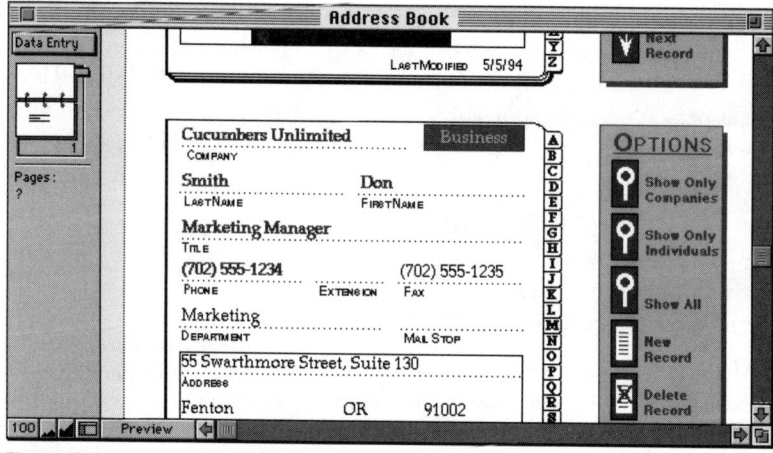

Figure 13-8: An Address Book layout in Preview mode.

In this view, dotted lines separate individual output pages. To see additional pages, click the book icon. Use the scroll bars to move around in the view and check its complete contents. If you want to find out the total number of pages in the report, drag the bookmark to the bottom of the book icon. (FileMaker Pro doesn't know how many pages the report contains until you perform this action.)

If your report looks satisfactory and you want a permanent copy of it, you can send it to the printer. If not, you have several options. If the problem is just a case of getting everything to fit, you may be able to cheat by adjusting the magnification in the Page Setup dialog box. This solution probably isn't the best choice for presentation copies of reports, however.

Chapter 13: Printing

For more serious Preview problems, you may need to go back to Layout mode and make adjustments. Omitting unnecessary fields is always a good idea; doing so provides more room for relevant data. Consult Chapter 12 for more information on the fine art of preparing reports, including tweaking the layout and creating new layouts that are report specific.

The following steps explain how to use Preview mode and what to do if a report is less than perfect:

1. **Prepare a report according to the steps listed earlier in this chapter in the section, "Selecting and sorting."**
2. **Choose Preview mode from the Select menu (or press ⌘-U).**
3. **Click the book icon to view the report's contents page by page.**
4. **Use the scroll bars to move around on each page if the screen isn't large enough to display it all.**

   You also can drag the window's size box to increase the available area.

5. **Review each page carefully to ensure that all data fits without running off the edge. Check for other problems.**
6. **Correct errors in Layout mode or by setting different options in the Page Setup dialog box.**

When the report appears satisfactory, you are ready to proceed with the next step, which is actually printing the report.

Printing

Printing itself should seem like a breeze after all the preparatory work you have done. In a perfect world, it would be. Alas, the world is not perfect — at least not insofar as humans are involved. Fortunately however, humans happen to be creative enough to solve most of the problems they create.

Curiously enough, you accomplish the actual act of printing a report in FileMaker Pro by issuing the Print command. You can find this command in the File menu. Or, as in most all Macintosh application programs, you can press ⌘-P to print.

The Print command

Choosing the Print command (or pressing ⌘-P) displays a dialog box that is similar to the one shown in Figure 13-9. The exact appearance of the dialog box may vary, depending on which printer you have chosen. We'll begin by examining the options that are presented for the LaserWriter printers.

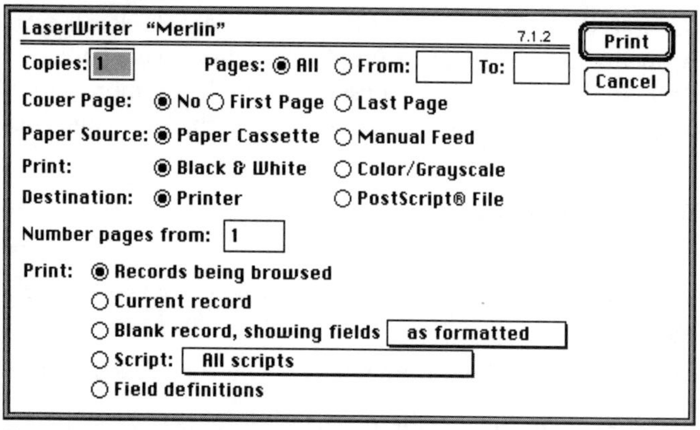

Figure 13-9: The Print dialog box for a LaserWriter.

In the upper-left corner is a text box into which you enter the number of copies that you want to print. Although this box may look as if it provides a handy way to make large numbers of copies for distribution, it isn't the best choice. Most printers aren't designed to function as demand copiers, and they tend to cost more than copiers to maintain and operate. You should normally limit the number of copies to 2 or 3 and make extra copies only for small reports (fewer than ten pages).

Next to the Copies text box are controls for designating which pages to print. Click the radio button of your choice and enter the appropriate numbers if you want to restrict printing to a particular range of pages (2 through 4, for example). Sometimes, to make doubly certain that everything is correct, you may want to print only the first page of a report. In that case, you enter **1** in both the From and To boxes.

Next come a series of radio button options that control how the print job is performed:

- *Cover Page:* You use this option to designate whether to include a cover page as part of the print job and whether to place the cover page before the report or after it. A cover page is useful if you're printing on a network printer and want to make sure that your print job is properly identified. Your user name, the name of the document you're printing, and the number of pages appear on the cover page.

- *Paper Source:* You use this option to designate whether paper will be drawn from the printer's internal paper cassette or fed by hand. The Manual Feed option is not useful for long reports, but you can use it to print a single envelope or piece of letterhead, for example. Envelopes are best fed manually unless you have a special envelope cassette.

- *Print:* Choose Black & White for text-only reports; it's faster. Choose Color/Grayscale if you're including graphics. Otherwise, they may come out looking like badly overexposed photographs.

Chapter 13: Printing

❖ *Destination:* Choose Printer to send the job directly to the printer that you have chosen. Choosing PostScript File creates a disk file into which the print job is spooled. You can send such a file to a service bureau for printing on a fancy image-setter.

At the bottom of the dialog box are options that are specific to FileMaker Pro. The first option enables you to enter the number to use for the first page of the printout. For example, you would enter a number other than 1 if you were preparing one grand document from several smaller reports. In this case, you would let FileMaker Pro know to begin numbering each report section where the previous section left off. Thus, if the first section you printed had six pages, when you went to print the second section you would enter **7** in this text box.

Finally, FileMaker Pro's Print dialog box has several radio buttons that control exactly what is to be printed:

❖ *Records being browsed:* Prints the current found set in the current sort order.

❖ *Current record:* Prints only one record; the one currently visible on the Macintosh screen.

❖ *Blank record, showing fields:* Prints an empty record. You choose from the pop-up menu to determine what kind of border to put around each field.

❖ *Script:* Choose which script to print from the pop-up menu. All scripts that are defined for the current database are shown.

❖ *Field definitions:* Prints the field definitions for this database.

When you have made all of your selections in the Print dialog box, click Print to print the material, or click Cancel if you change your mind.

The Print command — StyleWriter

The Print dialog box for a StyleWriter is different from that for a LaserWriter. When you are using a StyleWriter and you choose the Print command, you see a dialog box like the one in Figure 13-10.

Figure 13-10: The Print dialog box for a StyleWriter.

Many options are the same as those shown for the LaserWriter. In addition, the StyleWriter enables you to set the print quality. You use Best for high quality and Faster for lower quality but speedier printing.

The Print command — ImageWriter

The Print dialog box for an ImageWriter also is different from that for a LaserWriter. When you are using an ImageWriter and you choose the Print command, you see a dialog box like the one in Figure 13-11.

Figure 13-11: The Print dialog box for an ImageWriter.

Many options are the same as those shown for the LaserWriter. And as with the StyleWriter, you can set the print quality: Best for high quality and Faster for lower quality but speedier printing. The ImageWriter offers a third print quality option: Draft. The Draft option uses a built-in font and is very fast, but it can produce strange results. Use Draft only for tests. The ImageWriter also offers check box options that you can use to indicate whether you are using a color ribbon and whether you want the computer to spool documents to memory prior to printing. Spooling frees up the Mac to do other things.

Follow these steps to print a report after you finish setting options in the Print dialog box:

1. **Choose Print from the File menu (or press ⌘-P).**

2. *Optional:* **Enter the number of copies to print, if more than one.**

3. **Select whether to print the entire report or a range of pages.**

   If you do not want to print the entire report, enter the first and last page numbers of the range.

4. Select whether to include a cover page and whether it should come at the beginning or end of the print job (LaserWriter).

5. Select whether to restrict printing to black-and-white or to print in color/grayscale (LaserWriter).

6. Choose the destination for the print job: the chosen printer or a file on disk (LaserWriter).

7. Choose a print quality level (ImageWriter/StyleWriter).

8. Select a paper source.

9. Choose what to print by using the radio button options at the bottom of the dialog box.

10. Click Print.

Although using the Print dialog box involves many steps, you can bypass all of them if you want to. FileMaker Pro enables you to send off a print job without bringing up the Print dialog box. In this case, FileMaker Pro uses all of the dialog box's default choices, which are shown in Figure 13-9.

To bypass the Print dialog box and print directly, follow these steps:

1. Prepare and preview the report.

2. Press Option-⌘-P.

   An alert box appears briefly, telling you what's to be printed.

To cancel a print job as it's being sent to your printer (regardless of the type of printer you are using), press ⌘-Period (.). If your print driver supports background printing (a LaserWriter, for example) and you have selected that option in the Chooser, you need to press ⌘-Period (.) very quickly—before the print job has spooled to disk. If you aren't fast enough, you can use the PrintMonitor to cancel the print job.

Printing in the background with PrintMonitor

If you're using a laser printer and have chosen to print in the background, you will have occasion to deal with PrintMonitor. This Apple system software utility monitors printing while you go on with your work. PrintMonitor automatically runs when you send something to the printer. In System 7, it appears as a selection in and can be chosen from the Application menu, which is at the far right of the menu bar. (See Chapter 2 for more information about the Application menu.) Figure 13-12 shows PrintMonitor.

Part III: Working with Databases

```
┌─────────────────────────────────────┐
│ □            PrintMonitor           │
│              Printing               │
│  ┌───────────────────────────────┐  │
│  │ 🖨 FM00SS13.DOC @ Merlin     │  │
│  └───────────────────────────────┘  │
│               Waiting               │
│  ┌───────────────────────────────┐  │
│  │                              ▲│  │
│  │                               │  │
│  │                              ▼│  │
│  └───────────────────────────────┘  │
│   ( Cancel Printing )  ( Set Print Time... ) │
│  Printing Status: FM00SS13.DOC      │
│  Pages To Print: 15                 │
│  Waiting for LaserWriter "Merlin":  status: processing │
│  job                                │
└─────────────────────────────────────┘
```

Figure 13-12: PrintMonitor with a job in progress.

Note that PrintMonitor is used *only* in conjunction with background printing. Other printers that do not have drivers that support background printing must print in the foreground; that is, while a document is printing on such a printer, you must wait for it to finish before regaining control of your Mac. PrintMonitor is not available for such printers.

An area at the top of the PrintMonitor window shows which document is currently being printed, as well as the name of the chosen printer. Below this area is a list of any other documents that are waiting to be printed. If there are many jobs, you can use the scroll bar to examine them and their position in the list. The two buttons enable you to cancel a print job or set a specific time to have a job printed. Finally, a message area at the bottom of the window tells you what the printer is currently doing.

If you have any print jobs waiting, you can drag them into different positions to change the order in which they will be printed. To postpone a job until a specific time, select its name and then click Set Print Time. You see a dialog box like the one shown in Figure 13-13.

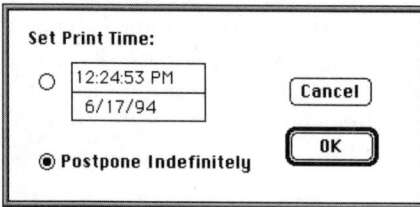

Figure 13-13: Setting a time for printing.

Enter the time and date that you want the document to be printed. You may want to choose a time when the office is closed if you're in a busy office, if you have trouble getting access to the network printer, or if don't need your printout right away. This option is especially good if you're printing a very large report. Delaying such a job until after hours shows consideration for the needs of your coworkers and avoids the problems caused by having the only network printer tied up for a long period of time.

In the Set Print Time dialog box, you also can postpone a job indefinitely. PrintMonitor will hold on to the job until you choose PrintMonitor from the Application menu again and select Set Print Time. The default time that comes up is always the current time, so you need only click OK to print the job.

Perhaps the most common reason to use PrintMonitor is to cancel a print job. To cancel a background print job with PrintMonitor, follow these steps:

1. **Choose PrintMonitor from the Application menu.**

2. **If the print job isn't the one that is currently printing, click to select the job.**

3. **Click the Cancel Printing button.**

   The Macintosh may take a few seconds to respond.

Printing More Effectively

The preceding information is all you need to know about run-of-the-mill printing. However, the following tips and tricks are useful if you want to get the most out of your printer. What's more, you will likely run into occasional problems. The section on troubleshooting outlines some of the most common problems and provides some solutions to them.

Tips and tricks

Every type of printer has its quirks. Understanding some of the more common idiosyncrasies and knowing how to deal with them not only can save you a great deal of grief, but also can help you achieve better results. The following basic hints apply to the most common kinds of printers:

Laser printers

- *Sunny side up:* Not many people are aware that most laser printer paper (and copier paper, which is the same thing and is frequently used in its place) has a good side and a so-so side. The paper's manufacturer intends for the paper to be printed only on the good side. You can achieve the best results by making sure that you do print on the good side.

  Sometimes, you cannot easily determine which side is the good side by just looking at the paper. The good side *may* be shinier. A better way to tell is to look at the package in which the paper came. In many cases, you will see an arrow or some other indicator that shows which side is meant to be printed on. When inserting the paper into your printer, be sure that the correct side is up. (Some printers expect paper to be inserted face up, while others print on the side of the paper that is face down. If you aren't sure which way you should insert paper into your particular printer, refer to the printer manual.)

- *We be jammin':* Everybody hates paper jams and misfeeds. You can't avoid them all, but you can cut down on their number and frequency. When you load a printer, grasp the paper firmly and "riffle" the edges with your thumb. Just draw your thumb down the edges as if you were flipping through the whole stack of paper. This action loosens the individual sheets from each other, lessening the chance that two or more pieces of paper will be drawn into the printer together.

- *Fontasies come true:* A laser printer takes a long time to do two things: construct a font for use on a document and prepare a graphic. To save time, use only fonts that are built into the printer at the factory (the printer doesn't have to construct these fonts). This tip is one to consider when you are designing a layout. Also, try to limit the number of different text styles that you use. Using too many fonts makes documents print slowly and can even, in extreme cases, crash the system or the printer.

- *You only go 'round once:* Several companies (such as Avery) make special labels for use in laser printers. Resist the temptation to use only a few labels from one sheet and then reuse the sheet later. After a few passes, the extreme heat of the laser printing process can cause a sheet of labels to warp and even partially melt or char, resulting in no end of expensive trouble. Try to do label printing jobs in large batches and throw away the unused labels from each batch (or find another use for them). The printer you save may be your own.

- *Is it just me, or is it warm in here?:* If your printer has been turned off, be sure to allow enough time for it to warm up. If you try to print on it immediately after you turn it on, you will likely see a message telling you that the printer isn't responding. Give it a minute or so before you try again.

Dot-matrix printers

- *Don't be uptight:* When you are using tractor-fed computer paper, make sure that the tension is adjusted correctly between the two feed mechanisms. Too little tension can cause the paper to jam and misfeed; too much tension can tear off the perforated edges and cause another kind of misfeed. Getting the tension exactly right is something of an art.

- *Back in the black:* Use only new ribbons and keep them well inked. Old ribbons can fray, resulting in ugly printouts and even damage to the print head.

Ink-jet printers

- *Ink-a-dink:* Avoid printing long reports that have a large number of graphics. Graphics consume a great deal of expensive ink and take longer to print.

- *Time on my hands:* To speed up printing, limit the number of fonts in the report. You also may want to select a lower print quality for jobs that you will not use for presentations.

Troubleshooting

Things go wrong. Here's what to do if you encounter a printing problem:

- *My printer doesn't do anything:* Is it turned off (the #1 cause of missed print jobs)? Are cable connections snug and secure? With printers such as the StyleWriter and ImageWriter, be sure that the correct port is selected in the Chooser.

- *The laser printer isn't visible in the Chooser:* Is your printer properly hooked up? Again, make sure that all cables are secure and tight. If you are printing to a network laser printer, see if it is connected correctly to the network. Is the printer on-line (turned on)?

- *Print quality seems poor:* Does a laser printer need more toner, does a StyleWriter need more ink, or does an ImageWriter need a new ribbon? Failure to print dense, even, black tones can be caused by low toner. You can temporarily correct this problem by gently rotating the toner cartridge a few times or increasing the print density setting on your laser (if it has one). With the StyleWriter and ImageWriter, see that print quality is set to its highest.

- *Laser printing is taking too long:* Is the printer hung up? If it's having trouble printing your job, it may have a glitch. Try turning off the printer, waiting a few seconds, and then restarting it. You will have to use PrintMonitor to restart the job.

    Occasionally, some print jobs may simply be too complex for your laser printer to handle. Try reprinting them with different print options, printing a smaller set of pages, or turning off background printing. You may be able to isolate the cause of the problem.

- *Fields are trailing off the page:* You need to change the magnification, select a new layout, or make layout changes to accommodate the fields. Be sure to use Preview before you print.

Part III: Working with Databases

CHAPTER 13 CONCEPTS AND TERMS

- Before you can print, you need to use the Chooser desk accessory to tell the Mac which printer you want to use. Once a print driver and printer have been selected, all future print jobs will be sent to that printer. If you have just one printer, you will only need to use the Chooser again if you reinstall system software or update to a new version, buy a new printer, or obtain a newer version of your printer's print driver. If you have several printers, you must revisit the Chooser whenever you want to send a job to a different printer.

- In the Page Setup dialog box, you set page options for the document you're about to print. These options include the kind of paper you want to print on, the amount of scaling to use, and whether to employ special effects, such as inversion or printing continuous sheets. Page Setup settings are document-specific and are saved along with the other information contained in the document.

- After setting up a page, you can use Preview mode to view a report on-screen. This mode shows how the report will look when you print it. You can correct problems at this stage before you waste time and paper.

- Printing is accomplished via the Print dialog box. In the Print dialog box, you can set the number of copies to print; which pages to print; whether to use color or gray if your printer can handle them; and exactly what database contents to print, including the current record, found set, scripts, and field definitions.

- To print directly (without using the Print dialog box), you press ⌘-Option-P.

- You can avoid many potential printing problems by setting up a printer correctly before you print. Checking the integrity of all cable connections, loading paper the right way, and restricting the use of fonts and graphics can ensure better results.

picture element (pixel or dot), is passed rapidly over a page, hammering out an impression through a ribbon.

ink jet
A type of printer technology in which ink is forced at high pressure onto the page. Ink-jet printers are frequently inexpensive, while being able to match the resolution and quality of many laser printers. The biggest drawback of ink-jet printers is their speed (or—more precisely—their lack of it).

laser printing
A type of printer technology in which laser light creates an image of a page on a rotating drum, magnetizing the drum. Toner particles adhere to the magnetized drum and are then transferred onto paper, where they are fused at high heat. This technology works like a conventional photocopier.

Preview
A FileMaker Pro mode that enables the user to see what a printed report or other document will look like prior to committing it to paper.

print driver
A software program that is used to control a specific printer. Macintosh print drivers are accessed in the Chooser.

PrintMonitor
A special Apple program that watches over and controls background laser print jobs.

bit-map
A collection of individual picture elements (pixels or dots) that together constitute a graphic item.

Chooser
An Apple desk accessory that tells the System which printer you want to use.

dogcow
An icon in the LaserWriter Page Setup Options dialog box that demonstrates the combined effects of various selected options.

dot matrix
A type of printer technology in which a print head that has many pins, each corresponding to one

Part IV
Intermediate Topics

CHAPTER FOURTEEN

Calculations and Computations

- Understanding Calculation fields and their uses
- Creating Calculation fields, including the use of algebraic and logical operations
- Learning about FileMaker Pro's built-in functions

For many purposes, being able to perform certain calculations on fields in a database is quite useful. For example, in an invoices database, where each record is an order, you may want to total all the prices for each item in an order, add in the sales tax, and then print the result. If the cost of shipping varies according to distance, you would want to be able to determine how much to charge each order, based on its state of destination. You may think that you need to do such calculations — and considerably more complex ones — manually, but FileMaker Pro offers a variety of computational and calculational capabilities through the use of its Calculation fields.

A *Calculation field* performs a specific operation or group of operations on specific data. The data is usually the contents of other fields in the current record. The operations that you can perform include the standard arithmetic functions, logical operations, and even special built-in operations that perform complex calculations on numbers and text.

About Calculation Fields

Like any field in FileMaker Pro, a Calculation field has two aspects: its definition and the data it contains. In the case of a Calculation field, the *data* consists of whatever result is obtained when the field's definition is evaluated. The *definition* specifies, in mathematical form, what manipulations to perform on the contents of one or more other fields in the current record. The results of these manipulations, or operations, are then displayed as the field's contents.

Consider a brief example. Suppose that you have an invoicing database that includes a field named Merchandise Total. You want to be able to compute the sales tax on this total and to display the Grand Total for the bill, which consists of the merchandise total plus the sales tax. You could use Calculation fields for both the sales tax and the grand total. The field definitions might look like this:

```
Sales Tax = .06125 * Merchandise Total (Multiply total by tax rate)
Grand Total = Merchandise Total + Sales Tax (Add tax to total)
```

Suppose that your current record shows a Merchandise Total of $20.00. In that case, the Sales Tax field would display 1.225, and the Grand Total would display 21.225. Of course, you would want to round this figure off to the nearest cent before presenting a bill; FileMaker Pro enables you to round it off easily, as you will see in the section on built-in functions.

You may think that Calculation fields are quite similar to Summary fields, and you would be right. These kinds of fields have one important difference, however, that has already been mentioned. Whereas Summary fields apply results across a *range* of records, the results of a Calculation field apply only to data in the *current* record. For example, if you want to compute the total sales for all the invoices issued over a certain span of time, you define a Summary field, but to calculate the merchandise total within one invoice, you use a Calculation field.

Calculation fields can do much more than just adding or multiplying the contents of other fields. Calculation fields also can manipulate the contents of Text fields and can perform tests on the contents of fields in order to determine which alternative course of action to select.

A formula in a Calculation field can contain several different components: field references, operators, constants, and built-in functions. You need to learn about these components in order to understand how to create Calculation fields.

Available operations

FileMaker Pro uses operators to specify how to manipulate data items. These operators fall into three broad categories. *Arithmetic operators* work with numbers, performing computations with them. *Logical operators* test to see whether specified conditions are true or false; this information can then be used to determine a course of action. *Text operators* work with text, extracting information from it or converting it into another form.

Arithmetic operations

The arithmetic operators perform the basic functions of arithmetic. Following is a list of these operators:

Chapter 14: Calculations and Computations

+   The plus sign performs addition. 2 + 3 means 5.

–   The minus sign performs subtraction. 3 - 2 means 1.

*   The asterisk indicates multiplication. 2 * 3 means 6.

/   The slash indicates division. 3 / 2 means 1.5.

^   The caret indicates exponentiation, or raising a number to a power. 3 ^ 2 means three to the second power, or 9.

Logical operations

The logical operators perform comparisons and, if necessary, combine the results into more complex tests. Basically, the logical operators are used to test the truth or falsity of some assertion. Consider a simple example:

`1 = 2 (one equals two)`

This statement is false; one does not equal two. Now consider another example:

`Bob's Sales > Anne's Sales (Bob's sales exceed Anne's sales)`

You don't know whether this statement is true because you don't know how much Bob or Anne sold. If Bob's sales equaled 1500 and Anne's sales equaled 1000, then the statement would be true. If the figures were reversed, with Anne earning 1500 and Bob limited to 1000, the statement would be false.

Why do you care? Because you can have a Calculation field perform additional steps that are based on whether a statement that you have entered is true or false. You might use the following formula in the Calculation field to present a different message (a Text result) depending on which salesperson closed the most sales:

`If (Bob Sales > Anne Sales, "Nice going, Bob!", "Nice going, Anne!")`

If Bob's sales totaled more than Anne's sales, the Calculation field displays the true condition for the test (that is, first message):

`Nice going, Bob!`

If Bob's sales were not greater than Anne's, the field displays the false condition for the test (that is, the second message):

`Nice going, Anne!`

You will learn more about putting logical operators together to perform tasks such as this as the chapter progresses, particularly when you get to the section on the IF function. See Table 14-1 for a list of logical operators and what they mean.

Table 14-1
Logical Operators

Operator	What It Means
=	Means "equals." The test is true if the items on either side of the sign are exactly equal in value. The statement 1 + 1 = 2 is true.
<> or ≠	Means "not equal to." The test is true if the items on either side of the sign are not equal in value. "Bob" <> "Anne" is true.
>	Means "greater than." The test is true if the item at the left of the sign exceeds in value the item to the right. 3 > 2 is true.
<	Means "less than." The test is true if the item at the left of the sign is smaller in value than the item to the right. 2 < 3 is true.
≤	Means "less than or equal to." 2.9 + 0.1 < 3 is true.
≥	Means "greater than or equal to." 2.9 + 0.1 > 3 is true.
AND	Used to combine the results of two separate tests. The result is true if, and only if, the results of both tests are also true. 3 > 2 AND 2 < 3 is true.
OR	Used to combine the results of two separate tests. The result is true if either, or both, of the tests are also true. 3 > 2 OR 2 > 3 is true.
NOT	Used to switch a test's result to its opposite. NOT 2 > 3 is true.

Text operations

The following are the three basic text operators:

-   &   Used to combine (or *concatenate*) two Text fields into one; "market" & "place" = "marketplace"

-   " "   Used to indicate a text constant. If you enter a text item without quotes, FileMaker Pro assumes that you mean the name of a field. "Anne " + Last Name = Anne Rice if Last Name contains Rice in the current record.

-   | Used to indicate a paragraph break within a text constant. If you want a constant to have more than one line, you need to use this operator to separate lines. "Anne|Rice" means
  Anne
  Rice

Creating an expression

Operators are combined with constants (numerical or text) and field names to create expressions. Think of an expression as a mathematical statement. From an earlier example, both of the following are statements:

Chapter 14: Calculations and Computations

```
Sales Tax = .06125 * Merchandise Total
Grand Total = Merchandise Total + Sales Tax
```

The sales tax rate, "0.06125," is a numerical constant; its value does not change. "Merchandise Total" represents the contents of that field in the current record; it may very well change from record to record. If you recall your high school or college algebra, you will recognize "Merchandise Total," or any valid field name, as a variable. Expressions consists of constants and variables that are separated by operators.

You can build complicated expressions if you wish. Of special use in this case are parentheses; you can use them to indicate the order in which to perform operations. For example, consider the following expression:

```
1 + 2 * 3
```

FileMaker Pro evaluates according to the standard algebraic order of operations, which specifies that all multiplications are done *before* any additions. The result for this expression is 7, not 9, which you might expect if all operations were performed strictly in left-to-right order.

To force FileMaker Pro to perform operations in the order that you want, you can use parentheses. Operations within parentheses are performed first, from innermost to outermost. You can nest operations within parentheses to gain further control. The following expression equals 18:

```
((( 1 + 2 ) * 3 ) * 2 )
```

Without parentheses, it equals 13. The standard order of operations is

> Exponentiation
>
> Multiplication and division
>
> Addition and subtraction

You also can use parentheses with logical expressions. The following expression is true:

```
(3 > 2 OR 2 > 3) AND 2 > 1
```

Creating a Calculation field

To create a Calculation field, you determine the results you want, create an expression that defines these results in mathematical terms, and then define the field. After you create the field in the Define Fields dialog box, you see an additional dialog box that is similar to Figure 14-1.

Part IV: Intermediate Topics

Figure 14-1: Defining a Calculation field.

The fields available in the current database appear in a scrolling list at the left. In the center are available operators. To the right are available functions. You learn more about functions in the next section. For now, you need to know only that a *function* is a predefined set of operations that work with specific kinds of data. A function operates on the data, known as the function's *arguments*, and then returns a result.

Below the Operations area is a large blank area. As you type a definition for the Calculation field, it appears in this area. You can type the definition directly or simply double-click the appropriate field names and single-click the operators. Below this area, a pop-up menu indicates what type of data the field's result should be. You need to be sure to select the correct result type.

As an example, the following steps show how to define a new Calculation field named My Sales Tax that calculates sales tax in Santa Fe county, where the rate is currently 6 1/8 percent:

1. **Choose Define Fields from the Select menu (or press ⌘-Shift-D).**

   The Define Fields dialog box appears.

2. **Type the name for the field,** My Field, **click the Calculation Field radio button (or press ⌘-C), and then click Create.**

   The Calculation Field dialog box (refer to Figure 14-1) appears.

3. **Double-click Product Subtotal in the Fields list and then click * .06125.**

   The result should be a number. Number is the default in the "Calculation result is" pop-up menu, so in this case you do not have to select a result data type. Be sure to select the correct result data type when you are creating other Calculation fields.

Chapter 14: Calculations and Computations

4. Click OK.

You return to the Define Fields dialog box, and the new Calculation field appears in the box.

You can examine a range of already-defined Calculation fields by looking at the template files that are included with FileMaker Pro. A particularly good template to examine is Invoices. With Invoices open, choose Define Fields from the Select menu (or press ⌘-Shift-D). The dialog box will show the definitions for all of the Calculation fields in the database.

About FileMaker Pro's Built-In Functions

Before you go begin to create your own complicated Calculation fields, you may be interested to know that FileMaker Pro comes equipped with a number of pre-defined calculations (see Table 14-2). Some of them can save you the expense of reinventing the wheel to solve a particular problem; others give you capabilities you wouldn't have otherwise.

Table 14-2
FileMaker Pro's Built-In Functions

Function Name	Purpose
Abs	Absolute value of expression
Atan	Arctangent of expression, in radians
Average	Compute average value of all values in a repeating field
Cos	Compute cosine of expression, expression in radians
Count	Count number of valid, nonempty entries in repeating field
Date	Convert numeric values into valid date
DateToText	Convert value in Date field to text
Day	Give day of month, 1 – 31, for given date
DayName	Print weekday name for given date
DayofYear	Give number of day, 1 – 366, for given date
Degrees	Convert value in radians into degrees
Exact	Return "true" if two text expressions match exactly, including case

(continued on the next page)

Part IV: Intermediate Topics

Table 14-2 *(continued)*	
Function Name	**Purpose**
Exp	Return antilog (base e) of expression
Extend	Make a nonrepeating field a repeating field, with the identical value in each place, for calculations with other repeating fields
FV	Given payment, interest rate, and number of periods, compute investment's future value
Hour	Give number of hours in a time expression
If	Perform logical test and do one action if it is true, another if it is false
Int	Return integer portion of numeric value
Last	Show last valid, nonempty entry in a repeating field
Left	Give leftmost part of given text string to indicated number of places
Length	Find number of characters in given text string
Ln	Compute natural (base e) logarithm of expression
Log	Compute common (base 10) logarithm of expression. Use 10 ^ *expression* for common antilog
Lower	Convert text string to all lowercase
Max	Give greatest value among those in a repeating field
Middle	Return middle portion of supplied text string, starting at given position and extending for specified number of characters
Min	Give smallest value among those in a repeating field
Minute	Return minute portion of time expression
Mod	Return remainder when an expression is divided by a given number
Month	Give number of month in date expression, range 1 – 12
MonthName	Give name of month in date expression
NPV	Using values in repeating field as unequal payment values, and given interest rate, find net present value of investment
NumToText	Convert numeric expression to text format
Pi	Return value of mathematical constant pi
PMT	Given principal, interest rate, and term, return loan payment
Position	Scan given text for given string starting at a certain position, return location of first occurrence of string

(continued on the next page)

Chapter 14: Calculations and Computations

Table 14-2 *(continued)*	
Function Name	*Purpose*
Proper	Convert first letter of each word in text string to uppercase; capitalize names
PV	Given payment, interest rate, and periods, calculate present value of investment
Radians	Convert degree value in radians, for use with trigonometric functions
Random	Generate random number
Replace	In a text string, start at given position, for a certain number of places, and replace existing text with supplied new text string
Right	Counting from right, return given number of characters in text expression
Round	Round off numeric expression to given number of decimal places
Seconds	Give seconds part of time expression
Sign	Examine numeric expression and return 1 for positive, – 1 for negative, 0 for 0
Sin	Compute sine of angle given in radians
Sqrt	Compute square root of numeric expression. Same as *expression* ^ 0.5
StDev	Examine all values in repeating field and give standard deviation
Sum	Total all values in repeating field
Summary	Extract value of given Summary field for current record range, field sorted by given break field
Tan	Compute tangent for given angle, angle expressed in radians
TextToDate	Convert text string into date format
TextToNum	Convert text string to numeric format, ignore alphabetic characters
TextToTime	Convert text string to time format
Time	Convert three given numeric values into time equivalent
TimeToText	Convert time value into text format
Today	Return current date from system clock
Trim	Strip supplied text expression of leading and/or trailing spaces
Upper	Convert text expression to all uppercase
WeekOfYear	Determine number of week in year, 1 – 52, for supplied date expression
Year	Return year part of given date expression

The functions fall into several categories, but they all work in the same way. A function performs operations on data and then returns a result. We call the data *arguments* to the function. The arguments are enclosed in parentheses directly after the function name. For example, in the expression

```
Round(Sales Tax, 2)
```

Round is the function name, and Sales Tax and 2 are the arguments.

A function expects certain types of data for each argument: numbers, text, or logical results. Failure to provide the correct types of arguments will result in errors. For example, although you can choose a Text field as an argument to the Round function, the calculation doesn't make any sense and simply results in a blank field. The kinds of data expected for each argument appear to the right of the function's name in the Calculation Field dialog box (refer to Figure 14-1).

Functions don't have to be the only component in an expression. They can be combined with constants or field references, as shown in this example:

```
Product Total + Round(Sales Tax, 2)
```

It shows an expression to define a Grand Total field, obtained by adding the Product Total to the results of rounding off the Sales Tax field's contents to two decimal places. The following example demonstrates that an expression also can be used as the argument to a function:

```
Round(Product Total * .06125, 2)
```

In this example, the Sales Tax field is replaced by an expression that yields the same result. The result of this expression is Sales Tax rounded to two decimal places.

Functions fall into nine categories, which are defined by the type of data with which the functions work. The following sections provide more details about all of FileMaker Pro's built-in functions. The functions are listed alphabetically under the category to which they belong. In addition to an explanation of each function's purpose and an example of how the function is used, the sections include a statement that shows how to phrase the function and its arguments. (The order for arranging the function and its arguments is called the *syntax* of the function.) Special notes and cautions, as well as references to other, related functions, are included in the explanations of some of the functions.

To use a function in a Calculation field definition, double-click its name in the Function list. Then replace its arguments with the appropriate field names or expressions.

Data conversion functions

These functions convert one type of data into another type. They are useful for achieving uniform results and for passing the results of one calculation on to another calculation that uses a different data type.

Chapter 14: Calculations and Computations

DateToText   NumToText   TextToDate
TextToNum   TextToTime TimeToText

DateToText

Purpose: Changes the contents of a Date field into text format. The result can then be passed on to another calculation that requires text input, or it can be printed directly. The text result appears in the form MM/DD/YY, so that September 2, 1994, appears as 09/02/94.

Syntax: DateToText (*date*), where
> *date* is a Date field or an expression yielding the date data type.

Example: The following expression defines a Calculation field, with text results, giving an invoice date after the text "The invoice was prepared on":

```
"The Invoice was prepared on " & DateToText(Invoice Date)
```

If the invoice date were October 1, 1994, the field would contain

```
The Invoice was prepared on 10/01/94
```

See Also: TextToDate

NumToText

Purpose: Changes the contents of a numeric field into text format. The result can then be passed on to another calculation that requires text input, or it can be printed directly.

Syntax: NumToText (*number*), where
> *number* is a number field or is a numerical expression.

Example: The following expression shows a field that tells a customer how much an order cost:

```
"Your order came to $" & NumtoText(Grand Total)
```

If the Grand Total field contained 99.95, the expression's value would be

```
Your order came to $99.95
```

See Also: TextToNum

TextToDate

Purpose: Changes a text date value directly into date format. The text supplied must be in the format MM/DD/YYYY for this function to work correctly.

Syntax: TextToDate(*text*), where
> *text* is a text constant or text expression in the form MM/DD/YYYY.

Example: The following expression converts a text constant into date format:

```
TextToDate("03/16/1960")
```

This expression yields the following result in date format:

```
03/16/60
```

See Also: DateToText, Date

Note: This function and the Date function are the only ways to enter a date constant into a formula that requires a date parameter, such as DayOfYear and DayName.

TextToNum

Purpose: Converts the number part of a text expression into numeric format. The alphabetic portion is ignored.

Syntax: TextToNum(*text*) where

text is a text constant or a text expression.

Example: The following defines a Calculation field in which non-numeric data such as a dollar sign and commas are stripped from a price:

```
TextToNum(Price)
```

If the Price field had been entered as $19,995.95, the Calculation field would contain

```
19995.95
```

See Also: NumToText

TextToTime

Purpose: Converts a text value or expression into time format. The results can then be passed on to a calculation that requires data in time format.

Syntax: TextToTime(*text*), where

text is a text constant or text expression. The date supplied must be in the form HH:MM:SS; seconds are optional. AM and PM may be used as suffixes.

Example: The expression

```
TextToTime(02:15pm)
```

yields 14:15:00 for use in time calculations.

See Also: TimeToText

Note: TextToTime and Time are the only ways to enter a time constant into a function or expression that requires data in time format.

Chapter 14: Calculations and Computations

TimeToText

Purpose: Converts a time format result into text format. The result may be printed directly or used in a text-based expression.

Syntax: TimeToText(*time*), where
time is a time format field or an expression yielding a time format result.

Example: The following extracts the time from a field and prints it along with a message:

```
"Your order was prepared at " & TimeToText(Time Entered)
```

If the Time Entered field contained 02:15:00, the field would read

```
Your order was prepared at 2:15:00
```

See Also: TextToTime

Date functions

Date functions are used to find out various facts about dates entered by the user, to determine the current date from the system clock, and to convert number data into date format.

Date	Day	DayName
DayofYear	Month	MonthName
Today	WeekofYear	Year

Date

Purpose: Determines the calendar date associated with three numbers, interpreted as days, months, and years, computed since January 1, 1 AD.

Syntax: Date(*month*, *day*, *year*) where
month is number of months
day is number of days
year is number of years (all are numeric expressions).

Example: In a database, the fields Month and Day specified the amount of time elapsed until an invoice is overdue. Year contains the year it was issued in. If the fields contain 19, 19, and 1990, then the expression

```
"Your invoice became overdue on " & Date(Month,Day,Year)
```

yields the result

```
Your invoice became overdue on July 19, 1991
```

See Also: Day, Month, Year

Day

Purpose: Returns a number from 1 to 31, which shows the number of the day in the month for a supplied date. The value returned is numeric.

Syntax: Day(*date*), where
> *date* is a valid expression with a date format.

Example: If the field Date contains the value 02/26/60, then the expression

```
Day(Date)
```

returns the following value

```
26
```

See Also: Month, Year

DayName

Purpose: Returns a text string with the name of the day of the week for the supplied date expression. The text returned is capitalized.

Syntax: DayName(*date*), where
> *date* is a valid date.

Example: The following expression could be used as part of a message in a form letter. The expression

```
"We missed you on " & DayName(Appointment Date)
```

yields the result

```
We missed you on Thursday
```

if the Appointment Date field contains 06/23/94.

See Also: MonthName

DayofYear

Purpose: Returns the number of days elapsed in the appropriate year since the date given. The result is a numeric value.

Syntax: DayOfYear(*date*), where
> *date* is a valid date expression.

Example: The following expression can be used to print a message about the Yuletide holiday:

```
"Only " & NumToText(358 - DayOfYear(Today's Date)) & " days
until Christmas!"
```

If the Today's Date field contains the value 12/23/94, then the expression yields

```
Only 2 days until Christmas!
```

See Also: WeekOfYear

Month

Purpose: Returns a numeric value in the range 1 through 12, corresponding to the month in the given date expression.

Syntax: Month(*date*), where
date is a valid expression in date format.

Example: If the Date field contains 03/16/60, then the expression

```
Month(Date)
```

yields

```
3
```

See Also: Day, Year

MonthName

Purpose: Returns a text value with the proper name of the month in the given date expression. The text returned is capitalized.

Syntax: MonthName(*date*), where
date is a valid date expression.

Example: If the field Date contains the value 02/16/60, the expression

```
MonthName(Date) & " was a good month! You were born."
```

yields

```
February was a good month! You were born.
```

See Also: DayName

Today

Purpose: Gets today's date, in proper date format, from the system clock. Obviously, the system clock in the Macintosh must be set correctly. Note that this function accepts no arguments.

Syntax: Today

Example: Use the Today function in a form letter layout to insert the current date (using the appropriate conversion):

```
DateToText(Today)
```

WeekofYear

Purpose: Calculates the number, in the range 1 through 52, of the given date in the year in which it occurred. Value returned is in numeric format.

Syntax: WeekofYear(*date*), where
date is a valid date expression.

Example: If the Date field contains the value 12/29/94, the expression

`WeekofYear(Date)`

returns the value

`52`

See Also: DayofYear

Year

Purpose: Extracts the year portion of a date expression. The value returned is in numeric format and can be used in calculations.

Syntax: Year(*date*), where
  date is a valid date expression.

Example: If the Date field contains the value 03/16/1960, then the expression

`Year(Date)`

yields the result

`1960`

The following expression yields the person's age after this year's birthday:

`Year(Today) - Year(Birthday)`

See Also: Day, Month

Field functions

Field functions are designed for use with values in repeating fields. Many of them perform statistical computations on these values. When a calculation is performed on a repeating field, only the repetitions that contain a value are included in the calculation. Note, too, that values that have entered for the repeating field but are not currently displayed are also included in the calculation.

Average	Count	Extend
Last	Max	Min
StDev	Sum	Summary

Average

Purpose: Computes the average value of all values in a repeating field. The average is found by adding all the values together and then dividing by the number of values so added. The result is a numeric value.

Syntax: Average(*repeating field name*), where
  repeating field name is the name of a valid, nonempty repeating field containing numeric values only.

Chapter 14: Calculations and Computations

Example: Suppose Prices is a repeating field containing the extended price of each item in an order. The following expression displays a message about the cost of these items:

```
"On average, the items you ordered cost $" &
NumToText(Average(Prices))
```

If Prices contains 5.00, 10.00, and 30.00, the expression yields

```
On average, the items you ordered cost $15.00
```

See Also: StDev, Max, Min

Count

Purpose: Determines the number of nonblank entries in a repeating field, returning the result as a numeric value.

Syntax: Count(*repeating field name*), where
repeating field name is the name of a valid, nonempty repeating field of any type.

Example: If the field Prices, formatted to contain up to ten values, actually contains 5.00, 10.00, and 30.00, then the following expression yields a message about the items ordered:

```
"You ordered " & Count(Prices) & " items. Thank you!"
```

In this case, the expression yields

```
You ordered 3 items. Thank you!
```

Extend

Purpose: Used to extend a nonrepeating field for use in calculations with other, repeating fields. Each value in the extended field is the same. Use this function when defining a repeating Calculation field that will work with repeating and nonrepeating fields.

Syntax: Extend(*nonrepeating field name*), where
nonrepeating field name is the name of a valid, single-entry field.

Example: The following expression defines the contents of the Calculation field Taxes, a ten-place field computed on item costs and a standard tax rate contained in the field Tax.

```
Prices * Extend(Tax)
```

Last

Purpose: Find the final entry in a nonempty repeating field. The entry is returned in the appropriate format.

Syntax: Last(*repeating field name*), where
> *repeating field name* is the name of a valid, nonempty repeating field of any type.

Example: If Prices is a numeric repeating field containing three values, 5.00, 10.00, and 30.00, then the expression

```
"The last item you ordered cost $" & Last(Prices)
```

yields the result

```
The last item you ordered cost $30.00
```

See Also: Max, Min

Max

Purpose: Finds the highest, latest, or greatest value among all values in a nonempty repeating field. The result is returned in the appropriate format.

Syntax: Max(*repeating field name*), where
> *repeating field name* is the name of a valid, nonempty repeating field of any type.

Example: Suppose that Dates is a ten-position repeating field containing dates of orders in an invoice record. Suppose, further, that it contains three values: 03/17/94, 04/18/94, and 05/19/94. In that case, the expression

```
"Your last order came on " & Max(Dates)
```

gives the result

```
Your last order came on 05/19/94
```

See Also: Min, Last

Min

Purpose: Scans a nonempty repeating field and finds the smallest, first, or earliest value in it. The result is returned in the appropriate format.

Syntax: Min(*repeating field name*), where
> *repeating field name* is the name of a valid, nonempty repeating field of any type.

Example: If Dates is a repeating field containing three values: 03/16/94, 04/17/94, and 05/18/94, then the expression

```
"Your first order came on " & Min(Dates)
```

gives the result

```
Your first order came on 03/16/94
```

See Also: Last, Max

StDev

Purpose: Computes the standard deviation for all values in a nonempty, numeric repeating field. The standard deviation gives a measure of how far the values in a range tend to depart from the average value.

Syntax: StDev(*repeating field name*), where
repeating field name is the name of a valid, nonempty repeating field containing numeric data only.

Example: If the field TestScores contains the values 98, 76, and 90, then the expression StDev(TestScores) yields 9.09, the standard deviation of these test scores.

See Also: Average, Max, Min

Sum

Purpose: Adds the contents of each nonblank entry in a numeric repeating field. The result returned is a numeric value.

Syntax: Sum(*repeating field name*), where
repeating field name is the name of a valid, nonempty repeating field containing numeric values only.

Example: If the repeating field Prices contains the values 5.00, 10.00, and 30.00, then the expression

```
"Your item total is $" & Sum(Prices)
```

gives the result

```
Your item total is $45.00
```

See Also: Average

Summary

Purpose: Used to obtain the value of a given Summary field for the current found set of records, when the database is sorted by a specified break field. This function is used to view the contents of a Summary field immediately in Browse mode, instead of waiting until Preview or Print time.

Syntax: Summary(*Summary field name, break field name*), where
Summary field name is the name of a valid Summary field, and
break field name is the name of a valid field by which the database is sorted.

Example: The expression

```
Summary(Total Sales, Salesperson)
```

breaks out sales by salesperson, showing subtotals of all sales for each salesperson entry in the database. The database must first by sorted by salesperson. The expression

```
Summary(Total Sales, Total Sales)
```
produces a single, grand total of sales for all records in the current found set.

See Also: Sum

Note: Refer to Chapter 5 for more information on Summary fields.

If the database is not sorted, a Calculation field defined with the Summary function will appear blank.

Because calculations based on the Summary function cover a range of records and values, they require much more time than calculations that restrict their computations to just the current record, especially in large databases.

Financial functions

These functions perform investment-related calculations. They are used to determine specifications of loans, how large investments will grow, and what investments are worth in constant money. They duplicate functions found on many financial pocket calculators.

FV   NPV   PMT

PV

FV

Purpose: Compute the future value of an investment, given the payment value, interest rate, and number of compounding periods. The result returned is a numeric value. The result is not the future value of an investment, starting with a certain balance; rather, it is the amount that accrues when equal payments are made over time to an account that bears a particular rate of interest.

Syntax: FV(*payment, rate, periods*), where
payment is a number representing the amount of each payment,
rate is a number giving the interest rate per period, and
periods is the number of payment periods.

Example: The expression
```
FV(100, .05/12, 360)
```
gives the value of an account if $100 payments are made each month for 30 years to an account that bears 5% annual interest.

See Also: NPV, PV

Note: Payments are assumed to be made at the end of a period. Be sure to give the interest rate per period. Divide the annual rate by 12, as shown in the example, to obtain the monthly rate.

Chapter 14: Calculations and Computations

A formula for the future value of a continuously compounded investment, assuming a certain starting value, is given by

```
Future Value = Present Value * Exp(Rate * Periods), where
```

Exp indicates the natural antilog of a number.

NPV

Purpose: Calculates the net present value of a series of unequal payments made regularly to an account bearing fixed interest per period over the life of the payments.

Syntax: NPV(*rate, repeating field name*), where
> *rate* is a numeric value indicating the interest rate per period, and
> *repeating field name* is the name of a valid repeating field containing the numeric value of each payment

Example: The expression

```
NPV(.03, Payments)
```

where Payments contains five values, representing an initial loan (expressed as a negative value) and four payments made once a year, gives the profit on the transaction in today's dollars if inflation is assumed to be 3%.

See Also: FV, PV

PMT

Purpose: Calculates the payment needed to fully amortize a loan, given the loan amount, the interest rate per payment period, and the number of periods.

Syntax: PMT(*amount, rate, periods*), where
> *amount* is a number representing the amount of the loan,
> *rate* is a number giving the interest rate per period, and
> *periods* is the number of payments.

Example: The expression

```
PMT(34,100, 10.99/12, 60)
```

gives a payment of 744.55, which is what is required to finance $34,100 at 10.99 percent annual interest over 60 months.

PV

Purpose: Calculates the present value of a series of equal payments, made at regular intervals, to an account bearing a fixed rate of interest.

Syntax: PV(*payment, rate, periods*), where
> *payment* is the numeric amount of each payment
> *rate* is the interest rate per period, and
> *periods* is the number of payments.

Example: The expression

```
PV(500, .03, 5)
```

gives the value of five annual $500 payments *in today's dollars*, assuming a 3% interest rate; in this case, $2,289.85.

See Also: NPV, FV

The IF function: making logical decisions

Purpose: The If function is used when you want to perform one of a set of alternative actions based on the results of a logical test. Normally, the If function is used to choose between two actions; however, you can include If functions within each other to add choices.

If you have had a little bit of programming experience, you should have no trouble with the If function. Otherwise, you may find it a bit tricky. This function would be a good one to experiment with extensively, testing the effects of various combinations.

The If function works with the other logical operators, such as less than, equals, OR, AND, and NOT. You combine these operators to create a test that is then evaluated for each record.

Syntax: If(*Test, Expression1, Expression2*), where
Test is a logical or numeric expression yielding a numeric or logical result,
Expression1 is an expression to be evaluated and whose value is assigned to the field if the test is true or is not equal to zero, and
Expression2 is an expression to be evaluated and whose value is assigned to the field if the test is false or is equal to zero.

Example: This function may seem a bit complicated, but it really isn't. Consider a simple example:

```
If(Number > 0, "The number is positive", "The Number is negative")
```

If the field Number contains 35, then the expression takes on the text value

```
The number is positive
```

If the field Number contains –11, the expression becomes

```
The number is negative
```

Remember, the function returns the value of the first expression if the test is true, and it returns the value of the second expression if the test is false.

Again, you can put Ifs inside Ifs (which is called *nesting*) to add choices. The following example, derived from the first, can handle the additional case where the value in the field Number is equal to zero.

```
If(Number > 0, "The number is positive", If(Number = 0, "The
number is zero", "The number is negative"))
```

Note: The test does not have to be a logical expression. If you use a numerical expression, the first action will be performed if the test result is not zero, and the second action will be performed if the test result is zero.

The values of the two expressions should be the values that you want for the field as a whole depending on which condition is met. For example, you can use the If function to define a Calculation field that gives the tax rate for mail order shipments. The expression

```
If(State = "NM", .06, 0)
```

assigns a tax rate of 6 percent to shipments within state if you're shipping from New Mexico. Otherwise, the rate is zero. If the Calculation field has the name Rate, you can use it in calculations like so:

```
Tax = Rate * Total
```

Sales tax is then automatically computed and added for in-state shipments and omitted from out-of-state shipments.

Mathematical functions

These functions perform a range of standard mathematical computations on numeric fields. Two of the functions, Pi and Random, do not accept arguments.

Abs	Exp	Int
Ln	Log	Mod
Pi	Random	Round
Sign	Sqrt	

Abs

Purpose: Returns the absolute value of a numerical expression. This function changes a negative value to a positive one and leaves zero and positive values alone.

Syntax: Abs(*expression*) where

expression is a numeric expression or the name of a field that contains a numeric value.

Example: If the field Difference contains –125, then the expression

```
Abs(Difference)
```

evaluates to 125.

See Also: Int, Sign

Exp

Purpose: Returns the natural antilog of the given numeric expression. This value is the result obtained when the constant e is raised to the power of the expression.

Syntax: Exp(*expression*), where
> *expression* is a numerical expression or a field that contains a numerical value.

Example: The following expression calculates what number has base *e* logarithm 2 (which is what's meant by the *antilog* 2.)

```
Exp(2)
```

This number, rounded to three decimals, is 7.389.

See Also: Ln, Log

Int

Purpose: Returns the integer portion of a numeric expression. This portion is the part to the left of the decimal point. The portion to the right, if any, is dropped.

Syntax: Int(*expression*), where
> *expression* is a numerical expression or a field containing a numerical value.

Example: The expression

```
Int(Pi)
```

is equal to 3.

See Also: Mod

Ln

Purpose: Returns the natural logarithm of the given numerical expression. The natural logarithm is the number which, when the constant e is raised to its power, gives the original number. In calculus, the natural logarithm of a number x is said to be the area under the curve 1/n evaluated between 1 and x.

Syntax: Ln(*expression*), where
> *expression* is a numeric expression or a field containing a numeric value.

Example: The expression

```
Ln(2)
```

has the value 0.693, rounded to three decimals.

See Also: Log, Exp

Chapter 14: Calculations and Computations

Log

Purpose: Computes the common (base 10) logarithm of the given numeric expression. Raising 10 to this power gives the original number. Thus, the log of 100 is 2, because $10 \wedge 2 = 100$.

Syntax: Log(*expression*), where
   expression is a numeric expression or a field containing a numeric value.

Example: The expression

```
Log(100 * 100)
```

has the value 4.

See Also: Ln, Exp

Mod

Purpose: Performs modulo arithmetic, which deals with what remains when a given number or expression is divided by another number.

Syntax: Mod(*expression*, *divisor*), where
   expression is a numerical expression or numeric field, indicating the number to be divided, and
   divisor is a numerical expression or numeric field, indicating the number by which to divide.

Example: The expression

```
Mod(10,3)
```

is equal to 1, which is the integer remainder left when 10 is divided evenly by 3.

See Also: Abs, Int

Pi

Purpose: Returns the value of the mathematical constant Pi. Pi is defined as the ratio of a circle's circumference to its diameter. It is a transcendental number whose fractional part neither repeats nor terminates. This function takes no arguments.

Syntax: Pi

Example: The expression

```
Pi * R ^ 2
```

is approximately equal to 12.57, if R is equal to 2. The expression gives the area of a circle with the radius equal to R.

See Also: Trigonometric functions

Random

Purpose: This function returns a random value in the range 0 to 1 inclusive. This function takes no arguments.

Syntax: Random

Example: The expression

`Int(52 * Random) + 1`

yields a random integer between 1 and 52 inclusive. Such a number might represent a card drawn from a standard deck.

Note: Any of the following conditions causes the generation of a new random number:

- A new record is created.
- The Random function is newly assigned to a formula.
- Data is changed in any of the fields that are refererenced by the formula containing the Random function.

Round

Purpose: Rounds off a numeric result to the specified number of decimal places.

Syntax: Round(*expression, places*), where
expression is a numerical expression or a field that contains a numerical value, and
places is a numerical expression that indicates how many decimal places to retain.

Example: The expression

`Round(Pi,4)`

gives the value of Pi to four decimals and is equal to 3.1416.

See Also: Int

Sign

Purpose: Returns one of three values, depending on the value of the given expression. If the expression is greater than zero (positive), Sign is equal to 1. If the expression is equal to zero, Sign is also equal to zero. If the expression is less than zero, Sign is equal to –1.

Syntax: Sign(*expression*), where
expression is a numerical expression or a field containing a numerical value.

Example: The expression

`Sign(123)`

has the value +1.

Chapter 14: Calculations and Computations

See Also: Abs

Sqrt

Purpose: Returns the square root of the given expression. The square root is the number which, when raised to the second power, equals the original expression.

Syntax: Sqrt(expression), where

expression is a numerical expression or a field containing a numerical value.

Example: The expression

```
Sqrt(9)
```

is equal to 3.

Note: Other roots can be extracted by using the exponentiation operator. In general, the nth root of a number is equal to that number raised to the reciprocal of n. Thus, the cube, or third root of 27 is given by the expression

```
27 ^ (1 / 3)
```

Text functions

Text functions are used to compare text strings and to extract pieces of text strings. They also can be used to insert text into a string.

Exact	Left	Length
Lower	Middle	Position
Proper	Replace	Right
Trim	Upper	

Exact

Purpose: Compares two text expressions or fields and determines whether they are exactly the same. The comparison is case sensitive, meaning that capitalization counts. The result returned is a logical value; true if the two strings are exactly the same, false if they are not.

Syntax: Exact(*first text, comparison text*), where

first text is a Text field, expression, or constant, and

comparison text is also a Text field, expression, or constant

Example: The expression

```
Exact(DayName(Today), "Monday")
```

is true if today's date is December 5, 1994. (Note that to create a text constant–such as Monday, in this example–you must surround it with quotation marks.)

See Also: Position

Note: You can adapt this function to perform a test that isn't case sensitive. Use either the Upper or Lower function to convert both text strings to all upper or lower case, as in this example:

```
Exact(Upper(Field1), Upper(Field2))
```

Left

Purpose: Returns a text result that equals the leftmost part of a given Text field or expression, counting from the specified number of characters.

Syntax: Left(*expression*, *number*), where

expression is a text expression or text from which the leftmost part is to be taken, and

number is a numerical expression or field specifying how many characters to take.

Example: The expression

```
Left("photocopy", 5)
```

is equal to photo.

See Also: Right, Middle

Length

Purpose: Returns a numerical result that indicates how many characters the specified expression contains.

Syntax: Length(*expression*), where

expression is a text expression, constant, or field that contains a text value.

Example: The expression

```
Length("photocopy")
```

is equal to 9.

See Also: Trim

Lower

Purpose: Converts the specified text string into all lowercase, yielding a text result.

Syntax: Lower(*expression*), where

expression is a text expression, constant, or field containing a text value.

Example: The expression

```
Lower("PrintMonitor")
```

is equal to

```
printmonitor
```

See Also: Upper, Proper

Middle

Purpose: Extracts a specified number of characters out of a given text string, starting at a certain position.

Syntax: Middle(*expression, starting at, number of characters*), where
expression is a Text field, text constant, or text expression,
starting at is a numerical value that indicates where to begin taking characters, and
number of characters is a numerical value that indicates how many characters to take.

Example: The expression

```
Middle("John Q. Public", 6, 1)
```

is equal to Q. (Remember that *spaces* are characters, too.)

See Also: Left, Right

Position

Purpose: Scans a given text expression in an attempt to locate the appearance of a search string, starting at a given position. Returns a numerical value equal to the position at which the search string starts within the larger string. If the search string is not found, the result is zero.

Syntax: Position(*expression, search, starting*), where
expression is a text constant, field, or expression in which to search
search is the text to search for, and
starting is a number that indicates at what character position to begin the search.

Example: The expression

```
Position("Clinton", "i", 1)
```

is equal to 3. The result of the Position function can be used with other functions, such as Right and Left, to extract individual words out of a text string. For example,

```
Left("Clinton R. Hicks", Position("Clinton R. Hicks", " ", 1))
```

extracts everything from the left up to and including the first blank. This result could then be used as a starting point when searching for the *next* word.

See Also: Left, Right, Middle

Proper

Purpose: Returns a text value in which the first letter of each word of the supplied text expression has been capitalized.

Syntax: Proper(*expression*), where
expression is a Text field, constant, or expression.

Example: The expression

```
Proper("SURF AND TURF")
```

is equal to

```
Surf And Turf
```

See Also: Upper, Lower

Replace

Purpose: Inserts a given text string into another text string, starting at a specified position and eliminating a given number of characters. The number of characters replaced need not be equal to the number inserted.

Syntax: Replace(*expression, starting, number, replace with*), where
expression is a Text field, constant, or expression in which to replace text
starting is a numerical value indicating at what position to begin replacing
number is a numerical value that indicates how many characters to replace, and
replace with is a Text field, constant, or expression to insert in the place of the specified characters

Example: The expression

```
Replace("Clinton R. Hicks", 9, 2, "Robert")
```

is equal to

```
Clinton Robert Hicks
```

See Also: Middle, Position

Right

Purpose: Starting at the right, extracts the specified number of characters from the given text expression.

Syntax: Right(*expression, number*), where
expression is a Text field, expression, or constant from which to take characters, and
number is a numerical value that indicates how many characters to take.

Example: The expression

```
Right("Rosanna", 4)
```

is equal to

```
anna
```

See Also: Left, Middle

Trim

Purpose: Removes leading and trailing spaces from a specified text expression or field.

Syntax: Trim(*expression*), where
expression is a Text field, constant, or expression.

Example: The expression

```
Trim("   Rosanna   ")
```

is equal to

```
Rosanna
```

See Also: Left, Right, Position

Note: Some programs and or systems other than FileMaker Pro on the Macintosh require a set number of characters per field. Unused spaces in such fields are filled with blanks. You can use the Trim function to remove these blanks when you import data from such systems.

Upper

Purpose: Converts a given text string into all uppercase.

Syntax: Upper(*expression*), where
expression is a Text field, constant, or expression.

Example: The expression

```
Upper("rosanna")
```

is equal to

```
ROSANNA
```

See Also: Lower, Proper

Time functions

The Time functions are analogous to the Date function described earlier in this chapter. You can use them to extract pieces out of a time expression or to convert number results into a valid time, even if the numbers don't fall into the 0 – 60 and 0 – 24 ranges normally required for minutes and hours.

    Hour   Minute   Seconds
    Time

Hour

Purpose: Extracts the hour part of a time expression, yielding a numeric result.

Syntax: Hour(*time*), where
time is a time field or expression.

Example: If Current is a time field containing 12:30pm, the expression

```
Hour(Current)
```

is equal to 12.

See Also: Minute, Seconds

Minute

Purpose: Extracts the minute part of a time expression, yielding a numeric result.

Syntax: Minute(*time*), where
time is a time field or expression.

Example: If Current is a time field containing 12:30pm, the expression

```
Minute(Current)
```

is equal to 30.

See Also: Hour, Seconds

Seconds

Purpose: Extracts the seconds part of a time expression, yielding a numerical result.

Syntax: Seconds(*time*), where
time is a time expression or field.

Example: If Current is a time field containing 12:30:15pm, the expression

```
Seconds(Current)
```

is equal to 15.

See Also: Hour, Minute

Note: The Hour, Minute, and Seconds functions can be used together to obtain the decimal equivalent of a time value. You would need to divide the Minute result by 60 and the Seconds result by 3600. An example of such an expression is

```
Hour(Current) + (Minute(Current) / 60) + (Seconds(Current) / 3600)
```

Time

Purpose: Returns a time value containing the specified number of hours, minutes, and seconds counted from 12:00 midnight. The function compensates for fractional values, extracting seconds from fractional minutes and minutes from fractional hours.

Syntax: Time(*hours, minutes, seconds*), where
hours is a numerical expression indicating the number of hours,
minutes is a numerical expression indicating the number of minutes, and
seconds is a numerical expression indicating the number of seconds.

Chapter 14: Calculations and Computations

Example: The expression

```
Time(13, 70, 71)
```

is equal to

```
2:11:11pm
```

See Also: Date

Trigonometric functions

This last group of function is used to work with triangles and with right angles. Note that the trig functions are designed to work in radians. There are 2Pi radians in 360 degrees. You can use the Degrees function to convert radian results into degrees.

Atan	Cos	Degrees
Radians	Sin	Tan

Atan

Purpose: Gives the arctangent of the specified expression; the result is given in radians.

Syntax: Atan(*expression*), where
expression is a numerical field, constant, or expression.

Example: The expression

```
Atan(Pi)
```

is equal to 1.2626, rounded to four decimals.

See Also: Tan, Degrees

Cos

Purpose: Gives the cosine of the specified expression, assumed to be given in radians.

Syntax: Cos(*expression*), where
expression is a numerical expression, field, or constant.

Example: The expression

```
Cos(Pi)
```

is equal to –1.

See Also: Sin, Degrees

Degrees

Purpose: Converts a value given in radians into degrees. There are 2Pi radians in 360 degrees.

Syntax: Degrees(*expression*), where
expression is a numerical field, expression, or constant whose value is given in radians.

Example: The expression

```
Degrees(Pi)
```

is equal to 180.

See Also: Radians

Radians

Purpose: Converts a value in degrees into radians, for use with calculations expecting a value in that form.

Syntax: Radians(*expression*), where
expression is a numerical field, constant, or expression containing a value expressed in degrees.

Example: The expression:

```
Cos(Radians(45))
```

is equal to 0.707, rounded to three decimals.

See Also: Degrees

Sin

Purpose: Returns the sine of the given expression, interpreted as an angle expressed in radians.

Syntax: Sin(*expression*), where
expression is a numerical field, constant, or expression given in radians.

Example: The expression

```
Sin(Pi)
```

is equal to 0.

See Also: Cos

Tan

Purpose: Gives the tangent of the specified angle, assumed to be expressed in radians.

Syntax: Tan(*expression*), where
expression is a numerical field, constant, or expression given in radians.

Example: The expression

```
Tan(Pi)
```

is equal to 0.

See Also: Atan

Chapter 14: Calculations and Computations

CHAPTER 14 CONCEPTS AND TERMS

- FileMaker Pro supports the use of Calculation fields. These fields perform operations on data in other fields. The results are displayed in the Calculation field as its contents.
- A Calculation field has two aspects: its definition, which is an expression that shows how the field's value is obtained, and its data, which is the result of evaluating the definition for the current record.
- Calculation fields are created within the Define Fields dialog box, within a separate dialog box that appears when a Calculation field is first defined or is later edited.
- A Calculation field's definition consists of a formula that is made up of mathematical expressions and functions.
- An expression consists of one or more operators that join fields or constant values. Fields are similar to variables in algebra.
- Operators include arithmetic, logical, and text operators.
- FileMaker Pro includes over sixty built-in functions. These functions perform data conversion, date, logical, mathematical, financial, statistical, text, time, and trigonometric calculations.

argument
A value supplied to a function, from which the function's value is calculated.

Boolean
A type of algebra in which expressions are evaluated for their truth value. Results are either true or false.

constant
A value that does not change. Pi, e, and 2 are all examples of constants.

cosine
For a right (90 degree) triangle, the ratio of an adjacent side to the hypotenuse (the side opposite the 90 degree angle) for one of the other two angles.

expression
A mathematical statement that consists of one or more operators, such as + or *, that join two or more variables or constants.

function
An operation performed on a value that yields a unique result for that value. The function of two different values can be the same, but the function of a given value can never differ from the original result.

operator
A symbol indicating that a certain mathematical process should be performed on the entities surrounding the operator symbol. Both + and > are examples of operators.

Order of Operations
Refers to the way in which algebraic expressions are evaluated. Exponents are done first, then multiplication and division, then addition and subtraction. Including parentheses in an expression can alter the order of operations.

sine
For a right (90 degree) triangle, the ratio of the opposite side to the hypotenuse for one of the other two angles.

tangent
In a right (90 degree) triangle, the ratio of the opposite side to the adjacent side for one of the two other angles.

variable
A value in an expression that may change, usually indicated by a letter or name. A field can be considered to be a variable, because its contents may change from record to record.

Part IV: Intermediate Topics

CHAPTER FIFTEEN

Automating FileMaker Pro

- Learning to use ScriptMaker to create FileMaker Pro scripts
- Attaching scripts to buttons
- Using QuicKeys with FileMaker Pro

When most people — particularly new Macintosh owners — see the term *script* or *scripting*, they think of programming. And when they think of programming, they quickly skip to the next section of the manual, assuming that this is a feature that was not meant for them. Unfortunately, in many cases, they're right. But FileMaker Pro provides an easier, kinder way to create scripts:

❖ Rather than type scripts in a word processing program or text editor, you design scripts in FileMaker Pro by choosing script steps from a list.

❖ You can create many scripting procedures simply by executing Sort instructions and Find requests and then telling FileMaker Pro that you want to use the identical procedures in a script. When you perform the important steps just before creating the script, FileMaker Pro often includes them for you as part of the default script. The general philosophy is "Set it up and then save it as a script."

To make it easy to design scripts, FileMaker Pro provides a script-creation utility called ScriptMaker. Using ScriptMaker, you can automate almost any FileMaker Pro function that you usually execute manually by selecting commands from the menus. Once defined, a script can be added to the Scripts menu and/or attached to a button in any layout, making it simple to execute the script any time you like.

Although this chapter is devoted primarily to explaining how to create and use scripts, you can automate FileMaker Pro functions in other ways, including the following:

❖ Creating auto-entry fields that are filled in for you whenever a new record is created or a record is edited (refer to Chapter 5)

❖ Setting a start-up script for a database (discussed in Chapter 7)

❖ Using a macro utility (QuicKeys, for example) to automate functions

❖ Using Apple Events and AppleScript to enable FileMaker Pro to interact with other programs

Using ScriptMaker

The majority of FileMaker Pro scripts are created in ScriptMaker. The commands used in the script are called *steps*. In most cases, the steps duplicate normal FileMaker Pro menu commands (see "Script Step Reference" later in this chapter for information about specific steps). As you read through this chapter, however, you will learn that script steps often are more powerful than the original commands that they represent. A step that acts on a field (Clear, for example) may be instructed to make a particular field the active one and then select the entire contents of that field before clearing its contents. When this action is attempted without a script, you must click the field and then manually select its contents (or use the Select All command) before choosing the Clear menu command. Thus, many steps frequently can be reduced to one.

The real power of FileMaker Pro scripts becomes apparent when you design an elaborate sequence of steps to carry out a complex function. With a script, you can be sure that the steps are executed in precisely the same manner each time. If you prefer, the same script can be designed so that the user can select *different* options each time it runs. For example, you could create a Find script that selects a particular group of records (all people in the database who are younger than 30) and then displays information about those records in a different layout. With only a minor modification, the same script can be designed so that the Find criteria could be changed by the user each time the script is performed. Similarly, a script designed to act on a specific field can be modified so that it simply acts on whatever field happens to be current. In that way, the script can be used with any field in the database.

Creating a script is not a complex process. Following are the basic steps:

1. **Open the database for which you want to define a script.**

   Scripts are stored with the databases in which they are created.

2. **Choose ScriptMaker from the Scripts menu.**

   The Define Scripts dialog box appears (see Figure 15-1).

3. **In the Script Name box, type a name for the script.**

   As soon as text is entered in the Script Name box, the Create button becomes available (that is, the button no longer is dimmed).

4. **If you do not want to list the script in the Scripts menu, click to remove the check mark from the Include in menu check box.**

   You can change the status of this check box at any time during the script-creation or script-editing process. A maximum of 52 scripts can be listed in the Scripts menu for any database.

Chapter 15: Automating FileMaker Pro

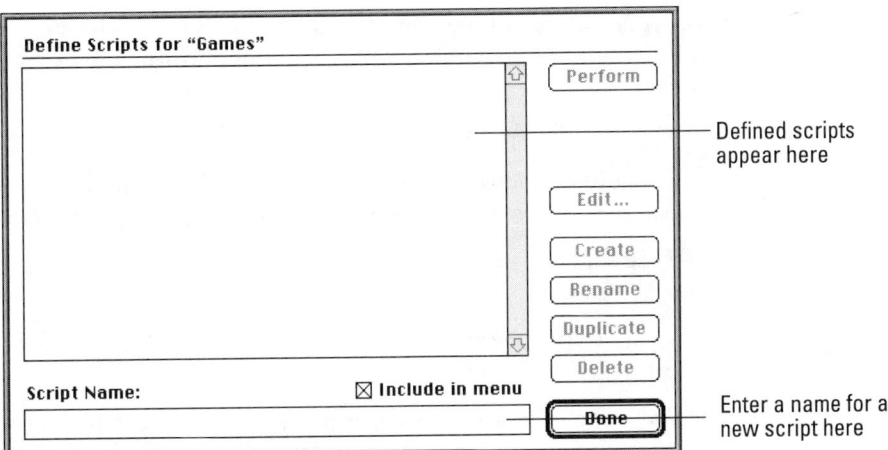

Figure 15-1: The Define Scripts dialog box.

The Script Definition dialog box appears, as shown in Figure 15-2. A standard set of script steps, based on FileMaker Pro's best guess of what you might want to do, is listed in the scrolling list on the right side of the dialog box. This is the initial version of the script.

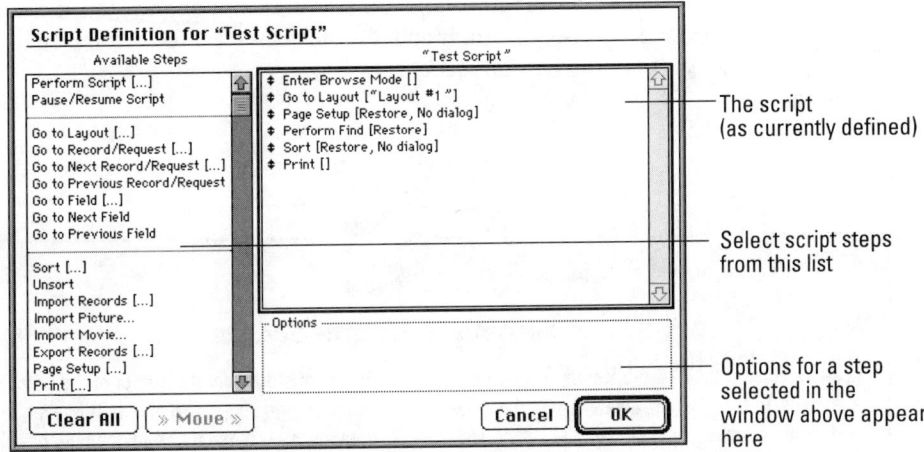

Figure 15-2: The Script Definition dialog box.

5. **Edit the contents of the script so that it contains only the steps you need and lists them in the correct order. You can perform any of the following actions:**

    ❖ To remove all steps from the script, click Clear All.

    ❖ To remove individual unwanted steps, select them in the script and then click Clear (the Clear button replaces the Move button when a step is selected).

    ❖ To rearrange the order of steps in the script, click the step and drag it to the desired position.

    ❖ To add a step to the script, select it in the Available Steps list and then click Move.

    ❖ To set options for a script step, begin by selecting the step in the script. Options that can be set for the step appear at the bottom of the dialog box.

6. **To accept the script definition, click OK. To ignore the changes that you made, click Cancel.**

Note that if a script consists of only one step, you may be able to avoid the script-definition process by assigning the step to a button (see "Attaching a Script to a Button" later in this chapter).

If you want a permanent record of a script, you can print it by issuing the Print command, clicking the Script radio button , and choosing the script you want to print from the pop-up menu. If you want to print *every* script for a database, choose All scripts from the pop-up menu.

Learning to Create Scripts

Learning to script can be facilitated by examining examples. In this chapter, elsewhere in this book, and in the databases included on the Macworld FileMaker Pro 2.0/2.1 Bible Disk, you'll find plenty of scripts that you can use as starting points. See an interesting action in a database? Choose Script-Maker from the Scripts menu, click the script that you want to examine, and then click Edit. You'll see the list of steps that the author of the database selected for the script. (Be aware, however, that some databases — those that you can buy, ones that are available for downloading from popular on-line services, and a few of the ones on this disk — are protected. Unless you know the necessary password, you may not be allowed to see or modify the scripts.)

Chapter 15: Automating FileMaker Pro

Listing scripts in the Scripts menu

As mentioned earlier, if the Include in menu check box is checked for a defined script, the script is assigned a place in the Scripts menu. Up to 52 scripts can be listed in the Scripts menu. The first ten scripts listed in the Define Scripts dialog box, however, are special. In addition to being listed in the Scripts menu, each of the first ten scripts is assigned a keyboard shortcut (⌘-1 through ⌘-0) so that you also can execute the scripts from the keyboard. To make it easy to remember and access the scripts that you need to use most often, be sure that those scripts are among the first ten.

You can rearrange the order of your scripts by dragging them to a new position in the script list in the Define Scripts dialog box, as shown in Figure 15-3. To change the position of a script, click the double-headed arrow icon that precedes the name of the script. The pointer changes to a larger version of the double-headed arrow. Then, while continuing to hold down the mouse button, drag the script up or down in the script list. When the script is in the correct position in the list, release the mouse button. Repeat this process for other scripts that you want to move.

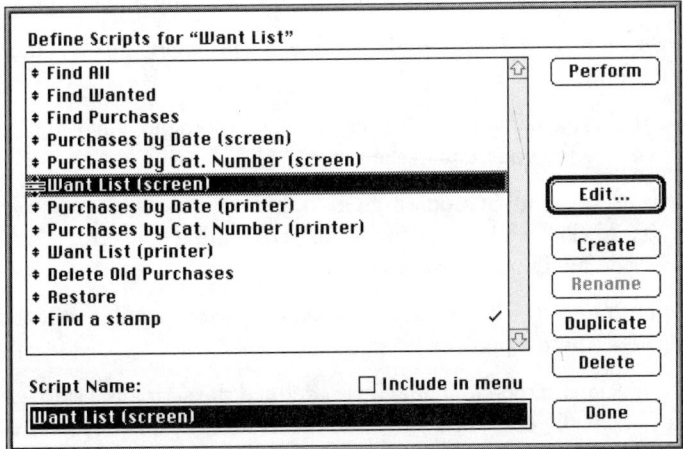

Figure 15-3: You can drag any script to change its order in the script list.

Make Your Own ⌘-Key Equivalents

As mentioned earlier, in any database, the first ten scripts you create that have the Include in menu check box checked are automatically assigned a ⌘-key equivalent (⌘-1 through ⌘-0). You also can use any of these first ten script slots to create ⌘-key equivalents menu commands for which FileMaker Pro does not provide keyboard shortcuts.

For example, you may want to create a one-step script that simply executes the normal Page Setup command (Page Setup [] or Page Setup [Restore]). As long as this script is one of the first ten scripts added to the Scripts menu, you can issue its command by pressing its new ⌘-key equivalent (⌘-3, for example). You can use this trick to add all your frequently used menu commands to the Scripts menu, such as Toggle View-As-List [], Save a Copy as [], and Spell Check Record.

Running a script

After you finish defining a script, you can execute it in any of several ways:

❖ Select the name of the script in the Define Scripts dialog box and then click the Perform button.

❖ Choose the script name from the Scripts menu (possible only if Include in menu was checked when you defined the script).

❖ Press the ⌘-key combination assigned to the script (possible only if Include in menu was checked when you defined the script and if the script is one of the first ten scripts defined for the database).

❖ Click a button to which you have attached the script (possible only if you assigned the script to a button).

❖ Open the database (possible only if you defined the script as a start-up script that runs automatically each time you open the database; explained in Chapter 7).

If you need to stop a script in progress, press ⌘-. (period). If a script is paused (by using a Pause step option or the Pause/Resume Script step), you can stop the script by clicking the Cancel button (instead of the Continue button, as you normally would).

As discussed earlier in this chapter, you can assign a script to the Scripts menu, attach the script to a button, make the script the start-up script, or set none of these options. The decision is entirely yours. You also can change a script or button assignment at any time by following the procedures outlined in this chapter. Note that the Perform button can be used with *any* script, regardless of the other ways (or lack of ways) in which the script can be accessed.

Chapter 15: Automating FileMaker Pro

Modifying a script

FileMaker Pro provides several methods for altering scripts, including renaming, duplicating, deleting, editing, and changing their order. These important script-editing techniques are discussed in the following sections.

Renaming a script

If you add a script to the Scripts menu by clicking the Include in menu check box in the Define Scripts dialog box (refer to Figure 15-1), whatever name you gave the script is what appears in the Scripts menu. (Otherwise, script names are visible only when you are editing scripts, assigning scripts to buttons, or setting a start-up action. In such cases, the specific script names aren't nearly as important because they normally are hidden from the user's view.)

If you decide to change the name, select the script in the Define Scripts dialog box, type a new name in the Script Name text box (or edit the existing name), and then click the Rename button.

Choosing Script Names

When you name or rename a script, it's always best to choose a descriptive name. Although you could follow the same naming conventions that FileMaker Pro uses for layouts (instead of Layout #1, Layout #2, and so on, you could use Script #1, Script #2, and so on), you'll have a miserable time later trying to determine what each script does. On the other hand, there'll be little possible confusion if you name your scripts descriptively — for example, Sort by State, Find Recent Purchases, and Print Aging Report.

Note, too, that there is no practical limit to the length of each script name. Before going overboard, however, and naming a script "Aging Report (designed for an ImageWriter printer in landscape mode) — to be printed only on the last day of the month," keep two things in mind:

❖ The Define Scripts dialog box does not expand to show all characters in an extremely long script name. FileMaker Pro displays only as much text as fits in the script list; the remainder is shown as ellipses.

❖ If a long script name is included in the Scripts menu, the width of the Scripts menu will expand as much as possible to display the longest script name — an arrangement that can result in a particularly ridiculous-looking pull-down menu. (I have two separate monitors attached to my Mac. When I assigned the long script name described earlier to the Scripts menu, the resulting pull-down menu extended off my main monitor and halfway onto a nearby two-page display!)

Duplicating a script

Rather than create every new script from scratch, you sometimes will find it easier to edit a copy of an existing script. For example, you may already have created a script that prints a certain report for you. If you want to have a similar script that displays the report on-screen instead, just create a duplicate of the script and change the Print [. . .] command to an Enter Preview Mode [. . .] command in the duplicate script.

To create a duplicate of a script, follow these steps:

1. **From the script list in the Define Scripts dialog box (refer to Figure 15-1), select the name of the script that you want to duplicate.**

   When selected, the name of the script appears in the Script Name box.

2. **Click the Duplicate button.**

   A copy of the script is created and is listed as *script name* Copy (for example, Print Sales Report Copy).

3. ***Optional:* Change the name of the duplicate script to something more descriptive by selecting the script in the script list, editing its name in the Script Name box, and clicking the Rename button.**

4. **Edit the new script as desired (click the Edit button).**

5. **Click Done when you finish working with scripts.**

Deleting a script

If you no longer need a script, or if you are approaching the limit of 52 scripts in the Scripts menu and need to make room for more, you can delete scripts.

To delete a script, follow these steps:

1. **In the Define Scripts dialog box select the name of the script that you want to delete.**

2. **Click Delete.**

   The dialog box shown in Figure 15-4 appears.

3. **Click Delete to remove the script or click Cancel if you change your mind.**

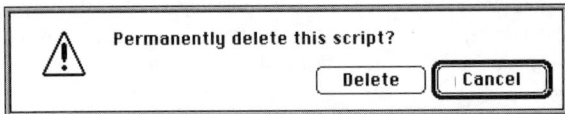

Figure 15-4: Deleting a script.

Chapter 15: Automating FileMaker Pro

Editing a script

Other editing actions that you can perform on a script include adding, removing, or changing the order of steps and replacing previously set options for steps. To change a script's appearance in — or omission from — the Scripts menu for the database, click the Include in menu check box in the Define Scripts dialog box. Like other check boxes, this one acts as a toggle; each time you click it, the state of the option is reversed.

Whenever you edit an existing script that includes a step that performs a Page Setup, Sort, Find request, or Import or Export operation, FileMaker Pro presents the dialog box shown in Figure 15-5. When you created the script, particular Page Setup, Sort, Find, Import, and Export options were in effect. If any steps relevant to these commands were used in the script, their settings also were saved as part of the script. If you included a Page Setup [. . .] step and had set the database for landscape printing, for example, that setting was saved with the script.

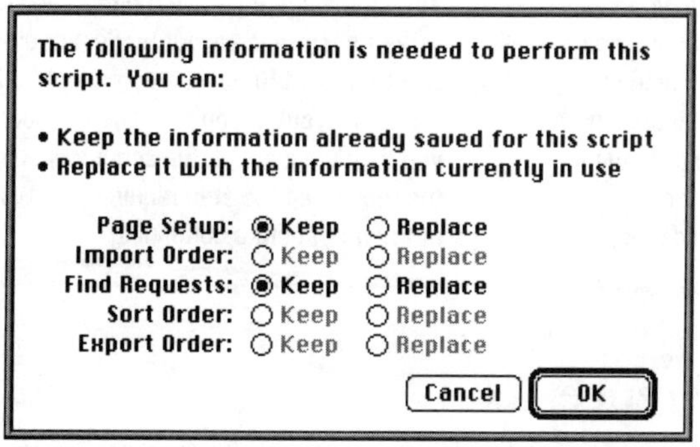

Figure 15-5: Keep or replace these settings.

When FileMaker Pro presents the dialog box shown in Figure 15-5, it wants to know whether you want to continue to use the previous settings that were saved with the script (the Keep radio buttons) or whether you want to replace those settings with the ones that are in effect at this moment (the Replace radio buttons). In Figure 15-5, the Page Setup and Find Requests settings can be kept or replaced. (The other options are dimmed because those steps were not used in the script.) If one of the reasons why you are editing this script is that you just created different Find Requests, for example, click the Replace button for Find Requests and then click OK.

Part IV: Intermediate Topics

Debugging a Script

When a script doesn't do what you intended it to do, you should check several things:

❖ Are the steps in the proper order?

A script is not executed en masse; its steps run in the order in which you placed them. If you need to set a printout for Landscape mode, for example, you normally would place a Page Setup [. . .] step before the Print [. . .] step.

❖ Should you have performed a preparatory action before executing the script?

If a step acts on a field, for example, you must somehow make the field the current one before running the script — or as part of running the script. If no field is selected, the step does nothing. Use a Specify field option as part of the step (if one is allowed); include a Go to Field [. . .], Go to Next Field, or Go to Previous Field step; or manually select the desired field before running the script.

❖ Have scripts or layouts been renamed?

Reexamine your scripts in ScriptMaker. If any Perform Script [. . .] or Go to Layout [. . .] step now reads unknown, it means that the database does not know what script or sub-script it is supposed to perform or the layout to which it is supposed to switch.

❖ Are you in the proper FileMaker Pro mode?

Although a script can be run from any mode, it cannot operate in Layout mode. For example, a Delete Record/Request step cannot be used to delete a layout. If you're in Layout mode when you execute a script, the script will switch to the mode that the step requires (Browse, Find, or Preview) before continuing.

Script step reference

Each element of a script is called a *step*. In this section, the step explanations are presented in the same order in which you'll encounter them in the Script Definition window. Figure 15-6 shows the entire set of script steps that are supported by FileMaker Pro 2.

Script step options

As you examine the different script steps in ScriptMaker, you'll notice that many of them include options that you can set. The options are individually explained within each step in this section, but here's a rundown of the effects of the most common options on their script steps.

Perform without dialog. Many script steps that normally are performed with an accompanying dialog box (enabling you to select a particular file, for example) can be performed without displaying the dialog box. Set the Perform without dialog option when, as part of the script step, you already have specified the file to be opened or other options to be performed, and you have no need to examine or change those options.

Chapter 15: Automating FileMaker Pro

```
Perform Script [...]
Pause/Resume Script

Go to Layout [...]
Go to Record/Request [...]
Go to Next Record/Request [...]
Go to Previous Record/Request
Go to Field [...]
Go to Next Field
Go to Previous Field

Sort [...]
Unsort
Import Records [...]
Import Picture...
Import Movie...
Export Records [...]
Page Setup [...]
Print [...]

Perform Find [...]
Find All
Refind
Omit
Omit Multiple [...]
Find Omitted

Enter Browse Mode [...]
Enter Find Mode [...]
Enter Preview Mode [...]

New Record/Request
Duplicate Record/Request
Delete Record/Request [...]
Delete Found Set [...]
Paste from Index [...]
Paste from Last Record [...]
Paste Current Date [...]
Paste Current Time [...]
Paste Current User [...]
Paste Literal [...]
Replace [...]
Reserialize [...]
Relookup [...]

Undo
Cut [...]
Copy [...]
Paste [...]
Clear [...]
Select All

Spell Check Selection [...]
Spell Check Record
Spell Check Found Set

Toggle Status Area [...]
Toggle View-As-List [...]
Toggle Window [...]
Home
Page Up
Page Down
End

Send Apple Event [...]
Help...
Open [...]
Close [...]
Save a Copy as [...]
Define Fields...
Quit
```

Figure 15-6: List of FileMaker Pro script steps.

Specify file. Click Specify file when you always want the current script step to operate on a particular file. This option often is used in conjunction with the Perform without dialog option. (Because you already have selected the file, there is little reason to present a standard file dialog box that enables you to choose a file.)

Specify record. Click Specify record when you always want the current script step to operate on a particular record. If you do not click this option, FileMaker Pro assumes that you (or another script step) will make the desired record the active one before this script step is executed.

Specify field. Some script steps operate on the contents of a field. Click Specify field if the script should always operate on a particular field. If you do not click this option, FileMaker Pro assumes that you (or another script step) will make the desired field the active one before this script step is executed.

Restore (import order, sort order, setup options, find requests, and others). The wording of the Restore option varies depending on the step to which it is attached. For example, in conjunction with a Sort step, it reads "Restore sort order." Set this option when you want FileMaker Pro to simply execute whatever settings were in effect for this procedure at the time the script was created. If neither Restore nor Perform without dialog is chosen, FileMaker Pro displays the appropriate dialog box when the script step is executed (enabling you to set options as you like).

Select entire contents. In script steps that deal with field contents (particularly the editing steps, such as Copy, Paste, and Clear), this step causes the entire contents of the chosen field to be selected. Otherwise, only the portion of the field that has been preselected by the user will be affected by the script.

Refresh screen. This option causes the screen to be redrawn when the step is reached.

Pause. This option adds Continue and Cancel buttons to the associated script step. The purpose of this option is to give the user an opportunity to perform an action (entering criteria in a Find Request or switching to Preview mode, for example) before continuing the current script.

Exit script after last. This option is available for relative record-navigation script steps (Go to Next Record/Request [...] and Go to Previous Record/Request [...]). When this option is selected, and the script tries to select a record that is outside the range of record numbers (choosing a record before the first record or after the last record in the current browsed set), the step is not performed and the script ends. When this option is not selected, and the script tries to select a record that is outside the range of record numbers, the step is performed on a record that *can* it reach (either the first or last record in the database).

Script step definitions

FileMaker Pro 2 provides more than 60 steps that you can use individually or in combination with other steps to form a script. Following are detailed explanations of each step, including the ways in which the available options affect the step. For additional information on a script step, refer to the chapter in which the equivalent menu command is discussed.

Perform Script [...]

Explanation: Use Perform Script [...] to execute another script from within the current script. When the execution of the other script concludes, the original script resumes automatically.

Option: Perform sub-scripts

Use the Specify pop-up menu to select the script that you want to perform. The name of every script that is currently defined for the database is listed in this pop-up menu. The final option in the Specify pop-up menu is External Script. Choose External Script if you want to execute a script in another FileMaker Pro database. When an external script is executed, its database is automatically opened in FileMaker Pro, and then the script runs.

Suppose, for example, that you have two databases: Invoices and Addresses. You could create a script in Invoices that — using the Perform Script [...] command — executed a Find request in Addresses (enabling you to locate a particular customer address or all addresses that include San Francisco in the City field).

Pause/Resume Script

Explanation: Use this script step to pause a script, enabling the user to perform some nonscript action during the execution of a script.

Option: none

When a Pause/Resume Script step is executed, the status area of the document window changes to show that the script has been paused (see Figure 15-7). After the user completes his actions, the script can be resumed by clicking the Continue button or pressing Enter. For example, you could alternate Go to Field [...] steps with Pause/Resume Script steps to walk a novice user through a data-entry routine.

Chapter 15: Automating FileMaker Pro

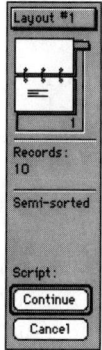

Figure 15-7: Click to continue or cancel a paused script.

Go to Layout [. . .]
Explanation: Use this step to switch to a particular layout that has been created for the current database (same as choosing a specific layout name from the layout pop-up menu in the upper-left corner of the document window).

Option: Refresh screen

The Specify pop-up menu must be used to select the layout that you want to display. In most cases, you will want to change to a particular layout; to do so, choose its name (Menu or Data Entry, for example) from the Specify menu. You also can switch to a layout based on a number in a field. (Notice that you *must* specify the field name if you choose this option.)

The Specify pop-up menu also has a special option, called Original layout, that is useful for ending a script. This option tells FileMaker Pro to switch back to whatever layout was current when the script was executed. For example, a Print Report script could be invoked from a layout named Data Entry. The script might switch to a report layout, print a copy of the report, and then — using the Original layout option — end by switching back to the Data Entry layout. The advantage of using Original layout rather than specifying the exact layout name (Data Entry, in this case) is that the script conceivably could be invoked from any layout and still return the user to that layout.

Go to Layout [. . .] is one of the most frequently used script steps. It's not unusual to begin a script with this step (to ensure that the correct layout is displayed, for example). In many databases (such as those found in the FM Pro Bible folder on the FileMaker Pro Bible Disk), this step is attached to navigation buttons that display a help or report layout.

Go to Record/Request [. . .]
Explanation: This step is used to display a particular record in the current found set or to enable the user to select one of these records to display. Go to Record/

Request [. . .] is frequently used to move directly to the first or last record in the database. (Specify 1 to go to the first record, and specify a very high record number — such as 9999 — to go to the last record.) When executed from Find mode, Go to Record/Request [. . .] displays a Find request page instead of a record.

Options: Perform without dialog, Specify record/request

If you want a *particular* record to be displayed, check the Specify record option and select the appropriate record. Because records can be selected only from the current found set, you usually will want to precede this script step with a Find request to ensure that the particular record of interest will indeed be available. If the record to be displayed could be different for each execution of the script, leave Specify record unchecked.

Remember that this step can also be used to display a Find request. If you want a *particular* Find request page to be displayed, check the Specify record option and select the appropriate Find request.

When Perform without dialog is not checked, the dialog box shown in Figure 15-8 appears. The wording changes to reflect the number of records in the found set (that is, the records currently being browsed) or the number of Find requests. When this option is checked, no dialog box appears; the script immediately displays the record or Find request that you've chosen with the Specify record option. (Perform without dialog normally should be chosen only when you also choose the Specify record option; otherwise, you'll have no control of the particular record that is displayed.)

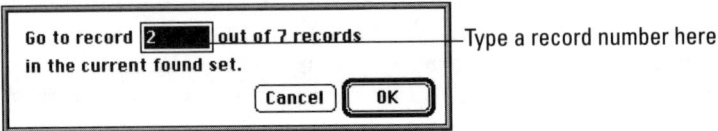

Figure 15-8: The Go to Record dialog box.

See also: Go to Next Record/Request [. . .], Go to Previous Record/Request [. . .]

Go to Next Record/Request [. . .]
Explanation: This step is used to display the next record in the current found set. The record considered to be "next" depends on the sort order (if any) that currently is in effect. When executed from Find mode, this script step displays the next Find request (if one exists).

Chapter 15: Automating FileMaker Pro

Option: Exit script after last

If Exit script after last is checked, the script halts if it attempts to display a record that does not exist — that is, a record or Find request number that is higher than the last record or Find request number.

See also: Go to Previous Record/Request [. . .], Go to Record/Request [. . .]

Go to Previous Record/Request [. . .]

Explanation: This step is used to display the previous record in the current found set. The record considered to be "previous" depends on the sort order (if any) that currently is in effect. When executed from Find mode, this script step displays the previous Find request (if one exists).

Option: Exit script after last

If Exit script after last is checked, the script halts if it attempts to display a record that does not exist — that is, a record or Find request number lower than 1.

See also: Go to Next Record/Request [. . .], Go to Record/Request [. . .]

Go to Field [. . .]

Explanation: Use this step to go to a particular field in the current layout.

Options: Select/play, Specify field

The Go to Field step enables you to move directly to any field in a layout. When a script includes steps that copy, cut, or paste information, you can use Go to Field to specify the appropriate field for each editing operation. Use the Specify field option to tell FileMaker Pro the field to which you want to go. (Note that if you do not specify a field, the script fails at this step.)

Set the Select/play option if you want to select the contents of a field (usually as a prelude to editing). If you set Select/Play and choose a Picture/Sound field that contains either a sound or a movie, the sound or movie plays.

See also: Go to Next Field, Go to Previous Field

Go to Next Field

Explanation: Use this step to move to the next field in the current layout. If no field is selected when a Go to Next Field step executes, you move to the first field in the current layout.

Option: none

After starting a script with a Go to Field [. . .] step to set the first field, you could use a series of Go to Next Field steps — each followed by a Pause/Resume Script step — to walk a new user through a data-entry layout. The beginning of the script might look like this:

Part IV: Intermediate Topics

```
Go to Field ["Last Name"]
Pause/Resume Script
Go to Next Field
Pause/Resume Script
Go to Next Field
```

See also: Go to Previous Field, Go to Field [. . .]

Go to Previous Field
Explanation: Use this step to move to the preceding field in the current layout. If no field is selected when a Go to Previous Field step executes, you move to the last field in the current layout.

Option: none

See also: Go to Next Field, Go to Field [. . .]

Sort [. . .]
Explanation: Use the Sort [. . .] step to sort the browsed records in a particular order (same as choosing Sort from the Select menu or pressing ⌘-S).

Options: Restore sort order, Perform without dialog

If Restore sort order is checked, the sort order defaults to the sort instructions that were in effect at the time the script was created. If Restore sort order is not checked, the sort order defaults to the most recently executed sort instructions for the database. If you want to be able to set different sort instructions each time the step executes, make sure that you do not check the Perform without dialog option. If, on the other hand, the sort instructions will not change from one execution of the script to another, or if you want to keep users from modifying the instructions, check Perform without dialog.

See also: Unsort

Unsort
Explanation: Use Unsort to restore records to the order in which they were entered into the database (same as clicking the Unsort button in the Sort Records dialog box).

Option: none

This script step is most useful when you have a database with records that were created in a purposeful order but now are sorted in some other order. Records in a checkbook database, for example, normally are created in date order; records in an invoice database are entered in order of invoice number. Unsort restores the records to their original order.

See also: Sort [. . .]

Chapter 15: Automating FileMaker Pro

Import Records [. . .]

Explanation: Use the Import Records [. . .] step to import data into the current database from another FileMaker Pro database or from a compatible data file (same as choosing Import Records from the Import/Export submenu of the File menu).

Options: Restore import order, Perform without dialog, Specify file

Leave all options unchecked to perform an import operation from scratch. When the step executes, FileMaker Pro displays a dialog box from which you select the file to be imported (see Figure 15-9).

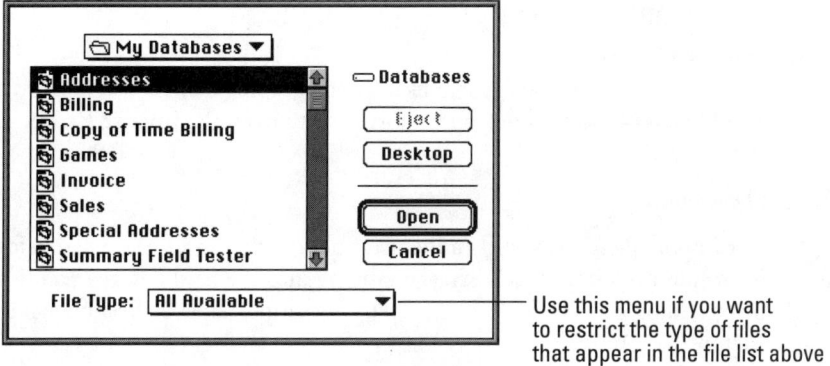

Figure 15-9: Select a file to import (optionally restricting choices to a particular file type chosen from the pop-up menu).

Next, the Specify Field Order for Import dialog box appears (see Figure 15-10). To execute the import operation, match the fields in the two databases as explained in Chapter 16, click a radio button to indicate that you want to Add new records or Replace data in current found set, and click OK.

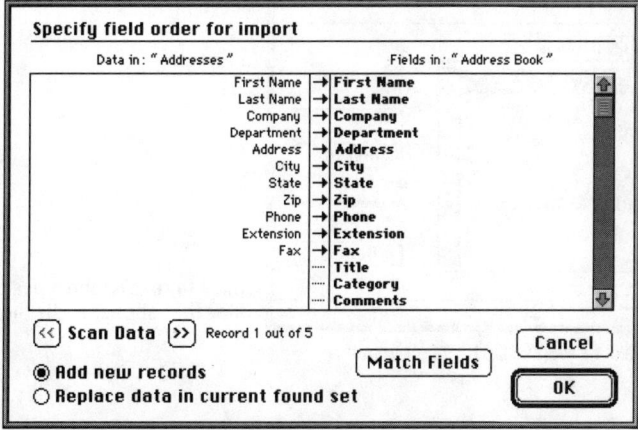

Figure 15-10: The Specify Field Order for Import dialog box.

If you previously selected the import file and the matching fields, you can click the Restore import order option to repeat the same import each time. For example, suppose that you periodically export new address records to a tab-separated text file called New Addresses. After importing these records into the Address Book database one time, you can create a script that uses the Import Records [. . .] step to import the new records automatically by using the same data file (set Specify file to select the New Addresses file) and the same import order (Restore import order) each time. In this case, you also could add the Perform without dialog option, because nothing would change that might require user intervention.

See also: Export Records [. . .]

Import Picture
Explanation: Use this script step to import a graphic from a disk file into a Picture/Sound field (same as choosing Import Picture from the Import/Export submenu of the File menu).

Option: none

For Import Picture to work, a Picture/Sound field must be selected before the step is executed — either by clicking or tabbing into the field before executing the script or by adding a Go to Field [. . .] step to the script that specifies the name of a Picture/Sound field.

When Import Picture is executed, a standard file dialog box appears (see Figure 15-11). Use normal navigation techniques (described in Chapter 2) to select the drive and/or folder in which the graphic file is stored. By clicking the Show pop-up menu at the bottom of the dialog box, you can restrict the files displayed to those of a specific graphic type, such as PICT or TIFF.

See also: Go to Field [. . .]

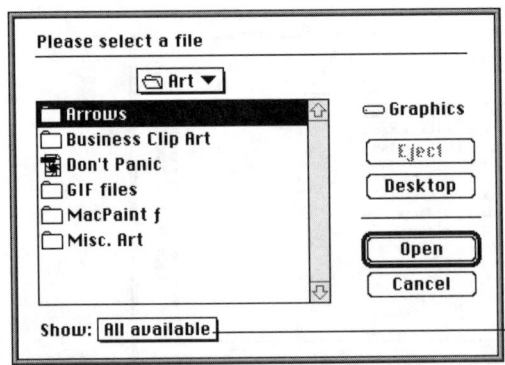

Figure 15-11: Select a graphic file to import from this dialog box.

Chapter 15: Automating FileMaker Pro

Import Movie

Explanation: This script step is used to import a QuickTime movie into a Picture/Sound field in the current record (same as choosing Import Movie from the Import/Export submenu of the File menu). When executed, this step displays a dialog box in which you can select a movie file to be imported (see Figure 15-12). If the Show Preview check box in the file dialog is checked, you can see a scene from each movie to help you choose the correct one.

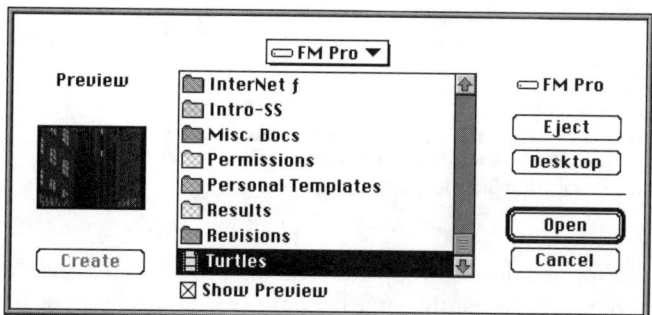

Figure 15-12: Select a QuickTime movie from this dialog box.

Option: none

For Import Movie to work, a Picture/Sound field must be selected before the step is executed — either by clicking or tabbing into the field before executing the script or by adding a Go to Field [. . .] step to the script that specifies the name of a Picture/Sound field. In addition, the QuickTime extension must be active.

Export Records [. . .]

Explanation: Use the Export Records [. . .] step to export data from the current FileMaker Pro database so that the data can be imported (read) into another FileMaker Pro database or another program (same as choosing Export Records from the Import/Export submenu of the File menu).

Options: Restore export order, Perform without dialog, Specify file

Leave all options unchecked to perform an export from scratch. When the step executes, FileMaker Pro displays a dialog box in which you name the new export data file and select a file type for the file (Tab-Separated Text, for example). Next, the Specify Field Order for Export dialog box appears (see Figure 15-13). To execute the export, choose the fields that you want to export, set options as explained in Chapter 16, and then click OK.

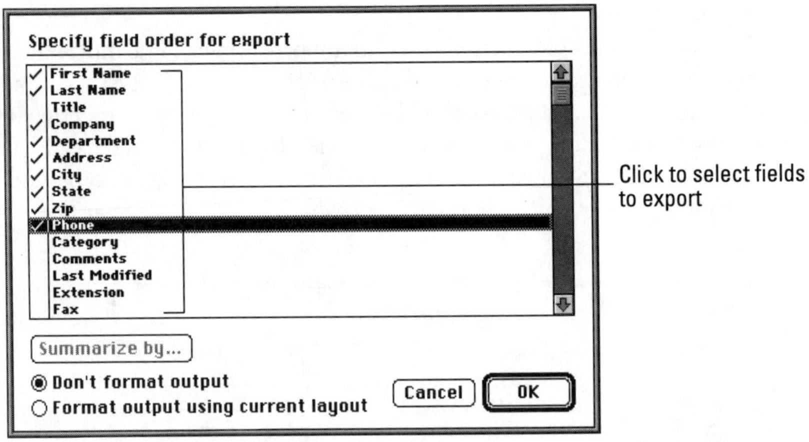

Figure 15-13: The Specify Field Order for Export dialog box.

If you have performed the export operation before, you can click the Restore export order option to repeat the same operation each time. Suppose that you periodically export new address records to a tab-separated text file called Addresses. After performing this export operation one time, you can create a script that uses the Export Records [. . .] step to export the new records to the same output file automatically. In this case, you also could add the Perform without dialog option, because nothing would change that might require user intervention.

Notice that Export Records [. . .] automatically exports data from all records currently being browsed. If you want to limit exports to a subset of records, use Find requests or related commands (or script steps) to select those records beforehand. See Chapter 9 for details on finding/selecting records.

See also: Import Records [. . .]

Page Setup [. . .]
Explanation: Use this script step to specify Page Setup options, such as paper size and orientation, for a print job (same as choosing Page Setup from the File menu).

Options: Restore setup options, Perform without dialog

See also: Print [. . .]

Print [. . .]
Explanation: Use this step to print according to the options set in the Print dialog box (same as choosing Print from the File menu or pressing ⌘-P).

Option: Perform without dialog

Chapter 15: Automating FileMaker Pro

Use the Print [. . .] step to send data to the printer or another output device, such as a fax/modem. By default, FileMaker Pro assumes that you want to use the Print options that were in effect when you last printed the database. If you want the chance to specify different Print options each time the script runs, leave the Perform without dialog option unchecked. When the script runs, you see the normal FileMaker Pro Print dialog box. On the other hand, if you always want to print with the same set of Print options (or don't want to give users an opportunity to select other Print options — inappropriate ones that might ruin the print job, for example), click Perform without dialog.

If special Page Setup options are necessary for a print job to print correctly (such as when you are printing labels on an ImageWriter printer or printing in Landscape mode), you will want to include Page Setup [. . .] as an earlier script step. Before including either the Print [. . .] or Page Setup [. . .] step in a script, start by printing the job correctly. Then, when you enter the Print [. . .] and Page Setup [. . .] steps in the script, FileMaker Pro will note the options that are set for these two steps and use those options whenever the script executes.

See also: Page Setup [. . .], Enter Preview Mode [. . .]

Perform Find [. . .]
Explanation: Use this step to execute the current Find request or requests (same as clicking the Find button in a Find request screen).

Option: Restore find requests

You must already have defined one or more Find requests to use this script step. You can do so by using the Enter Find Mode [. . .] step earlier in the script, by manually setting up the Find request(s) just before executing the script, or by executing a Find request just before creating the script and then checking the Restore find requests option.

See also: Find All, Refind, Enter Find Mode [. . .]

Find All
Explanation: This step makes all records visible (same as choosing Find All from the Select menu or pressing ⌘-J). Use Find All when you want to work with all records in the database, rather than with just a found set.

Option: none

See also: Enter Find Mode [. . .], Perform Find Request [. . .], Refind, Omit, Omit Multiple [. . .], Find Omitted

Refind
Explanation: This step re-executes the last Find request (same as choosing Refind from the Select menu or pressing ⌘-R).

Option: none

Part IV: Intermediate Topics

This script step is always performed by displaying a normal Find request on-screen.

See also: Enter Find Mode [. . .], Perform Find Request [. . .], Find All, Omit, Omit Multiple [. . .], Find Omitted

Omit
Explanation: This step omits (hides) the current record from the found set (same as choosing Omit from the Select menu or pressing ⌘-M).

Option: none

See also: Enter Find Mode [. . .], Perform Find Request [. . .], Find All, Refind, Omit Multiple [. . .], Find Omitted

Omit Multiple [. . .]
Explanation: This step omits (hides) the next *x* consecutive records from the found set (same as choosing Omit Multiple from the Select menu or pressing Shift-⌘-M).

Options: Specify record, Perform without dialog

When an Omit Multiple [. . .] step executes, a dialog box normally appears (see Figure 15-14) that asks the number of records you want to omit, beginning with the current record. If the Perform without dialog option is checked, the step defaults to omitting only the current record, just as though you had used the Omit step described earlier.

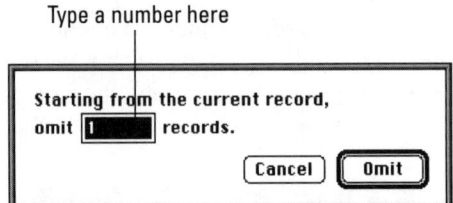

Figure 15-14: Specify the number of records to omit from the found set.

The Specify record option enables you to set the number of records that you want to omit (as always, beginning with the record that is current at the time the step is performed).

See also: Enter Find Mode [. . .], Perform Find Request [. . .], Find All, Refind, Omit, Find Omitted

Find Omitted
Explanation: This step swaps any records that currently are not included in the found set for those in the found set (same as choosing Find Omitted from the Select menu). The omitted records become visible, and the previously browsed records are hidden. Note that if all records are currently being browsed, this step has no effect.

Option: none

See also: Enter Find Mode [. . .], Perform Find Request [. . .], Find All, Refind, Omit, Omit Multiple [. . .]

Enter Browse Mode [. . .]
Explanation: Regardless of the active mode of the current database, this step switches to Browse mode (same as choosing Browse from the Select menu or pressing ⌘-B). You use Browse mode to enter and edit data.

Option: Pause

See also: Enter Find Mode [. . .], Enter Preview Mode [. . .]

Enter Find Mode [. . .]
Explanation: This script step switches the current layout to Find mode, enabling you to execute Find requests (same as choosing Find from the Select menu or pressing ⌘-F).

Options: Restore find requests, Pause

Select Restore find requests to start each Find with the criteria that were in effect when the script was created. If you prefer to start the Find request from scratch, leave this option unchecked. If additional steps follow Enter Find Mode [. . .], you also should select the Pause option — assuming that you want an opportunity to modify the Find request(s).

See also: Perform Find [. . .], Enter Browse Mode [. . .], Enter Preview Mode [. . .]

Enter Preview Mode [. . .]
Explanation: This step switches the current layout to Preview mode (same as choosing Preview from the Select menu or pressing ⌘-U).

Option: Pause

Preview mode often is used to display on-screen reports or to examine a layout before printing (commonly called a *print preview* in many Macintosh programs). When this step is followed by other steps, you may want to use the Pause option so that users of the database will have an adequate opportunity to examine the preview.

See also: Print [. . .], Enter Find Mode [. . .], Enter Browse Mode [. . .]

New Record/Request
Explanation: Use this script step to create a new blank record. When used in Browse mode, this step has the same effect as choosing New Record from the Edit menu (or pressing ⌘-N). When used in Find mode, this step has the same effect as choosing New Request from the Edit menu (or pressing ⌘-N).

Option: none

When scripting a data-entry routine to be used by novice computer users, you might well begin the script with a New Record/Request. In the Address Book database, this single step is attached to the New Record button (in the Data Entry layout) so that users can create additional records easily without having to know the ⌘-key sequence or the menu in which the command is located.

Duplicate Record/Request

Explanation: This step makes a duplicate of the current record (same as choosing Duplicate Record from the Edit menu or pressing ⌘-D). When executed from Find mode, the step makes a duplicate of the current Find request (same as choosing Duplicate Request from the Edit menu or pressing ⌘-D).

Option: none

Making a duplicate record and then editing the duplicate is a common data-entry shortcut for working with records that contain highly similar information. In a home-expenses database, for example, you undoubtedly would record expenses to the same companies over and over. If the only items that change are the amount and/or payment date, you can save time by finding a previous record for the same company (the electric company, for example), duplicating the old record, and then editing the record by typing the new dollar amount and transaction date.

See also: Paste from Last Record [. . .]

Delete Record/Request [. . .]

Explanation: This step is used to delete the current record (same as choosing Delete Record from the Edit menu or pressing ⌘-E) or the current Find request (same as choosing Delete Request from the Edit menu or pressing ⌘-E).

Option: Perform without dialog

Select Perform without dialog if you don't want the opportunity to confirm the `Permanently delete this record?` query that normally appears. Keep in mind, however, that as with other FileMaker Pro Delete commands, you cannot undo a record deletion.

See also: Delete Found Set [. . .]

Delete Found Set [. . .]

Explanation: Use the Delete Found Set [. . .] step to simultaneously delete all records that currently are being browsed (same as choosing Delete Found Set from the Edit menu).

Option: Perform without dialog

To make sure that this step is performed on the correct set of records, you first should issue appropriate Find commands or use a Find step, such as Perform Find [. . .], to select the group of records to be deleted. As with other Delete commands, you cannot undo a Delete Found Set [. . .] step.

See also: Delete Record/Request [. . .], Find All, Perform Find [. . .], Enter Find Mode [. . .], Refind, Omit, Omit Multiple [. . .], Find Omitted

Chapter 15: Automating FileMaker Pro

Paste from Index [. . .]
Explanation: This step enables you to paste information into a field by selecting the data to be pasted from the index for that field (same as choosing the From Index option from the Paste Special submenu of the Edit menu or pressing ⌘-I). When this script step is executed, FileMaker displays the index for the current field (see Figure 15-15) and allows you to select the index entry that you want to paste. This step is very helpful for ensuring the correct spelling and consistent wording of field entries.

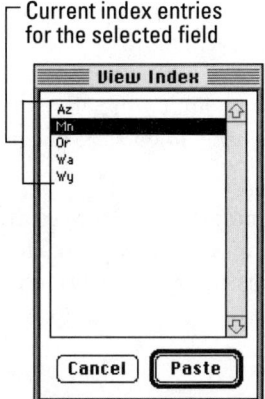

Figure 15-15: When Paste from Index [. . .] is executed, FileMaker displays the View Index dialog box for the current field.

Options: Select entire contents, Specify field

If you do not set the Specify field option, FileMaker assumes that you will preselect a field before executing this script step.

See also: Paste [. . .]

Paste from Last Record [. . .]
Explanation: This step pastes information from the most recently modified record into the selected field of the current record (same as choosing the From Last Record option from the Paste Special submenu of the Edit menu or pressing ⌘-').

Options: Select entire contents, Specify field

If the field to be used is not set with the Specify field option, FileMaker Pro assumes that you will select the field manually or as a previous script step before executing the Paste from Last Record [. . .] step. Because you generally will want to replace whatever is in the chosen field with the entire contents of that field from the last modified record, the Select entire contents option usually is chosen.

See also: Duplicate Record/Request

Paste Current Date [. . .]
Explanation: This step pastes today's date (according to your system clock) into the current field (same as choosing the Current Date option from the Paste Special submenu of the Edit menu or pressing ⌘--) or in a field specified as a step option.

Options: Select entire contents, Specify field

The date can be pasted into a field that is specified as a script-step option or into the current field, depending on whether the Specify Field option is used. The pasted date can replace the entire contents of the field (with Select entire contents checked) or can be added to the field at the insertion point (with Select entire contents unchecked). For the step to work, the chosen field must be of a proper type to accept a date.

If you do not already have an auto-entry field that automatically receives the current date when a new record is created or edited, you can use this script step to add a date stamp — such as a step in a data-entry or report-preparation script, for example.

See also: Paste, Paste Current Time [. . .]

Paste Current Time [. . .]
Explanation: This step pastes the current time (according to your system clock) into the current field (same as choosing the Current Time option from the Paste Special submenu of the Edit menu or pressing ⌘-;) or in a field specified as a step option.

Options: Select entire contents, Specify field

The time can be pasted into a field that is specified as a script-step option or into the current field, depending on whether the Specify Field option is used. The pasted time can replace the entire contents of the field (with Select entire contents checked) or can be added to the field at the insertion point (with Select entire contents unchecked). For the step to work, the chosen field must be of a proper type to accept a time.

If you do not already have an auto-entry field that automatically receives the current time when a new record is created or edited, you can use this script step to add a time stamp **command** as a step in a data-entry or report-preparation script, for example.

See also: Paste, Paste Current Date [. . .]

Paste Current User [. . .]
Explanation: This step pastes the name of the current user — according to the setting in the General section of the Preferences dialog box — into the current

Chapter 15: Automating FileMaker Pro

field (same as choosing Current User Name from the Paste Special submenu of the Edit menu or pressing Shift-⌘-N) or in a field specified as a step option.

Options: Select entire contents, Specify field

The user name can be pasted into a field that is specified as a script-step option or into the current field, depending on whether the Specify Field option is used. The pasted name can replace the entire contents of the field (with Select entire contents checked) or can be added to the field at the insertion point (with Select entire contents unchecked).

See Chapter 5 for instructions on setting or changing the current user name.

See also: Paste

Paste Literal [. . .]
Explanation: Use this step to paste a specific string (text or number) at the insertion point within the current field. Click Specify to indicate the string that you want to paste.

Option: none

This script step assumes that you have selected a field and positioned the insertion point before the step is executed. You can do this manually or by including a script step that selects the correct field, such as Go to Field [. . .].

See also: Paste

Replace [. . .]
Explanation: This step enables you to replace the same field in all records being browsed with the contents of the current field (same as choosing Replace from the Edit menu or pressing ⌘-=).

Options: Perform without dialog, Specify field

The Replace [. . .] step is very useful when you want a constant to be entered in a set of records. For example, you might issue a Find request that selects all New York ZIP codes and then use Replace to make sure that all the State fields contain the same information — presumably, New York or NY.

If you want to automatically use whatever information is in the selected or specified field of the current record, choose Perform without dialog. If you want to use the Replace [. . .] step to reserialize the records (assign serial numbers to the chosen field), do not check Perform without dialog. When the step executes, the dialog box shown in Figure 15-16 appears, enabling you to set a starting serial number and an increment. When the dialog box is on-screen, the user can use Replace [. . .] to perform the same actions as Reserialize [. . .].

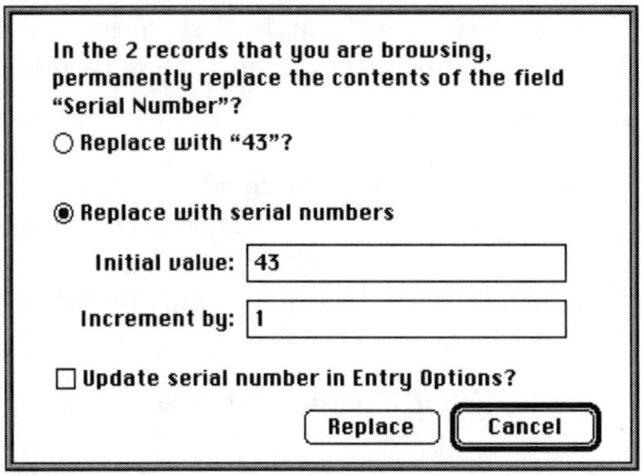

Figure 15-16: This dialog box enables you to set serial-number options or to simply replace the contents of the current field with a constant in all browsed records.

See also: Reserialize [. . .]

Reserialize [. . .]
Explanation: Use Reserialize [. . .] to assign serial numbers to a series of browsed records (same as choosing Replace from the Edit menu or pressing ⌘-= and then selecting the Replace with serial numbers option).

Options: Perform without dialog, Specify field

When this step is performed with the dialog box, you can use it to execute a reserialize *or* a replace operation.

See also: Replace [. . .]

Relookup [. . .]
Explanation: This step causes a relookup operation to be performed for the currently selected trigger field across all records being browsed (same as choosing Relookup from the Edit menu).

Options: Perform without dialog, Specify field

Use the Specify field option to select an eligible trigger field on which to base the relookup operation. If you do not set this option, FileMaker Pro assumes that you will select the field manually before executing the script.

To see an example of a script that performs a relookup, examine the Video Invoice database in the Macworld FileMaker Pro 2.0/2.1 Bible folder on the enclosed disk. The Relookup script is designed to run automatically each time the Video Invoice database is opened; the script updates all customer-address information.

Undo

Explanation: This step reverses (undoes) the most recent action performed in the database (same as choosing Undo from the Edit menu or pressing ⌘-Z). The "most recent action" conceivably could be another script step, if you want.

Option: none

Be aware that not all actions can be undone. Any command associated with deleting records, for example, cannot be reversed. When a command cannot be undone, the Undo command reads Can't Undo, and the Undo script step has no effect.

Cut [. . .]

Explanation: This step cuts the selected contents of a field to the Clipboard (same as choosing Cut from the Edit menu or pressing ⌘-X).

Options: Select entire contents, Specify field

Using the options alone or in combination, you can cut the entire contents of a field (Select entire contents), cut the selected contents of a particular field (Specify field), or cut the entire contents of a particular field (Select entire contents *and* Specify field). Information that is cut with this step is available for pasting elsewhere in the record, in a different record (enabling you to move existing information from one record to another), or in another program.

Note that cutting removes the selected text from the field. If your intent is merely to *duplicate* the information, use the Copy [. . .] step instead.

See also: Clear [. . .], Copy [. . .], Paste [. . .]

Copy [. . .]

Explanation: This step copies the selected contents of a field to the Clipboard (same as choosing Copy from the Edit menu or pressing ⌘-C).

Options: Select entire contents, Specify field

Using the options alone or in combination, you can copy the entire contents of a field (Select entire contents), copy the selected contents of a particular field (Specify field), or copy the entire contents of a particular field (Select entire contents *and* Specify field). Information that is copied with this step is available for pasting elsewhere in the record, in a different record (enabling you to duplicate existing information), or in another program.

See also: Cut [. . .], Paste [. . .]

Paste [. . .]

Explanation: This script step pastes the current contents of the Clipboard into the current field (same as choosing Paste from the Edit menu or pressing ⌘-V) or into a specified field.

Options: Select entire contents, Paste without style, Specify field

Data can be pasted into a field that is specified as a script step option or into the current field, depending on whether the Specify Field option is used. Pasted data can replace the entire contents of the field (with Select entire contents checked) or can be added to the field at the insertion point (with Select entire contents unchecked). If Paste without style is checked, any style formatting applied to the text (bold or italic, for example) is ignored. Otherwise, the pasted text includes whatever styles originally were applied to the text.

You should be aware of several common-sense restrictions when you use the Paste step. First, if the Clipboard is empty, nothing is pasted. Second, if the Clipboard contains data that is inappropriate for the selected field (such as a sound, picture, or movie that you are attempting to paste into a Text field, for example), nothing is pasted. Third, if no field is selected in the current layout and a field is not specified as an option for the script step, nothing is pasted.

Because the Clipboard is shared among all Macintosh programs, the material pasted conceivably could come from a program other than FileMaker Pro. For example, you could use a macro utility such as QuicKeys (discussed elsewhere in this chapter) to copy some text in a word processing program and then use the Paste step to transfer a copy of the text to a database field.

See also: Paste Literal [. . .], Paste from Last Record [. . .], Paste from Index [. . .], Paste Current Time [. . .], Paste Current Date [. . .], Paste Current User [. . .], Cut [. . .], Copy [. . .]

Clear [. . .]
Explanation: Clear removes data from the current field (same as choosing Clear from the Edit menu) or removes it from the particular field specified in the script step. Depending on the option selected, this step can delete all the data from a field or only the data that is currently selected.

Options: Select entire contents, Specify field

Clear can be used either on the currently selected field (leave Specify field unchecked) or on a particular field (click Specify field and then choose a field). To clear all data from a field, click the Select entire contents check box. To clear only the currently selected data from the field, leave Select entire contents unchecked. If the script step does not use the Select entire contents option, you must preselect text in the field before executing the script; otherwise, the step has no effect.

Unlike Cut [. . .], Clear does not save a copy of the data that has been removed; the data is not available for pasting. If you make a mistake, however, you can correct the Clear by immediately choosing Undo Clear from the Edit menu.

See also: Cut [. . .]

Select All

Explanation: Select All selects the entire contents of the current field (same as choosing Select All from the Edit menu, pressing ⌘-A, or quadruple-clicking a field).

Option: none

This command, like other script steps, cannot be used in Layout mode.

Spell Check Selection [. . .]

Explanation: Use the spelling checker to examine the selected text in the current field (same as choosing Check Selection from the Spelling submenu of the Edit menu).

Options: Select entire contents, Specify field

With no options set, this step can be used to spell-check selected text in any field of any layout. If no text is selected when the script executes, nothing happens — that is, no spell check is performed.

When only the first option (Select entire contents) is set, this step causes a spell check to be executed for the entire contents of the current field (the one that contains the cursor). If no field is current, the spell check is skipped.

If only the second option (Specify field) is used, the spell check is restricted to selected text within the particular field specified.

When both options are set, the entire contents of the specified field are checked. This method can be particularly useful for ensuring that the spelling is correct in a long text field (a Comments or Notes field, for example) or in a field in which you have composed a letter.

See also: Spell Check Record, Spell Check Found Set

Spell Check Record

Explanation: Use the spelling checker to examine every field in the current record (same as choosing Check Record from the Spelling submenu of the Edit menu).

Option: none

See also: Spell Check Selection [. . .], Spell Check Found Set

Spell Check Found Set

Explanation: This step performs a spelling check for every field in all records in the current found set — that is, the records that currently are being browsed. This step is the same as choosing Check Found Set from the Spelling submenu of the Edit menu.

Option: none

See also: Spell Check Selection [. . .], Spell Check Record

Toggle Status Area [. . .]

Explanation: This step enables you to toggle the state of the *status area* (the section of the document window that contains FileMaker Pro controls, such as the book icon and the Tool panel) or to specifically hide or show the status area. The Toggle version of this step has the same effect as clicking the status area control at the bottom of the document window.

Options: Refresh screen; Specify Show, Hide, or Toggle

To toggle the state of the status area (switching from Hide to Show or from Show to Hide), choose Toggle from the Specify pop-up menu. To switch to a specific state, whether the status area currently is shown or hidden, choose either Hide or Show from the Specify pop-up menu. You also can check Refresh screen if you want the screen to be redrawn at this step.

Toggle View-As-List [. . .]

Explanation: This step can be used to toggle the way records are displayed (one record per screen or as a continuous scrolling list) or to specifically set the database to one display mode or the other. The Toggle version of this script step is the same as choosing View as List from the Select menu.

Options: Refresh screen; Specify Show, Hide, or Toggle

To toggle the manner in which records are displayed (switching from showing one record per screen to showing the records as a list, or vice versa), choose Toggle from the Specify pop-up menu. To set the display mode to a specific state, regardless of the current display mode, choose either Hide or Show from the Specify pop-up menu. You also can check Refresh screen if you want the screen to be redrawn at this step.

Toggle Window [. . .]

Explanation: Depending on the option chosen from the Specify pop-up menu, this step can be used to hide (same as choosing Hide Window from the Window menu), zoom, or unzoom the current database document.

Options: Refresh screen; Specify Hide, Zoom, Unzoom

The Specify pop-up menu is not optional for the Toggle Window [. . .] step; you must choose an option. Choosing Hide results in hiding the current database. The name of the database is shown surrounded by parentheses in the Window menu — as (Sales), for example. To make the database visible again, select its name from the Window menu.

Choose Zoom to expand the document to the full size of the current screen. Choose Unzoom to return the document to its normal size and position on the screen. Note that repeated execution of either Zoom or Unzoom has no additional effect; the screen stays zoomed or unzoomed, as appropriate. To reverse the effect of a Toggle Window [Zoom] or a Toggle Window [Unzoom], add the opposite command as a new script step.

Chapter 15: Automating FileMaker Pro

Home
Explanation: This step is the same as dragging the box in the vertical scroll bar to the top position or pressing the Home key on an Apple Extended keyboard (displays the information and fields located in the top of the database window).

Options: none

Like their respective keys on the Apple Extended keyboard, the Home, Page Up, Page Down, and End script steps are used to scroll the database window up and down. These steps are very useful when you have designed a layout that exceeds the height of your monitor, enabling you to automatically scroll to show or view information that currently is off-screen (above or below it).

In an extremely long layout, you can use these script steps in combination to more accurately select an area for display. For example, if you have no control over when the script might be executed — and, hence, what portion of the screen currently is being shown — beginning the script with Home or End (and then following it with any necessary Page Up or Page Down steps) eliminates any possibility of error.

See also: Page Up, Page Down, End

Page Up
Explanation: This step is the same as clicking one time above the box in the vertical scroll bar or pressing the Page Up key on an Apple Extended keyboard (scrolls up one screen).

Option: none

See also: Home, Page Down, End

Page Down
Explanation: This step is the same as clicking one time below the box in the vertical scroll bar or pressing the Page Down key on an Apple Extended keyboard (scrolls down one screen).

Option: none

See also: Home, Page Up, End

End
Explanation: This step is the same as dragging the box in the vertical scroll bar to the bottom position or pressing the End key on an Apple Extended keyboard (displays the information and fields located in the bottom of the database window).

Option: none

See also: Home, Page Up, Page Down

Send Apple Event [. . .]
Explanation: If you are running System 7 on your Macintosh, you can use the Send Apple Event [. . .] step to facilitate interaction between FileMaker Pro and other programs.

Option: Specify

Apple Events — a feature of System 7 — enable you to send messages (commands and data) between programs. Acid Jazz, a shareware utility included on the *Macworld FileMaker Pro 2.0/2.1 Bible Disk*, uses Apple Events to add phone-dialing capabilities to FileMaker Pro. Although most users never will personally create a script that uses Apple Events, anyone can easily use this script step to launch other programs and documents from FileMaker Pro (discussed in "Using Apple Events," later in this chapter). And if you have QuicKeys (a commercial macro utility from CE Software), you can use this step to execute impressive macros (described in "Using QuicKeys with FileMaker Pro scripts," later in this chapter).

Help
Explanation: Displays the normal FileMaker Pro Help information (same as choosing Help from the Apple menu or pressing ⌘-?).

Option: none

Open [. . .]
Explanation: This step is used to enable the user to select a FileMaker Pro database to be opened (same as choosing Open from the File menu or pressing ⌘-O) or to open a specific database file automatically.

Option: Specify file

If a file is specified, that file is opened when the step executes. If no file is specified, a standard file dialog box appears, enabling you to select a database to open. In either case, a database opened with this script step becomes the current database. (If you intend to perform a script in another database, you don't have to open that other database first. Simply use the Perform Script [. . .] step, specify that an external script is to be used, and then select the database to open and the particular script you want to perform.)

See also: Close [. . .]

Close [. . .]
Explanation: This step closes the current file (same as choosing Close from the File menu or pressing ⌘-W) or closes another specific database file.

Option: Specify file

If no options are set, the Close step simply closes the current file (same as choosing Close from the File menu or pressing ⌘-W). If the Specify file option is checked, you can choose a particular file to close (Sales, for example).

The Close option is useful for ending a script that performs a final action for a database. You could, for example, use this step to sort the database in a specific way (to be sure that the database is ready for use the next day) and then close the file. If you have a database that works in conjunction with other databases (for an example,

Chapter 15: Automating FileMaker Pro

see the Callable Help Example folder in the FM Pro Bible folder on the enclosed disk), you can use the Close step to close the other file or files when they're no longer needed. (Closing unnecessary databases can free memory for other FileMaker Pro activities.)

See also: Open [. . .], Quit

Save a Copy as [. . .]
Explanation: This step is the same as choosing the Save a Copy As command from the File menu.

Option: Specify file

If no options are set for the Save a Copy as. . . step, the standard Save a Copy as dialog box appears when the script executes the step (see Figure 15-17). The dialog box enables you (or the current user) to name the copy, determine where on disk the file will be saved, and select the type of copy that is made (a duplicate, a compressed copy, or a clone). Click the Specify file option if you always want the file to be saved in a particular location, with the same filename and type.

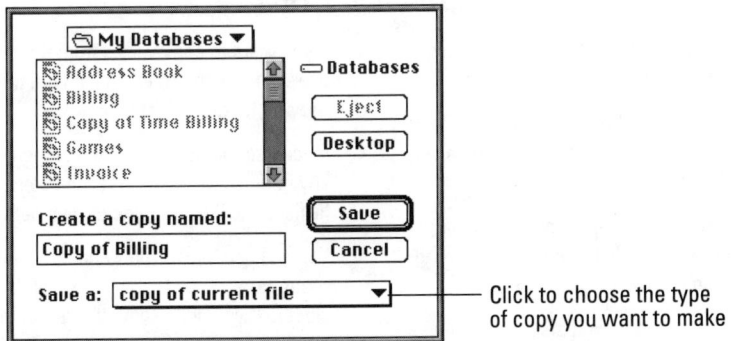

Figure 15-17: This dialog box appears when a Save a Copy as. . . step is executed.

An example of using the Save a Copy as. . . script step appears in the "Automatic Backups" sidebar in Chapter 3.

Define Fields
Explanation: This step displays the Define Fields dialog box for the current database, enabling you to create new fields, edit definitions for existing fields, delete fields, and set and change options for fields (same as choosing Define Fields from the Select menu or pressing Shift-⌘-D). See Chapter 5 for more information about defining fields.

Option: none

Quit

Explanation: This step quits FileMaker Pro and returns the user to the Desktop (same as choosing Quit from the File menu or pressing ⌘-Q). Any files that currently are open are saved automatically, if necessary.

Option: none

The Quit step can be extremely useful as a final command in a cleanup script. If you always print a report from a particular database as the final activity for the day, for example, you could define a script that does the printing and then ends by quitting FileMaker Pro.

See also: Close [. . .]

Scriptmaking Tips

Following are some useful script-making tips passed on by Max Pruden of Claris Technical Support:

❖ You can use the Go to Record/Request [. . .] step to go to the last record by specifying a very high record number, such as 9999.

❖ The Paste Literal [. . .] step works only if you first specify a target field for the paste by using the Go to Field [. . .] step.

❖ When you exit a Sort or Find step, you automatically switch to Browse mode, with the first record in the sort order or found set displayed. Thus, you don't need to include an Enter Browse mode [. . .] step or a Go to Record/Request [. . .] step to go to the first record.

❖ Two types of scripts can be executed by the Perform Script [. . .] step: *internal scripts* (scripts in the current file) and *external scripts* (scripts in other files). When you use Perform Script to execute an external script, you don't need to use the Open [. . .] step first to open the other database.

❖ If you want to copy values from Summary fields, use the Refresh screen option with the Enter Browse Mode [. . .] step.

❖ If you use the Copy [. . .] step without setting any options, the step copies the contents of all fields in the layout for the current record.

❖ You can use the Toggle Window [. . .] step to zoom the window to the full size of the current screen. If you don't know the size of the particular monitor that will be used with the database (as when you are distributing or selling your databases to others), this step can be very useful as part of a start-up script.

❖ A script executes in its own database. To perform procedures that affect two files, such as a Copy from one database and a Paste into another, you need two scripts: one in each database. For this example, you would create a script that copies the contents of a field in the current file and include a step to perform an external script (defined in the other database) that selects the appropriate field and then pastes.

Attaching a Script to a Button

As mentioned in earlier discussions of many of the templates included on the *Macworld FileMaker Pro 2.0/2.1 Bible Disk*, you can attach scripts to buttons or icons that you include in a layout. When a button is clicked, the script or script step attached to that button executes instantly — in exactly the same manner as though you chose the script name from the Scripts menu or clicked Perform in the Define Scripts dialog box.

Buttons frequently are added to layouts to make it easy and convenient for users to perform both simple and complex series of commands. By assigning the Go to Layout [...] step to a button, for example, you can quickly navigate to a particular layout, such as a help screen or a report layout. You also can attach a multistep script to a button that executes a Find request, performs a sort, prints a report, returns to the data-entry screen, and then restores the database to its state before the button was clicked. For several examples of buttons, examine the databases in the FM Pro Bible folder on the *Macworld FileMaker Pro 2.0/2.1 Bible Disk*.

Note that although graphic icons frequently are used as buttons, you can use *any* object as a button (including static text strings, for example).

To attach a script step or a script to a button, follow these steps:

1. **Switch to Layout mode.** (Choose Layout from the Select menu, press ⌘-L, or choose Layout from the Mode menu at the bottom of the database window).

2. **Select the icon, button, or other object that you want to make into a button.**

   When selected, an object has a *handle* (black dot) in each of its corners.

3. **Choose Define Button from the Scripts menu.**

   The Define Button dialog box appears (see Figure 15-18).

4. **To assign a single script step to the button, select the script step, set any options that appear for that step at the bottom of the dialog box, and then click OK.**

   — or —

4. **To assign a particular script to the button, select Perform Script [...], select the script to be executed from the Specify pop-up menu, and click OK.**

There is still more you should know about working with buttons, as follows:

❖ To remove a script or script step from a button (*undefine* it), perform Steps 1 through 3 (above), select one of the dotted dividing lines in the Define Button dialog box, and click OK.

Part IV: Intermediate Topics

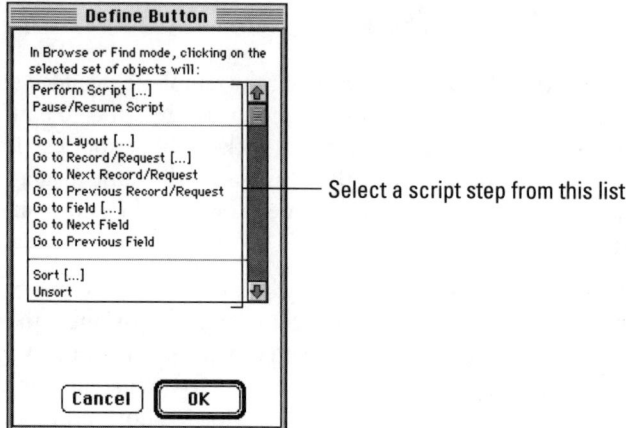

Figure 15-18: The Define Button dialog box.

- If you're having trouble identifying the particular objects in a layout that are buttons (as opposed to ordinary graphics, static text, and other objects), change to Layout mode, and choose Buttons from the Show submenu of the Layout menu. Each button will be surrounded by a gray outline.

- When you copy a button in a layout, that button's definition also is copied — that is, any script or script step attached to the button is attached to the copy. If you paste the button into another layout in the same database or a different one, the pasted button will attempt to perform the same function as the original button. You may need to edit the script or script step so that the duplicate now refers to the proper layout, field name, or whatever else the duplicate button references.

- To delete a button that you no longer need, switch to Layout mode, select the button, and then choose Cut or Clear from the Edit menu. Alternatively, you can simply press the Delete (or Backspace) key.

What Does This Button Do?

If you're curious about the script step or script that has been assigned to a button, there's a simple way to determine what the step or script does. Just switch to Layout mode, select the button, and choose Define Button from the Scripts menu. In the Define Button dialog box that appears, the step or script that is assigned to the button will be highlighted.

Chapter 15: Automating FileMaker Pro

Using Advanced Scripting Procedures

You can create many perfectly functional scripts by selecting single steps and by combining steps for commands with which you are very familiar, such as Go to Layout, Sort, Find, and Print. Some of the steps, step options, and system software features supported by ScriptMaker, however, can add extraordinary flexibility and power to FileMaker Pro. Although you may not immediately be interested in pursuing these power-scripting features, the following sections discuss them.

Executing other scripts from within a script

In FileMaker Pro, a script can be instructed to perform other scripts. These other scripts are known as *sub-scripts*. (In programming parlance, sub-scripts would be called subroutines.) To allow one script to perform another script (or *several* other scripts, for that matter), you simply set the Perform sub-scripts option when choosing the Perform Script [...] step. After running a sub-script, the original (or calling) script continues from where it left off.

Any script that is executed as part of a Perform Script [...] step — whether it is the object of the step or a sub-script — can be an internal or external script. An *internal script* is a script that is defined within the current database. An *external script* is a script in another database. When you run an external script, FileMaker Pro automatically opens the external database and executes the script. When the external script is completed, control returns to the original script and database, just as it does when a sub-script is performed.

To run an external script, follow these steps:

1. **When you define the script, choose Perform Script [...] as one of the steps.**
2. **With the Perform Script [...] step selected in the script, choose External script from the Specify pop-up menu.**

   The Specify External Script dialog box appears (see Figure 15-19).

Figure 15-19: The Specify External Script dialog box.

Part IV: Intermediate Topics

3. **Click Change File to select the database that contains the external script you want to execute.**

   A standard file dialog box appears.

4. **Select the database that contains the external script you want to execute, and click Open.**

   A modified version of the Specify External Script dialog box appears (see Figure 15-20).

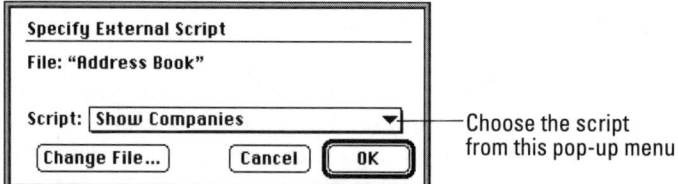

   Choose the script from this pop-up menu

   Figure 15-20: Choose an external script to perform.

5. **Click the Script pop-up menu, and select the script that you want to perform.**

6. **Click OK to record your choices.**

Using Apple Events

The Send Apple Event [. . .] script step allows you to send messages from FileMaker Pro to other programs. Although not all programs support the required and Do Script events, most programs should be able to respond to a request to launch or to open a particular document. This section describes how to perform these simple actions from within a FileMaker Pro database.

To create a program or document launcher by using Apple Events, follow these steps:

1. **Create a new script, choose the Send Apple Event [. . .] step, and click Specify.**

   The Specify Apple Event dialog box appears (see Figure 15-21).

2. **From the Send pop-up menu, choose Open application.**

   A standard file dialog box appears, in which you select the program that you want the script to launch.

   — or —

2. **From the Send pop-up menu, choose Open document.**

Chapter 15: Automating FileMaker Pro

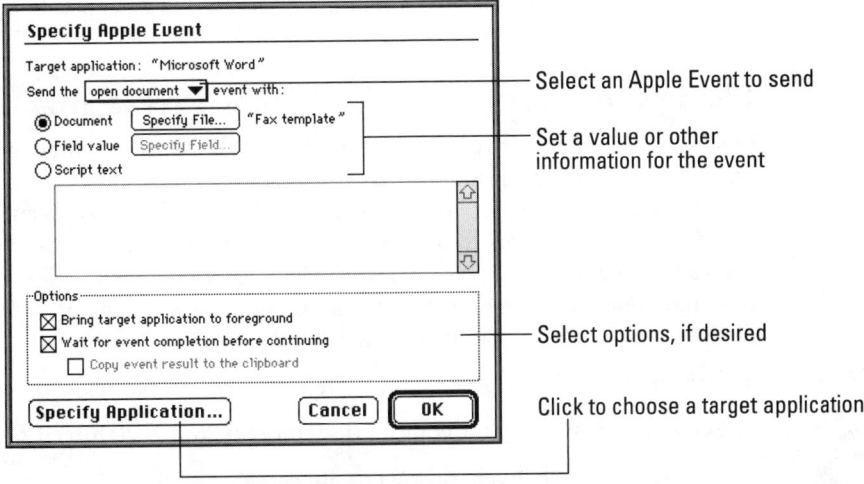

Figure 15-21: The Specify Apple Event dialog box.

Then click the Specify file button beside the Document radio button to choose a document.

3. **At the bottom of the Specify Apple Event dialog box, set any desired options.**

    In most cases, you will want to choose Bring target application to foreground; otherwise, when the program or document is launched, it may be hidden behind your FileMaker Pro database window.

4. **To save the script, click OK in this dialog box and then also click OK in the Script Definition dialog box.**

After defining a program- or document-launcher script, you can pretty things up by using a screen-capture utility such as Capture (Mainstay) to capture a picture of the program's or document's icon, paste the icon into your FileMaker Pro layout, and then use the Define Button command in the Scripts menu to make the icon into a button that launches the script. If you frequently use several utilities while running FileMaker (such as a calculator, clock, and address book, for instance), you can use this technique to create a string of buttons. Because these button definitions are not specific to one database, you can copy and paste the buttons into *any* database. As long as the databases are run on your machine and you don't change the locations of the programs or documents to be launched, the buttons should work fine.

To learn more about how FileMaker uses Apple Events, check out the Claris database named FileMaker and Apple Events on the *Macworld FileMaker Pro 2.0/ 2.1 Bible Disk.*

You can find additional information in the Apple Events Examples folder that comes with FileMaker Pro.

Using QuicKeys with FileMaker Pro scripts

QuicKeys is a general-purpose macro utility that allows you to automate complex functions in most Macintosh programs, desk accessories, the Finder, and so on. QuicKeys 2 and QuicKeys 3 can work in conjunction with Apple Events. Because FileMaker Pro 2 has a Send Apple Event [...] script step, you can use a script to invoke QuicKeys and execute any macro that you have defined. Following are the steps required to execute a QuicKeys macro; these steps assume that you have FileMaker Pro 2.0v4 or a more recent version.

To execute a QuicKeys macro from a FileMaker Pro script, follow these steps:

1. **Select the Send Apple Event [...] script step and click Specify.**

   The Specify Apple Event dialog box appears.

2. **Choose Other... event.**

   The Specify Event dialog box appears (see Figure 15-22).

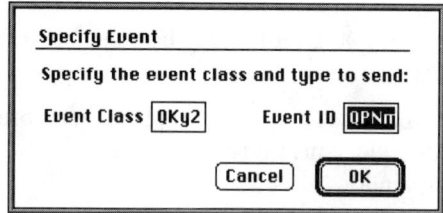

Figure 15-22: Enter the event class and type in this dialog box.

3. **For Event Class and Event ID, enter the following:** *QKy2* **and** *QPNm*. **Then click OK.**

   Be sure that the capitalization is correct; it must match exactly!

4. **If you have QuicKeys 2, click the Specify Application button, and then choose CEIAC in the Extensions folder of your System Folder.**

   — or —

4. **If you have QuicKeys 3, click the Specify Application button and then choose the QuicKeys Toolbox in the Extensions folder of your System Folder.**

Chapter 15: Automating FileMaker Pro

5. Click the **Script text** radio button and then type the name of the QuicKeys macro that you want to run (see Figure 15-23).
6. Click **OK** to finish the step definition.

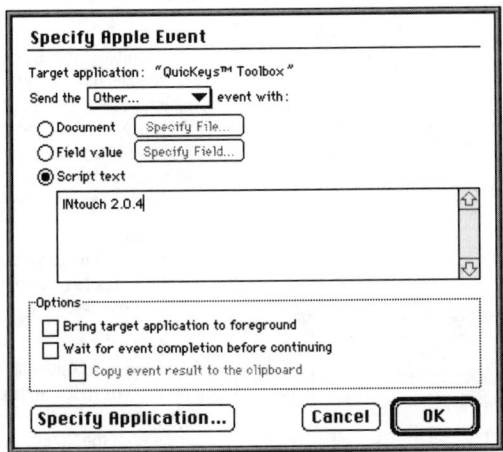

Figure 15-23: Using the Specify Apple Event dialog box to execute a QuicKeys 3 macro.

Figure 15-23 shows an Apple Event script that runs a QuicKeys macro called INtouch 2.0.4. This macro is a one-step macro that launches a commercial address book desk accessory. Because QuicKeys can automate almost any program function, you also could use it to create FileMaker Pro-specific macros — ones that perform a series of field-formatting operations, for example — and then use a Send Apple Event [. . .] step to activate each macro.

Using AppleScript

Available as part of System 7 Pro (Apple Computer) and also sold separately, AppleScript is a System 7-only, English-based programming/scripting language that you can use to integrate Macintosh programs and customize the way your Mac works. Unlike using the scripting feature in FileMaker Pro, using AppleScript really *is* programming.

If AppleScript is installed on your Mac, you can take a look at the AppleScript example provided with Acid Jazz, a shareware utility included as part of the *Macworld FileMaker Pro 2.0/2.1 Bible Disk.*

Part IV: Intermediate Topics

CHAPTER 15 CONCEPTS AND TERMS

- Using ScriptMaker, you can define scripts that automate procedures that you routinely perform in a particular database.

- Scripts can be attached to buttons, if you want. If added to the Scripts menu, the first ten scripts are assigned keyboard shortcuts (⌘-1 through ⌘-0).

- Like virtually anything else you define for a FileMaker Pro database, scripts can be edited, deleted, duplicated, renamed, or reordered.

- Most of the available script steps are intended to duplicate FileMaker Pro menu commands that you use in Browse, Find, or Preview mode. No steps affect work that you normally do while in Layout mode.

- A script step that performs a Find, Sort, Page Setup, Import Records, or Export Records procedure can remember the instructions set for that procedure simply by noting the settings that were in effect when the script was created.

- A script can consist of a single step. More complex scripts can have multiple steps and even can execute other scripts.

- Using the Send Apple Event [. . .] step, you can design a script that interacts with another program or executes a QuicKeys 2 or 3 macro.

Apple Events
Messages sent between applications that enable the applications to interact.

AppleScript
A System 7 macro-programming language from Apple Computer.

external script
A script in another database that is executed with the Perform Script [. . .] step. When an external script is performed in this manner, the database that contains the script automatically opens first.

handle
A black dot that appears at the corners of an object when it is selected (only in Layout mode). You can drag the handles to change the size of an object.

internal script
A script that is contained in and executed from the current database.

QuicKeys
A macro utility from CE Software that enables users to automate many functions in most programs. When you use the Send Apple Event [. . .] script step, QuicKeys macros that access other programs can be executed from within FileMaker Pro.

QuickTime
An Apple system extension that enables Macs to play specially designed movies.

script
A sequence of FileMaker Pro program actions that can be carried out in response to a button click or a choice from the Scripts menu.

step
A single action set for a FileMaker Pro script.

sub-script
Any FileMaker Pro script that is performed by another script.

CHAPTER SIXTEEN

Exchanging Data

IN THIS CHAPTER

- Understanding file formats
- Importing data from other programs
- Exporting data from FileMaker Pro
- Working with the Windows version of FileMaker Pro

As nice as it might be, you probably aren't going to spend your entire working life happily curled up inside FileMaker Pro. You likely work with many different applications, and perhaps you even stored your database-type information in some other program before you became a FileMaker Pro aficionado. Wouldn't it be great to be able to move all that stuff into, and perhaps even out of, FileMaker Pro? You may want to move your old address and phone-number data directly to FileMaker without retyping. You may want to move data from an Invoices database to a spreadsheet program so that you can check how you're doing and make predictions.

There are many reasons why you may want to move data. The good news is that you can do so without too much trouble, as this chapter explains.

Moving Data to and from Other Places

FileMaker Pro can work with data produced by a variety of other programs. FileMaker Pro also can work with data from other database application programs, such as dBASE. In fact, if the other program can save or export its data in one of half a dozen extremely common formats (such as tab-delimited text), FileMaker Pro can read and use the data. This data exchange is a two-way street: FileMaker produces data that these applications can use, and it can take data from those applications for use in a FileMaker Pro database. The former process is called *exporting*; the latter is called *importing*.

About importing and exporting

When you import data into FileMaker Pro, you bring that data in from some other program. You can import data from another FileMaker Pro document — even one created on a different type of computer. You can even import data from a remote network source, such as an SQL server. And you can use FileMaker Pro's import capabilities when you want to bring a picture or QuickTime movie data into a database.

Note: When you import data, you can choose to append the new records to your existing file or to use the new data to update existing records. When you import, FileMaker Pro copies data but does not copy layouts and/or field definitions. You cannot move new data into calculation and summary fields.

You also can make information from a FileMaker Pro database available for use in other applications. You might export the current found set of records to a word processing program, for example, for use in preparing a mass mailing. This process, called *mail merge*, is supported by virtually all the major word processing programs, including Microsoft Word and MacWrite.

Note that FileMaker Pro cannot export to remote sources; neither can you export data directly into another FileMaker Pro file. Instead of exporting directly into the target application file, you simply export the data to a temporary file and then import it using the target application's procedures to import data. The net effect is the same.

Although FileMaker Pro can work with data from many different applications, its capability is limited by the ways in which these applications store their data. The way that data is stored in an application is called the application's *file format*.

Understanding file formats

A file format specifies how an application's data is organized and interpreted. You can think of a file format as being a recipe for creating the finished file from its raw data (from the text that you type, for example). The instructions for interpreting a file format must be stored within the application program in which you want to use the data; otherwise, very strange and unsatisfactory results may occur.

FileMaker Pro supports the file formats discussed in the following sections. Notice that some formats are for importing data only and that others are solely for export purposes.

Tab-separated text
This format sometimes is called ASCII format (pronounced *askee*), but a few differences exist between the two formats. (*ASCII* refers to plain, unformatted text arranged according to an industry-standard coding scheme, and stands for American Standard Code for Information Interchange). In tab-separated text, tab characters separate fields in a record, and return characters separate records. Virtually all computer applications can interpret files that are in this format.

Merge
Merge is an export format that you use to create special documents used as the data portion of mail merges. Commas separate field values, return characters separate records, and the ASCII character 29 separates repeating fields. In this format, the first record is called the *header*; the header lists the field names contained in the file. Quotation marks surround field data.

Comma-separated text
This format is used for BASIC programming and in some applications. Commas separate field values, and return characters separate records. All field values except unformatted numbers are in quotation marks.

BASIC
This format is similar to comma-separated text but is designed for use with Microsoft standard BASIC.

SYLK
SYLK stands for *symbolic link* format. This is a spreadsheet format in which data is stored in rows and columns. SYLK can be used by Excel, WingZ, Resolve, and other applications. Each field is a column; each record is a row. Returns are output as spaces. Dates and times are output as text within quotation marks. Non-numeric data in a number field is suppressed. Fields are limited to a maximum of the 245 characters.

DIF
DIF is another spreadsheet format, used by older applications such as VisiCalc and AppleWorks. Each field is a column, and each record is a row.

WKS
WKS is a spreadsheet format used by Lotus 1-2-3. Each field is a column, and each record is a row.

DBF
DBF is dBASE III database format. Field names can be no more than 10 characters long, with a maximum 254 characters per field and 128 fields per record.

Edition file
This format, for use with the Macintosh System 7 Edition Manager, is an export-only format similar to tab-separated text. When you export data to this format, you're creating an edition file to which other users can subscribe. *Exporting in Edition file format is the same as publishing a record in other System 7 programs.*

Importing Data from Other Sources

You have several options when you import data from another source. You can combine information stored in several places in one master file; your master file might contain only selected fields from several similar files. You also can change the order in which records are stored. Recall that FileMaker Pro normally stores records in the order in which they are entered. When importing, FileMaker Pro copies records in sorted order. If you import data that includes repeating fields, you can split the latter values into separate records.

Format selection

When importing data, FileMaker Pro makes it easy to determine whether the import file is in an appropriate format. By default, the Import file dialog box lists only the files that FileMaker Pro understands (based on the XTND translator files that were copied onto your hard disk as part of FileMaker Pro's installation procedure). If the file that you want to import does not appear in the Import file dialog box's list of files, you may need to check the relevant application's documentation to determine what file format it uses. If FileMaker Pro doesn't support the standard file format of your source application, you'll need to have the application output a new data file in a format that FileMaker Pro *can* use. Many applications can output tab- or comma-separated text, for example.

FileMaker Pro supports the following formats for import purposes:

- FileMaker Pro
- Tab-Separated Text
- Comma-Separated Text
- SYLK
- DBF
- DIF
- WKS
- BASIC
- Merge
- Data Access Manager

Data cleanup

Data that you want to import may not be in tiptop shape. You may find, for example, that the match between fields in your source and target files isn't as clean as you had hoped, or that you don't have access to a supported file format. The procedures outlined in the following sections show you how to solve a couple of these problems.

Chapter 16: Exchanging Data

Cleaning up data in a spreadsheet

If you had your Mac for awhile before you bought FileMaker Pro, you probably also had one or more address or contacts files that you created in other programs—address data recorded in the Addresses with Audio HyperCard stack or in a desk accessory, for example. Rather than keep this information spread across a handful of programs and desk accessories, it's usually preferable to put all the data into *one* database, program, or desk accessory. Unfortunately, most of us don't plan for (or count on) the difficulties encountered when trying to create one composite file from two or more separate address files. In particular, the various files are likely to contain different fields. This section discusses some simple procedures you can use to clean up your disparate data before importing it into or exporting it from FileMaker Pro.

Following are two of the most common problems in importing address data:

❖ Address, phone number, and name fields in the file you want to import are split into two fields (address line 1 and address line 2, area code and phone number, and first name and last name), but the FileMaker Pro database contains only one field for the corresponding items, or vice versa.

❖ When exported, zip codes shorter than five digits may lose their leading zero (for example, 1276 rather than 01276).

Rather than import the data as it is and clean it up in the database afterward, you'll find it more efficient to use a spreadsheet application (such as the one included in ClarisWorks) to make the necessary transformations to the data. To do this, follow these general steps:

1. **Export the data from your database, spreadsheet, or address-book program as a tab-delimited ASCII text file.**

2. **Open the ASCII text file in a spreadsheet program; make the transformations to the data, creating new fields as necessary; and save the revised file as an ASCII text file.**

3. **Open the FileMaker Pro database into which you intend to import the data.**

4. **Use the Import Records command to import the ASCII text file into the database.**

The simplest way to make the transformations in the spreadsheet is to create additional columns on the right side of the spreadsheet. The following text explains how to accomplish this task within the spreadsheet environment of ClarisWorks (another popular program from Claris).

Each column must contain a formula that combines or converts one or more columns of the original data. Create the appropriate formula, and then use the Fill Down command (⌘-D) to copy the formula into the remaining cells in the column.

Part IV: Intermediate Topics

The simple spreadsheet shown in Figure 16-1 illustrates the formula needed to convert First Name and Last Name fields into a single Name field. Column A contains first names, column B contains last names, and column C contains the combined first and last names. The formula shown in the entry bar (=A2 & " " & B2) takes the first name in cell A2 (Jody), adds a space (" "), and then adds the last name from cell B2 (Privette) to the end of the text string. As mentioned above, you use the Fill Down command to copy the formula to all the rest of the cells in column C.

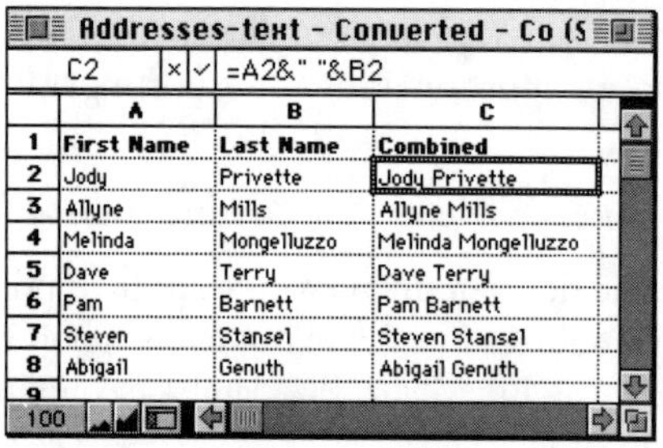

Figure 16-1: A formula to combine first and last names into a single name.

Suppose you have a database or other address file in which address information is split into two lines or fields and want to import that data into a file in which Address is only a single line or field. Some addresses in the original file, however, have only one line, while others in the file have two. In Figure 16-2, the equation =IF(B2<>"",A2 & ", " & B2,A2) checks to see whether the address has a second line (B2<>""). If the address has a second line, the formula combines the two portions, separating them with a comma followed by a blank, as in 251 Rock Road, P.O. Box 116. If the address has no second line, the formula simply copies the first address part (A2) into the cell.

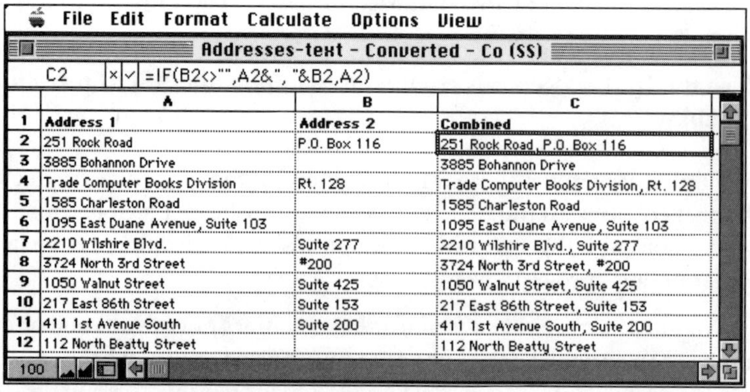

Figure 16-2: A formula to combine two-line addresses into a single address line.

Chapter 16: Exchanging Data

Because zip codes often are treated as numbers, the leading zero may disappear when the data is exported, resulting in an improper four-digit code. The lengthy formula =IF(LEN(A2)=4,"0" & A2,NUMTOTEXT(A2)) shown in Figure 16-3 checks to see whether the zip code is four digits long (LEN(A2)=4). If the zip code contains four digits, a leading zero is appended to the zip code ("0" & A2), which then is converted to text. If the zip code does not contain four digits, the zip code is converted to text and passed through unaltered (NUMTOTEXT(A2)).

Converting zip codes to text is necessary to display leading zeros and to handle blank zip code fields. If the formula ended simply with A2 rather than NUMTOTEXT(A2), a blank zip code would translate as 0 (zero).

Figure 16-3: A formula to check the length of the Zip code.

Converting return-delimited text

Another cleanup problem that you may encounter is data that has been exported in return-delimited format. In this format, fields are separated by return characters, and records are separated by two returns. You can convert this format to tab-delimited format, if you have access to a word processing program that can search for and replace hidden characters, such as the ASCII return and tab characters. Microsoft Word, MacWrite Pro, and ClarisWorks can perform this task, as can other applications.

To convert return-delimited text, follow these steps:

1. **Open the return-delimited file in your word processing program.**
2. **Choose the application's Find/Change command.**

    In Microsoft Word, for example, you would choose Replace from the Edit menu.

3. **Perform the following change operations:**

    ❖ Find all occurrences of two returns (^p^p in Word, for example) and change these characters to something else, such as *XXXX*.

Part IV: Intermediate Topics

❖ Find all occurrences of a single return (^p in Word) and change these characters to tabs (^t in Word, for example).

❖ Find all occurrences of *XXXX* and change these characters to single returns.

4. **Save the result as a text file.**

    The file now is in tab-delimited format.

How to import

When your data is cleaned up (if cleanup was needed), you're ready to import. To import data into a FileMaker Pro database, follow these steps:

1. **Open the destination database file in FileMaker Pro and switch to Browse mode.**

2. **Choose Import Records from the Import/Export submenu of the File menu.**

    The file dialog box shown in Figure 16-4 appears. At the bottom of the dialog box is a File Type pop-up menu where you can select the format of the file that you want to import.

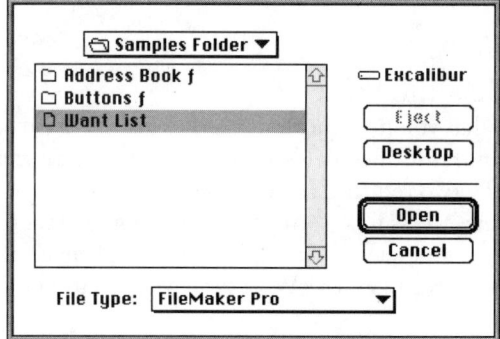

Figure 16-4: Choose a file to import from this dialog box.

3. *Optional*: **To limit the listed files to only those of a particular type, choose the appropriate file format from the File Type pop-up menu.**

    The default option in the File Type pop-up menu is All Available. This tells FileMaker to list in the file dialog box *every* file that it thinks it can read. In most cases, this is fine. However, if you're having a hard time finding the particular file you want to import, you can choose its specific type from the File Type pop-up menu.

4. **Select the name of the file you want to import.**

Chapter 16: Exchanging Data   455

5. **Click Open.**

   The Specify field order dialog box appears (see Figure 16-5). The purpose of this dialog box is to match fields in the source file with those in the destination file, as well as to pick the fields you want to import and the ones you want to ignore.

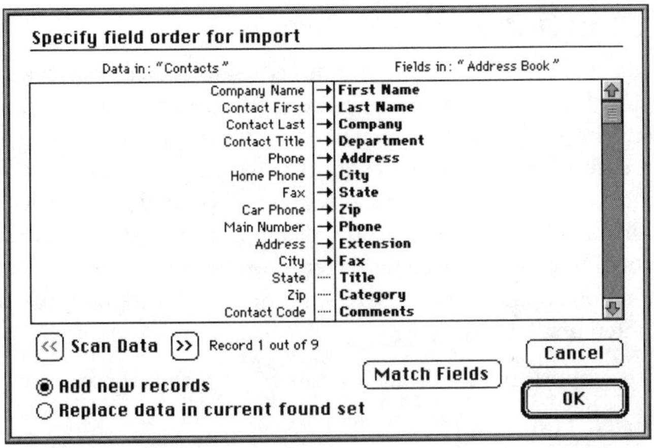

   ```
   Specify field order for import
         Data in: "Contacts"              Fields in: "Address Book"
                  Company Name   →  First Name
                  Contact First  →  Last Name
                  Contact Last   →  Company
                  Contact Title  →  Department
                          Phone  →  Address
                     Home Phone  →  City
                            Fax  →  State
                      Car Phone  →  Zip
                    Main Number  →  Phone
                        Address  →  Extension
                           City  →  Fax
                          State  ··· Title
                            Zip  ··· Category
                   Contact Code  ··· Comments

       << Scan Data  >>   Record 1 out of 9          Cancel
       ● Add new records              Match Fields
       ○ Replace data in current found set           OK
   ```

   Figure 16-5: The Specify field order dialog box.

6. *Optional*: **To expedite the field-matching process, click Match Fields (available in FileMaker 2.1 or higher only).**

   The Match Fields button pairs up any fields in the two files that have exactly the same name.

7. **Match the remaining fields that you want to import.**

   An arrow following a field name in the source file (left side of the dialog box) indicates that the field will be imported into the field to the right (in the destination file). If you don't want to import a particular field, click its arrow.

   Because fields in the two files can be in any order, it may be necessary for you to manually rearrange them so that they match. You can drag field names in the destination file (right side of the dialog box) to place them in a different order.

8. **Click the appropriate radio button to specify whether you want to Add new records or Replace data in the current found set.**

   Add new records simply appends the imported records to the destination file; Replace data in the current found set overwrites the records in the current found set. If you intend to use the latter option, you should first make a backup copy of the destination file. The Import command cannot be undone, so a mistake can have serious consequences for your data!

9. **Click OK.**

Exporting Data

When you export, you take FileMaker Pro data and change it to a format that another program can use. The process is virtually the same as importing, except that it operates in reverse.

Format selection

When you export records, you don't save directly into a document in another application; rather, you create a new document that the target application can open. As you do when importing records, you need to determine the file format of the destination program before you export data to be used by that program. You may need to check the relevant application's documentation to determine what file format(s) it can use. If FileMaker Pro doesn't support that application's standard file format, you'll have to instruct FileMaker to export a new data file in a format that the destination application *can* use. Many Macintosh programs can read tab- or comma-separated text files.

FileMaker Pro supports the following formats for export purposes:

- Tab-Separated Text
- Comma-Separated Text
- SYLK
- DBF
- DIF
- WKS
- BASIC
- Merge
- Edition file

Data cleanup

As you do when importing, you may need to clean up your data before exporting it. In particular, you may find unnecessary returns and spaces at the end of some records. These unneeded characters usually are the result of careless data entry and can cause trouble in your target file when you export data to it.

As a solution, you can define a new calculation field for each field to be exported. The definition of this field is a procedure that strips spaces and returns. Use the following definition:

```
If(Position(FieldName, "¶", 1), Trim (Left(FieldName,
Position(FieldName,"¶",1)-1)),Trim(FieldName))
```

Chapter 16: Exchanging Data

Replace "FieldName" with the name of the field that you want to strip. You must define a separate calculation field for each potential source field. Then export the calculation fields rather than the originals. *You should note that if you use this formula on a field that contains <u>intentional</u> returns (as might be found in a Comments field that contains serveral programs), the formula truncates the field contents at the end of the first paragraph - effectively deleting all paragraphs that follow.*

How to export

With data cleanup behind you (in the event that cleanup was necessary), you ready to export the data. Follow these steps to export FileMaker Pro data for use in another application:

1. **Open your source FileMaker Pro document.**

2. **Use Find mode to locate the set of records to export.**

   An export always consists only of records in the current found set. You also can use the Sort command to sort these records, if you want.

3. **In Browse mode, choose Export Records from the Import/Export submenu of the File menu.**

   A standard file dialog box appears, similar in appearance to the dialog box shown in Figure 16-4.

4. **Type a name for the destination file.**

5. **Choose a file format for the destination file from the File Type pop-up menu.**

6. **Click New.**

   The Specify field order for export dialog box appears (see Figure 16-6).

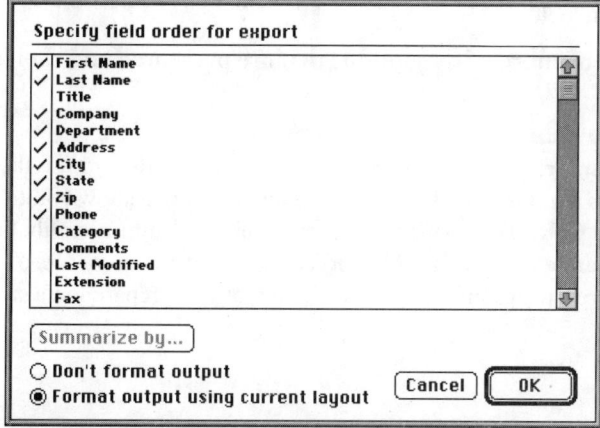

Figure 16-6: The Specify field order for export dialog box.

7. **Select the fields that you want to export.**

   Any field that is preceded by a check mark will be included in the export. Click on the check mark to deselect a field.

8. **Drag field names to change the export order of fields, if necessary.**

   Click to select the name of the field you want to move and then drag it to a new position in the field list. In most cases, you will want the order of the fields to match the order in which they appear in the destination file (assuming the destination file already exists).

9. **Click the appropriate radio button to specify whether you want to format the output.**

   Click the Don't format output radio button if you want the export to contain unformatted text. Click Format output using current layout if you want the data to be formatted to match the number, date, and time formats that you have assigned to the fields in the current layout.

10. **Click OK.**

    The target data file is created in the chosen format.

Exporting summary fields

If you like, it's also possible to export summary data from a FileMaker Pro database. The steps are as follows:

1. **Open your source FileMaker Pro document.**

2. **Repeat Steps 2 through 6 listed in "How to Export," above.**

3. **In the Specify field order for export dialog box, choose the Summary fields that you want to export and then click the Summarize by button.**

   The Summarize by dialog box appears, and lists the options by which you can summarize the field.

4. **Choose one or more of the options that are presented and then click OK.**

Performing a mail merge

As mentioned earlier, one common reason to export records is to use them in preparing a mass mailing. Many word processing programs allow you to design form letters into which personalized data can be entered automatically to generate a number of separate documents. This process is called a mail merge. You undoubtedly have received something in the mail that was prepared in a similar way.

Chapter 16: Exchanging Data

You can use FileMaker Pro to create mail merges of your own—informing valued customers that a special sale is coming up or letting friends know that you've moved, for example. The following general instructions show how to create a merge file in FileMaker Pro that can be used with Microsoft Word's Print Merge procedure:

1. **In FileMaker Pro, use Find and Sort to select records and prepare your data for exporting.**
2. **Choose Export Records, select the Merge file format, type the file name, and click New.**
3. **Specify the fields to be exported.**
4. **Click OK to create the export file.**
5. **Prepare a Word document that will receive and use the FileMaker Pro merge data.**

   By creating a merge form in Word and reserving spaces for the fields that are present in the merge data, you can create a series of personalized letters. A line from the merge form might look like this:

   Yes, «FirstName», we may soon be coming to «City» to award our $100 million megaprize!

   FirstName and City are names of fields in the merge data file. When the letter is printed, these field place holders are replaced with data from the FileMaker Pro export file — generating a separate form letter for each person in data file. See the Microsoft Word manual for additional details on creating a merge form and performing a merge.

6. **When you're ready to print, choose the Print Merge command from Microsoft Word's File menu.**

Exchanging Data with PCs

Because FileMaker Pro also runs under Microsoft Windows, you can move data to and from PCs as well. Keep two things in mind when you exchange data with a PC. First, you actually have to get data from your Mac to a PC, and vice versa; and second, you need to understand the differences between the Macintosh and PC versions of FileMaker Pro. The following sections explain.

Moving data to and from FileMaker Pro for Windows

You can share files between a Mac and a PC in three basic ways: you can use a network, which provides direct access to files; you can use the time-honored "sneaker net," meaning that you move files physically, on floppy disks, between machines; and you can transfer files electronically, using a modem or the serial ports on both computers. Here's how the three methods work:

- *Network.* Setting up a mixed network of Macs and PCs is a task for the experts. You can use AppleShare instead to make the task easier. For AppleShare, you need something like Farallon's PhoneNET Talk software, with a PhoneNet or Ethernet card for each PC. You can place the FileMaker Pro database files on an AppleShare server, on a host Mac, or on a host PC. See Chapter 20 for more information about using FileMaker Pro on a network.

- *Floppy disk.* You need a Macintosh with an Apple SuperDrive drive; all Macs sold since the late 1980s have these high-density (1.4MB) floppy drives. Use PC-formatted floppies to exchange databases between the two types of computers. (That's because your Mac can read PC floppies, but a PC can't read Mac floppies.)

  When moving a FileMaker Pro database from a PC to the Mac, you can use the Apple File Exchange program to transfer a readable copy of the database to your Mac's hard disk. Or you can use a utility such as DOS Mounter, Access PC, or PC Exchange to make PC disks visible on the Mac's Desktop. When moving files from a Mac to the PC, you can use the same utilities to enable you to transfer a copy of your Mac databases to a PC-formatted floppy. Then just take the floppy over to the PC and load the database into FileMaker Pro for Windows.

- *Serial communications.* You can transfer files by using a modem and the appropriate communications software. Alternatively, you can transfer files directly between the serial ports of the two machines by using a program such as MacLinkPlusPC.

However you transfer files, both the Mac and PC versions of FileMaker Pro can work with those files without any further ado; importing or exporting are unnecessary. You may, however, run into some problems caused by the differences between Macs and PCs, as well as minor differences between the two versions of FileMaker Pro.

Understanding the compatibility issues

In general, you should watch out for six potential problem areas when you move a Macintosh FileMaker Pro document to Microsoft Windows (or vice versa):

Chapter 16: Exchanging Data

- Character sets (refer to Figure 6-7)
- Fonts
- File names
- Colors
- Graphics formats
- Printing

The following paragraphs provide details on what you should look out for in these areas.

Character sets. Characters with ASCII values 0 through 127 (*low ASCII*) are the same in both systems. Characters with ASCII values greater than 127 (*high ASCII*) may be different, depending on the Windows font you're using. Some Macintosh high-ASCII characters are unprintable in Windows — for example, the bullet character (Option-8).

Figure 16-7 shows the characters that appear in two supposedly identical fonts on the Mac and the PC (Times, in this case). Only the shaded characters are actually the same; the others are different. Thus, if you enter text with special characters (the *é* characters in *résumé* are an example) on your Mac, you may get unexpected results that require messy (non-automatable) cleanup on the PC.

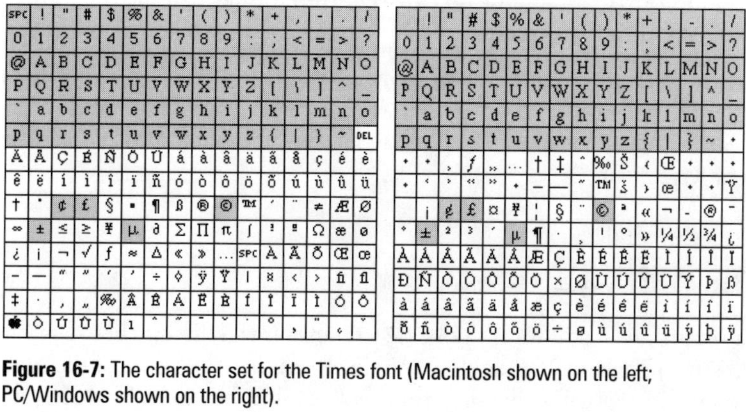

Figure 16-7: The character set for the Times font (Macintosh shown on the left; PC/Windows shown on the right).

Fonts. TrueType and Adobe fonts are available for both systems. Use the same technology on both computer systems, if you can. Otherwise, you're likely to encounter text-alignment problems in your layouts.

Part IV: Intermediate Topics

The Macintosh version of FileMaker Pro substitutes PC fonts as follows:

PC	Macintosh
MS Serif	Times
Times New Roman	Times
Times	New York
Tms Rmn	Times
Courier New	Courier
Courier	Monaco

File names. Macintosh file names can have up to 32 characters, but PC filenames are limited to eight characters plus a three-character extension. Macintosh files names are truncated (cut short) in the PC environment. You should also note that FileMaker Pro for Windows generally expects database names to end with a FM extension (as in SALES.FM, for instance).

Colors. Colors are organized into palettes. FileMaker Pro supports palettes of 8, 16, and 88 colors. Colors are not necessarily mapped the same way on the two systems, so you may see strange color effects on your PC when you open a Mac document.

Graphics formats. FileMaker Pro for Windows uses a PC file format to store pictures. You can, if you want, change this preference setting so that the Windows version stores graphics in PICT (Macintosh) format. For instructions, refer to your FileMaker Pro for Windows documentation.

Printing. Depending on the print driver you use on your PC, your PC results may differ from your Mac results, even when using the same printer. You may have to create two versions of each report layout: one tailored to the PC and the other for your Macintosh.

Working with a Newton

At press time, it still wasn't possible to transfer data directly between FileMaker Pro and a Newton MessagePad. Apple claims that Version 2 of the Newton Connection kit will make such transfers possible, however. You can call the company directly at 800-SOS-APPL for more information.

In the meantime, there's a workaround. The Newton's extra drawer features a Sharp application intended for use in sending information to a Sharp Wizard PDA. A HyperCard 2.1 stack called Newton Names and Notes DownLoader (NNND) lulls your Newton into the belief that it's exchanging data with a Sharp Wizard, when in fact it's talking to FileMaker Pro. The stack is free and is available on many information services.

Chapter 16: Exchanging Data

CHAPTER 16 CONCEPTS AND TERMS

- You can exchange FileMaker Pro data with other applications and with the Windows version of FileMaker Pro. FileMaker Pro supports a variety of popular file formats.
- FileMaker Pro can import data created in other programs, such as spreadsheets and other database programs.
- Converting selected FileMaker Pro data to another format for use in another application is called *exporting*.
- You can directly share data with the Windows version of FileMaker Pro, but certain results may differ, especially in terms of fonts, graphics, and colors.

ASCII
American Standard Code for Information Interchange. A code that associates a numerical value (0 through 255) with a character or control code.

exporting
Creating a special data file from the current document (a FileMaker Pro database, for example) that is intended to be read and used by another program.

file format
A standard specification for the way data is stored and interpreted.

header
A special first record that is frequently included as part of an export file. The header identifies (by name) all the fields that are present in the file and indicates the order in which they can be found.

high ASCII
Any ASCII character with a value higher than 127; the upper half of the ASCII character set. Special symbols and foreign language characters are found high ASCII.

importing
Reading data from another source into the current program. FileMaker Pro, for example, can read any tab-delimited text file — regardless of what program actually created the file.

low ASCII
Any ASCII character with a value less than or equal to 127; the lower half of the ASCII character set. Ordinary letters and numbers are found low ASCII.

mail merge
A program process in which the contents of a data file is combined with a standard document to create a series of documents, such as personalized form letters.

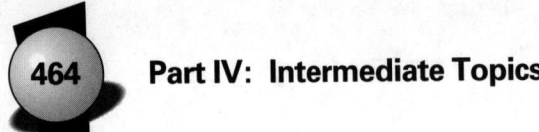

Part IV: Intermediate Topics

CHAPTER SEVENTEEN

Creating and Using FileMaker Pro Templates

- The difference between databases and templates
- Installing and reinstalling templates
- Making templates from your own databases as well as from other databases that you acquire
- Working with a new template

Up to this point, you have learned a great deal about designing and using databases. For some purposes, however, you don't need to go to all the trouble of designing a database from scratch. You may find a template that has been developed by someone else that you can use as is or easily modify to meet your needs. A *template*, in the case of FileMaker Pro, is a predefined and formatted database file into which you can enter your own data. More specifically, a *template* is a database without any records (and, conversely, a *database* is just a template that contains records).

When you install FileMaker Pro, the installation program copies seven FileMaker Pro templates to your hard disk. You can find them in the Templates folder inside the Example folder within the FileMaker Pro 2.1 (or 2.0) folder. These templates serve two purposes. First, they give you some databases with which you can safely experiment. Second, they are full-featured examples of practical databases that you may be able to use in running your business or home. For additional information on using and modifying these templates, refer to the "FileMaker Pro Templates Guide," included with your copy of FileMaker Pro 2.

This chapter discusses the techniques and commands you will need to know in order to work with *any* FileMaker Pro template, regardless of where you obtain it—whether it be from an on-line information service, a friend or colleague, or purchased as a commercial product from a member of the Claris Solutions Alliance (see Appendix D). For details on creating your own templates with the intent of giving or selling them to others, see Chapter 21.

Installing a Template

When you obtain one or more FileMaker Pro templates, there are several different methods that the database designers may have provided to enable you to install their templates. The precise method, however, is likely to vary from one database designer to another. Here are several of the most common procedures used to install templates or databases:

- *Run a special installer program.* This method is usually associated only with commercial packages, such as FileMaker Pro. When you run the installer program, you are given an option to install all or selected parts of the software—usually to any disk and folder that you choose.

- *Double-click a self-extracting archive.* To save disk space, templates (and other software) are frequently compressed into one or more self-extracting archives. A self-extracting archive contains compressed copies of the template—conserving disk space and reducing download time (for templates that are distributed through on-line information services). A self-extracting archive is called *self-extracting* because it includes a built-in file extraction program. When you double-click the icon of a self-extracting archive, a dialog box appears asking where you wish to install the files. After selecting a destination, the files are extracted from the archive, expanded to their normal size, and copied to the destination disk and folder. (The files on the *Macworld FileMaker Pro 2.0/2.1 Bible Disk* are all self-extracting archives created with a popular shareware program called Compact Pro.)

- *Extract the templates from a normal archive.* This is a variation of the previous distribution method. Instead of creating self-extracting archives, sometimes normal archives are created. The only difference is that you need a separate file-extraction utility (such as Compact Pro, StuffIt Deluxe, or StuffIt Lite) in order to extract the files. Both of these distribution methods are commonly used with templates, programs, and other materials that you'll find on on-line services, such as CompuServe and America Online.

- *Use the Finder to make a copy of the templates.* Many database templates are distributed as normal, uncompressed files. To install these templates, all you need to do is copy them to your hard disk—just as you would any other normal file or program.

Reinstalling a Fresh Copy of a Template

Like any other FileMaker Pro database, any changes you make to a template (entering or editing data, changing field definitions, rearranging fields on a layout, and so on) are instantly saved and become a permanent part of the file. Thus, when you are finished experimenting with a new template and are ready to begin enter-

Chapter 17: Creating and Using FileMaker Pro Templates

ing your own data, you'll want to start with a fresh copy of the template. There are two safe ways you can accomplish this:

❖ Re-run the installation program, double-click the self-extracting archive, or run the necessary file-extraction utility.

—or—

❖ For templates that are distributed as normal Finder copies, drag a fresh copy of the template from the distribution disk to your hard disk.

Saving a Database as a Template

FileMaker Pro templates also are referred to as clones. (These two terms are interchangeable.) A *clone* is an exact copy of a database, but without any records. The clone contains the same field definitions, layouts, and scripts as the original database. Because all the records have been removed, however, it is in a perfect state to receive fresh data.

There are several excellent instances in which you might want to create a clone of an existing database:

❖ *To create an archival copy of the structure of an important database—just in case.* Many of us tend to "tweak" a database as we use it: moving fields around, trying out new layouts, and testing additional scripts, for example. Because FileMaker Pro automatically saves *any* change that you make to a database, these little experiments have the potential to wreak havoc—causing scripts to stop functioning, Calculation fields to present the wrong results, and so on. If you've created a clone of the original database, you can get back to square one by simply importing the data from your current database into the clone.

❖ *To begin a new weekly, quarterly, or annual database.* Many databases are designed to be used only for a certain period of time and then started over again with new records. For example, I created a database in which I do my bookkeeping (tracking my business expenses and income). The IRS fully expects me to turn in an annual 1040 and Schedule C, so I need a new copy of this database at the beginning of each year. If you were to make a call-tracking database to be used by your department's receptionist to make a permanent record of incoming calls, you might want to start a fresh copy on a more frequent basis (monthly, weekly, or even daily, depending on the call volume).

❖ *To remove sample records and ready a commercial or shareware database for your own data.* Some templates—including many of the ones on the *Macworld FileMaker Pro 2.0/2.1 Bible Disk* and those that are included with FileMaker Pro itself— contain a small set of sample records, enabling you to get a feel for how the

Part IV: Intermediate Topics

database works without having to enter (or risk) your own data. As long as you restrict your experimentation to adding, deleting, and editing records, you can strip out all the sample records by simply making a clone of the database. Then you're ready to begin entering your own data.

❖ *To enable you to give the template away or sell it.* Unless your records are meant to be used as a sample, most people don't intentionally include their own personal or business data in a template. Making a clone strips that data out in one simple step.

To make a template/clone from any existing database, use the following procedure:

1. **Open the database in FileMaker Pro.**
2. **Choose Save a Copy As from the File menu.**

   A standard file dialog box appears, as shown in Figure 17-1.

3. **Choose clone (no records) from the Save a: pop-up menu.**

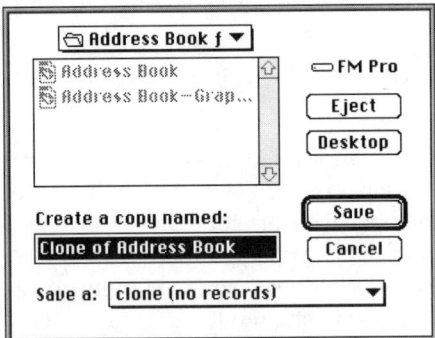

Figure 17-1: You can create a clone by selecting the proper option from this file dialog box.

The other two options in the Save a: pop-up menu are used to create

❖ A backup copy of the current database with all records intact; select copy of current file from the pop-up menu.

❖ A compressed backup copy of the current database with all records intact; select compressed copy (smaller) from the pop-up menu.

4. **Select a destination disk and folder using normal file navigation procedures (see Chapter 2 if you need help).**
5. **Type a name for the clone in the Create a copy named: text box.**

   If you're saving the file in a *different* folder/disk than the one where the current database is stored, you can use the same name as that of the original database. If

Chapter 17: Creating and Using FileMaker Pro Templates

you're storing it in the *same* folder/disk, you may want to use the default name proposed by FileMaker Pro; that is, Clone of *filename*.

Under no circumstances should you use the same name as the original database when saving the template in the same folder/disk location! Doing so replaces your original database with an empty template.

6. Click Save.

The clone is created but not opened. The original template file remains open in FileMaker Pro.

If you want to immediately begin working with the clone, close the original database (choose Close from the File menu or press Command-W) and then open the clone (choose Open from the File menu or press Command-O).

Working with a New Template

As mentioned previously in this chapter, the only difference between a database and a template or clone is that the latter contains no records. This presents one immediate problem for many users: When a template is first opened, the database window is likely to be *blank* (as shown in Figure 17-2). Because there are no records, there is nothing for FileMaker Pro to display — other than an empty database window.

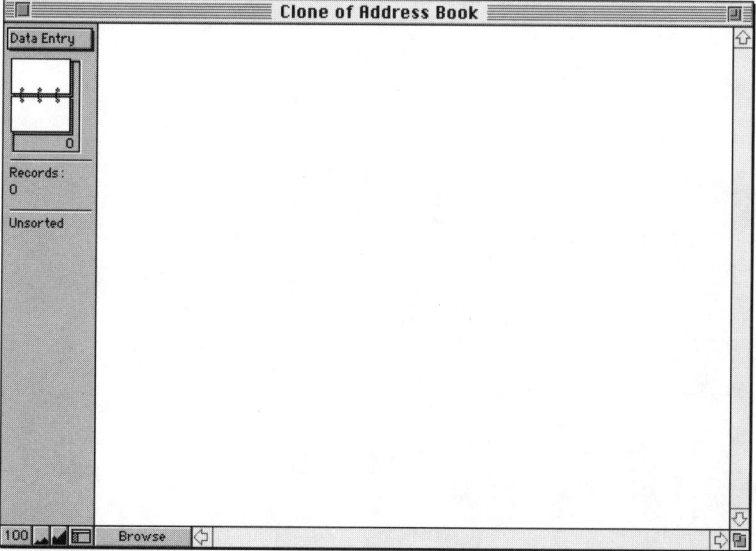

Figure 17-2: Opening a new template.

Part IV: Intermediate Topics

All that's necessary to do so that you can begin working with the template is to choose New Record from the Edit menu (or press Command-N). The opening layout immediately appears, and you can get down to business. Now if you ever see a blank database, you'll know what must be done to correct the situation.

Avoiding the Blank Look (in Your Templates and on Users' Faces)

There's nothing so potentially confusing to a new user as a blank screen. To avoid causing a panic, you can make one small modification to your template before handing or selling it to a user. Add a single new record and then close the file. When the user opens the file, he'll see whatever you originally intended him to see, such as a blank data entry form for record number 1 or an opening menu, for example.

Chapter 17: Creating and Using FileMaker Pro Templates

CHAPTER 17 CONCEPTS AND TERMS

- There are a number of methods that are used to install FileMaker Pro templates and databases that you obtain from others. The most common methods include running a special installation or file-extraction program, running a separate file-extraction utility, or making a copy from the Finder.

- To adapt a database for use as a template, you clone it by using the Save a Copy As command. The file dialog box has a clone (no records) option that omits records from the new copy. FileMaker Pro uses the terms *template* and *clone* interchangeably.

- When working with a clone/template, you may have to create the first record in order to make the various layouts appear.

archive
A compressed copy of one or more files. Archives can be created to save disk space, to reduce the time it takes to transmit (upload) and receive (download) the files by modem, or to serve simply as a backup copy (a personal safety net).

clone (or template)
An exact copy of a database—including all layouts, field definitions, and scripts—but *sans* records. A template (also called a clone by FileMaker Pro) is used as the basis for a new database.

download
To elect to receive a file (usually via a modem and phone line) from an information service, bulletin board system, or another user's computer.

installer
A special program provided to enable a user to easily copy a program, templates, and/or supporting files to their hard disk.

self-extracting archive
One or more compressed files that contain a built-in file extraction program. When a user double-clicks the icon of a self-extracting archive, a file dialog box appears that enables the user to select a destination disk and folder for the expanded (normal) files.

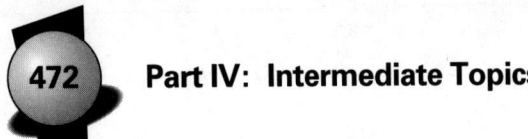

Part IV: Intermediate Topics

CHAPTER EIGHTEEN

Documenting and Designing Help Systems

IN THIS CHAPTER

- Deciding what information to include in a help system
- Learning about methods for documenting and providing help information

Do any of these scenarios sound familiar?

❖ You've just spent half an hour downloading an interesting-sounding FileMaker Pro template from CompuServe, America Online, or GEnie. After decompressing the template, you discover that it contains no instructions whatsoever — no Read Me file, no help screens, no descriptive text. Now what?

❖ Bill, one of your coworkers at XYZ Corp., is on vacation. While he's away, the boss asks whether you can fill in by entering customer orders, printing mailing labels, and generating daily reports. Although you know that Bill accomplishes these tasks with extraordinary ease, using a FileMaker Pro database that he custom-designed, you haven't got a clue as to how he does it.

❖ A couple of years back, you designed an elaborate database that has dozens of scripts and buttons. Recently you realized that, with just a few modifications, you can put the database to work again for a new task. Unfortunately, when you designed the database, documenting how it worked didn't seem very important. Now you can't remember what half the scripts were supposed to do or what that odd field named "Extra" was intended to do. It's surprising how easily you can forget.

❖ You've created a whiz-bang FileMaker Pro template that you think every Mac (or Windows) user will want for their very own. In your rush to share it with the world, you deposit copies of it on half a dozen bulletin boards and ask for a $10 shareware fee. Because you didn't bother to explain how the template works, it doesn't sell as well as you'd hoped it would, and the people who *are* sending you the shareware fee are also pestering you with questions.

Of course, not every database needs elaborate documentation. But if you spend a little time creating a simple help system or Read Me file, you can avoid some headaches later on. This chapter discusses appropriate (and sometimes essential) topics that you should include and suggests several different approaches that you can use to create help systems.

Suggested Help Topics

A help system that is carefully thought out anticipates user/customer needs. The better you anticipate, the happier the customer will be and the less time you will need to spend supporting or explaining the template. Here is a brief list of some material that is appropriate for inclusion in a help system or a Read Me file:

- A description of the purpose of the database

- An explanation of the purpose of each field, the type of data it should contain, and any restrictions/validation options that have been set (see Chapter 5 for more information on data validation options)

- An explanation of the purpose of each layout, as well as any special preparations that the user must make before using the layout (changing the Page Setup or printer selection, for example)

- An explanation of what each script does and how to execute the script (by selecting it from the Scripts menu or pressing a button)

- Suggestions for customizing the template (for example, selecting different fonts, changing screen colors, creating new reports and mailing labels, and adding features)

If you want people to treat your template as a serious business product rather than as something you just knocked together in a free moment, you need to make it look like a business product. Documentation or a help system is a must!

Choosing Help Topics

The types and quantity of help you provided should be dictated by need and common sense. If you are writing a help system for a database that will only be used by the Accounting Department in your company, for example, you should offer help with common data entry and report-generation questions that you expect will occur. But since everyone will be using the same version of the database, customization information may well be avoided.

When deciding the types of help to offer, try to put yourself in the place of a new user. Think about the terms that you've used for field labels that might not be immediately understood. When it could be unclear what type of information should be typed in a field, explain it. (If you're *really* smart, you'll actually give the database to some other people and ask them to tell you what kind of help they need.)

To get more ideas of the types of help that you may wish to include, you may want to *download* some of the shareware templates that are available on online services such as CompuServe, GEnie, and America Online. You're sure to find many excellent (and quite horrid) examples of help information.

Chapter 18: Documenting and Designing Help Systems

Different Approaches to Presenting Help Information

You can present help information and documentation in several ways. In choosing a method, consider who the intended reader of the information is (you, other developers and technical people, or end users and customers) and how often you expect the reader to refer to the information. For example, creating an elaborate on-line, context-sensitive help system for information that the reader will probably need to see only once doesn't make much sense.

Approach #1: A Read Me file

Creating a separate Read Me file in a word processing program or text editor is obviously the easiest way to document a template. And having the full text-formatting capabilities of a word processor at your disposal can make the writing go faster. As an added bonus (only a small one, however), writing the documentation as a separate file can help keep the size and complexity of the template to a minimum.

Arguably, this approach is best for providing information that is usually needed only once, such as installation instructions and minor customization notes, or for when you are creating the database only for your personal use or limited in-house use at your company. In the case of a personal template, if you later decide to share it with others, your notes can form the basis of an in-template help system.

When creating a database to be distributed as shareware, however, this approach to documentation is certainly better than nothing, but it is definitely *not* the best method. See Approaches 2 and 3 below for more appropriate means of providing help information.

If you want others to be able to read and print your Read Me file, you should give careful thought to the decision of which word processor or text editor to use in creating the file. Obviously, if you write the documentation in an obscure program, you will prevent many people from being able to open and read the file. The following sections offer some suggestions for creating a Read Me file.

TeachText and other text editors

TeachText is a text editor that Apple Computer provides with every version of the system software. Because everyone has system software installed on their Mac (it's what makes the Mac run), most people will either have TeachText on their hard disk or have ready access to it on the system software installation disks. And even if TeachText isn't installed on a user's system, the files created by TeachText are in Text-Only format, so virtually any word processing program can read them. These reasons are precisely why so many Read Me files are written in TeachText.

Note: TeachText has recently been replaced by Apple with a more powerful text editor called SimpleText. SimpleText also can be used to read files that were created with TeachText.

If you intend to distribute a document on on-line information systems and computer bulletin boards, creating the documentation in TeachText also will help keep the size of the material small. (No one wants to waste half an hour downloading a few pages of documentation that, because of the format selected, grow to several hundred K. See the following section on "Stand-alone documents.")

Stand-alone documents

If the primary method of distribution will be on disk, you can afford the luxury of using a program that can produce stand-alone documents (that is, documents that work just like programs). You don't need a separate program to open them; they're double-clickable!

If you scrounge around on-line, you're sure to find several utilities of this sort. DOCMaker, a shareware program from Green Mountain Software, is one of the best-known examples. It enables you to create stand-alone documents that include graphics and multiple fonts, styles, and colors (see Figure 18-1). In addition to being able to type and edit text within DOCMaker, you can use it to import text that was created in a variety of popular word processing formats. You can organize DOCMaker documents into chapters, print them, and search them. DOCMaker's only weaknesses are that the documents it creates tend to be large (over 100K) and that the program does not support tabs. A copy of DOCMaker is included on the *Macworld FileMaker Pro 2.0/2.1 Bible Disk.*

Several commercial programs are available for converting existing formatted documents into stand-alone documents. My current favorite is Common Ground from No Hands Software. To use Common Ground and most programs like it, you simply open a document in the word processing, desktop publishing, or other program in which you created it and then, using a special Chooser device supplied with the package, you print the document to disk. In the process, a *reader* is embedded in the final document. The reader enables other users to view the document by just double-clicking it. The advantages of using a program such as Common Ground are that it supports all of the normal formatting, graphics, and fonts and that the process of converting to a stand-alone document is totally painless. Note, however, that the size of resulting documents can be enormous.

Chapter 18: Documenting and Designing Help Systems

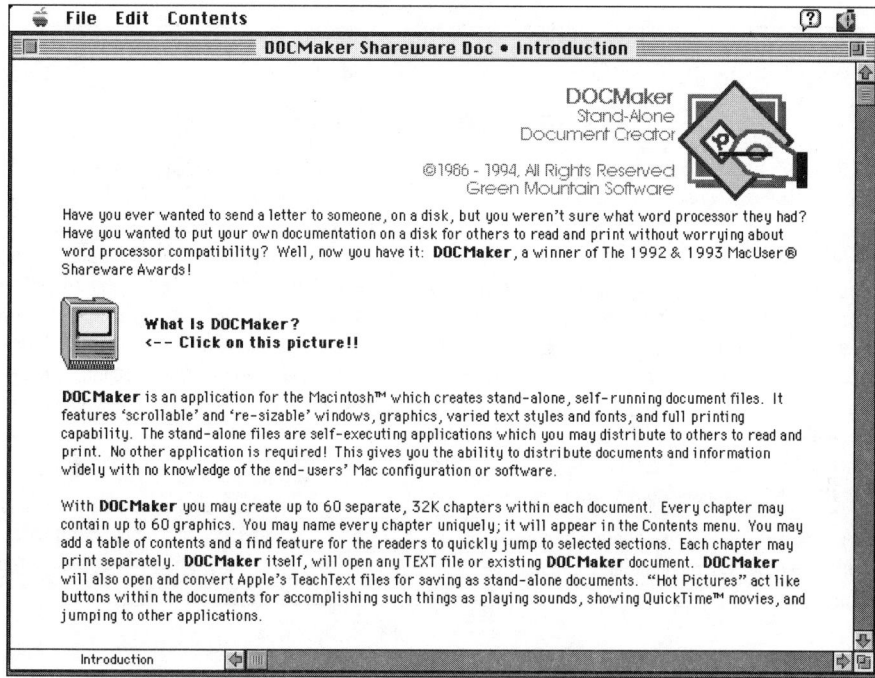

Figure 18-1: A DOCMaker stand-alone document.

Word processing programs
Using a standard word processing program (Microsoft Word, MacWrite, WriteNow, or WordPerfect, for example) is the least desirable method for creating documentation that will be distributed. (One exception to this general rule is when you develop a template solely for in-house use and the entire company is using the same word processing program.) Although many word processing programs can read documents that are created in other word processing programs, the possibility always exists that a sizable number of people will be unable to read the file. Authors who distribute documentation in word processing format can increase the odds that users can read it by including copies of the documentation in several different formats. Microsoft Word, MacWrite, and TeachText are some common choices.

Paper-only documentation
Of course, you may want to skip the compatibility issues altogether and simply include printed instructions with the template. You can distribute the template on information services but offer the printed documentation only to users who send in the shareware registration fee. Most authors who take this approach, however, are obliged to also include at least a stripped-down version of the documentation in a Read Me file. If you don't give users some idea of how the template works, they may not explore it sufficiently enough to determine whether it does something that's useful for them.

Part IV: Intermediate Topics

Using a Button to Summon Help

The script that is attached to each navigation button in the database consists of only a single line:

```
Go to layout <x>
```

You replace the `<x>` with the name of the data entry or help layout. (In the data entry layout, use the name of the help layout. In the help layout, use the name of the data entry layout.) Attach the command to each button by selecting the button on the layout and then choosing Define Button from the Scripts menu. (See Chapter 15 for more information on creating scripts and defining buttons.)

You should note that this approach can also be implemented with *multiple* help layouts. In a complex database, you may well want to have separate help screens for providing help with specific functions, such as data entry, performing Find requests and sorts, and printing reports. This serves several functions. First, it no longer forces the user to scroll through what—in many cases—may be multiple screens of information. Second, it more closely approximates the type of specific, context-appropriate help that users have come to expect from Mac programs.

Thus, the data entry screen may have separate buttons for data entry and sorting help, while the reports screen could have a single help button that summons help that is specific to preparing a report.

Approach #2: A help layout

Another method is to include the documentation or help information in the template itself. The advantages of placing this material in a FileMaker Pro template include the following:

- *No compatibility problems:* Because users need to have a copy of FileMaker Pro in order to use the template, by definition they have all the software they need to read the help text, too.

- *Ready access:* Users who need help don't want to have to hunt for it. When people need help, they usually want it right away. And because Read Me files take up disk space, users frequently toss them into the Trash after reading them, so such files aren't immediately accessible (or they may no longer be accessible *at all*).

Figure 18-2 shows an example of help text in a FileMaker Pro database. All the help information is contained in a single layout. If the information is too long to fit on a single screen, users can click the scroll bar to see it all.

As you can see in Figure 18-2, the Help layout contains no fields at all. When this layout is displayed, even if the user clicks the book icon to flip from one record to the next, the screen doesn't change. This is so because the help layout doesn't display any fields (field contents change from record to record). The help layout is constructed entirely of static text and graphics, so you never have to worry about the user inadvertently changing what's on-screen (by using the book icon, for example).

Chapter 18: Documenting and Designing Help Systems

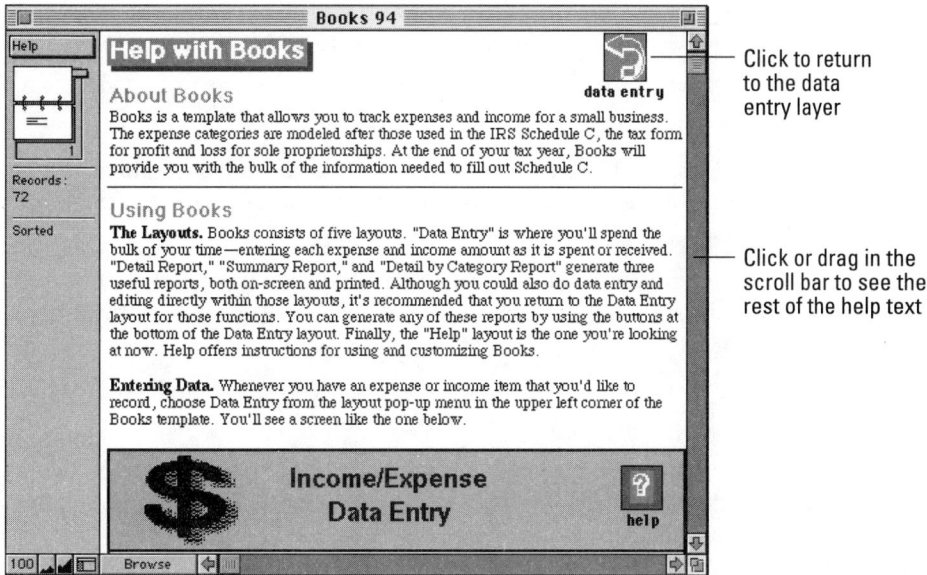

Figure 18-2: Help text as a separate layout.

To create a help screen that is similar to the one shown in Figure 18-2, do the following:

1. **In a new or existing database, change to Layout mode (choose Layout from the Select menu or press ⌘-L).**

2. **Choose New Layout from the Edit menu (or press ⌘-N).**

   The New Layout dialog box appears, as shown in Figure 18-3.

3. **Enter an appropriate name for the layout (Help, for example), select Blank as the layout type, and click OK to create the layout.**

   Because you don't often need fields in a help layout, choosing Blank saves time.

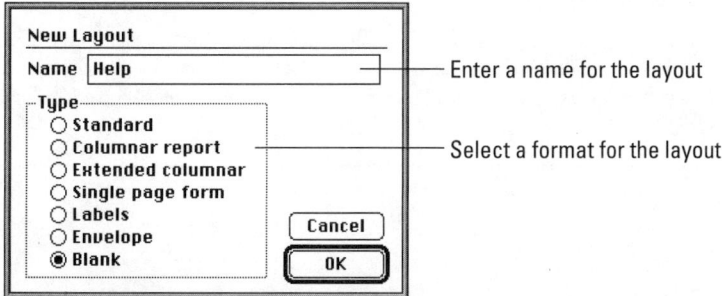

Figure 18-3: The New Layout dialog box.

Part IV: Intermediate Topics

4. **Select the Text tool (the uppercase *A*) from the Tool panel to add text blocks to the layout and resize the text blocks as necessary.**

   Note that if you have already prepared help text in a word processing document, you can copy and paste it into the layout.

5. *Optional:* **Add graphics by copying them from a graphics program or the Scrapbook desk accessory and then pasting them into the layout.**

   You also can import graphics directly into the layout by choosing the Import Picture command from the Import/Export submenu of the File menu. (See Chapter 6 for additional information on adding and importing graphics into a layout.)

6. *Optional:* **Create scripts that switch from the help layout to the data entry layout and vice versa (Go to Layout).**

   Although you can place the scripts in the Scripts menu, assigning them to buttons on the layout is more convenient. (See "Using a Button to Summon Help" and Chapter 15 for additional information.)

As you design the help layout, remember that you can mix fonts, styles, and colors in the same text block. When you are designing for other users, however, getting fancy with font choices doesn't pay. Unless the other users have the same fonts installed in their system, different fonts will be substituted. Also, although you can create the help text as one long text block, you may want to break it into a series of smaller, more manageable chunks. When you use this approach, you can easily intersperse graphics (such as screen captures, illustrations, and clip art) in the text.

Using Headers and Footers in Help Screens

If you want some help information to remain on-screen at all times, put it in the help layout's header or footer. As the user scrolls the window, the header and footer stay in place.

The figure shows a help layout from the FileMaker and Apple Events database (Claris Corp.) in which both a header and a footer keep critical information on-screen.

Chapter 18: Documenting and Designing Help Systems

Creating a Credits/Copyright Screen or a Shareware Registration Form

By using the same method that you use to provide in-template help, you can create a credits/copyright screen or a shareware registration form for a template. Without such a screen, you are likely to lose credit for the work you've done or miss out on shareware fees that are due you. In the case of a shareware template in particular, you want to make it as convenient as possible for the user to pay for your hard work. Creating the registration form as a separate layout ensures that:

❖ When ready to pay, the user never has to search his or her hard disk for a separate file that contains your name and address.

❖ The user is repeatedly reminded that the template is not public domain and that payment is expected.

❖ When the template is copied and given to others, the registration information is also copied.

The following figure shows two examples of layouts that provide credit/registration information and a registration form.

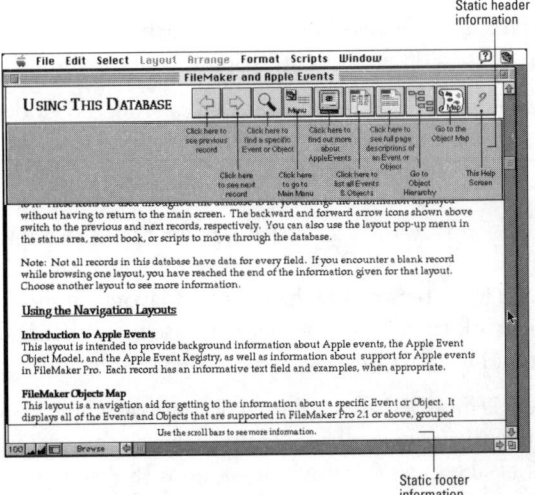

Static header information

Static footer information

Part IV: Intermediate Topics

Riting and Speling

Don't forget that FileMaker Pro 2 also has a built-in spelling checker. You may be a database whiz, but if your documentation or help text is riddled with spelling errors, your skills as a programmer/designer may also be questioned. To check spelling for the entire help layout, change to Layout mode, switch to the help screen layout, and choose Check Layout from the Spelling submenu of the Edit menu. See Chapter 11 for more information on using the spelling checker.

Approach #3: Script-guided help

FileMaker Pro scripts can make your help system much fancier and more helpful. By creating simple scripts and button definitions, you can design a series of help layouts that have the following features:

- *You can page through them.* Each left-arrow and right-arrow button can have an attached script that causes FileMaker to go to the previous or next layout.

- *You can access them through a main menu.* Each button or text string in the main menu can cause a different help layout to be displayed.

- *You can access them through an index.* You can link each index entry to a specific help layout, providing a help system that works in much the same way as FileMaker Pro's help system does.

The *Macworld FileMaker Pro 2.0/2.1 Bible Disk* has an example of this type of help system in the folder named Callable Help Example. Instead of forcing the user to jump back and forth between Help and other layouts in the database, Callable Help stores the help information in another database file. Because the help information is in a different file, you can view it while you are still working in the main database.

Callable Help is modeled after FileMaker Pro's own help system. Clicking the Help button in the main database (Help Caller, in this example) opens the help database (Books Help, in this example). Figure 18-4 shows the two database files.

You will notice that the help information in Books Help has absolutely nothing to do with the Help Caller database. In fact, it's some help text that I yanked out of one of my own databases and reformatted for this example. Don't let this bother you. What's important is that the files illustrate the mechanics required for you to implement a similar help system of your own.

Chapter 18: Documenting and Designing Help Systems

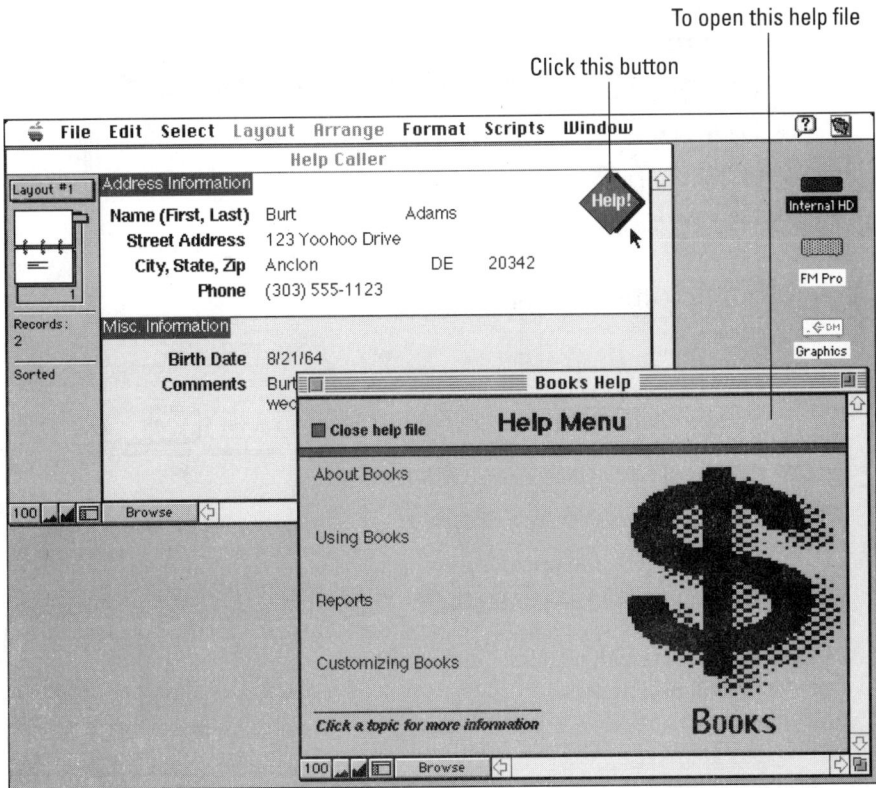

Figure 18-4: The help system consists of two FileMaker Pro databases: the Help Caller and the help file (Books Help).

Here's how the two databases interact. To access help, you simply click the Help button in the main database. Attached to the Help button is a one-line script that reads as follows:

```
Open ["Books Help"]
```

Although the script is simple, you cannot create it by just choosing the Define Button command from the Scripts menu and then choosing the Open command. Doing so causes a file dialog box to appear each time you click the Help button. Instead, you have to create the one-line script in ScriptMaker, specifying the help file when you choose the Open command (as shown in Figure 18-5). After you create the script, you then use the Define Button command to link the script to the Help button (Perform Script *script name*).

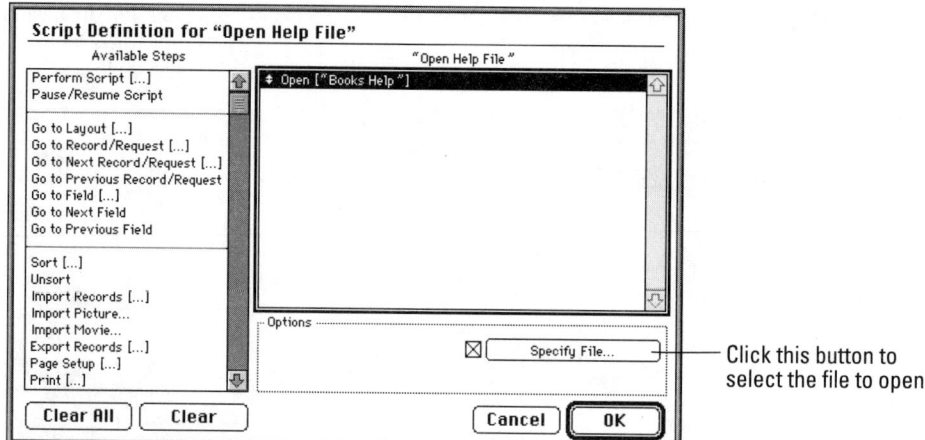

Figure 18-5: Creating the script that will open the help file.

When the help file opens, several actions that are set in the preferences for the document automatically occur (see Figure 18-6). The help database displays the first layout, called Help Menu, and the status area — the book pages and Tool panel — are hidden. (See Chapter 7 for more information on setting document and general preferences.)

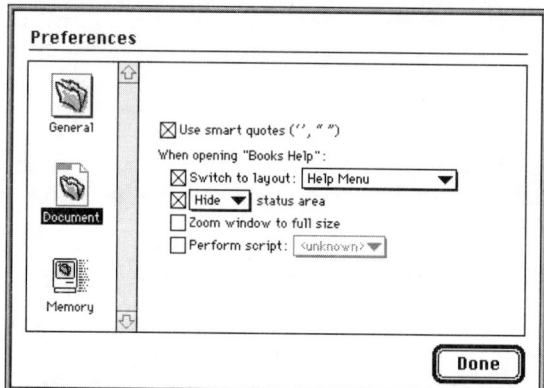

Figure 18-6: Startup actions are specified in the document preferences for the database.

Chapter 18: Documenting and Designing Help Systems

In Books Help, you move to a particular help topic by clicking the name of the topic in the Help Menu, which is the first layout (refer to Figure 18-4). In fact, every movement — whether to a help topic, to the main menu, or to a new page in the same help topic — is accomplished by using a Go to Layout script command. Clicking any of the four help topic text strings in the Help Menu layout causes a script to be executed and the appropriate layout to appear.

From one to three buttons are at the top of every help layout. In each layout except Help Menu, the upper-left button (Help Menu) returns the user to the Help menu. In the Help menu, the button in this location (Close help file) closes the help file in the same manner as clicking the close box.

In help topics that span two or more layouts, such as Using Books, one or two arrow buttons are in the upper-right corner of each layout (see Figure 18-7). Clicking an arrow causes a script to execute that switches to the previous or next layout for that help topic. As in the FileMaker Pro Help, the number of layouts for a help topic is indicated in the lower-right corner of each layout.

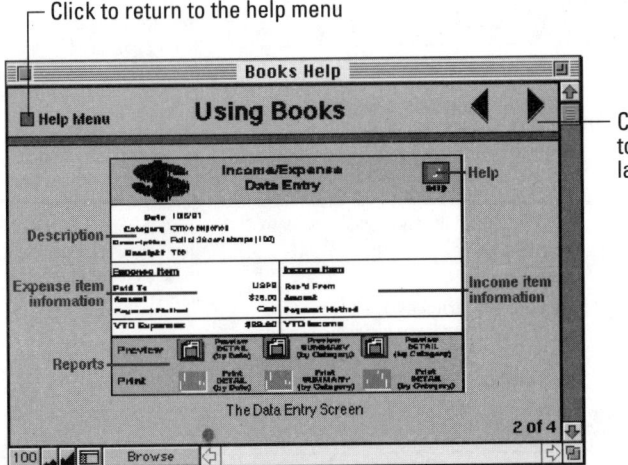

Figure 18-7: Click an arrow to navigate between multiple layouts for the same topic.

Part IV: Intermediate Topics

CHAPTER 18 CONCEPTS AND TERMS

- Even if you don't want to implement a formal help system for your database, you can easily create a Read Me file.

- You can add help, credit/copyright, and shareware registration screens to any database as separate layouts. You can use the Go to Layout script command to switch between any of these screens and the database's main menu or data entry layout.

- When you embed help information in layouts, you can create a single scrolling text screen or break the information into discrete chunks and place it in a series of layouts.

- In addition to using graphics objects as buttons, you also can use text strings as buttons. Clicking a text string in a help menu, for example, can cause a specific help layout to display.

- To keep a database as small as possible, you can create a separate help database that you call from a database and then dismiss when you no longer need it. Keeping the help separate from the main database also enables users to view the help at the same time that they are entering data, creating reports, or constructing new layouts.

button
An object, on a FileMaker Pro layout, to which a script is attached.

downloading
The process of using a modem to retrieve a program or document file from an on-line information service or a bulletin board system.

reader
A separate utility program that enables the contents of a document to be read, regardless of whether or not the user has his/her own copy of the program in which the document was created. A reader typically provides the user only with "read" privileges; that is, it can read documents created with a particular program, but does not allow users to "write" (create new documents of that type).

Read Me file
A text file that provides information about a program or template. Manufacturers of commercial programs often include a Read Me file on disk to inform users about important topics that are not covered in the program's manual. Although you do not have to name the file Read Me, such a filename encourages users to open the file and examine its contents.

stand-alone document
A document that contains its own reader and, hence, does not require the user to own any specific program in which to open and read the document. The document *is* a program.

text-only file
A document that contains only simple text — no formatting. Most text editors, such as TeachText, automatically save documents in this format. You can usually create such files by using the word processing program's Save As command and choosing Text-Only as the format. The point of creating a text-only file is to assure that the greatest number of people will own at least one program that can read the file.

uncompressing
To shorten the length of time required to download files from an information service, a special utility program is often used to compress the files (making them smaller). Uncompressing the files restores them to their original size and format.

Part V
Advanced Topics

CHAPTER NINETEEN

Linking Databases

- Linking two or more databases by defining lookup fields
- Specifying what FileMaker Pro should <u>do</u> when a match is not found
- Specifying what should happen when the field to be copied is blank
- Using the Relookup command to update lookup fields

As explained in Chapter 1, FileMaker Pro is a semirelational database. That is, you can set up fields that, when you enter data in them, cause FileMaker Pro to automatically look up information in another file and then copy that data into fields in the current file. This process is known as a *lookup*. Many people never use lookups — both because the concept is difficult to grasp and because applications for this feature aren't immediately apparent. The purpose of this chapter is to show you how lookups work and to offer you a simple example that illustrates the true power of the lookup.

How Lookups Work

Figure 19-1 shows three databases: Video Invoice, Customers, and Movies. Video Invoice — the main database — contains two key fields that, when you enter data in them, trigger lookups in the Customers and Movies databases. (All three databases are on the *Macworld FileMaker Pro 2.0/2.1 Bible Disk* in a folder named Lookup Example within the folder FM Pro Bible. A detailed description of how these databases work together is provided later in this chapter.)

To make some sense of lookups, you need to understand these important terms:

❖ *Current file:* The file in which the lookup is being requested.

❖ *Lookup file:* The file from which data will be extracted (that is, the file in which the data is looked up).

❖ *Trigger field:* The field in the current file that, when data is entered into it or its data is modified, triggers the lookup.

❖ *Match field:* The field in the lookup file that is compared with the contents of the trigger field.

❖ *Lookup field:* The field in the current file into which the looked-up data will be copied. (In order for a field to be treated as a lookup field, the data-entry option Look up values from a file must be set for the field.)

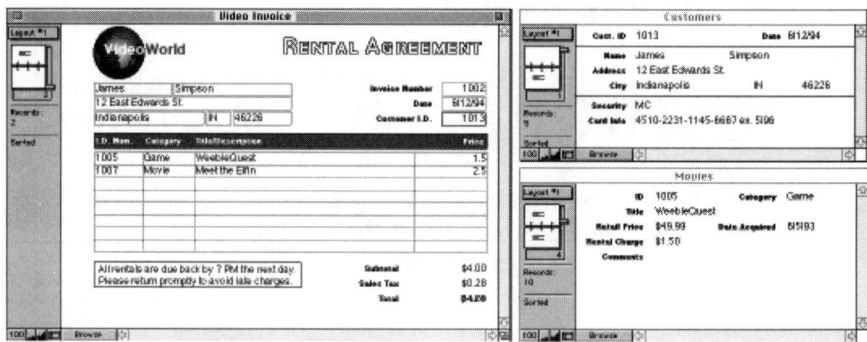

Figure 19-1: Three databases linked by lookups.

In order to execute a lookup, you need to have a pair of matching fields in two databases. Both fields have to store the same kind of information, such as customer I.D. numbers. In the database that requests the lookup, this field is the *trigger field*. (When information is entered or edited in the field and you press Enter or Tab, the lookup is triggered.) Although the trigger field's counterpart in the second database has no formal name, you can call it the *match field*. The trigger and match fields can contain I.D. numbers, social security numbers, part names, and so on. In general, the information in the match field should be different for every record (that is, the data should be unique). The moment that you enter or edit information in a trigger field, FileMaker Pro automatically performs all lookups that you have associated with that trigger field.

Often, a trigger field will trigger only a single lookup. For example, typing an inventory part number could result in a lookup of the part's price. You can also associate multiple lookups with the same trigger field. Entering an inventory part number could trigger lookups of the part name, color, description, and price, for instance.

Here's another example. Suppose that you have two databases that you want to link via the lookup feature. The first is an Orders database. The order form that serves as the main layout for Orders has a field in it called Customer Code. Customer information (including names and addresses) is kept in a separate database called Customers. A unique identification code, which is assigned when a customer first places an order, identifies each record in the Customers database. You define each of the name and address fields in Orders as lookup fields that are triggered by an entry in the Customer Code field.

Whenever a customer calls in a new order, a salesperson creates a new record in Orders and enters the customer's I.D. number into the Customer Code field. FileMaker Pro then checks the Customers database for a record that contains a matching I.D. If it finds a matching I.D., it automatically copies the name and address information for that customer into the current order form. As this example shows, nothing prevents you from defining several lookup fields that are all activated by the same trigger field — in this case, Customer Code.

Chapter 19: Linking Databases

Figure 19-2 shows an example of the Lookup Value dialog box in which you set options for a field that you're defining as a lookup field. To reach this dialog box, choose Define Fields (Shift-⌘-D) and click the Options button. In the Entry Options dialog box that appears, click the check box for Look up values from a file.

Figure 19-2: The Lookup Value dialog box.

In Figure 19-2, the current file is Billing (displayed on the right side of the dialog box), the lookup file is Address Book (shown on the left side of the dialog box), and the field that has been defined as a lookup field is Last Name. The following explanation describes what happens when you enter new data in the Client I.D. field:

1. When you enter new data in the Client I.D. field (the trigger field) of the Billing database (the current file), FileMaker Pro examines the lookup file named Address Book to determine whether its I.D. field (the match field) contains a value that matches the data entered in the Client I.D. field.

2. If FileMaker Pro finds a match in the Address Book, it copies that record's data for the Last Name field into the Last Name field in the Billing file.

— or —

2. If FileMaker Pro does not find an exact match for the data in the Client I.D. field, it does not copy anything into the Last Name field in the Billing file. The Last Name field is left blank.

By examining Figure 19-2, you can learn several important things about lookups. First, when you define a field as being a lookup field, you need to specify three pieces of information:

- The name of the field in the current file that, when data is first entered or is modified, will trigger the lookup (commonly referred to as the *trigger field*)
- The name of the field in the lookup file that FileMaker Pro will check for a match with the trigger field (the *match field*)
- The name of the field in the lookup file that FileMaker Pro will copy into the field in the current file

Second, the trigger field and its match field counterpart do not need to share the same name. The trigger field in the Billing file is named Client I.D., but the match field in the lookup file is named I.D. Similarly, although the field to be copied has the same name in both databases (both are called Last Name), they could have different names (Last Name and Surname, for example). Because the pop-up menus for the two files contain the names of all fields that have been defined for the respective files, the field names don't matter — you can pair up any two fields that you choose. You need to make sure, however, that you choose fields that make sense and that contain the appropriate data.

Third, the Lookup Value dialog box enables you to specify what should happen when FileMaker Pro does not find a match (see the lower-left corner of the dialog box). The default choice is to do nothing (don't copy). The next two choices (copy next lower value and copy next higher value) are often useful when you are performing lookups of numeric values. For example, when you want to determine the amount of postage that is necessary for a package, you could trigger a lookup in a postage rates database by entering a weight in the current database. Because postage is based on full ounces, you would use the copy next higher value option to take care of any weight that included a fraction of an ounce. Thus, entering **7.4** would return the value for 8 ounces.

The final option (use) enables you to specify a particular value or text string to enter when FileMaker Pro does not find a match. For example, if the lookup is supposed to return a consulting rate and you entered a new consulting code in the trigger field, you could instruct the lookup to return 100 (your usual hourly rate, right?). In the case of missing customer information, you could set this option to copy a message, such as New Customer or Client not found, into the field.

Fourth, sometimes FileMaker Pro finds a match, but the field that's to be copied into the current file is blank. (Using Figure 19-1 as an example, a clerk may have forgotten to complete the last name for a certain record — or maybe the clerk didn't know the individual's last name.) You can click the check box for Don't copy contents if empty (on the right side of the dialog box) to indicate what FileMaker

Pro should do if it finds a match but the field to be copied is blank. This option is useful if you have hand entered information into the current file and want to avoid having it replaced by blank data.

Finally, you can use the Set Lookup File button to change the lookup file. Although you will seldom need to use this option, if you rename the lookup database, change its location on disk, or replace the lookup file with a different one, you can click Set Lookup File to select the new database. (If you have other lookup fields in the current database that depend on the same lookup file, be sure to reset them for the new lookup file, too.)

Defining lookup fields

Follow these steps to define a lookup field in your own database:

1. **Open the database in which you want to define one or more lookup fields.**
2. **Choose Define Fields from the Select menu (or press Shift-⌘-D).**

   The Define Fields dialog box appears (see Figure 19-3).

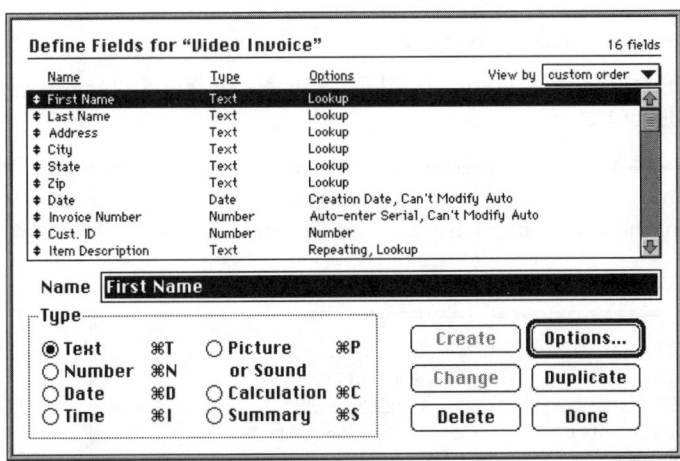

Figure 19-3: The Define Fields dialog box.

3. **In the field list, select the first field that you want to define as a lookup field and then click the Options button.**

   The Entry Options dialog box appears, as shown in Figure 19-4.

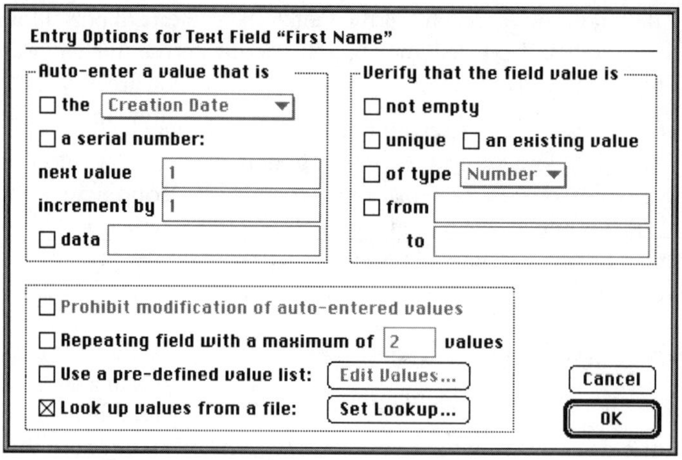

Part V: Advanced Topics

Figure 19-4: The Entry Options dialog box.

4. **At the bottom of the dialog box, click the check box for Lookup values from a file.**

    A standard file dialog box appears.

5. **Select the file that you want FileMaker Pro to look in for the new data and click OK.**

    A Lookup Value dialog box for the chosen field appears (see Figure 19-5). Information for the current file is shown on the right side of the dialog box; information for the lookup file is displayed on the left side.

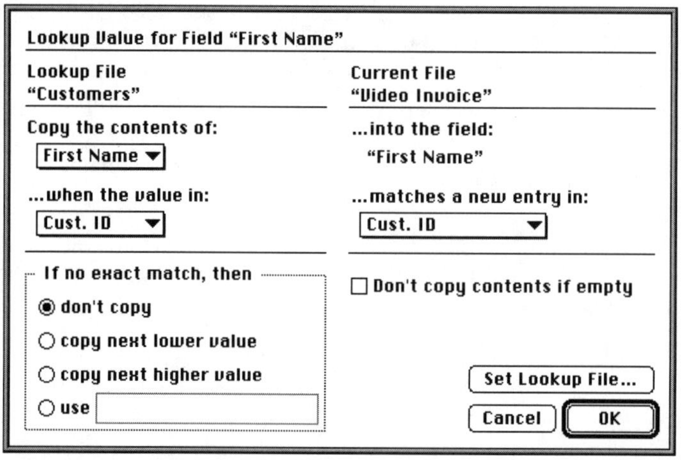

Figure 19-5: The Lookup Value dialog box for the field First Name.

Chapter 19: Linking Databases

On the left side of the dialog box, the Copy the contents of pop-up menu lists the fields in the lookup file. You use this menu to choose the field in the lookup file whose contents will be copied into the field that you are currently defining. (The name of the field that you are defining appears after "into the field" on the right side of the dialog box).

6. **Choose the field to be copied from the Copy the contents of pop-up menu.**

   As explained previously, the names of the two fields need not be the same. What's important is that they contain similar contents.

   Note that if the field that you want to copy data from is not in the Copy the contents of pop-up menu and you believe that the field is in a different file, you can select another lookup file by clicking the Set Lookup File button.

   The remaining pop-up menus enable you to specify the trigger field and the match field that will be compared when a lookup is triggered.

7. **Choose the trigger field from the current file (matches a new entry in) and the match field in the lookup file (when the value in) by selecting field names from the two pop-up menus.**

   As explained previously, the names of the two fields need not be the same. What's important is that they contain similar contents.

8. **Click a radio button in the lower-left corner of the dialog box to indicate how you want to handle instances in which FileMaker Pro does not find a match.**

   ❖ Select don't copy if you want FileMaker Pro to do nothing at all. (This option is the default.)

   ❖ Select copy next lower value or copy next higher value if you want FileMaker Pro to use the closest value it can find — either lower or higher (numerically or alphabetically). Be sure to use these options only in appropriate instances. Using it with the example shown in Figure 19-5, for example, can produce some very unusual and unintended results. (If FileMaker Pro can't find the matching I.D., would you really want it to copy the last name of the closest I.D. it can find?)

   ❖ Select use and type a value or text string (up to 254 characters) into the text box that follows it if you want to set a default piece of data to be copied into the field.

9. **To tell FileMaker not to copy a blank field into the current file, check the Don't copy contents if empty check box.**

Part V: Advanced Topics

Normally, if a lookup is performed and a match is found, FileMaker Pro copies the contents of the appropriate field into the field in the current file. Sometimes, however, the field to be copied from the lookup file is blank. If the field in the current file already contains data, this would delete the contents of the field. Clicking this option leaves the original data intact.

10. **To accept the options that you have set for the lookup field, click OK.**

— or —

10. **To ignore any changes that you have made to the field definition, click Cancel.**

You return to the Entry Options dialog box.

11. **To accept this field as a lookup field, click OK.**

The Define Fields dialog box appears.

12. **When you have finished defining fields and setting field options, click Done.**

If you ever want to change a field from a lookup field back to a normal field, choose Define Fields (Shift-⌘-D), select the field in the field list, click Options, and then click the Look up values from a file check box to remove the check mark.

Another Idea for Creating Trigger and Match Fields

When FileMaker Pro executes a lookup, it presents data from the first matching record that it finds. If, for example, you use Last Name as the trigger field and the lookup file contains five people who have the last name of Hamilton, FileMaker simply selects the first Hamilton record that it finds. Other Hamiltons in the database would never be located by the lookup. As you can see, a match field should normally contain unique data, such as an I.D. number, social security number, or phone number.

Unfortunately, many databases contain no such field. With a little imagination, however, you can create trigger and match fields that are composites of other fields. To do so, you create a Calculation field that concatenates two or more fields (adds them together). In an address database, for example, you could combine an individual's last name with the last four digits of his or her phone number to create an I.D. number such as Jones1247. Although this approach is not guaranteed to produce a unique I.D., the only people you would normally expect to share the same composite number would be members of the same family.

(continued on the next page)

(continued from the previous page)

In the file that triggers the lookup, you would need to ask for two pieces of information: the last name (Last Name) and the last four digits of the person's phone number (Last4). The Calculation formula for the I.D. field would read as follows:

```
Last Name & Last4
```

Set the result type to Text.

Because a matching field must also exist in the lookup file, you could create an I.D. Calculation field by using the following formula:

```
Last Name & Right (Phone, 4)
```

As in the first formula, the result type should also be Text. This formula assumes that you are already collecting a complete phone number (Phone) in the lookup file. The part of the formula that reads `Right (Phone, 4)` tells FileMaker Pro to consider only the last four digits of the phone number. Thus, you do not need to be concerned about whether some phone numbers in the database happen to contain an area code while others do not — nor about whether the phone number was typed with parentheses, dashes, spaces, or as a continuous string — because only the final four characters are used, and they will always be digits.

An extended example

Now that you understand the basics of performing a lookup, you may want to check the *Macworld FileMaker Pro 2.0/2.1 Bible Disk* for a working example. A folder called Lookup Example that contains three databases, Video Invoice, Customers, and Movies (see Figure 19-1), is in the folder named FM Pro Bible. These interrelated files were designed to show you how lookups are set up and how they work. These databases could easily serve as the starting point for a full-fledged video rental system. Here's how the files work together:

❖ The Video Invoice database has a single layout that is devoted to creating the rental statements that customers receive when they rent movies, games, or video-related equipment (such as VCRs, laser disk players, and video game systems).

❖ The Customers database contains customer-specific information, including a customer identification number, the date the customer record was created or last modified, name and address data, and information on the security deposit. The latter includes the form of the deposit (cash or a specific credit card) and a credit card number (if the deposit was made with a credit card). A unique customer identification number is automatically assigned whenever a new record is created; that is, when this information is taken from a new customer. (The Cust. I.D. field is an auto-entry field. A new serial number is assigned to each record by incrementing the previous record's serial number by 13. The numbers assigned to the sample records are 1013, 1026, 1039, 1052, and 1065. For more information on creating auto-entry fields, see Chapter 5.)

❖ The Movies database contains a separate record for every movie, video game, and piece of equipment that the store rents. Every item gets its own identification number which, like Cust. I.D., is automatically assigned when the record is created. (The I.D. field in the Movies database is also an auto-entry field. The I.D. numbers begin with 1000, and the number is incremented by 1 for each new record. The numbers assigned to the sample records are 1000 to 1009.) Other information that can be recorded for each movie, game, or piece of equipment includes a category (Movie, Game, or Equipment) that is chosen from a pop-up menu, a title (equipment can optionally be identified by a serial number), the retail price, the date acquired, the current daily rental charge, and comments.

All lookups are performed from the Video Invoice database. When a customer selects one or more items to rent, the clerk chooses New Record from the Edit menu or presses ⌘-N to create a new rental statement in Video Invoice. A new invoice number is generated by FileMaker Pro, and today's date is automatically entered on the form. Next, the clerk asks for the individual's customer number and enters it in the Customer I.D. field. If you want to try out the database, you can enter any of the following numbers into this field: 1013, 1026, 1039, 1052, or 1065.

Customer I.D. is the trigger field that has been specified for the following lookup fields: First Name, Last Name, Address, City, State, and Zip. The moment the clerk tabs out of the Customer I.D. field or presses Enter, FileMaker searches the Customers database for a record that contains a match in the Cust. I.D. field. If it finds a match, the customer's name and address information are filled in for the clerk. (If a match is not found, the clerk knows that the customer has an invalid number or that a search of the Customers database must be performed.)

After FileMaker Pro has copied the address data onto the form, it automatically positions the cursor in the first I.D. Num. field. When the clerk types the first item's I.D. number (for a movie, for example) and tabs to the next field, this action triggers another lookup. FileMaker Pro automatically searches the Movies database for a record that has a matching I.D. When it locates that record, it fills in the rest of the information for that item (category, title, and daily price). To assure that a match is found in the sample data, you can enter any number between 1000 and 1009.

If the customer wants to rent additional items, the clerk enters them in the same manner as the first item was entered. Because the body of the rental agreement is composed of repeating fields, every entry in the I.D. Num. field triggers a lookup for that particular rental item. As the clerk enters items, the subtotal, sales tax, and total are instantly updated. (In this example, the sales tax is 7% on all video rental items, so it is calculated by multiplying the subtotal by .07.)

Chapter 19: Linking Databases

"Opening" Lookup Files

Note that when FileMaker Pro checks for a match in the lookup file, it doesn't actually open the file. The file's name is displayed in the Window menu, surrounded by parentheses to indicate that a link has been established to it. If, for whatever reason, you want to examine the lookup file, you can choose it from the Window menu. The file opens just as it does when you choose Open from the File menu.

The point is that when you are working with lookup fields, you need to open only the current file. (The *current file* is the file that requests the lookup or lookups, and it is identified in the Window menu by a check mark.) You never need to open the lookup files themselves unless you have some other reason for opening them.

After checking the rental statement to make sure that it contains no errors, the clerk prints out the customer's copy by choosing the Print command from the File menu and selecting Current record as what should be printed.

Whenever the rental price of an item changes (charging less for older movies than for current ones is a common practice), the store owner simply opens the Movies database, locates the record, and then enters the new rental price. Similarly, if a customer moves or loses rental privileges, the owner or a clerk can edit or delete a customer's record in the Customers database.

Among other things, these databases demonstrate the following:

❖ *Multiple lookup fields can be activated by the same trigger field.* When a Customer I.D. is typed into a record in the Video Invoice database, all of the following lookups are triggered: First Name, Last Name, Address, City, State, and Zip. Each of these fields is defined as a lookup field that is triggered by Customer I.D.

❖ *A database can have multiple trigger fields, each one triggering one or several lookups.* The Video Invoice database contains two trigger fields: Customer I.D., which looks up the customer's name and address, and I.D. Num., which looks up category, title, and price information for each rental item.

❖ *A single database can look up information in multiple databases.* The Customer I.D. field triggers a series of lookups in the Customers database, and the I.D. Num. field triggers lookups in the Movies database.

❖ *When a repeating field is used as a lookup trigger, every instance of the field triggers another lookup.* In Video Invoice, an entry in any of the eight repetitions of I.D. Num. triggers a lookup for that invoice line.

❖ *When databases are linked by a lookup, you do not have to open the lookup files before you use them.* As long as the lookup files have not been moved and the disk is mounted, FileMaker Pro can access data in them.

More about lookups

As you can see, defining and using lookup fields is not difficult. When you are doing so, however, keep the following special features and restrictions in mind:

❖ *You can use the current file as the lookup file.* That's right. Rather than looking in an external file, you can copy values from other records in the same file. In the Video Invoice database, for example, the lookup field definitions could be changed so that when a Customer I.D. is entered, FileMaker Pro searches Video Invoice (rather than Customers) for a record with a matching Customer I.D. As long as a previous invoice for that customer exists, FileMaker can simply copy the address information from that invoice into the current one. If no match is found, you're talking to a new customer, and you can fill in the information by typing it.

❖ *When FileMaker Pro is determining whether it has found a match, it compares only the first 20 characters in the trigger and match fields.* Be sure that the I.D. numbers or text are not longer than 20 characters. If you have two records that differ only in the twenty-first character or later, FileMaker will simply select the first one of the two that it finds. Also, FileMaker Pro ignores the order of words, capitalization, and punctuation when it is performing the comparison. Thus, it considers crosby and Crosby! to be the same, and it considers Steve Simms and Simms, Steve to be the same. Finally, as it does when indexing a Number field, FileMaker Pro ignores text in numeric fields when it is checking for a match.

❖ *If possible, entries in a match field should be unique.* When FileMaker Pro checks for a match, it simply reports the first one that it finds. If there are several matches, the others will never be used. This is precisely why it is dangerous in most databases to use Last Name as a match field, for example. You can avoid duplication in match fields by defining the field as an automatically generated serial number and/or specifying that the field must be unique. (For more information about setting field definition options, see Chapter 5.)

❖ *You can edit the information in a lookup field just as you can in any other field.* However, a new lookup will occur only when you execute the Relookup command (discussed in the next section) or edit the trigger field.

❖ *If possible, avoid selecting a repeating field as one from which you are looking up data.* FileMaker Pro simply copies the first entry from the repeating field.

Performing a Relookup

Sometimes, information in your lookup file changes. You update parts descriptions and prices; and contact names, addresses, and phone numbers can change. You can bring any values in the current file up to date by simply tabbing or clicking in a trigger field and then issuing the Relookup command.

As an example, imagine that you have a small mail-order business that sells tropical fish. You may create a database called Catalog which can print an on-demand catalog that lists the fish you have on hand and their prices. Catalog performs its lookups by searching an Inventory database that contains description and price information for each type of fish that is currently in stock. As a small, specialized business, prices on particular fish may vary on a daily basis (depending on who your supplier happens to be today). Whenever a customer requests a catalog, you perform a Relookup to make sure that the prices are current.

You need to keep several important things in mind when you are executing a relookup:

❖ *A relookup is performed for all records that are currently being browsed.* You can restrict the affected records by first selecting a particular record or group of records.

❖ *Just as each trigger field in the current file triggers its own lookups, relookups are done only for the current trigger field (the one that contains the cursor when you choose the Relookup command).* Thus, if a file has several trigger fields, you can decide to perform a relookup for all or just some of the trigger fields.

❖ *You cannot use the Undo command to undo a relookup.* You may want to protect the integrity of the database by using the Save a Copy As command to create a backup of the database before you perform a relookup.

To perform a relookup, follow these steps:

1. **Open the database that contains the trigger fields and display the appropriate layout.**
2. **Select the records that you want to affect with the relookup.**

   Use normal record selection techniques, such as the Find, Find All, and Omit commands, to select the appropriate records.
3. **Tab into or click the first trigger field.**
4. **Choose Relookup from the Edit menu.**

   The dialog box in Figure 19-6 appears, showing the number of records that are currently being browsed.

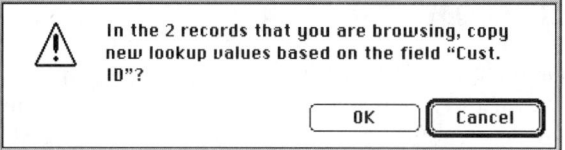

Figure 19-6: This dialog box appears when you are performing a relookup.

5. Click **OK** to replace the old values with new ones or click **Cancel** to leave the original values unchanged.

6. If you want to perform a relookup for additional trigger fields, repeat Steps 2 through 5.

You should always think carefully before executing a relookup. For instance, in an invoice database that pulls price information via lookup fields, performing a relookup on that field would effectively change the amounts due on outstanding invoices! Normal business practices dictate that you would seldom want to do a relookup on such a field.

If you want to see how Relookup works (rather than just read about it), you can try it out with the three databases in the Lookup Example folder (discussed above). First, select an existing invoice in the Video Invoice database. Then open the Customers and Movies databases, and change some of the values in the records that are currently being looked up. For example, to affect invoice 1001, you could change any of the name and address fields for customer 1052 in the Customers database, as well as the information for item 1000 and 1007 in the Movies database. Then simply follow the steps above to perform the Relookup.

Forcing a Relookup for a Single Record

As mentioned previously, a relookup normally affects all records that are currently being browsed, as well as all lookup fields that are associated with the current trigger field. Sometimes, however, you may want to update only a single record, rather than the entire database or a subset of it. Although you can use Find requests to limit browsing to the one record of interest and then choose the Relookup command, you can use an easier method to update one record.

Display the appropriate record, select the data in the trigger field, cut it (by choosing Cut from the Edit menu or by pressing ⌘-X), and then immediately paste it back into the same field (by choosing Paste from the Edit menu or by pressing ⌘-V). Remember that editing the contents of a trigger field always causes a lookup to be performed. Because FileMaker Pro knows only that something has been done to the field, this cut-and-paste procedure forces a lookup to occur. If the data that is looked up has changed, the new values will appear in the lookup fields. (Another way to force a lookup is to delete a single character and then retype it.)

Automating a Relookup

For certain types of databases, you may want to make sure that lookup fields are always up to date. Here are a couple of examples:

- Sales-related and marketing-related databases that use lookups to enter customer information, such as the contact name and address
- A catalog that is produced "on-demand" for customers and shows what products you currently have in stock, as well as their prices

Manually executing a relookup has several drawbacks, including the following:

- You may have a particular record-selection procedure that must be performed first.
- If you have several trigger fields, you may have to perform several relookups.
- You have to remember to do it.

A better approach is to automate the relookup by creating an appropriate script or set of scripts. As discussed in Chapter 7, you can set a script to execute automatically each time you open the database. To see an example of how to set up an automatic relookup, examine the Video Invoice file discussed earlier in this chapter. You can see the script by choosing ScriptMaker from the Scripts menu and then double-clicking the script named Relookup in the dialog box that appears. To see how the script was set to automatically execute each time the file is opened, choose Preferences from the File menu and click the Document icon in the left side of the Preferences Dialog box (shown in Figure 19-7).

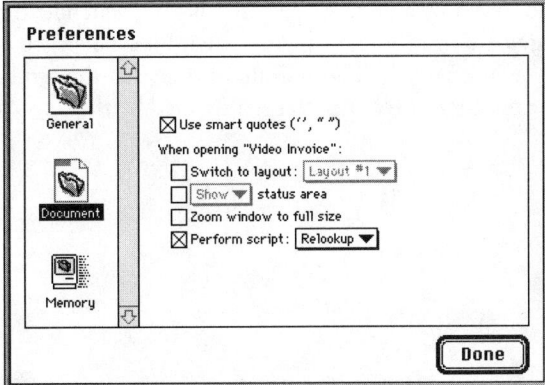

Figure 19-7: Use the Preferences command to specify a start-up script for any database.

The Relookup script (see Figure 19-8) is surprisingly simple. To execute a straightforward relookup, the script makes all records visible (Find All), moves the pointer into the Cust. I.D. field (the field that triggers the lookup of the customer name and address fields), and then performs the relookup (without showing a dialog box). If you wanted the relookup to restrict itself to a particular subset of records (rather than using all records, as in this example), you would execute the appropriate Find command before creating the script.

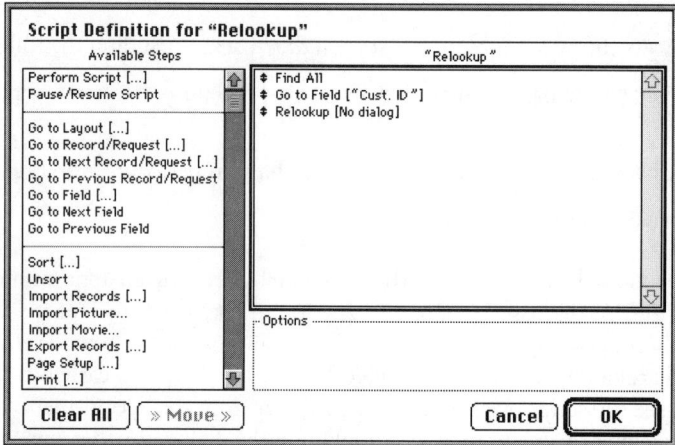

Figure 19-8: The Relookup script.

Remember that this script has been set to execute automatically each time the database is opened. When you open the database, you initially see a Command symbol cursor (⌘) followed by a blinking period. Like the watch icon that you see in many other programs, this symbol is displayed when FileMaker Pro is executing a process that cannot be interrupted. The amount of time that the symbol is on-screen depends on the number of records that are affected by the relookup.

Chapter 19: Linking Databases

CHAPTER 19 CONCEPTS AND TERMS

- By defining a field as a lookup field, you can pull its information from another database file, instead of having to type it each time.

- To trigger a lookup, simply type data into the trigger field or edit existing data in that field. Then exit the field by pressing Tab or Enter. FileMaker Pro checks the lookup file for a record that has matching data in the match field. If it finds one, it copies the appropriate data into the lookup field(s) in the current database.

- The names of the trigger and match fields in the two databases need not be the same. Similarly, the names of the lookup field and its counterpart in the lookup file also can be different.

- You can have one or many lookup fields that are associated with a single trigger field.

- To bring records in the current file up to date, you can select the appropriate records and issue the Relookup command. Doing so causes a lookup to be executed for each of the records that are being browsed.

- Every relookup is associated with a single trigger field. Only lookup fields that use that particular trigger field are affected by the relookup. Thus, if you have multiple trigger fields, you need to use multiple relookups to bring an entire record up to date.

current file
The file that requests the lookup.

lookup field
A field in the current database into which data will be copied when a lookup is triggered.

lookup file
The database in which data is looked up (in response to data being entered or edited in the trigger field in the current file).

match field
The field in the lookup file that is compared to the trigger field in the current field.

Relookup
A FileMaker Pro command that forces a lookup to occur for all records that you are currently browsing.

trigger field
A field in the current database that, when you enter data into it or edit data that is in it, causes one or more lookups to be performed.

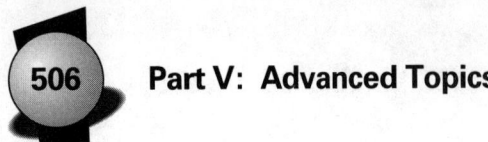

Part V: Advanced Topics

CHAPTER TWENTY

Sharing and Protecting Data

- Accessing a database as a host or a guest
- Sharing databases on a multiplatform network
- Setting passwords to protect a database

Not only is FileMaker Pro network-compatible, but it also includes features that enable it to manage network traffic and to control who in the company sees various databases and who can modify them (regardless of whether the database is on a network or is running in a single-user environment). This chapter explains how to use FileMaker Pro on a network, as well as how to password-protect and assign access privileges to sensitive data.

Running FileMaker Pro on a Network

Having your personal FileMaker Pro databases at your beck and call is great, but some data — particularly business information — is best shared with others. Back in the old days (before networks), employees spent an inordinate amount of time unnecessarily duplicating and hand-distributing data. When a colleague down the hall needed a copy of your sales spreadsheet, you made a copy of it on disk and carried the disk to his or her desk. Now that you're all linked via the company's network, you can simply share the data without physically having to move or copy it. Files can stay right where they are, regardless of whether they're located on your hard disk or on a file server.

Right out of the box, FileMaker Pro 2 is a network-ready program. When the program has been installed, FileMaker Pro databases can be shared among the users of any AppleTalk network. Using Farallon PhoneNET Talk network software and a compatible network connector card, PCs also can be part of the network, enabling users of Macintosh and Windows versions of FileMaker Pro to share the same databases. Because the software license requires it, and because failure to do so may cause your network to crawl, each user should have his or her own local copy of FileMaker Pro and run that copy when accessing shared databases. (There's an exception to this rule, however; see the discussion of FileMaker Pro Server in the "FileMaker Pro Server" sidebar.)

Part V: Advanced Topics

FileMaker Pro Server

In May 1994, Claris announced FileMaker Pro Server, a special server version of FileMaker Pro 2 designed to support up to 100 concurrent licensed FileMaker Pro Macintosh and Windows users over an AppleTalk network. According to a Claris press release: "Network-intensive tasks previously handled locally on a FileMaker Pro network, such as indexing, will be off-loaded to the FileMaker Pro Server, dramatically reducing the amount of data traffic that passes over the network." Using a newly designed database engine, Server reportedly is twice as fast as regular FileMaker Pro, yet maintains complete compatible with FileMaker Pro 2.0 and 2.1 for Mac and Windows.

FileMaker Pro Server is designed to take advantage of the new Power Macintoshes but requiring only a Mac II or higher. A Windows version of FileMaker Pro Server for Netware also is under development.

Hosts and guests

The person who opens a FileMaker Pro database and then declares it to be a multiuser database becomes the *host* for that database for the current session. (To open a database for sharing, choose Single-User from the File menu. The command changes to Multi-User.) The shared database can be located on your personal hard disk or on any hard disk on the AppleTalk network. Some networks use special file-sharing software, such as AppleShare (Apple Computer), to enable files to be used by others on the network. Contact your network administrator for details.

While the database is open, as many as 25 other users on the network can use the database. These users are referred to as *guests*. The specific privileges each guest has are determined by the designer of the database or, in some cases, the database administrator.

If the previous host was someone other than you, you will see the major changes made by that person, as well as any changes made to records by the host and guests. Because the host is in charge, only that person's changes to Sort, Find, and Page Setup commands are saved with the file. When you, as the new host, eventually close the database, *your* commands will be saved.

The host is in charge

Hosts and guests have different privileges and responsibilities. Following are some guidelines for being a host:

Chapter 20: Sharing and Protecting Data

- Any lookup files required by the database must be opened by the host.
- To avoid bringing the network to a standstill, the host should try to avoid running additional programs while he/she is serving as host.
- Only the host can define fields, change the order of layouts, save copies of the file, define groups, set access privileges, or change the database back to single-user status.

As you can see, the host is in charge of the big stuff: making certain that the database is ready to use, ensuring that his/her personal computer is not overburdened, and making major changes to the structure of the database. Reserving these major privileges for the host alone makes good sense. If any of the actions in the last point above were available to all users, no one would be able to get any work done. Imagine trying to enter a new record while the fields in a key layout were simultaneously being shifted around by several individuals.

In point of fact, if the host attempts any of the actions listed in the last point, FileMaker Pro automatically asks all guests to close the file. After the host completes the necessary changes and reopens the database as multiuser, guests can re-open the file and resume their work.

When you — as host — finish using the file and want to close it, you can choose Close, Quit, or Multi-User from the File menu. If any guests are using the database, FileMaker Pro asks that you notify them, requesting that they close the database as well.

To close a database (as host), follow these steps:

1. Choose Multi-User, Close (⌘-W), or Quit (⌘-Q) from the File menu.

If guests still are using the database, the Ask dialog box appears on the host's screen (see Figure 20-1).

Figure 20-1: The Ask dialog box.

Part V: Advanced Topics

2. **Click Ask to send each guest a message asking them to close the file.**

   A message appears on each guest's screen (see Figure 20-2), stating that the host wants to close the file and that guests must relinquish access to it.

3. **To acknowledge the message, guests click the OK button.**

   Guests who are running System 6 with MultiFinder may not see a message, however; they may hear a system beep instead.

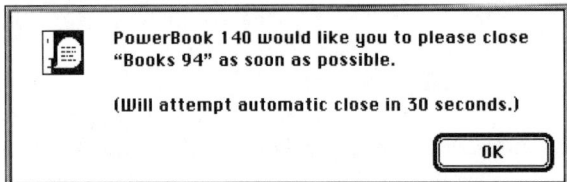

Figure 20-2: This message appears on guests' screens. While displayed, the message counts down to zero.

4. **After 30 seconds, FileMaker Pro automatically attempts to close the file.**

   If the file can be closed safely, FileMaker does so, regardless of whether guests have responded to the message. If the file cannot be closed safely, it remains open.

Setting a File as Single-User or Multiuser

When a host changes the status of a file from multi-user to single-user, or vice versa, that new status is saved along with the other database settings. If, for example, a host closes a file while it is still set as multiuser, the next time the file is opened, the file is automatically marked as sharable and is ready to receive guests. On the other hand, if the file is set to single-user status when it is closed, the next host — whoever that might be — must reset the file to multiuser (assuming that the file is still meant to be shared).

Chapter 20: Sharing and Protecting Data

Guest activities

To open a shared (multiuser) file as a guest, choose Open from the File menu (or press ⌘-O), click the Network button in the file dialog box that appears, and then choose a file from the Network Access dialog box (see Figure 20-3) and click Open. Only files that have been opened by a host appear in the file list. FileMaker also has a keyboard shortcut that you can use to go directly to the Network Access dialog box: just press Option-⌘-O.

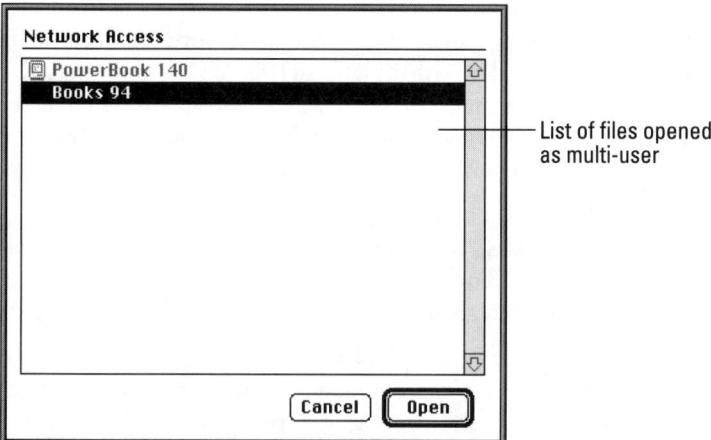

Figure 20-3: The Network Access dialog box.

If your network is divided into zones, the zones will be listed in a separate section at the bottom of the Network Access dialog box. In that case, you first must select a zone and then choose one of the shared files that appear at the top of the dialog box.

Forcing FileMaker Pro to Check Again

If you're certain that a particular file has been opened as multiuser, but you don't see it in the file list for the appropriate network zone, press the Option key as you click the zone name. This action allows FileMaker Pro more time to check for shared files.

Each guest may perform any action on the database that his/her privileges allow. At a minimum, each guest can browse the file (examine but not change data in the records). Other normal activities, such as editing, adding, and deleting records, also may be permitted. For details, see "Protecting Databases and Setting Access Privileges" later in this chapter.

Notes on cross-platform database sharing

As mentioned earlier in this chapter, both Macs and PCs can share FileMaker Pro databases on an AppleTalk network. In general, any typical task (such as entering and editing data, creating and deleting records, and sorting or issuing Find requests) can be performed on either platform (Mac or Windows). Data, graphics, and other elements that appear on one machine also appear on the other. Also, the program commands used to work with databases are the same whether the user is running the Macintosh or Windows version of FileMaker Pro. However, there are a few important differences:

- Platform-specific tasks can be performed only on the appropriate platform. A Windows user, for example, cannot play a QuickTime movie that's embedded in a Mac FileMaker database.

- Fonts occasionally can pose a problem. Common fonts, such as Times and Helvetica, are mapped to appropriate fonts when viewed on a different platform from the one on which the database was created. Unusual fonts may not translate so well and can cause field labels to spill over into fields or wrap to a new line, for example.

- Special symbols used in entering data or creating layout text can produce unusual or unexpected results when viewed on the other platform.

- File-naming conventions differ between the two platforms.

For information concerning other differences between the Mac and Windows versions of FileMaker Pro, as well as the mechanics of sharing databases between these two platforms *without* a network, see Chapter 16.

Protecting Databases and Setting Access Privileges

Some databases are designed to be shared equally by all users on a network. It is not uncommon for a department to have a shared business-contacts database, for example. At the very least, every member of the department should be allowed to view the records so that he or she can easily determine the name and phone number of the current contact at Optico, Inc., for instance. Allowing such a database to be shared can save considerable time and energy compared to having every department member maintain her or his own version of a contacts file.

Not all company information, however, is intended to be shared among all employees or even all members of the same department. A database that contains employee salary information, for example, may well be available only to members of the accounting department. And within that database, certain layouts and data may properly be modified or viewed only by the head of the department.

Other information often is meant for no one other than the person who designed the database in which it is stored. A manager, for example, may create a database that she uses to record comments about employee performance. Although the contents of this file may be extremely useful when the manager writes her semiannual employee evaluations, this highly sensitive information is not meant for public consumption; neither is the information intended to be viewed or edited by anyone else in the company.

FileMaker Pro anticipates the need for security and for assigning different types of privileges to different users. To this end, you can create passwords for databases, create groups, and associate access privileges and database *resources* (fields and layouts that can be viewed) with specific groups. The following information may help you better understand how these elements interact and how they are used:

- *Passwords and privileges.* Each password is associated with a particular set of *privileges* (what users can or cannot do with the database). Without a password, users can be prevented from even opening the file or can be granted minimal privileges, such as only viewing the data.

- *Groups and resources.* All group members are assigned passwords, which restrict the privileges of members of that group. Groups also can be associated with particular database resources (layouts and fields). You can prevent group members from seeing a sensitive report layout, for example, or stop them from modifying data in certain fields.

Creating passwords

The purpose of creating passwords is to restrict the types of activities that a user can perform on a database. (Examples of activities include browsing, adding, deleting, and editing records). The *master password* — normally held by the database designer or database administrator — provides complete access to the file, enabling the password holder to perform any desired design activity, including creating or changing layouts and editing scripts. The master password also is required when a user wants to set or change the access privileges of other people or groups.

The database designer or administrator also may create other passwords that allow fewer privileges. Depending on the content of a database, you may want to create a password that allows the user only to view the data (browse records), for example. This access is the minimum access any user can be given and is available to anyone who is able to open the database. You also can set privileges for users who have no password or have forgotten their passwords (described later in this section).

Part V: Advanced Topics

To create passwords for a database, follow these steps:

1. **Open the database for which you want to create passwords.**

   Every database must have its own passwords. There is no command with which you can create a "universal" password that works with all your databases.

2. **Choose Define Passwords from the Access Privileges submenu of the File menu.**

   The Define Passwords dialog box appears (see Figure 20-4).

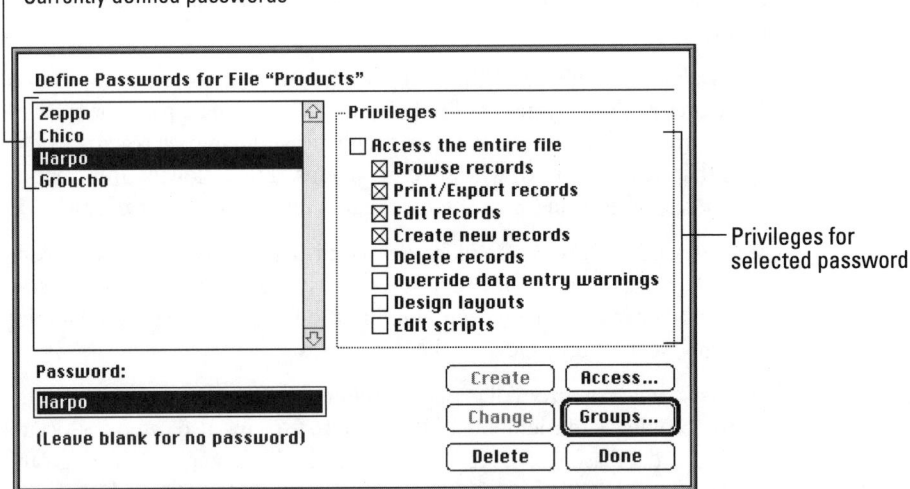

Figure 20-4: The Define Passwords dialog box.

3. **If you have not yet created a master password for this database, do so now.**

   In the Privileges section of the Define Passwords dialog box, check the Access the entire file checkbox. Type a new password in the Password box, and then click Create.

4. **If this is the only password you want to create at this time, click Done.**

   — or —

4. **Create the next password by typing it in the Password box, set privileges to be associated with the password by clicking check boxes, and then click Create.**

Chapter 20: Sharing and Protecting Data

5. **Click Done to save the new passwords for the file.**

    Before closing the Define Passwords dialog box, FileMaker Pro makes sure that you know the master password (and, hence, have the right to assign and modify passwords) by displaying the dialog box shown in Figure 20-5.

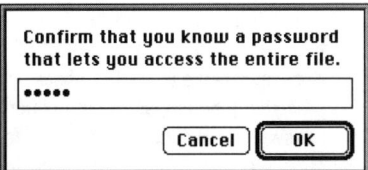

Figure 20-5: Enter the master password in this dialog box.

6. **Type the master password, and click OK.**

Creating True Number-Only Fields

The Define Passwords dialog box holds the key to creating true number-only fields. As discussed in Chapter 5, when you set a field type to Number, users still can enter any type of information in the field, including text. If you carry the definition a step further and set the Verify that the field value is of type Number option for the field, users receive a warning if they attempt to enter any non-numeric data in the field, as shown in the accompanying figure. Users are free, however, to override the warning whenever they want — an arrangement that defeats the purpose of having a number-only field.

To create a true number-only field, you must assign a password to the database and remove the check mark from the Override data entry warnings checkbox in the Privileges section of the Define Passwords dialog box. If a user with this password attempts to enter non-numeric data in the field, the dialog box shown in the following figure appears. The user cannot continue until the data is either entered correctly or removed. This technique works for all data-entry warnings that are related to the Verify that field value is options (entering a number outside the specified range or a value that is not unique, for example).

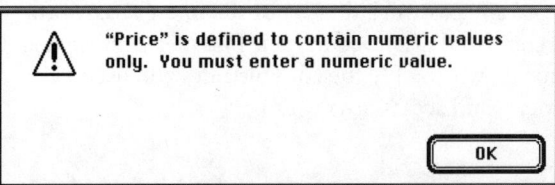

Part V: Advanced Topics

Passwords for Shareware Templates

One handy use for passwords is when you are developing shareware or commercial templates that you intend to sell to others. Before distributing the templates, you can create several levels of passwords that address different customer needs. The Following are some examples:

- *No password.* Create a blank password with limited privileges (browse records, print/export records, and edit records, for example). This technique allows a prospective customer to examine the database, print reports, and so on, but he or she is restricted to using whatever number of records you included in the database.

- *Second-level password.* In addition to the privileges available when no password is entered, this password allows a user to create and delete records. Offer to provide this password in exchange for a basic shareware fee. If they like your product, most customers will prefer this option.

- *Master-level password.* Check the Access the entire file option when specifying privileges for this password. This option gives customers complete freedom to modify the template as they see fit. Because it is the equivalent of selling the code for a computer program, you want to offer this master password for a substantially higher fee. (Recognize, of course, that giving a user full access means that he or she has more opportunity to break your scripts or to use the template in ways that you never intended, which can lead to support nightmares.)

Unless you see a reason to restrict access to certain layouts or fields, you probably don't need to create groups (described in "Creating and deleting groups" later in this chapter).

Passing out passwords

When the database designer or administrator hands out the passwords, the distribution is handled on a group basis (see "Creating and deleting groups,"). If the major groups are defined as departments, for example, the administrator is responsible for ensuring that every salesperson receives the same password. By distributing the passwords, the administrator is defining the group membership.

The group names, as well as their very existence, are of no concern to employees; only the person with the master password ever actually *sees* the group names. All users know is that they have a password that gives them particular rights—not whether others also have the same password and privileges. (People with lesser passwords — any password that is not the master password—have the Change Password command displayed in their File menu rather than the usual Access Privileges submenu, which only the administrator can use to view and change passwords, groups, and access privileges.)

Modifying passwords

If you have the master password, you can change or delete any password for the database. To alter a password, open the database by using the master password, and choose Define Passwords from the Access Privileges submenu of the File menu. When the Define Passwords dialog box appears, do one of the following things:

- *Delete a password* by selecting the password and clicking Delete.
- *Change a password* by selecting the password, typing a new password in the Password box, and clicking Change.

After deleting or altering passwords, it is your responsibility to let the affected individuals know about the changes.

Even if you do not have the master password for a database, you can change any password that has been assigned to *you*. For details, see "Changing a password" later in this chapter.

Creating and deleting groups

After you define passwords, the next step is to define groups and assign at least one password to each group. Because each password has specific privileges associated with it, you can be sure that all members of the group have identical privileges. (You should note that you are not *required* to create groups. If you simply want to prevent anyone else from opening a database that you designed, for example, all you need to do is create a master password with full access privileges. In this case, groups would serve no purpose.)

Each group is a cohesive class of users. Group membership can be based on employee rank, departments in your company, or anything else you like. In most cases, "need to know" is the most critical factor in determining group membership. The key thing to remember is that in addition to sharing a password, members of any given group have the same privileges in the database and can work with the same layouts and fields.

To define a group, follow these steps:

1. **If the database is not open, open it now and supply the master password when you are asked for it.**

   Only a person who knows the master password can create or modify groups.

2. **Choose Define Groups from the Access Privileges submenu of the File menu.**

   The Define Groups dialog box appears, as shown in Figure 20-6.

Part V: Advanced Topics

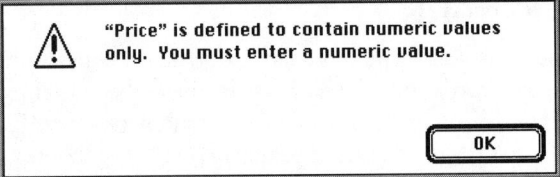

Figure 20-6: The Define Groups dialog box.

3. Type a name for the group in the Group Name box, and click Create.
4. To associate privileges and resources with the group name, click Access.

   The Access Privileges dialog box appears (see Figure 20-7).

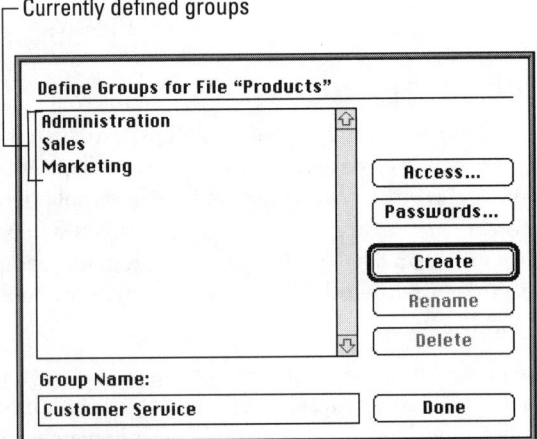

Figure 20-7: The Access Privileges dialog box.

5. Select the current group in the Groups column.
6. In the Passwords column, click the bullet next to each password that you want to associate with the group.

   Whatever privileges were assigned to the password(s) now are associated with that group. (Note that you can assign multiple passwords to one group, as well as associate multiple groups with the same password, if you like.)

   A solid bullet beside a password means that the password is associated with the currently selected group. A dimmed bullet means that the password is *not* associated with the currently selected group.

7. **To restrict access to particular layouts or fields, click the bullets that precede them in the Layouts and Fields columns.**

    A solid bullet means that the resource is accessible to the currently selected group. An open bullet means that the resource can be read but not altered by the group. A dimmed bullet means that the resource is not accessible by the group. (If a user attempts to display an inaccessible layout or a layout that contains an inaccessible field, FileMaker Pro covers the entire layout and displays the message `Access Denied`).

8. **Click Save to save the current settings, or click Revert to restore the original settings.**

9. **If you want to set passwords and resource privileges for other groups, select another group and repeat steps 5 through 8; otherwise, click Done to return to the Define Groups dialog box.**

10. **When you finish defining groups in the Define Groups dialog box, click Done to save your changes and return to the database.**

Any group that you create, you also can delete by selecting the group's name in the Define Groups dialog box and then clicking Delete. Before you delete groups for a database that currently is being shared, however, other users must close the file. When you choose Define Groups from the Access Privileges submenu of the File menu, the Ask dialog box appears immediately if other people are using the file. Click Ask, wait until the other users close the file or until FileMaker Pro closes it, and then delete the group.

Setting, changing, and examining access privileges

FileMaker Pro provides another method of setting, changing, and examining the relationships between assigned passwords, groups, and database resources. If you have the master password, you can choose Overview from the Access Privileges submenu of the File menu. The same Access Privileges dialog box that appears when you set group privileges also appears here. See the steps in the preceding section for instructions on changing or setting access privileges.

If you examine the various dialog boxes that appear when you choose a command from the Access Privileges submenu, you'll notice that you can click buttons that take you to any step in the protection-specification process: working with passwords, creating groups, or selecting available resources.

Part V: Advanced Topics

Another Use for the Access Privileges Dialog Box

Regardless of how you reach the Access Privileges dialog box, you also can use it for the following tasks:

❖ Determining which fields are displayed in any layout

❖ Determining all layouts in which a specific field appears

To see the fields used in a particular layout, select the layout name in the Layouts column of the dialog box. As shown in the following figure, all fields that appear in the selected layout are preceded by a solid bullet in the Fields column. To see all layouts that display a particular field, select the field in the Fields column. Associated layouts are preceded by a solid bullet.

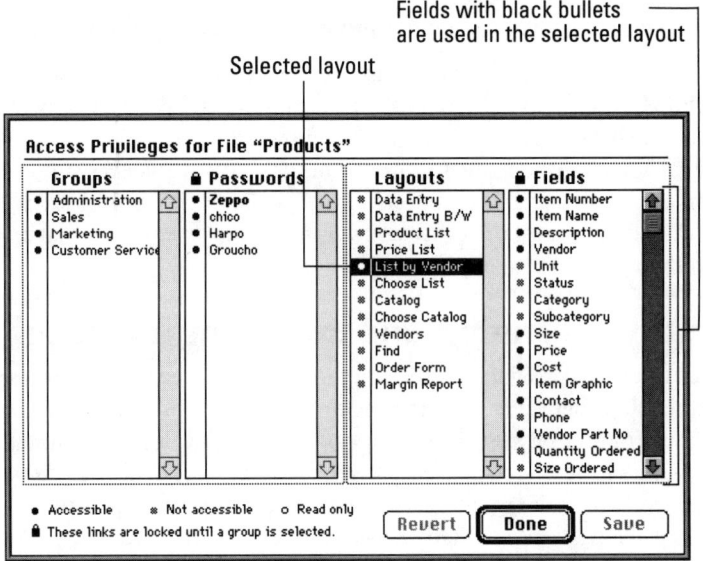

This information can make it easier for you to assign resources to different groups. In the Products database shown in the accompanying figure, for example, you may want to keep a certain group from seeing the contents of the Cost field. If you click Cost in the Fields column, you can quickly determine which layouts use that field and, hence, will be dimmed when a user from that group attempts to display those layouts. If the group members *must* see or work with a layout that is shown as currently including the Cost field, you can modify the layout by removing the Cost field, or you can make a new version of the layout that does not include this field.

Using a protected file

When you attempt to open a password-protected database — whether that database is on the network or on your personal machine — you immediately see the dialog box shown in Figure 20-8. As you type, the characters pressed appear as bullets in the dialog box. This extra bit of security keeps passersby from taking a gander at your password. If you make a mistake while typing the password, just press the Delete (or Backspace) key to remove the incorrect characters and then retype them.

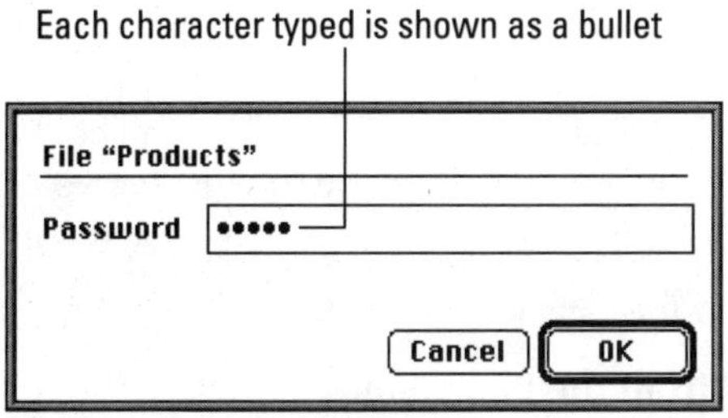

Figure 20-8: Enter your password.

When you finish, click OK, or press Return or Enter. If the password is correct, the database opens, and you are assigned the access privileges that are associated with the password.

If you mistype the password (or are simply entering a guess), FileMaker Pro displays a dialog box to inform you that the password is incorrect. If you click the OK button in this dialog box, the original password dialog box reappears (refer to Figure 20-8), and you can try again. If you don't know or remember the password, click Cancel. FileMaker Pro remains open, and you can select another database with which to work.

Opening a database without a password

If the person who assigned passwords also created a no-password option that enables users to open the database without having a password, a slightly different version of the password dialog box appears (see Figure 20-9). If you don't have a password, you can open the database merely by clicking OK or by pressing Return or Enter. As with actual passwords, a no-password user also has specific access privileges that have been assigned by the database designer or administrator.

Part V: Advanced Topics

```
File "Products"
Password [          ]
       (Leave blank for limited access) ——— This means that the file can
              [Cancel] [  OK  ]              be opened without a password
```

Figure 20-9: A password dialog box with a "no password" option.

Changing a password

After using any password (other than the master password) to open a database, you'll notice that the Access Privileges submenu of the File menu has been replaced by a new command: Change Password. Although you cannot alter your access privileges for the file, you can change your password whenever you want.

To change a password, follow theses steps:

1. Select Change Password from the File menu.

The Change Password dialog box appears (see Figure 20-10).

```
Change Password
Old password:
[                    ]
New password:
[                    ]
Confirm new password:
[                    ]
        [Cancel] [  OK  ]
```

Figure 20-10: The Change Password dialog box.

2. Type your current password in the Old password box.

3. Press the Tab key, and type the new password in the Next password box.

4. Press the Tab key, and type the new password a second time (to verify it) in the Confirm new password box.

5. Click OK to save the new password.

Although security experts suggest that you change your password regularly, this FileMaker Pro procedure has one big drawback. When you change a password for yourself, *you also are changing it for everyone else who uses the same password* — that is, all members of the group or groups to which the password has been assigned. It is your responsibility to see that all affected users of the database are informed of the password change.

Unless you are the sole user of a particular password, a better approach is to simply leave password changes to the database administrator. Because that person has complete access to the database and can view or alter passwords at any time (even if a user has already changed the password), the administrator is in a perfect position to handle this task. And because the administrator also knows the particular users who share each password, he or she can make sure that the new password is communicated only to the right people.

CHAPTER 20: CONCEPTS AND TERMS

- If you are working on an AppleTalk network, FileMaker Pro databases can be shared among users. Up to 25 users (plus the host) can simultaneously open and work in any shared database. Unless you have FileMaker Pro Server, however, each user should have his or own copy of FileMaker Pro.

- The first person to open a database for sharing during a computing session is called the *host*. Although guests (other users) can view and edit data in the file, only the host's Page Setup, Find, and Sort changes are saved when the file is closed. The host also is responsible for closing the database.

- If they are on the same network, users of the Windows version of FileMaker Pro can share their databases with Mac users, and vice versa.

- To protect a database or assign different privileges to different classes of users, you can assign passwords to the database, define groups that are associated with each password, and limit access to particular resources (layouts and fields).

access privileges
Activities that a user can perform when using a particular password.

guest
Any user who opens a shared database after the host has opened it.

host
The user who first opens a database and sets its status to multiuser, enabling other users on the network to share that database. In subsequent sessions, other users may become the host.

master password
A special password that provides complete access to a database, including permission to change the design of the database, set or change passwords and access privileges, and establish or change groups.

password
A string of characters that a user must type when opening a protected FileMaker Pro database. Different passwords often are associated with different privileges, specifying what a user can or cannot do with the database.

platform
A particular computer/operating system combination. The Mac/System 7 and PC/Windows are two common platforms, both of which are compatible with FileMaker Pro.

resources
Layouts and fields. When defining access privileges associated with a particular group, the database designer or administrator can prevent users from modifying or even seeing particular resources.

CHAPTER TWENTY-ONE

Developing Databases for Others

IN THIS CHAPTER

- Improving the usability and accessibility of templates you develop for others
- An introduction to FileMaker Pro SDK

N o database is an island.

Actually, this statement is only sometimes true. You will create plenty of databases for your personal use only — a home or business financial database or one that contains information about friends and business associates, for example. At times, however, you will want to share your examples of database wizardry with friends, business colleagues, or the public at large. Here are a few examples:

❖ *Sharing in-house business templates:* Your company doesn't have a network, so employees can't access a central shared database. However, when you or anyone else in the company has constructed a database that would be useful to other people in your department or to the company as a whole, you can distribute the template to everyone who needs it.

As a Sales Associate, John creates a contact database that he uses to track sales leads, make follow-up calls, and record his successes and failures with each customer. The department decides to standardize by providing a copy of the template to all of their salespeople so they can install it on their own Macs.

❖ *Sharing with friends:* Sam's club has an ongoing membership drive. Because several people on the membership committee have Macs and use FileMaker Pro, Sam creates a template to record information about each prospective or new member and then passes the template out to the other people on the committee. Each month, the members hand Sam a disk that contains a current copy of their version of the database. Sam clicks a button on the template that executes a script that identifies records that have been added or modified during the past 30 days and exports those records to a file. Sam then opens his master copy of the database and imports the records.

Part V: Advanced Topics

❖ *Sharing with the world:* After you develop a database to organize the contents of your wine cellar, record the results of your biweekly gambling treks to Atlantic City, or track your huge music CD and cassette collection, you may decide that the database is too good to keep to yourself. Because you're a member of an on-line information service (such as America Online, CompuServe, or GEnie), you decide to offer the template to others. Depending on your personal philosophy or degree of entrepreneurial spirit, you can post the template as freeware (free to anyone who wants it) or shareware (software for which you request a fee from all users who decide to keep it).

FileMaker provides two means of sharing templates. The usual method is to use the Save a Copy As command to create a clone of the finished database, stripping it of all records. Each user has access to the scripts and layouts you have painstakingly created, but your personal data stays with you.

The second approach is reserved for members of the Claris Solutions Alliance — bona fide third-party developers of commercial templates, add-ons, and training materials that are based on Claris products. Claris is now offering for sale a special product called FileMaker Pro SDK (Solutions Development Kit). Database templates that have been processed by SDK can be run as *stand-alone programs;* that is, the templates can be used on any Mac, even one that does not have a copy of FileMaker Pro installed on it. For anyone who is developing commercial templates, SDK provides the enormous benefit of vastly expanding the potential market for the templates. Instead of being able to address only the needs of other individuals who already own FileMaker Pro — or who can be convinced to buy a copy of the program so they can use your template — you can provide ready-made database solutions to anyone who has a Mac.

About the Claris Solutions Alliance

Members of the Claris Solutions Alliance include consultants, companies, and individual developers who offer commercial solutions to Claris customers. They provide such products and services as contract programming and database development, specialized and mass-market templates, and training programs or materials. You can learn more about the Claris Solutions Alliance by requesting a membership directory from Claris. See Appendix D for information on obtaining a free copy of the directory.

Chapter 21: Developing Databases for Others

Chapter 17 introduced you to the necessary procedures for creating a database template; this chapter carries the discussion further by doing the following:

❖ Suggesting techniques that you can use to improve the user interface for your templates

❖ Showing how to protect the structure of a template

❖ Explaining methods of restricting access to certain template features (for example, distributing templates with some key features disabled as a way of encouraging users to send in the shareware fee to obtain full access to features)

Creating Shareable Templates

Regardless of whether you are using the regular version of FileMaker Pro or FileMaker Pro SDK to create templates, you can use the following techniques and strategies to improve the appearance, functionality, and marketability of your work:

❖ Simplifying the interface with menus

❖ Providing buttons and scripts for common functions

❖ Designing for monitors of various sizes and color display capabilities

❖ Distributing shareware templates as demos or with selected sets of features disabled

Simplify the interface by using menus

For any database that contains more than just a simple data-entry layout, providing a menu to guide users to the different parts of the database is often a good idea. Menus can be particularly helpful for ensuring that computer novices and individuals who are unfamiliar with the database can easily find their way around and can reach the functions that they need to use at any given moment.

Menus are most useful when the database is divided into several different modes, each associated with a particular layout or set of layouts. In a parts inventory database, for example, you may have separate layouts for entering part sales, generating order forms when the inventory for a part drops below a critical level, and printing a status report that shows the optimal number, number on hand, and reorder level for every part. A simple menu that has three choices (Sales Entry, Order Parts, and Status Report) can help any user move directly to the section of interest.

Of course, the more logical sections your database contains, the more helpful (and appropriate) a menu can be. In databases that include dozens of layouts, you can create additional submenu screens as needed. For example, if you have created layouts for half a dozen different types of reports and labels, you may want to design separate Report and Label menus, placing each set of menus on a separate layout. (Don't overdo menu *nesting* of this sort, however. Although additional menus are helpful to novices and new users, the added time and button-clicking required to navigate through unnecessary menu layers can get old very quickly.)

Figure 21-1 shows a menu created as a separate layout in the New Buttons FM database. In this example, clicking any of the three buttons carries the user to a different layout in the database. Separate layouts are devoted to blank buttons, over-sized (large) buttons, and navigational buttons. (New Buttons FM is included on the *Macworld FileMaker Pro 2.0/2.1 Bible Disk*. It is patterned after the FileMaker Pro sample file named Buttons.) This same type of menu could enable users to select from several types of reports or to switch between several primary database functions, such as executing a Find request, generating mailing labels, or opening an associated database.

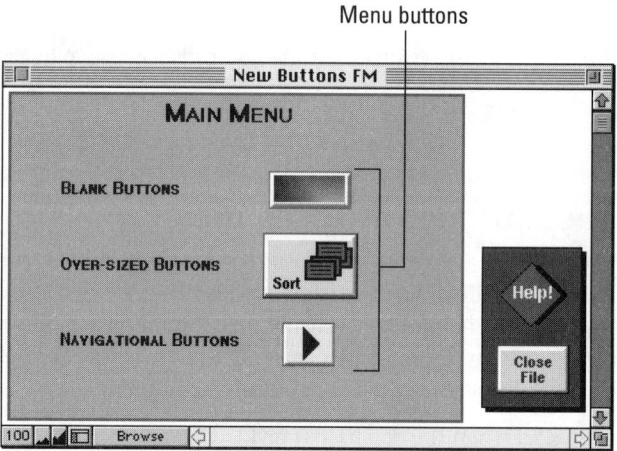

Figure 21-1: A menu created in its own dedicated layout.

In the Address Book database, the menu is incorporated into the Data Entry layout (see Figure 21-2). Because users spend the majority of their time in this layout, the menu palette enables them to simply click a button to perform a variety of functions that are related to data-entry. Note that several of the buttons duplicate menu commands but help novice users execute commands without having to remember the menu in which the command is located.

Chapter 21: Developing Databases for Others

Creating a Main Menu

If you want to use a main menu to control access to the different parts of a database, you can set the menu layout to be displayed automatically whenever the database is opened. To accomplish this, choose Preferences from the File menu, click the Document icon, and then in the section labeled When opening *"database name,"* click the check box marked Switch to layout and choose the name of your menu layout from the pop-up menu. To save the new Preference setting, click the Done button. From this point on, anyone who opens the database will immediately see the menu rather than the last layout used (the normal FileMaker Pro default).

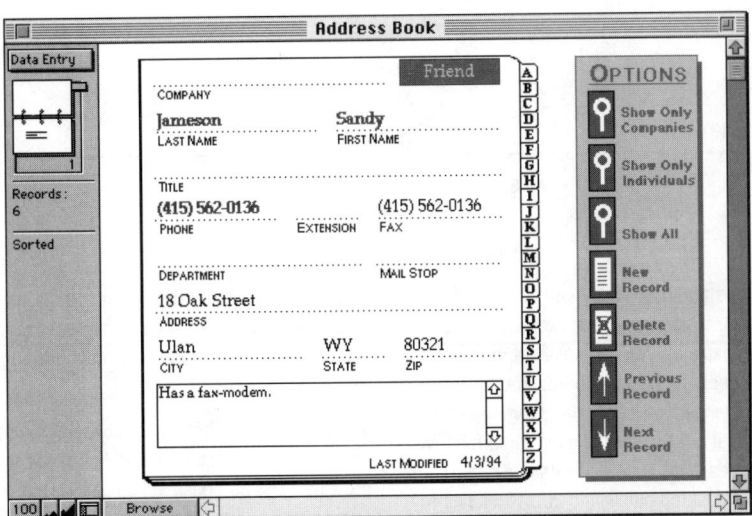

Figure 21-2: A menu palette.

The menu at the bottom of the Want List database (shown in Figure 21-3) is a variation of the menu palette displayed in Address Book. Instead of restricting itself to data entry functions, it presents all major functions that a user may want to perform with the database, including selecting specific subgroups, generating on-screen and printed reports, clearing out old records, and summoning help. Although this type of menu could easily have been created as a separate layout (as was the one for New Buttons FM), placing it in the most common layout (Data Entry) eliminates the necessity of having to add an additional layer of complexity to a full-featured database. (Parsimony is a good thing!)

Part V: Advanced Topics

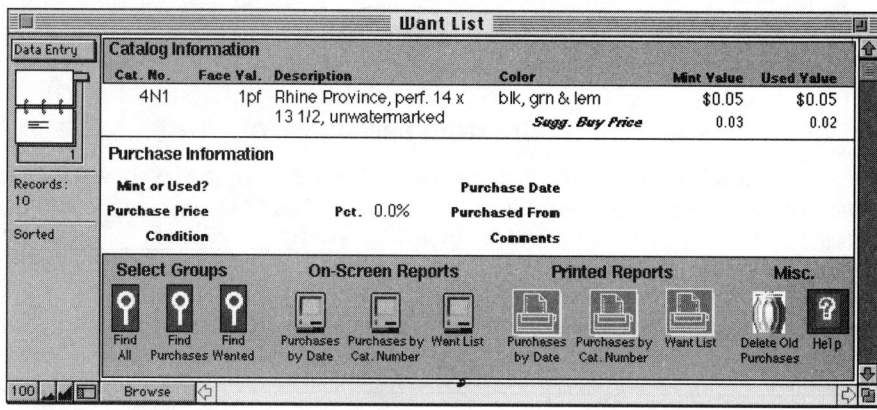

Figure 21-3: A menu incorporated into an existing layout.

Avoid Button Clutter

After you understand how easily you can assign actions to buttons (as the step-by-step instructions in this section explain), you can easily go button crazy. If you check the bulletin boards and on-line information services, you'll find many templates that have layouts that contain two or even three full rows of button. Just as using a dozen fonts in a document can make your desktop publishing effort look like a ransom note, presenting too many buttons in one place can slow the user down because finding the correct button for a function is difficult. Bad programming. . . .

If you really need that many icons, either find a logical way to group them by function (as was done in the Want List database in Figure 21-3) or think seriously about creating a series of menu layouts.

Creating a Navigation Menu

As mentioned throughout this book, buttons — such as those used in these menu examples — gain their functionality by having ScriptMaker scripts or a script step attached to them. The following series of steps explains how to design a navigation menu like the one used by the New Buttons FM database.

To create a navigation menu, do the following:

1. **Open the database and switch to Layout mode (by choosing Layout from the Select menu or by pressing ⌘-L).**

Chapter 21: Developing Databases for Others

2. **Create a new layout to hold the menu by choosing New Layout from the Edit menu (or by pressing ⌘-N).**

   As an alternative, you can create the menu as part of an existing layout as shown in Figures 21-2 and 21-3. If you decide to do so, go directly to Step 3.

3. **Paste, import, or create the graphics that will serve as the buttons.**

4. **Color and arrange the buttons on the layout as desired.**

5. **Select a button by clicking it once and then choose Define Button from the Scripts menu.**

   The Define Button dialog box appears (see Figure 21-4).

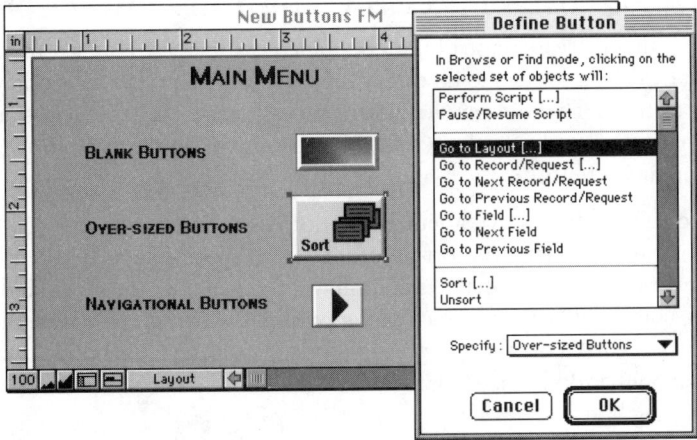

Figure 21-4: Defining a menu button.

6. **Choose the Go to Layout [...] option from the scrolling list and, from the Specify pop-up menu at the bottom of the dialog box, select the layout that you want to go to (see Figure 21-4).**

7. **Repeat Steps 5 and 6 for each menu button that you want to define, selecting a different layout to go to for each button.**

8. **If you haven't already done so, name the menu layout by choosing Layout Options from the Layout menu, typing a name in the Name text box, and clicking OK (see Figure 21-5).**

9. *Optional:* **If you always want the menu layout to appear first when you open the database, see the "Creating a Main Menu" sidebar, earlier in this chapter.**

Part V: Advanced Topics

Figure 21-5: Naming a layout.

Providing instant access via buttons and scripts

Anything that increases ease of use simultaneously increases the worth of your templates. Why ask users to do things the hard way (manually selecting various sets of Sort instructions, for example), when you can create scripts and buttons that will accomplish these tasks for them if they just choose a command from the Scripts menu or click a button?

Think carefully about how others will want to use your template. If you know that users will perform common sort procedures, that specific subgroups are of interest to many of them, or that many users will want to generate the same kinds of reports, you should create layouts and appropriate scripts to automate these elements. To make the scripts accessible, assign them to buttons, list them in the Scripts menu, or do both. See Chapter 15 for more information on creating scripts and defining buttons.

More Button Basics

Label Those Buttons!
Although the Mac is a graphically-oriented computer and icons are a common part of its user interface, you may frequently be tempted to design menu buttons and other types of buttons as unlabeled icons. Resist at all costs! Although the meaning of a button may be obvious to you, it may not be apparent to other people who will use your database or template. (A new Macintosh user may not even understand the use of a question mark as a Help button.)

When you are designing a template for others, you should avoid anything that slows people down by causing them to guess what you had in mind, search for the help file, or reach for a manual. As the examples in Figures 21-1 through 21-3 clearly show, adding a label to a button takes little screen space.

(continued on the next page)

Chapter 21: Developing Databases for Others

(continued from the previous page)

Not All Buttons Must Be Icons

Although buttons are cool and lend a professional appearance to most databases, not everyone is a graphics wizard. Nor is everyone an icon lover. In FileMaker Pro, *any* object can be a button.

For example, in Layout mode, you can use the Text tool (the uppercase *A*) to create static text that you can use as a button (refer to Figure 21-6). Follow these steps if you want to use static text to create text buttons, instead of using a graphic:

1. Switch to Layout mode (⌘-L) and select the Text tool.

2. Choose an interesting font for the text (Helvetica Bold, for example).

3. Type the text strings.

4. Select each text object and choose a fill color for it.

— or —

4. Draw a filled object to serve as a background for the text strings (a rectangle, rounded rectangle, oval, or rounded oval), choose a contrasting color for it, and then move a copy of the object behind each text string.

5. Assign an action to each button by selecting the button and then choosing the Define Button command from the Scripts menu.

The following figure shows an example of three text buttons.

[Find] [Sort] [Reports]

Consider color and screen space

Fortunately, the days of sterile-looking *monochrome* (black-and-white) monitors are almost gone. Adding color to layouts can make them more attractive, easier on the eyes, and more pleasant to use. Unfortunately, many Macs that have monochrome displays (such as the Mac Plus, SE, Classics, Portable, and several models of the PowerBook) are still in use. In addition, the sizes and shapes of monitors and built-in displays vary. When creating templates, you obviously want to accommodate as large an audience as you can. To do so, you need to make two important decisions:

❖ Should you support color, monochrome, or both?

❖ Should the templates fit on the smallest possible screen, be optimized for one standard size of display, or be offered in several sizes?

Color

You can safely include color in a template in two ways:

❖ Select colors that contrast appropriately whether users display them on a color, gray scale, or monochrome monitor.

❖ Provide two versions of the template: one color and one monochrome.

If you want to support all monitor types simultaneously, do the design work in color. After you create a layout, use the Monitors control panel to change the display to the Black & White setting (see Figure 21-6). Make sure that the chosen colors do not obscure any text that is attached to the icons and fields and that the text and other elements are still clearly visible when you're doing data entry or viewing reports. If you find any problems, use Monitors to switch back to the original color setting, make changes, and pop back into Black & White mode to see how the new colors work out. After finalizing your color choices, you may want to make an additional check by using Monitors to cycle through all the Colors and Grays settings that are available. (Normally, the monitor and display card can show the same number of grays as they can colors. When switching from colors to grays, the display card simply substitutes an equivalent gray shade for each color that you have used. As a result, if a display is readable and attractive in color, it should be equally readable and attractive in gray scale.)

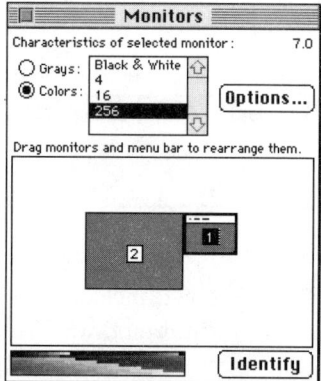

Figure 21-6: To display the Monitors control panel, choose Control Panels from the Apple menu and then select (System 6) or open (System 7) Monitors.

Because different users will have different display cards that govern the number of colors they can see, you may simply settle for handling only a few of the most basic monitor/display card setups. Monochrome, 8-bit color, and gray scale will cover most of your potential audience, so you can reduce the amount of "colorization" work that you have to do by supporting only two Monitors settings: 256 colors and Black & White. Or, if you want to avoid this hassle entirely, you can simply supply two different versions of the template — one optimized for 256 colors and another for Black & White. (Note that there's another, slightly more complicated, way of handling this issue. In the Invoices template, a sample template included with FileMaker Pro, Claris provides two versions of each critical layout: one designed for color and another for black-and-white. The user can click a button that determines which of the two layouts is displayed.)

Chapter 21: Developing Databases for Others

Screen real estate

When you are designing for other users, you also need to consider the different sizes of their displays. For example, users who have a full-page or two-page display commonly design layouts that fill the screen. Unfortunately, when such templates are opened on a Mac Classic or a PowerBook, significant portions of the window will be off-screen.

As with color templates, you have a few options:

* Restrict the template dimensions to fit the smallest screen size that you want to support.

* Assume that a user who has a small screen will be willing to scroll to reach parts of any layout that are off-screen.

* Provide several versions of the template, each optimized for a particular display.

* Divide a large layout into several smaller ones and switch between the different layouts using menus or buttons.

Database Associates Inc. included an interesting option in its AddressTrak template (shown in Figure 21-7) that you may want to use in some large templates. Programmed for a standard 13-inch monitor, AddressTrak contains some layouts that require more than a single screen to display fully. To help you move from the top to the bottom of the display (and vice versa), the template includes buttons that are defined as the script steps Page Down and Page Up (or End and Home), respectively. (The button for Page Up/Home is at the bottom of the database window—currently off-screen in Figure 21-8). A demo version of AddressTrak is included on the FileMaker Pro Bible Disk.

Protecting a template

When you design a template for in-house use, you may want to prevent others from changing it. For example, regardless of whether the person who is changing the locations of fields in a data layout is an expert or a novice who selected the Layout menu by mistake, you may want to prevent changes to the field locations. Similarly, if a database contains sensitive information, such as salary information, you may want to prevent other users from accessing the database or restrict who has access rights to the layout that contains the sensitive information.

By choosing the Access Privileges command from the File menu, the designer of any FileMaker Pro database can set passwords, define specific groups of users for the database, and set privileges that are allowed with each password. Figure 21-8 shows the basic process of setting a password for a database. For more information, refer to Chapter 20. Note that although access privileges are more commonly associated in people's minds with products that are installed on a network, you can

Part V: Advanced Topics

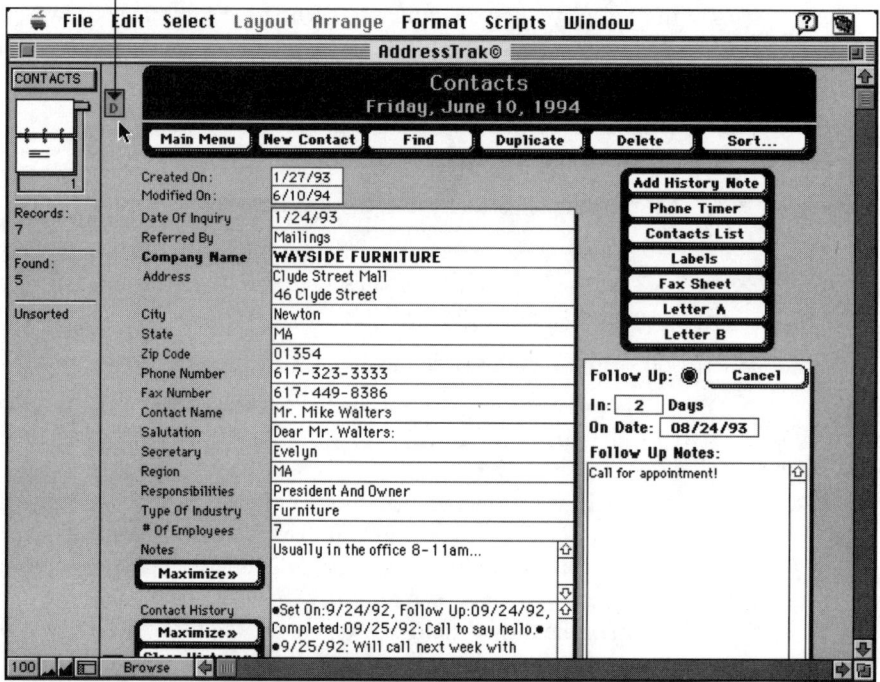

Figure 21-7: The Contacts layout from AddressTrak.

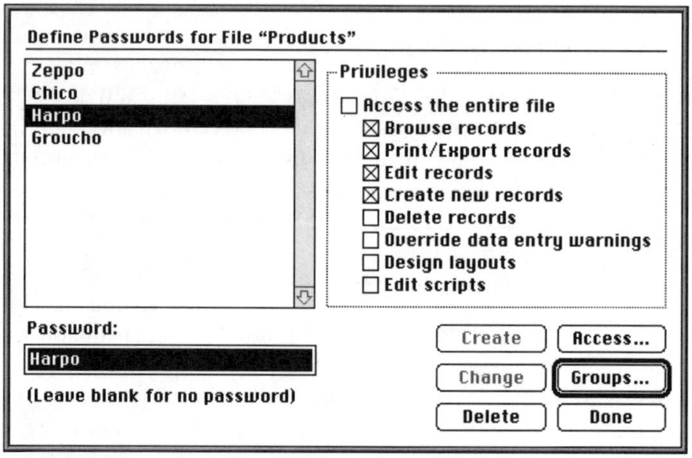

Figure 21-8: Setting access privileges.

Chapter 21: Developing Databases for Others

set access privileges for any FileMaker Pro database — including databases that are running on stand-alone Macs.

Restricting access to features of shareware templates

In addition to protecting the template from unwanted changes, you can restrict access to certain features when you create a demo or shareware version of a template. To restrict access, you assign one or more passwords for the database, each limiting the particular features that are available to the user (as shown in Figure 21-8). By taking this approach, you give users an added incentive to buy the full version or to pay the requested shareware fee.

For example, if I were offering Address Book as a shareware template, I could define three different passwords for it. At the lowest level, I would restrict access to all advanced features, allowing users only to browse and edit the sample records included in the database. This level of access provides the equivalent of a demo, giving the user a feel for the database's capabilities but not enabling any of its real functionality. I would supply this password in the documentation included in the version of the template that is uploaded to the on-line services.

As an alternative, FileMaker Pro also allows you to define a "no password" password. To do this, you simply leave the password box in Figure 21-8 blank, select privileges, and then click Create. When new users open the file, they can then leave the password dialog box blank and will then be granted access to the minimal privileges that you assigned to this condition.

On receipt of a basic shareware fee, I would supply a second password that enables the user to print/export records, create new records, delete records, and override data entry warnings. Assuming that the user is happy with the way that the database is designed (as I hope most will be), this level of functionality will be all the person requires. For an additional charge, I may offer a master password that enables the user to also modify the structure of the database (changing and designing layouts, as well as editing scripts). Advanced users may want to take advantage of this ultimate password so they can freely customize and modify the template in ways that make it more useful to them.

Note that FileMaker Pro provides an additional level of protection that can sometimes be useful. By defining groups (collections of users who share the same password), you can restrict access to particular fields and layouts. In making a demo, for example, you could use this feature to keep users from ever seeing one or more reports. For more information on creating groups, see Chapter 20.

Using FileMaker Pro SDK

As mentioned at the beginning of this chapter, FileMaker Pro SDK (Solutions Development Kit) is a special programming tool that compiles FileMaker Pro templates, changing them into stand-alone programs. If you intend to create commercial templates, using FileMaker Pro SDK offers several direct benefits when compared to creating normal FileMaker Pro templates:

- *It increases the size of the potential market.* To use a normal template, an individual must already own or be willing to buy a complete copy of FileMaker Pro. When you are selling an expensive vertical-market database (such as a video store rentals database), customers may consider the cost of a full copy of FileMaker Pro to be a drop in the bucket. When you are attempting to sell an inexpensive, general-purpose template, on the other hand, you cannot expect customers to shoulder the cost of a program just so they can use the template.

- *It presents a simplified interface.* A normal template can use FileMaker Pro techniques for restricting access to certain features, but the entire set of FileMaker Pro menus is still presented (even though some items may be dimmed). SDK restricts menu options to those required by the template. When customers are not FileMaker-savvy, eliminating unnecessary FileMaker Pro features can make the template easier for them to understand and use.

- *It protects your investment while preventing tampering.* Providing an unprotected FileMaker Pro template to customers is tantamount to handing them the source code for your product. If you have used special techniques to create the template, SDK keeps them safe from prying eyes and prevents customers from inadvertently or deliberately modifying the way the template works.

When you become a member of the Claris Solutions Alliance (CSA), you are eligible to purchase the SDK CD-ROM for $499. With it, you can produce royalty-free, stand-alone FileMaker Pro databases that will run on the Mac or in Windows.

Chapter 21: Developing Databases for Others

CHAPTER 21 CONCEPTS AND TERMS

- Templates that are "good enough" for you may not be good enough to market commercially or to give to others. You need to take many considerations into account when you are designing templates for distribution.
- When developing templates for the widest possible audience, you can easily add features that enhance ease of use and enable it to be used on a variety of monitors and display cards.
- Shareware and demo templates can use FileMaker Pro's password feature to restrict access to parts or features of the template.
- If you are interested in becoming a commercial template developer, you should investigate the possibility of becoming a member of the Claris Solutions Alliance and purchasing a copy of FileMaker Pro SDK.

freeware
Programs or templates that are offered to users free of charge.

gray scale
Objects and text are displayed in shades of gray rather than in color. As with color, most gray scale displays can support multiple numbers of gray shades (4, 16, and 256, for example).

monochrome
Refers to a two-color display (usually black-and-white).

shareware
Programs or templates that are distributed to users on the honor system. If you decide to keep the program or template, you must send the author the requested fee.

source code
In a computer program, source code is the set of instructions that makes a program do what it was intended to do. The instructions are in a human-readable form (usually in a programming language such as Pascal, C, BASIC, FORTRAN, or assembly language). In a FileMaker Pro template, script definitions, and Apple Event instructions may be considered the equivalent of source code.

stand-alone program
After FileMaker Pro SDK is used to compile a template, it becomes a program. It can be run on any Mac, and it does not require that a copy of FileMaker Pro be installed.

ět

Part VI
Appendixes

APPENDIX A

Installing FileMaker Pro 2

If you've just purchased FileMaker Pro 2, the first thing you'll want to do—after filling out the registration card, of course—is to install it on your Macintosh. Follow the instructions below.

System Requirements

To install and run FileMaker Pro 2.0 or 2.1, you need the following:

- ❖ Macintosh Plus or a more recent model

    FileMaker Pro will not run on a Mac 128K or Mac 512K.

- ❖ Macintosh system software, Version 6.0 or later

    FileMaker Pro also can run under AU/X 2.0 or later.

- ❖ At least 1MB of memory for System 6 and 2MB for System 7

    You should note that to run most Macintosh programs under System 7, 4MB of memory is usually considered a more realistic minimum.

    You can determine which version of system software you're using by choosing About This Macintosh or About the Finder from the Apple menu.

- ❖ An internal or external hard disk with at least 1.2MB of free space (if you are installing only the application) or 4MB of free space (for the complete installation including the Help file, utilities, and sample files)

- ❖ A printer that FileMaker Pro supports: the Apple ImageWriter, LaserWriter, and StyleWriter; the GCC Personal Laser Printer; the Hewlett-Packard DeskWriter and DeskJet; or a compatible printer.

Using the Installer

To install FileMaker Pro 2.0 or 2.1, you need to run a special Installer program. (If you've installed any version of the system software in the last few years, you'll recognize the Installer.) Using the Installer — rather than installing by hand — assures that FileMaker Pro and its support files will be correctly installed, uncompressed, and ready to run.

Begin by locking each of the FileMaker Pro master disks to protect them from inadvertent changes. (To lock a floppy disk, slide the tab in the upper-right corner of the disk so that the tiny window is open.)

Next, insert the disk labeled Install 1 and, if the disk window is not open, double-click the disk's icon. (If the disk contains a Read Me file, double-click the file's icon to view late-breaking news about the program and/or the installation process. After you read and, optionally, print the Read Me document, choose Quit from the File menu. You'll return to the desktop.)

Before you begin the installation, turn off any active antivirus program, system extensions (INITs), and control panels. Antivirus software, in particular, can interfere with the installation process. (Note that if you are running System 7, you can temporarily turn off these utilities and programs by holding down the Shift key as you start up or restart the Mac.) If you aren't sure how to turn off an antivirus utility, check its instruction manual. You also should quit other programs that you are running and close any open desk accessories and control panels.

Performing an Easy Install

When running the Installer, you need to do only the following:

❖ Decide whether to perform an Easy or Custom Install.

❖ Select the hard disk on which to install the software.

An Easy Install copies the program and all support files to the hard disk of your choice. A Custom Install copies only the program components that you select.

Most users should use Easy Install to install FileMaker Pro to the *start-up hard disk* (the one that contains the System Folder that is used to start up the Macintosh). If you think that you may want to perform a Custom Install or install FileMaker Pro on a disk other than the start-up hard disk, read the sections in this chapter called "Performing a Custom Install" and "Selecting a different hard disk" before proceeding with the installation.

To install FileMaker Pro by using Easy Install, do the following:

1. Double-click the Installer icon (see Figure A-1).

   The opening screen appears, as shown in Figure A-2.

Appendix A: Installing FileMaker Pro 2

 — Double-click to begin the installation

Figure A-1: The Installer program icon.

Figure A-2: The opening screen.

2. **To continue, click OK (or press Return or Enter).**

    The Easy Install dialog box appears (see Figure A-3). You use it to set installation options and install FileMaker Pro 2.

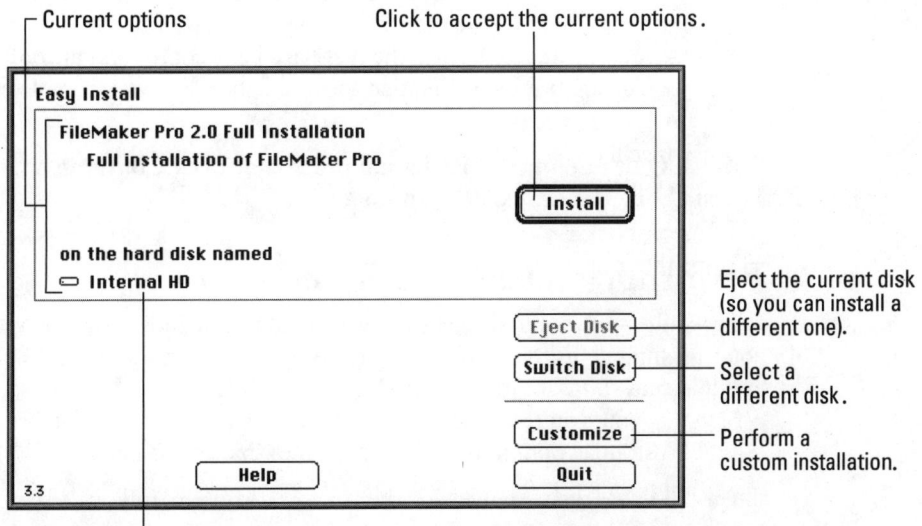

Selected hard disk

Figure A-3: This dialog box enables you to set installation options and install FileMaker Pro 2.

Part VI: Appendixes

The default procedure for the Installer is to perform an Easy Install on the startup hard disk. (An Easy Install is a complete installation of FileMaker Pro, its supporting files and utilities, and sample files.)

3. **Be sure that the correct hard disk is selected and then click Install.**

   Because you are installing FileMaker Pro 2 on the startup hard disk, Installer requires that any open programs, desk accessories, and control panels be shut down. If it detects that any of them are running, FileMaker displays the dialog box shown in Figure A-4. To quit any open programs, click Continue; to save files before you continue with the installation, click Cancel.

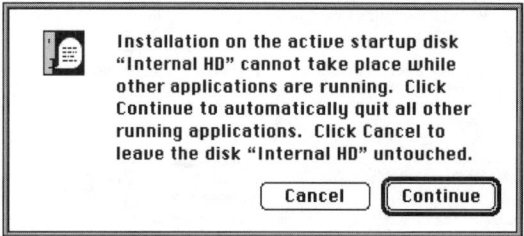

Figure A-4: Shut down current applications?

   If you click Cancel, the Installer will quit, and you can save the files. After saving them, quit the programs and begin again at Step 1.

4. **Insert the different floppy disks as they are requested.**

   Installer copies the files to the hard disk (see Figure A-5) and uncompresses them (or *unstuffs* them; see Figure A-6), indicating how much of the unstuffing process it has completed. After the files have been copied and uncompressed, you see a dialog box indicating that the installation has been completed (see Figure A-7).

5. **Click Quit to end the installation process or click Continue if you want to install FileMaker Pro 2 on another disk.**

Performing a Custom Install

Why would you want to do a custom installation? The most common reason is that you have limited disk space (this problem often occurs on PowerBooks, for example) and you want to make FileMaker Pro fit on the hard disk. Also, if you're certain that you won't need some of the files, such as the sample databases, you can use the Customize option to copy only the files that you *do* need.

To install FileMaker Pro by using the Customize option, follow these steps:

1. **Double-click the Installer icon.**

   The opening screen appears.

Appendix A: Installing FileMaker Pro 2

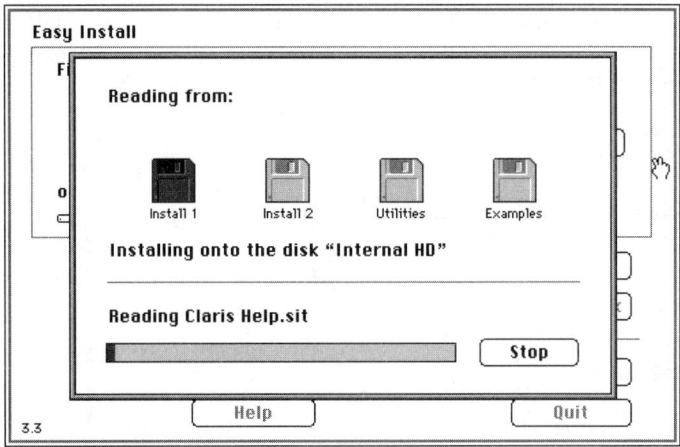

Figure A-5: The installation process.

Figure A-6: Many of the files that Installer copies to your hard disk are compressed. At the end of the installation process, they are automatically expanded to full size.

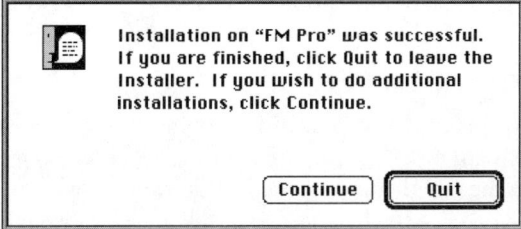

Figure A-7: The installation is complete.

2. **To continue, click OK (or press Return or Enter).**

3. **Click Customize.**

    In the screen that appears (see Figure A-8), you select program components from a scrolling list.

4. **Select the FileMaker Pro components that you want to install.**

    Click to select an individual item. Shift-click to select more than one item.

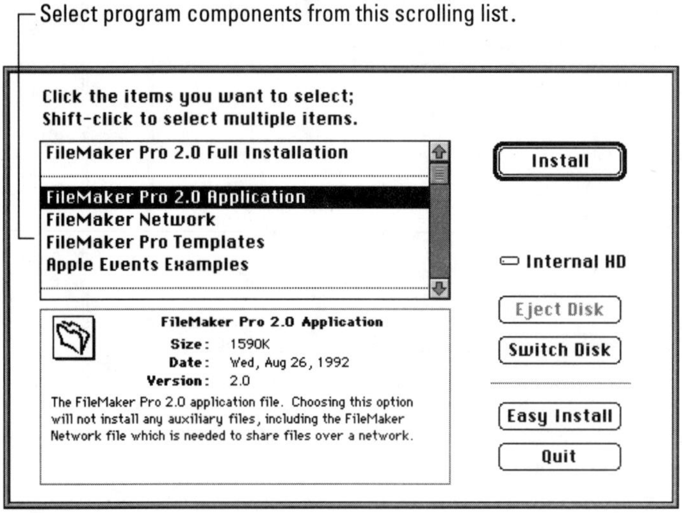

Figure A-8: Selecting custom options.

Before selecting the final set of items, click each one individually. A help message appears in the lower half of the screen. The message explains the purpose of each item, displays the item's version number, and shows how much disk space is required to install the item.

5. **Click Install.**

   As described for Easy Install, the Installer proceeds with the installation, requesting new floppy disks as they are needed.

Selecting a different hard disk

Regardless of whether you perform an Easy or Custom Install, you can install FileMaker Pro onto any hard disk that has sufficient space. To install it on a different hard disk from the one that is proposed, click Switch Disk (see Figure A-3). Each time you click the button, the Installer cycles through the mounted disk drives, displaying the name of the next one in line. Stop when you see the name of the correct drive. You should note, however, that selecting any drive other than the start-up hard disk will not result in a proper installation.

Here's the problem. During an installation to the start-up hard disk, critical Claris files are copied into the System Folder. Installer also makes sure that only the newest versions of these files are copied. For example, it prevents an older copy of

Appendix A: Installing FileMaker Pro 2

the Claris Help System from replacing a more recent one. When you choose a different hard disk, on the other hand, the Installer copies all files to that disk and completely ignores the start-up disk and System Folder. To complete the installation, you have to manually move the proper files into the Claris folder on the start-up hard disk.

Of the two solutions to this problem, one is easy and one is hard. The easy way is to install FileMaker Pro onto the start-up hard disk and then move the FileMaker Pro folder to the other hard disk. The hard way is to install directly onto the destination hard disk and then move the essential files back into the System Folder on the start-up hard disk. (Please note that the only good reason to attempt the hard method is because you have insufficient disk space on your start-up hard disk to allow you to use the easy method.)

To install FileMaker Pro on a different hard disk using the easy method, follow these steps:

1. **Use the Installer to install FileMaker on the start-up hard disk, as described in the section "Performing an Easy Install."**
2. **When the installation is done, drag the newly created FileMaker Pro folder from the start-up hard disk to the hard disk of your choice.**

   Doing so creates a copy of the folder and its contents on the destination drive.

3. **Drag the original FileMaker Pro folder from the start-up hard disk into the Trash.**
4. **Choose Empty Trash from the Special menu.**

   This action deletes the FileMaker Pro folder that was on the start-up hard disk.

To install FileMaker Pro on a different hard disk using the hard method, follow these steps:

1. **Double-click the Installer icon.**

   The opening screen appears.

2. **To continue, click OK (or press Return or Enter).**
3. **Repeatedly click Switch Disk until the destination hard disk is selected.**
4. **Perform an Easy or Custom Install as described previously.**

   Following the installation, a new folder named FileMaker Pro will appear on the hard disk that you selected in Step 3. Inside the folder, you'll see an array of files and folders like those shown in Figure A-9.

Part VI: Appendixes

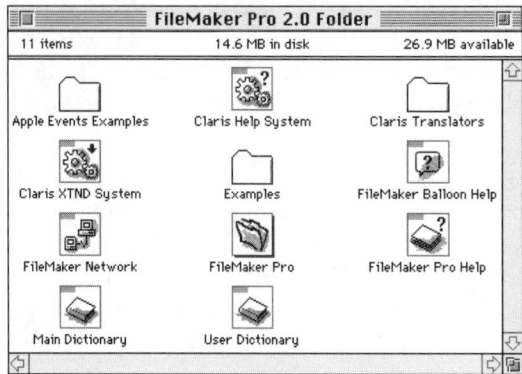

Figure A-9: The contents of the FileMaker Pro folder.

5. **Double-click the System Folder on the start-up hard disk.**

   The folder opens.

6. **Choose by Name from the View menu.**

7. **Look inside the System Folder window for a folder named Claris.**

   If you own a previous version of FileMaker Pro or have installed any other Claris programs, you should see the Claris folder.

   The remaining steps depend on whether the Claris folder already exists in the System Folder.

8. **If the System Folder does not contain a Claris folder, choose New Folder from the File menu.**

   A folder named untitled folder or Empty Folder is created for you.

9. **Rename the folder as Claris.**

10. **Open the FileMaker Pro folder on the hard disk where you just in stalled FileMaker Pro.**

11. **Within the FileMaker Pro folder, Shift-click to select all files and folders except the following:**

    ❖ FileMaker Pro

    ❖ Examples

    ❖ Apple Events Samples

12. **Drag the selected files onto the icon of the Claris folder.**

    This action copies the files into the Claris folder.

Appendix A: Installing FileMaker Pro 2

13. Go back to the FileMaker Pro folder and Shift-click to select the same items again.

14. Drag the items to the Trash, and then select Empty Trash from the Special menu.

— or —

8. If the System Folder contains a Claris folder, open the FileMaker Pro folder on the hard disk where you just installed FileMaker Pro and Shift-click to select the following files and folders:

   ❖ FileMaker Pro Help

   ❖ FileMaker Balloon Help

   ❖ FileMaker Network

9. Drag these items to the Claris folder inside the System Folder on the start-up hard disk.

   (If you see a message informing you that you're about to replace some older files, click OK.)

10. If you haven't already done so, open the Claris folder and set the View for both the FileMaker Pro and Claris folders to by Name.

    To set the View, click anywhere inside each folder, and choose by Name from the View menu.

11. Expand the two folder windows so that you can see the Last Modified date for each file and arrange the windows one above the other or side-by-side so you can see them both at the same time.

12. Visually compare the Last Modified dates for the following files in the two folders:

    ❖ Claris Help System

    ❖ Claris XTND System

    ❖ Main Dictionary

    If the date for any of these files in the FileMaker Pro folder is more recent than the date for the same file in the Claris folder, drag the new file into the Claris folder (replacing the old file). Similarly, if any of these files is not already in the Claris folder, drag it there.

13. If the Claris folder does not contain a User Dictionary file, drag that file to the Claris folder from the FileMaker Pro folder.

14. Open the Claris Translators folders on both disks and compare the Last Modified dates as you did in Step 12.

15. If any translator in the FileMaker Pro folder is more recent than the same file in the Claris folder, drag the new file into the Claris Translators folder inside the Claris folder (replacing the old file).

— or —

15. If any new translator file is missing from the start-up disk, drag it there.

— or —

15. If you do not find a Claris Translators folder within the Claris Folder, drag the entire folder there.

16. Return to the FileMaker Pro folder; drag all files and folders — except FileMaker Pro, Examples, and Apple Events Examples — into the Trash; and choose Empty Trash from the Special menu.

17. If you replaced any old translators with new ones in Step 15, open the Preferences folder (found inside the System Folder), drag the file named XTND Translator List into the Trash, choose Empty Trash from the Special menu, and then restart the Mac by choosing Restart from the Special menu.

The next time you launch FileMaker Pro 2 (or any other Claris program), the XTND Translator List will be rebuilt based on the new translators.

As you can see, the easy method is the preferred approach, and you should definitely use it if you have sufficient free space on the start-up hard disk — unless, of course, you *like* doing things the hard way.

Registering FileMaker Pro 2

The first time that you run your newly-installed copy of FileMaker Pro 2, a registration screen appears (see Figure A-10). Enter your name, company name (if you have one), and the serial number for the program (found on the product registration card). Press the Tab key to move from field to field. Click OK to begin the program or click Cancel to halt the registration and return to the desktop.

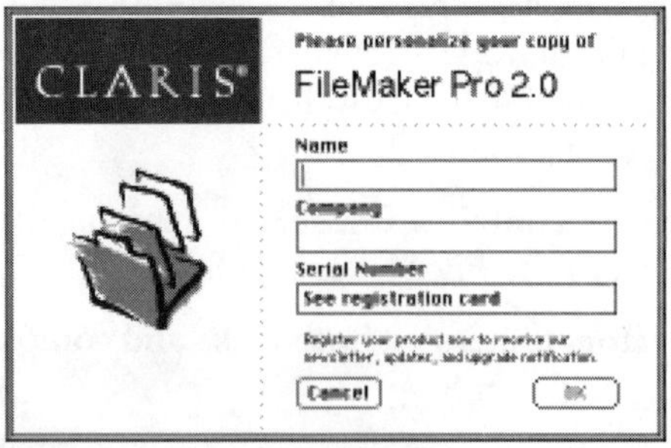

Figure A-10: The registration screen.

APPENDIX B

Installing FileMaker Pro Updates

If you're using FileMaker Pro 2.0 or an early release of 2.1, you can update to the current release by running a special FileMaker Pro Updater utility that you can find on and download from most major information services, such as America Online and CompuServe. Claris routinely issues new copies of their Updater — both to correct minor bugs and to add small enhancements to FileMaker Pro 2. This appendix explains how to install an update, using the FileMaker Pro 2.1v2 update as an example. Although the fixes and enhancements will obviously differ in later updates, the installation procedure should remain the same.

Updating to FileMaker Pro 2.1v2

The FileMaker Pro Updater folder for FileMaker Pro 2.1v2 contains two updater utilities. You use one to update your copy of FileMaker Pro to Version 2.1v2. The other is for installing the current MacIPX software (Version 1.1), and is intended only for users who are running FileMaker Pro on a Novell Netware network and are sharing databases among Macs and PCs that are running Microsoft Windows.

FileMaker Pro 2.1v2 includes the following changes and program enhancements:

❖ It corrects some Apple Events problems.

   These changes are of particular interest if you are using AppleScript or want to use FileMaker Pro scripts to interact with other programs.

❖ It adds a Match Fields button to the Import Mapping dialog box.

   This feature enables you to more easily import data from a FileMaker Pro database that is the same version as the one you are using. It automatically pairs up fields in the two files when they have the same names.

Part VI: Appendixes

See the file named Release Notes, 2.1v2, within the FileMaker Pro Updater folder for additional details. Refer to the file named Update Read Me if you also need to install the MacIPX software. Follow these steps to update to FileMaker Pro 2.1:

1. **Quit FileMaker Pro and any other programs that are currently running, and disable any antivirus utility that is installed on the Mac.**

2. **Open the FileMaker Pro Updater folder.**

    The file named Update Read Me contains instructions for installing both updates. You can read the file by double-clicking it. (Be sure to choose Quit when you are through looking at the file.)

3. **Open the FileMaker Pro 2.1v2 Updater folder (see Figure B-1) and double-click the icon marked FileMaker Pro 2.1v2 Updater.**

    The opening screen appears, as shown in Figure B-2.

Figure B-1: Contents of the FileMaker Pro 2.1v2 Updater folder.

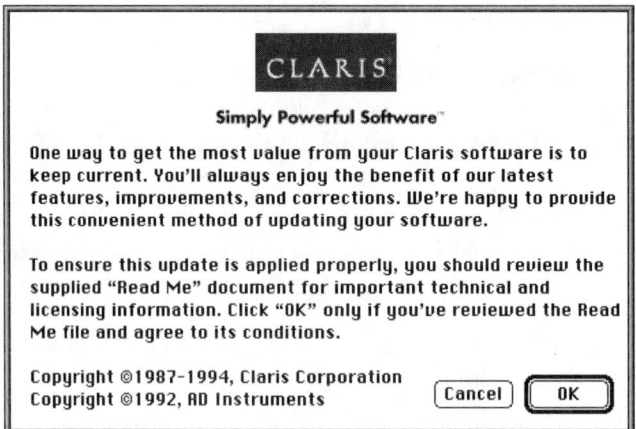

Figure B-2: The opening screen.

4. **After reading the information that is presented to you, click OK to continue with the update.**

    The UpdateMaker 2.2 dialog box appears (see Figure B-3).

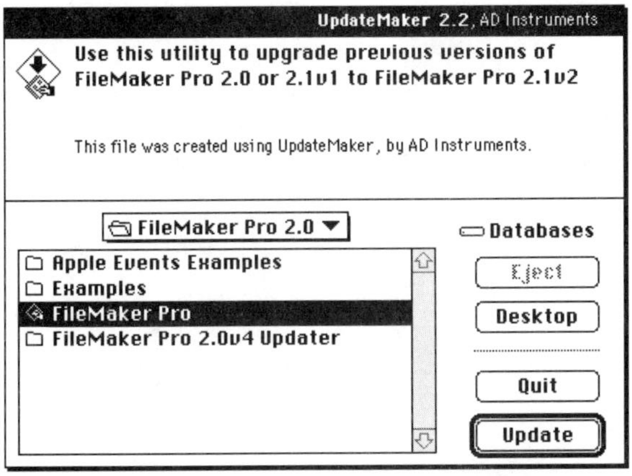

Appendix B: Installing FileMaker Pro Updates

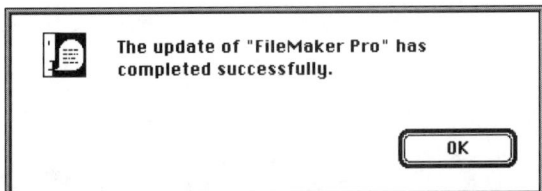

Figure B-3: Selecting the copy of FileMaker Pro to update.

UpdateMaker attempts to locate your copy of FileMaker Pro.

5. **If UpdateMaker doesn't automatically find and select your copy of FileMaker Pro, use normal navigation techniques to select it.**

6. **With your copy of FileMaker Pro selected in the file list, click Update.**

   The update proceeds. When it is done, you see the dialog box shown in Figure B-4, which tells you that the update is complete.

Figure B-4: The update is complete.

To protect your original copy of FileMaker Pro, Updater renames it as Old FileMaker Pro and leaves it in its original state.

7. **After running your newly updated copy of FileMaker Pro, you can safely delete Old FileMaker Pro by dragging it into the Trash and then choosing Empty from the Special menu.**

8. **To complete the installation, drag the file named FileMaker Network into the Claris folder (located in the System Folder on your start-up hard disk).**

   (If you are asked whether you want to replace a file with the same name, click OK.)

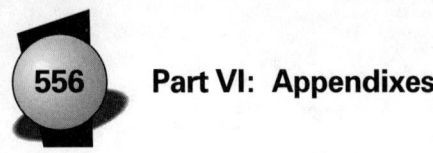

Part VI: Appendixes

APPENDIX C
Keyboard Shortcuts

This appendix contains keyboard equivalents for a large number of FileMaker Pro commands and actions. These commands are organized according to the various kinds of tasks that you may want to perform.

**Table C-1
General Commands**

Command	Key	Menu	Comments
Cancel any operation	⌘-Period (.)		
Clear	Clear		
Close	⌘-W	File	Also can click the close box on the document window
Define Fields	Shift-⌘-D	Select	
Help	⌘-?	Apple or Balloon Help	
Network Access	⌘-Option-O		Also available by clicking Network in the Open dialog box
Open	⌘-O	File	
Print	⌘-P	File	
Print direct	⌘-Option-P		Bypasses the Print dialog box
Quit	⌘-Q	File	

Table C-2
Mode-Selection Commands

Command	Key	Menu	Comments
Browse	⌘-B	Select	Also can be selected from the Mode pop-up menu
Find	⌘-F	Select	Also can be selected from the Mode pop-up menu
Layout	⌘-L	Select	Also can be selected from the Mode pop-up menu
Preview	⌘-U	Select	Also can be selected from the Mode pop-up menu

Table C-3
Window controls

Command	Key	Menu	Comments
Resize window	Shift-⌘-Z		
Scroll to top of current record or preview page	Home		
Scroll to bottom of current record or preview page	End		
Scroll up one page in current record	Page Up		
Scroll down one page in current record	Page Down		
Scroll to first record with View as List option checked	Home		
Scroll to last record with View as List option checked	End		
Scroll up one page	Page Up		
Scroll down one page	Page Down		
Select a record by number	Esc		
Status area (toggle on and off)	⌘-Option-S		Also available by clicking Status area control

Appendix C: Keyboard Shortcuts

Table C-4
Layout Mode Commands

Command	Key	Menu	Comments
Align Objects	⌘-K	Arrange	
Alignment	Shift-⌘-K	Arrange	
Align to Grid	⌘-Y	Layout	Works as an on/off toggle
Align to Grid off while resizing	⌘-drag a handle		Allows object sizes other than those provided by the grid
Align to Grid off while dragging	⌘-drag the object		Allows object positioning other than locations provided by the grid
Bring Forward	Shift-⌘-F	Arrange	
Bring to Front	⌘-Option-Shift-F	Arrange	
Constrain lines to vertical/horizontal	Option-drag		
Constrain ovals to circles and rectangles to squares	Option-drag		
Constrain resizing to vertical/horizontal	Option-drag a handle		
Date Format	Double-click a Date field		Same as choosing Date Format from Format menu
Delete Layout	⌘-E	Edit	
Display object's format	Double-click the object		See also specific object and field types listed in this table
Drag selected layout part past an object	Option-drag		
Duplicate Selection	⌘-D (or Option-drag the object)	Edit	
Field Borders	⌘-Option-B	Format	
Field Format	⌘-Option-F	Format	

(continued on the next page)

Table C-4 *(continued)*

Command	Key	Menu	Comments
Group	⌘-G	Arrange	
Lock	⌘-H	Arrange	
Move selected object one pixel	Arrow keys		Moves in direction of arrow key
New Layout	⌘-N	Edit	
Number Format	Double-click a Number field		Same as choosing Number Format from Format menu
Picture Format	Double-click a Picture/Sound Format field or graphic object		Same as choosing Picture from the Format menu
Redefine field on layout	Option-double click the field		
Reorder selected layout part	Shift-drag the part		
Reorient part labels	⌘-click label		
Reset default format based on current object	⌘-click object		
Select All	⌘-A	Edit	
Select objects by type	⌘-Option-A		An object must be selected first
Send Backward	Shift-⌘-J	Arrange	
Send to Back	⌘-Option-Shift-J	Arrange	
Square the object being resized	Option-(resize object)		
Text Format	Double-click a Text field or label		Same as choosing Text Format from Format menu
Time Format	Double-click a Time field		Same as choosing Time Format from Format menu
T-Squares	⌘-T	Layout	Works as an off/off toggle
Ungroup	Shift-⌘-G	Arrange	
Unlock	Shift-⌘-H	Arrange	

Appendix C: Keyboard Shortcuts

Table C-5
Text Formatting Commands

Command	Key	Menu	Comments
Align Center	⌘-\	Format⇨Align Text	Layout mode only
Align Left	⌘-[	Format⇨Align Text	Layout mode only
Align Right	⌘-]	Format⇨Align Text	Layout mode only
Bold	Shift-⌘-B	Format⇨Style	
Italic	Shift-⌘-I	Format⇨Style	
Justify	Shift-⌘-\	Format⇨Align Text	Layout mode only
Outline	Shift-⌘-O	Format⇨Style	
Plain	Shift-⌘-P	Format⇨Style	
Next larger point size	⌘->	Format⇨Size	
Next smaller point size	⌘<	Format⇨Size	
One point larger	⌘-Option->	Format⇨Size	
One point smaller	⌘-Option-<	Format⇨Size	
Select All	⌘-A	Edit	
Shadow	Shift-⌘-S	Format⇨Style	
Subscript	⌘-+	Format⇨Style	
Superscript	⌘— (hyphen)	Format⇨Style	
Underline	Shift-⌘-U	Format⇨Style	

Table C-6
Data Entry and Editing Commands

Command	Key	Menu	Comments
Copy	⌘-C	Edit	
Cut	⌘-X	Edit	
Delete next character	del		Located above arrow keys on Extended keyboard

(continued on the next page)

Table C-6 *(continued)*

Command	Key	Menu	Comments
Delete next word	Option-del		Located above arrow keys on Extended keyboard
Delete previous character	Delete (or Backspace)		
Delete previous word	Option-Delete (or Option-Backspace)		
Next field	Tab		
Nonbreaking space	Option-spacebar		
Paste	⌘-V	Edit	
Paste Current Date	⌘— (hyphen)	Edit⇨Paste Special	
Paste Current Time	⌘-;	Edit⇨Paste Special	
Paste Current User Name	Shift-⌘-N	Edit⇨Paste Special	
Paste without text style	⌘-Option-V		
Paste From Index	⌘-I	Edit⇨Paste Special	
Paste From Last Record	⌘-'	Edit⇨Paste Special	
Paste From Last Record, move to next field	Shift-⌘-'	Edit⇨Paste Special	
Previous field	Shift-Tab or Option-Tab		
Select All	⌘-A	Edit	
Spell Word	Shift-⌘-Y	Edit⇨Spelling	Option to Spell as you type must be on
Undo	⌘-Z	Edit	

Table C-7
Commands for Working with Records

Command	Key	Menu	Comments
Copy found set	⌘-Option-C		
Delete Record or Request	⌘-E	Edit	Command is mode-specific
Delete immediately	⌘-Option-E		Bypass confirmation dialog box
Duplicate Record or Request	⌘-D	Edit	Command is mode-specific
Find All	⌘-J	Select	
New Record or Request	⌘-N	Edit	Command is mode-specific
Next record, request, or layout	⌘-Tab		Command is mode-specific
Omit	⌘-M	Select	
Omit Multiple	Shift-⌘-M	Select	
Previous record, request, or layout	Shift-⌘-Tab or ⌘-Option-Tab		Command is mode-specific
Refind	⌘-R	Select	
Replace	⌘-=	Edit	
Sort	⌘-S	Select	

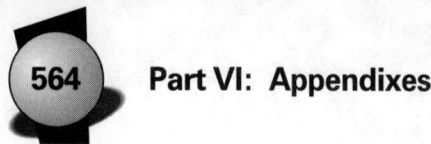

Part VI: Appendixes

APPENDIX D

Resources

In addition to using this book and the material that came with your copy of FileMaker Pro, you can turn to many other resources for more information about the product. These resources can help you accomplish any of the following:

- Learning new database programming techniques and tricks
- Working around or discovering solutions to problems that you have encountered in using FileMaker Pro
- Finding out about upcoming versions of FileMaker Pro, as well as utilities that enhance the program
- Purchasing ready-to-run FileMaker Pro templates that are designed for your particular business
- Hiring a specialist to create a database template especially for you
- Trying out free and inexpensive templates

Technical Support/General Help

If you need help with a problem that isn't explained in this book or in the *FileMaker Pro User's Guide*, the best source of information is the Claris Technical Support Department (408-727-9054 for Macintosh questions; 408-727-9004 for Windows questions). Have your FileMaker Pro serial number handy when you call.

If you have a fax machine or fax modem, you can obtain a wealth of technical information, troubleshooting notes, and programming tips by calling the Claris FAX AnswerLine. Dial 800-800-8954 from a touch-tone phone and request that a catalog of document listings be faxed to you. After you receive the catalog, you can call the same number to request that as many as five additional documents be faxed to you. (If you need more than five, you can make multiple calls.) Although the FAX AnswerLine is impersonal when you compare it to speaking with a live technical support representative, it does provide answers to many common (and not-so-common) FileMaker Pro questions. And, best of all, it's completely free!

If you have a modem inside your Macintosh or one connected to it, you can get in touch with Claris in several other ways. The company maintains technical support accounts on several major information services, including CompuServe (76004,1614), AppleLink (CLARIS.TECH), and America Online (Keyword: CLARIS; e-mail: CLARIS). If you search the special interest group sections offered by these information services, you will also find freeware, shareware, and demo versions of FileMaker Pro templates that you can download to your Mac and try out; sections devoted exclusively to troubleshooting and programming tips; and scores of dedicated users who — if you ask nicely — may be able to offer a solution to your FileMaker Pro problem *du jour*.

Custom Programming and Vertical Applications

Because FileMaker Pro is such a popular database program, you probably won't be surprised to learn that some individuals and companies make their living by providing after-market materials, such as database templates, custom programming, and training materials.

In April 1993, Claris began publishing a guide to third-party companies who provide FileMaker Pro solutions and who support other Claris products. You can obtain up to five free copies of the *Claris Solutions Alliance Directory* free from Claris by calling 408-727-8227, and you can purchase additional copies for a nominal fee.

If your intent is to provide some FileMaker Pro solutions of your own, you can currently join the Claris Solutions Alliance program for an annual fee of $249 by calling the same phone number.

News Sources

Currently, *MacWEEK* — published 48 times per year — is the only major Macintosh-industry newspaper. *MacWEEK* is unquestionably the best source of up-to-the-minute news about Macintosh software and hardware — whether still in the development stage or recently released — and it also provides information concerning corporate doings, changes in Apple's system software, and so on. It's a "must-have" for individuals who want to keep up with the goings-on in the Macintosh world.

Subscriptions to *MacWEEK* are free to qualified candidates (*MacWEEK* determines who qualifies), or you can purchase a subscription for $125 per year ($225 for Canada/Mexico; $350 international). To obtain a subscription application, contact

Customer Service Department
MacWEEK
c/o JCI
P.O. Box 1766
Riverton, NJ 08077-7366
609-786-8230

Magazines: Additional Sources of Tips

Several good computer magazines occasionally provide FileMaker Pro tips and techniques. In addition to featuring in-depth reviews of new versions of programs (such as FileMaker Pro), they occasionally publish brief user tips and feature articles that explain how to get more out of your copy of FileMaker Pro.

Macworld and *MacUser* magazines focus primarily on the needs of business users. *Macintosh Home Journal* caters more to novice users and the needs of individuals who have Macs at home. You should be able to pick up a copy of any of these magazines at a local newsstand, or you can contact the magazines directly for subscription information at the following addresses:

Macworld
Subscription Department
P.O. Box 51666
Boulder, CO 80321-1666
(800-288-6848 in U.S.; 303-447-9330 outside the U.S.)

MacUser
P.O. Box 56986
Boulder, CO 80322-6986
(800-627-2247 in U.S./Canada; 303-447-9330 all other countries)

Mac Home Journal
P.O. Box 468
Mt. Morris, IL 61054
(800-800-6542)

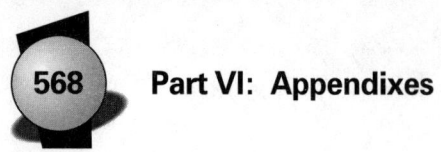

APPENDIX E

FileMaker Pro Limitations

Unless you have an extremely large project in mind or anticipate that several dozen network users will need access to your database simultaneously, you normally don't need to be too concerned about bumping into limitations imposed by FileMaker Pro. The most important restrictions are listed in Table E-1. For a complete list of limitations, refer to Appendix D of the *FileMaker Pro User's Guide*.

Table E-1
FileMaker Pro Limitations

Item	Limit or Specification
Maximum file size	32MB
Number of files open simultaneously	16 (System 7); 14 (System 6 with MultiFinder)
Number of records per file	Limited only by disk space or maximum file size (32MB)
Number of fields per record	Limited only by disk space or maximum file size (32MB)
Number of layouts per file	Limited only by disk space or maximum file size (32MB)
Maximum field name length	Up to 60 characters
Number of field repetitions	1,000 per field
Text field contents	Up to 64,000 characters per field
Maximum sort levels	Up to 10
Simultaneous network guests	Up to 25 per file with FileMaker Pro; 100 with FileMaker Pro Server
Import file formats	FileMaker Pro, tab-separated text, comma-separated text, DBF (dBASE III), DIF, WKS, BASIC, Merge, SYLK
Export file formats DIF, WKS, BASIC, Merge, SYLK, Edition	Tab-separated text, comma-separated text, DBF (dBASE III),
Picture file formats for import	EPS, TIFF, PICT, MacPaint, QuickTime movies

Don't be overly concerned if you aren't familiar with some of the file formats that are mentioned in the table. All you really need to know is that FileMaker Pro can readily handle most popular Macintosh database, spreadsheet, and graphic formats — at least the ones that you are most likely to need or want to use. For more information on supported file formats, see Chapter 16.

APPENDIX F

Installing and Using the Macworld FileMaker Pro 2.0/2.1 Bible Disk

Included with the FileMaker Pro Bible is a high-density (1.4MB) Macintosh disk that contains an assortment of hand-picked, ready-to-run FileMaker Pro database templates, technical information about the program, add-on utilities, and demos. This material is stored on the floppy as a series of self-extracting archives created with Compact Pro (Cyclos). When you double-click any archive, you are given an opportunity to choose a destination disk (usually a hard disk) for the expanded files. Then the files are automatically extracted from the archive and copied to the destination disk.

To use the *Macworld FileMaker Pro 2.0/2.1 Bible Disk*, you need the following:

❖ A high-density floppy drive (also known as an Apple SuperDrive)

❖ 3.3MB of free hard disk space (if you want to extract all files)

All Macs manufactured during the past several years come equipped with a SuperDrive. If you have an older Macintosh that can read and write only 800K floppies, on the other hand, find a friend, colleague, or dealer who will let you copy the files on the *Macworld FileMaker Pro 2.0/2.1 Bible Disk* to two 800K disks.

To extract files from the *Macworld FileMaker Pro 2.0/2.1 Bible Disk*, do the following:

1. **Insert the *Macworld FileMaker Pro 2.0/2.1 Bible Disk* into the Macintosh's floppy drive.**

    The disk window shown in Figure F-1 appears.

Part VI: Appendixes

Figure F-1: The contents of the disk.

2. **Locate an archive of interest.**

    The disk contain seven separate archives, some exposed and some within folders. You open folders to expose the archive of interest. The contents of the various archives are described later in this appendix.

3. **Double-click the archive's icon.**

    The extraction program launches, and the Select Destination Folder dialog box appears (see Figure F-2).

Figure F-2: Select a location for the extracted files.

4. **Use normal navigation procedures to select the disk and folder to which you want to copy the contents of the archive.**

    Be sure to select a disk other than the *Macworld FileMaker Pro 2.0/2.1 Bible Disk* — the hard disk, for example. Treat the *Macworld FileMaker Pro 2.0/2.1 Bible Disk* as you would treat any master disk. If you ever need to reinstall any of the software, you can use the original disk to do so.

5. **Click the Extract button.**

    The Extracting dialog box in Figure F-3 appears. The files are extracted one-by-one from the archive and are copied to the destination disk and folder that you selected in Step 4. When all files have been extracted, you are automatically returned to the desktop.

Appendix F: Installing and Using the FileMaker Pro 2.0/2.1 Bible Disk

Figure F-3: This dialog box shows the name of each file as it is extracted from the archive.

To extract the contents of additional archives, repeat Steps 2 through 5.

Disk Contents

The material on the *Macworld FileMaker Pro 2.0/2.1 Bible Disk* is divided into four categories:

❖ *FM Pro Bible archive:* Templates, databases, examples, and other materials created especially for this book.

❖ *Demos:* A folder containing a working demo of a commercial database template.

❖ *Freeware:* Templates and completed FileMaker Pro databases.

❖ *Shareware:* A pair of Macintosh utilities that you can use to enhance FileMaker Pro and document your templates.

Table F-1 provides a brief description of what is on the disk.

Table F-1
Disk Contents (by Archive/Folder Contents)

Disk Location	Filename(s)	Description
FM Pro Bible archive	Address Book _	Address Book template
FM Pro Bible archive	Buttons _	Menu-driven database containing buttons that you can use in your own templates
FM Pro Bible archive	Callable Help Example	Shows how to call a Help database from another database
FM Pro Bible archive	Mac Dictionary	Special user dictionary (spelling) with more than 300 Macintosh company names, product names, and industry terms
FM Pro Bible archive	Summary Field Tester	Test file that you can use to see how different Summary field functions work

(continued on the next page)

Part VI: Appendixes

Table F-1 *(continued)*		
Disk Location	**Filename(s)**	**Description**
FM Pro Bible archive	Want List	Template for recording stamp purchases and "wants"; easily modified for use with other collectibles
Demos _	AddressTrak Demo	Demo version of commercial contact management template
Freeware _	DayPlan 1.0	Set of interrelated templates that form a personal information management (PIM) system
Freeware _	FileMaker and Apple Events	Claris-provided explanations of using AppleEvents with FileMaker Pro
Freeware _	oTechInfo Pro 1.0v1r	Claris-provided tips and tricks for using FileMaker Pro
Shareware _	Acid Jazz 1.2v1	Utility that adds phone-dialing capabilities to FileMaker Pro (as well as to other programs) via AppleEvents
Shareware _	DOCMaker	Utility that enables you to create stand-alone documents that contain multiple fonts, color, and graphics

Note that the contributed software (found in the Demo, Shareware, and Freeware folders) often includes documentation that explains how best to use and install the necessary files. In general, you can use Apple's TeachText or SimpleText programs, or any other word processing program, to read the documentation. Be sure to look through this documentation before using any of the templates.

Protecting the Originals

Because FileMaker Pro automatically saves any change that you make to a database or template, making a backup copy of any template before you use it for the first time is always a good idea. All files on the *Macworld FileMaker Pro 2.0/2.1 Bible Disk* are stored as archives and cannot be run until after you have extracted them, so you don't have to worry about inadvertently changing the originals. If you need additional unaltered copies of any file, you can simply extract another copy from the master disk.

Floppy disks, however, occasionally develop errors that make them partially or totally unusable. The *Macworld FileMaker Pro 2.0/2.1 Bible Disk* is completely copyable, so you may want to make a backup copy of the disk, extract files from the backup, and put the original disk away for safekeeping.

Appendix F: Installing and Using the FileMaker Pro 2.0/2.1 Bible Disk

About Shareware and Freeware

If you're new to computing, the concept of shareware is probably new to you. *Shareware* programs or templates are computer products that you can "try before you buy." If you like the software, you're requested to send a fee to the author of the program. In order to insure the widest possible distribution of shareware, the authors frequently post copies of their masterpieces on computer information services (such as CompuServe and America Online), enabling users everywhere to download the programs, try them out, and decide for themselves whether the programs are useful.

Shareware is distributed on the honor system. Shareware authors are trusting you to do the right thing. That is, if you decide to keep and use their program or template, you should send them the small fee that's requested. If you decide that the program is not for you, on the other hand, you should remove it from your hard disk. Usually, shareware authors encourage you to share their programs with your friends and colleagues. See each program's documentation for any special distribution instructions that the authors may have included.

The *Macworld FileMaker Pro 2.0/2.1 Bible Disk* includes two shareware utilities: Acid Jazz and DOCMaker. In my opinion, these two utilities represent the best of the currently available shareware products for FileMaker Pro. Acid Jazz adds phone dialing capabilities to FileMaker Pro. DOCMaker enables you to create standalone documents, so it is the perfect tool for documenting your own shareware database templates. The following pages have reproductions of the registration forms for this pair of shareware products. If you decide to keep and use these utilities — as I hope you will — please fill out the appropriate form (or use the one included within the program files) and send the requested fee to the author.

Freeware, on the other hand, comes with few strings attached. No fee is requested for keeping and using a freeware program or template, but normally you must abide by the author's distribution instructions. For example, the author may allow you to give a copy of the program or template to friends on the condition that you make sure that the copy has not been altered in any way and that it contains all the original files — including the documentation.

Shareware Registration Forms

ACID JAZZ (1.2v1)
Acid Jazz is not a free program.

You may evaluate the program for a period not exceeding 15 days. If you want to continue using the program, please send $15 (US) to the following address:

P.O. Box 1645
San Jose, CA 95109-1645
U.S.A.

Make your checks payable to: Kevin J. Jundt

Acid Jazz is NOT public domain software. It is released as Shareware (Copyright © 1993, 1994 - Kevin J. Jundt), so feel free to distribute it to anybody who may find it useful as long as you do not charge for it. Acid Jazz cannot be distributed for profit without the prior written approval of the author. Unmodified copies of this document as well as all sample files MUST be included with the application whenever it is distributed.

Disclaimer

Use the Acid Jazz application at your own risk. The author (Kevin J. Jundt) makes no warranties, either express or implied, regarding the fitness of the Acid Jazz application for any particular purpose. The author claims no liability for data loss or any other problems caused directly or indirectly by use of the Acid Jazz application.

Requirements

Acid Jazz requires System 7.0 or greater. Older versions of the operating system do not support AppleEvents.

In order to use AppleScript to control Acid Jazz, you must have AppleScript installed on your machine. The included AppleScript example file is an AppleScript Script Editor document and will not open unless you have this application installed.

In order to control Acid Jazz from FileMaker Pro, you must have version 2.0 or greater (2.1 is recommended).

In order to control Acid Jazz from HyperCard, you must have version 2.1 or greater.

In order to control Acid Jazz from QuicKeys, you must have version 2.1 or greater. You must also have the Apple Events Extension installed.

In order to dial the phone using a modem, you must have a Hayes-compatible modem properly connected to your computer.

Appendix F: Installing and Using the FileMaker Pro 2.0/2.1 Bible Disk

DOCMaker v4.1
Order Form

Green Mountain Software
9404 Valley Lane
Huntsville, AL 35803-1326

Dear Green Mountain
Software Folks,

Please add me to your loyal shareware supporters list and send me the latest DOCMaker disk and the Users Manual.

Where I found DOCMaker _____

Name _____

Address _____

City _____ State _____ Zip _____

Country _____

Location	Quantity		Price (each)		Total
USA _____	_____	X	$25.00	=	$ _____
Out of USA	_____	X	$30.00	=	$ _____

Call or write for information on Group Discounts, Site Licenses, and Localized Versions.

❏ Send 1.4mb High Density Diskette

❏ Send 800k Double Density Diskette

ALL NON-USA Orders: Please pay with US Currency or Money Order. No personal checks please!

Send payment to:
    Green Mountain Software
    9404 Valley Lane
    Huntsville, Alabama 35803-1326   USA
    205 883-7910

Or you may order DOCMaker from the MacShareware Catalog service using your credit card. The number is:
    1-800 368-5195
for overseas orders:
    303 872-8651

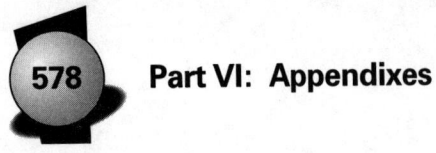

Part VI: Appendixes

Index

—A—

A (add or edit) tool, 87, 88
Abs function, 389
Access PC utility, 460
access privileges
    and data protection on networks, 512—523, 524
    for sharable templates, 535—537
Acid Jazz, 445, 576
active program, 52
addition, 369
Address Book database example
    choosing Phone Directory, 238
    defining fields, 98—103
    defining start-up actions, 142—144
    described, 95—97
    designing Data Entry layout, 104—122
    designing Report layout, 123—129
    in Find mode, 271
    in Preview mode, 354
    writing scripts, 129—142
Address Book—Graphics database, 105
alert boxes, 41, 44
algorithms for sorting, 295, 312
aliases
    creating, 67
    as icons, 29, 68
aligning
    keyboard shortcuts for, 559, 561
    objects in layouts, 112—118, 219
Alignment dialog box, 114, 127—128, 219

Align to Grid command, 112, 212
alphanumeric data, 268
ampersand (&) as text operator, 370
AND as text operator, 370
AND searches, 273
angle brackets (<>)
    as Find symbols, 274
    as logical operators, 369, 370
Apple Events, 446
    in scripts, 442—444
Apple menu, 29, 68, 91
    About the Finder/About This Macintosh commands, 51
    Chooser, for printer selection, 54—55, 344—346
    Control Panels command, for adjusting double-click speed, 37
    for selecting programs, 52
AppleScript, 445, 446
AppleShare, 460, 508
AppleTalk, 507
    See also networks
Application menu, 29, 31, 68, 91
applications, 30
    See also programs
archiving compressed copies of databases, 80, 471
arguments, 372, 401
arithmetic operators, 368—369
Arrange menu
    Alignment command, 114, 127, 219
    Bring Forward command, 220

Bring to Front command, 220
Group/Ungroup commands, 220
Lock/Unlock commands, 220
Send Backward command, 121, 220
Send to Back command, 220
Tab Order command, 220—221
arrow (cursor-control) keys, 246—247, 268
arrows for hierarchical menus, 87
ascending sort order, 293, 312
ASCII file formats, 448, 451, 463
Ask dialog box, 509
asterisk (*)
   as Find symbol, 275
   for multiplication, 369
   as wildcard, 278
Atan function, 399
at sign (@)
   as Find symbol, 275
   as wildcard, 278
auto-entry fields, 145, 169
auto-incrementation for data entry, 12, 24, 168—169
automatic backups, 81—84
automatic lookups, 503—504
Average function, 382—383
Average (summary function), 159—160
Avery labels, 199, 222, 362

— B —

BACKGROUNDER icons, 4
background printing, 359
Backspace key for deletion, 39
backups
   automatic, 81—84
   by duplicating databases, 79—81
   described, 91

importance of, 28, 61—62, 78—79
See also saving
balloon help, 29, 30, 68
baselines (underlining), 214
BASIC file formats, 449, 569—570
batch mode, 313
batteries and penalties of disk operations on laptops, 230
binary sorts, 295
bit-maps, 364
blank layouts, 193
body part of layouts, 19, 20, 190, 205—206, 222, 338
boldface, keyboard shortcut for, 129
bomb icon, 28
Book, 86, 88, 90
book icon, 239, 268
Boolean algebra, 401
bootable disks, 30
borders
   on Data Entry layout fields, 110
   on fields in layouts, 213—214
bounding boxes, 113
boxes around fields, 121
Browse mode
   changing magnification level, 243
   choosing layouts, 238—239
   choosing records within databases, 239—243
   creating new records, 244—245
   deleting records, 266
   described, 20, 85, 235—236
   editing records, 264—266
   entering data, 245—248
      copying and reusing data, 261—263
      current date/time/username, 263—264

Index

date fields, 250—251
number fields, 249
Picture/Sound fields, 251—257
QuickTime movies, 252, 255
special characters, 248
text fields, 249
time fields, 249
from value lists, 257—261
showing/hiding status area, 244
spell checking, 267
switching to, 77, 236
tools and functions for, 237—244
browsing, 19
bubble sorts, 295
buttons, 45, 68, 145, 486
assigning scripts to, 140—142, 439—440
caution on proliferation of, 530
importance of labeling, 532—533

—C—

caches, 74, 230, 232
Calculation fields, 151, 155, 187, 367—368
creating, 371—373
with expressions, 370—371
types of calculations, 368—370
See also functions
calculations
caution on field contents, 180
described, 12, 367
using time values, 167
canceling
scripts, 408
sort operations, 300
See also closing
CanOpener 2 (Abbott Systems), 329—331

capitalization functions, 395—396, 397
caret (%&) for exponentiation, 369
Change Password dialog box, 522
changing data. *See* editing
character sets and Windows/FileMaker file compatibility, 461
check boxes, 45, 68, 258
Chooser
described, 54—55, 68, 364
for printer selection, 54—55, 344—346
circles tool, 87, 88
keyboard shortcuts for, 559
Claris FAX AnswerLine, 566
Claris Folder, considerations for FileMaker Pro installation, 548—552
Claris Solutions Alliance, 526, 538, 566
Claris technical support, 565—566
Clear (script step), 432
clicking mouse, 32—33, 68
Clipboard, 39, 68, 341
clones
described, 70, 80, 91, 468, 471
See also templates
close boxes, 41, 42, 69
Close (script step), 436—437
closing
FileMaker Pro, 74
files/databases, 77
See also canceling
colors
choosing for sharable templates, 533—534
for Data Entry layout field text, 108—109
for graphics boxes, 121
tools for selecting, 87
and Windows/FileMaker file compatibility, 462

columnar layouts, 193, 195—199
columns for report layouts, 124
Command key combinations
    for entering special characters, 248
    for selecting options from menus, 36
    ⌘-; (semicolon) for current system time, 264
    ⌘-= for Replace command, 289
    ⌘-A for Select All command, 120
    ⌘-B for Browse command, 236
    ⌘-C for Copy command, 40, 265
    ⌘-D for Delete Request command, 281
    ⌘-D for Duplicate Request command, 279
    ⌘-D for duplicating files, 63
    ⌘-E for deleting records, 266
    ⌘-F for Find command, 131, 270
    ⌘-G for Group command, 220
    ⌘-H for Lock command, 220
    ⌘- - (hyphen) for current system date, 263
    ⌘-J for Find All command, 299
    ⌘-K for Align Objects command, 128
    ⌘-L for Layout mode, 120
    ⌘-M for Omit command, 285
    ⌘-N for creating new records, 90
    ⌘-N for New Layout command, 124
    ⌘-O for opening files or databases, 75
    ⌘-O for opening programs, disks or folders, 72, 73
    ⌘-Option-Esc for emergency quitting of programs, 28, 69
    ⌘-. (period) for canceling dialog boxes, 44
    ⌘-. (period) for canceling sort operations, 300
    ⌘-P for Print command, 355
    ⌘-Q for quitting, 74
    ⌘-R for Refind command, 280
    ⌘-S for Sort command, 132—133, 296
    ⌘-U for Preview command, 354
    ⌘-V for pasting, 40, 265
    ⌘-W for closing boxes, 41
    ⌘-W for closing files, 77
    ⌘-X for Cut command, 40, 265
    assigning scripts to, 408
commands, issuing, 84—86
comma-separated file formats, 449, 569—570
Comments field, 111
Common Ground utility (No Hands Software), 476
compressing/uncompressing files, 80, 486
concatenation of text fields, 370
constants, 401
copying
    databases, 79—81
    fields, 181
    files as backups, 63—66
    found sets, 287
    keyboard shortcuts for, 561—563
    and reusing data in Browse mode, 261—263
    scripts, 410
copyright/credits screens, 481
Copy (script step), 431, 438
Cos function, 399
cosine, 401
Count function, 383
Count (summary function), 160
cover pages, 60, 356
crashes, 28, 62, 69
creation date/time as auto-entry value, 166
creator name as auto-entry value, 166

Index 583

credits/copyright screens, 481
current field, 245, 268
current files (for lookups), 489, 499, 500, 505
current record, 268
cursor-control (arrow) keys, 246—247
customizing
    for automatic script execution, 83
    with document-specific preferences, 226—230
    FileMaker Pro installation, 547—548
    keyboard to avoid keystroke conflicts with FileMaker Pro, 86
    layouts, 16—17
    mouse double-click speed, 37
    with Preferences dialog box, 223—226
    with save-at-interval preferences, 230—231
Cut/Copy/Paste commands, 265
    keyboard shortcuts for, 561—562
Cut (script step), 431

—D—

Dantz Development Corp., 66
database (management) programs, 9, 13—14, 24
databases
    advantages, 12—13
    archiving, 80
    closing, 77
    creating, 75—77, 97—98
    creating templates of, 79—80
    defined, 9, 24
    designing, 97
    duplicating, 79—81

flat-file, 14
importance of backing up, 28, 61—62, 78—79
limitations of paper records, 11
linking. *See* lookups
navigating, 239—243
opening, 75
opening at program startup, 73
performing scripts at opening of, 227, 230
relational, 14—15
spell checking, 267
See also Address Book database example; Browse mode; files; Layout mode; *Macworld FileMaker Pro 2.0/2.1 Bible Disk*
data conversion expressions, 376—379
data entry
    auto-incrementation, 12
    keyboard shortcuts for, 561—562
    See also Browse mode; field entry options; layouts for data entry
data protection on networks, 512—523
data transfers. *See* exporting; importing
data type. *See* field types
Date fields, 151, 152—153, 250—251
Date Function, 379
date-stamping, 128—129
date/time, 263—264
    in searches, 281—282
    setting for background printing, 360
DateToText function, 377
Day function, 380
DayName function, 380
DayofYear function, 380
DBF file formats, 449, 569—570
defaults

advantages of setting, 12
described, 24, 232
setting for text formats in Layout mode, 123
Define Button dialog box, 140—141, 439, 531
Define Fields dialog box, 76—77, 98, 148—149, 493
Define Fields (script step), 437
Define Groups dialog box, 517—518
Define Parts dialog box, 104, 206—207
Define Passwords dialog box, 514, 515, 517
Define Scripts dialog box, 133—134, 405
Degrees function, 399—400
Delete Found Set (script step), 426
Delete key, 265
Delete Record/Request (script step), 426
deleting
　caution on, 78
　fields, 182—184, 216
　files, 32
　Find requests, 280—281
　found sets, 288
　layout parts, 210—211
　layouts, 204—205
　records, 266
　scripts, 410
　text, 39—40
descending sort order, 293, 312
desktop
　backing up files from, 63—64
　described, 28—32, 69
　starting FileMaker Pro from, 71—73
devices, removable, 31
dialog boxes

changing order of fields listed in, 152
described, 41, 43—46, 69
for file handling, 46—50
modal and modeless, 46
dictionaries. *See* spell checking
DIF file formats, 449, 569—570
dimmed menu options as unavailable, 35, 85, 237, 268
directories. *See* folders
disk caching, 74, 230, 232
DiskFit Direct (Dantz Development Corp.), 66
DiskFit Pro (Dantz Development Corp.), 66
disk icons, 29, 31
disks
　aliases of, 67
　mounted, 31
　selecting from dialog boxes, 47—50
　See also floppy disks; hard disks; *Macworld FileMaker Pro 2.0/2.1 Bible* Disk
division, 369
DOCMaker utility (Green Mountain Software), 476, 577
document icons, 72
dogcow icon, 364
DOS Mounter, 460
dot-matrix printers, 362, 364
dots (ellipses ...), 87
double-clicking mouse, 36—37, 69
downloading, 471, 474, 486
dragging objects with mouse, 34, 69, 113
Duplicate Record/Request (script step), 426
duplicates
　creating. *See* copying
　searching for, 283

—E—

Easy Install dialog box, 545
editing
   described, 12
   Find requests, 279—280
   keyboard shortcuts for, 561—562
   picture/sound fields, 264
   records, 264—266
   scripts, 411—412
   text, 38—41
   undoing changes, 78
   See also spell checking
Edition File formats, 449
Edit menu
   Clear command, 265
   Copy command, 40
   Cut/Copy/Paste commands, 265
   Delete Found Set command, 288
   Delete Request command, 281
   Duplicate Layout command, 203, 339
   Duplicate Record command, 263
   Duplicate Request command, 279
   New Layout command, 124, 192, 194
   New Record command, 80
   Paste command, 40
   Paste Special submenu, 217
      Current Date/Time/User Names commands, 263
      Date Symbol command, 129
      From Index command, 262
      From Last Record command, 263
      Page Number command, 129
   Relookup command, 179, 187, 501—502
   Replace command, 289
   Select All command, 120
   Spelling submenu, 267, 315—317
      Install Dictionaries command, 319, 325, 326
      Spell Word command, 318
      User Dictionary command, 322, 323
   Spell Options command, 314
   Undo command, 78
ejecting floppy disks, 49
ellipses (...), 87
   as find symbol, 275, 281
emergency quit command (⌘-Option-Esc), 28, 69
End (script step), 435
enlarging/reducing printed output, 57
Enter Browse Mode (script step), 425
Enter Find Mode (script step), 425
Enter key for accepting dialog box default option, 44, 101
Enter Preview Mode (script step), 425
Entry Options dialog box, 165, 494
envelope layouts, 193, 202—203
envelopes, 56
EPSF file formats, 255
EPS file formats, 255, 569—570
equal sign (=)
   as Find symbol, 165, 275
   as logical operator, 369, 370
Exact function, 393—394
exclamation point (!), as Find symbol, 165, 275
Exp function, 390
exponentiation, 369
exporting
   cleaning up data, 456—457
   described, 13, 24, 333, 447, 456, 463
   file formats for, 456, 569—570

how to perform, 457—458
for mail merges, 458—459
to PCs, 459—462
user dictionaries for spell checking, 324
See also importing
Export Records (script step), 421—422
expressions, 370—371, 401
creating, 370—371
Extended Columnar layouts, 193, 196
Extend function, 383
external and internal scripts, 438, 441, 446
external hard disks, 25—26

—F—

Farallon PhoneNET Talk, 507
Field Borders dialog box, 11
field entry options
auto-entry, 163, 165—169
data validation, 163, 170—174
setting for existing fields, 184
value lists, repeats and lookups, 163, 174—180
Field Format dialog box, 175—176, 215, 216
Field Format for "Comments" dialog box, 111
field functions, 382—386
fields, 10, 24
adding to layouts, 211
auto-entry, 145
borders, 110
borders for, 213—214
creating from scratch, 180—181
defining, 98—101, 148—149, 180—181, 184—185

defining order of advance for Tab key, 220
deleting, 182—184, 216
design considerations, 150
duplicating, 181
fill patterns, 214—215
labels for, 108
moving/sizing in layouts, 212—213
naming, 148—149
renaming, 182
repeating, 172—174, 187, 216
required, 12, 24, 102, 145, 187
scroll bars on, 216
searching for empty, 282
setting data entry options, 101—103
sizing, 112, 126
sorting, 298—300
text attributes, 107—109
Text type versus Numeric, 99—100
underlining with baselines, 214
See also data entry; finding; layouts; sorting
Field tool, 87, 88
field types, 12, 24, 145, 147—149, 187
Calculation, 155
changing, 184—186
Date, 152—153
Number, 151
Picture and Sound, 154—155
Summary, 156—163
Text, 150
Time, 153
file dialog box, 72, 75, 79, 91
file formats, 448, 463, 569—570
for sound and graphics, 255

FileMaker Pro
   advantages, 1
   basics, 15—23
   home and business uses for, 22—23
   limitations, 569—570
   quitting, 74
   starting, 71—74
   upgrades from previous versions, 1, 6
   version upgrade features, 553—555
FileMaker Pro installation
   with Customize option, 546—548
   with Easy Install option, 544—546
   hard disk selection, 548—552
   and registration, 552
   system requirements, 543
   for version upgrades, 553—555
FileMaker Pro SDK (Solutions Development Kit), 526, 538
FileMaker Pro Server, 508
File menu, 34, 77
   Access Privileges submenu,
      Define Groups command, 517
      Define Passwords command, 514
   Change Password command, 522
   Close command, 41, 77
   for creating word lists from existing databases, 327
   Duplicate command, 63
   Import/Export command, 218, 251—252, 451, 454, 457
   Make Alias command, 67
   New command, 75—77, 97, 148
   Open command, 72, 73, 75
   Page Setup command, 55—59
   Preferences command, 142—143, 223—225
      Document options, 226—229
      General options, 225—226
      Memory options, 78, 230—231
      for specifying automatic script execution, 83
   Print command, 53, 59—61, 355—359
   Quit command, 27, 74, 77
   Save a Copy As command, 48, 65, 79—81, 468
   Save As command, 64
file names and Windows/FileMaker Pro file compatibility, 462, 512
files
   aliases of, 67
   deleting, 32
   described, 29, 30, 69
   FileMaker Pro's size limitations, 569
   handling with dialog boxes, 46—50, 51
   importance of backing up, 28, 61—62, 78—79
   opening, 50
   opening at program startup, 73
   saving, 48, 77—78
   See also databases
file transfers. *See* exporting; importing
Fill control tool, 87, 88
Fill palette, 88
fill patterns for layout fields, 214—215
Find All (script step), 423
Find Businesses script, 136—137
Find button, 89, 90
Find feature, 12, 24
Find Friends script, 137

finding, 291
    Address Book database example scripts for, 130—138
    advantages of displaying multiple records, 240
    advantages over browsing, 269
    and found sets, 266, 272
    with lookups, 15, 24, 176—180
Find mode
    described, 20, 270
    finding non-matches, 284—285
    finding records, 272—273
    matching all criteria, 172, 273—275
    matching one criterion or another, 275—276
    matching special items, 281—285
    matching text, 276—278
    switching to, 270
    Symbols pop-up menu, 271
    tools and functions available in, 89—90, 270—271
    See also found sets
Find Omitted (script step), 424—425
Find Relatives script, 137—138
Find requests, 272
    advantages of sorting after, 305
    creating, 279
    deleting, 280—281
    form, 131—132
    repeating and editing, 279—280
Find symbols, 165, 274
flat-file databases, 14, 24
floppy disks
    ejecting, 49
    icons for, 29, 31
focus of programs, 1

folders
    aliases of, 67
    described, 29, 30, 69
    selecting from dialog boxes, 47—50
fonts
    keyboard shortcuts for, 561
    selecting for Data Entry layout fields, 108
    tips for speeding printing, 362
    and Windows/FileMaker Pro file compatibility, 461—462, 512
footers. *See* headers/footers
Format menu
    Field Borders command, 11, 213, 214, 215
    Field Format command, 111, 175—176, 216
    Text Format command, 109
formatting
    headers/footers, 127—129
    See also layouts
forms, advantages of FileMaker Pro for creating, 22
found sets, 266, 272, 291, 341
    copying, 287
    deleting, 288
    omitting records from, 285—287
    replacing values in, 288—290
    sorting, 337
    swapping omitted records with, 287
Fraction of Total (summary function), 162
freeware, 539, 573, 575—577
function keys, 36
functions, 373—375, 401
    data conversion, 376—379
    date, 379—382
    field, 382—386

Index 589

financial, 386—388
IF, 388—389
mathematical, 389—393
text, 393—397
time, 397—399
trigonometric, 399—400
FV function, 386—387

—G—

Go to Field (script step), 417
Go to Layout (script step), 415
Go to Next Field (script step), 417—418
Go to Next Record/Request (script step), 416—417
Go to Previous Field (script step), 418
Go to Previous Record/Request (script step), 417
Go to Record/Request (script step), 415—416, 438
grand summaries, 19, 206, 338
graphics
    adding to Data Entry layouts, 105—106
    adding to layouts, 217—218
    grouping/ungrouping, 121—122
    and Windows/FileMaker Pro file compatibility, 462
grayed-out (dimmed) menu options as unavailable, 35, 85, 237, 268
gray scale, 539
grouping/ungrouping
    graphics, 121—122
    keyboard shortcuts for, 560
    of objects, 145
    objects in layouts, 220
    of records, 12

groups of network users, 517—520
guests on networks, 508, 511—512, 524

—H—

handles, 33, 105, 113, 116, 145
hard disks
    backing up, 61—62, 66
    external, 25—26
    required for FileMaker Pro, 543
    selecting for FileMaker Pro files, 548—552
    start-up, 544
    SuperDrives, 460
head crashes, 62
header records, 449, 462
headers/footers
    deleting, 104
    described, 19, 20, 190, 206
    formatting, 127—129, 338, 339
    on help screens, 480
    See also title headers/footers
help
    from balloon help, 29, 30, 68
    designing systems for, 473—485
    using buttons to summon, 478
Help (script step), 436
hierarchical menus, 35, 69, 87, 91
high ASCII file formats, 463
highlighting of menu commands, 85
Home (script step), 435
hosts on networks, 508—510, 524
Hour functions, 397—398

— I —

I-beam mouse pointer, 32
icons
    bomb, 28
    book, 239, 268
    described, 32
    in dialog boxes, 45
    for documents, 72
    dogcow, 364
    for FileMaker Pro, 72
    floppy disks, 29, 31
    Installer, 544—545
    for page orientation for printing, 57
    for SCSI port, 26
    Trash can, 29, 32
    used in this book, 4
IF function, 388—389
ImageWriter printers, 57, 358
    Page Setup for, 351—352
    Print dialog box for, 358
    selecting, 345
importing
    and cleaning up data, 450—454
    described, 13, 24, 333, 447—448, 463
    file formats for, 448—449, 450
    graphics into layouts, 218
    how to perform, 454—455
    from PCs, 459—462
    user dictionaries for spell checking, 323—324
    See also exporting
Import Movie dialog box, 252
Import Movie (script step), 421
Import Picture dialog box, 252
Import Picture (script step), 420
Import Records (script step), 419—420
incrementing serialized data entry, 168—169
indexes
    by field type, 151, 187
    by phrases or groups of values, 245
    described, 268
    entering data from, 262
    importance in searches, 278, 295
ink-jet printers, 362, 364
insertion point, 245, 268
Installer icon, 544—545
installers, 471
installing
    dictionaries for spell checking, 318
    Macworld FileMaker Pro 2.0/2.1 Bible Disk, 571—573
    templates, 466
    See also FileMaker Pro installation
internal and external scripts, 438, 441, 446
international sort orders, 307
Int function, 390
invalid data, 284, 291

— J —

Jundt, Kevin J., 576

— K —

keyboard
    entering special characters, 248
    function keys, 36
    navigating from, 246—247
    and utility keystroke conflicts with FileMaker Pro, 86
    See also Command key combinations

Index

keyboard shortcuts
    for data entry and editing, 561—562
    described, 36, 69, 85, 91
    for editing, 265
    for handling records, 563
    list of, 557—563
    for selecting mode of operation, 558
    for text formatting, 561
    for use in Layout mode, 559—560
    for window control, 558
    See also Command key combinations
Key Caps (Apple Computer), 248
KeyFinder (Norton Utilities for Macintosh), 248
keystroke equivalents, 84

—L—

label layouts, 193, 199—202
labels
    for layout fields, 108
    for layout parts, 210
    for use in laser printers, 362
Label Setup dialog box, 200
landscape (sideways) orientation, 57, 126, 352
Langth function, 394
laptops and penalties of disk operations, 230
laser printers, 362, 364
LaserWriter printers, 58—59
    Page Setup for, 347—350
    Print dialog box for, 356
    selecting, 345
Last function, 383—384
launching. *See* starting

Layout menu
    Align to Grid command, 112, 212
    Define Parts command, 208
    Layout Options command, 119, 198
    Ruler Lines command, 212
    Rulers command, 212
    Ruler Settings command, 212
    Show submenu, Text Objects command, 112
    Size command, 112
    T-squares command, 212
Layout mode
    described, 20, 85, 91, 190
    keyboard shortcuts for, 559—560
    switching to, 191
    tools available in, 86—89
Layout Options dialog box, 119, 198
layout parts, 145
Layout pop-up menu, 86, 88
layouts, 16—20, 145, 189, 222, 268
    copying, 203
    creating, 192—193, 205—221
    for data entry,
        adding boxes, 121
        aligning/moving objects on, 112—118
        designing, 104—106
        grouping/ungrouping graphics, 120—122
        naming, 119
        setting field attributes, 107—111
        setting field dimensions, 112—118
        sizing, 120
        specifying as start-up screen, 142—143
    for data entry standard, 103
    deleting, 204—205

deleting parts, 210—211
for help topics, 478—480
limitations on number per file, 569
moving parts around, 209—210
predefined, 193—194
    columnar, 195—199
    for envelopes, 202—203
    for labels, 199—202
    standard, 194—195
rearranging, 203—204
renaming, 204
for reports,
    designing, 123—126, 335, 336
    duplicating, 339
    headers and footers, 127—129
    selecting recrods to include, 335, 337
    sizing fields, 126
    transferring between databases, 339—340
specifying for start-up, 226—227
See also fields
leading/trailing summaries, 206
Left function, 394
line tool, 87, 88, 217
line width control tool, 88, 89
list views, 268
list windows, 42
Ln function, 390
logarithmic functions, 390—391
Log function, 391
logical operators, 369
lookup fields, 489, 505
lookup files, 489, 500, 505
lookups, 15, 24, 176—180, 187
    automating, 503—504
    defining fields for, 493—497
    example, 497—500
    how to perform, 489—493, 501—502
    restrictions, 500
Lookup Value dialog box, 177—178, 491, 494
low ASCII file formats, 463
Lower function, 394

—M—

Macintosh computers
    models required to run FileMaker Pro, 543
    penalties of disk operations on laptops, 230
    shutting down, 27—28
    starting up, 25—26
Macintosh Home Journal magazine, 567
MacPaint file formats, 255, 569—570
macros. *See* scripts
MacUser magazine, 567
MacWEEK newspaper, 566—567
Macworld FileMaker Pro 2.0/2.1 Bible Disk
    Address Book database example, 97
    Address Book—Graphics, 97
    button examples on, 439
    Callable Help Example, 482
    Customers database, 489, 497
    list of contents, 573—574
    Movies database, 489, 497, 498
    New Buttons FM database, 528
    protecting, 574
    scripts on, 406
    Video Invoice database, 489, 497
Macworld magazine, 567
magazines with FileMaker Pro tips, 567

Index

magnification level, 243

mail merges, 448, 458—459, 463

marquees, 33

master passwords, 513, 524

matches. *See* finding

match fields (for lookups), 489, 490, 492, 496—497, 505

mathematical functions, 389—393

mathematical operations. *See* calculations

Max function, 384

Maximum (summary function), 161

memory
    required for FileMaker Pro, 543
    See also RAM (random access memory)

menu bars, 29, 69

menus
    described, 69
    designing for sharable templates, 527—532
    dimmed as unavailable, 237, 268
    grayed-out items on, 35, 85
    hierarchical, 35, 69, 87, 91
    option selection with keyboard shortcuts, 36
    option selection with mouse, 34—35
    pop-up, 35, 45, 69, 91
    sample for navigation in sharable databases, 530—531
    selecting commands from, 84—86

Merge file formats, 449, 569—570

Middle function, 395

Min function, 384

Minimum (summary function), 161

minus sign (-) for subtraction, 369

Minute function, 398

modal and modeless dialog boxes, 46, 69

mode selector, 88, 89

modes of operation
    described, 20—21, 91
    keyboard shortcuts for selecting, 558

modes of operations, *See also* Browse mode; Find mode; Layout mode

Mod function, 391

modification date/time, as auto-entry value, 166

modifier keys, 85, 91, 248, 268

modifier name, as auto-entry value, 166

monochrome monitors, 539

Month function, 381

MonthName function, 381

Moov file formats, 255

mounted disks, 31

mouse
    for dragging objects, 113
    how to use, 32—37
    for menu option selection, 85

Mouse control panel, 37

mouse pointer, 29, 32, 69

moving
    cursor (navigating) in Browse mode, 239—243
    cursor with arrow keys, 246—247
    fields in layouts, 212—213

MultiFinder
    described, 69, 91
    for switching programs, 51—52

multiplication, 369

— N —

naming
    copies of databases, 80

databases, 76
fields, 148—149, 182
layouts, 119, 204
scripts, 81, 404—405, 409
navigating
in Browse mode, 239—243
with cursor-control (arrow) keys, 246—247
Network Access dialog box, 511
networks
access privileges and data protection, 512—523
with AppleShare, 460
hosts and guests, 508—512
PC-Mac file sharing, 460—462, 512
printers, 345, 346
running FileMaker Pro on, 507—508
New File dialog box, 75—76
New Layout dialog box, 119
New Record/Request (script step), 425—426
Newton MessagePads, data transfers, 462
NOT as text operator, 370
NPV function, 387
nudging objects, 114
Number fields, 151, 249
true number-only fields, 515
numbering pages. *See* page numbering
NumToText function, 377

Omit Multiple dialog box, 285
Omit Multiple (script step), 424
Omit (script step), 424
omitting, 291
online services
posting templates as shareware, 526
for technical help, 566
Open dialog box, 46, 47
opening
databases, 75
described, 91
files, 50
Open (script step), 436
operators, 401
Option-Command key combinations
Option-⌘-B for Field Borders command, 213, 214
Option-⌘-F for Field Format command, 216
Option-dragging objects with mouse, 113
Options for Field "xxx" dialog box, 156—157
Options for Summary Field "xxx" dialog box, 158
OR as text operator, 370
OR searches, 275
Order of Operations, 401
orientation of pages for printing, 57, 126, 352
ovals tool, 87, 88, 217
keyboard shortcuts for, 559

— O —

objects
aligning/moving on Data Entry layouts, 112—118
pasting, 41
Omit check box, 89, 90

— P —

Page Down (script step), 435
page numbering, in footers, 129
Page Setup dialog box, 56, 346—352
Page Setup (script step), 422

Index

Page Up (script step), 435
palettes, 86—90
paper size, 56, 57, 352
paper source, 60, 356
Part Definition dialog box, 207
part label controls, 88, 89
parts of layouts, 19
Part tool, 87, 88
passwords, 524
   changing, 517, 522—523
   creating, 513—516
   distributing, 516
   for group access privileges, 517—520
   opening databases with no-password option, 521—522
   for sharable templates, 535—537
Paste Current Date (script step), 428
Paste Current Time (script step), 428
Paste Current User (script step), 428—429
Paste From Index (script step), 427
Paste From Last Record (script step), 427—428
Paste Literal (script step), 429, 438
Paste (script step), 431—432
pasting text or objects, 40—41
Pattern palette, 88
Pause/Resume Script step, 414
pausing scripts, 413
PC Exchange utility, 460
PCs, importing/exporting from/to, 459—462
pen control tool, 87, 88
Perform Find (script step), 423
Perform Script step, 414, 438, 441
Phone Directory, 123
   creating preliminary layout, 124—126

Phone Directory by Company script, 139—140
Phone Directory by Last Name script, 138—139
PhoneNET Talk, 507
PICT file formats, 255, 569—570
Picture fields, 151, 154—155, 187, 251—257
   sorting on, 311
pictures
   advantages in databases, 154
   file formats supported for import, 569
Pi function, 391
"pipe" character (|), as text operator, 370
pitch, horizontal and vertical (for labels), 201
platforms, 524
   and cross-platform transfers, 459—462
plus sign (+) for addition, 369
PMT function, 387
pop-up lists, 258
pop-up menus, 35, 45, 69, 91
portrait orientation, 57
Position function, 395
PowerBooks
   battery saving with automatic saves, 78
   caution on shortened battery life with FileMaker Pro, 74
precedence (Order of Operations), 401
preferences, 232
Preferences dialog box, 83, 142—143, 145, 223—225
   Document options, 226—229
   General options, 225—226
   Memory options, 78, 230—231
   for specifying automatic script execution, 83
Preview mode, 20, 123, 354—355, 364

Print dialog box, 60
    for ImageWriter printers, 358
    for LaserWriter printers, 356
    for StyleWriter printers, 357
printer drivers, 69, 344, 364
printers
    ImageWriters, 57
    LaserWriters, 58—59
    on networks, 345, 346
    required for FileMaker Pro, 543
    selecting, 56, 344—346
    setup from Page Setup dialog box, 56, 346—352
    specifying at printtime, 357
    tips for saving wear and tear, 362
printing, 53—61, 337—338
    in background, 359—361
    with landscape (sideways) orientation, 57, 126, 352
    previewing documents in Preview mode, 20, 337—338, 354—355
    with Print command, 355—359
    with PrintMonitor, 359—361
    report preparation, 343, 353—355
    setting up for, 343, 344—352
    troubleshooting, 344, 363
    and Windows/FileMaker Pro file compatibility, 462
    See also reports
PrintMonitor, 359—361
Print (script step), 422—423
privileges for access on networks, 512—523
programs
    described, 29, 30
    launching with aliases, 67
    for making backups, 66
    switching between, 50—53
Proper function, 395—396

protecting
    data on networks, 512—523
    sharable templates, 535—537
Pruden, Max, 438
publishing (Edition File) formats, 449
PV function, 387—388

— Q —

question mark (?), as Find symbol, 275
QuicKeys with scripts, 444—445, 446
QuickTime movies, 252, 255, 446, 512, 569—570
QUICK TIPS icons, 4
Quit (script step), 438
quitting FileMaker Pro, 74
quotation marks
    "smart" quotes option, 226
    straight quotes, 228
    as text operators, 370

— R —

Radians function, 400
radio buttons, 45, 69, 258
    selecting multiple with Shift-clicking, 176
raising to power (exponentiation), 369
RAM (random access memory), 230, 232
    saving with disk caching, 74
Random function, 392
range checking, 12, 24
ranges of records, 368
readers, 476, 486
Read Me files, 475, 486
records
    defined, 9, 24

deleting, 266
editing, 264—266
keyboard shortcuts for handling, 563
limitations on number per file, 569
order of storage, 293
ranges of, 368
unsorting, 310
rectangles tool, 87, 88, 217
keyboard shortcuts for, 559
Refind (script step), 423—424
registration of FileMaker Pro, 552
relational databases, 14—15, 24
relation functions (lookups), 176—180
relookups, 501—502, 503—504, 505
Relookup (script step), 430
removable devices, 31
renaming scripts, 409
reordering layout parts, 209
Repeating fields, 172—174, 187, 216
sorting on, 311
Replace function, 396
Replace (script step), 429
reports
described, 13, 335
designing, 335—336, 338—339
in Preview and Layout modes, 20
See also layouts for reports; printing
required fields, 12, 24, 102, 145, 187
Reserialize (script step), 430
reset switch, 28, 69
resources, 333, 513, 524
technical support, 565—566
restoring original (unsorted) record order, 310
Retrospect (Dantz Development Corp.), 66
Return-delimited text files, 453—454

Return key for accepting dialog box default option, 44, 101
Right function, 396
root, 325, 333
rounded rectangles tool, 217
Round function, 392
Ruler Lines command, 212
Rulers command, 212
Ruler Settings command, 212
running programs. *See* starting

— S —

Save a Copy As dialog box, 65
Save a Copy As (script step), 437
Save As dialog box, 46, 47, 64
saving
databases as templates, 467—468
files, 48, 91
files on laptops, 230
See also backups
scaling of printed output, 57
schedule creation with FileMaker Pro, 22
scientific notation (exponentiation), 369
screen
script for refreshing, 413
size considerations for sharable template design, 535
Script Definition dialog box, 81—83, 134, 405
ScriptMaker
described, 403
how to use, 404—406
scripts
advantages, 91, 129, 145, 230, 232, 403, 446

with AppleScript, 445
assigning to buttons, 140—142
assigning to Command key combinations, 408
attaching to buttons, 439—440
for automatic backups, 81—84
for automatic lookups, 503—504
canceling, 408
copying, 410
defining, 130—131
deleting, 410
editing and debugging, 411—412
executing from within other scripts, 441—442
for finding and sorting within Address Book database example, 131—140
for help topics, 482—485
internal and external, 438, 441
listing in Scripts menu, 407
naming, 81, 404—405, 409
performing at opening of databases, 227, 230
with QuicKeys, 444—445
renaming, 409
running, 408
for sorting, 311
step reference, 412—438
using Apple Events, 442—444
utilizing user name, 226
Scripts menu
Define Button command, 140, 439, 531
listing scripts in, 407
ScriptMaker command, 81—84, 91, 404
scroll arrows, bars and boxes, 42, 43, 69
on layout fields, 216

scrolling
keyboard shortcuts for, 558
through lists of files, 51
SCSI (Small Computer System Interface) devices
described, 26, 69
turning on/off, 26, 27
searching. *See* finding
Seconds function, 398
Select All (script step), 433
selecting
with mouse, 33—35
output device, 54
paper size, 56, 352
printers, 56, 344—346
programs, 52
text, 38—39
selection tool (arrow pointer), 87, 88
Select menu
Browse command, 236
Define Fields command, 148, 372, 493
Find All command, 299
Find command, 131—132, 270
Find omitted command, 287
Layout command, 119
Omit command, 285
Omit Multiple command, 285
Preview command, 123, 354
Refind command, 280
Sort command, 132—133, 296
View as List command, 242
semi-relational programs, 15, 24
Send Apple Event (script step), 435—436, 442

Index

serializing data entry, 168—169
Set Field Order dialog box, 125, 196—197
shareware, 539, 573, 575—577
    posting templates as, 526
Shift-Command key combinations
    Shift-⌘-B for boldface, 129
    Shift-⌘-D for Define Fields command, 148, 372
    Shift-⌘-F for Bring Forward command, 220
    Shift-⌘-G for Ungroup command, 122
    Shift-⌘-H for Unlock command, 220
    Shift-⌘-J for Send Backward command, 121, 220
    Shift-⌘-M for Omit Multiple command, 285
    Shift-⌘-Y for Spell Word command, 318
Shift-dragging objects with mouse, 113
Shift-Option-Command key combinations
    Shift-Option-⌘-F for Bring to Front command, 220
    Shift-Option-⌘-J for Send to Back command, 220
Shift-Tab key for moving to next field, 247
Show All script, 136
Show Companies script, 131
Show Individuals script, 135
Shut Down, 69
sideways (landscape) orientation, 57
Sign function, 392
SimpleText, 476
sine, 401
Sin function, 400
Single Page Form layouts, 193
size boxes, 41, 42, 69
Size windoid, 112, 115, 209

sizing
    fields, 112
    fields in layouts, 212—213
    layouts, 120
slashes (//)
    as date symbol, 129
    as find symbol, 275
slash (/) for division, 369
"smart" quotes option, 226
SND 1/SND 2 file formats, 255
Sort by Company, Last Name script, 138
sorting, 12, 24, 293, 312
    Address Book database example scripts for, 138—140
    canceling, 300
    creating sort order, 296—298, 304—305, 312
    fields in dialog box lists, 152
    layouts in pop-up menu lists, 203—204
    with modified sort specifications, 303—305
    in multiple sorts, 303
    on international sort orders, 307
    on one field, 298—300
    on several fields, 301—303
    on summary fields, 308—310
    for reports, 335, 337, 353—354
    restoring original record order, 310
    with value lists, 306
Sort Records dialog box, 132—133, 296—298
Sort (script step), 418
Sound control panel, 256
Sound fields, 151, 154—155, 187, 251—257
    sorting on, 311
Sound Record dialog box, 253

source code, 539
special characters, 248
Special menu, 27
    Set Startup command, MultiFinder option, 52
    Shut Down command, 26, 27, 69
Specify Apple Event dialog box, 443
Specify Event dialog box, 444
Specify External Script dialog box, 441
Specify Field Order for Export dialog box, 457
Specify Field Order for Import dialog box, 419
Spell Check Found Set (script step), 433
spell checking, 267, 313
    adding words to dictionaries, 321—324
    creating spelling lists from existing databases, 326—329
    extracting dictionaries from other programs, 329—331
    help files, 482
    installing dictionaries, 318—320
    on request, 315—318
    on the fly, 313, 318
    restricting to subsets of fields, 332
    setting options, 313—314
    with stand-along programs, 331
    user dictionaries, 317, 320—326
Spell Check Record (script step), 433
Spell Check Selection (script step), 433
Spelling Options dialog box, 314
spreadsheet imports, 451—453
Sqrt function, 393
squares tool, 87, 88
    keyboard shortcuts for, 559
stand-alone documents, 476—477, 486
stand-alone programs, 526, 538, 539
Standard Deviation (summary function), 161
standard layouts, 103, 193, 194—195
starting FileMaker Pro, 71—74
starting up your Macintosh, 25—26
start-up actions, 142, 230
start-up hard disks, 544
stationery documents, 48, 70, 80
status area
    controls, 88, 89
    specifying show/hide preference, 227, 244
StDev function, 385
STEP-BY-STEP icons, 4
step reference for scripts, 412—438, 446
straight quotes, 228
StyleWriter printers
    Page Setup for, 350
    Print dialog box for, 357
    selecting, 345
subdirectories. *See* folders
submenus, 35, 91
sub-scripts, 441, 446
sub-summaries, 19, 20, 206, 339
subtraction, 369
Sum function, 385
Summary fields, 151, 156—163, 187, 206, 222
    exporting, 458
    sorting, 308—310
Summary function, 385—386
summary parts of layouts, 190, 206
SuperDrives, 460
SYLK file formats, 449, 569—570
symbols. *See* icons
Symbols menu, 89, 90
Symbols pop-up menu, 271

System Folder
    considerations for FileMaker Pro installation, 548—552
    described, 29, 30
system software, 51, 69
    required for FileMaker Pro, 543

—T—

Tab key for moving to next field, 247
Tab Order dialog box, 220—221
tab-separated text, 448, 451, 569
Tan function, 400
tangent, 401
tape drives, iconless, 31
TeachText, 475—476
technical support, 565—567
templates
    of databases, 79—80, 467—469
    described, 48, 70, 465, 469—470
    installing, 466
    restricting access to features of, 537
    sharable,
        advantages, 525—526
        buttons and scripts for accessibility, 532—533
        color considerations, 533—534
        designing menus, 527—532
        with FileMaker Pro SDK (Solutions Development Kit), 526, 538
        protecting from changes, 535—537
        screen size considerations, 535
text
    adding to layouts, 217
    deleting, 39—40
    editing, 38—41
    pasting, 40—41

text boxes, 45, 70
Text fields, 150, 249
text files, 329, 333
Text Format dialog box, 109
text formatting
    keyboard shortcuts for, 561
    selecting defaults for, 123
text functions, 393—397
text-only files, 486
text operators, 370
TextToDate function, 377—378
TextToNum function, 378
TextToTime function, 378
Thunder 7 (BaseLine Publishing), 331
TIFF file formats, 255, 569—570
time, setting for background printing, 360
Time fields, 151, 153, 249
Time function, 398—399
time functions, 397—399
TimeToText function, 379
title bars, 41, 42, 70
title headers/footers, 19, 206, 338
Today function, 381
Toggle Status Area (script step), 434
Toggle View-As-List (script step), 434
Toggle Window (script step), 434, 438
Tool palette, 87, 88
tools
    described, 86—90
    setting preferences for defaults, 225
Total (summary function), 159
trailing/leading summaries, 206, 339
transferring files. *See* exporting; importing
Trash icon, 29, 32
trigger fields (for lookups), 178, 187, 489, 490, 492, 496—497, 505

trigonometric functions, 399—400
Trim function, 397
troubleshooting problems caused by incorrect shutdown procedures, 27
truncation of data on reports, 126
T-squares command, 212
turning on/off
    Macintoshes, 27—28, 69, 74
    SCSI devices, 26, 27

—U—

uncompressing files, 486
underlining. *See* baselines (underlining)
undoing edits, 78
Undo (script step), 431
unique fields, 187
unsorting records, 310
Unsort (script step), 418
unstuffing, 546, 547
UpdateMaker dialog box, 554—555
Upper function, 397
User Dictionary dialog box, 322
    See also spell checking
user interface, 1
user name prompts, 225
utilities
    for hard disk repairs, 28
    and keystroke conflicts with FileMaker Pro, 86

—V—

validation of data entry, 170—180
value lists, 174—176, 187, 257—261, 312
    sorting with, 306
values
    replacing through searches, 288—290
    searching for greater/less than, 282—283
variables, 401
"Verify that the field value is..." options, 170—172
vertical lines (|), as text operators, 370
View Index dialog box, 262
View menu, sort options, 284
virus protection with backups, 62

—W—

"watch" icon mouse pointer, 32
WeekofYear function, 381—382
wildcard characters in searches, 278
windoids, 41, 42, 145, 209
windows, 29, 30, 41—43
    setting preferences for size, 227
WKS file formats, 449, 569—570

—Y—

Year function, 382

—Z—

zoom boxes, 41, 42, 70
zoom controls, 88, 89
zooming
    in Browse mode, 243
    in Find mode, 270
zoom percentage box, 88, 89

Notes

Notes

Notes

Notes

Notes

Notes

Notes

Notes

Notes

Notes

Notes

Notes

Notes

Notes

IDG BOOKS' ... FOR DUMMIES™ SERIES

Find out why over 6 million computer users love IDG'S ...FOR DUMMIES BOOKS!

"I laughed and learned..."
Arlene J. Peterson, Rapid City, South Dakota

DOS FOR DUMMIES,™ 2nd EDITION
by Dan Gookin

This fun and easy DOS primer has taught millions of readers how to learn DOS! A #1 bestseller for over 56 weeks!

ISBN: 1-878058-75-4
$16.95 USA/$21.95 Canada
£14.99 UK and Eire

 INTERNATIONAL BESTSELLER!

WINDOWS FOR DUMMIES™
by Andy Rathbone

Learn the Windows interface with this bestselling reference.

ISBN: 1-878058-61-4
$16.95 USA/$21.95 Canada
£14.99 UK and Eire

#1 BESTSELLER!

THE INTERNET FOR DUMMIES™
by John Levine

Surf the Internet with this simple reference to command, service and linking basics. For DOS, Windows, UNIX, and Mac users.

ISBN: 1-56884-024-1
$19.95 USA/$26.95 Canada
£17.99 UK and Eire

 NATIONAL BESTSELLER!

PCs FOR DUMMIES,™ 2nd EDITION
by Dan Gookin & Andy Rathbone

This #1 bestselling reference is the perfect companion for the computer phobic.

ISBN: 1-56884-078-4
$16.95 USA/$21.95 Canada
£14.99 UK and Eire

 NATIONAL BESTSELLER!

MACs FOR DUMMIES,™ 2nd Edition
by David Pogue

The #1 Mac book, totally revised and updated. Get the most from your Mac!

ISBN: 1-56884-051-9
$19.95 USA/$26.95 Canada
£17.99 UK and Eire

#1 MAC BOOK

WORDPERFECT FOR DUMMIES™
by Dan Gookin

Bestseller Dan Gookin teaches all the basics in this fun reference that covers WordPerfect 4.2 - 5.1.

ISBN: 1-878058-52-5
$16.95 USA/$21.95 Canada/£14.99 UK and Eire

 NATIONAL BESTSELLER!

UPGRADING AND FIXING PCs FOR DUMMIES™
by Andy Rathbone

Here's the complete, easy-to-follow reference for upgrading and repairing PCs yourself.

ISBN: 1-56884-002-0
$19.95 USA/$26.95 Canada

 NATIONAL BESTSELLER!

WORD FOR WINDOWS FOR DUMMIES™
by Dan Gookin

Learn Word for Windows basics the fun and easy way. Covers Version 2.

ISBN: 1-878058-86-X
$16.95 USA/$21.95 Canada
£14.99 UK and Eire

 NATIONAL BESTSELLER!

WORDPERFECT 6 FOR DUMMIES™
by Dan Gookin

WordPerfect 6 commands and functions, presented in the friendly ...For Dummies style.

ISBN: 1-878058-77-0
$16.95 USA/$21.95 Canada
£14.99 UK and Eire

 NATIONAL BESTSELLER!

1-2-3 FOR DUMMIES™
by Greg Harvey

Spreadsheet guru Greg Harvey's fast and friendly reference covers 1-2-3 Releases 2 - 2.4.

ISBN: 1-878058-60-6
$16.95 USA/$21.95 Canada
£14.99 UK and Eire

 NATIONAL BESTSELLER!

EXCEL FOR DUMMIES,™ 2nd EDITION
by Greg Harvey

Updated, expanded—The easy-to-use reference to Excel 5 features and commands.

ISBN: 1-56884-050-0
$16.95 USA/$21.95 Canada
£14.99 UK and Eire

 NATIONAL BESTSELLER!

UNIX FOR DUMMIES™
by John R. Levine & Margaret Levine Young

This enjoyable reference gets novice UNIX users up and running—fast.

ISBN: 1-878058-58-4
$19.95 USA/$26.95 Canada/ £17.99 UK and Eire

 NATIONAL BESTSELLER!

For more information or to order by mail, call 1-800-762-2974. Call for a free catalog! For volume discounts and special orders, please call Tony Real, Special Sales, at 415-312-0644. For International sales and distribution information, please call our authorized distributors:

CANADA Macmillan Canada 416-293-8141

UNITED KINGDOM Transworld 44-81-231-6661

AUSTRALIA Woodslane Pty Ltd. 61-2-979-5944

IDG BOOKS' ... FOR DUMMIES™ SERIES

"DOS For Dummies is the ideal book for anyone who's just bought a PC and is too shy to ask friends stupid questions."

MTV, Computer Book of the Year, United Kingdom

"This book allows me to get the answers to questions I am too embarrassed to ask."

Amanda Kelly, Doylestown, PA on Gookin and Rathbone's PCs For Dummies

"If it wasn't for this book, I would have turned in my computer for a stereo."

Experanza Andrade, Enfield, CT

CORELDRAW! FOR DUMMIES™
by Deke McClelland

This bestselling author leads designers through the drawing features of Versions 3 & 4.

ISBN: 1-56884-042-X
$19.95 USA/$26.95 Canada/17.99 UK & Eire

QUICKEN FOR WINDOWS FOR DUMMIES™
by Steve Nelson

Manage finances like a pro with Steve Nelson's friendly help. Covers Version 3.

ISBN: 1-56884-005-5
$16.95 USA/$21.95 Canada
£14.99 UK & Eire

NATIONAL BESTSELLER!

QUATTRO PRO FOR DOS FOR DUMMIES™
by John Walkenbach

This friendly guide makes Quattro Pro fun and easy and covers the basics of Version 5.

ISBN: 1-56884-023-3
$16.95 USA/$21.95 Canada/14.99 UK & Eire

MODEMS FOR DUMMIES™
by Tina Rathbone

Learn how to communicate with and get the most out of your modem — includes basics for DOS, Windows, and Mac users.

ISBN: 1-56884-001-2
$19.95 USA/$26.95 Canada
14.99 UK & Eire

1-2-3 FOR WINDOWS FOR DUMMIES™
by John Walkenbach

Learn the basics of 1-2-3 for Windows from this spreadsheet expert (covers release 4).

ISBN: 1-56884-052-7
$16.95 USA/$21.95 Canada/14.99 UK & Eire

NETWARE FOR DUMMIES™
by Ed Tittel & Denni Connor

Learn to install, use, and manage a NetWare network with this straightforward reference.

ISBN: 1-56884-003-9
$19.95 USA/$26.95 Canada/17.99 UK & Eire

OS/2 FOR DUMMIES™
by Andy Rathbone

This fun and easy OS/2 survival guide is perfect for beginning and intermediate users.

ISBN: 1-878058-76-2
$19.95 USA/$26.95 Canada/17.99 UK & Eire

QUICKEN FOR DOS FOR DUMMIES™
by Steve Nelson

Manage your own finances with this enjoyable reference that covers Version 7.

ISBN: 1-56884-006-3
$16.95 USA/$21.95 Canada/14.99 UK & Eire

WORD 6 FOR DOS FOR DUMMIES™
by Beth Slick

This friendly reference teaches novice Word users all the basics of Word 6 for DOS

ISBN: 1-56884-000-4
$16.95 USA/$21.95 Canada/14.99 UK & Eire

AMI PRO FOR DUMMIES™
by Jim Meade

Learn Ami Pro Version 3 with this friendly reference to the popular Lotus word processor.

ISBN: 1-56884-049-7
$19.95 USA/$26.95 Canada/17.99 UK & Eire

WORDPERFECT FOR WINDOWS FOR DUMMIES™
by Margaret Levine Young

Here's a fun and friendly reference that teaches novice users features and commands of WordPerfect For Windows Version 6.

ISBN: 1-56884-032-2
$16.95 USA/$21.95 Canada/14.99 UK & Eire

For more information or to order by mail, call 1-800-762-2974. Call for a free catalog! For volume discounts and special orders, please call Tony Real, Special Sales, at 415-312-0644. For International sales and distribution information, please call our authorized distributors:

CANADA Macmillan Canada 416-293-8141

UNITED KINGDOM Transworld 44-81-231-6661

AUSTRALIA Woodslane Pty Ltd. 61-2-979-5944

IDG's bestselling ...For Dummies Quick Reference Series provides a quick and simple way to remember software commands and functions, written in our down-to-earth, plain English style that guides beginners and experts alike through important commands and hidden troublespots.

Fun, Fast & Cheap!

"Thanks for coming up with the simplest idea ever, a reference that you really can use and understand."

Allison J. O'Neill, Edison, NJ

ILLUSTRATED COMPUTER DICTIONARY FOR DUMMIES™
by Dan Gookin, Wally Wang, & Chris Van Buren

This plain English guide to computer jargon helps with even the most techie terms.

ISBN: 1-56884-004-7
$12.95 USA/$16.95 Canada
£11.99 UK & Eire

WINDOWS FOR DUMMIES™ QUICK REFERENCE
by Greg Harvey

The quick and friendly way to remember Windows tasks & features.

ISBN: 1-56884-008-X
$8.95 USA/$11.95 Canada
£7.99 UK & Eire

DOS FOR DUMMIES™ QUICK REFERENCE
by Greg Harvey

A fast, fun, and cheap way to remember DOS commands.

ISBN: 1-56884-007-1
$8.95 USA/$11.95 Canada
£7.99 UK & Eire

WORDPERFECT FOR DOS FOR DUMMIES™ QUICK REFERENCE
by Greg Harvey

With this guide you'll never have to worry about deciphering cryptic WordPerfect commands again!

ISBN: 1-56884-009-8
$8.95 USA/$11.95 Canada
£7.99 UK & Eire

WORD FOR WINDOWS FOR DUMMIES™ QUICK REFERENCE
by George Lynch

End your stress over style sheets, mail merge, and other pesky Word features with this quick reference. Covers Word 2.

ISBN: 1-56884-029-2
$8.95 USA/$11.95 Canada

1-2-3 FOR DUMMIES™ QUICK REFERENCE
by John Walkenbach

Keep this quick and easy reference by your desk and you'll never have to worry about forgetting tricky 1-2-3 commands again!

ISBN: 1-56884-027-6
$8.95 USA/$11.95 Canada
£7.99 UK & Eire

EXCEL FOR DUMMIES™ QUICK REFERENCE
by John Walkenbach

A fast, fun and cheap way to remember bothersome Excel commands.

ISBN: 1-56884-028-4
$8.95 USA/$11.95 Canada
£7.99 UK & Eire

WORDPERFECT FOR WINDOWS FOR DUMMIES™ QUICK REFERENCE
by Greg Harvey

The quick and friendly "look-it-up" guide to the leading Windows word processor.

ISBN: 1-56884-039-X
$8.95 USA/$11.95 Canada/£7.99 UK & Eire

For more information or to order by mail, call 1-800-762-2974. Call for a free catalog! For volume discounts and special orders, please call Tony Real, Special Sales, at 415-312-0644. For International sales and distribution information, please call our authorized distributors:

CANADA Macmillan Canada 416-293-8141   UNITED KINGDOM Transworld 44-81-231-6661   AUSTRALIA Woodslane Pty Ltd. 61-2-979-5944

IDG BOOKS' MACWORLD SERIES

"This is the perfect book for the way I think and work."
Chris Rosa, Operations Mgr., South San Francisco, CA on Macworld Macintosh SECRETS

"Lon obviously 'sweated the details' when he compiled this excellent System 7.1 reference. The unusually detailed table of contents makes finding items a breeze!"
James F. Steffy, Syscon Corporation, Middletown, RI, on Lon Poole's Macworld Guide To System 7.1, 2nd Edition

"This was an incredible book. It truly made learning Word 5.0 quick and easy."
William Levin, Chicago, IL, on Macworld Guide to Microsoft Word 5

"An essential guide for anyone managing Mac networks."
Reese Jones, President, Farallon Computing, on the Macworld Networking Handbook

"Should've put it in a wire binder, I am continuously using it!"
Ric Rivera, Seattle, WA on Lon Poole's Macworld Guide To System 7.1, 2nd Edition

MACWORLD GUIDE TO SYSTEM 7.1, 2nd EDITION
by Lon Poole

Take an extensive tour of System 7.1 software, with *Macworld* columnist Lon Poole's insider tips and troubleshooting help.

ISBN: 1-878058-65-7
$24.95 USA/$33.95 Canada/£22.99 UK & Eire

MACWORLD GUIDE TO MICROSOFT WORKS 3
by Barrie Sosinsky

This complete guide to Works 3 gets you up and running with Microsoft's popular integrated software—fast.

ISBN: 1-878058-42-8
$22.95 USA/$29.95 Canada/£21.99 UK & Eire

MACWORLD GUIDE TO CLARISWORKS 2
by Steven Schwartz

NEW IDG BOOKS

Learn with step-by-step quick tips how to integrate the powerful modules and features of this popular top-selling integrated package.

ISBN: 1-56884-018-7
$22.95 USA/$29.95 Canada/£21.99 UK & Eire

MACWORLD GUIDE TO MICROSOFT EXCEL 4
by David Maguiness

Create powerful spreadsheets right away with this clear and extensive step-by-step guide to Excel 4.

ISBN: 1-878058-40-1
$22.95 USA/$29.95 Canada/£21.99 UK & Eire

MACWORLD GUIDE TO MICROSOFT WORD 5/5.1
by Jim Heid

This is the complete guide to Word 5 & 5.1, with step-by-step tutorials and timesaving tips for creating impressive-looking documents with Word.

ISBN: 1-878058-39-8
$22.95 USA/$29.95 Canada/£21.99 UK & Eire

MACWORLD NETWORKING HANDBOOK
by Dave Kosiur & Nancy E.H. Jones

Mac network management from the inside out! This insider's guide won the Society of Technical Communication's "Award of Excellence."

ISBN: 1-878058-31-2
$29.95 USA/$39.95 Canada/£26.99 UK & Eire

For more information or to order by mail, call 1-800-762-2974. Call for a free catalog! For volume discounts and special orders, please call Tony Real, Special Sales, at 415-312-0644. For International sales and distribution information, please call our authorized distributors:

CANADA Macmillan Canada
416-293-8141

UNITED KINGDOM Transworld
44-81-231-6661

AUSTRALIA Woodslane Pty Ltd.
61-2-979-5944

IDG BOOKS' MACWORLD SERIES

"The time this book is going to save Mac users will pay them back about fifty times over."

Doug Hamer, DS Hammer Design, Wakefield, MA, on Deke McClelland's bestselling Macworld Photoshop 2.5 Bible

"The 8MB of software legitimately ...smokes the covers off... any book/collection I have found to date."

Earl Wirth, Account Mgr., Calgary, Alberta, Canada, on Macworld Macintosh SECRETS

"Great 'behind the scenes' information on Macintosh hardware and software."

Kevin Garrison, Sales, Mt. Pleasant, SC on Macworld Macintosh SECRETS

"Found information in this book that I have seen nowhere else."

Michael K. Riggs, Moscow, ID on Macworld Macintosh SECRETS

MACWORLD MACINTOSH SECRETS™
by David Pogue & Joseph Schorr

Hundreds of the latest expert tips on Mac hardware, software, multimedia, networks, and much more are revealed by *Macworld* magazine's, "Desktop Critic" David Pogue, with coauthor and *Macworld* magazine's contributing writer Joseph Schorr! Includes over 8MB of commercial software and shareware.

ISBN: 1-56884-025-X
$39.95 USA/$52.95 Canada/£36.99 incl. VAT UK & Eire

MACWORLD PHOTOSHOP 2.5 BIBLE
by Deke McClelland

Packed with tips & techniques on electronic painting, photo retouching & special effects by *Macworld* Contributing Editor Deke McClelland, this is the complete reference to image editing. Now covers version 2.5.1

ISBN: 1-56884-022-5
$29.95 USA/$39.95 Canada/£26.99 incl. VAT UK & Eire

MACWORLD QUARKXPRESS 3.2/3.3 BIBLE
by Barbara Assadi & Galen Gruman

The definitive guide to QuarkXPress 3.2 and 3.3 explains page layout, graphics, and color prepress. Includes FREE disk with QuarkXPress XTensions and scripts.

ISBN: 1-878058-85-1
$39.95 USA/$52.95 Canada
£36.99 incl. VAT UK & Eire

☞ ALL NEW!

MACWORLD PAGEMAKER 5 BIBLE
by Craig Danuloff

Stuffed with insider tips & techniques, the ultimate guide to page layout is here, plus 2 disks of PageMaker utilities, templates, fonts, and clip art.

ISBN: 1-878058-84-3
$39.95 USA/$52.95 Canada
£36.99 incl. VAT UK & Eire

MACWORLD COMPLETE MAC HANDBOOK PLUS CD, 2nd EDITION
by Jim Heid

This is the ultimate guide to using, mastering, and expanding the Mac. Includes CD-ROM with software, demos, QuickTime movies, & more!

ISBN: 1-56884-033-0
$39.95 USA/$52.95 Canada
£36.99 incl. VAT UK & Eire

☞ REVISION OF NATIONAL BESTSELLER!

For more information or to order by mail, call 1-800-762-2974. Call for a free catalog! For volume discounts and special orders, please call Tony Real, Special Sales, at 415-312-0644. For International sales and distribution information, please call our authorized distributors:

CANADA Macmillan Canada 416-293-8141
UNITED KINGDOM Transworld 44-81-231-6661
AUSTRALIA Woodslane Pty Ltd. 61-2-979-5944

Order Form

Order Center: (800) 762-2974 (8 a.m.-5 p.m., PST, weekdays) or (415) 312-0650

For Fastest Service: Photocopy This Order Form and FAX it to: (415) 358-1260

Quantity	ISBN	Title	Price	Total

Shipping & Handling Charges

Subtotal	U.S.	Canada & International	International Air Mail
Up to $20.00	Add $3.00	Add $4.00	Add $10.00
$20.01-40.00	$4.00	$5.00	$20.00
$40.01-60.00	$5.00	$6.00	$25.00
$60.01-80.00	$6.00	$8.00	$35.00
Over $80.00	$7.00	$10.00	$50.00

In U.S. and Canada, shipping is UPS ground or equivalent.
For Rush shipping call (800) 762-2974.

Subtotal _____
CA residents add applicable sales tax _____
IN and MA residents add 5% sales tax _____
IL residents add 6.25% sales tax _____
RI residents add 7% sales tax _____
Shipping _____
Total _____

Ship to:

Name _____
Company _____
Address _____
City/State/Zip _____
Daytime Phone _____

Payment: ❑ Check to IDG Books (US Funds Only) ❑ Visa ❑ Mastercard ❑ American Express

Card# _____ Exp. _____ Signature _____

Please send this order form to: IDG Books, 155 Bovet Road, Suite 310, San Mateo, CA 94402.
Allow up to 3 weeks for delivery. Thank you!

IDG BOOKS WORLDWIDE LICENSE AGREEMENT

Important — read carefully before opening the software packet(s). This is a legal agreement between you (either an individual or an entity) and IDG Books Worldwide, Inc. (IDG). By opening the accompanying sealed packet(s) containing the software disk(s), you acknowledge that you have read and accept the following IDG License Agreement. If you do not agree and do not want to be bound by the terms of this Agreement, promptly return the book and the unopened software packet(s) to the place you obtained them for a full refund.

1. License. This License Agreement (Agreement) permits you to use one copy of the enclosed Software program(s) on a single computer. The Software is in "use" on a computer when it is loaded into temporary memory (i.e., RAM) or installed into permanent memory (e.g., hard disk, CD ROM, or other storage device) of that computer.

2. Copyright. The entire contents of this disk(s) and the compilation of the Software are copyrighted and protected by both United States copyright laws and international treaty provisions. The individual programs on the disk(s) are copyrighted by the authors of each program respectively. Each program has its own use permissions and limitations. You may only (a) make one copy of the Software for backup or archival purposes, or (b) transfer the Software to a single hard disk, provided that you keep the original for backup or archival purposes. To use each program, you must follow the individual requirements and restrictions detailed for each in Appendix F of this Book. Do not use a program if you do not want to follow its Licensing Agreement. None of the material on this disk(s) or listed in this Book may ever be distributed, in original or modified form, for commercial purposes.

3. Other Restrictions. You may not rent or lease the Software. You may transfer the Software and user documentation on a permanent basis provided you retain no copies and the recipient agrees to the terms of this Agreement. You may not reverse engineer, decompile, or disassemble the Software except to the extent that the foregoing restriction is expressly prohibited by applicable law. If the Software is an update or has been updated, any transfer must include the most recent update and all prior versions.

4. Limited Warranty. IDG Warrants that the Software and disk(s) are free from defects in materials and workmanship for a period of sixty (60) days from the date of purchase of this Book. If IDG receives notification within the warranty period of defects in material or workmanship, IDG will replace the defective disk(s). IDG's entire liability and your exclusive remedy shall be limited to replacement of the Software, which is returned to IDG with a copy of your receipt. This Limited Warranty is void if failure of the Software has resulted from accident, abuse, or misapplication. Any replacement Software will be warranted for the remainder of the original warranty period or thirty (30) days, whichever is longer.

5. No Other Warranties. To the maximum extent permitted by applicable law, IDG and the author disclaim all other warranties, express or implied, including but not limited to implied warranties of merchantability and fitness for a particular purpose, with respect to the Software, the programs, the source code contained therein and/or the techniques described in this Book. This limited warranty gives you specific legal rights. You may have others which vary from state/jurisdiction to state/jurisdiction.

6. No Liability For Consequential Damages. To the extent permitted by applicable law, in no event shall IDG or the author be liable for any damages whatsoever (including without limitation, damages for loss of business profits, business interruption, loss of business information, or any other pecuniary loss) arising out of the use of or inability to use the Book or the Software, even if IDG has been advised of the possibility of such damages. Because some states/jurisdictions do not allow the exclusion or limitation of liability for consequential or incidental damages, the above limitation may not apply to you.

3 1/2", 800 K Disk Format Available.

The enclosed disk is in 3 1/2" 1.44MB, high-density format. If you have a different size drive, or a low-density drive, and you cannot arrange to transfer the data to the disk size you need, you can obtain the programs on 3 1/2", 800 K low-density disks by writing: IDG Books Worldwide, Attn: *MacWorld FileMaker Pro 2.0/2.1 Bible*, IDG Books Worldwide, 3250 North Post Road, Suite 140, Indianapolis, IN 46226, or call 800-762-2974. Please specify the size of disk you need, and please allow 3 to 4 weeks for delivery.

IDG BOOKS WORLDWIDE REGISTRATION CARD

RETURN THIS REGISTRATION CARD FOR FREE CATALOG

Title of this book: Macworld FileMaker 2.0/2.1 Pro Bible

My overall rating of this book: ❑ Very good [1] ❑ Good [2] ❑ Satisfactory [3] ❑ Fair [4] ❑ Poor [5]

How I first heard about this book:

❑ Found in bookstore; name: [6] _____

❑ Book review: [7] _____

❑ Advertisement: [8] _____

❑ Catalog: [9] _____

❑ Word of mouth; heard about book from friend, co-worker, etc.: [10] _____

❑ Other: [11] _____

What I liked most about this book: _____

What I would change, add, delete, etc., in future editions of this book: _____

Other comments: _____

Number of computer books I purchase in a year: ❑ 1 [12] ❑ 2-5 [13] ❑ 6-10 [14] ❑ More than 10 [15]

I would characterize my computer skills as: ❑ Beginner [16] ❑ Intermediate [17] ❑ Advanced [18] ❑ Professional [19]

I use ❑ DOS [20] ❑ Windows [21] ❑ OS/2 [22] ❑ Unix [23] ❑ Macintosh [24] ❑ Other: [25] _____
(please specify)

I would be interested in new books on the following subjects:
(please check all that apply, and use the spaces provided to identify specific software)

❑ Word processing: [26]

❑ Spreadsheets: [27]

❑ Data bases: [28]

❑ Desktop publishing: [29]

❑ File Utilities: [30]

❑ Money management: [31]

❑ Networking: [32]

❑ Programming languages: [33]

❑ Other: [34]

I use a PC at (please check all that apply): ❑ home [35] ❑ work [36] ❑ school [37] ❑ other: [38] _____

The disks I prefer to use are ❑ 5.25 [39] ❑ 3.5 [40] ❑ other: [41] _____

I have a CD ROM: ❑ yes [42] ❑ no [43]

I plan to buy or upgrade computer hardware this year: ❑ yes [44] ❑ no [45]

I plan to buy or upgrade computer software this year: ❑ yes [46] ❑ no [47]

Name: _____ **Business title:** [48] _____ **Type of Business:** [49] _____

Address (❑ home [50] ❑ work [51] /Company name: _____)

Street/Suite# _____

City [52] /**State** [53] /**Zipcode** [54]: _____ **Country** [55] _____

❑ **I liked this book!** You may quote me by name in future IDG Books Worldwide promotional materials.

My daytime phone number is _____

IDG BOOKS

THE WORLD OF COMPUTER KNOWLEDGE

☐ **YES!**
Please keep me informed about IDG's World of Computer Knowledge. Send me the latest IDG Books catalog.

BUSINESS REPLY MAIL
FIRST CLASS MAIL   PERMIT NO. 2605   SAN MATEO, CALIFORNIA

IDG Books Worldwide
155 Bovet Road
San Mateo, CA 94402-9833